Charlene Gagon,

HOTEVILLA
HOPI SHRINE OF THE COVENANT

MICROCOSM
OF THE WORLD

By

THOMAS E. MAILS AND DAN EVEHEMA

Illustrations by Thomas E. Mails,
with assistance by Ryan F. Mails, and
with some drawings from the
Traditional's newspaper, *Techqua Ikachi*.

Published by
Marlowe & Company
in association with the
TOUCH THE EARTH FOUNDATION.

HOTEVILLA: HOPI SHRINE OF THE COVENANT—MICROCOSM OF THE WORLD
COPYRIGHT © 1995 BY THOMAS E. MAILS

Published by
Marlowe & Company
632 Broadway, Seventh floor
New York, NY 10012

Published in cooperation with the Touch the Earth Foundation.

Text design by Juddesign
Illustrations by Thomas E. Mails

FIRST HARDBACK/PAPERBACK EDITION PUBLISHED IN 1995

Library of Congress Cataloging-in-Publication Data
Hotevilla: Hopi Shrine of the Covenant—Microcosm of the World
Thomas E. Mails co-authored with Dan Evehema, 1st ed.

p.   cm.
ISBN 1-56924-810-9 PB; 1-56924-835-4 CL
1. Indians of North America—Hopi History 2. Indians of North America— Hopi Prophecy
3. Indians of North America —Hopi Ceremonialism, Mails, Thomas E.

Table of Contents

CHAPTER 1   Running Where the Brave Dare Not Go
— the Gritty Elders of Hotevilla. 1

CHAPTER 2   The Emergence. 38

CHAPTER 3   Migration and Heritage. 74

CHAPTER 4   The Lull Before the Thunderstorm 131

CHAPTER 5   The Thunderstorm 205

CHAPTER 6   The Aftermath. 257

CHAPTER 7   Two-Hearteds: Progressive Hopi and
The Government. 308

CHAPTER 8   Two-Hearteds: The Peabody Mine,
Missions, and Navajo Relocation. 357

CHAPTER 9   Two-Hearteds: The Tribal Council 396

CHAPTER 10   The One-Hearteds and Hope 467

CHAPTER 11   Prophecy and Our Response 523

BIBLIOGRAPHY   574

APPENDIX   577

June 1, 1993

Chief Dan Evehema

I, Dan Evehema, being the eldest of our tribal leaders, hearby grant to author Thomas E. Mails exclusive rights to publish and write a book telling the history of the traditional Hopi people of the village of Hotevilla Arizona. Including general events, and especialy the prophecy given to us in ancient times regarding the end of the world's fourth cycle and the beginning of the 5th cycle, including the vital roll the traditional Hopi people are playing in this crucial time.

We have been looking for many years for someone with a true heart to come to help us tell this story. It is my belief that Thomas E. Mails is this person. He will help us share our message of prophecy, peace and harmony with all the peoples of the world.

_____ Dan Evehema
Chief Dan Evehema

_____
Title
___Roadrunar & Greaswood
Clans

_____6-1-93_____
Date

Susie Lomatska
Witnessed / Susie Lomatska

Dedication:

To The Covenant!

Running
Where the Brave
Dare Not Go—

The Gritty Elders
of Hotevilla

Is it possible, probable, even logical, that an endangered species without Federal protection — five elderly native people, supported by perhaps fifteen younger men and women, living the simplest of lives in a remote village in Northern Arizona — hold in their hands the fate of the Americas, and perhaps even of the entire world? For that, based upon astonishing prophecies they received nearly a thousand years ago, is what they claim. And they say that their village, Hotevilla, is a shrine — the Shrine of the Covenant — and a microcosm of the world.

Implausible as it seems, this little village may at this moment — and for a long time to come — be the most important place in the world. It is not the regular kind of shrine like Lourdes where miracles happen, although some have at Hotevilla. But it is a very holy place, and its holiness has been hammered out by sacrificing people for all of its years. As such it is a most special shrine to visit and to live in, for it brings benefits and opportunities to those who do that nothing else in the world can match. Do I sense skepticism? Bear with me. If these five and their supporters have lost their minds, so did every generation of their ancestors. The more you learn about this stalwart group, the more logical, legitimate and encompassing their fantastic claim becomes.

Hotevilla, 1930

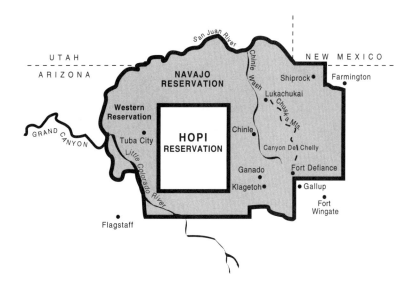

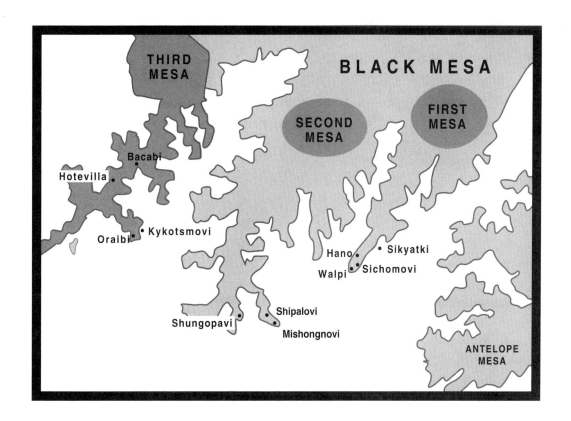

The Hopi Villages

When a declaration so impressive as this is made, you will want to know who exactly the speakers are.

If you drive north in Arizona from Flagstaff to Tuba City and then head south on Highway 264, you will shortly find yourself within the Hopi Indian

Reservation and following a two-lane road that cuts cleanly through mainly flat and sparsely vegetated country. After travelling about 30 miles the countryside will break into mesas, you will see Hopi farming sites, and you will come to Hotevilla.

As you turn west toward the village, you will pass a small sign that reads: "Welcome to Hotevilla. Not permitted for all non-Indian visitors:
1. sound recording
2. photography
3. sketching
4. removing objects
5. loitering near kivas and shrines."

No belligerence is intended by the sign. Every Hopi village has had problems with tactless outsiders. Its primary purpose is to protect the privacy of the residents and the sanctity of their religious festival days. The people learned the hard way that once their religious practices were known, some outsiders would want to stop them and replace them with their own spiritual beliefs. Of all the Hopi villages, so long as the restrictions are observed visitors are the most welcome at Hotevilla, and on dance days everyone can share in its wondrous moments. Dan Evehema says, "We are welcoming all people from all over the world to see dances at Hotevilla. The Men's Society are the fathers of every human. We have a welcoming heart to all people."

Hotevilla is a place where ancient history is alive. Indigenous peoples are carrying on an enchanting spiritual lifeway that has continued for thousands of years. Along with other Hopi villages and Pueblo tribes in Arizona and New Mexico they are unique, even among Native American tribes, in that they live today much as their people always have, although they face imminent cultural extinction from a collaboration of powerful forces.

What you will first see in Hotevilla is on the surface a typical Hopi community going about its daily business. But the people, village, and farming lands are not typical. The point of mentioning the sign now is to establish that our story, except for some supporting evidence, does not come from scientists such as historians, anthropologists, archaeologists or even ethnologists. It is not a story any outsider, including myself, could ferret out. It could only come from the Hopi people who have lived it for the whole of their lives. Because of their wisdom, loyalty to tradition, experience, and venerable ages that border on 100 years, we will call them in this book "the Elders." Out of profound respect, other Traditionals refer to them as "the Elderly Elders." How there came to be so few is one of the intriguing questions you will want answered as the chronicle progresses… and it will lead us into truly Machiavellian situations that involve a myriad of shadowy incidents and people.

As you continue to drive along the bumpy dirt road that leads from the highway into the village, you will come to a country-type store and post office. In 1993, if you had observed carefully while entering there, you would have noticed that except for extending to the modern school building a short distance away, the electrical poles and wires ended there. Perhaps you would have wondered why. It had something to do with the Covenant. Next you would pass a tall water tower whose sculptured metal form and gray color, courtesy of the United States Government and the Hopi Tribal Council, are a deliberately tart contrast to the homes you are about to see. You might have wondered why they did this. The tower has been battered by constant desert winds and is presently in need of repair. You would have assumed that it served the village, but except for the school and the tiny community of Bacobi across the highway, it did not. Water mains were in some of the Hotevilla roads, but only a few of the houses were connected to them. There was a reason for this, and it too had something to do with the Covenant.

Moving into the main part of the village with its irregular pattern of narrow streets you will still see a pastoral mixture of stone, adobe, wooden and concrete block houses of small to medium size that harmonize in shape and color with the reddish-brown landscape and enclose a ceremonial dance plaza. Interspersed among the homes and close to the plaza are six ceremonial kivas that are rectangular in shape and are usually subterranean rooms. You can identify the kivas by the stout ladder that extends several feet above the hatch opening in each kiva roof. Although at this very moment in 1994 something intensely dramatic is happening to change all this, at the end of 1993 there were few telephones in the village proper, and no water or sewer lines. Each different area had its own cluster of clean outhouses set off by themselves and kept locked. Propane tanks supplied the fuel for cooking. Wood and coal stoves and fireplaces provided the heat. Many of the homes used solar panels and gas generators to supply their television sets and limited lighting. House interiors are neat, tastefully furnished, and cheerful. The center of everything is the dining table, where every guest is invited to eat. The food includes traditional Hopi dishes, but when they can afford it, market items supplement the diet. Some of the villagers have second homes that are closer to their distant farming plots. In the case of the Elders, they observe at these second homes all of the self-imposed limitations just noted. A Hopi village encompasses its people, village proper, and its farming lands. All of these things are considered one. And when they speak of their "land," and especially of "losing it," everything is included. Take it, and you have taken everything.

Hotevilla, located on the third of three mesas that house a dozen villages, is by destiny among the youngest of them, yet it has the look and feel of an ancient place. The ghosts of its past visit regularly, and when the Kachinas have returned to dance and the ceremonies are being performed in the kivas, the spirits of the cloud people and the underworld people are hauntingly present.

When the full-time residents are at home, the village numbers something more than 400 residents, and even on most of its days of celebration it is serenely quiet. Perhaps it is the quietest then, as returning family members swell the population to 600, and groups ranging from hundreds to thousands of visitors watch with bated breath while the excitingly painted and beautifully costumed Kachinas dance and sing their aboriginal chants. The guttural tones roll up from a mysterious underworld, and accompanying them are shaken tortoiseshell and gourd rattles that call down rain from other Kachina spirits who have arrived overhead as cotton clouds that wander slowly in a placid blue sky.

Although it is popular to think that the dances are dying out, if you were one of the 2,000 or so visitors watching the Hotevilla Homegoing Dance on July 23, 1993, you would have been profoundly impressed by the number of participants. Where a knowledgeable visitor might have expected 30 or fewer Kachinas, there were 70 of the cherished Long Hairs. And before the dance ended, 60 other villagers magnificently costumed in ancient attire, making a grand total of 130, emerged from the kivas to meld with them. They did this with a special intensity, as with consummate grace, patience, and attention to detail they moved in stages through the village, some returning to their sacred homes in the underworld, and others to the towering San Francisco Peaks 60 miles away. Plainly, this was not just any Homegoing Dance, and it was certainly not a last farewell. It was more like the throwing down of a special kind of gauntlet at a critical moment in time. I could see why author Mischa Titiev wrote in his book, *Old Oraibi*, that after separating from Oraibi Village and holding fast to tradition, Hotevilla became the spiritual center of the Hopi world.

Katherine Cheshire, my eldest son, Ryan, and I felt engagement too…the tremendous contest that since the Hopi Emergence has been and still is afoot…and never, not even when I wrote at his request the life story of my eminent friend, the Sioux holy man, Fools Crow, have I undertaken anything so significant or urgent as this. The need to communicate the message of the Elders to the entire world is overwhelming, and it does not help to know that others, including the Hopi Elders themselves, have with only minimal success sought for nearly eighty years to do this. The glowing red core of the message, first given to their ancestors nearly a thousand years ago, is that when the close of the present Fourth Cycle and the opening of a new Fifth Cycle of the world is at hand, the number of survivors and the manner of its transition from one cycle to the other will be determined by two things: first, by what the Hopi Elders and their supporters are able to continue doing during the change, and second, by how the world's citizens respond.

Considering the importance of the message, you will be puzzled and wonder why the Elders have failed in their efforts to be heard. Of course, the conditions have not been right yet, and that has had something to do with it. But there are many other reasons, and some are not something the perpetrators, including government, corporations, and acquisitive individuals can be proud of. These include Hopi who, even though it is a matter of justifying their own positions, refuse to listen and do everything they can to impede, embarrass, and put an end to the Elders. Meanwhile, the moment of change from one cycle to the other approaches, and time and opportunity for the Elders to do what they must are swiftly running out.

In 1976, a certain scholar whose interest has for a long time centered on the Hopi wrote — and I trust he does not mean this the way it sounds — that there are now many who feel that an Indian can do no wrong. "For these individuals," he declared, "the Hopi are mystic sages, hoarding profound and esoteric wisdom acquired through the centuries, a not unflattering role which some Hopi have been quick to seize upon…The most recent view of the Hopi is that of a poor, deprived group in desperate need of political and social assistance which will, of course, be provided through the infinite wisdom of outsiders with little knowledge of Hopi realities…They (the Hopi) are masters of passive resistance, of discussion and deception, and are proficient at involving others in conducting their battles for them…Those traditionalists who wish to return to pre-government ways are a tiny but very vocal percentage who, by the nature of their resistance to the government, destroy that which they prize."

Although from personal experience I would be the last to tell you that Native Americans can do no wrong, it is clear that the writer is pointing a finger at people like myself and the Elders, indicating that neither of us has good sense; the end of the culture is here and there is nothing we or anyone else can do to change this.

"Despite their adamant resistance to change," he goes on, "the Hopi are being subverted at an ever-increasing rate. They are acutely aware that their culture is not well but there is little they can do. Moreover, members of the dominant culture do not assist the transition either mercifully or intelligently… Although there will always be Hopi, the cheerfully determined, peaceful people will vanish as they merge into the mainstream of American life. That which will remain to mark the passing of yet another culture will be the Hopi's unique art and their superb crafts."

In light of a present circumstance he could not have known about, the author may prove to be right about the demise — although he has its manner wrong. But doesn't the coldness of this make you shudder? It is an epitaph! Reality being what it may, he is not only selling all Hopis short, he is saying exactly what the enemies of the traditional culture want to hear and to happen, and the diminishment of the Elders is treated as a natural, inevitable, and proper consequence of life as it happens… a shrugging of the shoulders and a 'sad, but that's the way it is' attitude. Candles of inestimable worth, the last and only fully informed and qualified teachers in Hotevilla, and surely among the finest in the Americas, are about to be deliberately snuffed out! The final curtain is being drawn upon the last of the fully functioning magnificent native cultures of the Americas. Already the sands of time are beginning to blow over its ruins. I do not want to turn away listeners by overstating this too forcibly. If I do so, I hope you will understand why and forgive me. But what I am saying must not be ignored. Unless the course is changed, the consequences are just too great for all of us!

Think about this: Where the way they once lived is concerned, except for the Pueblos, every last one of the other great cultures is virtually gone — almost eradicated, nearly extinguished. What we read about that so fascinates us is only there in photographs and literary reconstructions, and anyone who needs to be convinced of this should go where the natives live today and see for themselves how appallingly little remains of what once was.

Oh, true enough, you can still find the Sun Dance among the Plains tribes, and you can find the Sunrise Ceremony among the Apaches. Nearly every tribe still has one or more small facet, some remnant of the ancestral life, that they continue to practice, and since it is their only way of retaining identity, they do this with consuming intensity. But as a rule, what they do is only a ghost or shadow of what once was, only a smattering of what formerly made the individual cultures so great, and from which we could have, were it otherwise, learned so much. In its place we find gambling casinos with their mixture of blessings and curses, the exploitation of oil, ores, and minerals by outside sources, dumping grounds for waste materials so hazardous outsiders want nothing to do with them, and on far too many reservations economic and health conditions so appalling that our Government, out of fear for what they would need to do if they did acknowledge its existence, does the least they can get by with.

I do not mean to diminish the wonderful contributions of present day Native Americans in all facets of American life. They have moved into the mainstream with laudable competence. But when we look at the books about Native Americans being published today, we quickly see which time periods and what things are actually being featured about them. Examine the films being produced in Hollywood. Some are about the Native American cultures as they currently function, but most are about the superb cultures of the past. Publishers feature the Incas, Mayas, Aztecs, Mound Builders, and the ancient tribes of North America. With only a few noteworthy exceptions, writers and the media center their interests elsewhere, in such movies and books as *Dances With Wolves*, *The Last of the Mohicans*, *Geronimo*, *The Broken Chain*...

Of all that once was, only the Hopi, especially Hotevilla — and to a varying extent the Pueblos of Zuni, Acoma, Laguna, and the Rio Grande — remain.

There is no mention whatsoever by the writer just referred to of the fact that the diminishment of the Hopi Traditionals has come from an orchestrated onslaught of unrelenting pressures by external and internal forces — such as the Tribal Council, not one of whose members are nearly as qualified as the Elders are to teach anyone about ceremonial things — who are devoid of fairness and utterly amazed that in response the true Traditionalists haven't simply rolled over on their backs like frightened animals and played dead.

Some other scholars, in analyzing the relationships between the Elders and those who oppose them, attribute the differences in Hopiland to nothing more than personal approaches aimed at accomplishing the same end. This is in no wise true. The end is not the same, and the devious tactics employed by all of the opponents make this painfully clear. In this regard, Dan and I will be the first to admit that our book is a one-sided presentation. We do not think anyone should expect it to be otherwise. We are not, however, alone in doing this. For decades now the amply funded opponents we consider herein have themselves actively pursued and scornfully argued only their own case, constantly demeaning the Elders, achieving relatively easy victories, acquiring a feeling of invincibility, and never expecting to be confronted in a book by Maasaw's true representatives.

Of course, the Elders know what has transpired, and they do not think of themselves as perfect and above reproach. It will be seen that they repeatedly confess to their own shortcomings. They have lived in the midst of this tenuous and divisive situation for a full century. They know better than anyone else what it can do to people, and that they face extinction momentarily. Moreover, they make these facts excruciatingly clear herein. But we must ask ourselves whether their extinction is what we will want to happen — especially when we learn why they have clung so tenaciously as they have to their position for such an incredibly long period of time. The Elderly Elders have run where the brave dare not go for reasons that merit their being rooted for, supported and preserved! Most of all, this message to the world comes with a twist: The powers that be may eradicate them, but in doing so will have sealed their own doom. A preposterous position, of course, but a position nevertheless taken! On the other hand, if they rescue them, the saviors will have assured their own success.

Contrary to accusations about their "deceptiveness" and being "users," it is heartbreaking to see how naive the Elders have been in their expectations. They believe so fervently in what they are doing that it never occurred to them that some of their own people, let alone people in the outside world, would turn a deaf ear to their message. After all, isn't the saving of the world as important to everyone as anything could possibly be? So, beginning years ago they passed the word to visitors — a word that centered in prophecy but was also about self-determination, self-government, and human rights. A mild curiosity was expressed, but nothing of significance happened. They turned then to issuing over a period of eleven years a free local newsletter. In the face of extremely limited distribution, a lack of writing and publishing skills, and what people considered to be greater concerns, that didn't accomplish what they hoped for either. Partially because of the way it has been distributed and an inadequate understanding of the Hopi culture by non-Hopi readers, a free booklet by Chief Dan Katchongva of Hotevilla has excited only a mild response. (We are featuring the newsletters and the booklet in a new way here, and trust they will have a far greater impact.) At various times, the Traditionalists have enlisted the aid of a few outsiders who wrote, and are still writing, articles to spread the word. That too has not stirred a reaction of any consequence. A couple of films have been produced, and while these have stuck in the minds of some who have seen them, the daily personal tasks of the viewers appear to have pushed the films' messages off to one side. Long letters have been written to presidents, senators, congressmen, bureau chiefs, and state leaders. The responses are few, and assaults have continued. Delegations of representatives from several of the Hopi villages have gone, as it was prophesied they should, four times to the United Nations, where to their dismay they have received only a cursory reception.

Does all of this bewilder you and make you wonder whether the message is really worthwhile? It shouldn't. You know as I do that government leaders and U.N. delegates, even though they might wish it were otherwise, have been and are far too occupied with what they consider to be more pressing problems than those offered by a microscopic delegation of mostly elderly people representing a little tribe of people with no political clout and living in the middle of nowhere.

During this eighty-year period when the Elders have sought to communicate their message, the United States has dealt with two World Wars, the Vietnam and Korean wars, a national depression, the Cold War with Russia, civil rights problems, racial divisions, drugs and excessive violence, an evolving global economy, worldwide needs of every kind, political and personal self-interests, poverty, immigration and more. As for the U.N., it was bad enough for it to be handling the Cold War, let alone what it is confronted with now as countries fragment, internal wars rage, starvation and disease spread, and it is beset with funding shortages and lack of political cohesion and will. Just now the Opinion section of the Sunday *Los Angeles Times* carried a major article asking whether the United Nations organization is "in a free fall." "The world's safety net," it said, "is fraying — At the height of its greatest opportunity to realize its long-envisioned global mission, the United Nations is in danger of going into free fall. The world body is presently stretched beyond its financial resources, bogged down in noble humanitarian expeditions and threatened by the squeamishness and inconstancy of its strongest members." By the time the U.N. has recovered and is ready to listen, its moment to act will be gone.

A major problem the Elders have made for themselves as they have sought to communicate their central revelation about the closing and the opening has come from the fact that they have buried the magna-message in a list of difficulties they face, which in some instances are faced by the Hopi in general. There are so many of these, each with its own urgency, that they obscure the vastly more important prophecies and warnings. It is as though they have placed their priceless jewel on a tabletop, and then covered it over with successive layers of coarse cloth — one layer for each problem.

These individual issues — especially because most of them impact and impede the fulfillment of the Covenant — are certainly important; even, as you will see, vital, and as such they are discussed fully in the chapters ahead. But the point is that they must be viewed in their proper place and independently, for when everything is lumped together outsiders see only the personal dilemmas of the Hopi, and in comparing them to other national and international urgencies find them, on a scale of one to ten, relatively unimportant — measuring about a three. The usual response from others is "We all have problems...would you like to hear about mine?"

So, the Elders are left desperate and reduced to begging for someone to listen. "How can we," they cry out, "do what we are called to do if what we need to accomplish it is taken away from us?" The question is a fair one, even paralyzing in light of something that is in the process of happening right now at Hotevilla. But they should not be begging. It is everyone else who should be begging them. Another part of the problem is that they have been going to the wrong people for help. They must turn to ordinary, typical people who will listen, and whose cumulative strength, once it is unleashed, can, as history (even Hopi history itself) has shown, remove any legislative mountain and stunningly alter the course of any cause — or, in particular this: *prophetic fulfillment.*

Our book came into being in the strangest of ways when an incident in which Leigh Jenkins, who heads the Office of Cultural Preservation as an employee of the Hopi Tribal Council, surprisingly became the unwitting catalyst for my getting to know the Hopi Elders of Hotevilla — whose own problems with the Council and Mr. Jenkins, it may surprise you to learn — are legendary.

My friend, Katherine Cheshire, who as of 1993 has for nine years maintained a close relationship with the Hopi Elders at Hotevilla, earned their trust, and has been adopted by one of their families, was deeply concerned about the situation and discussed it with them. This is not something I could have done on my own. During the three years when I was producing my two-volume series, *The Pueblo Children of the Earth Mother*, published in 1983, I spent considerable time in Hopi country and became friends with a number of individuals. But all of these lived in First Mesa villages, and most are now deceased. I had not been to the reservation for ten years, had no contacts, was busy with other things, and knew little of what was going on there. As it turned out, there was plenty. Katherine's friends responded quickly. In short order I received two long telephone calls and the following letter, dated May 25, 1993 from Manuel Hoyungowa, who is the recently chosen leader and spokesperson among the group of younger but strongly traditional people at Hotevilla who support the Elders, and spokesperson also for some of the True Traditionals of the other mesa villages.

> *Dear Thomas,*
>
> *It was a pleasure to talk with you last Thursday. I have heard many good things about you and your work. It was very encouraging to know that you also understand that the Hopi Traditional Message to the world, that the Elders have been trying to communicate, can't be done by the Hopi people alone. The time has come for true hearted people to know the truth of what has been going on. Please find enclosed a copy of our current Hopi constitution. You have already been sent other documentation that the Hopi Elders have distributed to the U.S. Government. I hope that this will create the foundation for our work together.*
>
> *We, the Traditional Hopi, do not recognize those who would call themselves Hopi Council. It seems to us that this group should be spending their energy on protecting our home land. It has been our spiritual instruction to protect and provide the proper ceremonies to keep this world in balance. This is what our traditional way of life is.*
>
> *The Hopi Council, and other native american councils, were set up as puppet bureaucracies created by the U.S. Government to control the people and land use. The Elders' beliefs are that other world factions are manipulating these puppet governments for greed and gluttony of world resources.*
>
> *The Traditional Hopi have never signed any agreement with the U.S. Government. When this council was created it was voted in by the Tewa, people from New Mexico at First Mesa. This does not represent the other Hopi villages. To us, the government that Mr. Jenkins and the Tribal council represents is not legal. This Hopi Puppet Council has very*

strong words and makes much trouble for the future of all Hopi People. We, the traditionalists, are sad that our own people act this way out in the world. The Tribal council speaks of prophecy and taking care of our spiritual laws, but seems to only have empty words and no action or power to bring about the change that we all know must happen at this time to protect the land and life of our Earth Mother. I want to take this opportunity to say I have read some of your books and know that you speak the truth that you are a friend to the Native American. In particular, the Pueblo Children of the Earth Mother.

I know it is time that we must in any way possible make people aware of the Hopi Prophecy and way of life in this creation world. It is through the sharing of this spiritual truth that our world will be saved from a terrible destruction. If the Hopi Traditionalists and the true hearts that have given this promise to the creation fail to carry this message to the world, this day may come soon. So we do need your help to carry this message to the winds. I am pleased to invite you to speak in person and meet with the other traditionals. I hope you will accept this invitation at the earliest date possible.

Best Wishes…Manuel

Four days later, Katherine picked me up at the Phoenix airport and took me to the Hopi Reservation and the home of Dan Evehema, where we met that night with Dan, Manuel, Dan's granddaughter, Susie Lomatska, and a fourth person. The meeting, thanks to this unnamed person who did most of the talking, was not as promising as I had expected. But there was a second visit where Manuel, Susie, and Katherine were present, and then several more meetings with Dan, Susie, and Katherine over the next two days, for Dan was busy planting corn, which is almost as important a thing as any traditional Hopi can do. During these conversations, where Susie often served as translator, we got to know each other, friendships bonded, I learned a great deal about the concerns of the Elders, and things changed dramatically. We found that we thought a great deal alike, had similar goals, and that we shared a mutual friend in Oscar Sheyka, the former kiva chief at Zuni. At Dan's request, before I left to return home, Katherine prepared the following letter. Dan signed it, and Susie witnessed the signing. A copy of the original is in the front of the book.

June 1, 1993

Chief Dan Evehema

I, Dan Evehema, being the eldest of our tribal leaders, hereby grant to author Thomas E. Mails exclusive rights to publish and write a book telling the history of the traditional Hopi people of the village of Hotevilla, Arizona, including special events, and especially the prophecy given to us in ancient times regarding the end of the world's fourth cycle and the beginning of the fifth cycle, including the vital role the traditional Hopi people are playing in this crucial time. We have been looking for many years for someone with a true heart to come to help us tell this story. It is my belief that Thomas E. Mails is this person. He will help us share our message of prophecy, peace, and harmony with all the people of the world.

In addition to his letter, Dan prepared for me in the sacred Hopi way a prayer feather. It is to bring me spiritual guidance as I write. To purify and protect me, Dan also gave me a pouch full of sacred white cornmeal, and some of the sacred tobacco that is smoked only in the kivas. All of these items sit by my side while I work at my computer and are used in special ways to bless what I do.

While I was delighted with Dan's confidence in me, I was also troubled by the portents and responsibilities involved. I knew from the first moment that treating this entire subject would lead me into deep and murky waters where, as has already been indicated, powerful opponents lurk. I am not so heroic as the Elders are, but I have found that, with innocent conviction, they are warm, wonderful, and convincing people. Being with Dan and Susie and their families evokes a special kind of happiness and special thoughts about achievement, struggle, and heroic effort. With the exception of Fools Crow, I have never experienced such an absence of greed, such a willingness to live in the simplest of lifestyles. I profoundly appreciate what the Elders have done and are doing. Since opportunities and appeals like this seldom come along in anyone's lifetime... I will not "walk away" and am ready to accept the risks. And I am even more grateful than before to Katherine, who has continued from that very first moment to render invaluable and heroic assistance to the preparation of the book.

Regarding the risks: As a World War II veteran and one who has always supported our country and respected our Government, I am unwilling to believe that it acts maliciously. Yet I do know that when the Government feels it is right in a given instance, it has repeatedly shown that it does not take affronts lightly, and with the unlimited backing of taxpayers' funds it can outlast anyone in achieving its vindication. The Elders themselves have learned the hard way that there is always the possibility — or probability — of retaliation. Sooner or later it will come. In this instance we hope that the end will be different, that the Government will do what is right. There have been such times in history to celebrate and savor. Adding this one would be wonderful!

As the statements of the Elders and their newsletters indicate, the Hopi Traditionals have for a long time looked for "one" who in this crucial time would come to help them. I make no claim to being this person. Nor is it important to me that anyone think of me as such. All I hope is that whatever I do will be helpful.

One day, I asked Dan what he thought I could do that would benefit the Elders the most. He looked steadily at me for a moment and blinked as though he was attempting to hold back tears. "Tell our story, then even when we old ones are gone it will still live," he said. He turned his head to gaze out the window at the rust-colored land he loves so dearly, and I thought about his response for a few minutes. It would not be a simple task, and it was a daunting challenge. Dan had no interest in a biographical sketch. He wanted "our story" told, the story of the Hopi of The Sacred Covenant. This would mean pulling in everything connected to it, and a working time whose length I could not predict. We writers also like accounts that can be developed into seamless presentations that readers can easily follow. In this case it would not be possible. The information needed to accomplish that would not be available. So the story has bumps and glitches — but it says what the Elders, particularly Dan Evehema, want it to say.

"And what," I asked him, "if readers are still not willing to believe the prophecies, and continue to feel there are worse problems to deal with in the world than those revealed by the Traditionalists?"

He turned back to me and replied with intensity, "Just tell our story, and let people all over the world decide for themselves what they will do about it."

And what, in substance, is this extraordinary story? Dan and the others tell us that about A.D. 1100, after a millennia(s)-long period of special preparation while they were migrating, a group of their ancestors found Maasaw, the awesome Guardian Spirit of the Earth, at his dwelling place called Oraibi.

Here at Oraibi, an agreement — the Sacred Covenant — was made between Maasaw and the people. Afterward, Maasaw bestowed upon them the dubious honor of placing in their hands, together with the sharing of this responsibility with certain of the ancient peoples in other lands — so that the Covenant was global in scale — the fate of a world they did not yet know anything about, save those things the Guardian Spirit described to them in his prophecies. In other words, the Hopi at Oraibi, half of whom after an agonizing split in 1906 moved and founded Hotevilla, were expected to become part of what is today an ever dwindling network of loyal servant people. Their special charge, later extended by Maasaw to all of the Hopi villages, was North America. It was and is a stunning responsibility, and with the passing of time it has become an even greater one as other Hopi have made unacceptable concessions, and the aboriginal loyalists to the Covenant in other lands either have become or are becoming extinct. Now the Elders must cover for those people and countries too — which is another matter that will be considered in greater detail in subsequent chapters.

In a sense, the Elders believe that Hotevilla is the pivot point upon which the fate of the world will turn.

All of the whys and wherefores of this legendary Covenant and the struggle to keep the faith to the end are the heart and core of our book, *Hotevilla, Hopi Shrine of the Covenant, Microcosm of the World*. Although Dan Evehema is the co-author, our book is not a biographical sketch of his life, and it reveals absolutely nothing about Hopi kiva rites or religious secrets. His express request is that we do not include any illustrations of kiva rituals or paraphernalia. He does not want other Hopis to think he reveals such information. Even the drawings and paintings of Hopi Kachinas I do include are adapted from photographs taken nearly a century ago during public performances at several villages. To see the actual dances, you will need to go to Hotevilla on a festival day. In fact, nothing about Hopi life that is not germane to the book's purpose is included in it. Just as it was for his ancestors during proceeding generations, Dan's abiding concern and that of the other Traditionalists is the keeping of the Covenant, nothing more, which requires, among other things, that when, as is the present case, the prophesied signs clearly show the end of the Fourth Cycle of the world's existence is near, the Hopi Elders of Hotevilla must make known to everyone who will listen certain information about it first given to them by Maasaw.

A responsive audience for this is at last forming, although Native Americans are all too often among the last spokespersons outsiders will listen to. Even though experience recommends otherwise, it has not been our habit to give credence to anything that does not originate with us, is rooted in faith, or that does not come from some prestigious or influential source.

Amazingly, it has been the very quest of the Hopi to grow in grace, find Maasaw, and keep the Covenant that explains most of the mysteries concerning them since their first appearance on the surface of the earth. The Elders say that their resolute stands against foreign intrusion, their annual cycle of rituals, their manner of daily life, their political views, their factionalism, and their migrations have all grown out of their commitment to the Covenant.

Until recently, the Hopi have done nothing to document their migration myths. They accept them at face value, trust their oral tradition, and find documentation unnecessary. Over the past century, however, Anglo scientists in the archaeology, anthropology, and ethnology branches have sought diligently to learn all they can about the fascinating Anasazi, forebears of the Hopi and other Pueblo peoples, and especially why they appear to have migrated so continually and, the scientists think, moved from one location to another as frequently as they did. Literally thousands of habitation sites — a few of the 15,000 and more are described in Chapters 2 and 3 — have been discovered throughout the greater southwest area, so many that, except for the reprehensible pot hunters and looters that seem to go everywhere, at least half have not even been explored. The most commonly advanced reasons for Anasazi/Hopi movements include exhausted resources, droughts, overburdened facilities, enemy pressures, and more recently the idea that factionalism is a common and ongoing Hopi trait that has led to frequent partings.

But the scientists may be looking in the wrong places and not listening to the right people. The Elders say that Hopi movements came from the suggested reasons only as secondary causes. The primary cause in each instance was the keeping of the Covenant that laid out for them a pattern of life to follow. Its goal was to keep the world in balance and to prepare them to act in a special way when the Fourth Cycle of the world approached its end and the beginning of the Fifth Cycle was at hand. In support of this position, it has been discovered by the scientists that during some extended droughts the Hopi did not move at all, and with their dry farming techniques in fact survived remarkably well. Maasaw also warned the people that staying too long in some places might lead to an easy life that fostered corruption and an eventual breakdown of the society. The Hopi migration story given in Chapters 2 and 3 illuminates this warning.

Little evidence exists to prove that enemies drove the Hopi out of their stone dwellings. And, if factionalism is indeed a prime cause, then we must ask how, as researchers have also discovered, it happened that more often than not many of the Anasazi/Pueblo villages were occupied for impressively long periods of time. . . some of them for hundreds of years. It seems more likely that the Hopis moved when, in their kiva meetings, the leaders determined that Maasaw wanted them to. Of course, the command to "migrate" in itself implies continual movement.

Dan and the others describe the migration years and those at Oraibi and Hotevilla as a Maasaw-directed time of sinking down roots into Earth Mother, during which they progressively merged in an ever deeper and continuous way with She, Maasaw, and Muyingwa, the Hopi god of germination — all of which has helped to keep the world in balance and prepared them for their vital role in time — which, expressly, is this present, precarious moment.

MAASAW AND THE ELDERS

"The content of this message was determined by elders of the Hopi village, Hotevilla. It was selected and translated in the village over a period of twenty years at the request of former and present village leaders. The intention is to provide a document of and for Hopi people.

We do this to document our culture for future Hopi children and for all of our friends. Maybe two or three will understand why our elders have tried to keep the true Hopi culture alive and the

Hopi Nation free from foreign control. They have resisted foreign powers and their laws, because the law we follow never changes. We believe Hopi life is good. But since many of us have failed to listen to the wisdom of our leaders, our way of life as Hopi is about to disappear. Our late chief, Kachongva, requested that this story be told. At last we can fulfill his wish.

Here elders of our village tell what was handed down, including prophesies and warnings of coming events. They tell the history of the Hopi people, especially of Hotevilla village, how it was founded, and why we still resist the interference of the [White] people we call Bahanna. This influence is evident. Soon we will have destroyed our way of life. We speak our language less and less. We are forgetting the meaning of our ceremonies. Our world view has become so recklessly mixed with alien thinking from outside our culture that soon we won't even know who we are. We have failed to listen to the warnings and wisdom of our leaders. We have created our own misfortune and downfall. We are unhappy children. What kind of life awaits you? What will happen to the land? Your own experience will tell you whether the elders were right or wrong. Think about it!"

This brief opening statement is wracked with sadness. The number of warriors has dwindled year by year and is almost down to nothing. There is little strength or time left to fight or tell the story, and the desperate hope is that before it is too late someone, if even no more than a few, will listen and do something about the grave situation. You will find that this reference applies to the Hopi of Hotevilla, to the other Hopi villages, and to outsiders. Notice that in their minds the storytellers believe they share the blame for what has come to pass, possibly because it is their nature to feel they could have done more and fought harder against the outside influences that, however well-meaning, have inexorably altered and brought the ancient pattern of Hopi life to the brink of extinction. One by one the storytellers run down the list of Hopi losses, most of which they attribute to White intrusion, although some are charged to the Hopi themselves. Despite the fact that it is a shrine, the reality is that, like the rest of the world today, Hotevilla is no longer the harmonious place it once was. Changing times and continuing pressures have altered the people. Where economic matters are concerned, the differences are acute. Some young people are disillusioned and understandably want to exchange their seeds and digging sticks for the comforts and advantages of the modern age. Ceremonial life, with qualifications to be noted, still reigns, although the Elders and the mature leaders must again contest with young people who, like their peers everywhere, want to demonstrate their competence and independence. The concluding questions posed by the Elders reach beyond the Hopi Reservation to make known that we all share in the consequences and had better think about it! The entire statement centers in a line that will often be repeated herein — "the law we follow never changes." This law and the Covenant are the same.

I do not want to recklessly build suspense, but when my writing was well under way at the end of 1993, I could — lest we jump to incorrect conclusions and let the differences at Hotevilla influence our thoughts in a negative way — have said that we should remember that despite unrelenting efforts by the Tribal Council and Progressives to modernize the village and turn it away from the Elders, almost no modernization has taken place...and that despite the variety of differences that exist, allegiance to the ancient vows continued to reign. *I could have said that then, but today I tell you with more profound regret than anyone could imagine, I no longer can. For if what the Elders say about what is happening is true, the course of the world has as of this moment irrevocably turned toward its close.*

There are several reasons why this is so. Despite their heroic efforts, the ranks of the keepers of the Covenant have dangerously thinned. The once-stout rope has been abraded down to a tattered string. And now, those who have managed to keep the agreement with Maasaw are at further risk because of advanced age. All of them are considerably beyond the average Hopi lifespan and could depart at any moment. Regardless, some of those persons with ulterior motives would like, if they could, to speed that departure along. Not only are the Elders regularly criticized by Tribal Council members at meetings and in the Tribal press, a short while ago word came that the Tribal Council was sending out employees to look for elderly citizens "who might be better off if they were placed in homes where others could properly care for them." Since the Hopi have always respected and cared for their own family members of any age, the search was a thinly veiled attempt to threaten those who differ with the Council and those it represents. Other and worse pressures continue, and you will soon see what these are. And why do they? Because the Elders are a mirror which exposes them for what they really are and want, and the exposed are afraid that other people will see the unpleasant reflection too. The fact is that, in spite of everything they have attempted in their efforts to eliminate the Elders, this handful of gritty little servants of Maasaw remains an ever-present embarrassment to them.

None of this is imagined, and the chapters ahead will make this exceedingly clear. I saw the same thing happen with Sioux holy man Fools Crow and the tribal council that was in office at Pine Ridge in the mid-70s. He stood in their way because he was everything they should have been in life, and all of the residents of the Pine Ridge Reservation knew it. So the tribal chairman in particular did everything he could to get rid of Fools Crow, even to having his hired "goons," as they were commonly called, burn down the holy man's house. It didn't work, but only because most of the people rallied to Fools Crow's support. So, too, the Elders must be defended against their detractors, and we must rally to their side. For not only is what is being done to them wrong, if the time to react to the approaching end is short, the time for the Elders to work for us, speak to us, and teach us is shorter still.

Even the fact that the Council and others impede the fulfillment of the Covenant has not deterred the Elderly Elders from their chosen course. I have also learned from Dan that in the case of Hotevilla, where the Elders have fought valiantly (and successfully until this very moment when the situation is changing) to prevent utility trenches from being cut and utilities installed, there is an "unseen" and incredibly powerful factor to consider.

While this particular issue is addressed more fully in Chapter 9, a glimpse into history is necessary here. The village of Oraibi, referred to today as "Old Oraibi," and from which the founders of Hotevilla split in 1906, was known in ancient times as the "Mother Village," the anchor and fountain that gave sustenance to the other villages of Black Mesa. This form of identity is commonly known to Hopis and scientists, and it indicates that in the ancient Anasazi past there were many such mother villages which formed the center of larger communities. Chaco Canyon was undoubtedly one such place where a mother village existed. But what is not commonly known is that this Mother Village, Oraibi, has — as probably all mother villages did — a "marker" whose nature was ordained by Maasaw, and which was planted in the village and within the bosom of Mother Earth shortly after the time of its founding. Maasaw's instructions concerning it were that if this object was ever disturbed, it would bring about the spiritual end of the village, render it devoid of energy, and in truth seriously affect the existence of the entire world. Old Oraibi's marker was different in that it had the added power to affect the way the world would close its Fourth Cycle.

Only some Elders, and now I and three other trusted people, know that sometime after Hotevilla was founded, the power of the Oraibi object was transferred to it when the Kikmongwi, Yukiuma, together with a few other leaders, fashioned and secretly buried with appropriate ritual in the ground someplace in the village a similarly specially prepared and holy object, whose nature I will not divulge, but upon which the functioning of the village, its existence, and that of the world assuredly depends. Whoever cuts into this object for whatever reason will bring to pass the end of Hotevilla as it is constituted today, the shocking chastisement of the perpetrators, the shaping of the final stages of the Fourth Cycle of the world, and set in place the way the cycle will close. Note that there are qualifications regarding this that are discussed in the book. *Perhaps*, and you must believe me when I say I hope that is the operable adverb, this is precisely what is coming to pass at this very moment, April 16, 1994. The opponents may, as of now, have messed around too long and gone too far.

I do not want to include the documentation for this accusation here, but you will find it at the end of Chapter 9. For reasons that are explained there, the Tribal Council and the Bureau of Indian Affairs, with assistance from Progressive Hopis, have probably committed the one unpardonable sin that will bring to pass a fatal change for themselves, and also for the village of Hotevilla as a shrine and fortress. For a century, the Elders have desperately hoped this would not happen, but it has. And now, the ramifications for the world are grim. At least, that is what the Elders say Maasaw warned them would happen, and as you read the prophecies He handed down and compare them to what is taking place today you will be hard pressed to conclude otherwise. How concerned should we be? If all of this is nothing more than an elaborately concocted melodrama, it will pass away and be scornfully dismissed. If not, though…

Aptly named Thomas, the "doubter," I had this quality shattered more than once when I saw Fools Crow quietly work curing miracles that, had they witnessed them, would have brought awed legions to their knees. Yet this quality of mine has a dogged nature. In our scientifically oriented world of hard facts I still feel a little foolish as I tell you these things about the ending of this Fourth Cycle of the world and the beginning of the next. Yet I vividly remember that some of those who witnessed the explosion of the first atomic bomb uttered, after a moment of stunned silence, "My God, what have we wrought!" Their answer came shortly thereafter at Hiroshima and Nagasaki, and the world has quivered ever since. So, too, it may well be that something far greater than those bombs and their nuclear godchildren is taking place at a quiet little village in Hopi Land, and that its more than dreadful consequences will follow in the near future.

During all of these years when protests have been made about putting in utility lines, people who have not known about this buried object I just described have concluded that objections to utilities were based mainly upon their improperly invading and injuring Mother Earth, destroying shrines, or cutting across sacred ritual pathways. Those things are of consequence. But digging ditches is not really the main issue. The energies involved as the utilities go to work and what might be encountered and destroyed is the issue. We were told what this object is — but only a few of the Elders know where it is. Can you imagine their concern as the ditch-diggers move ever closer to the site. It is no wonder that they are in the kivas and praying fervently! Can the energies be affected? If so, to what degree? Has the object been struck? If not, how close to it are they?

Is this revelation simply an attempt to frighten opponents off? I am sure not, for it would bring temporary relief at best. When Dan related the story he was calm, resolute, and focused. He made no effort to convince us. The object is there, all right, and those who have wanted to see modern progress in Hotevilla will soon wish they had known about it and borne it in mind. Why has this dramatic secret not been revealed before? Information like this remains with the religious leaders. It is not bandied about. Hopi people respect that. But also because the Elders did not believe it was needed, and because ground in Hotevilla has previously been broken without serious incident. The Elders had no obligation to tell others about it — especially those who have scorned them. They have pleaded with people to keep the Covenant, and that in itself would have been enough. Covenant Keepers would not be putting in utilities. Dan says that in previous attempts the intruders have so far lucked out and not hit the object.

I don't, but the Hopis do, believe in witchcraft and curses. Can this word about the object be placed in the category of a curse that should be put to a test, or perhaps be relegated to the category of "old wives' tales"? Recently, after examining the famous yarns that claim a curse killed Lord Carrianvon and possibly 25 others who violated warnings and entered the Egyptian King Tut's tomb, an Italian doctor decided that a mold bacteria — not a curse — was the real culprit.

Something else in the ongoing case of Old Oraibi should be borne in mind, however. It is intriguing, is it not, to know that immediately after the fracturing of the village, the original "mother" began to decline while the new village of Hotevilla prospered. What do you suppose accounted for this amazing difference? Oraibi had as many residents, it was established and prominent, it retained its kivas and as many if not more ritual items than the Hotevilla people did, and it had the supposedly happy support of the affluent Bahannas who caused the division. Still, its power waned, it collapsed slowly and painfully in upon itself, and today Old Oraibi is but a hollow, moaning shell of its formerly royal being. Just so, as the utilities are turned on at Hotevilla, the power of the great rituals will be sapped like they were at Old Oraibi, and if the object itself is damaged or destroyed our only hope will be a circumscribed survival. The specter of this single ogre has completely changed the tone of our book from what it was when I started to write it.

Remember, though, that it has never been the nature of the Traditional Elders to give up. Issue No. 13 of the Elders' newsletter, *Techqua Ikachi*, "Land and Life," concludes with this short, symbolic tale entitled, "The Fearless Small Moves The Mountain." It is an appeal to every young person in the Hopi villages, and especially to those at Hotevilla, who should read it and think about its meaning as they decide what to do with their lives. When they have finished, surely some will look around them at the land and the houses of their villages, and, fully cognizant of the stakes involved, with a gleam in their eyes and taking a deep breath will vow fiercely to themselves that they will not let the Covenant and their great culture, for which others have worked so long and so hard, become extinct.

"A long time ago," the story goes, "there was once a village with many people high up on the mesa. For many years they lived happily, and multiplied to great numbers. Until one day, when a big old bear moved into their village. He moved there because he had eaten all the eatable sources everywhere he had been. He was always hungry, and wanted to eat only meat. At first they fed him by hunting, but soon the game became scarce and the hunters had great difficulty in bringing anything for him to eat. Thus this caused him to become hungrier and meaner. The people began to miss their children, who went out then never came back home. Then the older people began to decrease. Their village chief was worried and concerned. He became suspicious of the old mean bear, so he assigned his good warriors to get rid of him, but they too disappeared, until not too many were left. They were all afraid of the mean old bear. Concerned and worried, the chief would smoke and pray for help every day, just any help to get rid of the bear.

"And then one night while the chief smoked and prayed for help, he heard a tiny little voice saying: 'Oh, Chief, I can help you get rid of the bear.' The old chief looked around, but could not see anyone. 'Where are you, and who are you?' asked the chief. 'I'm here behind your ear, I'm a tick,' answered the tiny voice. But what can this little tick do to harm the bear, for he is as big as a mountain, thought the chief. 'But what can you do,' he asked, 'the mean bear is so big and powerful?' 'Just leave it to me,' answered the tick, who was out of its wits in its passion to get rid of the mean bear. Maybe this tiny tick had some power, so the chief gave permission. That very same night the tick reached the bear, climbed inside his ear, and began biting with all its might. The mean bear began to scratch his ears. Within three days he was going crazy. Finally, he ran down to the edge of the mesa and jumped down into the deep canyon, thus killing himself, his guts bursting open.

"The chief and the people were very happy, and repaid the tick by roasting the old mean bear for the tick to eat off of for the rest of his life, and so the people continued their humble way of life happily ever after."

The white mans greed + treatment of NATIVE American will come back to haunt him -

"This story," the writers add, "goes to show us that the smallest of us can move mountains with faith and courage. The story also shows us how every one of us can be brave and competent and beloved."

Quite probably, you have in considering the story noted that the people endured a great deal of misery from the bear before the tick came forward to solve their problem. You might wonder why they had to suffer this delay and about the eternal mystery of why bad things happen to good people — the "why me?" syndrome kicking in — which, of course, should cause anyone to also ask why good things also happen. You will notice, however, as we move ahead the Elders, are closer to termination, despair than ever before, yet still without bitterness in thought, word or deed. They know that faith is always tested, and that the testing has a purpose. It keeps our minds centered upon what really matters, upon our relationship with the One who alone can guarantee our survival.

SOURCES

Parts of this book appear in bold italics and begin with the words THE ELDERS. These were contributed by fifteen Hotevilla Hopis. Of them the major contributors by far are, using the names they are most commonly known by, Dan Evehema, who in 1994 is 101 years old, Titus Lamson, who is between 95 and 98, and Caroline Tawangyama, who is 88. Dan and Caroline are siblings. She was the first child born in Hotevilla after it was founded in 1906. Dan and Titus are brothers through their membership in the Men's Society, which was formed in 1910 when government officials took their fathers off to jail. Dan, Titus, and Paul Sewemanewa are the only living members of the original Society. The bold type sections provide our central story — an overview that organizes and supports the rest of the material.

In addition, Dan Katchongva (ca. 1865-1972), Sun Clan member and son of the famous Yukiuma who will receive prominent mention herein, told in 1970 his own personal story in the booklet previously referred to, *From the Beginning of Life to the Day of Purification: The Hopi Story*. Portions of this material are also set forth in bold italics and headed in each instance with the title KATCHONGVA. Dan Evehema, as well as the other Elders, was close to Katchongva, and because of the urgency feels that since it complements the Elders' account we should include his information in our book.

The third primary source we have drawn upon are the issues of the newsletter, TECHQUA IKACHI, "LAND AND LIFE." The way the village leaders who wrote them began the newsletters evokes wonderful images. After nearly 70 years of for the most part quietly enduring losses and abuses as they sought to preserve the traditional life and Covenant, in desperation they decided it was vital to make a bolder approach and go public with their views. Most of the things the Government, Tribal Council, and Progressives were doing had to be contested. Since numerous attempts had already been made by the Tribal Council to silence them, between 1975 and 1986 they met clandestinely 45 times at the remote Evehema ranch, where they built a ramada on top of its mesa and close to the ancestral stone homes. With the (surprising) aid of four government agency people — two White men who translated the Elders' statements into English and two agency White women who typed the information as it was received — the newsletters came one by one into being. While Tribal Council police and members sought without success over this eleven-year period to locate their meeting place, 44 issues plus one special bulletin were hammered out and published. Dan did not say where they were printed. David Monongye served as the editor, and they are an exceptionally rich kind of information that is not otherwise available in Hopi literature, since they tell us firsthand what the unyieldingly Traditional Hopi themselves have felt, thought, and done as this momentous last century has passed by. Those who read them with care will find rare insights into the true Hopi life cycle. Done primarily to communicate with other Hopis, the copies have been mislaid and are amazingly hard to find today. By diligent searching and by good fortune, however, Katherine, Dan, and Susie managed to recover for my use 42 of them and the bulletin. Only a few are dated, although the content allows us to fairly well pin most of them down. Issues range from four to six pages in length, are in an 8 1/2 x 11 inch format, and all are done on typewriters. The total number of pages, allowing for the two missing issues, is 190. Issue No. 1 was published in August 1975, "in," as they put it, "the traditional village of Hotevilla in the Hopi Independent nation…It represents the viewpoint of the village leaders David Monongye, Jack Pongyayesva, Paul Sewemanewa, Dan Evehema, and Amos Howesa," and it begins as follows:

THE TRADITIONAL VIEWPOINT
INTRODUCING TECHQUA IKACHI, LAND AND LIFE…

This newsletter is the first of its kind. It is a periodical which speaks from the viewpoint of the Traditional Hopi. It is printed for thinking people, especially those concerned about the future and fate of the Hopi in today's world and as an educational help for the young people of the Hopi and all other native nations.

We shall attempt to set straight the things that have been said and printed about the Traditional Hopi by people who oppose the Hopi way of life and are working hard to modify the ageless Hopi teachings. We hope this will bring more insight into Hopi life and help the children of today to understand their elders and not to hate them. We shall not attempt to indoctrinate, but merely to bring out the teachings that have enabled the Hopi to survive for centuries and organize their minds for full efficiency.

There are many questions that must be clarified. To most people this will all sound rather foolish. The Hopi do not force people to take everything literally. There are limits to everything, and very few things can be taken to extremes. But one may learn something from it… TECHQUA IKACHI, *Land and Life, is published by traditional leaders in the village of Hotevilla in the Hopi Independent Nation. Questions and comments are welcome. Since all people of the world are one in their traditional roots, we gladly consider articles and messages from other villages and nations on issues concerning the continuation of the traditional way of life and world peace. The shield symbol [used for a logo] means: "Together with all nations we protect both land and life and hold the world in balance." This publication is made possible through voluntary contributions. Send us your name and address for future editions. Subscriptions may become available at a later date.*

In his book, *Pages from Hopi History*, p. 219, Harry C. James mentions that since the leaders of Hotevilla have never closed their doors to outsiders, more than a few who came at different times between 1950 and 1975 have presumed to become spokespersons for the Traditionals, and in pleading various cases became, in the minds of reputable conservative groups, the authoritative voice, when in fact they were not.

In this book, however, that is not the circumstance. Here the highest and best informed of the Traditional Elders of Hotevilla speak directly for themselves. The voice in most of the book is first person, and its content describes that which has been both personally received and experienced. The charm of the Elders' own manner of presenting views is preserved for you, which certainly offers more than any restatement for literary purposes and quality than I — or any other writer for that matter — could manage.

Putting these sources together provides us with a rare document, a textbook account in fact, of how one of the greatest and the last of the native cultures in America has been systematically extinguished. In these pages we watch it happen, and then, besides seeking to cope with what will come of it, we will one day ask ourselves what might have been had our Government handled the Traditional Hopis differently.

For the most part, the newsletters deal with situations that were current at the time written, and in any given issue several topics might be treated without regard to sequential presentation. There is, therefore, no helpful order. The Elders simply addressed whatever circumstance was going on or whomever their target might be — groups, children, or individual adults — saying with remarkable candor and insight whatever they thought was necessary to meet the emergency of the moment or the day. It is clear that the stated information was what was being routinely discussed over longer periods of time in the kivas and homes, and therefore represents the cultural thoughts and climate of the Traditionals as a whole. As such, I pass it along pretty much as the Elders themselves put it. There were more than a few times, when for any one of a dozen reasons — distractions, weather, differences of opinion as to how to state something, etc. — as they sat up there on the mesa top composing an article, it came out as a garbled and seemingly hastily contrived statement, one not worked over to assure clarity. It may be there were also moments when the staff said, in effect, let's quit fussing with it and let it go as is. Readers will understand that. Some fault may also lie with the interpreters and stenographers, who, as we can easily understand, had the difficult and often tiresome job of seeking to meld statements together that did not at first make sense. But they kept the secret and they helped. That is what matters. We can forgive them for now and then just giving up and allowing a passage to float on its own.

In deciding what I should do with the newsletters, my choices were to let the passages stand, delete what was difficult to comprehend, or edit them. I changed some of the punctuation and deleted what did not seem pertinent to the book. Some of the material did not need any editing at all. I edited the rest and reassembled the material in categories for greater effectiveness and easier reading. Dan approved of this and is confident that the final version we have here is what it ought to be. You will encounter different spellings for Maasaw and some other Hopi words, but rather than change the different authors' usage I have left their spelling as it is. In all of these instances the person, place, or object referred to will still be obvious.

You will notice that many of the letters are marked by sadness. This is understandable. The authors were more often than not frustrated, tired, and anxious. Writing was not something they were good at or really wanted to do, and they were continually fighting tremendous odds — the Agency, Tribal Council, schools, financial needs, and the unhappy problem of having to persuade people who should have needed no persuading. Always, too, there was the more pleasant mandate to fulfill the ceremonial cycle, to till their fields, and to be with their families and friends.

Because there are so many parts to be woven together, I have adopted a legend to help you know who is saying what in the different chapters. Each article and illustration taken from one of the *Techqua Ikachi* newsletters is introduced with the capital letters TI followed by a dash. Material beginning with the letters TEM followed by a dash is my personal comment, guided by my consultations with Dan. The letters DE followed by a dash are Dan's own statements, sometimes edited for clarity, other times not. Any material that does not begin with a prefix has its author identified.

David Monongye has put on the cloud mask. I did not get to meet him, but I wish I had. Katherine Cheshire is his adopted daughter. Dan Evehema is now the senior religious statesman of Hotevilla, and he has provided me with both inspiration and most of the material needed to flesh out our account. Born on an unknown day in the village of Oraibi in 1893, at 101 years of age Dan stands today only a shade over five feet tall and may weigh a hundred pounds. Yet in every way he is a giant of a man. He is alert enough to follow and to participate in any conversation, sharp and energetic enough to function as the highest of the kiva Fathers, and in 1993 was chosen by the members of his kiva to lead the important Soyal and Niman ceremonies at Hotevilla. He has a hearty appetite, makes his way about unaided, and still lives at and farms his ancestral lands. He is up at sunrise for his daily prayers and can stay up as late as is necessary. He shares in every aspect of Hopi life in the village and at his home. His voice is strong. He speaks fluent Hopi, surprisingly good English, and can read English. He is a charismatic, respected, and established leader, one of a handful who can still say they have remained throughout their lives totally faithful to the Covenant made with Maasaw.

His reddish-brown face and his hands are as rugged as the mesa that borders his home, and his head is topped by a mantle of long silver hair so soft the desert winds whip it constantly into the wildest of patterns. His black eyes have softened somewhat. They are not so penetrating as they once were — although they lock tightly onto yours when he engages you in conversation, and they sparkle with joy when he laughs. He at times appears to doze off when a group conversation is going on, yet you always find out later that he has missed very little. A few years ago, cataracts rendered him blind. Modern surgery and eyeglasses freed him of that misfortune to once again be a full partner in the life and land he loves. Above all, the restored vision has enabled him to continue his Herculean battle. He deeply appreciates this Bahanna contribution to his well-being and wishes everyone to know that when he and the other Elders chastise Bahannas in their public statements, their reference is to those who have without right or justification transformed and ravaged the Hopi culture. Outside this, his warm feelings for Bahanna friends is readily apparent to all who know him.

White man

His mother's name was Honvenka, and his father was Kootsvayoema. They did not have English names, and he does not know the years they died...something that is not surprising once you learn that the Hopi do not keep calendars of years and by custom prefer not to mention the dead by name. He had three brothers, two of whom died and one who is living, and four sisters, two of whom died and two who are living. He was married, and his wife has also gone to live in the Underworld. They had no children. While his parents were alive, the family dwelt in a mesa-top stone house whose ruins are still standing. After a sister and a brother married, stone houses were also built for them and their spouses on the sloping side of the mesa, close to and just below the main house. Those ruins are present too. "The family," Dan says, "always lived here, even before the Oraibi split in 1906; it was the ranch house where our crops were, and we could see Navajo enemies from up on top when they came to steal from us." Photographs of one of these traditional houses, which are surprisingly small and have six-foot ceilings, are included in this chapter. Dan's present home at the foot of this same mesa is illustrated in Chapter 11.

In 1907, for refusing to accept the White man's ways and to send his children to the Government school, Dan's father, along with other Hopi men, was taken away by soldiers and imprisoned "for a long time" at Keams Canyon for the first of what ultimately would be four occasions. At this same time, Dan and his brothers and sisters — as well as all other Hopi children of school age — were forced to attend schools at this and other locations. During his three years at the Agency site, Dan often saw his own father and the other Hopi men walking about in chains. After this initial schooling, Dan returned home, and then was forced to spend another three years at a school in Phoenix. At these schools, he was not allowed to speak the Hopi language, was lectured to about the advantages of the White world and the disadvantages of being a Hopi, learned to read and write a limited amount of English, was introduced to simple mathematics, and was required to listen to Bible stories, memorize the Ten Commandments, and sing Christian hymns. After he returned home to stay, he worked at the family ranch planting corn and other vegetables and herding sheep. His life has been spent as a farmer and rancher, although all he does today is farming. His ranch is located about 12 miles from Hotevilla village and borders a poorly graded dirt road that runs east from Highway 264 as it passes Kykotsmovi. He states with some satisfaction that he has never worked for the government and that he is happier here [at the ranch] today than ever in his life. Susie Lomatska, his sister's daughter, takes care of him, and is a staunch Traditional. She is a joy to know and has helped enormously with the preparation of our book.

All of the Elders and the rest of the traditionalists at Hotevilla along with those at other Hopi villages are remarkable people, but neither Dan nor they would tell you they think they are. Other than when they are joking, it is not the Hopi way to brag or to put oneself forward. Whatever is done by anyone is simply an expected part of the fabric of Hopi life and not to be boasted about…another reason why the amazing message of Hotevilla and the Covenant has a ring of resounding truth. Were the same information to come from someone who seeks status or personal gain it would immediately be suspect and taken with the proverbial grain of salt.

In a statement made in a *Land and Life* issue entitled "About Ourselves," we are given a sense of what the Elders are really like: "Greetings," they say, "Thank you for your patience, we apologize for the delay of our publication and wish to explain the delay to our readers…We are experiencing great strain from the pressures of outside forces, feeling discouraged and weary while we carry out our sacred duties. Like many others, we depend on outside help and encouragement which gives us the strength to continue. We find that we cannot communicate without funds and technology, and we would like to thank all you good people who have given us your helping hands. In addition to the communications we do many other things which are just as important. We must continue our ceremonials and tend our fields. We face difficulties when it comes to writing, handicapped by illiteracy and a lack of knowledge of grammar. Therefore our message does not reach you as fast as we would like it to…In spite of all the obstacles we are satisfied that we are able to, in a small way, inform the outside world with our message...We do not compare with other publications. Consider that we are in a remote area and barely manage to hang on...We hope that with your help 'Techqua Ikachi' (Land and Life) will survive and continue to bring the traditional Hopi message to the outside world. We thank you."

The fifteen or so mature people who stand solidly with the Elderly Elders are ready to go on. There may be more. Because it is not the Hopi way to ask people to declare themselves, no one can know for certain how many, and discussions about this do not occur — even in the kivas. Manuel Hoyungowa has taken his position. You will appreciate Dan's comments regarding him given in Chapter 10. Other stalwarts include Martin Gashweseoma, Thomas Banyacya and Emery Holmes. Susie is remarkably well informed and strong. Her children are being raised in the old ways. But the Elders are praying that all of the younger people at Hotevilla will think long and hard about this and hopefully decide not to exchange their priceless heritage and opportunity for any Covenant-damaging thing the outside world has to offer. Surely, as the previously mentioned Homegoing Dance indicates, there are some who in considering it have already within themselves stepped forward and picked up the faded and frayed but more precious than ever mantle of the Covenant. Our hope must be that a continuing succession will do the same. The rest of us cannot, for only they by birthright can.

Beyond this, the Elders remind their descendants that while their way of life may lack the Bahannas' material goods, it does offer independence, self-sufficiency, and identity. People who adhere to Tradition know who they are and have a sense of solidity and belonging. On the other hand, what is happening to the Hopi now, let alone what is coming, clearly shows that where choice is concerned the alternative is to become completely dependent, to be indebted without the ability to pay, and to drift away from the villages and into a vast sea of Bahannas. Dan also cautions that once a Hopi has fallen entirely off the balance bar that must be walked, this person can never get entirely back on it. This extends to all Hopis who participate in the ceremonies and dances in any of the villages, for only those with "one heart," and not the "two hearted," can fully achieve what the rituals offer to the Hopi and can accomplish for humankind.

In talking with Dan, he did not seem to believe there are at present any besides the group at Hotevilla that are holding fast to the Covenant. There are indications that this is not true. I was given recently copies of two issues of a newsletter that indicate otherwise and offer additional hope. They are written by a group of young Hopis, who for a time at least were headquartered in Flagstaff. They called themselves "The Hopi Epicenter for International Outreach," and although they represented at least certain of the religious leaders of Mishongnovi and Shungopovi, everything they wrote was rooted in the Hotevilla prophetic message. They even used the shield symbol the Elders did for their *Land and Life* newsletter. The Epicenter staff wrote with uncommon intelligence and clarity, and provided excellent insights into both the evolution of and current activities, problems, and needs of the Hopi. An interesting statistic cited in their initial issue, published in the spring of 1987, is that according to Hopi leaders, "20% of the Hopi are Traditionals, 25% are staunch progressives, while the remaining 55% vacillate between the two, choosing to take the best from both worlds." The numbers of once fully Traditional Hopi of old have eroded greatly. It is illuminating to see how this has happened.

I hoped the Epicenter newsletters would continue, but with regret must tell you that the last time I was in Flagstaff I looked through the telephone directory and found no listing for them. It may be they relocated elsewhere, but it appears they did not survive the inevitable reactions sure to come from the Tribal Council and others.

There is other positive news to place alongside the lamentable negatives. Some of the aggressive things the Tribal Council and Government are doing in Hopi Land are getting everyone's attention, stirring them up, and making them wonder whether the Elders haven't been right all along. Some are ready to rethink the situation and join the Elders. You will be pleased by the reactions of some religious leaders at Shongopovi. Besides this, after viewing the century-long transformation of Hopi Land, I found to my surprise that while Dan is a biting realist, he in several regards remains optimistic. One of these is that he holds fast to the escape valve found in Maasaw's option for choice that can lead to change. Directions can be altered, the pace of time can be affected, and although its kind must be defined, there is still hope for the Hopi — and us. In one of our discussions, Dan pointed out that shortly after the first White missionaries came to the villages, people were appalled at what was happening, and like Yukiuma did in 1906 at Oraibi, drew a line in the sand. What followed was a passionate strengthening of the ancient religious cycle. Just so, Dan thinks that in the near future there will be another reaction and girding up of the Traditional life. There is further precedence for this. At least twice during this century when incidents have jeopardized the existence of the ceremonial cycle, the Hopi have rallied and made their practices stronger. Is this important to the rest of the world? Indeed it is. Our fates are linked to those of the True Hopi, and as the deterioration of the world progresses, we outsiders will learn to appreciate in the profoundest of ways any resurgence of Hopi Traditional life. This book will tell you in detail why this is so.

Thus Dan tells us that in the midst of chaos, there is hope for the Hopis, and therefore for us. Be glad that he does. Somewhere along in the book you will find yourself asking whether we really do have hope, and if so, where it lies. Any suggestion of overpopulation, environmental demise, or a holocaust or apocalypse is frightening. It colors everything in an unpleasant way, and, wanting desperately to remain optimistic, we react and turn away. I have just read that interest in environmental magazines is waning. Most of us want to bury our heads in the sand and not listen. It's easier, it's cheaper, and it's less stressful. Sometimes it works. In this case it won't. In the end it will be hard, far more costly, and infinitely stressful. Even those who do listen wrestle uneasily with feelings about trying to exist in a confined, threatening, or out-of-control environment and world scene. They gingerly address the question of how to cope with overwhelming world events, and wonder whether there actually is anything to look forward to.

Since the Hopi prophecies are similar in some ways to those of many other prophets, at first they will not seem helpful here. But they must be read carefully — looking between the lines as well as at them — for they are significantly different in how they can work out. They are apocalyptic, but it is an apocalypse with a shining and realistic confidence nestled in its core. The Traditional Hopi have worked to assure this truth more than any other since the day they first settled down in Hopi Land. They haven't fought to watch it end, they've fought to keep it going. They tell us what is wrong, but they also show us what is right and the way out. Survival is the very essence of everything the Elders have to say. Their work, their ritual, their resistance — everything they have done and want to continue doing has their continued existence and that of the whole world in mind.

It is common for prophets to speak of the "end" of the world. Yet you have probably noticed that in connection with Hopi prophecy I use instead the adverbs "close" and "closing." My reason for doing this is a good one, for where hope is concerned the difference is enormous. While the Elders themselves use the term "end" in their articulation of prophecy, what they speak about is in no wise terminal. Notice also that in one sense the story you are about to read ends here. When the Elderly Elders are gone, there will be no one left who can tell us these things from personal experience.

But to understand fully this exalted story of the Covenant and its ramifications, we must begin even before the beginning, at a time when, according to the ancient myths, the ancestors of the peoples of the Americas — including those who became the Hopi — still lived in the Underworld. We meet them there, follow them as they emerge from the Underworld onto the surface of the earth and encounter Maasaw, and then migrate for untold centuries as they look for him again.

Our focus, naturally, will be upon history as Dan and the others present it. But we can only see it materialize as we view certain data gathered by scientists. This illuminates the Hopi claims in general, and specifically those of the people of Oraibi and Hotevilla. Once we know who the Hopi are, have in hand an overview of their impressive accomplishments, endurance, and loyalty, and then understand what was going on as they migrated and settled down in Hopi Land, we are prepared to move on and deal with the concerns of today and tomorrow.

Thomas E. Mails, Canyon Lake, California, April 1994

This Land and Life shield symbol means:

"Together with all nations we protect both land and life and hold the world in balance."

TI— The Shield symbol used as the logo for the Elders' newsletter

The authors

TI— *He who knows not, and knows not that he knows not, is a fool — shun him.*

He who knows not, and knows that he knows not, is a child — teach him.

He who knows, and knows not that he knows is asleep — wake him.

He who knows, and knows that he knows is wise — follow him.

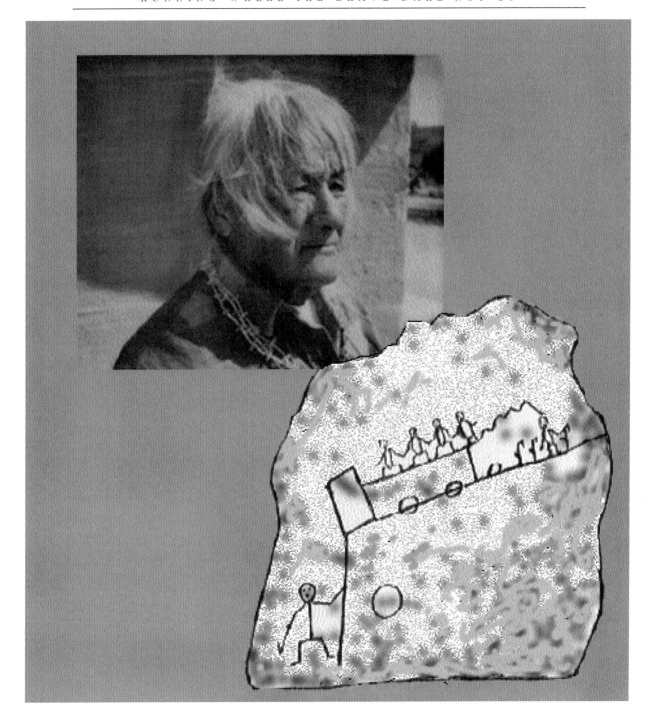

DAN EVEHEMA AND THE PROPHECY ROCK

"I have nothing here. My life is simple. All I have is my planting stick and my seeds. If you are willing to live as I do, and follow my instructions, the life plan I shall give you, you may live here with me and take care of the land. Then you shall have a long, happy and peaceful life. (Maasaw)"

The interior and exterior of the ancient Evehema family residence.

The farming plots are in the distance and at the foot of the mesa.

CHAPTER 2

THE EMERGENCE

Harold Kuebler, an astute Doubleday senior editor who became a cherished friend, once said to me when he found me arguing a point in one of my books, "Just state the evidence, and let readers make up their own minds." It was a valuable lesson that has served me well over the course of a dozen books, and for the most part the Elders and Dan Katchongva present their own case, as from this point forward we examine in greater depth their statements regarding the Sacred Covenant and its incredible consequences. It is here, naturally, that the "rub" of the book sets in most strongly, for there is bound to be a general hesitation to accept the idea that, if indeed the earth and we creatures who inhabit it are in such peril as the Elders and scientists suggest, God would place our salvation in the hands of such a remote and simple place as Hotevilla. Of course, as we see the history of the Hopi unfold, we will find they have been an extremely talented, profoundly spiritual and capable people. We will also see that Hotevilla is not actually a simple place, and that its religious practices are as complex as those of any people in history. Still, we are faced with a dilemma: We must either accept that someone in the outside world can deliver us from our mushrooming problems, do nothing, or entrust ourselves to the Elders.

In considering this, I have asked myself countless questions that others will ask, and for each of them I have received answers and drawn what for me are positive conclusions. For example, it is fair to ask whether any of the Covenant's earliest details can be proven. In the scientific sense, of course not. What we are dealing with is a matter of faith. Yet we cannot ignore the fact that the Elders' accounts are strongly supported by history. I also know that people can read into accounts what they wish to see and doctor them accordingly. But when the predicted things continue to happen, the evidence weighs more heavily than ever in the storytellers' favor. If the argument is advanced that many of the warnings and prophecies are so loosely stated they could apply to any number of instances, their fulfillment compensates for this by sharpening, clarifying, and crystallizing them permanently in time and place. Moreover, we must always bear in mind that most of the prophecies are kinds whose fulfillments take place over a period of time. It is not single events tied to a day or hour that the prophecies are pointing to.

Those who wish to detract from the prophecies and warnings might hope they can play upon the idea that they are being proclaimed after the fact. But oral tradition, the migration patterns, and the site markings negate this completely as they testify eloquently to a prehistoric origin. We also know that oral tradition demands truth. To violate this rule is to lose any power associated with whatever is revealed. Under such circumstances, what would anyone gain by concocting a fabrication?

We can also weigh the seemingly mythical references of the Elders and Katchongva by seeing how they have played out in the lives of the people. If someone does continuously and conscientiously over an amazingly long period of time exactly what they say they were told to do, it lends stronger and stronger credence to the fact of the original commands and their source.

Finally, anyone who wants greater assurance regarding the Elders' and Katchongva's testimonies about the end time can easily have it. Considering what is predicted, we do not want to believe it, do we? In the United States and many other places in the world extreme things are happening as nature lashes us in countless ways, but most of the time beauty still abounds, and folks are going on with life in the blasé belief that nothing is going to happen that will derail them in any grievous or permanent way. But all they need do is watch and wait. If Princeton Professor Henry W Kendall (who is referred to in Chapter 11), environmentalists in general, or the Hopi leaders are bluffing, mistaken, or fabricating information, then nothing will come of it and life will go on much as it has before. If, on the other hand, what they have to say is true, then the evidences will all too soon be undeniable and everywhere present.

THE ELDERS

We had a beautiful life in a world below this one, but we became careless and spoiled it. The wisest knew of the guardian of this world, Maasaw, who lived at Oraibi. They sent a bird to him as a messenger to ask permission for us to come up into his world. He said we could come if we were willing to live humbly as he does.

Our elders have told this story through the ages: "We came from the underworld, where corruption made life impossible. We failed to follow our original law. Selfish desires guided our actions. We lost our respect for women and our leaders. All life was thrown off balance.

"The few remaining wise people came together and decided to leave their corrupted world. They had heard someone walking up above. Their messenger learned that this was Maasaw, whom he asked whether we could come. Maasaw answered, 'They may come, but I live simply. All I have is my planting stick and seeds. If they are willing to live as I do, they are welcome here.' We climbed up through a reed, and emerged at the bottom of the Grand Canyon. Through the Sipapuni we came onto this earth.

"Here, Maasaw was waiting for us. To test our wisdom and truthfulness, he put before our leaders several ears of corn, then he asked them each to choose one. Most of them greedily took the longest ears of corn. Only a short one was left for the leader who waited to choose last. He and his people were given the name 'Hopi.' Then Massaw instructed us to migrate in all directions and build houses. He said, 'Don't stay, only long enough to grow and store food for the journey ahead. Break your pottery when you leave. Leave markings on the rocks as your land claim. Build sacred shrines. In this way, the earth will receive spiritual roots and you will hold the land together in balance. All this will keep you aware of the true law.'"

TEM— Since Katchongva has gone into considerable detail regarding the Beginning and the Emergence of the Hopi people, the Elders give only the briefest version of the account. They emphasize those things that provide the necessary groundwork for dealing with what has happened since Bahanna laid siege to the Hopi lifeway. The Elders want to establish the longevity of the Hopi, the Covenant, and the preexistence of Maasaw at a place named Oraibi.

Writers spell Maasaw in several different ways. Masau'u is a common usage. Maasaw is how the Elders write it and how it is pronounced. Katchongva spells it Maasauu. Except for his account, I use Maasaw throughout the book. You have seen that Maasaw was already present when the first people emerged from the underworld onto the North American upper world, and that he is the Guardian, or overseer, for the Creator, who remains the true owner. It is said that due to a tragic accident Maasaw's features are grotesque and that he does not reveal them to anyone, although he wears a mask that displays his true appearance. However forbidding he looks, Maasaw is the most versatile of the Hopi deities, for he fills many roles. He is the god of fire and death, he is master of the underworld of spirits, and as he moves around he resides in different rock shrines

that are near each of the Hopi villages. He is an uneasy nightwalker who carries a firebrand and watches over the people while they sleep. I mentioned previously that he also makes daytime appearances.

The nature of people in the underworld becomes fixed when we see their "fallen" side as they spoil a beautiful existence. This human characteristic is a constant that will surface frequently throughout history, and we should not be surprised when it does. Among the people are wise individuals who know there is a better way to live, and who do not wish to be corrupted. So they petition Maasaw to let them and their few remaining followers escape. Immediately the Elders stress that the basis for acceptance is a willingness to live humbly, as Maasaw himself does. This is a key and abiding provision of the Covenant. There is no projected time at which any other way of life will be acceptable, for pride and greed lead inevitably to "corruption." The people violated this original law. We will see the specific behavior that is cited repeating itself in history among the Hopi and in our outside world. "Selfish desires guided our actions," the Elders say. "We lost our respect for women and our leaders. All life was thrown off balance." As we continue on with the statements of the Elders and Katchongva, we will return to these behavioral patterns. It will help us understand what the Elders mean when they use the word "balance," and why losing it "throws off all life."

Maasaw was "walking up above." He is a worrier and a pacer; constant motion is his nature. He is not a remote deity, he is always around and in the center of things. At this point, his instructions clarify part of what it means to live humbly. They call for a simple life that centers in planting and harvesting done by the most rudimentary means. It is a good enough way for Maasaw, and it will be good enough for his true followers.

The people "climbed up through a reed." Katchongva will enlarge upon this concept and clarify its purpose. The place of emergence is established as the Grand Canyon, and more narrowly defined as the "Sipapuni," which is a small hole in the ground. The Hopi have pinned this site down, and visit it annually. A replica of this opening is made in the floor of every kiva used by the Hopi for religious purposes, and is accepted as a pipeline through which direct communication may be carried out with those who have departed and live in the underworld. When you die, your spirit returns to the Underworld through the emergence Sipapuni.

The Elders describe how Maasaw was waiting for the people and ready to test their wisdom and truthfulness by having them choose between varying lengths of corn ears. Those gathered there include more than one race, and more than the wise leaders and their few followers are among them. We see that their fallen nature has emerged with them. They are still greedy. The last to choose is the least greedy, although the only ear left for him is the short one. His absolution comes only in his willingness to be the last to choose. For this humble decision and meek demeanor he and his followers are given the name "Hopi." Katchongva will define the full meaning of the tribal name for us, and we will see that it means far more than "peaceful," which is the usual cryptic definition assigned to it.

The Elders wisely do not assign dates for the emergence and this first meeting with Maasaw. Attempting to pin it down would lead to fruitless arguments that have nothing to do with the Covenant. We are not, however, left with an entirely abstract concept, since a long period of verifiable testing and preparation is set into motion. The people are to migrate in all directions and to build houses. But they must not stay in any one place. Notice that they are to continue moving because of the Covenant, and not because of drought, enemies, factionalism, or other reasons. They are to keep journeying, and to break their pottery when they leave. Why? I would like to think it was because it would have foiled pot hunters or made traveling easier, but I suspect it was to cut any ties with the place where they had been living. They did not, in any case, break it all, which is fortunate in that it has enabled us to learn about their magnificent craftsmanship, but unfortunate where looters are concerned. They were also to leave markings on the rocks as land claims, and they certainly did this abundantly. Sadly, only some of the inscriptions can be interpreted, and many remain mysteries. The matter of land claims and the proper understanding of the subject will assume considerable importance as we move into historic times. The journeying people were also to build sacred shrines. The inclusion of this practice establishes the spiritual base of the people as existing at an early date, and we will examine the matter and nature of Hopi shrines in future chapters.

And what will the migrations accomplish? According to the Elders, three things: The earth will receive spiritual roots, the land will be held together in balance and harmony, and all of this will keep the people aware of the true law, which is to keep the Covenant — whose full breadth we have thus far in the book only begun to picture and understand. This understanding is not necessary for the Creator and Maasaw, who remain current with the people as time progresses. But it is for the people themselves. They have been given an assignment that is far greater than they know. Maasaw intends to continually test, and thereby to reinforce, their will to endure. They need to discover for themselves what stuff they are made of…whether and how well they will stand up to the testing, and they also need to discover the special rewards that come to those who measure up to the task. With this process will come self-esteem and confidence, and the Creator's purposes will be accomplished.

KATCHONGVA...
THE BEGINNING OF LIFE

Somewhere down in the underworld we were created by the Great Spirit, the Creator. We were created first one, then two, then three. We were created equal, of oneness, living in a spiritual way, where the life is everlasting. We were happy and at peace with our fellow men. All things were plentiful, provided by our Mother Earth upon which we were placed. We did not need to plant or work to get food. Illness and troubles were unknown. For many years we lived happily and increased to great numbers.

When the Great Spirit created us, he also gave us instructions or laws to live by. We promised to live by his laws so that we would remain peaceful, using them as a guideline for living happily upon that land where he created and placed us. But from the beginning he warned us that we must not be tempted by certain things by which we might lose this perfect way of life.

Of course we had advantage of many good things in this life, so by and by we broke the Creator's command by doing what he told us not to do. So he punished us by making us as we are now, with both soul and body. He said, "From now on you will have to go on your own. You will get sick, and the length of your life will be limited."

He made our bodies of two principles, good and evil. The left side is good, for it contains the heart. The right side is evil, for it has no heart. The left side is awkward but wise. The right side is clever and strong, but it lacks wisdom. There would be a constant struggle between the two sides, and by our actions we would have to decide which was stronger, the evil or the good.

We lived in good ways for many years, but eventually evil proved to be stronger. Some of the people forgot or ignored the Great Spirit's laws and once again began to do things that went against his instructions. They became materialistic, inventing many things for their own gain and not sharing things as they had in the past. This resulted in a great division, for some still wanted to follow the original instructions and live simply.

The inventive ones, clever but lacking wisdom, made many destructive things by which their lives were disrupted, and which threatened to destroy all the people. Many of the things we see today are known to have existed at that time. Finally immorality flourished. The life of the people became corrupted with social and sexual license, which swiftly involved the Kikmongwi's wife and daughters, who rarely came home to take care of their household duties. Not only the Kikmongwi but also the high religious leaders were having the same problem. Soon the leaders and others with good hearts were worried that the life of the people was getting out of control.

The Kikmongwi gathered the high priests. They smoked and prayed for guidance toward a way to solve the corruption. Many times they gathered, until finally someone suggested that they move, find a new place, and start a new life.

EMERGENCE INTO THE PRESENT WORLD

Now they had often heard certain thumping sounds coming from above, so they knew that someone might be living there. It was decided that this must be investigated. I will describe this briefly, for the whole story would take much space.

Being gifted with wisdom, they created birds for this purpose.

I will name three. Two which are known for their strength and swiftness are the kisa [hawk] and the pavowkaya [swallow]. The third was a moochnee [related to the mockingbird]. His flight is awkward, but he is known to be wise. They were each created at separate times by magic songs, tobacco smoke and prayers, from dirt and saliva, which was covered by a white cape [ova]. Each was welcomed respectfully and given instructions for his mission, should he succeed.

The first two failed to reach the top side of the sky, but the third one, moochnee, came through the opening into this world.

The new world was beautiful. The earth was green and in bloom. The bird observed all his instructions. His sense of wisdom guided him to the being he was instructed to seek. When he found him it was high noon, for the being, Maasauu, the Great Spirit, was preparing his noonday meal. Ears of corn lay beside the fire. He flew down and lit on top of his kisi [shady house] and sounded his arrival. Maasauu was not surprised by the visitor, for by his wisdom and sense of smell he already knew someone was coming. Respectfully he welcomed him and invited him to sit down. The interview was brief and to the point. "Why are you here? Could it

be important?" "Yes," said Moochnee, "I was sent here by the underworld people. They wish to come to your land and live with you, for their ways have become corrupted. With your permission they wish to move here with you and start a new life. This is why I have come." Maasauu *replied bluntly, but with respect, "They may come."*

With this message the bird returned to the underworld. While he was gone the Kikmongwi and the leaders had continued to pray and wait for his successful return. Upon his return with

the good news of the new world and Maasauu's permission for them to come, they were overjoyed.

Now the question was how they were to get to the top, so again they smoked and prayed for guidance. At last they agreed to plant a tree that would grow to the top and serve as a pathway. They planted the seed of a shalavee [spruce tree], then they prayed and sang magic songs. The tree grew and grew until it reached the sky, but its branches were so soft and so many that it bent under the heavy earth pressure from the top, so it did not pierce the sky. They planted another seed, this one to be a louqu [pine]. It grew as they sang their magic songs. This tree was stout and strong. "Surely this one will go through," they thought. But it was unsuccessful, for its branches also bent upon contact with the solid object. Again they planted a seed. This time it was a lgakave [reed]. Since it had a pointed end it pierced the sky up into the new world.

Meanwhile all of this had been kept secret. Only proper

righteous and one-hearted people were informed of the plans to leave the corrupt world. They were prepared to move out, so as soon as they knew it was successful they started to come up on the inside of the plant, resting between the joints as they worked their way up to the opening.

When they got to this world, everything was beautiful and peaceful. The land was virgin, unmolested. They were very happy. They sang and danced with joy, but their joy was short-lived, for that night the chief's daughter died suddenly. Everyone was sad and worried. People looked at one another suspiciously. An evil spell had been enacted. This caused great concern that a witch or two-hearted person might be among them.

Now the Kikmongwi had great power, which he must use to settle the concerns of his people. He made a small ball out of cornmeal, which he tossed up above the group of people. The one upon whose head it landed would be the guilty one. It landed upon the head of a girl. A quick decision was made to throw her back through the opening into the underworld. The wickedness must be gotten rid of, for they wished to live peacefully in this new land. But the witch girl cried out for mercy, telling them that on their long journey they would face many obstacles and dangers of every description, and that her services would become useful, for she had power to fight evil. She invited the Kikmongwi to look back down into the underworld. He looked and saw his child playing happily with the other children in the underworld, where upon death we will all return. The witch girl was spared, but they left her there alone, perhaps hoping that she would perish by some unknown cause.

THE FIRST MEETING WITH THE GREAT SPIRIT IN THIS WORLD
It was here that the Great Spirit first appeared to them on this earth, to give them the instructions by which they were to live and travel. They divided into groups, each with its selected leader. Before them he laid ears of corn of various lengths.

They were each instructed to pick one ear of corn to take with them on their journey, for their subsistence and their livelihood. One by one they greedily picked out the longest and most perfect long ears until only the shortest was left. They did not realize that this was a test of wisdom. The shortest ear was picked by the humblest leader. Then the Great Spirit gave them their names and the languages by which they would be recognized. The last picker of short corn was named HOPI.

HOPI means not only to be peaceful, but to obey and have faith in the instructions of the Great Spirit, and not to distort any of his teachings for influence or power, or in any way to corrupt the Hopi way of life. Otherwise the name will be taken away.

He then gave them instructions according to which they were to migrate for a certain purpose to the four corners of the new land, leaving many footprints, rock writings, and ruins, for in time many would forget that they were all one, united by a single purpose in coming up through the reed. Now that we were on top we were each to follow our own leaders, but so long as we did not forget the instructions of the Great Spirit we would be able to survive. We were now bound by a vow to live by these instructions and to complete our pattern of migration. Massauu told us that whoever would be the first to find him would be the leader of those who were to follow, then he disappeared.

AN ACT OF PROPHETIC CONSEQUENCE

We migrated for many years to every corner of this continent, marking our claim as we traveled, as these markings clearly testify up to the present day. On our way we stopped for rest near the great river now known as the Colorado. We had traveled far and gained a great deal of knowledge, not forgetting our instructions. The group leader was of the Bow Clan, a great chief with wisdom. But it was here that this great chief disappeared into the dark night. After putting his family to sleep he left in search of the Earth Center, where clever, ingenious people from all nations meet to plan the future. By some means he found the place and was welcomed with respect. It was a beautiful place with all manner of good things. Good food was laid before him by most beautiful girls. It was all very tempting.

Until today we did not know the significance of this action. It had to do with the future. By this action he caused a change to occur in the pattern of life as we near the end of the life cycle of this world, such that many of us would seek the materialistic world, trying to enjoy all the good things it has to offer before destroying ourselves.

Sacred Instructions (handwritten, top right margin)

Those gifted with the knowledge of the sacred instructions will then live very cautiously, for they will remember and have faith in these instructions, and it will be on their shoulders that the fate of the world will rest. The people will corrupt the good ways of life, bringing about the same life as that from which we fled in the underworld. The sacred body of the female will no longer be hidden, for the shield of protection will be uplifted, an act of temptation toward sexual license, which will also be enjoyed. Most of us will be lost in all the confusion. An awareness that something extraordinary is happening will develop in most of the people, for even their leaders will be confused into polluting themselves. It will be difficult to decide whom to follow.

The Hopi knew all this would come about. All these aspects of today's life pattern were planned. So today we must stand fully on our belief in order to survive. The only course is to follow the instructions of the Great Spirit himself.

The Mission of the Two Brothers

This Bow Clan chief had two grown sons. When they learned of their father's misdeed they were very sad. Their knowledge of the teachings which they had received from him was all in order. Now they were left alone to lead their people, for the very next day their father died.

They asked their mother to permit them to carry out the order of their instructions for an event of this nature. She replied that it was up to them, for their knowledge was complete. Upon agreement, the younger brother was to continue in search of Maasauu, and to settle where he found him. There he would await the return of his older brother, who was to travel eastward toward the rising sun, where he would rest briefly. While resting, he must listen for the voice of his younger brother, who would expect him to come to his aid, for the change in the life pattern will have disrupted the way of life of his people. Under the pressure of a new ruler they will surely be wiped off the face of the earth unless he comes.

Maasauu (handwritten, right margin)

So today we are still standing firmly on the Great Spirit's instructions. We will continue to look and pray toward the East for his prompt return. The younger brother warned the elder that the land and the people would change. "But do not let your heart be troubled," he said, "for you will find us. Many will turn away from the life plan of Maasauu, but a few of us who are true to his teachings will remain in our dwellings. The ancient character of our heads, the shape of our houses, the layout of our villages, and *the type of land upon which our village stands, and our way of life. All will be in order, by which you will find us."*

X *Before the first people had begun their migrations the people named Hopi were given a set of stone tablets. Into these tablets the Great Spirit inscribed the laws by which the Hopi were to travel and live the good way of life, the peaceful way. They also contained a warning that the Hopi must beware, for in time they would be influenced by wicked people to forsake the life plan of Maasauu. It would not be easy to stand up against this, for it would involve many good things that would tempt many good people to forsake these laws. The Hopi would be led into a most difficult position. The stones contain instructions to be followed in such a case.*

The older brother was to take one of the stone tablets with him to the rising sun, and bring it back with him when he hears the desperate call for aid. His brother will be in a state of hopelessness and despair. His people may have forsaken the teachings, no longer respecting their elders, and even turning upon their elders to destroy their way of life. The stone tablets will be the final acknowledgment of their true identity and brotherhood. Their mother is Sun Clan. They are the children of the Sun.

So it must be a Hopi who traveled from here to the rising sun and is waiting someplace. Therefore it is only the Hopi that still have this world rotating properly, and it is the Hopi who must be purified if this world is to be saved. No other person anyplace will accomplish this.

The older brother had to travel fast on his journey, for there was not much time, so the horse was created for him. The younger brother and his people continued on in search of Maasauu.

On their way they came to a land that looked fertile and warm. Here they marked their clan symbols on the rock to claim the land. This was done by the Fire Clan, the Spider Clan, and the Snake Clan. This place is now called Moencopi. They did not settle there at that time.

TEM— Katchongva tells us that people were created by the "Creator," and, like the Biblical Adam and Eve, they lived joyfully in what can only be described as a paradise. There was equality, oneness, a spiritual center, and life was everlasting. Peace and happiness reigned. But with these gifts came responsibility and the need to be wise. He gave them laws, which were guidelines, and the people promised to live by them. This was more than simple obedience. It was a lifeway to which the people committed themselves. Therefore, a Covenant existed from the very beginning. But the people had to have free choice, which was logical since the Creator could not have a true and loving relationship with them in any other way. He had to allow them to be tempted by things that might lead them to break their promise, which is exactly what happened. Here again, we have a foretaste of what is to come in the historic period. Prepare yourselves, Katchongva is saying, for you will see human nature and history repeated again and again all over the world and among the Hopi.

The punishments for breaking the rules are carefully spelled out. The idea encapsulated in the body made of good and evil principles is a most interesting one that ought to be pursued by psychiatrists. It recognizes that from our inception we are made with conflicting thoughts and emotions. The right side serves as a continual test of our wisdom and resolve, and it should not be thought of as an unfair complication, since it reminds us that it is not wise to stray away from the Creator and into dangerous places. As Katchongva articulates the struggle between the left and right sides, we learn that actions determine which side is stronger. In other words, more than a mental contest is involved…there is the choosing of a way of life to which each person commits their entire being. When the right side dominates, people begin to live just as most do today, although there will always be some who hold fast to their agreement. Destructive substances are produced, lives are disrupted, and things are created and desired. "Finally immorality flourished," including even the women in the Kikmongwi's (the title of the chief of a Hopi village today is "Kikmongwi") family and those of the other religious leaders. At last, the alarmed leaders did what they still do in such instances today. They smoked and prayed for guidance. The answer that came to them was to find a new place and start a new life. *Repentence*

Katchongva introduces us now to the manner of emergence, the new world, and to Maasaw. Scientists would dispute the idea of Maasaw having corn in North America at this particular time, for maize seems to have originated either in ancient Peru or Mexico and then to have migrated north from tribe to tribe, reaching the Anasazi around A.D. 1. (Qualifications regarding the dating of corn are given at the end of this chapter.) These ancestors of the Hopi, although not identified as such as yet by the scientists, were in existence long, long before that time. But corn is so central to the lifeway of the people and the Covenant it is natural to think of it as having always been available.

The concept of the reed emphasizes a direct path and a closeness that fosters unity — perhaps only the fond wish of Maasaw. It is worth observing that reed plants, particularly cattails, still play a prominent part in the gifts given away by the Kachinas during their plaza dances. The new world the emerging people arrived in was wonderful — unspoiled and beautiful — the way the Creator and Maasaw intended it to always be. The people celebrated their good fortune! But their joy was short-lived, for a witch was among them. Remember that a witch is a two-hearted person, as opposed to one-hearted people who keep the Covenant. We will watch for further manifestations of witchcraft performed by two-hearted people in historic times, although an extensive treatment of the subject is not germane to the book.

Katchongva injects here some momentary confusion. Where the Elders make it clear that Maasaw met the people when they emerged, Katchongva states that the Great Spirit appeared to them. Farther on, he uses the two titles as though he understands them as being different designations for the same person. And yet, in his opening paragraph he makes it clear that the Great Spirit creates, while Maasaw is up above on the surface of the earth. I suspect that Katchongva, or his translator, inadvertently confuses this coupling by calling Maasaw "Great Spirit," rather than his correct title, "Guardian Spirit." Katchongva affirms the Hopi belief in life after death by revealing that the Kikmongwi's daughter was seen to be playing happily with other children in the underworld, and he stresses that all Hopi return there at death.

Katchongva's account of the first meeting includes more details than that of the Elders. The people are divided into groups, each with its selected leader. The corn ears are of various lengths, and they are to be taken along for subsistence and livelihood. In other words, the people are to plant and harvest the kernels, and corn is to be their staple food. The choice of ears is a test of wisdom, and will reveal the humblest leader. Maasaw prizes humility, and as the story progresses, we will understand why. After the selection is made, and differences between groups are apparent, tribal names and languages are assigned. Since tribes existed in the Americas long before the year One, the emergence has to extend back to that distant time period too.

We receive a further articulation of what the tribal name, Hopi, means…"not only to be peaceful, but to obey and have faith in the instructions of the Great Spirit, and not to distort any of his teachings for influence or power, or in any way to corrupt the Hopi way of life." Katchongva implies that the admonitions apply both to the early people and to succeeding generations. Once they are established, the Covenant terms will remain in force.

Now come the instructions to migrate to the four corners of the new land, *for a certain purpose*. In other words, the migration period will accomplish certain necessary things. They are to leave footprints (which are only made by walking), rock writings, and ruins that will help them remember that when they emerged they were all one and united by a common goal. As the Elders have pointed out and will say again, the migration and lifeway will be a time of sending down spiritual roots that unites them totally with Earth Mother. The significance of this will become most apparent when we discuss the end times. These qualities are what Maasaw hoped for, and what he is still hoping for today as we come to the end of the Fourth Cycle and the beginning of the Fifth. Each group is to follow its own leaders and will be able to survive so long as Maasaw's instructions are remembered and obeyed.

The migration will also establish the Hopi claim to ownership of the land they have occupied and put their shrines on. This is something whose value could not have been known to them at the beginning, but its need would become painfully evident once Bahanna intruded.

We return again to the Covenant. *"We were now bound by a vow to live by these instructions and to complete our pattern of migration."* One day, when the time is right, one of the groups will find Maasaw again, and this group will be the designated leader of those who will arrive in the same place later on.

"We migrated for many years to every corner of this continent," Katchongva says. While the Hopi can certainly support their claim to have gone everywhere in the greater Four Corners area that includes Utah, Arizona, New Mexico, and Colorado, I doubt they have pictographic evidence to support travel to every part of the Americas. But the reference may be to all of the groups who migrated. "We," however, does include the Hopi, since Katchongva narrows his account down to them, and in particular to the group leader who is of the Bow Clan, whose personal meandering led to a change in the pattern of life and a kind of materialism that has more than become the hallmark of our modern world; it is destroying us!

Katchongva, telling his story in 1970, foretells now the Elders of 1993 when he states that *"Those gifted with the knowledge of the sacred instructions will then live very cautiously, for they will remember and have faith in these instructions, and it will be on their shoulders that the fate of the world will rest."* See how unerringly he runs down the reoccurrence in the end times of the dominance of the right side of the person, when he asserts that "The people will corrupt the good ways of life…The sacred body of the female will no longer be hidden…an act of temptation toward sexual license, which will also be enjoyed…Most of us will be lost in all the confusion…An awareness that something extraordinary is happening will develop in most of the people, for even their leaders will be confused into polluting themselves…It will be difficult to decide whom to follow."

An excellent picture of today's world, don't you think, with confusion, corruption, heightened awareness that things have gone badly wrong, and sexual license nearly out of control and spreading its incredible consequences like a plague? Don't you like his respect for "the sacred body of the female," and wish that all of us still held that concept firmly in mind?

"The Hopi," Katchongva says, "knew all this would come about." So it was prophesied by Maasaw at the beginning, and warnings were issued at the same time. "All these aspects of today's life pattern were planned." This does not mean it is the way things have to be. The planning includes the possibility of alternate developments and options. Free choice still reigns. But the consequences of breaking the Covenant are foretold. "So today we," those who are one-hearted and know what is right, "must stand fully on our belief in order to survive. The only course is to follow the instructions of the Great Spirit himself."

Katchongva moves quickly to a story that has clear present-day ramifications — that of the two sons of the Bow Clan chief. The oldest of the two is to travel eastward toward the rising sun, where he will rest and listen for the voice of his younger brother. The younger brother is to continue his search for Maasaw. When the predicted changes disrupt the lifeway of the Hopi people, as is the present case, the older brother will hear the younger brother's cries for help and come to his aid. For "Under the pressure of a new ruler" — which Katchongva and the Elders believe is the United States Government and those bodies through whom it works — "they will surely be wiped off the face of the earth unless he comes." How long does he have? Those who calculate the progress of the strip mining going on at Black Mesa and the erecting of other power plants in the Four Corners area give it 10 years. The final chapter addresses this problem.

Katchongva clearly believes that the absent brother is Hopi, but according to different sources there is some confusion as to whether the brother is Hopi or of the White race. Later you will learn that the Elders and Katchongva are also looking to other peoples to come and help them in their struggle to survive and to fulfill the Covenant.

Understandably, Katchongva in his time and Elders today have fervently looked and prayed for this older brother to return. Maasaw knew that at least a few of the Hopi who would be true to his teachings would remain loyal and keep the Covenant. They will be known by "The ancient character of our heads," which refers, Dan says, not to cranial structure, but to the maiden whorl hairdo once worn by young women to signify their traditional preparation for marriage, and to the long hair of the men with the trimmed bangs on the forehead. They will also be known by their rectangular and properly oriented houses, by the layout of the villages, which cluster around the ceremonial plaza and the kivas, by the mesa and wash type of land, which are historically Hopi farming and hunting areas, and by the way of life that has been repeated year in and year out for millennia. It is this annual cycle of religious ceremonies that marks the Hopi for who they truly are. "All will be in order," the brother promises, "by which you will find us." The description is of Hotevilla, whose men are still known by their hairstyles, and whose Elders and their supporters, so few now, are the glue in this stellar affirmation. Without them, the older brother would have a very difficult time locating his ancestral home. This leads me to wonder how, unless Maasaw with his divine understandings could look ahead and know it would be so, we can otherwise account for the fact that the Hopi and other Pueblo Indians would be the only ones to maintain virtually their entire traditional culture from the beginning until today, and thus be available for him to work through in an uninterrupted manner. To put this another way, suppose he had chosen some other tribe, the majority of whose traditional culture has been lost. Where would we be now?

Katchongva refers to a barb that remains current and sticks in the side of the Elders — the set of stone tablets given to the Hopi group by Maasaw before their migrations were begun. Both Mischa Titiev and Frank Waters were shown one or more of the tablets possessed by the Oraibi people, and describe them in some detail in their books. Since the tablets are so sacred and meaningful to the Hopi, I illustrate the most prophetic one in chapter 10. They are approximately eight inches wide, ten inches long, and one-and-a-half inches thick. They weigh about eight pounds each. The symbols inscribed on them are quite plain, although the Hopi can read a great deal from them. They have figured prominently in land claim dealings with other tribes and the state and federal governments, and are especially important to the Elders at the present time.

Since the tablets contain instructions to be followed when the Hopi are influenced by wicked people and forsake the laws of Maasaw, it is most unfortunate that the people of Hotevilla do not possess them. The older brother has a small piece of one, and the other has recently been hidden away in a secret place by someone whose identity is suspected, but not positively known to the Elders.

Will the elder brother hear this plaintive cry and come soon? The Elders certainly hope so. His younger brother is in a state of hopelessness and despair, especially over what has just happened regarding utilities in Hotevilla. As predicted also, and thanks to the persuasion and intrusion of the Bahanna, many of the younger people have forsaken the teachings, are no longer respecting their elders, and even turning upon their elders to destroy their way of life. The coming together of the broken tablet will reunite the brothers and reveal their true identity and brotherhood.

How essential is this reunion? *"Only the Hopi still have this world rotating properly, and it is the Hopi who must be purified if this world is to be saved. No other person anyplace will accomplish this."* That puts the answer plainly, doesn't it? The earth's rotation and balance are interrelated and will be treated later, as will the matter of purification. All of these are directly associated with the end times.

Nearly 900 years ago, the younger brother and his group came tantalizingly close to Maasaw at a place now called Moencopi. They marked the land with clan symbols, but "they did not settle there at that time." It looked "fertile and warm," making one wonder what Hopi country's actual appearance was in those ancient days.

As stated in Chapter 1, the Elders describe the migration period as a time of putting down spiritual roots, and Katchongva adds that the roots interweave with

Mother Earth to produce a seamless spiritual blanket which, having been woven over so long a time, became strong enough to survive the rigors of existence. The idea has a parable-like quality. Intriguingly, the roots appear to have remained in fluid state, only solidifying when the people settled at Oraibi, whose name means "place where the roots solidify." Dan makes it clear that as the Covenant is kept these roots continue to be sent down and into the blanket. How long has the period from emergence until today lasted? Thirty years ago, speculators set it at 10,000 years. Some have now moved it closer to 20,000 years. None of this speculation deals however, with the important point, which is that we must recognize the woven roots concept before we can begin to look at and feel the blanket — which is, of course, the Covenant and all of its ramifications. Once this happens, we see everything in an entirely new light. The migration period becomes understandable, and we know why the people embraced their lifeway so ferociously — until White pressures, persuasions and complications made it impossible. We also understand why the Hopi did not appreciate the efforts of intruders to take even any part of their lifeway away from them and replace it with their own, and have reacted as they have. Worse still, when we realize that destroying their lifeway destroys at the same time our own possibility of survival, taking their lifeway away becomes irrational. Hopi unwillingness to roll over and play dead has not been a matter of stubbornness or lack of comprehension. They have not had a choice. It was, and it is, utterly presumptuous and self-serving to expect the Hopi to walk away from a Covenant that has been kept for so long that no one actually knows its length. They have been keeping a promise that is vital to themselves and to the entire world. How could they break it solely because strangers who cared nothing about it arrived with a culture they believed was so superior that the Hopi must welcome it immediately, unquestioningly, and with open arms?

We are about to look at only a small, yet impressive portion of what the Hopi accomplished during their evolution under the Covenant. When the sciences first began to examine the stunning evidences of the culture that had flourished for so long in the Four Corners region, they were in awe and could only wonder who had created it. It was the grandest of mysteries as to who these people were and how, with only their minds, hands, and the simplest of tools, they were able to do what they did.

Now we know, don't we. They were determined loyalists who, even though the process went on for centuries, crafted everything they did with loving devotion. It was prayed into existence and endowed with fertility. That's why it was, and still is, so beautiful. They were keeping creation in harmony and balance, and the aura of that knowledge carried them along like a flowing wind. The structures they lived and worshiped in, the items they fashioned and used, and the costumes they wore were painstakingly sculptured to serve the Covenant in the best way possible as it was kept and moved forward year after year. Only after the meeting with Maasaw at Oraibi were they able to get the sense of the full dimensions of the Covenant's purposes, and even then it would be a long, long time before the fog lifted to the point where the end could be more clearly seen.

Even though members of the sciences did not recognize the underlying importance of the Covenant, piece by piece the "Anasazi" puzzle came together. Finally, their research made it clear to them that the Anasazi and the living Pueblos were one and the same — ancestor and descendant — and the lifeway being practiced at Hopi and the other Pueblos was the very lifeway that had evolved and been practiced for untold centuries. Thrilling? Of course it was! At last real people could be seen where before they could only be imagined. Chills went up and down their spines as they learned it then, and when we are among the Pueblo people today, especially on ceremonial occasions, they still do. To walk where they live is to experience the pulse of an ancient creation still alive.

As word of this dramatic discovery went out, Anglos swarmed into Hopi country: curious, impetuous, dripping — why, I don't really understand — with arrogance, and devious and scornful of native rights to life and lands. It surprised and baffled them to encounter believers more staunch than any others they had seen in their march across North America. Yet as our story tells you, even these believers could not forever hold every line against them. The strengths were not even. The pressures and odds were unrelenting and much too great. The blanket, or mantle, became beaten and frayed, and even at Hotevilla it has come down now to a tiny fragment of what it once was.

What it was...

Thanks to a carefully preserved oral tradition, the older Hopi know more than is generally thought about their history, but they have never had reason to survey and document the Southwestern ruins of their ancestors. You see, even though certain warnings were given to them, they did not, until now, let themselves believe that their wonderful culture would end.

Fortunately, then, we can turn to the sciences for this information, since without it we could only listen to the narratives and try to piece together in our imaginations the evidences and shapes of what happened. The Hopi are content without this, but lacking it we could never understand its magnitude, or care, or help them and ourselves in this crucial time of need. And without this information, even the Hopi children for whom the Elders have such hope, and who have been so progressively removed from it by exposure to the White world and its enticements, have no way of knowing how magnificent their ancestors have been and how special their Elders are.

While it is hard to imagine today, the disdainful Spaniards who entered the Southwest in the sixteenth century cared little about the cultures of the native peoples they encountered. Instead they searched for gold, property, and slaves. Explorers came upon great ruins and thriving villages, but thought them worthy of no more than passing mention. The early Mexicans and Americans who followed the Spanish did about the same, being far more concerned with their own precarious future than they were with supposed primitives of little consequence. It would not be until centuries later that the mining and power industries of the United States learned that under the unassuming soil of Hopi land lay vast and valuable resources of coal and minerals.

Not until the end of the 1800s did views about cultures begin to change. Various world conditions and Charles Darwin's theory of evolution combined to bring about a new interest in the story of mankind as a whole, and no more promising area for field research was available than the southwestern part of North America. American explorers, government surveyors, and private citizens entered the region and quickly returned with such glowing reports that U.S. government and private eastern museums sponsored repeated expeditions to the Southwest to gather information and to collect such artifacts as were available.

Their earliest efforts were spent in southern Arizona territory. Then, when the great cliff ruins of Mesa Verde, Colorado, were discovered by Richard Wetherill in 1888, already-whetted appetites shifted quickly toward the Four Corners area, where the borders of Arizona, Utah, Colorado, and New Mexico meet, and within a few years hundreds of spectacular ruins were being examined.

Unfortunately, the first archaeologists to work there had little concern for recording the locations and relationships of artifacts. Excavations were indiscriminate, and findings were poorly tabulated. Artifact collectors in general were quick to loot where they could. It was a misfortune that continued for twenty-five years or more and resulted in endless assortments of artifacts separated from their essential data. By 1915, however, the portentous differences in many of the ruins had become so apparent that far more attention was being paid to the sites and associations of items found, although a coordination and a chronology of findings were still lacking.

Almost by accident, the summer of 1927 brought to pass a key development. The Pecos Ruin in New Mexico was being explored by Alfred Vincent Kidder, and a group of forty or so avid Southwestern archaeologists gathered there to share their experiences and viewpoints. As they talked, it became apparent that the time had come to formulate a chronological classification of findings. Before the conference ended, they had hammered out a time and information structure known as the Pecos Classification, which, although it has been refined, is still in use by archaeologists today.

It seems they were now able to determine that by 300 B.C., at the latest, several major and minor cultures in what is now the southwestern United States had developed to the point where remains they left behind could, with some assurance, be associated with them through archaeological research. They were identifiable peoples and could be traced through the various stages of their development — from their appearance to their disappearance, or through their mergers with other cultures.

DAN EVEHEMA

FIRST: CHIEF
of the SUN CLAN
Son of "YUKIUMA"
D-1972

DAN KATCHONGVA

DAVID MONONGYE

TITUS QUOMAYOMPTEWA (LAMSON)

JAMES POYUNGAMA

CAROLINE TAWANGYAMA

Susie Lomatska

KATHERINE CHESHIRE

Snake gatherers leaving the kiva at Oraibi

Walpi Village

Priest seeking solitude at a sacred place

Antelope House ruin in Canyon del Muerto

Mummy Cave in Canyon del Muerto

Chaco Canyon's Pueblo Bonito Ruins

Two of the major cultures, the Hohokam and the Mogollon, faded from sight by A.D. 1400 or 1500. The third, known today as the Anasazi, never vanished and is recognizable in the Pueblo peoples living today in Arizona and New Mexico.

The makeup of the Anasazi was the primary concern of the archaeologists at Pecos. At the time of the 1927 conference they were beginning to wonder about the relationship of what they believed were two successive cultures who had occupied a common homeland in the Four Corners area: a foraging people designated as "Basketmakers," because they left behind an abundance of basket remains, and a later people the Spanish called "Pueblos" because they were sedentary in nature and lived in permanent stone or adobe villages.

At Pecos the two were arranged in a rough chronological order, as follows:

Basketmaker I	400 or 300 B.C. to 100 B.C.
Basketmaker II	100 B.C. to A.D. 500 or 700
Basketmaker III	A.D. 500 to 700 or later
Pueblo I	A.D. 700 to 900
Pueblo II	A.D. 900 to 1100 or 1150
Pueblo III	A.D. 1100 or 1150 to 1200 or 1300
Pueblo IV	A.D. 1300 to 1598
Pueblo V	A.D. 1598 to the present

Subsequent findings and conferences, however, corrected the Pecos impression that the Basketmakers had been succeeded by later pueblo-building arrivals. Careful examinations of cultural affiliations all but proved that the Basketmakers and the Pueblos were, and still are today, the same people going through successive cultural phases.

Thus a more unifying term for the evolving culture became necessary, and by good fortune the Navajo had already provided it. Knowing that the stone ruins in the canyons they came to occupy after A.D. 1500 were not those of their own ancestors, the Navajo called the builders of the stone dwellings "Anasazi," which means something like "enemy ancestors" or "ancient ones." Having no better name at hand, archaeologists adopted the Navajo term.

Other knowledge that subsequently came to light included the ability to posit the times when different architectural, physical, social, clothing, and pottery styles came into being. It was also discovered that not everyone among the Anasazi did everything at the same pace or time; that while one area clung to old ways, another would be adopting a new material culture and social and religious ideas. Amazingly enough, although much has been accomplished, the surface of Southwestern archaeology has only been scratched. Although more than fifteen thousand sites have been located, fewer than 50 percent of them have been explored.

A modification of the Pecos Classification, called the Roberts Classification, came into being in 1935, and it is frequently used by professionals as an alternate to the Pecos order. When it is compared to that of Pecos, it can be seen that Roberts's classification is more descriptive. One can follow the chronological developments simply by interpreting the titles of each stage, which are:

Basketmaker	A.D. 1 to 550
Modified Basketmaker	A.D. 550 to 750
Developmental Pueblo	A.D. 750 to 1100
Great Pueblo	A.D. 1100 to 1300
Regressive Pueblo	A.D. 1300 to 1600
Historic Pueblo	A.D. 1600 to present

Helpful as the Pecos and Roberts classifications have been in permitting the assignment of Anasazi developments to specific periods, it remains that data regarding these cultural stages cannot be assembled in neat compartments. As this remarkable people passed from one period into the next, certain changes did take place, and archaeologists employ these changes to identify the transition. For example, they can say a given custom was not practiced before. Yet certain other customs were continued. They might be polished and reshaped, but they were kept and carried over into subsequent phases. So true was this that it is probable the Anasazi were never aware of phases in the sense that the archaeologist is.

Pueblo groups in the Southwest continue to build structures of ancient type, to produce certain timeless material culture objects, and to practice ceremonies undoubtedly similar to ancestral customs. With information obtained from ethnographic studies of the Hopi and other Pueblos, certain comparisons may be made to tell us what life must have been like in ages past. We need, of course, to illuminate this information with what the Elders and Dan Katchongva have to say.

While archaeologists have not yet identified any culture that they would unhesitatingly call Basketmaker I, this much is certain: Agriculture, and particularly the cultivation of maize, or corn, made the ultimate difference for the Anasazi. Giving no credit as the Hopis do to Maasaw for this gift, the sciences do recognize that it was the fuel that launched the Anasazi on to the course they followed from that time forward. It solidified them as a recognizable people whose existence could be traced from that point forward.

With archaeology as our docent, we pick up their story in the Basketmaker II Period, in the San Jose drainage basin, about A.D. 215. The manner of life at that point was mainly nonagricultural, although some agriculture was practiced. Whenever Basketmaker II remains have been found, varying amounts of corncobs, squash rinds, and other agricultural products have been found with them.

Recent discoveries far to the south make it all but positive that the Basketmakers were not the first to cultivate corn. The queen of crops was being cultivated in Mesoamerica and South America long before the Basketmakers knew of it, and it was already the mainstay of the earlier Mogollon and Hohokam. So reason, with the help of a few hints from archaeology, tells us that corn was first brought to the

Southwest to the Hohokam and Mogollon, and was passed by their hands on to several cultures, including the San Juan Basketmakers. Why then do the Hopi speak of corn as being present among them from the emergence? Because it is so vital to their lives that they cannot conceive of a time when it was not their staple food!

Geographic expansion came about slowly. There was no need to hurry, and the people were careful to send down their spiritual roots as Maasaw instructed them to do. So the Anasazi thought in seasons, not in minutes and hours. The Four Corners region, home of the earliest Basketmaker Anasazi, remained the territorial center during the years of village beginnings. In fact, the early and late Basketmakers occupied about the same territory, with this significant difference: Early Basketmaker remains are few and far between outside the Four Corners region, while those of Late Basketmakers are plentiful in areas seldom used before.

The reason for this is clear. As the sedentary lifeway took over, the population grew rapidly. Where once there were few villages, soon there were hundreds. It was expansion of an interesting kind, though, and it merits special attention, for it seems not so much the result of an increase in the Basketmaker birthrate as the result of an influx of new people, who, seeing the advantages of farming and sedentary ways, moved in with the Basketmakers and took up the good life. Physical evidence points toward these new folk as being of several different tribes. A variation in head form between the mummies of Falls Creek Cave, Colorado, and those found in sites farther west is but one indication that they were undergoing salient changes in culture. Perhaps these new people brought with them the hard wooden cradleboard that was familiar in Pueblo times and accounted for the slightly flattened skulls marking the Basketmaker Period's end.

Before the Basketmakers and their immediate Pueblo descendants ran their course, they had spread their villages over a vast territory and left behind them thousands of ruins. An extensive occupancy, with Basketmaker village sites spaced only a few miles apart, occurred in southern Nevada along the lower valleys of the Virgin and Muddy rivers. In Utah there were cave and hilltop villages as far north as the Great Salt Lake, although the main occupancy was at the southeastern end of the state. The southwestern quarter of Colorado was virtually covered with Basketmaker villages.

Southward in New Mexico there are numerous Basketmaker village sites in the valley of the San Juan and its tributaries — the Animas, La Plata, and Chaco. Shabik'eshchee Village marks the southeastern frontier of late Basketmaker land. Arizona has a number of Basketmaker cave sites in Kayenta, particularly in Canyons de Chelly and del Muerto, in the Lukachukai Mountain region, and in the Red Rocks Valley.

There might even have been a southerly extension into the mountain belt of central Arizona and western New Mexico. This was "likely territory," whose well-watered valleys were occupied by Indians in Basketmaker days. But no archaeologist as yet knows whether the occupants were Basketmaker, Mogollon, Hohokam, or some regional blend of small groups.

Timewise, Basketmaker III would embrace the greater portion of the sixth, seventh, and eighth centuries, at least in the central Four Corners area. The frontier villages would lag behind, as is natural. Communication was poor, and resistance to change was stronger in some regions than in others. At the end of the chronological period, though, the Basketmakers would flow so smoothly into Pueblo I that anyone living in those exhilarating days would not have noticed it was happening.

By the end of the Basketmaker III Period in A.D. 750, Anasazi leagues of real significance were established and progressing at varying rates in three principal regions known today as Chaco Canyon, Kayenta, and Mesa Verde. Besides these, three lesser communities were beginning to form, one north and one south of Kayenta, and the other east of Chaco, along the Rio Grande. Pueblo settlements in the Northern Peripheral District (the Virgin Region) were gradually abandoned during the Pueblo II and III periods, and their inhabitants helped to increase the population in the San Juan area to the south. While the basic lifeway of the Basketmaker III Period was still followed, each of the forming leagues began to develop, at its own pace, certain practices and characteristics that made it in time somewhat different from the others. The differences are important to those who want to know the Anasazi well, since it is here we find the true genius of the Anasazi culture in full measure, and here we begin to understand why the individual Hopi villages have always differed slightly from one another in the way they have managed their religious and political affairs. These are distinctions that evolved during the migration period, and as such they are not easily put aside. For Katchongva, the Elders, and Old Oraibi/Hotevilla in particular, the matter of the Covenant would be uppermost in any decisions that were made.

Of all the Indian nations whose descendants live today, the Pueblos of Arizona and New Mexico seem at first glance to be the least influenced by other cultures. Much of the outside interest in them is precisely because of that. It is profoundly moving to see what appears to be the pure and ancient past still present and unaffected. To walk among the Pueblo villages and people, and in particular to watch the dances, evokes the strangest sensations imaginable. As a result, it is common for writers to attribute to the Pueblo Indians enduring qualities of life and wisdom and a purity of race seldom granted to others.

How much of that is valid and how much exists only in the imagination may never be known, but the lives and wisdom of the Elders and Katchongva are persuasive. This much is certain: Whatever the Anasazi ancestors actually were, and whatever the Pueblo descendants are today, they are in some part the product of neighboring cultural influences that have helped shape their way of life. From their earliest beginnings the Anasazi have not lived in a cultural vacuum, and they can be appreciated fully only when they are studied in that light.

Many specialists support this. Within the Southwestern area itself, grains of early influence carried over from the Hunting and the Cochise peoples. Next, and more important still to the developing Anasazi, were the Hohokam, Mogollon, Sinagua, Salado, and Cohonina.

Moreover, it is reasonably certain that some of the cultures influencing the ancient Anasazi eventually merged with them to produce a new culture that is, as of now, truly the child of them all.

Most anthropologists believe that the present-day Pueblos are a combination in greater part of the Anasazi of the Four Corners area; in a lesser part of the Mogollon, who may have physically merged with the Anasazi in several regions after A.D. 1300; and to a lesser extent still of the Sinagua, who may have merged with the Anasazi about A.D. 1200 to produce at least some of those who are known today as Hopi. A few specialists even speculate that the Mogollon and Sinagua split over an extended period of time into numerous small groups that joined various Anasazi groups, so that descendants of the Mogollon and Sinagua are everywhere present among the Pueblos today. Beyond this physical alloy lies the influence of cultures that, while they did not, so far as is known, merge physically with the Anasazi, nevertheless had cross-cultural relationships with them, each to some extent influencing and being influenced in turn. Accordingly, any proper study of the Anasazi must include an overview of those cultures that played so important a part in their world.

Mesoamerica, and perhaps even Peru, also had their part in molding the Anasazi. In speaking of the Mesoamerican demise at the hands of the Spanish, Arthur H. Rohn states: "Spanish invaders would come and lay waste to the native cultures. But long before then, something of the Mesoamerican tradition had filtered to the distant north, into the wilds of the North American Southwest and as far east as the Mississippi Valley and beyond. There, in attenuated form, many of the customs, rituals, handicrafts, and living patterns of preconquest Mexico found a new birth and vitality."

Campell Grant declares that, in the Pueblo III Period, "the Anasazi now came under the influence of the so-called Mesoamerica civilizations, either directly or by way of the Hohokam tradition. It is from Mesoamerica that the people of the great pueblos obtained the custom of making mosaics, copper bells, and, increasingly, the use of life forms in art." Clarifying this, he adds that during the misnamed Regressive Pueblo Period "both the polychrome pottery and mural paintings in the kivas show a number of new life forms, such as birds, mythological beasts, and masked dancers, which John O. Brew (1944, pp. 242-245) attributes to influence from the Tlaloc religion of central Mesoamerica. He suggests, further, that this is the source of the Kachina cult among the modern Pueblo Indians." Dan Evehema would not accept that. Oral tradition indicates that the Kachina rituals came into being among the Anasazi themselves, either during life in the underworld, early on in the migration period itself, or, as Dan thinks is more likely, beginning with the founding of Oraibi and the pattern of life laid out by Maasaw.

Florence H. Ellis and Laurens Hammack state that "the concepts, personnel, and categories of rites in Pueblo religion certainly make up one of our most marked evidences of continued prehistoric contacts between Mexico and the

Southwest…comparisons suggest that the traits were strained less through a net of time than regionally determined at their source and regionally modified after reception…our living Pueblo people still are perpetuating on this northern periphery their derivative form of basic concepts once common to all Mesoamerica."

Since dates become important in such a pursuit as this, it should be noted that whenever we turn to archaeological literature a surprising variation in dates for the Mesoamerican and Southwestern nations occurs. I could not cite them all, so I use those dates that make an effective chronology, and they should be taken only for what they are: possible times.

The earliest pottery found to date in the New World comes from the coasts of Ecuador and Colombia and is dated at ca. 3000 B.C., or nearly five thousand years ago. This would seem like a promising place to begin, but it isn't. The ruins and burial places of the four "Lands of Gold" in Central and South America — southern Nicaragua, Costa Rica, Panama, and Colombia — have been completely looted by native treasure hunters, and in consequence it is almost impossible to date anything with precision. In addition, the trade routes linking the higher civilizations of the north and south led directly through the region, and even if artifacts could be found along the route, it would be difficult to say for certain just what did originate in the Lands of Gold and which of their cultural customs came from Mexico and Peru.

The situation is quite different in Mexico and Peru. While not enough is known, sufficient discoveries have been made to allow specialists to envision civilizations and to speculate with qualified assurance about their cultural diffusions. Maize, or corn, is clearly the most important of the discoveries.

In the late 1940s archaeologists working in the debris of Bat Cave, Catron County, New Mexico, discovered tiny ears of cultivated maize, at least 5,500 years old. Questions arose immediately about where they had come from, for this particular corn required a wild ancestor that was capable of reproducing itself. Never in prehistoric times had corn spread north or west of Anasazi territory, so the obvious direction to look for the ancestor was south. Finally, in the 1960s, archaeologist Richard S. MacNeish of the University of Alberta found the elusive ancestor in a Tehuacán Valley cave southeast of Mexico City. Plants discovered there — including tiny ears of wild corn — dated back to between 5200 and 3400 B.C., and in trash layers above the one containing the tiny wild corn were subsequent deposits bearing progressively larger ears of cultivated corn, with the highest level dating between A.D. 500 and 1000, a total time span of as much as six thousand years!

The conclusion was inescapable: People were cultivating corn as early as the dates of the discovered ears, and society was already evolving into a farming complex. The Indian civilizations of Mesoamerica and North America were founded on corn, and corn itself was a native of the New World, a development from wild plants found only in the Americas. By 3000 B.C. corn cultivation was spreading rapidly throughout Mesoamerica and had already made its way in infant form into

North America, offering new possibilities for people to sustain themselves and to develop other skills. Wherever it arrived it became the staple crop, and today corn has become the most valuable crop grown in the United States. Along with wheat, rice, and potatoes, it ranks as one of the four most important crops in the world. Its importance as a culture-diffusing item is overwhelming, and it became a miraculous transforming power that enabled sedentary cultures to develop in amazing ways. Not surprisingly, it has in the minds of the Pueblo Indians become something that always existed, is holy and sacred, and it plays a central part in every CORN ceremonial act.

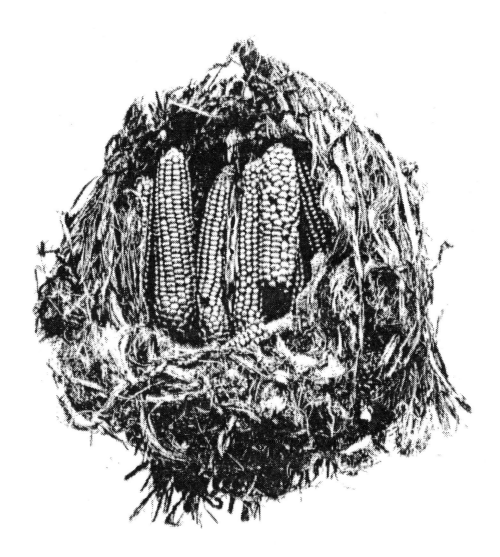

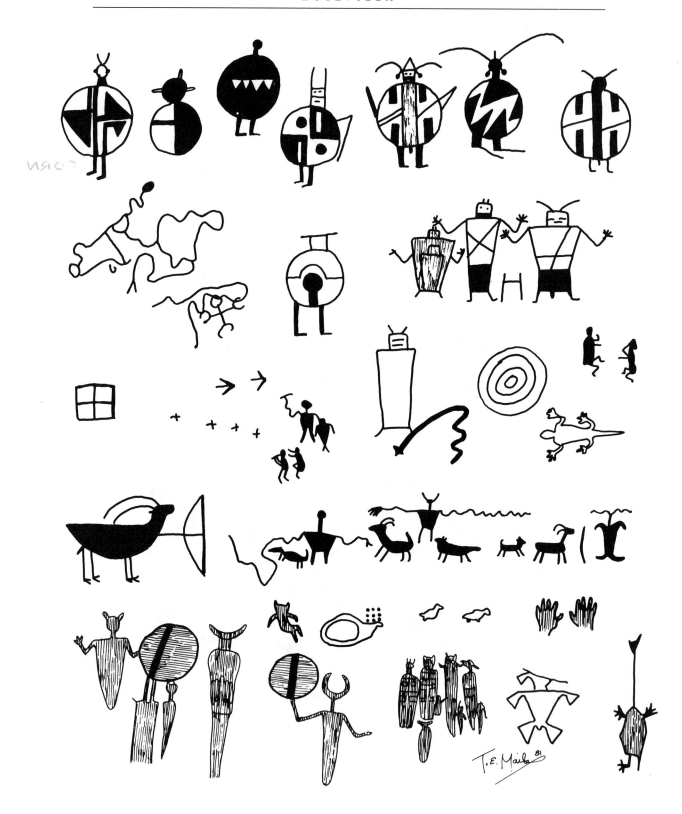

ANASZAI ROCK ART ABOUNDS IN UTAH. *Pictured above are only a few of the petroglyphs and pictographs reported by Neil M. Judd and Julian H. Steward from White and Cottonwood canyon sites, and from near the Colorado River north of Moab.*

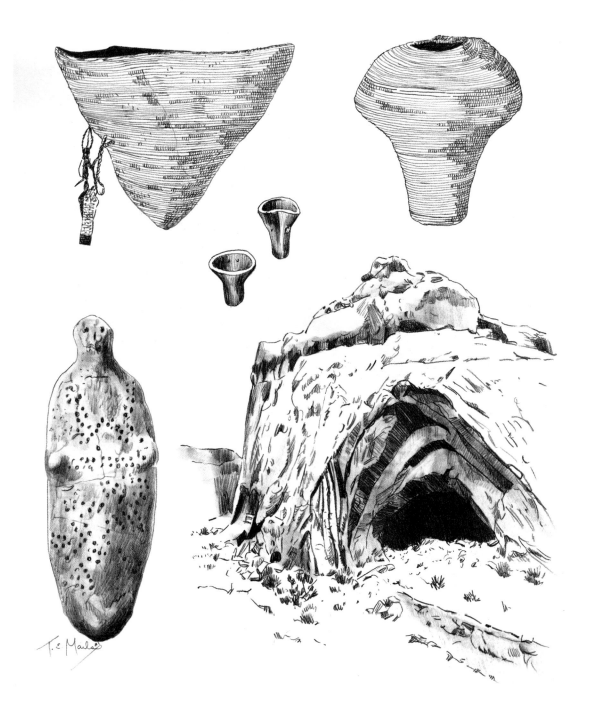

Top left, *Basketmaker II conical carrying basket from White Dog Cave, Arizona. From Peabody Museum, Harvard University.* Top right, *Basketmaker II water-carrying basket from Marsh Pass, Arizona.* Center, *Basketmaker III unfired clay cornucopia-like objects from Tsegi Canyon, Arizona.* Bottom left, *Basketmaker III figurine of unfired clay from northeastern Arizona. From Kidder and Guernsey, 1919, and Earl H. Morris, 1925.* Bottom right, *White Dog Cave, where many Basketmaker II remains were found.*

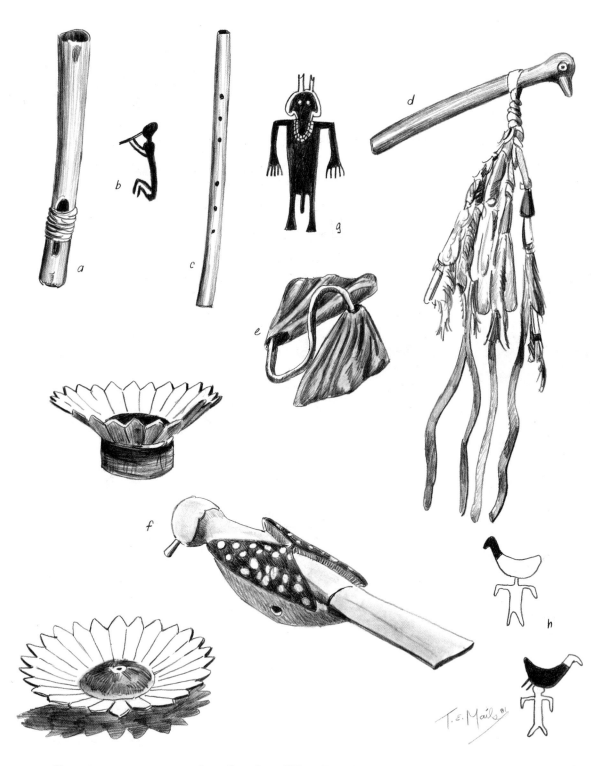

CEREMONIAL ITEMS: a, *bone flute from White Dog Cave, Arizona.* b, *pictograph of hump-backed flute player.* c, *30-inch-long wooden flute found in Big Cave in Canyon del Muerto.* d, *ceremonial wand with bird head found in White Dog Cave.* e, *Basketmaker II deer-hoof rattle from White Dog Cave.* f, *painted wooden bird and two of many wooden sunflowers found in a cache in Sunflower Cave, Arizona.* g, h, *unidentified pictographs.*

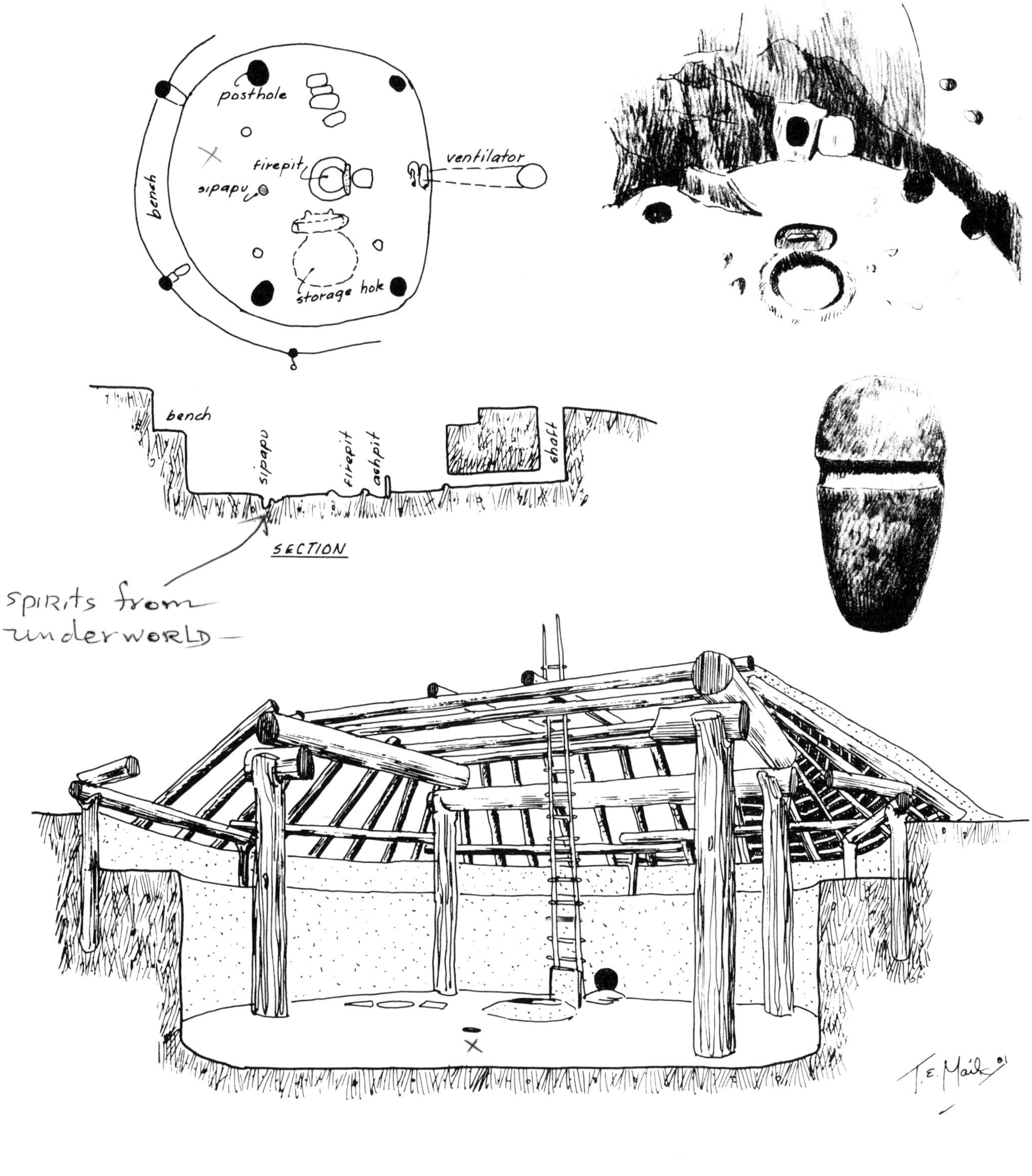
posthole
ventilator
firepit
sipapu
bench
storage hole
bench
sipapu
firepit
ashpit
shaft
SECTION
spirits from
underworld —
T.E. Mails '91

WHITEWATER. Top left, *plan and section of pithouse.* Top right, *pithouse view showing stone collar used for aperture of ventilator shaft.* Center right, *stone axhead.* Bottom, *postulated reconstruction of framing method for pithouse shown top left. From Roberts, 1939.*

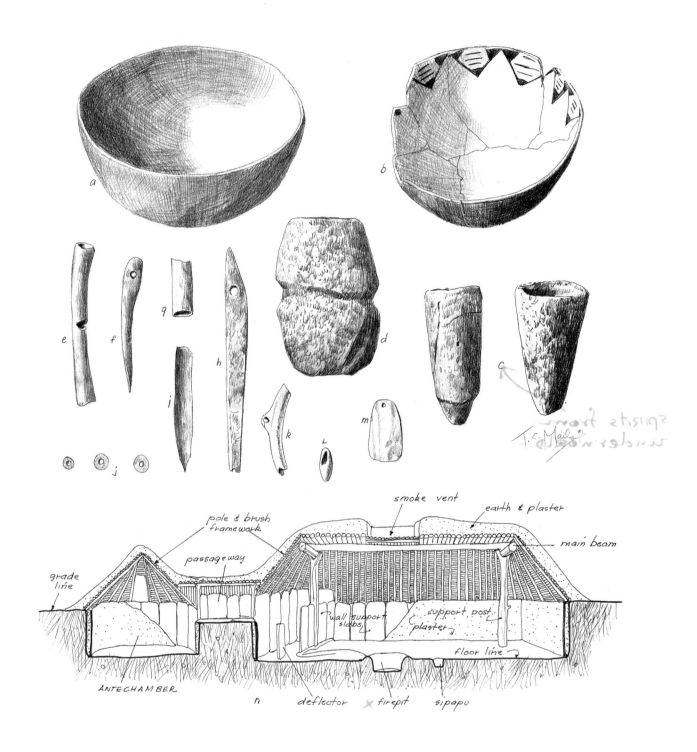

SHABIK'ESHCHEE VILLAGE. a–m, *typical lesser material culture items found in the village:*
a, *bowl with polished black interior.* b, *bowl with painted design.* c, *clay cloud-blower pipers.*
d, *stone maul.* e, *bone whistle.* f, *bone needle.* g, *bone bead.* h, *bone bodkin.* i, *bone awl.*
j, *shell beads.* k, *shell pendant.* l, *shell from necklace.* m, *shell earring or pendant.*
n, *section through pithouse showing postulated structural details. From Roberts, 1929.*

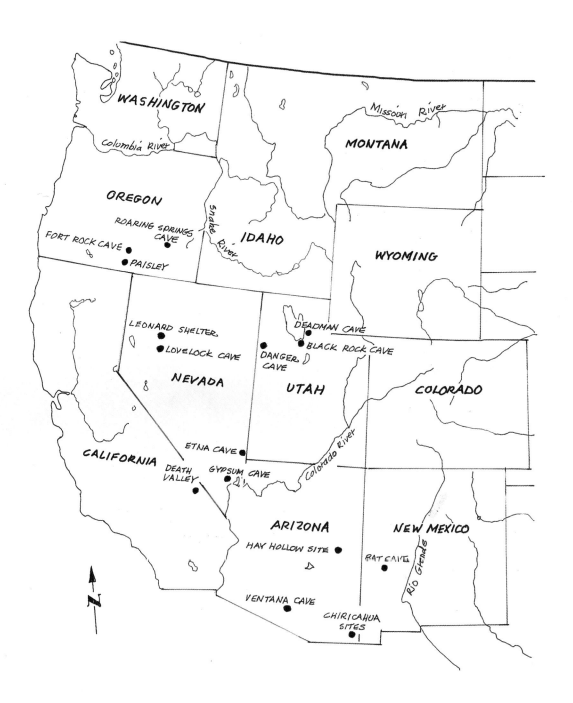

Some sites of the Desert Culture. Redrawn from Martin and Plog, 1973.

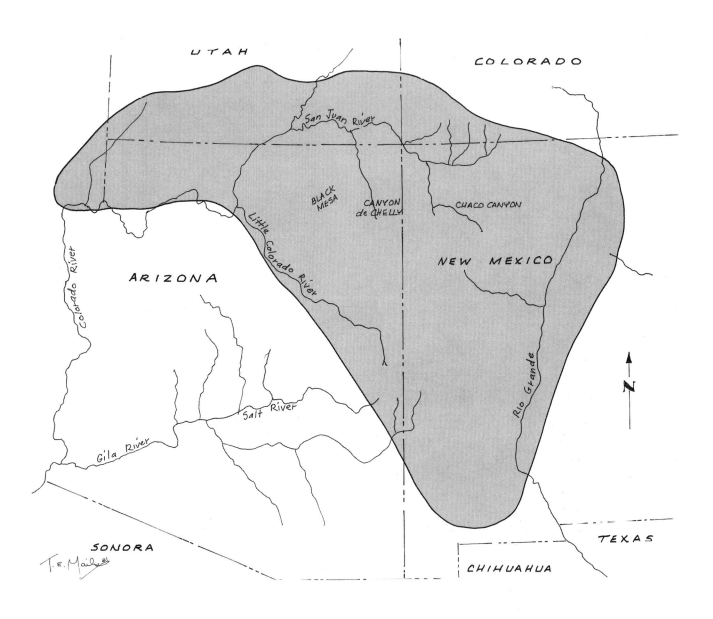

Map showing approximate area occupied by the Anasazi Basketmaker culture prior to the formation of the six major regions. The extension into the southwestern corner of New Mexico must allow for an overlapping and mixture of the Anasazi and Mogollon.

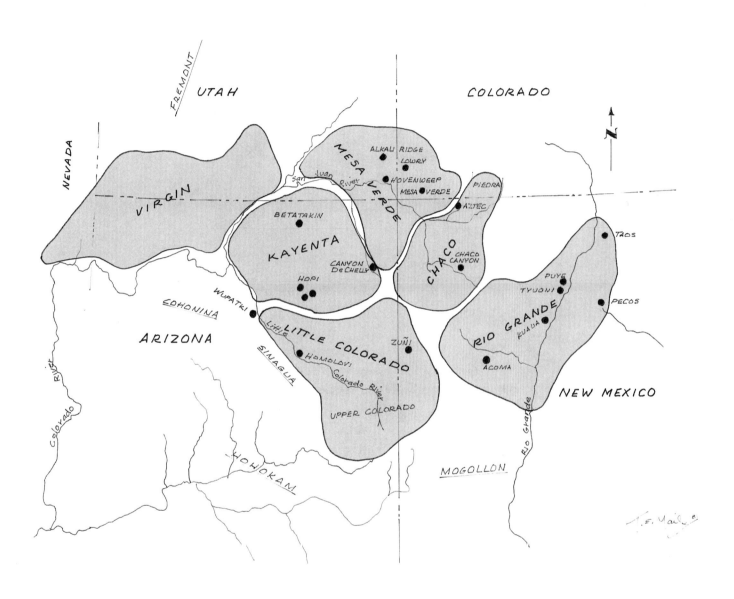

Map showing the approximate geographic areas of the six Anasazi regions.

CHAPTER 3

MIGRATION AND HERITAGE

THE SCIENCES AND THE CENTRAL LITTLE COLORADO SECTION

Archaeologists and anthropologists can tell us other things that support the claims made by the Elders and Katchongva. From what they have learned thus far, it appears that the Hopi Region at the southern end of Black Mesa was not occupied during Basketmaker II times, though there were scores of cave sites in the adjacent Kayenta Region. The earliest occupancy of the Hopi country is represented by a few pithouse sites in the Basketmaker III Period of A.D. 500–700 and by many sites in the Basketmaker III–Pueblo I transition period of A.D. 700–800. During the latter period the pithouses were enlarged, and isolated slab-lined storage chambers were arranged as contiguous surface units. The villages grew larger and more complex, and there is clear evidence their inhabitants were influenced by the Mogollon in architecture, in ceramics, and perhaps in religion.

The well-known cliff dwellings and immense stone pueblos of the Anasazi excite the praises of everyone who visits them, and as you examine the illustrations at the end of this chapter, you will see that even as the precursor pithouses evolved, the Anasazi developed a kind of architecture so sophisticated it would do credit to even our modern craftspeople. When the archaeologists discovered them, they found that, even though 700 years had passed, enough of the well-constructed ruins were still present and standing to allow them to reconstruct the pit buildings.

The form of Pueblo I Period culture in the Hopi region from A.D. 700 to 900 is not as clearly definable as the development sequence in the San Juan region. Until about A.D. 900, north of the Little Colorado River, the Anasazi in Northern Arizona seemed to have had a more or less uniform culture, Kayenta Branch. During this period there was considerable change: The bow and arrow replaced the atlatl, and there were improvements in metates and manos. Cotton was added to the other sources of textile fibers, and beans augmented the corn and squash crops.

With the advent of Pueblo II, ranging from A.D. 900 to 1100, the Hopi culture assumed an individuality that has resulted in its being given a separate archaeological classification, the Tusayan Branch. During this period there was an increase in the number of sites and an appreciable increase in population. The Hopi pithouses of this time strongly resembled the Pueblo II pithouses of the San Francisco Mountain district, and there was an infusion of Tusayan wares from the Kayenta area. The masonry-lined pithouses varied in form from circular to rectangular to D-shaped, and a D-shaped kiva developed from the house types. The sites were still small, consisting of from two to nine rooms, and they were located both on the rim of hills and on the river benches.

The essentially barren terrain in the Central Little Colorado section is quite similar to that of renowned Chaco Canyon. Flat areas abound. Elevations above sea level range from 4,500 feet on the Little Colorado River to 6,500 feet on some of the higher buttes. Precipitation averages eight inches a year, and much of it is quickly lost as runoff. It contrasts sharply with the Upper Little Colorado section, which is mountainous, tree-covered, and far wetter. The earliest archaeological work in the central section was done by Jesse Walter Fewkes, who was there several times between 1896 and 1904. Walter Hough was in the central section in 1901 as part of the Museum-Gates Expedition, but he concentrated mainly upon exhuming burials associated with large Pueblo IV sites. Harold S. Colton made some sporadic site surveys in 1939 and added what he learned to the reports of Fewkes and Hough to make his own report on the area. Nothing further happened until a few limited excavations were carried out in the late 1940s and early 1950s. In the early 1960s, William Wasley performed salvage archaeology along the proposed route of Highway 66 in eastern Arizona, and at that time he confirmed that an Anasazi-Mogollon blending had taken place in the Puerco and Little Colorado valleys. In 1949 Fred Wendorf, under the auspices of the Museum of Northern Arizona, had excavated a pithouse village on the Flat Top site, which is located on a high mesa at the southern end of the Petrified Forest National Park. Thought to be Mogollon, the dwellings were slab-lined, with an entrance oriented toward the northeast. The pottery suggests that until the middle of Pueblo II the Lower Little Colorado section was mainly Mogollon territory.

Then in 1966 the Museum of Northern Arizona performed two series of excavations, one in the southwestern Hopi Buttes locality and the other several miles east of Holbrook. Eleven sites were dug in all, and in the Hopi Buttes locality a survey recorded 211 sites in a 25-square-mile area. Also in 1966, two pre-ceramic, pre–A.D. 500 pithouses were excavated near Dilkon. These established the first positive Basketmaker II presence in Central Little Colorado. The Hopi Buttes survey recorded three Basketmaker III sites, only one of which was excavated. Most of the pottery was Lino Black-on-gray, revealing a Kayenta influence, and it dated the sites somewhere between A.D. 600 and 800. The three Basketmaker dwellings were circular surface rooms that appear to have had the familiar four-main-post-and-beam support system, covered with brush and earth. Floors were finished with a coating of clay and had central clay-lined firepits. In addition to the dwellings, two roasting pits and a slab-lined storage pit were unearthed.

PUEBLO I — A.D. 700–900

A single Pueblo I site consisting of three pithouses was excavated at Hopi Buttes, along with two Pueblo I dwellings at other locations. Kana-a Black-on-white pottery places the Buttes site within the Kayenta range of cultural influence and dates it in the A.D. 800–950 period. The three pithouses differed enough from one another to suggest a Mogollon and Anasazi relationship. The first pithouse was circular, with an eastward-oriented ramp entryway of Mogollon vintage. The second pithouse was also circular, but had the typical Anasazi bench, ventilator, and partitioned floor. The third pithouse was more rectangular, with a northward-oriented alcove, and it lacked the typical roof support pattern.

Two other pithouses of the Pueblo I Period were excavated in the Hopi Buttes area. These were circular and had northeast-oriented ventilator shafts, partitioned floors, and the four-post roof-support system. One had a dual ventilator shaft similar to those of the early Kayenta pithouses. A Pueblo I site near Winslow was excavated in 1956 and 1957. Archaeologists feel that the Pueblo I Period in the Central Little Colorado section was strongly influenced by the Kayenta Region. Its architecture and pottery were Kayenta in style. The two regions probably formed a uniform subculture during Basketmaker III, Pueblo I, and early Pueblo II. Little Colorado variations from the Kayenta culture are explained "by the necessary adaptation to the more arid environment and to the high degree of interaction with the Mogollon people to the south."

PUEBLO II — A.D. 900–1100

The Pueblo II Period in the Central Little Colorado section spans the years A.D. 900–1100, but it is best understood when it is divided into two phases. During the first phase, from A.D. 900 to 1075, it continued to be strongly marked by Kayenta influence. The second phase opened in A.D. 1075 with the introduction of Holbrook Black-on-white pottery. This was the beginning of the Winslow branch, which marked a time of movement away from Kayenta influence.

Five unexcavated sites at Hopi Buttes represent the early part of Pueblo II. All the painted pottery is Black Mesa Black-on-white. A single site excavated near

Holbrook represents the Winslow branch. This was an L-shaped five-room pueblo with adobe walls. A short distance to the east was a D-shaped pithouse, with a firepit, ventilator, and a four-post roof-support system. The Little Colorado ceramic tradition had been established, but the pottery characteristics were still Kayenta Anasazi. Ultimately, Little Colorado wares unique to the area would develop out of Kayenta styles.

The reason for the change is not certain, but a dramatic increase in sites at Holbrook in early Pueblo II indicates that considerable population growth was taking place. Whether this growth was due to an influx of new people or to a shift of Little Colorado residents is not known. While it is possible that the Central Little Colorado inhabitants had become in time a distinct sociocultural group, they continued to maintain a high level of interaction with Anasazi to the north and Mogollon to the south. As has been seen in earlier chapters, the latter part of the Pueblo II Period was for the Anasazi a time of unrest and a beginning of movement. Departures were already taking place from Aztec and the Virgin regions to the north, and from Chaco Canyon to the west. Presumably the Little Colorado and Rio Grande regions began to receive some of these migrants, along with their cultural influences.

Holbrook Phase sites were relatively small. They consisted of two or three pithouses and a surface storage room that was rectangular and crudely built. It had a foundation of basalt or sandstone slabs that probably carried mud or jacal upper walls. The pithouse entrances were ramped, the pits were rectangular, and a four-post roof-support system was employed. Interior details included circular firepits and various other pits used for pot rests and storage. No kivas were found, but that may be because of the limited number of Pueblo II excavations carried out.

PUEBLO III — A.D. 1100–1250

Pueblo III at Central Little Colorado dates from A.D. 1100 to 1250 and is known as the McDonald Phase. In the Hopi Buttes survey mentioned earlier, sixty sites were assigned to the early part of the McDonald Phase and eighty-one to the late part. This indicates another increase in area population after A.D. 1175. Pueblo III sites in the Central Little Colorado section remained small, although somewhat larger than those of Pueblo II. A typical village consisted of four or five pithouses and several surface dwellings. Some of the sites included kivas, and some did not. No large cluster was found. Instead, little settlements were scattered over all parts of the area to take advantage of the numerous arroyos and dunes that made the best farming places and of the limited water sources needed for everyday purposes.

Some Pueblo III pithouses still had the shallow rectangular pits and ramped side entrances that reflected Mogollon influence and were common to Pueblo II. But deeper pits with square shapes and roof entrances became in time the more dominant form. Instead of the familiar four-post support system, two main posts were recessed into the walls like the posts in a pithouse found at Chaco Canyon.

Other interesting deviants from the norm included ventilator shaft openings placed at or in the room corners and perforated sandstone slabs used for roof smoke holes and for ventilator shaft openings. In the 1960s, pithouses identical to the later and unusual forms just described were excavated at Neskahi Village on Paiute Mesa near Navajo Mountain in southern Utah. These were dated A.D. 1000–1100, and as such were somewhat earlier than those of Central Little Colorado. The surface structures of Pueblo III at Central Little Colorado also varied in form and construction. Most of the surface rooms were rectangular, but other room shapes were devised to conform to topographical demands. A typical building consisted of five contiguous rooms and clay walls that were inset with small sandstones to slow down deterioration. At the Sundown site near Holbrook, a clay-walled kiva was built within a masonry room. Masonry walls of the McDonald Phase varied. Depending on the site, they were either dressed sandstone or crudely laid unshaped basalt rock. Kivas of this phase were D-shaped, keyhole-shaped, and rectangular, with platforms at one end like those of present-day Hopi. At the Hopi Buttes Plaza site a rectangular Great Kiva was discovered that was 35 feet (10.5 m) wide. The Sundown site included a shallow, circular, and benched Great Kiva measuring 40 feet (12 m) in diameter. Both sites were beautifully constructed, had several clan-sized kivas enclosed within the room blocks, and had walled plazas. It is assumed they served as greater community centers, the kind the Hopi call "mother villages." When Fajada Butte and Sun Temple are described further on, it will be apparent that the Pueblo were, as a whole, greatly skilled in astronomical knowledge and its applications to cyclical ceremonial and agricultural life.

ORAIBI!

In A.D. 1120 we arrive at one of the most propitious moments in Hopi history. The people have for a very long time been migrating, leaving footsteps and markings, and obediently sinking down their spiritual roots. From a distance, Maasaw has been watching over them and is anxiously awaiting their arrival at Oraibi to begin a new phase in the Covenant process. And now, the first of the Hopi groups arrive where he is, and the heralded meeting takes place. The Elders and Katchongva, telling their story long after the fact, describe the reunion with no discernible emotion. They know and we know, however, that it had to be a momentous event for the people who were there, for their ancestors and they had worked so long and so hard to keep their promises that the victory must have been sweet. Did the word concerning this go out to the other migrating groups immediately? It appears so, for we learn they began to arrive at Oraibi "from all directions." We see in the continuing statements of the Elders and Katchongva that oral tradition includes intriguing information about this historic meeting and its consequences.

Scientists say that the original, or Old, Oraibi was founded by the Bear Clan around A.D. 1120, although Katchongva gives the original credit to the Bow Clan, who relinquished it to the Bear Clan, whose name is connected with a rock called "orai." Oraibi will become the oldest continuously occupied town in the United States. It undoubtedly began as a small cluster of dwellings, but by historic times had evolved into a sprawling community. The center of Old Oraibi consisted of two main multistoried, masonry buildings located on the east and west sides of a long, narrow plaza, with slightly smaller room clusters situated at the north and south ends of the plaza in such a way as to complete the plaza enclosure. An additional thirty or more small-house clusters were grouped about the main buildings, each cluster being so laid out as to provide for a village with seven streets oriented north and south. At one time the village had thirteen rectangular kivas that were detached from the dwelling units.

Today, most of Old Oraibi is in ruins. Yet when Victor Mindeleff examined it in 1882 and 1883, he discovered that it was the largest of all the Hopi villages and contained half of the entire Hopi population. In 1899 George A. Dorsey spoke of Old Oraibi as the largest and most ancient of all Hopi pueblos, and in many respects the best preserved and most interesting community in the world. It was a proud village without a church, spurning the advances of the U.S. Government, and separated from its nearest neighbor by a broad, deep valley. There was only one White man within 20 miles, and the nearest trading post was 35 miles away. In 1929 Lyndon L. Hargrave found ample evidence that Old Oraibi was very old. Beneath the town were the remains of dwellings, room on top of room. Some years before, the edge of a road had been cut through a trash mound at the bottom of which were found the buried remains of older and better houses.

Old Oraibi remained the largest of the Hopi towns until 1906, when dissension over changes that would affect the keeping of the Covenant — matters like schooling, leadership, government pressures in general, and Christianity — split the community and brought about the founding of Hotevilla. The withdrawal of other residents from Hotevilla led to the founding of Bacobi in 1907, and to the establishment of New Oraibi at the foot of Third Mesa in 1910. New Oraibi was to become, in terms of the adoption of White ways, the most progressive of the Hopi villages. It has at least three Christian churches, is the headquarters of the Hopi Tribal Council, has accepted more White man's innovations than any other village, and it has abandoned many Hopi customs. Although the village is still quite small, many of its houses are more modern than usual, having electricity and up-to-date furnishings. Well and piped water is even available, and there are indoor toilets.

The residents of New Oraibi, as have all of the Hopi villages, have adopted White people's dress for daily purposes. Children play baseball, basketball, and the like. But except for the prosperous and modern Tribal Council enterprise, the economic life of New Oraibi parallels that of other villages. While no Kachina initiations are held at the village, some vestiges of the Kachina cult are still present.

By 1932 the population of Old Oraibi had been reduced to 87, and the cere-monial organization had suffered a serious decline. Then the population increased some, reaching 167 in 1968, but Old Oraibi became until recently a bitter place insofar as its attitude and spiritual energies were concerned. Today a sign at the village entrance tells Whites flatly to "Keep Out." It was not always so. In his report on Kokopnyama in 1929, Hargrave says there was hardly a room, either above or below ground, in Oraibi or the villages of Second Mesa, that at some time he had not been permitted to enter.

Old Oraibi in 1950

THE ELDERS

We finally completed our migrations in Oraibi. There we met Maasaw again. He gave us warnings and prophecies, and instructions on the pattern of Hopi life. Different clans arrived from all directions. As each one asked to be admitted into the village, they had to tell what they could contribute to nourish the people and make them happy. If they spoke boastfully, they were rejected and told, "Go to the next mesa where your kind of people live." Only humble people received permission to settle in Oraibi. They belonged to various clans, each with knowledge and wisdom of its own. Together, we established our mother village as a sacred shrine, and started our yearly cycle of ceremonies.

KATCHONGVA

While the people were migrating, Maasauu was waiting for the first ones to arrive. In those days he used to take walks near the place where he lived, carrying a bunch of violet flowers (du-

Old Oraibi, 1900

Old Oraibi, 1919

kyarn-see) in his belt. One day he lost them along the way. When he went to look for them he found that they had been picked up by the Hornytoad Woman. When he asked her for the flowers she refused to give them back, but instead gave him her promise that she would help him in time of need. "I too have a metal helmet," she told him, (possibly meaning that certain people with metal helmets would help the Hopi when they get into difficulty). Often Maasauu would walk about a half mile north of his du-pa-cha (a type of temporary house) to a place where there lay a long rock which formed a natural shelter, which he must have picked as the place where he and the first people would find each other. While waiting there he would amuse himself by playing a game to test his skill, the name of which (Nadu won-pi-kya) was to play an important part later on in the life of the Hopi, for it was here that the knowledge and wisdom of the first people was to be tested. Until recent times children used to play a similar game there, something like hide-and-seek. One person would hide, then signal by tapping on the rock, which would transmit the sound in a peculiar way so that the others could not tell exactly where the tapping was coming from. (Some years ago this rock was destroyed by government road builders.) It was here that they found Maasauu waiting.

THE MEETING WITH MAASAUU NEAR ORAIBI

Before the migrations began Maasauu had let it be known, though perhaps not by direct instructions, that whoever would find him first would be the leader there. Later it became clear that this was a procedure by which their true character would be specified. When they found him the people gathered and sat down with him to talk. The first thing they wanted to know was where he lived.

He replied that he lived just north of there at a place called Oraibi. For a certain reason he did not name it fully. The full name is Sip-Oraibi, meaning something that has been solidified, referring to the fact that this is the place where the earth was made solid.

They asked permission to live there with him. He did not answer directly, for within them he saw evil. "It's up to you," he said. "I have nothing here. My life is simple. All I have is my planting stick and my corn. If you are willing to live as I do, and follow my instructions, the life plan which I shall give you, you may live here with me and take care of the land. Then you shall have a long, happy, fruitful life."

Then they asked him whether he would be their leader, thinking that thus they would be assured a peaceful life. "No," he replied, "the one who led you here will be the leader until you fulfill your pattern of life" (for he saw into their hearts and knew that they still had many selfish desires). "After that I will be the leader, but not before, for I am the first and I shall be the last." Having left all the instructions with them, he disappeared.

THE FOUNDING OF ORAIBI VILLAGE

The village of Oraibi was settled and built in accordance with the instructions of the Great Spirit. The Bow Clan chief was the father of the ceremonial order. They remained under the leadership of the Bow Clan for some time, perhaps until corruptions set in. As you recall, the Bow Clan chief of the past had contaminated his standing by taking part in the changing of the life pattern.

Later the Bear Clan took over. This might have been because the bear is strong and mighty. There may have been other reasons too, such as a prophecy which told that a bear, sleeping somewhere in the northern part of what is now called Europe, would awaken at a certain time and walk to the northern part of this country, where he would wait. This group is called Bear Clan because they came across a dead bear at the place of the shield symbol. Most of the important people claimed to be of the Bear Clan, including the Bluebird and Spider Clan people.

For some reason the Coyote Clan, who migrated from Shgotkee near Walpi, were considered bad people, though very clever. At first they were not permitted to enter but, in accord with our custom, on the fourth request they were admitted, on agreement that they would act as a protection and in time speak for the chief should difficulties arise. But they were warned to be cautious, though faithful ones might remain true to the last. So it is with all clans, for along the way most of us will deceive our leaders for glory, which will tend to pollute our ways and jeopardize our beliefs. The last group to be permitted into Oraibi was the Grey Eagle Clan. When they had finished their migrations, they first settled in what is now called New Mexico. Being warlike and troublemakers, they were evicted by the Pueblo Indians. When they came to this area, they first settled in Mishongnovi on Second Mesa, on the agreement that they would not cause trouble. Should they break their agreement, they were to leave without resistance.

They made trouble in Mishongnovi so they left as promised. They went by way of Oraibi, where they asked to be admitted. After several attempts they finally gained entry, promising as they had in the other village that they would leave voluntarily should they create trouble. According to this agreement the chief of Mishongnovi would then consider whether to receive them again at Second Mesa or send them back to New Mexico, where the Pueblo people could deal with them as they saw fit.

TEM— The Elders see the migration period as coming to an end in Oraibi as the ancestors meet Maasaw again. The time, as close as archaeologists can determine, is somewhere between A.D. 1100 and 1120…more than 800 years ago. The Elders state simply that he gave them three things: warnings, prophecies, and instructions on the pattern of Hopi life. These are the essences of the Covenant, although it is only as we read on that we come to recognize them as such. Since they will be mentioned in connection with numerous fulfillments and behavior tendencies as the narrative proceeds, they do not define or elaborate upon them here. In particular, Dan articulates for us in specific terms this sacred pattern of Hopi life, and he will explain the course (assuming that the Elders and their supporters are able to carry on) it will take as we approach the end of the Fourth Cycle. For the moment, you should know that it consists of daily prayers, working with the land every day, carrying out the annual ceremonial cycle, making special prayers for land and life, and sending runners to the directions — in particular obtaining sacred water from the San Francisco Peaks.

Oral tradition tells the Elders that soon after the meeting different clans began to arrive from all directions. The time lapse was minimal. They came from north, east, south, and west, excited also about the long-awaited meeting with Maasaw. While the Elders do not say so, we can be certain that the newcomers wanted to know everything about the meeting, in particular about the details of the Covenant. Documents I refer to later demonstrate that people in all of the villages that evolved know about it, and that their ancestors subscribed to it. Reading between the lines for the rest of the statement, we can see how the fulfillment began to manifest itself. The founders of Oraibi knew they were on to something big, although its fullest proportions could not be known to them then. They did know it could not thrive if all of the residents did not contribute positive things and share the communal happiness that would be essential to success. The welfare of the group came first. Humility was the most desired virtue, since without it factionalism and individualism would once again rear its ugly head and defeat everything the founders knew they had to accomplish. There must be complete willingness to follow the guidance and protection of the Creator and his Helpers. Those who met these basic tests were welcomed, and thereafter made their individual contributions to the whole, so that nothing was missing and every side was considered in regard to everything done. Working together, they established Oraibi as *a mother village and a sacred shrine*. And they started their yearly cycle of ceremonies. I mention the beginning of the cycle elsewhere, but want to emphasize here that Dan thinks the annual cycle of ceremonies the Hopi follow today began with the founding of Oraibi — which would suggest that the other villages obtained at least some of it from them. The rituals were most certainly in embryonic form throughout the Anasazi villages long before Oraibi came into being, but the finished form of what is presently done came only after the founding. And its focus — that which it revolves around and centers in — has always been the Covenant.

Katchongva is consistent in his approach. He includes things in his account that set up what should be looked for as time passes and the warnings and prophecies are fulfilled. Maasauu, as Katchongva spells it, was "waiting" impatiently for the first ones to arrive. When he sensed it was about to happen, he took daily walks to an unusual rock where he expected to meet them. The story of Hornytoad Woman sets up Katchongva's expectation of help from another nation when the Hopi are in dire need of rescue.

Rock of Maasaw

As were many ancient Native American games, the game Katchongva describes was an instructional one. Important lessons were learned by playing it, and Maasaw used it to test their knowledge and wisdom. The peculiar sound emitted by the stone when it was tapped made it difficult to tell where it was coming from. Obviously, Maasaw gave them clues about the sound, so that only the wisest and knowing ones would be able to read it and thus could find him and be with him. It appears that the migrants who did find him heard him tapping on the rock and honed in on it like an owl who is stalking its prey in the dark of night. Therefore, they found Maasaw waiting, and the anticipated meeting took place. Interesting, isn't it, that after hundreds of years of effective use this historic and functional rock would in typical fashion be — as is so much of the rest of Hopi life — wantonly destroyed by a bulldozing and couldn't-care-less employee of the United States Government. The symbolism is inescapable.

Notice now that Katchongva distinguishes between indirect and direct instructions where Maasaw is concerned. Not everything is prophesied. Some things were "let drop" during conversations soon after the emergence and before the migrations began. He was testing the people to see which of them were listening to him and which were caught up in the beauty and conquest of their new world. It was a procedure by which their true character and leadership qualities would be known.

Everyone could see that he did not make the rock his paramount home, and wanted to know where he did live. He answers with only part of the name, perhaps because he has read them carefully and knows the real reason they want to come and live with him…security and no responsibility. That would be too easy. They need to face up to some critical demands that go with the territory. It is your decision, he says, and you had better know what you are getting yourself into. All they will have is the barest essentials, and they must follow his instructions and take care of the land. He does not put a time limit on this. It is the way it is always going to be for those who want to live where he lives, be one of his own, and be his servants to the world. He knows, you see, that to stray away from this will be to open oneself up to intrusive thoughts and temptations. There are rewards for the sacrifices. Those who stick with him will have a long, happy, and fruitful life.

The Elders are the living example of the truth of this, and they are perfectly content to live without the advantages of modern life that the rest of us dote on and take for granted. People wonder why they use outhouses and do without running water, sewer lines, electric lights, and telephones. They gladly trade utilities and conveniences for independence, simplicity, relative peace, and the joy of an intertwined service-relationship with Mother Earth and the rest of the Creator's creation. After all, their ancestors and they managed surprisingly well for nearly seven hundred years before any of these advantages became available, and there is nothing that they do use they would not gladly jettison if it would rid them of the other things that came with it and have nearly sacked the culture.

Human to the core and awed by the responsibilities portended, the anxious people did at the meeting what all of us would do. They looked for the easy way out. If Maasaw would just be their leader, it would relieve them entirely of responsibility. No way, he replied, they were going to learn that those who had listened and guided them to him have the knowledge and wisdom to lead them. Perhaps this would show them what people can be when they measure up. At the proper time, he would become their leader. That was among the things ordained. But the time had not been set by the Creator, and Maasaw could not say when it would be.

It was time to let them mull all of this over and make their decisions, so Maasaw simply disappeared — for the moment, that is; He didn't abandon them.

The clan chiefs with the right stuff went to work and, following Maasaw's instructions, began to build the village of Oraibi. With only their hands, digging sticks, and seeds they put up their houses and kivas, laid out their farming plots, and began to work the silken sands as they tilled the fertile soil. The ceremonial order was set into motion.

Despite all of their energies and hopes, it was not long before the true nature of man's two sides began to assert itself. It seems this is the way it will always

*my Quest!
seek the
just
necessities*

be. The Bow Clan chief had, in effect, set the stage, and the players marched mindlessly in. Hence the Bear Clan took over. This was another fulfillment of prophecy, and its happening told the discerning people they could expect the rest of the warnings and prophecies to be fulfilled too. The nature of clans becomes a parable for Katchongva as he plays upon his theme of an easily corrupted human nature. He is saying again what we do when we advise our child to hold tightly to our hand as we cross a busy and dangerous street...don't wander off or think you can make it on your own...the Creator and his Helpers are the only ones who can keep you safe.

Notice that the oral tradition cited by Katchongva includes knowledge that, even in the earliest years of Oraibi's existence, the mother village knew other Pueblo peoples were living in villages as far away as present-day New Mexico. The Hopi were neither isolated nor failing to interact with their cousins. This was true of their relationships with other cultures as well.

The Scientists

Archaeologists have determined that toward the end of the Pueblo III Period, somewhere between A.D. 1200 and 1300, the Anasazi population distribution of the Central Little Colorado section experienced a pronounced contraction. Most of the area was abandoned as the section's inhabitants began to accumulate in ever-expanding pueblos along the Colorado River and on the Hopi mesas. Reasons given for this include changes in climate, an increasing number of refugees, and pressures by marauding invaders. It is stated that the seemingly defensive nature of some locations supports the last-mentioned idea, or that a combination of the problems caused the contraction. More likely, it was the keeping of the Covenant that caused it. I find it significant that not just parts of, but entire areas were abandoned in a single move. Not one person stayed behind. The Elders have made it perfectly clear that the people were to continue migrating until they found Maasaw. Who would want to be left behind when that was going on?

From a practical point of view, scholars wonder why the Anasazi migrating from other areas would even come to the arid Central Little Colorado Valley. A settled existence was precarious, especially at a distance from the Colorado River Valley. Perhaps they came because Anasazi relatives were already living there and surviving. Pertinent to this, John T. Hack inserts a perceptive note, stating that the Hopi region seems, when first one experiences it, to be nothing but a barren, windswept desert. But, paradoxically, it is this very barrenness that gives it superiority. Its exposed position and broad valley flats enable windstorms to pile up great mounds of sand that inhibit arroyo cutting, allow floodwater to spread, and provide a permanent groundwater supply in or beneath the large dune areas. A few scholars say the valley was the only alternative to the Rio Grande Region, but more likely it was because Maasaw was beckoning to them, and they had not found him yet.

Evidence shows that some of the first migrants actually made their way past Hopi country and south into the Upper Little Colorado section, where accommodation with the Mogollon people would not have been a problem. But the Apache and Navajo decided they wanted the territory, and that might have given the Anasazi in the Little Colorado Region any remaining impetus they needed to move to the Hopi mesas. Maasaw was there. It was an almost secure place to settle down, and despite the intrusions and circumscriptions by Spanish, Mexicans, and Anglos, the Hopi have survived at that sacred place ever since.

PUEBLO IV — A.D. 1250–1540

Pueblo IV in both the Little Colorado and Rio Grande regions is known to the anthropological subsciences as the period of redistribution and the establishment of new communities. It has two phases. The first covers the time of instability, migrations, and the inauguration of new cultural centers. It extends from A.D. 1250 to the time just preceding the arrival of the Spaniards in A.D. 1540. The second phase is of shorter duration and spans the interval from the appearance of the first explorers to the final subjugation of the Pueblo peoples in 1692, when their temporarily successful revolt against the Spaniards, which began in 1680, was ended. Early Pueblo IV was formerly referred to in the literature as a period of regression or cultural decline. But subsequent study has shown that the designation is no longer appropriate.

Because of a lack of archaeological information, it is difficult to name Little Colorado ruins that are solely representative of the earliest Pueblo IV Phase. Distinct sites on the border between the Central and Upper parts include Puerco, Chevelon, Homolovi, and Chavez Pass. There are, however, many other examples that had their beginnings early in Pueblo IV and continued on to practically the end of the phase. And in the Hopi country of Arizona there are many Jeddito Valley sites that date to this period.

Later stages of the early phase are represented by Sikyatki in the Hopi area, or district, and perhaps by whatever associations can reasonably be made with the more southern Casa Grande villages.

The second phase of Pueblo IV is regarded as the early historic. It is best represented by Awatovi in the Hopi district and by Hawikuh near the present-day village of Zuni, New Mexico. These were thriving villages long before the Spaniards arrived in A.D. 1540, and they continued to function for some time thereafter. Hawikuh was not abandoned until A.D. 1670, and Awatovi was, for reasons soon to be described, destroyed — either in the autumn of A.D. 1700 or in early 1701.

Hopi Buttes

A single Pueblo IV site, located on top of a precipitous cone-shaped volcanic plug named Chimney Butte, was excavated during the Hopi Buttes survey mentioned earlier. It consisted of one rectangular room whose walls were of double-coursed, unshaped basalt boulders. There was no finished floor and no definite firepit. Pottery shards indicated occupation of the butte as early as Pueblo II, giving it a possible date range of A.D. 900–1350. The inaccessibility of this 6,553-foot-elevation ruin that rises 1,000 feet above the surrounding plain prompted George J. Gumerman and S. Alan Skinner to suggest it was a shrine. Supporting this idea are the frequent mention of Chimney Butte in Hopi legend and the fact that it is regularly associated with present-day Second Mesa ceremonies.

Kin Tiel

A number of large and interesting ruins, which must have been spectacular places during their occupation period and that show Hopi affinities, are located within the Central Little Colorado section of the Pueblo IV Period. One of these is Wide Ruin, or Kin Tiel as the Navajo call it. A village plan is included in the illustrations at the end of this chapter. The ruin is on an upper and eastern tributary of Leroux Wash called Wide Ruin Wash, 18 miles north of Chambers, Arizona. On early maps Kin Tiel is designated as Pueblo Grande, and it first became known through the work of Mindeleff and Fewkes. It is dated about A.D. 1264–85.

In 1929 Hargrave, in search of datable beams for Dr. Andrew E. Douglass, excavated at Kin Tiel, and also at Kokopnyama, which is on Antelope Mesa about a mile east of the Jeddito trading post. In looking at the Kin Tiel ruin itself, and at a reconstructed floor plan, one can easily see why it was called Pueblo Grande and Wide Ruin. It was an immense pueblo, sometimes referred to as the "Butterfly Ruin," because it formed a compact assemblage of rooms that in plan were shaped like a butterfly.

Hargrave reports that, unlike other ruins in the immediate area, Kin Tiel had an outer wall unbroken except for narrow passageways. As in the case of Pueblo Bonito at Chaco Canyon, terraced dwelling rooms looked down upon open courts. The courts were separated by a stream channel that appeared to have been crossed by extensions of the outer wall of the village. As with the Show Low and Pinedale ruins, local settlers had removed virtually all the Kin Tiel wall stones for their own building purposes. In consequence, no primitive masonry stands above ground today. The ruin has been leveled, and all that remains is a low, widespread mound of sandstone blocks and adobe mortar.

The significant thing is that the Kin Tiel kivas represent what are believed to be the earliest and most easterly examples of kivas of Hopi character. Both were built in A.D. 1275 or 1276. It is remarkable that Hopi-style kivas should occur so far from what has been regarded as the Hopi homeland. Of course, one of the even more distant rectangular Pinedale kivas is Hopi in style and dates between A.D. 1293 and 1330.

The Hopi type of kiva chamber is divided by a rise in floor elevation into what is called the kiva room proper and the platform, or alcove. The kiva room is the larger portion. It contains the altar appropriate to each ceremony, and the ritual is enacted there by the society members. The platform space, along with side benches, is reserved for spectators who are permitted to witness certain parts of ceremonies, and for novices during the tribal initiation ceremony. Both kivas at Kin Tiel seem to have followed this pattern. Pueblo custom also decrees that the kiva be partly, if not wholly, underground.

Where villages stand on solid rock, kivas are built on lower ledges or set into crevices so that the side of the kiva that is against the cliff permits in essence the fulfillment of the subterranean aspect. The kivas at Kin Tiel were subterranean. Entrance was by means of a ladder that extended through a hatchway and whose butts rested on the platform floor.

Of particular interest to Hargrave were two parallel rows of small holes drilled in the flagstone floor of both kivas. In his opinion, the holes were used to anchor the lower end of looms, since it is well known that Hopi men have always woven blankets in their kivas.

Pottery recovered from the fill in both kivas is described as black-on-white, black-on-orange, and corrugated, indicating the period to be one of transition from Pueblo III to Pueblo IV.

Puerco

Puerco was once a very large pueblo. It included about 125 rooms arranged in a rectangle, with three kivas situated in a plaza in front of the rooms. The kivas were rectangular, and each had a bench at its south end. The pottery was mainly a development of Homolovi, but the Hopi influence was greater than that of Zuni. The pueblo appears to have been built as a unit rather than in stages, and it is dated A.D. 1250–1350.

Homolovi

The Homolovi ruin was partially excavated by Fewkes in 1896 and by Gordon G. Pond in 1965. This was an especially large masonry pueblo, having two plazas surrounded by dwelling rooms, into which were incorporated several ceremonial structures. The original building was two stories in height, and many of the lower-floor rooms were paved with sandstone slabs. A rectangular kiva inspected by Pond featured a slab-lined bench and wall murals. Pond also reports that a large number of Hopi pottery types were found. Homolovi shards are indistinguishable from those of Awatovi. Possible dates for the Homolovi site are A.D. 1200–1300. Hopi informants recognize Homolovi as a Hopi site, and they support their assertion with legends referring to the village, which say that the founders of the Hopi village named Shipaulovi once lived there.

Chevelon

The Chevelon ruin was excavated by Fewkes in 1896. It is 15 miles east of Winslow and south of the Little Colorado River. Large amounts of shell were unearthed at Chevelon, suggesting it had trade and ties with the Hohokam.

Pottery was similar to that of Homolovi. Burial methods were identical to those of Homolovi.

HOPI

Archaeologists are not able to say when exactly the next Hopi villages after Old Oraibi were begun. But we know from the accounts of the Elders and Katchongva that certainly a few of them were in embryo form shortly thereafter, and that when the contraction of the Little Colorado Region of the early 1200s got under way, many villages that still exist today began to grow at an appreciable rate. Adding to the difficulty of pinning down their original locations is the fact that a considerable shifting about of sites took place. This should be expected. The Hopi were and are sedentary people, but in typical Anasazi fashion, sedentary did not mean stationary. They continually reconstructed and added to sites and sometimes moved entire villages to one or more new locations. At Hopi, this became especially true after the Pueblo revolt erupted in 1680 and they feared the consequences.

The scientific assessment and description of the Hopi culture, once improperly identified as "Moki," could not commence until the advent of the historic period in A.D. 1540. But we have seen that the Hopi story really begins in A.D. 1100–1120, at the end of the Pueblo IV Period, when the pueblo, or village, known as Old Oraibi was founded. Since excavations are not permitted by the Hopi, no one knows for sure what the exact date of founding is.

The Hopi language is Uto-Aztecan (Shoshonean), and thus connected with those of the Ute and Comanche. The town of Hano is the single exception, as it maintains its Tewan dialect. As we have learned, the name Hopi, or Hopitu Shinumu, means considerably more than just "the Peaceful People." It includes several aspects that have to do with the keeping of the Covenant. But the Hopi could and would stand up to a challenge, and could become contentious and violent if in their view the situation justified or demanded it. While the Hopi had "a horror of wanton killing" and were rarely the aggressors in warfare, it was their custom to go on the warpath each fall after the harvest was gathered. Upon returning, they would celebrate by dancing with the scalps they had taken, and even when their war parties ceased they continued to perform either the Kaleti, or Warrior Dance, or the Howina'aiva, or Market Dance.

Ultimately, the Hopi towns, forming an overall community first identified by the Spanish as the Province of Tusayan, came to occupy three high and virtually barren mesas that are the southwesternmost extensions or spurs of Black Mesa, known by scientists today as the Central Little Colorado section. Since Old Oraibi, on the westernmost mesa, was the earliest settlement, the Hopi considered these mesas, beginning there, as the first, second, and third mesas. But after the Englishman Thomas V. Keam established a trading post east of the mesas in 1878, and the U.S. Government built its agency at Keams Canyon in 1887, the mesas were numbered from east to west, and they are so known today.

The names of the Hopi villages and other Hopi words occur fairly often in the following chapters, and it might be helpful to explain here that Hopi is always written precisely as it is spoken. Most of the letters in the English and Hopi alphabets stand for the same sounds, and Hopi letters are always pronounced the same, although there are differences in dialect between mesas. For example, the present-day Hopi villages and their pronunciations are as follows:

First Mesa
Walpi (Wahl-pee)
Sichomovi (Seet-chew-moh-vee)
Hano (Hah-no)
Polacca (Poh-lah-ka)

Second Mesa
Shipaulovi (She-paul-oh-vee)
Mishongnovi (Mee-shong-noh-vee)
Shongopovi (Shung-oh-po-vee)

Third Mesa
Old Oraibi (Oh-rye-bee)
New Oraibi (New Oh-rye-bee)
Hotevilla (Hoh-tah-vill-ah)
Bacobi (Bah-ko-bee)

Other village
Moencopi (Moh-en-koh-pee)

There are three villages on First Mesa: Walpi, Sichomovi, and Hano. Polacca sits at the foot of the mesa on the eastern side.

Walpi, the most interesting of the villages to any visitor because of its dramatic setting on the tip of a stark, 600-foot-high mesa, was built about A.D. 1300. Its name means "Place of the Gap." Walpi has five kivas. One is enclosed within a house block, and the other four are detached.

Sichomovi, alternatively spelled *Sichimovi*, "Place of the Mound Where Wild Currants Grow," lies between Walpi and Hano, and it is separated from Walpi only by a narrow bridge of rock. The present village was begun about A.D. 1750 by a group from Walpi, said to be the Patki, Lizard, Wild Mustard, and Badger clans. After being devastated by a smallpox epidemic, the Sichomovi people moved to Tsegi Canyon and to Zuni. Later, though, they returned and resettled in Sichomovi. The present village has two kivas, placed back to back in a plaza.

Hano is a Tewa village that was founded sometime after A.D. 1696 by people who fled the Rio Grande country after the reconquest of the pueblos by the Spanish. The people of Hano still consider themselves Tewa, even though they have adopted many Hopi customs and intermarried. Hano and Sichomovi are contiguous in appearance, but the Tewa and Hopi are keenly aware of an un-marked boundary line that separates the two villages.

Polacca is named after Tom Polaccaca, a Hano-Tewa who built the first store below the mesa. The village grew up around the First Mesa day school in the 1890s. It has had no political or ceremonial status, but so many people have now moved down to it from Walpi that the venerable mesa-top village is virtually abandoned as a dwelling place. Ceremonies are still held up in Walpi, and the kivas remain, but important political changes have been made. By ancient custom, ceremonies will always be held at Walpi, because it is the ceremonial center for First Mesa by virtue of its length of residence.

Second Mesa is 12 miles west of First Mesa, and it is split at its extreme end into two spurs. Shipaulovi (sometimes spelled Shipolovi) and Mishongnovi are on one spur, and Shongopovi is on the other.

Shipaulovi is the word for a small fly or gnat, whose petroglyph was on a stone brought to the village by a Kachina and preserved in a shrine. Harold S. Colton and others subscribe to a legend that says the founders of Shipaulovi once lived at Homolovi and were driven out by swarms of mosquitoes; hence, to Colton, the petroglyph is a mosquito and the name means just that. The beams taken from the old Franciscan mission at Shongopovi argue that people from there settled Shipaulovi after a schism. Shipaulovi has three detached kivas.

The name *Mishongnovi* means "Place of the Black Man." The reference is to a chief named Mishong, who was a member of the Crow Clan. Mishong led his followers from the San Francisco Peaks region, near Flagstaff, to Shongopovi. They were not allowed to settle there, but were permitted to begin a village below the shrine at Corn Rock, a prominent sandstone pillar at the end of Second Mesa, on condition that the Mishongnovi would forever protect the shrine from dese-cration. Archaeologists believe that Mishongnovi was occupied from A.D. 1250 to 1800, and that it moved to its present site on the end of the mesa (from the lower position near Corn Rock shrine) during the 1700s. The present village has four detached kivas. A Franciscan chapel was established at Mishongnovi in 1629, and it was cared for by a priest from Shongopovi until 1680.

Shongopovi, or *Shungopovi*, means "Place by the Spring Where the Tall Reeds Grow." According to tradition, it is actually the oldest of the Hopi villages, but the original site was not where the present one is today. Shongopovi was esta-blished by the Bear Clan. According to Bertha P. Dutton, Shongopovi people built a new pueblo on top of Second Mesa in 1680. An excellent spring, named Gray Spring, is said to have been the result of the ceremonial prayers of the Cloud Clan. It is walled in with masonry and has been used by the villagers for several centuries. The original site of Shongopovi was just north of Gray Spring. Pottery shards found there by Colton led him to conclude that it was established before A.D. 1250 and then occupied until the early part of the 1400s. The Franciscan mission of San Bartolomo was built on a ridge about 500 yards above the spring, and from 1629 to 1680 a substantial portion of Shongopovi was situated near the mission. Following the Pueblo revolt of 1680–92, the present village was built, and some of the mission beams were incorporated within it. It has five detached kivas.

Third Mesa is 10 miles west of Second Mesa. Old Oraibi sits on the tip of the spur, with New Oraibi at its base. Eight miles or so beyond Old Oraibi and on top of the mesa is Hotevilla, and a half mile northeast of Hotevilla is Bacobi, or Bakabi.

Hotevilla means "skin the back." The original reference was to a low cave housing its main spring. The entrance was so tight that persons using it usually skinned their backs on the rough cave roof. It was founded in 1906 by Yukiuma and his followers after the schism at Old Oraibi. Since we will consider this schism and its ultimate meaning in coming chapters, only a brief summary is needed here. Because of his commitment to the Covenant, Yukiuma, the man who became the Kikmongwi of Hotevilla, together with his followers, stubbornly refused most of the demands of Bureau of Indian Affairs officials, and the village has remained one of the most conservative of the Hopi. It is said by some who write about the event that part of the ruined condition of Old Oraibi is explained by the fact that when the dissenters moved away they literally took their houses with them, but the Elders and Katchongva dispute this and say it is not true. They were not allowed to take anything save what they were wearing, and even some of their garments were torn off them. Considering how important to mankind the sacredness of the mother village and the keeping of the Covenant is, outsiders may find it hard to understand how such an unpleasant division could take place. This will be explained, and you will find that it actually makes very good sense.

Bacobi, "Place of the Jointed Reed," was established in 1907. It appears that a small group of people who came reluctantly away with the Hostiles decided not to stay. When the Friendlies at Oraibi refused to accept them, they moved on and founded Bacobi, which is just across the highway from Hotevilla.

Moencopi (also spelled *Moenkopi*) means "Place of the Flowing Stream." It is about 40 miles north of Old Oraibi and is a colony of the ancient town. It is built in the midst of sites said to have been occupied by the migrating Hopi clans of early days. Moencopi was founded about 1870 by an Old Oraibi chief named Tuba, or Toovi, and the traditional Hopi people who live there still recognize the authority of the village chief of Old Oraibi. Moencopi is actually two communities: Upper Moencopi is the more modern one, and it surrounds a day school in the old village; Lower Moencopi is a traditional community. Not far from Moencopi, the U.S. Government established an agency that was run by Mormon missionaries. This has become a fairly large and active center, named Tuba City, but Mormon efforts to convert the Hopi have met with only limited success.

The *Jeddito Valley*, a few miles east of the Hopi mesas and not far south of Keams Canyon, became, like the Hopi villages proper, an important culture center in prehistoric times. Natural water reservoirs and broad valleys filled with alluvial deposits, together with herbs, grasses, shrubs, timber, sandstone, and clay and coal deposits, combined to make the area one of the most desirable for dwelling places in the Central Little Colorado section. The remains of ancient habitations are found tucked in considerable number under the mesa rims. Pithouse sites in the valley date from A.D. 670 to after 800, but the excitement of archaeologists has centered in the large pueblo ruins of Awatovi, Kawaika-a, Chakpahu, Pink Arrow, Nesuftonga, Kokopnyama, and Kululongturqui. Victor Mindeleff mapped the five largest Jeddito ruins in 1882 and 1883.

Awatovi, alternatively spelled *Awatobi*, a place where ironically as it turns out — sublime artistic beauty abounded, was situated on the old trail that connected the villages of Cibola (the Zuni area) and the villages of Hopi. Consequently, it was the first to be discovered, in 1540, by Tovar and Cardenas. Espejo visited the Jeddito Valley in 1583, Onate in 1598, and de Vargas in 1692. In the first half of the seventeenth century a Roman Catholic Franciscan mission was established at Awatovi, and it remained in operation until its destruction during the Pueblo Revolt of 1680. In 1700 an attempt was made to reestablish the mission. But it collapsed when the Awatovi pueblo was abruptly terminated by traditional Hopi under circumstances that were almost inevitable and reprehensibly sad. Historic blame has rested with the Hopis for perpetuating the act, but missionaries cannot always be proud of what they set into motion.

The story is told that during the winter of 1700, after the people of Awatovi had permitted the Franciscan priests to return and to reestablish their mission, a swarm of angered Hopis from other mesas — Mischa Titiev claims most were from Oraibi — with the chief of Awatovi as an accomplice, attacked Awatovi. They trapped and burned most of the men, who had been asked by their chief to meet in their kivas before sunrise, captured the remaining men, abducted the women and children, and then tortured and dismembered the Awatovi male captives and some of the women and children at a place near Second Mesa. The documentation for this is given in nearly a dozen publications, but for a vivid and heartrending account I recommend that of Harry C. James, *Pages from Hopi History*, pages 61–64.

From 1935 to 1939 an expedition from the Peabody Museum did extensive work in the Jeddito Valley area. Twenty-one sites were excavated entirely or in part; they dated from the sixth century A.D. to the early part of the eighteenth. At these sites approximately 1,500 rooms were uncovered, 1,300 of them at Awatovi and the rest at other sites on Antelope Mesa and in the Jeddito Valley. Two of the earliest sites were of particular note: The first was a Basketmaker III–Pueblo III site near the Jeddito trading post. It consisted of subterranean and surface ruins whose history could be traced for at least six hundred years. The second was a village about a quarter of a mile long, situated on a point that projected out into the Jeddito Valley below Kawaika-a. Its main occupancy was Basketmaker III–Pueblo I, with pithouses, slab-lined storage rooms, outdoor firepits, and one Pueblo II house built inside an earlier pithouse. Especially interesting was the fact that the site exhibited traits comparable to Basketmaker III–Pueblo I sites of the San Juan area, and to contemporary sites of the Upper Little Colorado section along the Mogollon Rim.

As for Awatovi itself, the only walls still standing in 1935 were those of the southeast corner of the old mission. Elsewhere nothing but great mounds of building debris lined the former plazas. But by the time the Peabody Museum archaeological investigations ended in 1939, Awatovi had proved to be the ruin of a large pueblo that once had covered 23 acres on the rim of Antelope Mesa overlooking the Jeddito Valley. Its occupancy period ranged from Pueblo III to the early part of Pueblo V, and more expressly to the moment of the heartrending massacre. Besides the pueblo, there was the ruin of the seventeenth-century mission, San Bernardo de Aguatubi, although according to Brew, Anasazi occupation of the site had reached its peak in the fourteenth and fifteenth centuries and was already in decline when the mission was founded.

As at Old Oraibi, trenching revealed room built upon room, one house being built on the ruins of another after the earlier ruins had been filled in and smoothed over with trash. The buried rooms, happily enough, had actually been preserved by the topping process, and their walls were still in excellent condition. In addition to the dwelling and storage rooms, five rectangular kivas were excavated in 1935. Four were in open plazas, and one was incorporated in a large building. The first kiva was the most elaborate encountered in the history of Anasazi archaeology, save the Great Kivas at Chaco Canyon and a few other places. The remains of two domestic sheep found on the floor made it clear that the chamber belonged to the later, or Spanish mission, period; and of the kivas uncovered, it most closely resembled the modern Hopi kiva. The other kivas were all slab-lined, but had benches on only one wall.

Many artifacts were discovered in 1935, including bone and stone implements and beads made of clay, bone, stone, and shell. Unusual were pottery imitations of shell that were painted and pierced for use as beads, pendants, and earrings. There was also a "surprisingly frequent" occurrence of life forms in the pottery decoration. Especially gratifying to the archaeologists was the discovery of Kachina portrayals and what seemed to be representations of ceremonial dances. In their sum, these finds alone promised that some of the modern Hopi ceremonials might now be traced "into the archaeological past."

In 1936, the "Western Mound" of Awatovi was excavated, and testing was done elsewhere on the site. Almost immediately, differences in construction and pottery indicated the excavators were into an earlier period. None of the brilliant Sikyatki and Mission polychrome wares were present. All of the pottery was characteristic of the latter part of the Pueblo III Period. Moreover, walls were double-coursed and well laid. Many rooms contained two firepits, and it was clear that coal was being burned in these prehistoric times. Early in the second month of the season, pieces of painted wall plaster were found in a kiva fill. Intensified examination revealed many painted layers on the kiva walls. Anticipation heightened appreciably, and it was by no means misplaced, for this was to become one of the most remarkable and valuable discovery times in the history of Southwestern archaeology, as spades sank deep into kiva after subterranean kiva in Awatovi and

Kawaika-a. Until this moment came to pass, most information regarding ancient ceremonial life could only be guessed at. Archaeologists had speculated about what uses were made of mute artifacts, they read backward from modern times after observing present Pueblo customs, and they studied petroglyphs. But there was no written language to assist the guesses they made, and hints of wall paintings, wherever they were found, tantalized them and encouraged them to continue searching for more informative murals.

It would be worthwhile and instructive to reexamine the murals today in terms of what they have to say about the making and keeping of the Covenant.

A few examples of other murals are the following: At Alkali Ridge, in the westernmost section of the Mesa Verde Region, fragments of murals were found in a Pueblo II site. At Mesa Verde proper, a few geometric designs and simple representative bird figures — I'm sure you remember the part the three birds played in the emergence story — still remained in fragmentary form on some kiva walls. Paul S. Martin discovered geometric kiva paintings at Lowry Ruin in Colorado. Then, after the Museum-Gates Expedition was concluded in 1901, Walter Hough published in the annual report of the National Museum for that year a description of an illustrated mural at Kawaika-a, in the Jeddito Valley.

All of these murals were exciting to the discoverers, for the immense artistic talents of the Pueblo people came proudly into view. Now, though, twenty-three more paintings were found on those famous first-kiva walls at Awatovi. The mesmerized searchers moved on to an adjoining kiva, and then on to another. Soon the mural total was forty-one. The archaeologists and their Hopi crew were ecstatic. Yet these findings were only a sample of what was yet to come, for remnants of what must once have been absolutely spectacular murals were to be discovered in eighteen kivas in Awatovi and Kawaika-a. Archaeologist John Otis Brew noted that surprising variations were to be found in subject and technique. Depictions included pure geometric designs, realistic human figures, and formalized bird and animal representations much like those on Sikyatki pottery. He was convinced that a study of these, along with pottery paintings, would add much to our knowledge of the history of Pueblo art. Beyond this, it seemed probable that some of the figures could be identified with modern ceremonies and legends. And since the paintings occurred on kiva walls, it might also be possible to obtain information from them regarding the societies or clans by whom the kivas were used.

Every mural element was carefully photographed and a scale drawing made. The color was then recorded as closely as possible by comparing it with a color dictionary that was being compiled as they went along. Black, white, reds, and yellow were the most common colors, but orange, green, blue, and pinks also augmented the brown of the adobe plaster background. As far as could be determined, the mural paintings were done with an unknown kind of brush and the fingers on reasonably smooth masonry and mortar walls that were plastered over. Since entry was through the roof, unbroken walls were available for the murals. At Awatovi, some of the mortar had been reinforced with a matting of reeds or grass, as at

murals

Hopi and Zuni. Several finish coats of a fine-textured reddish brown plaster completed the job and provided the working surface for the murals. The paint was mixed with a mordant and uniformly done on dry plaster in the manner called fresco secco (as opposed to fresco, which is done on wet plaster that bonds and holds the paint).

It is provocative to see how discoveries of magnitude and what the Traditional life produces seem to parallel and augment one another. The simultaneous discoveries of the relationship of Basketmaker and Pueblo types and the excavations of Great Kivas have already provided us with typical examples of this. Now, while archaeologists probed for long-sought murals in the kivas of Awatovi and Kawaika-a, the same thing was happening over in New Mexico. In 1935, during the excavation of Kuaua, near the town of Bernalillo, other important murals were found in a single kiva. They are treated in the book *Sun Father's Way* by Bertha Dutton, as well as in numerous other reports. According to Watson Smith, as of the time of his 1952 report on Awatovi, the Kuaua murals were better preserved than those of Jeddito, and because of their broad content they constituted by far the most valuable and extensive collection of prehistoric mural art outside Awatovi and Kawaika-a. In 1975 Frank C. Hibben's book *Kiva Art of the Anasazi at Pottery Mound* was published about the splendid murals painted on the walls of kivas found in a ruin known as Pottery Mound, in central New Mexico. This village was occupied between A.D. 1300 and 1475, placing it in the same period during which Awatovi reached its florescence.

In his summary remarks on the general history and distribution of kiva mural paintings, Smith sees wall painting as a persistent trait in Pueblo cultural development. It began, simply at least, as early as Pueblo II, perhaps in the middle San Juan area, and grew gradually in complexity as it spread throughout the entire Anasazi realm. It flowered in Pueblo IV, at the same time that ceramics and architecture reached their climax of vigor. After that a decline in all three media of expression began, and only ceramics and wall art, now translated to easel art, have experienced within this century any kind of renaissance. Chalk it up to intruding peoples, who took away the isolation and peace the Hopis had once known, and which enabled them to produce such magnificent works.

Smith's extensive book *Kiva Mural Decorations at Awatovi and Kawaika-a, with a Survey of Other Wall Paintings in the Pueblo Southwest* (1952) must be ranked with the finest publications available on the Anasazi. It reads easily, but it is utterly perceptive and thorough about Pueblo life in general during the Pueblo III, IV, and V periods.

At Awatovi twenty-three kivas were either excavated or tested. At Kawaika-a twelve more were excavated. Smith's report contains diagrams for most of these, together with sections and photographs that spell out in careful detail the final transitional step from the earlier circular kiva to the rectangular modern kiva. Smith concludes that all the kivas were constructed and occupied during the Pueblo IV Period, and more expressly between A.D. 1300 and 1630. All but one of the kivas were characterized by a predominance of Pueblo IV black-on-yellow pottery found on the floor and in the fill. This does not mean there were no earlier kivas at Awatovi or Kawaika-a. It means only that further excavation would be required to uncover the earlier kivas "almost certainly there."

The kivas were apparently subterranean or partly so, but it was not possible to determine whether the roofs were level with the grade or, as at modern Hopi, had their entryways projecting a few feet or so above grade. Some kivas appear to have been located in plazas; in many instances they were built in clusters. At least three clusters at Awatovi were located on the cliff edge, just as so many are at modern Hopi, so that the rear walls were almost entirely above ground and exposed to the elements.

Generally speaking, the kivas at Awatovi and Kawaika-a conformed to prescribed pattern in architecture and function. Their style remained constant for three centuries, and the modern Hopi kivas resemble them closely. Smith decided, on the basis of his kiva studies, that "the basic pattern of Hopi ceremonial life was well established during early Pueblo IV times and has changed little since."

Kawaika-a, or *Kawaikuh*, so often referred to in the Awatovi material, is dated A.D. 1350–1469 and is the largest pueblo ruin in the Jeddito area. It is on the southwestern edge of Antelope Mesa, about three miles east of Awatovi. The pueblo was of irregular arrangement, having a number of kivas and plazas or courts enclosed by room clusters of various sizes.

Walter Hough visited the ruin in 1901, in conjunction with the Museum-Gates Expedition, and recorded a wall elaborately decorated in color: The painted wall showed part of a human figure and a bird, both done in yellow, green, and white. However, the far more significant work at Kawaika-a was done by Watson Smith and the Peabody Museum expedition of 1935 to 1939.

Sikyatki has also been mentioned several times. It holds a prominent place in legends still told at Walpi. Its ruins are about 2 miles north of Polacca, and its primary renown comes from the extraordinary pottery created there. According to legend, the village was founded by the Kokop, or Fuel, people at a time when Walpi was possibly the only other town on First Mesa. Rivalry and disputes between the two pueblos escalated, leading a Walpi man to cut short the hair of a Sikyatki youth. Later, the humiliated and headstrong youth, while participating in a ceremony at Walpi, took a knife and went looking for his enemy. When he couldn't find him, he cut off the head of the man's sister instead. He escaped and ran along the cliff top boasting of his deed. In reply, the infuriated men of Walpi waited until the men of Sikyatki were out in their fields, then attacked the village and destroyed it.

These are troubling acts for those who insist upon thinking of the Hopi as always perfectly peaceful people. We see now, however, that in a given instance, they, like most other people in the world, can and do behave badly at times when they believe it is necessary. Remember, though, that they are a microcosm of the rest of humanity and as such can identify with the rest of us, knowing what we think and feel, and how and why we behave as we do in certain circumstances. They also know what antidotes to apply, especially in this contracting end time.

Having addressed this situation, I think it should be pointed out that, with only a handful of other exceptions where deaths occurred, the Awatovi affair was the only one of consequence to physically mar the peace during the last thousand years of Hopi existence. If the rest of the world could match that record, think how secure and serene life would have been and be for everyone.

In the summer of 1895 Fewkes and his crew of Hopi workmen excavated some parts of the infamous Sikyatki ruin. Only the slightest traces of the village remained above ground. The roofs had collapsed, sand had drifted into and filled the open spaces, and sagebrush and other desert plants had taken root in the debris. Modern melon and squash fields covered part of the ruin area. There was little to suggest that just below the surface were ceramics that would rank with the finest ever created. Even Hopi who came to visit while work was in progress were transfixed by the beautifully decorated vessels that came to light. In fact, the finest potter of the mesa, a woman from Hano named Nampeyo, proclaimed that her best work was inferior to the worst by the women of Sikyatki, and she begged permission to copy some of the designs for her own use. Lesou, her husband, helped decorate the pottery that resulted and assisted her further by gathering shards to be used for inspiration. In this way a whole new era in Hopi ceramics was begun.

As the ruin itself was exposed, it proved to be rectangular in plan, with its northern and western buildings being much higher than the southern and eastern units. Among the lesser material culture objects obtained by Fewkes were prayer sticks, properly called pahos. They were numerous and of different kinds, varying in form from wooden slats to pencil-like rods bearing carved ferrules. Most were painted in green and black and resemble those used today by the Flute Fraternity at Walpi. Fewkes believed this resemblance supported the claim of the fraternity that their ancestors were among the first to settle in Hopi country and were among those who once populated Sikyatki pueblo.

Coal was not used only as fuel; in the form of lignite it was polished and shaped for jewelry. Turquoise beads gave evidence of trade with Rio Grande Anasazi, and shell indicated trade contacts with Gulf peoples. The most common form of necklace was made of short pieces of bird bones strung together and stained green. Slabs of mica and selenite were drilled and shaped to make pendants and earrings.

Many of the pottery bowls contained smooth stones similar to those still employed to polish pottery. Also found were concretionary quartz crystals like those used by medicine men, stalactite fragments, one fossil cephalopod, white kaolin disks, and a cylindrical clay corn fetish.

By all odds, though, the most artistic of the objects found at Sikyatki was the pottery, and its forms were so symmetrical that Fewkes could hardly believe they were done without a potter's wheel. He thought it "not too much to say" that the Sikyatki collection included ceramics more finely made and elaborately decorated than any ceramic work of any aboriginal tribe of North America, and that it compared favorably with the best work of Mesoamerica. It was vastly superior to pottery being made in the adjacent pueblos in 1895, in form, in fineness of parts, and in beauty of decoration. It was ornamented with an elaborate and symbolic polychrome decoration that differed in character from that of any pueblo near or far. Beyond its surpassing beauty as an art form, there was knowledge to be gained from its symbolic decorations, for never before had such a variety of ancient picture writing been discovered in any one ruin in the Southwest. Fewkes was certain that if anyone could interpret this Pueblo pictography correctly, our understanding of the ancient Pueblo mind and acts would be vastly enriched and enlarged.

Kokopnyama, dated A.D. 1269–1430, is situated 1 mile northeast of the Jeddito trading post and a few miles south of Keams Canyon, on the north side of the Jeddito Valley. Lyndon L. Hargrave did some work there in 1929, the same year he investigated Kin Tiel. He reported that a surface survey indicated a ruin about 10 acres in area, with architectural features "not unlike those of modern Hopi pueblos, if recent influence in the latter is disregarded." The general plan was essentially the same, with house groups that were two or more stories in height enclosing open courts. In addition to having a main quadrangular plaza surrounded by room blocks, the pueblo stretched north for nearly 600 feet along the mesa's edge. The Pueblo III dwellings and the Pueblo IV kivas were on the slope below the mesa edge. Entrance was most often made through the roof, and until the early 1900s practically all first-floor rooms of historic Hopi pueblos were entered in this way. Mealing bins were also found in Kokopnyama rooms.

Hargrave reports the finding of four kivas, and he excavated three of these. Two were virtually identical to those of Awatovi and Kawaika-a in size and features. Exceptions were that neither contained a foot drum or a sipapu, and one had a fireplace unique for this area in addition to its square subfloor firepit. In essence this fireplace resembled an upholstered armchair without legs. The deflector constituted its back, and a sandstone extension at each side its arms. Between the arms was a fireplace that had two levels. Fireplaces like this are also found in the kivas of the Rio Grande pueblos.

The third kiva excavated was unusual only in that it was almost square and had no rear bench. Its ventilator shaft entered the rear wall at floor level and then intersected a vertical circular shaft within the core of the masonry wall itself.

MESA VERDE

Mesa Verde, whose period of occupation lasted from ca. 1100 to the late 1200s, is located in southwestern Colorado and is known the world over for its spectacular cliff dwellings. Thousands of tourists come every year to marvel at the stone construction skills that are displayed and to wonder about the people who lived there — in particular, at Cliff Palace, Mug House, Long House, Spruce Tree House, Balcony House, and Square Tower House. In addition to the cliff dwellings, there is an intriguing Fire Temple, and on the mesa top above the dwellings are the tantalizing ruins of solar towers and Sun Temple, plainly showing the worship patterns of the people.

While no one knows for certain where all of the Mesa Verde villagers went when they abandoned the mesa in the late 1200s, many scholars believe that some portion migrated to the northern tip of Black Mesa, and then on to Hopi Land, where their descendants live today.

CHACO CANYON

The first professional archaeologist to work at awesome Chaco Canyon was George H. Pepper of the American Museum of Natural History in New York. Since 1905 extensive work has been done by the School of American Research, Santa Fe, New Mexico; the National Geographic Society, in conjunction with the Smithsonian Institution; and the University of New Mexico. The Chaco Canyon National Monument was established on March 11, 1907, and the National Park Service has since performed regular research in association with its Chaco Center on the University of New Mexico campus. Stabilization work to preserve the ruins from weeds, sand, rubble, and the elements goes on continually. So far, four of the thirteen major village ruins have been excavated and are being maintained: Pueblo Bonito, Chetro Ketl, Pueblo del Arroyo, and Kin Kletso. Several Hosta Butte sites have also been excavated and kept up. All the major ruins have received some stabilization, with special care being taken not to alter the appearance of the original walls.

Pithouses

Fewkes believed that the caves in the area were selected for habitation not because they could be better defended than surface pueblos but because of their constant creek-water supply and the associated land patches that could be cultivated. Small numbers of marauding Indians could have raided the Anasazi cornfields, but the cliff dwellers kept enough food in store to last more than a year, and even a prolonged siege could not have run them out or caused their surrender. Nor could the high cliff villages have been successfully assaulted. The defenders were too securely in place.

In 1920 Neil M. Judd, curator of American archaeology at the U.S. National Museum, went on a reconnaissance trip to Chaco in preparation for a National Geographic expedition at Pueblo Bonito that would begin actual work in 1921. Probing in the area, his workmen came upon the first of two pithouses they would find. These were not by any means the earliest dwellings in the Chaco area, but they were the first documented evidence of Basketmaker presence there, and as such constituted exciting finds. In 1927 a Late Basketmaker village 9 miles east of Pueblo Bonito was excavated by Frank H.H. Roberts.

Fajada Butte

The accomplishments of archaeologists working at Chaco Canyon have long been impressive, yet some of the truly monumental discoveries have just recently come to light. In 1978 and 1979 astonishing secrets were revealed by aerial photography. Infrared sensors have disclosed a Chaco metropolis whose scope dwarfs the canyon community previously known. They have also revealed a vast roadway system that crisscrosses the entire region. And then there is Fajada.

On June 29, 1977, Anna Sofaer, one of a group of amateur archaeologists cataloging rock art in Chaco Canyon, made a serendipitous find that, to put it mildly, has excited the entire scientific community.

High up on a rattlesnake-infested butte named Fajada, she paused about midday at a mysterious, although already known, group of three mammoth stone slabs that fronted two spiral-shaped petroglyphs on the cliff face beyond them. A beam of light that passed through an opening between two of the slabs caught her eye, and she watched in utter fascination as it first struck and then made its way slowly across the surface of one of the petroglyphs. Before its course was run, she realized she was seeing in operation a unique sun calendar that had been constructed by Chaco priests a thousand years before. Specialists and photographers were hurriedly called in to check it out.

After working for two years to solve and record the exact workings of what proved to be an amazingly accurate midday sun calendar, archaeoastronomers were convinced that Fajada, as they named the device, ranks in precision, accuracy, and functional versatility with the best astronomical structures yet found in the Old and New worlds.

Fajada is unique among time clocks. In contrast to other ancient time devices that use architectural features for alignment and take their orientation from points on the horizon where the sun rises and sets, Fajada uses sunlight itself as the indicator and employs the three great stones as directional channels. These are sandstone slabs ranging in height from 6 to 9 feet (0.8–2.7 m) and in thickness from 8 to 18 inches (20–45 cm). They weigh about two tons each. Their back edges lean against the cliff, they are set roughly parallel to one another, and they are spaced a few inches apart, so that two narrow, pointed shafts of sunlight pass through the gaps and strike the petroglyphs, marking the seasons in this manner by singling out the equinoxes and solstices. Not only does the calendar divide the year into the four quarters, posting a unique pattern to mark the beginning of each, it also gives a rough idea of the number of days elapsing between the beginning points. In addition, it can predict lunar eclipses.

The larger spiral petroglyph has nine coils. The smaller spiral has three coils, with the outer line extended to make the whole look like a coiled snake. At winter solstice, December 21, the shortest day of the year, the two shafts of light frame the large spiral exactly. At midday one band rests on the left edge and the other band rests on the right edge. At summer solstice, June 21, when the sun is at its zenith, one beam strikes the exact center of the large spiral. At midday on the autumn and spring equinoxes marking the midpoints between the summer and winter solstices, one light beam precisely bisects the nine turns on the larger spiral's right side, and at the same moment the other wedge of light descends through the precise center of the smaller spiral.

Adding to the fascination of the stone shafts is the fact that their surfaces are double-curved. Thus, at the summer solstice, when the sun is moving horizontally in the sky, the slabs' upper edges play their own special role by translating the light into a beam that progresses vertically across the spiral petroglyph.

Fajada has taken its place today as the first midday solar calendar on record, the only one known to make use of its peculiar geometry. The skill required to build it is evident, and specialists are learning that the Anasazi and other ancient peoples of North America were far more sophisticated and knowledgeable than previously thought. Without question, this new and portentous discovery, along with others being made at Chaco Canyon, has prompted archaeologists, archaeo-astronomers, and other professionals to look again, and with particular keenness, for similar wonders at Anasazi ruins everywhere, and in consequence, a number have been discovered.

BLACK MESA

As part of an ongoing training project carried out in 1968, 1969, and 1970, an archaeological investigation team from Prescott College, Arizona, excavated and surveyed parts of Black Mesa in the western Kayenta area. The team findings to date have been summarized in two excellent volumes published by the Prescott College Press, and these contribute greatly to our knowledge concerning this hitherto minor but unknown segment of the Anasazi culture.

Black Mesa lies between the Kayenta-Marsh Pass region and the historic Hopi pueblos. It is one of the few large areas of the Southwest that have not been extensively explored by archaeologists, probably because there are only a handful of the dry caves that could hold substantial amounts of perishable material. It also lacks the scenic grandeur of other Anasazi locations, and it is at best a marginal area of Anasazi development.

After excavating nine sites and surveying 193 more, researchers have determined that the prehistoric cultural tradition on the mesa is indeed Kayenta Anasazi, dating from A.D. 500 or before to ca. A.D. 1200, when the area was entirely abandoned.

To establish a chronology for the area, a series of time phases were delineated. The earliest of these has been entitled the Dot Klish Phase, and it is associated with Basketmaker III. Dot Klish Phase village sites were scattered and small, a condition that would remain constant during the occupation of Black Mesa. "The primary social unit was most likely the extended family or several extended families which occupied a single site." No pattern of village orientation or architectural style was followed, and they did not duplicate the linear villages of other Basketmaker III sites. Dwellings were usually shallow oval pithouses or small jacal structures. Storage rooms were either slab or masonry-lined and semi-subterranean.

Manos held in one hand were the usual grinding tools. There is evidence that coal was used for some firing of pottery and for home fuel. Charred corn and the bones of animals were found, and it appears that two types of agriculture were practiced: floodwater farming and dry farming.

Another phase, the Tallahogan, is equivalent to the Basketmaker III–Pueblo I transition period. It ended around A.D. 852. Building sites were located on slightly higher terraces than in the Dot Klish Phase, possibly to allow use of the former building areas for farm plots.

Dinnebilo Phase settlements, covering the approximate years A.D. 875–975, evidenced yet another shift in location. Kayentans still lived along the main drainages, but the movement now was to the uplands. Specialized activity sites were in use by now, as different parts of the mesa were employed at different times for hunting, collecting, and farming. Some sites were so small and poorly arranged they can hardly be called villages, while others evidence a classic Pueblo I unit village kind of orientation.

The Wepo Phase, dating from ca. A.D. 1000 to 1050, saw a fourth shift in areas of occupation and the first kivas. After nearly half a millennium of occupation, the Kayentans of Black Mesa moved away from the confines of the Moenkopi and its major tributaries and up to the upland region. Now there was an increased reliance on dry farming. Village plans began to stabilize, marking a transition from subsurface to surface structures that varied to a marked degree in either their arrangement or their lack of it. One village might have surface dwellings on the north side of the site facing south, a kiva in front of these, and a trash deposit out in front of the kiva. Another village might have kivas, storage rooms, and dwellings—consisting both of pithouses and of jacal structures—scattered all over the site. Considerable experimentation in architecture is apparent. Jacal and masonry were combined, and pithouses were Mogollon-like in style, consisting of shallow pits, rectangular rooms with rounded corners, and ramped entryways. Large, sometimes circular, multi-room jacal structures were common. Kivas were circular and occasionally masonry-lined. They varied in banquette or recess style, and sometimes had what might have been a foot drum located behind the firepit. There was a high ratio of kivas to dwellings.

The Lamoki Phase, covering the years from A.D. 1050 to 1100, was a time of population increase. Occupation of the uplands continued, along with dry farming. In addition, the northeast corner of the mesa was now inhabited, and a relatively large cliff dwelling, Standing Fall House, was begun. The village plan that would also characterize the following Toreva Phase was adopted. It consisted of a masonry room block fronted by a kiva, and beyond that the trash heap. Site orientation was generally along an east-west axis. More masonry was employed than previously, although it is assumed that jacal structures were attached to the masonry.

The Toreva Phase, lasting from A.D. 1100 to ca. 1200, ended the prehistoric occupation of northeastern Black Mesa. It was attended by an increased shift of villages to the uplands. There was also a decided clustering of sites in certain locations, particularly around the edges of low sage-covered flats suitable for dry farming. The change in settlement pattern was due, apparently, to the environmental situation. Sites were now of two kinds: primary villages with dwellings, storage rooms, and kivas; and secondary sites with "habitation rooms and limited activity areas." Artifacts continued to resemble those of earlier phases, although most manos were now two-handed, "hinting at the possibility of an increase in dependence upon cultivated and noncultivated plant foods."

For reasons yet to be agreed upon by anthropologists and archaeologists, the Anasazi began to move out of Black Mesa, and it was entirely abandoned by the end of the Toreva Phase in A.D. 1200. Everything of value was taken along by the migrating people, and the discovery of a whole artifact is rare. Even the heavy stone metates were removed, suggesting that the Kayentans of Black Mesa did not plan to move far. Surely it is no coincidence that the pueblos of the modern Hopi are only thirty miles south of Black Mesa.

As a final note, the Prescott College team has concluded that the Black Mesa Anasazi were in "continual interaction" with other Kayenta peoples, a fact testified to by the remarkable similarity of pottery design style and design attributes. Isolation or a lack of relationship would have led to greater differences in pottery techniques, shape, and design.

Pueblo IV, dated by archaeologists from A.D. 1300 to 1600, was the first culture phase sufficiently known and comparable to the modern to be labeled Hopi, although anything must begin with Oraibi. As the fourteenth century began, there was an impressive increase in the size of some sites and at the same time a contraction in their number while the overall population continued to grow. The San Juan Region was abandoned, and many southern migrations took place coincidentally with the great drought of A.D. 1276–99. Later, all or part of the Kayenta population moved south to join their cultural relatives on the spur tips of Black Mesa. *Hopi Land* Later still, another population influx came from the Winslow area. New pottery types were developed from intrusive models. Large masonry pueblos came into being, with rectangular kivas of the historic type. As evidenced by the magnificent kiva wall paintings of Awatovi and Kawaika-a, a religious life similar to present-day practices characterized the period, although sometime after A.D. 1500 the Jeddito area was gradually abandoned, with Awatovi surviving until A.D. 1701.

An approximate dating for the Jeddito and Hopi area villages is as follows for the Pueblo III, IV, and V periods: Looking at their impressive time spans causes me to wonder whether the idea of constant factionalism is a tenable one, especially when we know that some of the moves from one site to another had nothing at all to do with internal arguments. Why am I stressing this? Because

Dan and I have not found anything to support the idea that the Hopi are naturally contentious. More often than not they go to great lengths to get along, and we believe that will, in the end, prove to be the case where the Hotevilla Elders and the other villages are concerned.

JEDDITO

Awatovi	*A.D. 1200–1700 (500 years)*
Kokopnyama	*A.D. 1269–1430 (161 years)*
Kawaika-a	*A.D. 1350–1469 (119 years)*
Sikyatki	*A.D. 1300–1500 (200 years)*

HOPI

Old Oraibi	*A.D. 1120 to–present (786 years before the split in 1906)*
original Shipaulovi	*A.D. 1200–1680 (480 years)*
late Shipaulovi	*A.D. 1680–present (314 years)*
original Mishongnovi	*A.D. 1250–1800 (550 years)*
late Mishongnovi	*A.D. 1800–present (194 years)*
original Shongopovi	*A.D. 1250–1680 (430 years)*
late Shongopovi	*A.D. 1680–present (314 years)*
original Walpi	*A.D. 1300–1700 (400 years)*
Hano	*A.D. 1696–present (298 years)*
Sichomovi	*A.D. 1750–present (244 years)*
Moencopi	*A.D. 1870–present*
Tuba City	*A.D. 1870–present*
Polacca	*A.D. 1880–present*
Hotevilla	*A.D. 1906–present*
Bacobi	*A.D. 1907–present*
New Oraibi	*A.D. 1910–present*

POPULATION FIGURES*

	1889	*1932*	*1948*	*1968*
Old Oraibi	903	87	199	167
Shipaulovi	126	123	152	142
Mishongnovi	244	266	298	530
Shongopovi	225	307	423	475
Walpi	232	163		80
Hano	161	309		241
Sichomovi	103	315		364
Moencopi			640	710
Tuba City				
Polacca				
Hotevilla			644	
Bacobi			176	
New Oraibi			590	401

*Estimated total population of the reservation in 1976 was 6,000, and in 1994 it is between nine and ten thousand. Considering themselves to be a sovereign people, the Hopi have refused to allow a census, although there are currently differences of opinion about this.

*The 1889 and 1968 figures are taken from Harry C. James, *Pages from Hopi History* (p. 16), and the 1932 and 1948 figures are from Stanley A. Stubbs, *Bird's-Eye View of the Pueblos*, pp. xv and 95-117.

It is time now to look at some of the visible evidences of Anasazi migration and accomplishment. Of these, it is not easy to prove which of them is of Hopi origin, or another of the Anasazi/Pueblo peoples, but most have characteristics that show Hopi affinities. However it may be, the nature of Hopi culture as seen by the first outsiders to come to Hopi country, and to a remarkable degree still present today, is alive to the perceptive viewer in all of these dwellings.

BETATAKIN

AZTEC

AZTEC RUIN, NEW MEXICO. *View from within the court looking north at the center of the north wing where, after excavation, the walls were the highest. The Great Kiva, since restored, is shown in the foreground. From Earl H. Morris photograph.*

KIN TIEL PUEBLO

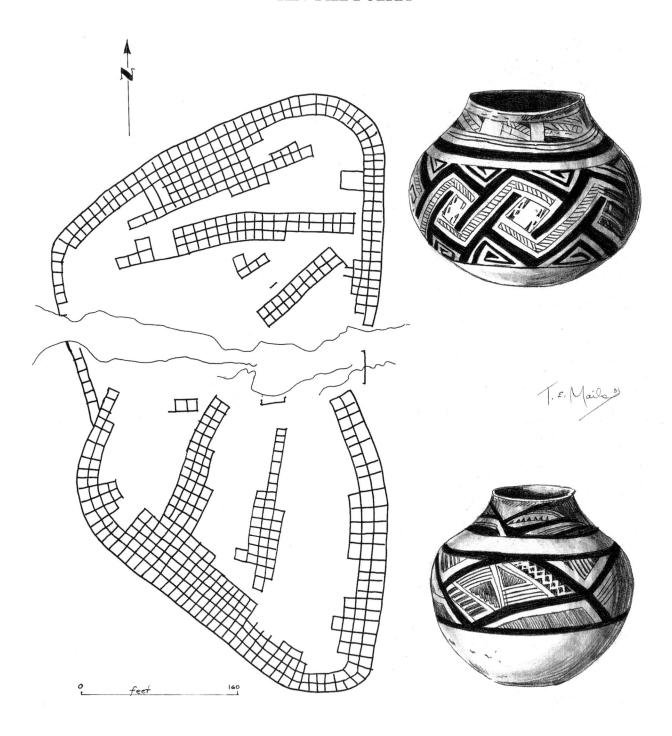

THE GENERAL PLAN OF KIN TIEL PUEBLO. *The pueblo included Hopi-style kivas, surprising archaeologists over finding these so far from the Hopi homeland.*

ANTELOPE MESA

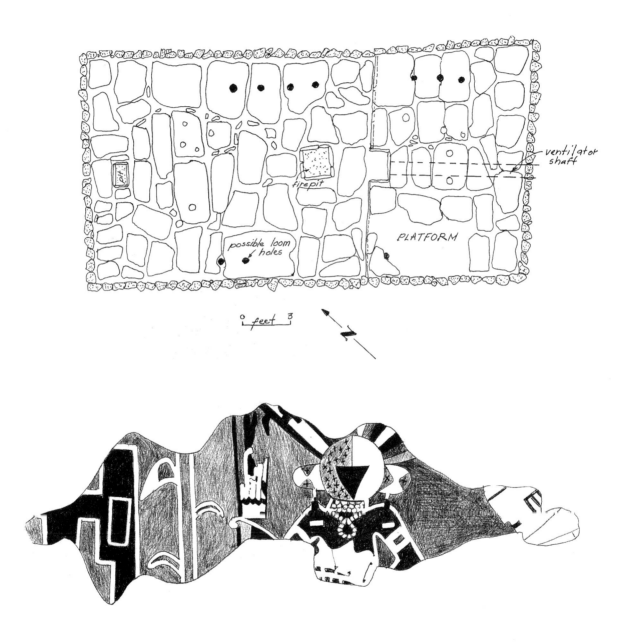

Top, *Hopi style kiva.* Bottom, *kiva mural fragment depicting Ahola Kachina, who appears at the Powamu Ceremony and symbolizes the coming of the sun.*

Antelope Mesa kiva
mural fragments

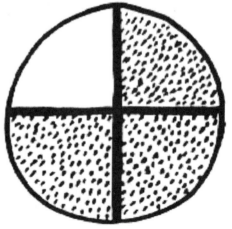

*Antelope Mesa kiva
mural fragments*

BLACK MESA

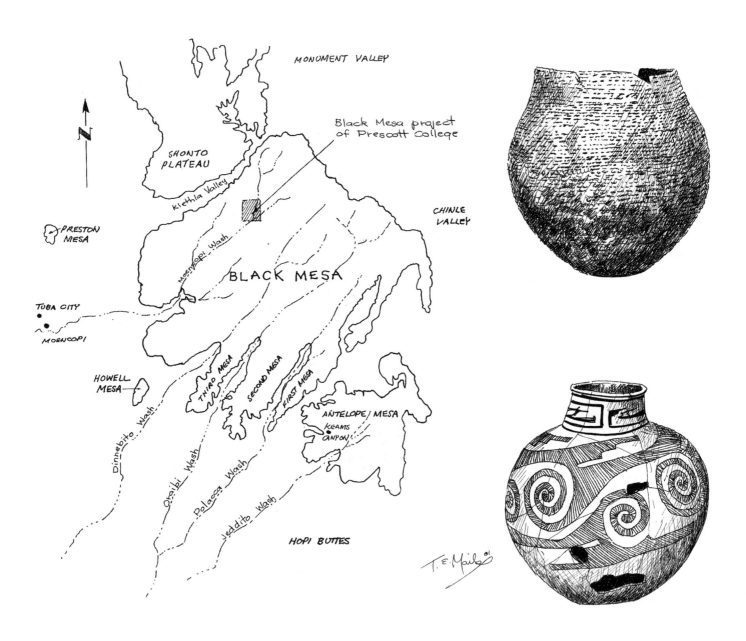

Left, *map showing location of Black Mesa*. Top right, *Tusayan Corrugated.*
Bottom right, *Dogoszhi Black-on-white. From Gumerman, 1970.*

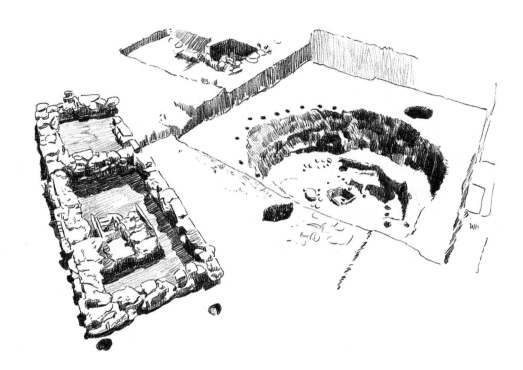

Partially excavated Toreva Phase site showing pithouse, and a two-room masonry structure for storage that was converted to a mealing room.

View of Black Mesa from the northeast at the mesa's highest elevation, about 1000 feet above the desert floor below.

Cast shadows at the Sacred Mesa which reveal to the Elders the forms of the Creator and his helpers.

The Hopi Sacred Mesa

INSCRIPTION HOUSE

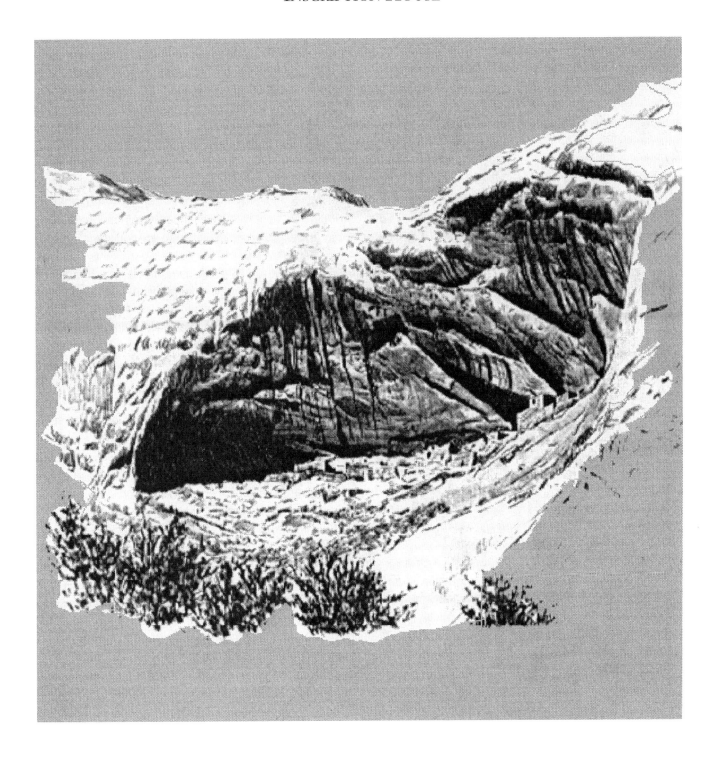

MESA VERDE

Mug House

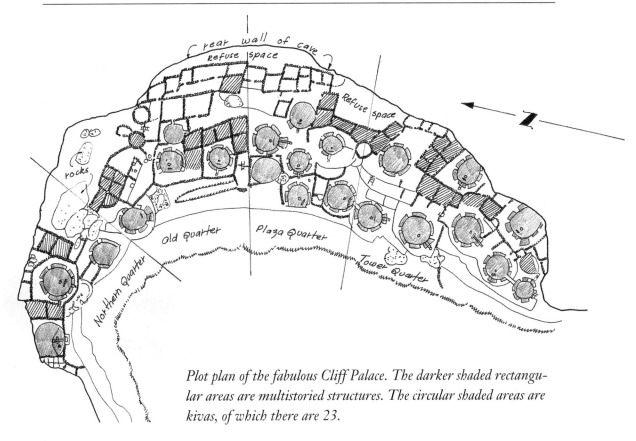

Plot plan of the fabulous Cliff Palace. The darker shaded rectangular areas are multistoried structures. The circular shaded areas are kivas, of which there are 23.

Cliff Palace

Bins for grinding corn in upper cave of Fire Temple House.

Western end of Fire Temple Court.

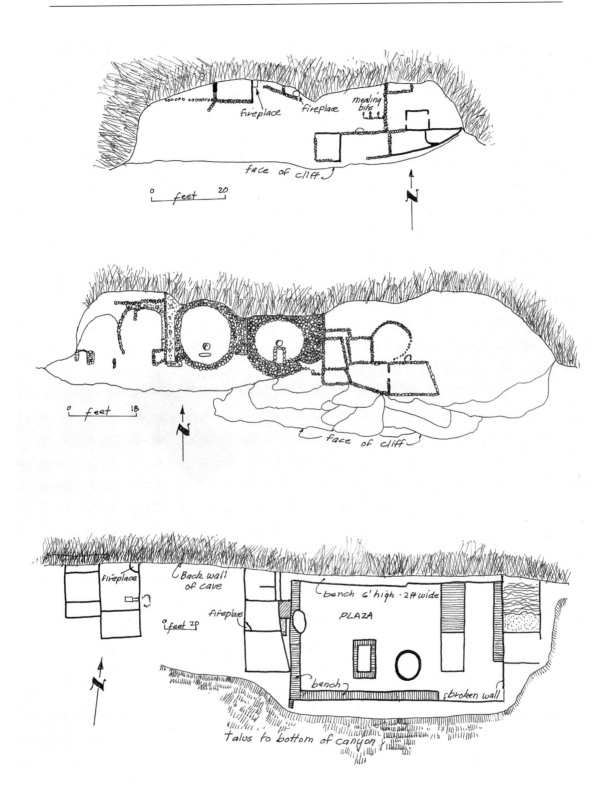

Top, *ground plan of Upper Cave of Fire Temple House;* Center, *ground plan of Lower Cave of Fire Temple House;* Bottom, *ground plan of Fire Temple House central court.*

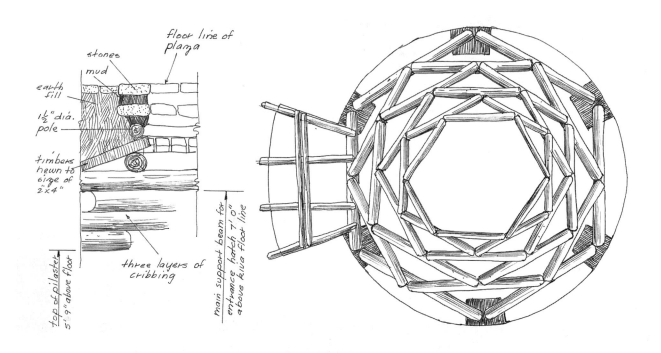

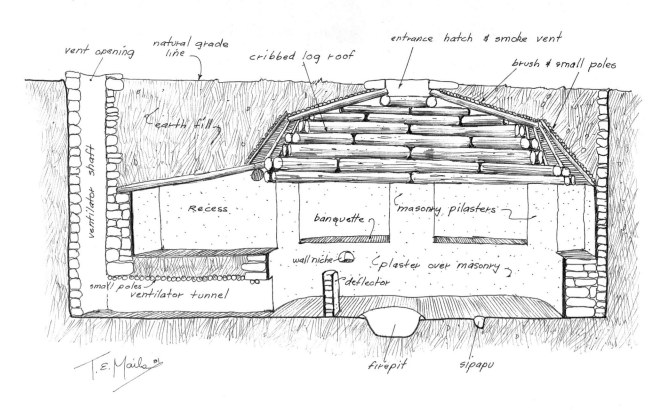

Top left, *section showing details of entrance hatch framing of kiva at Spruce Tree House;* Top right, *top view showing typical method of framing a kiva;* Bottom, *section showing postulated construction of the "pure type" crib-roof kiva.*

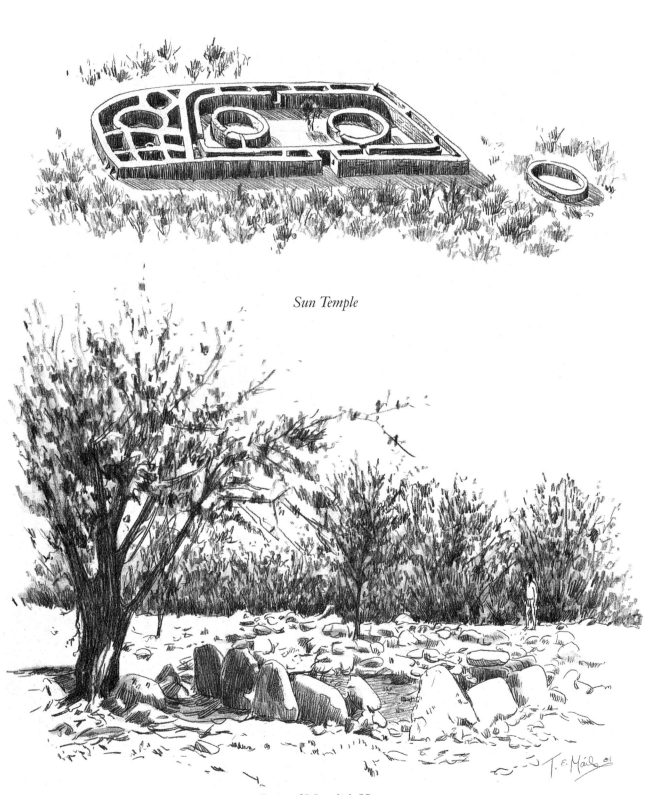

Sun Temple

Ruin of Megalith House

CHACO CANYON
A Macaw and ceremonial objects

CHACO CANYON POTTERY: a, *Old Bonitian ladle;* b, *Old Bonito corrugated cooking vessel;* c, *decorated pitcher;* d, *cylindrical vase;* e, *bird-shaped bowl with T-shaped opening;* f, *beginner's bowl;* g, *olla, or water jar, from Late Bonito phase;* h, *rare clay pottery-maker's stamp.*

PUEBLO BONITO. *Pueblo Bonito is one of the ruins in Chaco Canyon.*

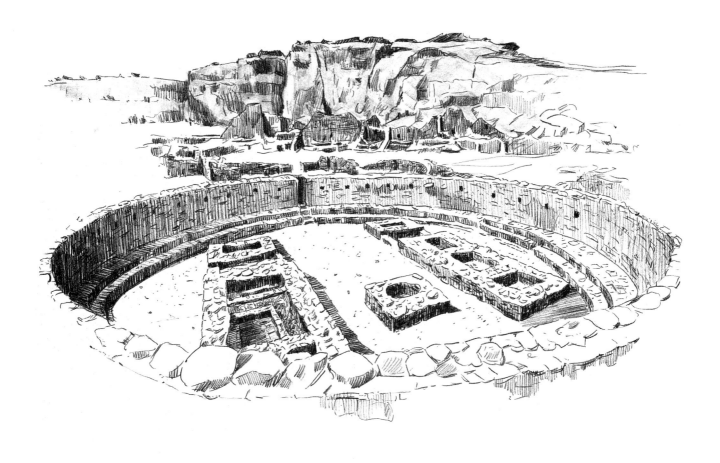

RUINS OF PUEBLO BONITO'S MAGNIFICENT GREAT KIVA. *Diameter at the outside wall above the benches is 51 feet. One great kiva at Chaco measured 65 feet in diameter.*

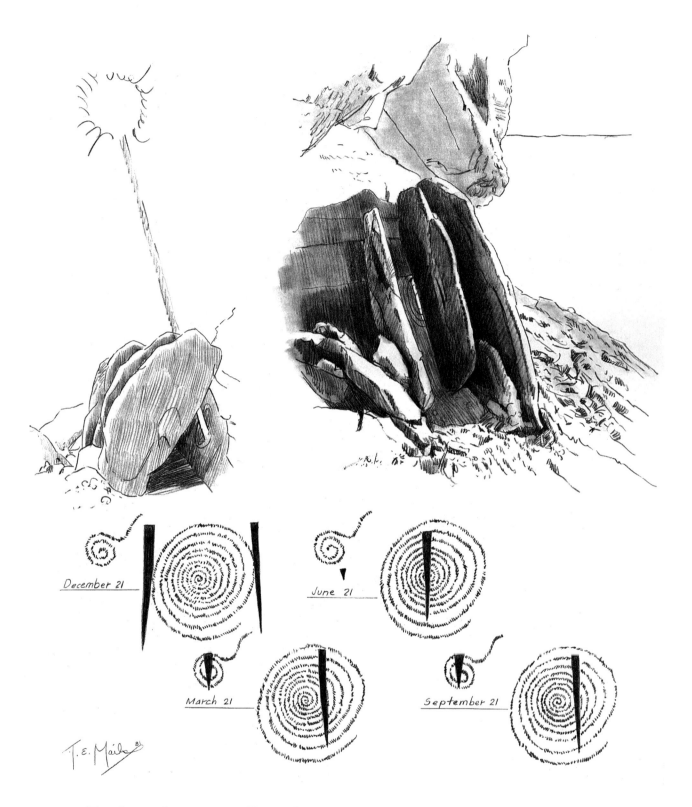

THE SOLAR CALENDAR ON FAJADA BUTTE: Top, *perspective views showing how the sun rays penetrate between the stone slabs to strike the petroglyphs and mark the solstices and equinoxes.* Bottom, *dagger-shaped lines show where the spirals are intersected at the critical dates.*

CHAPTER 4

THE LULL BEFORE THE THUNDERSTORM

THE HOPI AND PUEBLO V — THE LULL BEFORE THE THUNDERSTORM!

Toward the end of the nineteenth century, and especially after A.D. 1882 when the Hopi Reservation was founded, Americans began to visit these intriguing people on their towering southwestern mesas. To their utter surprise and delight they discovered there in the very midst of a burgeoning and modernizing United States life as it was when the first emissaries of Coronado arrived in Hopi Land more than 300 years earlier. It was like stepping magically back into ancient time and a rare and astounding experience. Almost nothing had changed. All but a few of the Hopi continued to love and preserve their ancient culture in an amazing way. And for those visitors who already knew about the stunning ruins of the Anasazi civilization, the absolutely wondrous thing was that the mists of time were penetrated, and the human element of the greater Anasazi/Hopi world came sweeping into view! More amazing still, as we reach the end of the twentieth century, is the fact that the traditional customs and architecture are still present to an astonishing degree. Here and here alone on the North American continent can Natives be found who in many ways live as their ancestors did a thousand and more years ago. Credit this to the Traditional Hopis as a whole, and especially the Elderly Elders of Hotevilla. Without their stubborn adherence to the Covenant, it would not be so. Very few evidences of it would be left.

Since the observations of outsiders fill in gaps that are important to those of us who are curious about the Hopi, we will look first at what the Bahannas found when they arrived there in the late nineteenth century. As we do so, please bear in mind that while this view through the window has its particular worth, what those who live inside the house have to say about their lives and thoughts is more valuable still. Observers must, by the very nature of the situation, deal mainly with externals, and can tell us little about how the Hopi themselves felt when the occupation took place and settled in. So in this chapter and others that follow, Katchongva and the Elderly Elders tell us their fascinating side of the story. However biased it may be — and it would be impossible for it to be otherwise — they pass on to us a priceless combination of their first-hand experiences, thoughts, and information personally obtained from clan and family members — some of whose lives date back to the late 1600s. They are also masters of oral tradition, the ancient practice of handing down memorized information from elders to descendants. As they speak, remember that what they say comes from inside the house, from fully within the ancient tradition. More than once when Dan Evehema and I talked, he reminded me that what he was telling me was precisely what had been handed down to him.

THE ELDERS

The cycle begins with the making of prayer feathers so all land and life may prosper. This makes life beautiful. We had plenty of food and were happy together. At that time, everything was in balance. We had rain and flowers. We loved each other, and lived in peace. No one was anxious about losing the land. No thoughts about the Bahannas troubled us, since the white people were not here yet.

KATCHONGVA

The vow which we made with the Great Spirit obligated us to follow his way of life. He gave the land to us to use and care for through our ceremonial duties. He instructed us and showed us the road plan by which we must govern our lives. We wrote this pattern on a rock so that we would always be reminded to follow the straight road. The Hopi must not drift away from this road or he will take this land away from us. This is the warning given to us by Maasauu.

Oraibi village was settled firmly. Migrating people were now gathering there and asking to be admitted into the village. The Kikmongwi and the high priests would always consider their request and base their judgement upon their character and wisdom. Those who showed signs of boastfulness were turned away and told to go to the south mesas, where their kind of people lived.

BALANCE

Top: *Placing prayer feathers*
Bottom: *Balance*

Only good people, humble and sincere in their prayers, were admitted.
Among the ceremonies of each group the prayer for rain was important in order for the crops to grow and produce an abundance of food. The people depended on this for their livelihood. Boastful people were not admitted so that the prayers would not be polluted. Oraibi was now finally established. The pattern of the religious order was established. Cycle by cycle we paid respect to our Mother Earth, our Father Sun, the Great Spirit, and all things through our ceremonials. We were happy, for we were united as one.

TEM— "Readers who are unfamiliar with the situation as it has been on the Hopi Reservation will wonder why the Hopi are so upset and fearful about the Bahannas, or Whites. To understand this and the White effect upon the keeping of the Covenant, you will need to read the entire book. But to begin with, it is only necessary to understand what life as they lived it was like before the second wave of Bahannas came, and why the traditional Hopi so fiercely resented the loss of it. Their unhappy memories of the Spanish had been dulled by several hundred reasonably peaceful years, and life had returned to normal. While the next Bahannas were prophesied and expected, the Hopi could not have imagined that these invaders would be fueled by an even more acquisitive and arrogant nature. Although prophecy cautioned otherwise, they assumed that if they were fortunate, life after this Bahannas' coming might consist of joyful sharing, with the left side of humanity prevailing and a live-and-let-live philosophy like their own in effect. So they began the meeting with an open mind. It did not take long for them to learn they were mistaken. Fortune was not good, and they were in real trouble.

Before dealing with that, however, the Elders lean back, close their eyes, and nostalgically begin to dream about life when it was not complicated by outside pressures and about the annual cycle of religious ceremonies — especially how they begin. They see the women happily at work and the children who will inherit and carry on all of this. They see themselves in the musty subterranean kivas at the beginning of the cycle, when the making of very special prayer feathers takes place. These are fashioned by the hundreds to be placed out in shrines where Sun will pick up their spirits and take them to the Divine Beings as Hopi requests for prosperity throughout the land and life of the entire world. There is no narrowness in this. At Hotevilla, they do this kind of a prayer feather, or paho, only once each year, and it is a most sacred and solemn duty they must perform. Other prayer feathers are made for certain occasions, such as those that are given to the Kachinas at the end of the Homegoing Dance. Outside of this, Dan, because of his position, is the only person at Hotevilla who is properly authorized to make prayer feathers whenever he feels there is a need to do so.

But the love, reverence, and hope that accompany the fashioning of these first prayer feathers is very special, and the act itself calls in blessings that make life beautiful. For nearly a thousand years the Hopi at Old Oraibi and then Hotevilla have been fashioning these, and in doing so have been obedient to the Covenant, keeping in balance everything that is essential to the world's stability. We didn't know this was the case, did we? We thought other forces were taking care of us. Prayer feathers are not complicated, and most are quite simple in their makeup. The feathers of various kinds of birds are used, but small eagle feathers are preferred for these, and to their quills are attached the tiny feathers of other birds by binding them on with a short length of white cotton string. While the work goes on, sacred smoking is done, and constant prayers are chanted or said that infuse themselves into the feathers and are carried by the spirits of the feathers to the divine beings. Even our imagining what it is like to do this brings a deep sense of peace and a feeling of profound satisfaction.

Prayer feathers

It is time now to understand what the Elders mean by "balance." Balance is, Dan explains, like walking along the blade of a knife, so that you walk straight ahead toward a goal and seek to not fall off to either side. It is not a keeping of things in balance by avoiding excesses or by equally distributing weight, nor is it a matter of leaning too heavily toward one side or the other. As will be seen later on, walking the straight path does, however, keep the natural forces in harmony with one another and the world rotating properly. In this context, it is like a key that keeps the earth locked in its universal pattern.

Notice how rich Hopi life was before it was interfered with: There was plenty of food, and people were happy together. They loved each other and lived in peace. They had rain and flowers, and they were not anxious about losing the land. But that was because the White people were not there yet.

Is it hard to understand why the Elders would like to go back or to at least hold the line where it is?

Katchongva too centers his remembrances in the cycle of ceremonial duties that were essential to following the way of life and road plan that would preserve the land Maasaw had placed in their care. Without the land, how would they keep the Covenant? See how Katchongva spells out the matter of balance by reminding the Hopi that the ancestors had even written this pattern on a rock so they would see it and never forget to follow "the straight road." The Hopi are warned that they must not drift away from this, else the land will be taken away from them. Remember what I said earlier, that the word "land" includes the people, their farming plots, and the village itself. Note here that Katchongva does not say that Maasaw or the Creator will personally take away the land. That won't be necessary. Someone else will do it…the United States Government and the power industries with both the *XY* knowing and unknowing help of the Tribal Council…which is precisely what is happening today because too many Hopis have ignored the prophetic warnings and drifted away from the tradition that was their strength.

Katchongva stresses what the Elders do, that only humble people who were sincere in their prayers would be able to hold fast to the Covenant. This would enhance the prospects for a united community of people who would survive to keep it…which meant offering up purified prayers that were not polluted by self-centered thoughts. He confirms Dan's opinion that the religious cycle we presently see was begun at Oraibi. "The pattern of the religious order was established. Cycle by cycle we paid respect to our Mother Earth, our Father Sun, the Great Spirit, and all things through our ceremonials." It would not bother the Elders in the least to learn that anthropologists would dispute their position regarding the beginning time for the Kachina cycle, since from what I have read, it appears that most scientists believe it was worked out over a long period of time. Assuredly, additions were made from time to time, and some things were dropped. But Dan accepts that the core began with Oraibi and remains a constant today. He should know.

As the Year 1900 Came to Pass, the First White American Visitors Were Arriving in Hopi Country…

They found that in general, the Hopi were quite small in stature. Most of the men were only a smidgin over five feet tall, and the women were shorter still. Constant physical activity and a sparse diet kept everyone lean, and a surprising number lived to 100 years of age and more. Even in recent times many of the spiritual leaders have lived beyond the century mark. Their skin color was reddish-brown, and their eyes were jet black, as was their hair — except for the elders, whose hair ranged from silver to white.

For everyday purposes, some of the Hopi men of A.D. 1900 were beginning to wear the White man's style of clothing, but others clung to the old-style home-made cotton trousers and either plain white or brightly colored shirts of calico or velvet. The trousers usually extended no lower than the shin, and they were slit open at the seam on the outer side for about the lower half of their length. Footless stockings, homespun, dyed, and knitted, were sometimes worn. These were held up by woven garters at a point just below the knee. A colorful bandanna was wrapped around the head at forehead level to hold the hair in place. At work in the fields or while hunting, the men wore considerably less, only a G-string made of hide or cloth and a pair of plain moccasins. It was comfortable attire for the Southwest climate, and the hot desert sun did not burn their dark skins so easily as it did that of White men. During ceremonies the Hopi men wore traditional moccasins and apparel, some of which you will see in the illustrations included in the book. A visual portrayal of Hopi life is included at the end of this chapter, and ceremonial costumes are shown in color plates at the end of Chapter 11.

Most of the women, especially the older ones, still dressed just as their immediate ancestors did. They wore beautiful woven blanket dresses, generally blue with a white border, or white with a red and blue border. Every dress would last its maker a lifetime. A shawl of calico or of native weave was thrown over the shoulders to complete the outfit. The dress itself was made so that the left shoulder was left uncovered, and the hem came a little below the knee. A woven belt pulled the dress in at the waist. By 1900, though, many of the women and girls were being encouraged by the government and prudish missionaries to wear a calico slip under the dress, so that arms and shoulders were well covered. Women did not wear stockings, and it was common for them to go about barefoot. But buckskin moccasins with rawhide soles were worn now and then. There was a plain white high-topped style for daily wear in the village that sometimes had a black sole, and there was a white wraparound legging-moccasin combination whose primary use was for weddings and ceremonies. For travel and field work, some women topped their daily-wear moccasins with a separate buckskin leg-wrapping, so that the combination looked about like the one-piece wraparound type just described. It was left a natural color and offered protection when it was necessary to go to the desert where cacti, chollas, prickly shrubs, sharp rocks, and reptiles abounded.

Jewelry in the year 1900 consisted of earrings, bracelets, necklaces, belts, and rings. Earrings of pure turquoise were common, but there were also wooden disks and rectangles with wonderful turquoise and shell mosaics appended on one side. Necklaces were fashioned of silver, turquoise, coral, shell, glass, and amber. Belts, rings, and bracelets were adorned with silver obtained in trade, although limited work had recently begun in copper.

Before they were eligible for marriage, some girls wore their hair loose and much in the manner of boys, except that it was parted. Others, Dan says, had a small bun done up on each side of the head. Girls of marriageable age had their hair done up in traditional large whorls called nash-ni, with one whorl on each side of the head. Some writers — myself included — say this was an imitation of the squash blossom, the Hopi symbol for purity, and that after marriage the hair was hung in two side coils to represent the long squash, a coiffure intended to symbolize fruitfulness. Others describe the whorls as representing butterflies, which they say, depending upon the authority, is either a symbol of virginity or fertility.

Dan says that the whorl was a "silent statement" of the girl's showing, in the traditional way, that she was ready for marriage. This, in itself, made her feelings sufficiently known. He adds that the whorl had nothing to do with the butterfly or squash blossom.

To make the whorl, the hair was parted in the middle and then gathered into long rolls at the side. Each roll was wound over either a corn-husk form or a large U-shaped branch of wood, forming two semicircles that joined to produce a single disk with a diameter of approximately 8 inches. Whorls like this were depicted in ancient pictoglyphs and in the murals at Awatovi.

Married women parted their hair in the middle, cut it fairly short, and then gathered it into two thick queues or rolls, one at each side of the head. The queues were then wound with a hair string for approximately 4 inches, and the ends were left loose in a fan shape. The methods of winding varied slightly. Polingaysi Qoyawayma says that when she was a child in the 1890s, hair combings and cuttings were saved and made into a hair cord to be employed ceremonially, as in tying the maiden's whorl.

Regarding the Hopi wedding ceremony, the artist E.A. Burbank says, "After the Ne-man-Kachin'ea there is what they call 'Obeek-ne-ak,' where young boys and girls take their food and go for a picnic out beyond the mesa. There is where the lovemaking takes place. They usually select the one they want, more for riches or industry than for love. After that the girl tells her mother that she wants a certain lad; if agreeable to the mother, they grind a lot of meal, make a stack of piki (bread), and invite his relatives in. They all give advice on what a good husband should be, admonishing him to raise plenty of corn, get plenty of wood, and so on. Then the groom-to-be takes meat over to the girl's home and it is accepted with many thanks. At this point more advice is given and more food is served. They visit back and forth, taking presents of piki and meat until time for the wedding ceremony, which takes place usually after most of the winter ceremonies are over. Meantime the girl, her mother, and all of their clan women grind bushels of corn into meal that is just as fine as our flour, until they think they have more than the amount that was prepared for the last wedding. Then the groom's mother is notified that on a certain night they will bring the promised bride. The girl begins to grind and keeps grinding for three days and nights. On the second day of grinding there is a battle of mud slinging between boys and girls, relatives of the couple. This is all in fun, of course. On the third day the hair is dressed. A new pottery bowl is set in a circle of sand, the soap weed and fresh water are made into suds, and the boy's mother washes the bride's hair, which is then fashioned into beautiful whirls like a married woman's. The bride's mother then washes the groom's head."

During the Home Going Dance at Hotevilla in July 1993, a young woman came out of a kiva dressed in a traditional white wedding outfit, and with her was a little girl who was similarly attired. Both had their hair fixed in whorls. After them came thirty other young women wearing traditional bordered blankets. When I asked Susie Lomatska what this signified, she answered that the women were advertising their readiness, or desire, to be married. The thirty women proceeded to sprinkle white cornmeal on the dancers, obviously asking these Kachinas to, when they returned home, carry their prayers for a husband and a good marriage to the deities.

"As for the men," Burbank continues, "while the women are busy making piki, they usually kill ten or more sheep. They card and spin cotton until they have enough for two dresses and a long belt. They make two large white blankets, and a smaller one with dark red and blue borders, a white belt with long streamers, and moccasins of deerskin. If they are especially happy over the wedding, they also make a dark woven dress for everyday wear. The girl and her relatives bring meal often to the cave where the men are working, almost a wagonful of meal at a time.

When all is finished the bride is bathed and dressed in the large white blanket and belted down. At sunrise the mother-in-law takes her back to her own home, and the groom comes when it is time to eat.

Each woman guest is supposed to bring a plaque of corn and meal with which to make pudding called 'Pee-gum-eh,' which is baked overnight in the ground. Then there is another big meal.

Only once do they wear their white dress after they come home, and that is at the Ne-man-Kachin'ea, and then the large white blanket is laid away for her burial robe. So you see it takes almost a year to really get married the Hopi way."

The hairstyle of the Hopi male child of 1900 was the same as that of his father, except that the father's was washed and combed oftener. Men did not part their hair, letting it fall long and loose to flow down their backs and trimming it across the forehead to make bangs. Sometimes they pulled it into a bun at the back of the head and wrapped it with yarn in the chongo style. Those influenced by Whites began to crop the sides evenly just above the shoulders, and then fixed it in place with a cloth band.

Outside persuasion has changed Hopi attitudes considerably, but in 1900 it was still a serious offense for men or women to cut their hair in any way not pre-scribed by ritual rules. Babies received a first, ritual haircut at the time of the February Powamu, and there are many symbolic references to hair in the myths and customs. For instance, the silken strands that lay across the ripened corn husks are really "hair" that will fall away when the life cycle of the ear is completed.

Life was a cycle and the year was a cycle. For all things in the universe there was no beginning and there was no end. A Hopi died, but only to be born again in an Underworld where life went on much as it did on earth, and where a close rela-tionship between those in the Underworld and Upper World continued on. In this comforting knowledge the Hopi found a general security and every reason to fol-low month by month the ancient Way and Covenant that promised them always a fulfilling existence. Things were never easy on the harsh mesas, but as we have already seen the ancestors knew even that was best, for comfort brought pride, and pride brought dissension, and dissension assured division. The welfare of the vil-lage came first, the individual came last, and each village had the strength of its whole upon which any one Hopi could depend. Prayers and acts were multiplied by the number present, and even those who lived "below" had ways of adding their strength to that of the people on earth. Deities watched over every aspect of life, and they provided man with all he needed to know toward obtaining their help in proper season. It was and it still is a good Life Way, and outsiders who went to the villages at the turn of the century were profoundly impressed by these people who were immersed in an existence that had continued without serious deviation for untold centuries. The impression was, however, not sufficient to keep people from attempting to convert the Hopi to White ways.

The annual change of seasons had a consistency that conveyed a sense of security, with Mother Earth holding them like a cherished child in her folded arms. After the harvest, when "Indian summer" was gone and the cold winds began to buffet the mesas, the Hopi stayed in their houses and moved close to their wood- or coal-fed fireplaces. It is interesting to visit Hopi ranches today and find outcroppings of coal nearly everywhere. Fortunately, the first visitors did not realize the extent and worth of this "black gold." Otherwise, the industrial assault would have come sooner than it did.

The change of season brought a kind of reunion, for until this moment the entire family had been preoccupied with the concerns and pleasures of outdoor summer life. Now the men had time to repair their dancing costumes. There were always moccasins to be made. The woodcarvers spent more time on their Kachina dolls, and the weavers were busy at their looms. The basketmaker took out her stock of split yucca leaves, twigs, and grass. Only the potter looked for other things to do. Her craft awaited the coming again of warmer months.

In general, the woman's daily work remained the same in all seasons. There was always corn to grind, food to be prepared, water to be carried up the steep trails, and walls to be whitewashed. Food for the coming winter had to be protected against mice and vermin. Whenever possible it was moved onto the roof to be sunned. But women could take their time, and everyone from the littlest child to the oldest grandparent lent a helping hand.

Late fall in Hopi country was enjoyable in many ways, for the sun was often bright and the sky was often clear. Snowfalls were as rare as the rains of summer. The cold at night might be intense, but the days were crisp or mild. There was little change in the landscape. Few trees were around to lose their leaves, and the desert plants seldom altered the appearance of the earth. Their tiny, thin leaves and somber colors were most often lost among the painted rocks and sweeping plains. Now and then the winds roared and whirlwinds undulated across deserted cornfields. The sun sank lower and lower in the southwest, until at last the Hopi grew properly concerned lest it depart entirely and leave them forever in the grasp of a winter hard at hand. But they also knew that after every winter the correct rituals would draw the sun back. The societies "owned" the ways, and after the Soyalufia Ceremony at winter solstice anyone with "eyes to see" acknowledged that the sun wandered no farther away.

Before September ended, the Lakon would perform their ceremony, and those errant Hopi who had not laid in a sufficient supply of wood went to gather it in a hurry. Usually they regretted their delay, for the trees used for supplemental fuel were far off, and the day was hardly long enough to go there, load a burro, and return home. Each morning, also, the sheep and goats had to be prodded out of their corrals under the mesa ledges to feed on leafless brush.

October was called the "Harvest moon," and it was the time of the Marau and Oaquil ceremonies. Crops were gathered, and everyone feasted and rejoiced in the village. In November, called the "Neophyte moon," youths of proper age were initiated into the Kachina societies. In even years the great ceremony of the New Fire was enacted, with its enthralling rites of fire worship that had been handed down for centuries. In odd years the Na-a-ish-nya Ceremony was performed by the New Fire Society.

By December, Hopi country was held tightly in the grip of winter, but as the evil spirits were also held fast beneath the frozen ground, they could do no harm to anyone who mentioned them. So, many legends and stories were told around the glowing coal and piñon fires that warmed the Hopi houses. Meanwhile, anticipation began to grow for Soyalufia, in many respects the most important ceremony in the Hopi calendar, for it marked the time when the Kachinas would return from resting and sleeping in the underworld and the San Francisco Peaks. December was called the "Hoe moon," because tradition dictated that in this month the farmlands were to be cleared and leveled for spring planting. The wind had already done its share in removing debris from the fields, but men must cooperate by smoothing over the surface.

January, called the "Prayer-stick moon," brought the ceremony of the Horn Society with their great horned headdresses. More and more Kachinas arrived at Hopi. It was an exciting and promising time.

February was called the "Getting-ready moon," and weatherwise it was the hardest month of the winter season, although it was in this very month that the Kachina people had found melons and green corn growing near the San Francisco Mountains. So the Powamu Ceremony was held to celebrate what could not be seen, yet was known, and beans were planted in the kivas.

In March, the first shoots of green appeared. This month was called the "Prickly-pear moon," and it was the only month named for a natural object. March weather was often the most disagreeable of the year, for fierce winds came laden with dirt and sand to pile in great heaps against the mesa sides and to penetrate every crack in the houses on the mesa tops. Still, it was part of the Covenant Plan, and the Hopi made the most of it. Important ceremonies were enacted by the societies, and leaders met to discuss how things were going and what needed to be done. Kivas were places where agreeable company could be found to work and talk with. At home around the fireside there was always good company, and enthralling stories were told and told again. Men hunted if it was necessary and sometimes made journeys to trade or to observe ceremonies in other places, such as the Zuni Shalako. Usually, but not always wisely, the Hopi disdained the cold. Their clothing remained the same as for other seasons, except that a blanket or rabbit-skin robe might give added protection. If a man had an outdoor errand, he simply ran all the way there and back. When kiva ceremonies ended, the men usually climbed from the subterranean chamber wearing little more than a breechclout or G-string. In consequence, pulmonary diseases were common and were often made worse by the close, overheated, and badly ventilated dwellings.

Most visitors to Hopi country saw it at its best season — April. The cornfields were green, and the few cottonwoods were in full leaf. The desert was glowing, the people were well fed, and everyone was happy. A rebirth of Nature occurred every April, just when the farmers were cutting away the last of the brush and establishing windbreaks to protect the new crops. Sometimes, though, a capricious Nature sent frosts and lashing winds to destroy all but the native plants, which had some special concert with her that granted them immunity. Even the precious peach crops would be lost. Yet the people had prepared for just

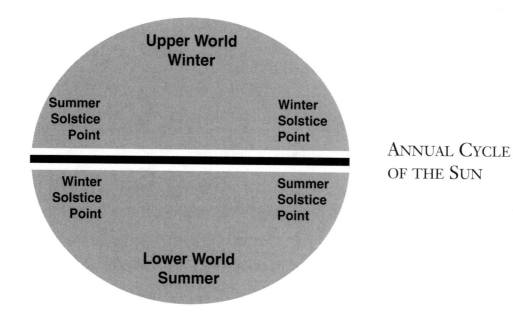

ANNUAL CYCLE
OF THE SUN

CEREMONIAL CYCLE

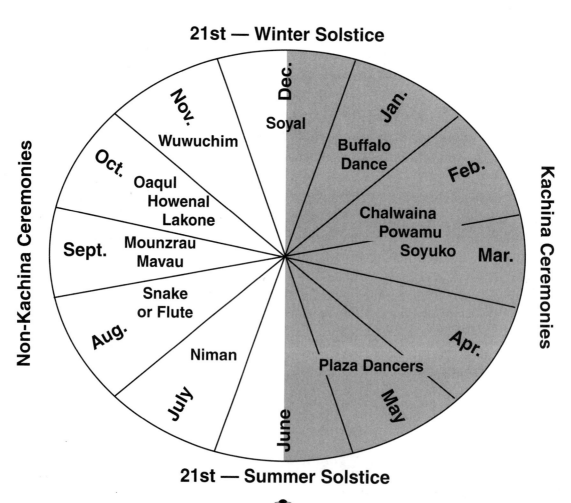

such a time, and emergency stores put aside in other years were called upon to fill the gap.

May was known as the "Waiting moon," and the fields hummed with activity and anticipation. The sweet corn was planted, and the Hopi became once again an outdoor people. The cycle had returned to where we first encountered it. The winds were slacking off, and the sun was moving closer day by day. Despite the unceasing work to be done, there were countless minor celebrations by masked Kachinas and great ceremonies to be performed. After all, this was the season of awakening life.

June and July were especially happy times for the Hopi. Now more than ever it was clear to them that animal life was inseparably linked with growing things, and every word and act illustrated the oneness of mankind with an unseen but living world of mind and matter. The dances celebrated this.

When the sun paused in its path at the summer solstice, the Hopi in gratitude spent the time making prayer offerings of thanksgiving to send with the Kachinas as they returned to their Underworld home. Now a new segment of ceremonies would get under way. Dancers would perform such beautiful yet mesmerizing dances at this time as the Flute or the Snake-Antelope rituals, and the ceremonies of the three women's societies would take place, while everyone in the village prepared to enjoy them in a special way.

By late August the pueblo was settling down again. If all had gone as it should, the moon of September watched over a scene of tranquility in Hopi Land. Once the crops were harvested, when "Indian summer" was gone and the cold winds began to buffet the mesas, the Hopi stayed in their houses, moved closer to their fireplaces... and the yearly cycle unfolded once more.

Most of this sounds quite ideal, and when kept in its proper context it is. But no visitor to Hopi in 1900 could avoid commenting upon what were believed to be negative aspects of life. None of the villages had even the equivalent of an outhouse then, and none had adequate water — let alone running water. The water for some villages had to be hauled on the back up a 500- or 600-foot cliff, and it was always a scarce commodity. When we discover that the Elders still live happily with some of these same conditions today, we always want to know "why in the world" they both do it and prefer it. The *Techqua Ikachi* newsletters answer the question for us.

Hopi children seen by the early visitors were described as excellent examples of adaptation to environment, able to care for themselves in most ways as soon as they could crawl. In fact, the manner in which tiny children could climb up and down ladders to their homes was marvelous. They played on the roofs, and they sat on the brinks of the mesa precipices hundreds of feet high without exciting the least fear in their mothers. Their canine pets, of which there were a great number, could easily run up and down the ladders with them.

At home, boys and girls wore nothing until they were eleven or twelve, although on festival days they were dressed in their finest attire. Visitors said that generations of desert- and mesa-bred ancestors, plus an active life in the open, endowed the young people with "figures rivaling those of the statues of young Greek gods."

Hough says that "as of 1896 it was rare to see a parent strike a child. Instead, there was kindness and affection worthy of the highest praise. It was refreshing for someone who had seen so much of the opposite to observe the close association of children with their parents or near relatives, and how quiet and obedient they were." Further on, Burbank adds his observations about this same thing.

The Hopi children had teachers at home or in the fields who explained to them the things they needed to know to become essential members of the community. It surprised visitors to discover how much small children had learned about birds, plants, and other aspects of nature and about duties at home, in the fields, and in the village. Through "play-work" had come a kind of "know-how."

Little boys scarcely able to walk had tiny bows and arrows pressed into their hands, and were encouraged by adults to shoot at brush targets, who applauded heartily whenever they knocked one over. It was common to see several little armed "warriors" on the rooftops guarding the pueblo. Girls played house with the aid of a few stones and considerable imagination. When rain fell and filled the water holes, the children dived immediately into them, splashing around and immensely enjoying the rare treat.

Wherever the adults went, the children followed along, searching for the seeds of wild plants or for berries, gathering grass and yucca for baskets, watching the cornfields, gathering the crops, and always having some small share in the work. When a house was being built, they worked almost as hard as their elders, carrying in their little baskets loads of earth or stones "with an earnestness that could only be admired." Newsletter accounts that begin at the end of this chapter give us an enlightening view of daily life from the Hopi perspective.

After the government school was established at Keams Canyon in 1887, Hopi training methods were interfered with substantially as attempts were made to compel attendance. For a time, many of the Hopi parents — and particularly some of those at Oraibi — refused to cooperate in the move to turn their children into Whites. To counter this, armed force was used by the Government, and unspeakable methods were inaugurated, such as sometimes tying the children's hands with barbed wire while their hair was cut — with Christian missionaries standing by and approving.

In their contacts with government agents and schoolteachers, the Hopi soon learned that whenever questions arose concerning differences in moral behavior, their position would invariably be adjudged wrong, and severe punishment would follow. In the matter of sexual behavior this became a particular problem, for while modesty prevailed in public, sex was an open aspect of Hopi family life. With everyone sleeping in the same room, marital relations were neither concealed nor embarrassing. As an instructive device teaching lessons about the blessings of fertility in all aspects of life, including creativity, sacred clowns performed

Beginning of the End.

what seemed to haughty — and uninformed or misinformed — missionaries to be obscene acts, and fertility symbols were commonly included in altar sand paintings. Premarital affairs were taken for granted and readily condoned. Eventually, because of the Christian reaction and furor, the Hopi opted for a dual manner of life, behaving one way for the Whites and secretly continuing the old preferred ways at home. The fact was that in the Hopi mind the use of fertility symbols and acts perpetuated and provided for a blessed future. But the prudish missionaries and other Christians made no effort to learn about and appreciate this truth.

Visitors to Hopi country found that some of the Hopi religious ceremonials included athletic sports. Foot racing, for example, was purely religious, and George Wharton James reported that they got "much fun out of some of their semi-religious exercises. A game they were very fond of, and one that required considerable skill to play, was we-la. Several players, each armed with a leather covered dart, or ma-te'va, would rush after a small hoop made of corn husks or broom corn well bound together — the we-la — and throw their darts so that they stuck in it. Racing along in the dance plaza, or streets, or down in the valley on the sand, the youths laughed, shouted, gesticulated, every now and then stopped for a moment, jabbered over the score, then eagerly followed the motion of the thrower of the we-la so as to be ready to strike the ma-te'va into it, and then suddenly let them fly, making a picturesque and lively sight. The hoop was about a foot in diameter and two inches thick; the ma-te'va was nearly a foot long. Each player had his own color of feathers on his dart, so that he could tell when he scored."

In 1921, Earl Forrest was able to photograph boys about the age of twelve playing with large homemade wooden tops, which they spun in the manner followed by all boys with tops and kept in motion by whipping. The Fred Harvey collection includes such Hopi items as tops and whips, a ring-and-dart game, and counters and gaming pieces.

When Wayne Dennis made his study of the Hopi child in 1937 and 1938 in New Oraibi, he found that after the children's assigned work was finished, they were free to amuse themselves. Evenings especially were times for play, and on moonlight nights it went on long after sunset. Play was always carried on outdoors, wherever in the village the children chose. However, girls and boys seldom played together, and initiated children did not play games with the uninitiated.

There was unorganized play and organized play. The former consisted of girls playing "house," and boys playing "farmer" and "hunter." Made-up games with odd items fitted also in this category. Organized games included shinny, a kind of hockey game; tops; a stick-throwing game; a snake game employing a long twisting line of children; a girls' grinding party; archery; darts; pachisi; a gambling game; and a hidden-object game.

Until recently, when the wheel replaced walking and the conditioning that came from this, foot racing played an important part in the religious life of the Hopi. Males were trained for this from childhood, and they often ran for miles across the broiling desert without resting. Many of the fields were long distances

Running

from the villages, and although pickup trucks are now in vogue, a few farmers still make the round trip to their fields and back on foot in a single day. In former times, a sixty-year-old citizen of Old Oraibi had a cornfield 40 miles away. During the planting and growing season he camped at the field, and whenever he made the journey home for supplies he ran the entire distance, going both ways in less than twenty-four hours. George Wharton James on several occasions engaged a young man to take a message from Old Oraibi to Keams Canyon, a distance of 72 miles. The youth ran all the way, delivered the message, and brought back an answer within thirty-six hours. One Old Oraibi man of James's acquaintance ran more than 90 miles in one day. Fred Volz, a trader at Canyon Diablo and Oraibi, once hired a number of the best Hopi runners to round up wild horses for him. They gathered in not only the horses, but also deer and antelope.

Dan Evehema himself excelled as a runner and frequently participated in races that involved other Pueblos and tribes. Many of these extended over distances ranging from 60 to 100 miles, and he won most of them. He laughed heartily when he told me that he had beaten our friend, Oscar Sheyka of Zuni, every time they raced together. But he added that Oscar was a great runner and wonderful person, which of course I already knew. On one of two trips Dan made to San Francisco, he was coaxed by Bahannas into taking part with several other Native Americans in a race from San Francisco to Portland, Oregon — a distance of 600 miles. "That one was too long," he sighed. Although they made it into Oregon, none of them could run all the way to Portland. The Bahannas who accompanied them in automobiles to see how they would do were not pleased and reluctantly brought them back to San Francisco. "All of these Bahannas," he said, "got winded just trying to keep up with us Indians as we walked around the hilly city."

From earliest childhood the Hopi were taught to be honest, obedient, and industrious. As a result, visitors in the year 1900 found their ethical standards to be extremely high. Murder was almost unknown among them. They were scrupulously honest. Robbery was very rare, and a liar was held in contempt by everyone. No judicial courts were needed.

The Anasazi compiled no books or written language, only the petroglyphs found on the cliff faces, the paintings on pottery, and the wall murals. Perhaps this explains why the Hopi began by example and involvement the education of their children in the customs and beliefs of their people at an early age. In the ceremonial sphere, from the time the children were a few months old they were taken to see every public ritual that took place in the village. The child grew up with the Kachinas, and the Kachinas and life were always understood as one.

The Government agents quickly saw this as an opportunity to divide families and irreparably fracture the culture. They devised boarding schools for the children that were located many miles from most of the family homes. Not only were the children separated from their families for most of the year, they had no opportunity to grow up within the cocoon of the religious cycle, hence had no training in it. It is not difficult to imagine what this cost the Hopis, and what it did to growing up in the traditional lifeway.

Hopi history was told in traditions and myths that described life before emergence from the Underworld, the manner of the exit through the sipapu itself, the long years of wandering before the Hopi settled permanently, and finally the origins of their many religious ceremonies. These were handed down by word of mouth from one generation to another by elderly men versed in the lore of the Anasazi. Children were taught until they could repeat each legend with amazing accuracy. Some stories told recently have been compared with those recorded by the Spanish in the sixteenth century and found to be the same, even in the minutest details.

In 1900 the most important phase of the child's education still commenced when boys and girls were initiated into the tribe's Kachina Cult. A few years later the second step was taken as they joined one or more of the several secret societies. Then, on achieving adolescence, the boys took the third and climactic step by passing through the Tribal Initiation and being admitted to the Soyal Rite, which opened the annual cycle of ceremonial observances.

The steady immersion into the religious life infused and circumscribed Hopi existence. Within this sphere the major portion of adult education would take place, and an encompassing and marvelous education it was, full of the unexpected, the mysterious, and the miraculous. Yet it was not an aspect the Hopi of any age asked questions about, for its efficacy lay in the fact that it had always been done in a prescribed way; through this Way the people had survived and kept the Covenant from their beginning.

To complete our outsider's view of Hopi life, we need at least a glimpse into their religious beliefs and practices. As stated earlier, however, Dan and I agreed that the ritual acts, views, and paraphernalia that govern the day-to-day Hopi world were private and not pertinent to our book, so the general information that follows, except for an insertion or two, does not come from him. You will see that some of his offhand comments contradict several of the statements, and traditionalists frequently say that only those Hopi who are properly initiated and trained are in a position to know and teach the truth. Even with the help of informants, the best anyone else can achieve is something that gives us a limited sense of what is, in actuality, a very complex spiritual situation.

In the view of Anglo scientists — which is only an approximation of the actual situation and open to error — it has been deduced that there are seven principal deities who possess the root power that regulates and sustains life. Co-tuk-inung-wa is the all-powerful one who created the earth. Muingwas is the one who controls germination, lives in the Underworld, and is the guardian of life. Gna-tum-si is the creator of life. Baho-li-konga is a great serpent who controls lifeblood, vegetal sap, and especially water. Maasaw is widely known as the one who controls death, but you will learn that in the Elders' minds his place is far greater and more detailed than this. Omau is the force that controls clouds and rain. Dewa is the sun, or father. The Kachinas are intermediaries, serving as messengers and as bearers of blessings. Some nonhuman beings serve as messengers, as do pahos, or prayer sticks, and other ritual paraphernalia. Stripped to its essence, the Hopi religious position is that all created things, human and nonhuman, have individuality, and each individual has its proper place in relation to all other phenomena, with a definite role in the cosmic scheme. Whereas the nonhuman individuals fulfill their obligations more or less automatically, man has specific responsibilities that must be learned and fulfilled in the traditional Way, and much of the child's training is devoted to learning this Way.

In broad terms, the Way consists of the manner of acting, feeling, and thinking in every role that a human being is required to assume in the life cycle from birth to death; the welfare of the tribe and the individual, in that order, depends upon the responsible and wholehearted fulfillment of the role. In narrow terms, the Elders describe the Way as fulfilling "the Pattern," or Law to which they have subscribed in the Covenant relationship with the Creator and Maasaw. Responsibilities increase with age, and they reach their peak in ceremonial participation, with the heaviest burden being carried by the village chief or kikmongwi, and the next heaviest by the clan chiefs, although the matriarch plays her consistently vital role in the all-important matrilineal system. As one might assume, the Traditional Way, as it was followed prior to White intrusion, taught young people to respect their elders and to look to them for the solutions to a happy and productive existence. In it, elders were not "put out to pasture." They were, and remained so until death, in every respect essential to the fulfillment of traditional life.

It is entirely correct to say that every aspect of Hopi traditional life is infused with religion. According to George Wharton James, the religious life of the Hopi in 1900 consumed anywhere from two to sixteen days out of every month. Dan confirmed that as being accurate for the past, and said it still does — sixteen is an accurate figure. The total number of spiritually occupied days for each year is close to 200, leaving only 165 for other matters. Besides the ceremonies, there are the countless individual religious acts that accompany the major events in life and the conduct of life each day. How is someone supposed to hold a regular wage-paying job and do this? The fact is that they cannot. But they can live the Traditional life and do it.

As Laura Thompson and Alice Joseph point out, the rules for ritual observance have two aspects, the physical and the psychical, and "If either aspect is neglected, or any regulation broken, failure will result." Participants in ceremonies must perform the proper acts and observe the tabus, and they must exercise control over their emotions and hearts, keeping a good heart, and exulting only at those moments when it is traditionally appropriate, as when the snakes are ritually purified in the Snake Ceremony. Such control comes to a person through a life of ceremony and prayer.

In the scheme of control, prayer is thought of as a form of willing something into being. Hence, by ritual acts that include prayer, the Hopi believe that human beings, in conjunction with the Kachina spirits, can control nature to a limited extent, and that if man fails to carry out his responsibility in this wise the earth will become unbalanced and even its rotation will be affected. The universe itself will undergo severe changes. The movement of the sun, the coming of the rain, crop growth, and reproduction as a whole are all linked to man's correct, complete, and active carrying out of the rules. If the Hopi wish these things to happen, they must fulfill their roles individually and collectively.

In this connection, Mischa Titiev mentions that at Old Oraibi, while particular emphasis was placed upon individual freedom, Hopi behavior was checked by fear of nonconformity. Public opinion was so important in the closely grouped villages that a person seldom dared to depart from the conventional modes of behavior.

An interesting sidelight in the Hopi scheme of behavior patterns is witchcraft. Whenever a situation assumes the proportions of a crisis, such as a drought, an epidemic, or a particular mode of behavior, the Hopi assume that one or more individuals have, for personal reasons, worked against the common good. These individuals, often described as "two-hearted," are considered to be witches who are allied with ants, owls, crows, and the like. They have an animal heart and a human heart. They are organized into a secret society, and they even seek to recruit sleeping children. Witches are greatly feared, even though difficult to identify. But manufactured charms and certain colors, such as turquoise, can turn witches away, and such charms and colors are always present in the home and on the person.

Why the TURQUOISE

Very little is known about the medical practices of the Hopi outside the fact that each society has its cure for a specific illness. Early visitors to the reservation found that children were being educated in the use of herbs for medicinal purposes, and some of the ethnologists who lived among the Hopi were themselves treated by medicine men, usually not because they believed the medicine men could really heal them, but out of sheer curiosity as to what the healers could truly accomplish.

In conjunction with the agency, when Caucasian doctors and nurses first arrived at the reservation they were met with mixed reactions, and they still are, even though health conditions among the Hopi have never met outside standards. Sanitation has been a persistent problem, and drought and famine have made their sporadic contributions. European invaders brought entirely new diseases, against which the Hopi had no immunity, leading to several epidemics. The combination of all these factors, plus the ordinary risks of daily life on the high mesas, kept the Hopi ever mindful of the perils of life, and they feared illness or a serious injury more than death. Death was only a transition from life in one world to life in the next, but illness or the loss of limbs could reduce the victim to a state of utter dependency. Even worse, his failure to fulfill his role might disrupt the organized household group in all its aspects.

Once their fears were allayed somewhat, the younger Hopi responded reasonably well to the medical offerings of the Government health care workers, but the conservative elders, with exceptions, remained firm in their adherence to ancient curing ways. This is to some extent because those who achieve a natural death often lived — this is less so now — to a surprising old age. Why change the Traditional way? say the Elders even now, although they welcome the fact that Bahanna physicians are able to treat them for health problems which were not present before Whites arrived in North America.

Walter Hough said there were few Hopi who did not know the "herbs and simples," and that even the children knew many of the herbs. The plants they used in medicine "would stock a primitive drug store." Bunches of dried herbs, roots, and other plants hung from the ceiling beams of every house and were made into teas and powders for every sort of illness. Hough encountered medicine women as well as medicine men, the best known of the women being Saalako, the mother of an important Snake priest. She brewed the dark medicine used for the Snake Dance emetic and, Hough asserted, she guarded the secret antidote used for snakebites. Dan still uses herbs for curing and says he knows the proper way to apply all of those that are available in Hopi country.

Curings by society officers ordinarily took place in the kivas, and if the cure was successful, the males or females who were cured were expected to join the respective societies that healed them. Individual treatments by medicine men usually occurred in the home.

H.R. Voth knew a certain "Homikini who was probably the best Indian physician in Oraibi. He is a splendid botanist, and has good knowledge of the medicinal properties of the various herbs, viewing the matter from the Hopi standpoint."

Jesse Walter Fewkes described another society, the Yayawimpkia, or Yaya, who were fire priests who healed by fire. They were experts in the art of making fire by drilling with a stick on a bit of wood, and they performed this act in the Sumaikoli or Little New Fire Ceremony. Few of them remained in Fewkes's time, however. Their services were sometimes called for when a burn or some such matter was to be treated, and they did perform wonderful feats of juggling and magic, especially in winter, when abbreviated ceremonies were held. In consequence, the Hopi were renowned as jugglers and had a reputation extending far and wide over the Southwest.

It appears that Hopi medical practices, including their views and approaches, closely parallel those I have experienced personally with Sioux, and in a lesser way with Apache, medicine men. No doubt all of the native cultures, working in like environments, developed similar thoughts and procedures.

Since the Underworld plays such an important role in Hopi life, we need to understand how a Hopi enters it.

As he did with everything else, Mennonite missionary H.R. Voth, about whom you will learn more in Chapter 5, commented on Hopi burials and, holding back nothing as sacred, even took a number of photographs of Hopi burial places. While some of the family and close relatives might cry and mourn over a death, he said, they do not lament and scream, and the Hopi do not wish to talk about the deceased. The Hopi have good and personal reasons for this, but Voth did not listen to them.

At death, Voth said, the remains of the deceased were immediately prepared for burial, and there was no embalming. Nor was there any rule as to who did the preparation, although it was most often the father and a relative. A prayer offering was tied to the hair in front, and the face was covered with a masklike layer of cotton. Openings were provided for eyes and nose, and the mask was tied on by a string that passed around the head at forehead level, "to hide themselves in." To this string were fastened a number of prayer feathers that the deceased would wear in the Underworld. Fewkes stated that as the mask, called the "cloud mask," was put on, the deceased was addressed as follows: "You have become a Kachina. Aid us in bringing the rain, and intercede with the gods to fertilize our farms." Black marks were made under the eyes, on the lips, forehead, cheeks, the palms of the hands, and the soles of the feet. Prayer feathers, sometimes a little food, and a small container of drinking water were placed on the chest. The body was then wrapped in several blankets, which were secured by ropes. It was then carried on the back of the father, some relative, or on a horse or burro, to its final resting place. Fewkes said it was carried by the oldest man in the clan.

Dead children who have not yet been initiated into any religious society were placed in one of the numerous crevices along the edge of the mesa on which the village is located. A covering of stones was placed over the body.

The bodies of grown persons who had been members of societies were buried in a graveyard that was usually situated on the slope of a mesa or on a hilltop. Graveyards were scattered around the mesas and were neither marked nor taken care of. There were no tombstones, but insignia indicating the society to which the deceased belonged were sometimes placed on the graves.

Most of these traditions are continued today — at least those that missionaries and health officials have not been able to interfere with.

I insert here that the Hopis expect outsiders to respect their burial places and to stay away from them. In no wise is anything on or near a burial or a shrine to be touched, picked up, or taken. Nor should anything be added to a grave or a shrine. These are private to the Hopi, hallowed, and must remain so.

Other authorities add that on the third day after the burial, a last meal and the final prayer offerings are prepared. The meal is fixed by the mother, wife, aunt, or other near relative, and it consists of piki, cooked beans, corn, meat, herbs, and other foods. All this is put in a bowl. The one who has prepared the body for burial makes a double-stick paho with painted green sticks and black points, one single black paho, and a puhu, or road, consisting of an eagle-breath feather. To this are tied two cotton strings. Six other prayer offerings are also fashioned. In the evening the paho maker takes these and the bowl to the grave site, placing everything except the puhu on top of the grave. At a place west of the grave he places the "road" pointing westward. Then he sprinkles a cornmeal line farther westward, denoting the continuation of the road. At sunrise the next morning the breath or soul of the deceased rises from the grave, partakes of the food in the bowl, mounts the single black paho, and then travels along the "road" to the Underworld, carrying with them the double-stick paho. Hopi religious leaders go to the San Francisco Peaks and join the Kachinas already there.

Dan describes this journey of the dead as "passing on to the next life." According to Fewkes, the reason the body faces east is that the deceased will see the sun when it rises and be able to emerge from the grave in time for the trip, which will take a minimum of four days.

The exception to the making of this journey is the uninitiated child. In this case the string-and-meal road points toward the child's former home, to which the soul of the child returns and where it is reincarnated in the next child born in the family. Until then, its soul is believed to hover above the house. Whenever the family hears an unusual noise it thinks the soul is moving about, and the mother may secretly deposit a pinch of food for the soul to eat. In the event no other child is born to the mother, when she dies and goes on her journey to the Underworld she takes the little soul with her.

As a final note to his observations, Voth stated that the dead are sometimes remembered by prayer offerings and food in such ceremonies as the Soyal and Marau. He also said that offerings prepared for ceremonial use are afterward deposited in shrines and other places "where the dead come and get them." [Actually, they come and get the "spirit, smell, or breath" of the offerings, which do not themselves disappear.] Those who find none are said to be very sorry and cry. In one Hopi legend, a visitor to the Underworld received complaints that certain of the prayer feathers hanging before the faces of the dead were very old and that their friends were forgetting to prepare new ones for them."

E.A. Burbank, widely acknowledged in his time as one of the greatest painters of the American Indian, visited 128 indigenous tribes in the period between 1890 and 1900. He was among the Hopi in 1898. A book about his experiences, *Burbank Among the Indians* was published in 1944 by The Caxton Printers, Ltd., Caldwell, Idaho. It contains some of the few firsthand observations we have from outsiders concerning Hopi life at the turn of the century. For Hopi thoughts and feelings, we will listen after this to the Elders themselves. Burbank was one of the few visitors who were openly interested in the Hopi as human beings, although he too, as you will see in Chapter 5, was a devout Christian who believed that all Indians must be converted. After staying with them for some time, he decided that the Hopis were the most interesting of all the Pueblo Indians. He described them as "industrious natives," and said he had "never known a more charming, hospitable, and peace-loving people." They named him "Many Brushes." But his writings make it evident that he was another of those painters who believed the Hopi culture would soon be extinct, and so must be recorded on canvas.

Several years prior to Burbank's arrival, the government, "in the interest of good health," he said, offered to build new stone-walled and furnished homes if the Hopis would agree to move down from the mesas to the lowlands. Many of the Hopi accepted this offer, and a number of houses were built at Polacca. But few of the people lived in them. Instead they rented them to tourists and lived on the proceeds. Burbank rented one of the houses for five dollars a month, and converted it into a comfortable studio. It was just as the government had built and furnished it, except that the springs of the beds were gone. When he complained about this, the Hopi owner explained that he needed the bedsprings to dry peaches in the sun.

Burbank concluded that Hopi life in 1898 was exceedingly hard, having to be wrested from the barren soils of the southwestern deserts, yet he thought it "a strange enigma that the greatest advance toward civilization made by any primitive American people was achieved by the Pueblos, of which the Hopis were the most advanced and prosperous."

Recurrent droughts had taught the Hopis to store their grain, usually enough for two years, against the dry years. There were few other foodstuffs to depend on, and theirs was a harsh, "unfriendly" land that produced only when the weather conditions were exceptionally good. (Memories of sparse harvests are never absent from the minds of the elderly people, and even today, whenever there is extra money, it goes for kinds of foods that can be stored away.)

Their lands for growing crops had been handed down from generation to generation for hundreds of years. Their farms were the joint property of the people of the village. Each village had its own farmlands, some of them quite distant from the village itself. Burbank was told that the men who farmed the lands belonging to the village of Moenkopi sometimes ran 40 miles to their work in the morning, worked all day in the burning sun, then ran 40 miles back home at night. This was only one of "the difficulties under which this amazing people carried on their agriculture." All of the Pueblos were stocky people of short stature, but of great physical strength.

The Hopi principal crop in 1898 was, as always, corn. Because of the frequent sandstorms, farmers had to be very careful about the way their corn was planted. First they would dig a hole in the sand, place a few grains in the hole, then build a fortification of dirt around the hill on the side from which the prevailing winds blew. This protected the young shoots from the sandstorms, and by the time the corn grew above the fortification, sandstorm season had passed. (Dan still plants his corn in this manner, and it is moving to see how deftly he does it. Detailed references to Hopi agricultural practices and their spiritual dimension in regard to the keeping of the Covenant are made in this and future chapters.)

That did not end the Hopi's worries over his cornfield. Crows and ground rats and other wildlife hovered about, waiting for a chance to eat the corn stalks. At the edge of each field a hut was built, and there a Hopi stayed all day long watching for invaders. If bird or beast entered his field or that of his neighbors he stood sentinel to drive them away. (This situation has not changed either.)

Corn was raised in three colors: red, yellow, and blue. They also grew squashes and melons, and produced the finest peaches Burbank ever ate. It was a custom to allot each peach tree to a little girl whose duty it was to care for the tree for as long as she lived.

Although the Spanish do not mention finding turkeys among the Hopis, by 1900 every Hopi village had its flock. These were not raised for food. Their feathers were highly valued for use in ceremonial rites. At dance time, the turkeys presented an odd appearance as they strutted around with their tail feathers plucked. Many Hopi villages had golden eagles, which were captured young and raised in cages. They were especially prized for their feathers.

Burbank found the Hopi villages to be in many ways women's worlds. They seemed to dominate the affairs of each pueblo. They owned the property, including the pueblo itself. The family line was traced through the women. They had the final say-so in most village affairs. Some non-Indians who "knew the Pueblos" said it was the conservatism of the women that was largely responsible for the lack of change in the four centuries that the Pueblos had been exposed to the White man's civilization.

The men were the farmers in each Hopi village and were the warriors if the village was attacked. They conducted most of the ceremonial dances. The women, on the other hand, took charge of the food when it was produced, and stored it. They were the cooks, the pottery and basket makers, and the rug weavers. It always seemed to Burbank that in spite of the fact that they were the bosses of the pueblo, the Hopi women took on much more of the work than did the men.

Their most important job was that of grinding the corn into fine meal. This was done by pulverizing the grain between two stones. It was a tedious operation, and it required a long time to get a little meal. Hopi girls were put to work at this job as soon as they were old enough to hold a grinding stone in their hands. When they were grinding corn they would sing and all had "sweet voices."

As soon as they were in their teens they learned to make a bread called "piki." Many times Burbank watched them at this fascinating operation. Their stove consisted of a flat stone 2 feet long and 1 foot wide. It was propped up at each corner with smaller stones. Underneath it a fire was built. The cornmeal was mixed with water and lye to make a batter. When the stone was heated just right they spread this batter over it with their hands. It cooked very quickly, and when it was done it was removed from the hot stone in sheets as thin as paper. It ranged in color from bluish black to pink.

[Piki making is another of the ancient skills that is passing away. Only a handful of the women at Hotevilla can make it now, and it is one of the very special gifts that a few fortunate spectators will receive from the Kachinas at giveaway time during a dance. Susie can make it, and its taste and smell is wonderful. Katherine and I were among those fortunate people who received some from the Kachinas at the July Home Going Dance in 1993, and my son Ryan was given a ceremonial bow and arrows. We were delighted.]

Burbank found piki to be very nourishing and healthful. When rolled up it was most convenient to dunk it into coffee or soup, and he became very fond of it. When he first arrived at Polacca he also enjoyed the corn bread made by the natives. "But I enjoyed it, too, only until I saw them make it. A group of Hopi women would gather around a large bowl. They filled their mouths with cornmeal and began to chew. When the meal was thoroughly mixed with saliva each woman would deposit her contribution in the bowl. When a sufficient amount had been accumulated it was put in the oven to bake... It was," Burbank says, "a well-known fact that saliva mixed with cornmeal sweetens it in a chemical change. Many primitive people have used this method. I must admit that the Hopi corn bread was tasty, but after witnessing its preparation, I could no longer stomach it." (Today, the saliva is omitted by most corn bread makers.)

Burbank thought the Hopis were among the finest cooks he discovered in his years among the Indians. He never ate better corn, soup, or meats than those which they prepared. They were particularly skillful at cooking mutton and beef.

The Hopi had an ingenious way of catching small fowl known as winter birds. They tied several loops of horsehair to a stick about a yard long and placed it where the birds congregated on the snow. The birds invariably managed to get their feet tangled in the loops of horsehair, and then the Hopi boys caught them. Pulling the quill from one of the tail feathers, the Hopi would pierce the snowbird's gizzard, killing it instantly. These birds were roasted over hot coals, stringing about a dozen on a stick, and were laid away for future consumption.

The climate was hot in the summer and quite cold in winter in most of the Hopi villages. But as a rule, the little Hopi children went around as naked in the winter as they did in the summer. Burbank spent December, January, February, and March at Polacca and saw naked children up to six years of age playing in the snow.

Thanks to the cold, the Hopi could keep cooked food for a long time; likewise the melons, which they kept from one season to another. They had a trick for opening watermelons with their thumbs. They would make a nick at each end and then drop the melon to the ground from a height of about two feet. Invariably it would split lengthwise, exactly in the center. If a visitor were present when the melon was cracked, the Hopi would hand him one half and eat the other half himself. Fingers were used to scoop out the center of the melon, then rolled-up piki was used to sop up the juice.

One of the principal jobs of the Hopi women was carrying water in big earthen jars to their homes on the mesa. At Walpi the pueblo was 700 feet above the surrounding territory, and all the water they had was carried up the trail by the women — usually without their losing a drop.

The Hopis told Burbank they had known the art of weaving rugs, belts, and material for their clothes since ancient times. They said that a dress woven by a Hopi woman would last for a lifetime with all kinds of wear. Some of the men had taken up rug weaving and had become very skillful at it.

From the Tewas the Hopis had learned the art of making pottery that was artistic and decorative as well as useful. The finest pottery of all, Burbank believed, was made by the Tewa woman named Nampeyo. The Tewas had long since learned to develop colors for their pottery by pulverizing different colored stones. Green was obtained by allowing water to stand in tin vessels until verdigris formed, and yellow came from boiling the yellow desert flowers. In their spare time the Hopis often busied themselves carving small images of wood, which they called "katcins." These were originally made for the Hopi children, but when the

Hopis discovered that Kachina dolls could be sold to tourists, a thriving industry in wood carving was developed.

Burbank found that the Hopis as well as the other Pueblos were very fond of music. He thought that many of them, especially the girls, had wonderful singing voices. The Hopis seemed particularly devoted to their children, whom they never punished, yet they extracted the greatest obedience from them by kindness alone. The discipline of the youngsters, he said, was amazing. Burbank painted pictures of several of the children and reports they sat as patiently as did the older people.

During this 1898 period Burbank decided that North American Indian children were perhaps the happiest in the world. "For some reason" the Indian father and mother trained their children in "psychological principles which only recently the white man has discovered."

While modern psychologists had only begun to advise parents to "Be slow and gentle with children; suddenness, either mental or physical, will confuse them. Let their life fall into a routine. Let them feel they are part of the family. Let them develop as individuals, and do not repress, but guide their natural interests." This was already the policy of the Indians as the painter observed them.

"Nowhere were children more charmingly treated than among the Pueblo Indians. It was rare to hear a Pueblo child cry or to hear him quarrel with his playmates. I think I never saw a Pueblo Indian strike or punish a child. And the children were polite, gentle, and happy."

"How," Burbank asked, "did the Indian parents accomplish this miracle? First by affection. Then, both men and women, young and old, always had time for the youngsters. The interests of the children were woven smoothly into the routine of the home. If the mother was making pottery, she gave the little child a piece of clay to work with. Then she never said, 'No, no, you're doing it wrong. Make your pot this way.' She simply let the child learn by trial and error and by watching her skillful hands."

As soon as the pots were ready to be fired, a host of children showed up with ears of blue corn. The firing was done out-of-doors, without a kiln, using a bonfire. After the blaze died down, the mother always had time to shell the blue corn and rake some of the embers into the sand, so that the children could drop the kernels among the hot coals and pop them.

Little girls were encouraged to balance on their heads small pots that were cracked or had turned out badly in the fire. If they broke the pots, nothing was said. Soon they would bring up water from the river or the spring, though among the Hopi Indians the older women did most of the water carrying.

Every Pueblo child could dance almost as soon as he could walk. At sundown it was common to see a Pueblo father, after a long day's work in the fields, pick up a tiny thing perhaps only three months old and hold the baby carefully against his breast while he chanted a song and went through the steps of a dance. Indian rhythms were thus literally danced into the babies.

When the Pueblo Indians put on a dance, the tiny tots followed along after their elders, dressed in ceremonial clothes just like the grown-ups. They brought up the rear of a long line of dancers, patting out the rhythm with tiny feet in buckskin shoes. Seldom did they err in the tempo, though the detail of the step might be a little vague. But again, no one corrected them or criticized them. It was assumed that they had their part in the tribal ceremony, and that they were doing well. They learned in their own way.

Observing from the outside through Anglo eyes, Burbank said with obvious warm feelings that the turn-of-the-century life of the entire pueblo was slow and gentle and quiet. The bright sun rose, and work in the fields and in the house went on. There was clay to play with. There were playmates and dogs and good foods. And one day was much like another. Adults spoke to each other quietly and courteously. Voices were seldom raised, and people were seldom inconsiderate in their speech. These habits were quickly picked up by children.

There was always a grandfather or aunt or big sister ready to cradle the sleepy child; always an old man singing an ancient song or telling an ancient tale out in the plaza, in the shade of the house. Sleepy babies swung happily in cradle swings suspended from the roof beams. They were securely tied in, and one good push kept them swinging for many minutes.

It seemed to Burbank no wonder that Hopi children were happy, good, and always ready to enjoy themselves and play tricks, especially on the adults.

Nevertheless, ominous signs of change were already present in Burbank's time. "In every Pueblo village," he said, "I found one or more churches. Some of them were old churches built a century or more ago by the early Catholic missionaries. Some were newer churches built by the Protestants. Indians had adopted some of the missionaries' teachings, but they clung to their own ideas of how the world was made and of the hereafter."

The Hopis would never believe Burbank when he told them what a lot of white people there were in the world. "While I was among them, a delegation of Hopis went to Washington. They decided to count white men and see whether or not I was lying. The Santa Fe gave them a private car, in which the Hopis stationed a man at each window to count white people. From Holbrook to Albuquerque, they had no trouble, but by the time they reached Kansas City the white people were so thick they decided to count houses. They counted houses all the way to Chicago, and then began counting towns. That kept them busy until they reached Washington, where they held a powwow (council meeting) and decided that Many Brushes had not lied to them, after all."

The foregoing descriptions of Hopi culture help us understand something of why the Elders and Katchongva describe life before White intrusion as having been "beautiful" and "good." But as I suggested earlier, observers who can only view the Hopi from a Bahanna perspective cannot know exactly how the Hopi themselves feel about the past and present, or what their understandings were. An outsider's view is always limited to a window whose cloudiness varies according to training and good fortune. In this and following chapters, though, much of the cloudiness is cleared away as in surprisingly intimate ways our aged informants tell us in wonderful detail some of what they personally have been taught, felt, and experienced during this cataclysmic past century. We can, therefore, move closer to them than anyone has been able to before, and even the best-informed scholars will find valuable new information about traditional Hopi life and thought. Just a few words in the middle of a line, an idea expressed here and there, can bring entirely new understandings and correct or redirect many impressions previously held. "Tell our story," Dan said, and now, in their newsletters and otherwise, the details of this story begin to emerge. You will see immediately, as they tell us about the life cycle, that the Bahanna views gathered at the turn of the century are mostly devoid of the human dimension, and will not have taken us into the traditional Hopi heart and mind… It is our great fortune, then, to be taken on this wondrous journey.

The Life Cycle And Ceremonial Cycle — Maasaw's Life Plan

TI— "I have nothing here. My life is simple. All I have is my planting stick and my seeds. If you are willing to live as I do, and follow my instructions, the life plan I shall give you, you may live here with me and take care of the land. Then you shall have a long, happy and peaceful life."

TEM— In discussing with Dan the first meeting at Oraibi of Maasaw and the people, I pointed out to him their stories said that Maasaw, in setting forth what they must limit themselves to if they wanted to remain at Oraibi, specified a digging stick and some seeds. I had read, however, that other Hopi mentioned they were also given a jug of water. "Is this true?" I wanted to know. Dan replied that Maasaw did indeed give them water, but not in a jug. He gave them springs of water that gushed forth from basins and the mesa sides, and for everyday purposes these places were where the Hopi were to obtain it. He also, Dan added, was wearing a simple black-colored cloak and indicated they too must be satisfied with simple clothing. So the complete picture as to what the people must settle for if they wanted to stay at Oraibi and be the keepers of the Covenant is that they must depend upon four things: a digging stick, seeds, natural water from springs, and the simplest of clothing. Consider this when the Elders criticize others for violating the Covenant by wanting more.

TI— "Massau, the Great Spirit, has marked out this part of the land for the Hopi to live upon. We will not forget His spiritual knowledge and wisdom by which the Hopi are to take care of the land and feed His children while communicating with the natural forces for their health. The Hopi must plant his seeds and watch them grow; he must pay attention to the signs of change in natural order.

He must watch with close attention to the behavior of all life on earth. Any change or odd behavior will be the sign that the natural order of the earth is getting out of balance. Hopi believe that Hopi land is the Spiritual Center where changes will be visible to the trained mind and sight.

This life cycle is also known as the ceremonial cycle. An ending and beginning, or an ending of a time and a new life. When this cycle ends we give thanks to our guiding spirits and Mother Earth for their care. We give thanks for our health and nourishment, for completing the cycle with all life, and we pray and ask for the same during the coming new cycle. We often hear our Grandmothers and Grandfathers saying, "Thank you. Thank you, my guiding spirit for the care in making it possible for me to complete this cycle. I wish to be here next year." This Thanksgiving is not only for ourselves, it includes all life. We must all keep strong and pray that we all reach the end of this year's cycle with good health and peace."

PRAISE

The Elder's Prayer to the Great Spirit:
O' Great Spirit
whose Voice I hear in the Winds
and whose Breath gives Life to all the World

Hear me
I am small and weak. I need your
Strength and Wisdom

Let me walk in Beauty, and make my eyes
ever behold the Red and Purple Sunset

Make my Hands respect the Things You
have made
and my Ears sharp to Hear Your Voice

Make me Wise so that I may Understand the
Things You have taught my People

Let me Learn the Lessons You have Hidden
in every Leaf and Rock

I seek Strength
not to be greater than my Brother,
but to Understand my greatest Enemy — myself

Make me always ready to come to you with
Clean Hands and Straight Eyes

So when Life fades as the fading Sunset,
my Spirit may come to You
without shame.

To Celebrate Thanksgiving

TI— "In our last issue we spoke a little of the origin and meaning of Thanksgiving. It must be understood we spoke only of its origin in this land. We know that other lands have their own ways of celebrating Thanksgiving."

Ka-mu-ya — December

TI— "Two moons have passed. Let us go back to the sacred month Ka-mu-ya (December) when the Father Sun has reached his winter home and then begins his journey back to his summer home. Bahannas call this the solstice. The Hopi Soyal ceremonial is performed and the germs of seeds are planted within Mother Earth's womb. The Hopi believe the Earth is a living Mother to all life and nourishes all of her living children. This planting is done with ritual and blessings in order for these seeds to form normally and perfectly.

The month demands respect and happiness, and cheerful wholesome words must be spoken. There must be no disturbing loud behavior or running. No digging of the ground is permitted. This is the time to sit back during the cold nights and tell tales of the past, of our history, and to review the divine laws the Great Creator has given us. It is a time to review the conduct and attitudes of people. This is also the time when plans for the coming year are made. The priests in the kivas pray for prosperity in food, health, happiness, and for protection against evil for all land and life. The Kachinas visit to bring happiness and joy for young and old. The Kachinas bring the rain of loving care upon the cornfields and deliver our messages of desire to the Rain Gods. The Creator, nature, and spirits, controllers of movement, plan both good and bad for the coming year depending upon the behavior of mankind. They say that even the wicked and the witches devise a scheme designed to destroy the morals of people and separate them from the Creator's divine laws, leading them to self-destruction. This has been a glimpse into the sacred month."

In Pa-mu-ya the Water Month (February)

TI— "The Kachinas, the messengers between the Hopi and the cloud spirits, now come to bring food and happiness to both young and old. This part is activated by the religious groups — by the religious and spiritual leaders of every phase of the ceremonials. No ceremonial is complete without the proper leaders, who are the religious priests.

One can hear the boom, boom of the drums, the sound of rattles and turtle shells throughout the kivas if one is fortunate enough to be in one of the villages. Now the seeds within our Mother Earth begin to stir into life with the blessings of the people and the Kachinas. This is a time of social dancing for both sexes, of singing and dancing for happiness and prosperity. Po-wa-mu, the purification, will now put things in order. A perfectly healthy environment is required in order to receive the new life seed into the world. The purification ceremony is performed which cleanses away the impurities that have been spread upon and into Mother Earth. The rest is very complex and sacred and also closely guarded. We hope you have followed us up to this point through your own spiritual guidance.

On the 16th day the new life comes into our world. It comes in the form of food (bean sprouts) which symbolizes that our labor and prayers have borne fruit. From each kiva the Kachinas deliver the new food to each household. There are also gifts of bows and arrows and rattles for boys. For the girls there are Kachina dolls and rattles to bring joy and happiness. During the day many visiting Kachinas go through the village repeatedly to bring more gifts and spread happiness among the children. This continues until sundown. This is not the end of the ceremonial. More singing and dancing follows from midnight until dawn. These dances are different and unique. The dancers are lined up according to age. The youngest begin the movements, which then pass to the center and through the middle group of the dancers out to the ends where the oldest are. The movements, which are repeated until the song ends, symbolize the life cycles of Life and Earth and the rebirth of old age to new age, portraying over and over again the ancient teaching that this life must continue on the Earth and continue its cycle from season to season. Should we forget and stray from these great laws of the Creator we all will face time's end, when a New Age will appear as all civilizations disappear. This will be the consequence if, through our recklessness, we continue to abuse the Earth and no longer deserve to have the use of it. After the end comes, a new age and new life forms will appear to make the Earth bloom once more. It is the duty of the Hopi to keep all cycles continuing. Would any open-minded and thinking person permit our way of life to die in the midst of civilization? Does anyone know how our way of life may be saved and protected from harm?"

Po-Wa-Mu-Ya, or Purification Month

TI— "Here we are again after some months of absence. We give you our blessing and thank you all once again for being patient. We are just like anyone else, we have to hustle around to keep our family from going hungry and to keep them warm. Also we have to meet many expenses, needs to which we have become attached in our changing world. In addition, especially during the fall and winter months, the ceremonial is a must and must be honored in the proper order so that it will be effective in keeping the world and natural order in balance.

This purification month has an important part in our yearly cycle. There are many parts and dramas which are spiritually meaningful that complete the ceremonial. We need not explain much of it because the word itself, purification, is clearly explanatory to those with an open mind.

Not all the village members can participate...only those who are members of the sacred Po-wa-mu-ya Society. This ritual takes all day with the songs or chants, praying, blessing, and the purification of the land all life on it. Praying they may be successful so men on earth will improve their conduct and behavior. Improve to the very best from the past year toward good health and happiness.

The deeper thoughts in the prayers are that purification must be fulfilled as prophesied to a new dawn of time so the world will bloom into peacefulness."

The Stone Racer

TI— "Once again let us explore our past. One of the sports which has died out is the "stone race," as it has been called by outsiders. For those who are unfamiliar we will describe the "stone" briefly. The stone is made out of pitch, or resin, from the pine tree. It is boiled at a high temperature, and some animal hair is added to hold it together. Dark sand is then added for color, and then it is shaped into a cube roughly the size of a baseball. When the mixture cools it becomes as hard as stone. The stone can be thrown a great distance with a scoop-like motion of the foot.

The stone race begins on the fourth day after the Bean Ceremonial (Powamu). Every able-bodied man and boy could participate, so that each kiva was represented. The race was repeated four times. Each morning an elder would run from kiva to kiva announcing the race to be held that day, the old animal hooves around his waist clanking as he ran in the early dawn. He would complete four rounds: the first to prepare the body paints, the second to commence painting, the third to dress up, and the fourth round to be on your way to the start of the race. Each kiva's members dressed differently. The first race was held in a small circle about 5 miles in circumference. Each day the circle was increased until at least 25 miles are run.

The enactment of the stone race meant many things. Its chief meaning is the Commemoration of the Migrations of the Hopi clans by which our land was claimed. The last, the largest circuit symbolizes the claiming of the whole continent for its Native People and wildlife.

At the time when the stone races were being held the Hopis were good runners and the different kivas challenged each other. Sometimes the races were done for Clan mothers and their father's Clan mothers. At the end, the Kachina racers would come to challenge the men and boys of the village. It was a time of fun for everyone but still it had a mysterious meaning. It was as if we used ordinary, everyday language to address the spirit world.

No doubt many of our readers will wonder why this meaningful ceremonial has died out. Let us say it is because of one aspect of Bahanna's modern technology, the wheel. The wheel which caused our feet and legs, and our bodies too, to be dependent on being carried by wheels. Where we once used to walk and run long distances, we now use wheels to reach places both near and far. We hope you have enjoyed this look into our past with us."

wheel

Renewal And The Changing Climate

TI— "Greetings. First of all we thank our readers for the support and encouragement you give that we must hold fast to our ideals, no matter how gloomy our future looks. We appreciate your love and your unselfish giving and sharing with us, not taking, so we can continue to share our message and knowledge with you. We appreciate your concern that our ways must survive. Through your encouragement we have gathered much strength to struggle on for our rights, to live the way that is best for us.

In spite of all the world problems we must put them aside and be happy that the season for earth renewal has arrived. We should be eager to be active outdoors in our gardens and fields. By the warmth of our Father Sun the germs of seeds will stir within our Mother Earth and come forth and clothe her with the garments of green meadows, flowers, and crops for the nourishment of all life. This will be so if the time plan of the yearly cycle is in balance.

We are much concerned about the climate. No one seems to be able to predict the weather accurately from day to day. However, we know according to our time markers that it is past due for certain seeds to be planted at their proper time. This spring we are reluctant to plant due to the late snow and cold weather.

Once more maybe our ancient Prophecy is right, that one day we will plant wearing finger sacks (gloves) clearing away snow with our feet before planting. The summers will become shorter for maturing the corns for harvesting. The result is anybody's guess."

Our Waning Farms

TI— "Greetings. Spring is here. The time for hard work is fast approaching. It will be a relief to go out into the wide-open spaces, surrounded by the mesas, hills, and mountains after the long winter months. We missed our fields and are anxious to once again work the land and plant. Other people around the country with green thumbs will be turning their best efforts toward self-sufficiency. The right direction, we say. We wish them luck.

Meanwhile, we here in Hopi Land wonder how our crops will be this year. Will there be enough moisture in the soil to bring the young plants to the surface? Will it rain so the plants will grow strong and healthy for a good harvest? These are our main concerns because we live in an arid land. No matter, Hopi will plant to keep culture and tradition alive. Sadly, up to this time, Hopi life in many ways has been hooked into the materialistic society along with the rest of the Bahanna countries. Those who have adopted materialistic ways desire a hard-cash income in order to keep up with the Joneses. This attitude also robs most Hopi of the ambition needed to farm. So also goes the educated Hopi who is not willing to help the Traditional Hopi without cash payment. If this situation continues the fields will lie idle when the devoted Traditionals pass on.

without Recompense

Land banks

Most of us don't know how important winter is in Hopi Land. We shiver and complain when our houses fail to warm up the way we want. Perhaps we begin to run short on coal and firewood. Soon we begin to complain to the snow clouds to stop dumping snow on us. In this we are acting silly; snow is a must. Without snow the spring months will be dry and can cause problems in planting. So we were concerned and sad when snow failed to come. This winter has been mild and spring-like. The fruit trees bloomed a month early, a beautiful sight they were. We had hoped the weather would not turn cold and ruin the fruit. Sadly, we lost out to a more powerful force than man — that is, our Mother Nature. We take it as though she has boxed our ears for being deaf to her environmental laws. She has snatched the food from our mouths as punishment. For four days and nights now a freezing cold wind has been beating on our doors and windows.

Most people will not think much about this kind of incident, but to the Hopi this means much in the light of traditional prophecy. For one thing this cold spell could continue late into spring. This is unusual and would shorten the growing season. It is said we will clear away the snow with our moccasins before we plant and finger sacks (gloves) will be worn. This prophecy may sound impossible, so let us wait and see if Grandpa's prediction will come to pass. The question is: Will this occur the world over? This would depend on the geographical areas; in the regions with different climate, things will happen in different ways. For instance, tropical land could become a land of ice; the Arctic region could become tropical. This may occur due to a pole shift according to Bahanna's concept. But this need not happen if we, the people, get our leaders to do something about the harmful things being done to the environment.

No Safety

Greenhouse effect

XXX

While we are on this subject, let us review some of the ancient teachings passed on to our ancient fathers from the Great Spirit. These teachings say we were put on this land to protect or defend it from harm so that it will always be here to nourish us. As time passed on things became clearer. The Great Spirit was right when He said we have many evil ambitions in our hearts that we would pursue throughout our long journey through life. At this age one need not go far to see the evidence of this. Some of these ambitions are harmless, and others are harmful, so the Great Spirit says we must be aware of this and avoid pitfalls."

Our Spiritual Thoughts

TI— "The spring is here. Summer is just around the corner. This is a good time to pass on our greetings to our loved ones with thoughts of good health and happiness. It is a time which gives us good feelings of strength, so we hustle around readying our gardens and fields for planting. With our blessings the seeds are put into the soil, the womb of our Mother Earth. She too feels the warmth of our Father Sun. She begins to stir; with the power of her kindness she commences her duty of glorifying the land with a green coating of meadows and flowers. Let us be in harmony, for we are one.

We have called to Mother Nature with our prayers: 'May your creations come up strong and healthy so there will be abundance of food and beauty for all.'

Some of us will be busy working our fields, planting, blending with nature, putting in our seeds, watching them appear. It makes us proud that we too are creators. We pamper our plants, sing and pray so they will grow healthy and strong. They will grow and grow to produce food for our nourishment in return for our kindness and care so that we will stay strong and healthy. The plants will be happy for the duty they have done; both we and the plants will be happy to be part of nature."

The Delights Of Planting

TI— "Some of us like to raise our own food. It gives one great pride just to see the seed you put into the soil which comes up. 'Miracle,' you whisper to yourself. Then you feel even more delighted when you get a meal from it.

Often we receive letters regarding the Hopi farming methods of raising Hopi corn. There are no ready answers as to how it is done. The Traditional way we do our planting is very complicated. Much of it is connected to the concepts of spiritual bases and our ceremonials. This we feel would not be understandable to non-Hopi. However, we can say freely that corn can be grown almost anywhere that the climate and soil is right. Since Hopi Land is arid, we neither irrigate or fertilize our fields. The fact is that Hopi Land is like anywhere else. There are soil differences, but by long experience the Hopi are able to find fertile land which can best be suited to each crop.

Since not all Hopis know the traditional ways of growing things, especially younger Hopi, it is now up to the elders to teach them some wisdom in growing corn and other crops. Herein is a brief view. The elders would say that growing things is important and sacred. It holds the significance of many things, that without food there would be no life. Someone must provide food so that all life will continue on with good health and happiness. One must be willing and put his heart into it. That way, one will gradually blend with the fields so that he will work in harmony. When planting one must be in a good humor — no anger or sad thoughts. One must sing and talk to the seeds, encourage them to come to the surface with joy. When they surface, thank them and encourage them to keep strong. As they grow, you thank them and also the unseen spirits who helped make

my shoshoni Charlene taught me this — x

Planting the corn with the digging stick, and "Singing" up the crop.

Planting is not the end of the work. Predators must be kept away, and weeds have to be pulled. The plants must be prayed over and sung to…

it possible for the harvest which will provide food. These are a few sides of the wisdom for growing crops.

The Traditional way of planting is unique. The environment and Natural Order must be considered. Seeds are planted in rows, at least four or five steps apart. The same distance apart for corn and melons, two steps for beans and other crops.

Since no source of water is available for irrigation this method lets moisture in the soil equalize to reach each plant for growing and rooting deeper until the rain comes. A planting stick of wild desert oak is used in making the holes by hand for the seed. A large field is finished in a week or more. At least eight to twelve kernels are planted so that they will surface with strong energy. Later they will be thinned to four or five stalks depending on whether pests are more or less bothersome. The task can be easier if it is a wet spring; the moist soil is near the top. A foot or more down is dug during a dry spring. The pests, wind, and drought are considered for protection of the plants. Our prayers and ceremonials are important in helping our plants to grow."

Following the Sun or Time of Planting

TI— "Here is another subject often asked about. When is the right time for Hopi to plant? Nowadays most people plant by a calendar or almanac. Hopi use their own system, a wisdom that all things are activated and stir to life through space and time upon times of their own. It is a knowledge to be aware of — a sign will show when Natural Order is out of balance.

As spring approaches, the time markers are closely watched which can be any landmark which is stationary. As the sun travels along to his summer house (summer solstice), the sun will rise from a certain landmark that means the beginning of spring. Hopi then begin to plant. Sweet corn first, which is fast growing for special purposes. Next come the slower plants such as lima beans and melons. From there on the other crops are planted. The main crop of corn follows in bigger fields. Then once again the sweet corn is planted. This closes the planting season. By this time the sun will reach his summer home.

Hopi also watch and observe the flowering of certain desert plants which bloom according to their own timetable. By giving attention to all these the Hopi know the earth is still stable and in balance. They say each marker represents where certain things will occur or begin to show itself according to the timing of nature. Knowing this we know if the clock is ticking awkwardly. Our ceremonial cycle also serves other purposes. Sadly it is waning. This may mean something.

Why all this hocus-pocus raising our corn? Our concepts may not mean much of value to most people. But Hopi are proud to have a spiritual guide to lead them on."

Healing Those Who Are Ill

TI— "In our last issue we described some of our planting methods. Here is another subject often asked about by outsiders: the Hopi way of healing illness.

The fact is that before Bahanna came there were few sicknesses common to the Hopi. Since the modern world came, many new diseases and illnesses were introduced. Healing became more difficult for the Hopi medicine man. Now, often the Bahanna doctor and Hopi medicine man depend on one another. When the Bahanna methods fail the sick can go to the Hopi methods and vice versa. By tradition not anyone can be a medicine man. There are religious orders which usually heal by ritual. One group cannot use the methods which belong to others, for they are closely guarded. By tradition the Badger Clan are general healers but can recommend to other healers those conditions that they can't handle. Herb medicines are also closely guarded. Home remedies can be used by anyone if one recognizes the right herbs. Then there is the bone doctor who fixes broken and dislocated bones. The Hopi medicine man does not go to school to learn. They are gifted and well recognized. Therefore the quack medicine man is uncommon. It is hard for any outsider to learn about this. Often wrong information is given just to get rid of a too-persistent student. Good luck when you try to learn about it."

Spring and Summer Activities

TI— "One can barely see the three figures moving about in the distance. The land is bare, dry, and empty, as if no one could survive there. Not a speck of moisture is visible on the surface. One who expects green meadows would be disappointed. This is Hopi Land.

In this large sandy field, the three men are busy working, each with a planting stick, a bag of seeds and thoughts of food for tomorrow and winter months. (This past winter brought less snow, which Hopi depend on for spring moisture.) Planting could have been easier, but the wind and hot sun has dried up much of the moisture. So they must go down quite deep to place the seeds below the surface of wet soil. In our traditional way, each hopes and prays it will rain soon so the planting will be quicker and easier. As he works, the eldest softly hums encouragement and blessing to his seeds. Now and then he shyly glances westward where the rain clouds are building.

A short distance west of them, another group is busy working at a dam site, hurrying to complete their job before it rains. 'Stop your rain songs, Joe, until we finish this job,' yells the foreman jokingly to his Bahanna Hopi employee, trying hard to be heard above the earth-moving machine. This land they are working on is land the Hopi Tribal Council chairman fenced off for his own stock, even though this area is very dry; hardly anyone could call it grazing land. However, there could be a different kind of wealth underneath the surface, as was foretold in the prophesies, so it has been leased without traditional approval to an oil company for exploration.

Suddenly there is a cloudburst of heavy rain, and the workers employed by the Council and oil company scramble for cover. It lasts just a few minutes and puddles began to flow. 'You should not have stopped me, boss,' mocks Joe, boastfully adding, 'drumbeats and foot stomping aren't necessary to make rain so I can drink!'

Outside the fence, the men are disappointed. In spite of the disapproval of the traditionals, who blame both themselves and the dam builders, the dam was approved and built at the insistence of the Hopi Tribal Council chairman.

But the dam greatly disturbs our prayers. Perhaps it will rain much harder next time. Hopefully, these and other earth dams in Hopi Land and elsewhere will break down and be a waste of time and money.

So the time passes on into summer, and men tend their plants like newly born infants. We will face all the challenges of nature, wind, animals, and insects, plus keep the weeds removed, or the soil will be sucked bone dry.

Now is the time for Kachinas' ceremonial dances, for rain and blessings, for people's happiness. Clowns usually participate, not only filling the people with laughter, but also to imitate people's behavior, so they can correct their ways. This sacred drama is not understood by many.

As the day nears its end, warrior Kachinas of different characteristics signifying different races of people appear as clowns to check if there are any corruptions. Very near the end of the ceremony the clown chief will admit the wrongdoings and request that this be accepted as purification for his children by the warriors, who will return to whip and douse the clowns with water. The clowns then have to sing and dance of their sins or wrongdoings, clowning in the opposite meaning while under the watchful eye of the warrior Kachinas. Someday we too will have to do this as prophesied, and it will be up to the purifier what is to be done with those of us who have become traitors to our beliefs. We might have our ears boxed, or even lose our right to the land."

Summer and the Sweet Corn. Kachinas Come in with Beauty. Time to Love One Another.

TI— "Summer is here, the fields are green with growing crops, ears of corn begin to appear on the stalks, melons and beans appear on the vines. As you walk among the plants, talking and singing, a good feeling of pride and happiness fills your heart. You can now say the labor you put into it will produce some harvest which will keep the wolf away from your door.

There is the sweet corn that was planted earlier, which is ready for a good meal, but you don't dare touch it yet because you know this is for a special occa-

SOYAL: *In mid-December, Abalani and his two sisters, Blue Corn Girl and Yellow Corn Girl, appear beside the Chief (Mong) Kiva at Walpi. They come to bless the corn crop for the coming year. The sisters carry distinctive corn as they sing and slowly process through the village. Pictured here is the Yellow Corn Girl sister. From a Joeseph Mora photograph.*

sion which is only a few days away. Everyone hustles around preparing for the Niman Ceremonial (home dance). Women are readying the food to feed the guests. Maybe for relations or friends from neighboring villages, maybe even from faraway cities. The men folk spend much time in kivas, smoking and praying for success (that their efforts are not in vain).

Both young and old are waiting anxiously, especially the children. They were told that if their behavior is good the Kachina friends will bring them gifts of melon, fresh corn, dolls, or bows and arrows.

Finally the day has arrived. Kachinas come in with beauty. The children receive their gifts with joy and happiness. In like manner the grown-ups are happy to enjoy the day watching and listening to songs. This is the time when all hateful moods and attitudes are forgotten. Time to turn to love one another. This closes the Kachina dances for the summer. Good day."

The Snake Ceremonial

TI— " 'Look, the snakemen are coming out from their kiva now!' shout the children as they stand on the housetops and call to each other. Yes, the children always used to wait for the snakemen's departure and arrival, knowing that the main dance was near at hand because the snake priests and their helper had been out several days gathering their little brothers, the snakes, from all directions.

This important ceremony, lasting only about an hour, attracts many visitors from all parts of the world, people of all religious sects, plus writers, anthropologists, and the curious. One group which is absent is the Hopi people who have converted to other religions, and one may well wonder why this is so.

The ceremonial dance is performed by two societies, Antelope and Snake. Antelope members are the leaders. The day before the main dance, the races at sunrise occur, in honor mainly of the Antelope Society but also for those in the Snake. This event is not run for prize money, but for good health and food in the coming year, as well as for the land and all life. No fee is charged visitors, because care is taken not to commercialize this sacred ceremony. At one time this dance was closed to the non-Indian public because of its sacred quality, but the decision to make it public was reached by the high priests. As one older priest said, 'If only one, two, or three spectators with good hearts and good thoughts merge with our thoughts of prayer to accomplish our success, that is good' (Lololma).

The snake dance is also an occasion for a reunion of all the friends and relatives who come from afar. It is a time for a four-day feast of fresh corn, melons, and fruits right off the vines and trees. And after the dance the ladies of all ages have some good fun by challenging the men and boys to a chase in the streets for special prizes. But this was how it used to be.

Today, this unique celebration is beginning to wane, to become extinct. Instead of enjoying these few days in the old way, some young people use it as an opportunity for immoral behavior and to be out of control. This affects the people in an adverse way, sometimes making them cross and frustrated, and always causing worry to the Traditionals that the ceremony at present is losing effectiveness with nature. The cycle this year is very poor, there is very little rainfall, insects on our crops are many — because in our food is the only moisture to satisfy their thirst and hunger. We are sad that they too are suffering.

"Surely there is something wrong. We must look within ourselves and take care in our movements. We seem to be in doubt of the Great Laws that govern the earth. We are in doubt of the words of old.

"*It has been told to us that there are two water serpents coiling the earth, from North to South pole. On each of the poles sits a warrior god on the serpent's head and tail, now and then communicating messages of our conduct and behavior toward each other; now and then releasing light pressure which causes the great serpents to move, resettling earth movements — a message also commanding nature to warn us by her actions that time is getting short and so we must correct ourselves. If we refuse to heed the warning, the warrior gods will let go of the serpents and we will all perish. They will say: we do not deserve the land given to us because we are careless.*

This sounds much like fantasy. We might believe the old ones' stories then, but it will be too late. There is another 'fantasy' that is often mocked: that the Hopi ceremonials, with all their foot thumping and singing praise of the earth, cannot produce rain, while the white man's country has much rain without the use of any ritual.

The old ones say our earth is like a spotted fawn, with each spot having a duty to make the body function. Hopi Land we hold to be the center of the earth's body. It is the

spot of power, with the duty to foretell the future by comparing the actions of mankind with the prophecy told to us. Hopi teaches caution and awareness. This much we know."

Let Us Talk of Happiness and Sharing

TI— "Greetings, for some time now we have been silent. We delayed our message in order that we may bring you new information about much that is going on, or not going on, in most of the activities in Hopi Land. At this time we are wishing you all happiness and good health. Your support is very special, and we want to thank you for being patient in hearing from us. As usual, we are very busy in our fields and with the many other things which keep our life cycle complete.

First let us talk of happiness. The Hopi still practice many things which bring happiness to people. Hopi have not yet commercialized the native dances, so anyone who is fortunate enough to be in Hopi Land at the right moment can share with us our joy. An exception is during the Sacred Ceremonial; most of it is barred to outsiders. Most dances are in the summer months. These dances bring together our relatives and friends from neighboring villages and from distant places. We also get to see our youngsters from faraway schools whom we may not have seen for months, even years. We laugh with joy to see how our children and grandchildren have grown. We, the elders, tease one another about our age. We look back over our younger days and on to our long-gone grandmas and grandpas in an effort to find our family tree. There may be a new addition in our relatives who have been away a long time. In this case a small Hopi naming ceremonial is done by the women folk. This is done so our relationship and identity may be closely knitted. At this time our corn, melons, and other things are ready to eat, so there is lots of food. People sit by the open fire outdoors, roasting their corn during the evening hours. Passersby are invited to share, or relatives will get together to enjoy their meal and exchange the latest news and stories.

When harvest time comes, harvesting is hard work but can be fun. If the harvest is good one can be eager. A satisfying reward for the relatives who help with the harvest is a meal of good stew and corn bread (piki). This is our thanksgiving for the reward we have received for our labor from our Mother Earth and the other unseen spirits who made this possible.

The harvest time is important; this is the time when we look within the hearts and thoughts of ourselves and others. If the harvest is good we are happy that our prayers are successful, but if the harvest is poor, something is very wrong with us."

But There Are Alarming Changes

TI— "As part of our pattern of life in Hopi Land, ceremonials were held in each village. Prayers for rain and fruitful crops once again were accomplished, bringing happiness and surprises to relatives and friends, changing our facial expressions and physical appearances.

But sadly, alarming changes have come to pass because of our disrespectfulness and competitive tendency in overdoing Kachina and wedding ceremonials.

This year, social dances were held before the sacred snake and flute ceremonials, when it is proper to wait four days after they are over.

Hopi Land was very dry this summer. Our crops were poor, many plants dried out, and rainfall was spotty, as foretold by our elders. This is a time when our thoughts and prayers stray due to pressing problems, which make us forgetful of nature's presence. The changing of our ceremonial pattern could be a proof of our prophecy."

The Rewards for Our Labors

TI— "Greetings, the harvest in Hopi Land is over; all the crops are in. The men now breathe in relief. Since spring much of their time has been spent in the fields caring for the crops and protecting them from pests. Now they deserve to sit back with pride and happiness and plan for the winter months. It is now the women's duty to care for the harvest, which is stacked outdoors to dry then is stored away indoors for winter use. Many things we do during the growing season to make all this possible. It is hard work, but if one has good willing friends or neighbors to help there is no problem. The togetherness creates good spiritual feelings. We join in a thanksgiving to the spirits who made all this possible.

Now is the time the reward for our labors is measured and a time to look into our hearts and the hearts of others. Most of the people will have a good harvest, others less, and some none. A good harvest means your prayers have been answered, that your heart and mind have been wholesome and sound in spirit, devoted to working the land for food. Thus you, the earth, and the universe are blended and in harmony to be self-sufficient. Later we will refer to the people who have less to harvest, or none at all.

The following is the fact predicted for this period of changing times where western ways or lifestyles are affecting the Hopi. In many ways the Hopi are forgetting the important factor of self-sufficiency. Let us ask Grandpa why he keeps insisting that we must learn to be self-sufficient and be independent.

'Well, if you want to know,' and scratching his head in thought continues, 'I fear for your future. When I was your age, strong and full of vigor, I did everything with my hands. I worked and my field grew anything that is good to eat. I could do this and that which is needed without complaint or being told. I respected my elders. Nowadays you are all lazy and brainless. How do you expect to feed your family when you get married? Of course you are growing in a different world, your ideas are changing, not like the old Hopi ways. Nowadays you depend much on Bahanna's world; you now partake of the goodies brought in by Bahanna. As long as you earn your wages by hard work and pay with your own earnings, that is better than depending on someone else. Still, this will change your whole way of thinking. It is important that you must always practice self-sufficiency.' Changing to a more comfortable position, he continues, 'Suppose one day the world will have problems with food shortages. The Bahanna people will be worried and uncomfortable. Even though Bahanna is skillful and intelligent his house or structure is without spiritual foundation. A structure without this must sooner or later fall. There are spiritual and universal laws higher than that which man has made for himself. One of these principles is self-sufficiency. Suppose one day that hunger strikes the whole world. It might not affect us so much, but we will still suffer as much. Throughout centuries we have practiced the true principle law of self-sufficiency and thus have continued to survive. But also throughout our history we have suffered food shortages and hunger several times because of corruption caused by our own ambition. Hopis say the true principles don't change, so the higher universal laws are as good as they always were unless we bring problems on ourselves by forgetting them.'

This grandfather knows the wisdom, the key to self-sufficiency. We must plant, we must grow food, we must keep the wisdom of our ancients alive and not let our fields lay idle."

Maasaw and the Harvest Season

TI— "We are now into harvest season. Our youngsters and adults take it just like any other season — it has some important meaning. It changes the life pattern of all land and life. We Hopi look at ourselves as we are.

The amount and quality we harvest reflect our ways of life in the past years. If the harvest is good, our mind power was strong and clear — in harmony with nature and spirit through prayers. This is faithfulness and happiness. If the harvest is poor, our power of mind strayed because it was not clear — the prayers did not connect to accomplish the desire. This is sadness and worry.

This season is also a harvest of unknown mystery. Only nature and spirit know what kind of life we did harvest, what they store away for us for the coming year, what most of us will see.

Let us step back to our past, before our way of life was disturbed. Our life was of happiness; our activities, entertainments, and ceremonial patters were complete. Let's take a glimpse at one of the ancient ones.

Long ago, when the first Hopi met Massau, or Great Spirit, they asked for his permission to live with him in Old Oraibi. Massau would watch activities from his house top.

Perhaps, for some reason, he thought of the idea of getting the people together to make them happy during the harvest season. He gathered the leaders and explained what he had in mind. He made a request that was announced from the house top: that during four days the people would harvest for him; women would prepare the meals, while girls, boys and men together would harvest his cornfields.

On the fourth day, they gathered and went below the mesa. There, they formed two groups at one-fourth of a mile from each side of the field. At a signal they ran toward the field while shouting and whooping. Boys and girls worked side by side, shy at first until they began to laugh and talk. They had great fun and took advantage of this occasion, for at that time, girls were respected so that one could not talk to a girl just anywhere or at any time.

Suddenly, Maasaw would pop out of the corn pile and start chasing the men around. Everybody would be laughing, hollering, and, at the same time, fearful of him, for his face looked ugly, horrible and bloody with the look of death. This ended the harvesting, and they returned home.

After the meal, Maasaw entered the plaza, where men were dressed in different costumes to tease and challenge him. Finally, he would knock out one of his victims with his weapon, a drumstick. He acted like a clown and would strip his victims, who pretended to be dead. He would then dress himself up with that costume in the opposite manner of him who he stripped. Dressed like that, Maasaw would chase the men around, and everyone would laugh and have a good time. It would end with them killing him with a hot torch to the mouth. Then he was carried to the outskirts of the village, where he was dumped. But he came alive when they hollered and shouted.

Those were days when men communicated openly and verbally with spirit beings, when animals, birds, and men could talk and understand each other. At that time there were no 'animals of burden.'

Then, Maasaw was part of the ceremonial cycle until he hid himself from men. Later, he was impersonated. Finally, not long ago, this was discontinued. Is it possible that this has meaning the Great Spirit himself has drawn up?"

More Harvest Memories

TI— "This is the season of happiness and joy, abundance of food, and no lack of appetite. There is hard work for men and women, as well as children old enough to help their parents. Each boy also helps his uncle, who will in turn help him when he is old enough to become a man. Each girl helps her clan relations and aunts with the same hope for the time she enters marriage.

First, peaches must be brought in, split and dried on the housetops or on rocky places. Some people even build small sheds of stone where they stay to look after their fruit in case it rains. Men bring muskmelons and watermelons on their backs or on donkeys, and nowadays on wagons. Beans are gathered, winnowed, and cleaned.

Navajos come to the villages with mutton for trade, and the Hopi go into Navajo country to trade for mutton or even live sheep. Three or four melons will get a head, including free fresh mutton roasts at every hogan they visit. Everyone has a good time, happy to share their harvest again. Corn harvesting begins, with many people living by their fields until it is finished. Some will bring their corn on donkeys and wagons and even on their backs for many miles. When everything is gathered the housetops and yards look colorful beyond description, outer walls covered with drying food such as roasted sweet corn, muskmelon, and beans, even jerky meat from the Navajos, for use during winter. These are just a few glimpses of yesteryear, when our thoughts were one.

'That's past, why talk about it! Today is today!' the younger set would reply with a frown. 'Yes,' we agree, 'but we are only humans like anybody else. Memories often drift back of the beautiful things as well as bad experiences of the past. Perhaps we would still walk in beauty if we had not made mistakes.'

We don't have to look far to find it within us. It might not be too late. Beauty and happiness can be renewed when we find our way and abide as closely as possible to the Great Creator's laws. Harvest time is very sacred. There is not only food for thought, but a blessing for the coming year. What we harvest is also a spiritual matter. Will we reap obstacles in the coming year, or perhaps some advantage by which to survive? No one knows but the Creator. Let us all pray that today's harvest is good health and happiness to all people on earth."

Thanksgiving Day in Hopi Land

TI— " 'Thanksgiving Day is one of the occasions to which I look forward,' said one Hopi elder, 'because it is the day when the whole family comes together. After stuffing ourselves with turkey, pumpkin pies, and other goodies, we sit back and review the history of our ancestors and cover other subjects we think are important to pass down from generation to generation. Maybe other friends and relatives whom we seldom see will be dropping by from towns and cities away from Hopi Land, wishing us good health. They are usually carrying in or towing new additions to the family. The children are mischievous, but even so I love them and pat them. When trouble arises among them taming them can be useless because they cannot understand my loving words to them in Hopi. I then remember and pity them for losing their original language before their time. I scold the mothers to use more Hopi language while their children are growing so we can communicate. Well, I say to myself, our ancient ancestors are right — times will change.'

The Bahanna have their way of celebrating Thanksgiving. Hopis do observe Thanksgiving, but not only by feasting on turkey or pumpkin pies. First, let us go back to the question of how the tradition of Thanksgiving Day originated. It seems no one has an absolute answer. Versions we have learned from books or were taught by Bahanna teachers say that the Indians and Pilgrims (a group of white religious people who landed at Plymouth Rock) feasted together to thank the gods for the food they ate. One version is that this feast in actuality was a going-away party for the Pilgrims given by the Indians, because they were ready to return to their own land due to hardships, starvation, sickness, and deaths. After the feast the Pilgrims realized the Indians had more food stored than they had thought, so they never left. There are still other versions, but let us add our own.

Our version is more a story based on prophecy, one so long that it would take many pages to relate. Here we shall briefly outline the tale for you to judge. As remembered by our wise men the so-called 'Turkey Feast' landing of Pilgrims on this continent was a fulfillment of a prophecy for Bahanna (white men) to come. In this case great care and caution must be taken by the Indians according to the Great Spirit's instructions. Tests must be taken to screen out the bad from the good. Are the newcomers in proper order to be accepted by the native people of the land so that they may settle?

Somehow the Pilgrims must have passed some of the tests. Mainly they were not warlike. They were well mannered and strongly religious in their duties to the Great Spirit and the unseen. Their beliefs appeared closely related to the native religion. The natives would readily accept them, but only one thing was lacking. They never asked permission to settle upon the land. So at the end of four years, perhaps four months or four days as is customary in mystic counting, the command was given for the Pilgrims to leave.

Perhaps they then met in council and resolved the misunderstanding and were accepted to settle permanently, but not before a resolution was made and sealed with the blood of both parties. Vows were made: that settlers will obey the Natural Laws of the land. That they would not in any way hinder the way of life of the natives, and not extend beyond the boundaries of the land given them to use into land not given to them. So someone is right that actually the Pilgrims celebrated to give thanks for the land in which they were allowed to settle. Partly the celebration may have been to give thanks for the turkeys, corn, and pumpkin the natives threw in, which completes the origin of Thanksgiving Day.

Of course we have no written documents to prove that this is true. It is possible Bahanna may have the documents, but no doubt glorifying the event in order to cover up their wrongdoings. This could be the first broken treaty, this much we know. We know that most Indian tribes have some form of celebrating the Thanksgiving Day with dances and feasts in traditional ways to give thanks for abundant harvest. Hopi have our own way of thanksgiving during this time of the year based on ancient concepts. Hopi believe all life on our earth lives and goes by life cycles; therefore all must rest and renew for the coming cycle. Whatever it may bring, either good or bad, in some part rests on man's behavior."

The Dark Side and the Bright Side

TI— "Sometimes our emotions are swollen by depressing problems. There  is not much one can do about this. But the next best thing is to take to the field and sing with Nature among the plants. This is often a sure cure in forgetting our problems. However, we have not much choice; because of our age we become feeble. Besides, there is not much help from the educated Hopi who have left for greener pastures. We like to hear about other people and events amidst the confused world. We, the Hopi people, are in the same boat. We are trying to create a better world for our coming children. *key*

We had several good rains during the summer growing season. Our crops are fairly good because we had less pests to deal with. So we had plenty of fresh things to eat, besides sitting in the plaza, enjoying the Kachina Ceremonial dances with our relatives and friends from distant places.

The harvest was good. It is now stored away for winter use, such as for weddings and ceremonials, and of course for eating. All these things have created happiness for us. We give our thanks to the Unseen Spirit for help in producing the food. As part of our pattern of life in Hopi Land, ceremonials were held in each village. Prayers for rain and fruitful crops once again were accomplished, bringing happiness and surprises to relatives and friends, changing our facial expressions and physical appearances."

We have before us now a description of Hopi life as it was long ago, has been for the Elders over the past century, and of how the Elders feel about it. We can certainly sense the quiet richness of the lifeway. From the moment of White intrusion, however, with every passing day thunderclouds of trouble were building up in size and power, turning blacker and blacker as they rumbled ominously. Then they crackled so loud it hurt the ears, and the wind began to blow across the mesas, sending stinging sand into Hopi eyes and forcing the people to struggle harder than they ever had before to stand upright.

Hopi maiden in handwoven dress, blanket, and wraparound boots, native costume of 1900. From a Museum of Northern Arizona photograph.

HOPI BRIDE, 1930. *She carries the reed mat, which is wrapped around the rain sash and white robe. Behind her are an oval ceramic jar with a Polik Mana (Butterfly) Kacina design and a metal wash bucket. Both are filled with cornmeal, which serves as part payment for her bridal outfit. Adapted from a Southwest Museum photograph.*

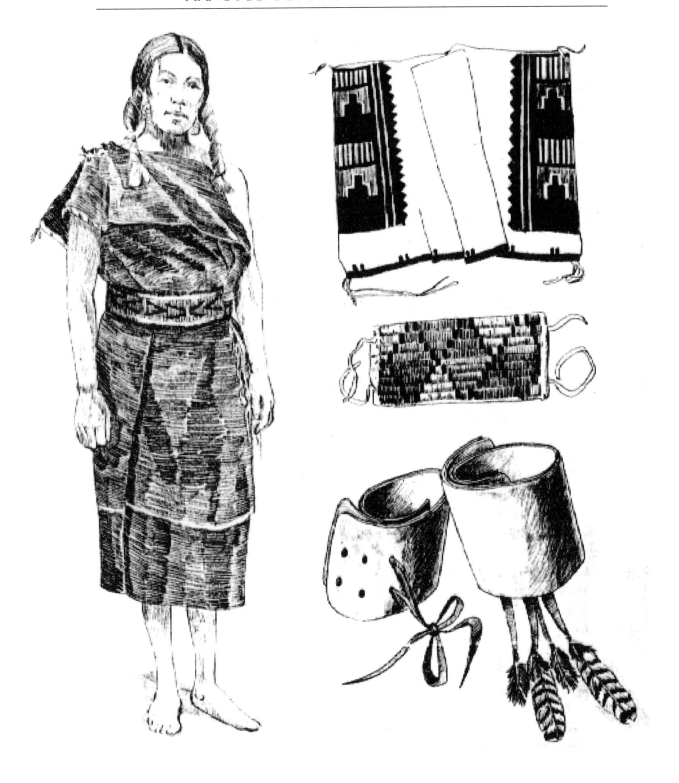

Left, *woman in native woven dress and belt sash.* Top right, *men's brocade dance kilt.*
Middle right, *anklet (or ankle band) rawhide, canvas cover and thread design.* Bottom right,
pair of men's dance armbands, double thickness of rawhide painted turquoise blue.

Male clothing in 1900

The Hopi-style cradle board

Man working at the vertical loom

Children's attire

Rabbit hunter with throwing stick

Making a rabbit-skin robe. From an E.H. Allcutt photograph, 1899.

Left, *farmer with typical corn plant*. Right, *wooden farming implements: pitchfork, digging stick, hoe, beater.*

Maiden using mano and metate to grind corn.

Sorting corn

Top, *cooking corn in an outdoor ground oven.* Middle left, *section showing construction of ground oven and smaller flue.* Middle right, *rolled piki bread.* Bottom, *making piki bread;* left, *spreading the batter on a hot stone;* right, *peeling the bread off the stone.*

Peach orchard

Cultivating melons

Below the mesa-top pueblo of Walpi, women filled their earthenware jars at water holes and then carried the heavy load on their backs up the steep foot trail to their homes.

BASKETMAKER

POTTER

KACHINA DOLLS — *The oldest styles are the simplest, newer styles feature details*

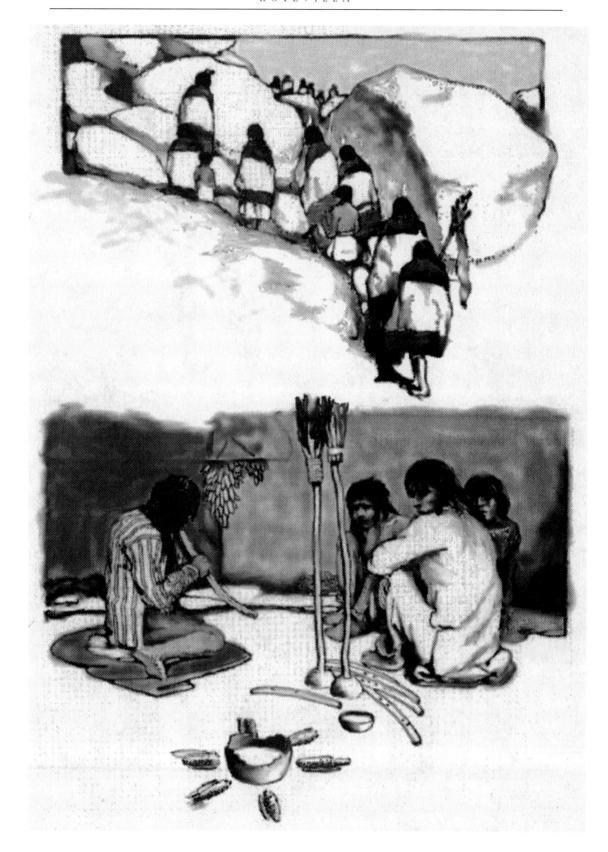

RITUAL

NIMAN

AHOLI

YELLOW CORN GIRL

HOWENAI MANA

TU-UQTI, UNCLE OF THE KUWAN HEHEYA KACHINAS

A corn meal thank offering to Earth Mother

THE THUNDERSTORM

THE SPANISH BAHANNAS

Into the beautiful, calm, and harmonious life of the Pueblo Indians in A.D. 1540 marched the militant Spaniards on their probing expeditions. The natives were apprehensive, but they were not hostile. Maasaw's prophecy had prepared them. It was possible that these newcomers, however different their appearance and mannerisms, could be their expected brothers come to help them. And even if that should not be the case, the Hopis were willing to share what they had until the newcomers moved on. The sharing would prove to be a two-way street, as the Spanish introduced them to numerous things that would prove beneficial to the Hopi...horses, sheep, cattle, new fruits and vegetables, metal tools, and more. But religion was something else in the Spanish mind. Priests and soldiers ruthlessly destroyed everything they considered heretical or hostile to the "true" Christian faith. Nothing was spared — not the sacred places, not the holiest objects, not the sacred rites and ceremonies, and any future Hopi religious practices were absolutely forbidden.

For a while, the villagers were bewildered. They did not know how to handle this. They had learned that other tribes did not worship in the exact way they did, but a contest between religions or any type of religious war was unknown to them. Worship was a celebration of the eternal mystery of life and the blessings that accompanied it. It was a Divine gift to be shared by all peoples, but each in their own way. Had Christianity contented itself simply with exchanging and enriching the variety of possible expressions for the salutary reverence of the Hopi and other Pueblos, it would have been welcomed.

But Spanish religious fanaticism made no such allowances, and Pueblo resistance was inevitable. Anger and hostility flamed into violence as religious bigotry continued to assert itself. In 1680, an uncharacteristically savage and successful revolt by all of the Pueblo peoples in the Southwest drove the astonished Spaniards, pompous victors in Peru, Central and Middle America, entirely out of Indian lands.

When the chastised but unrepentant losers returned a few years later, it was with an entirely new plan for conquest. They rooted their foundling communities once more among the pliant Rio Grande pueblos and villages, which were skilled at absorbing punishment and continuing on, and they used greater discretion in how they dealt with the people.

That succeeded, and the Rio Grande Indians responded by sharing their vast knowledge of desert living. They taught the Spaniards all of their unique skills necessary to sustain life in the Southwest desert — how to successfully grow corn, how to build adobe houses, how to dry chili peppers, how to preserve meat, how to obtain fruit and liquid from cactus, how to keep drinking water cool in clay ollas, and what herbs and roots to use for food and medicines.

The success of this limited reconquest was secured, but the generosity of the Indians did not end the religious problems for them. The attempt to suppress ceremonials and religious practices continued. Crossing, recrossing, and settling on ancient tribal lands, the Europeans urged the pueblo and mesa dwellers to embrace the new and liberating "Christian" life, and a certain degree of success was achieved. For the most part, however, the Pueblos closed their kivas to outsiders and practiced their ancient rituals, making certain that their religious beliefs and practices would accommodate, but never again be replaced by, Christianity.

THE ELDERS

This changed suddenly when a Spanish missionary came. He settled in Oraibi and started to convert us. He controlled us and treated us like slaves. He prohibited our yearly ceremonial cycle. Then it stopped raining. Starvation made us think of our original ways.

We decided to get rid of this Spaniard. One of the clans accepted the task of killing him. Then with our prayers, it started raining again. This restored our faith in the Hopi way. We wanted never again to be led astray.

We see from this terse statement of the Elders, and the one that follows by Katchongva, that the ancestors had passed along to succeeding generations their bittersweet remembrances of how it had been when the Spanish attempted to take over the Hopis.

In particular, they remembered Awatovi...how the Spanish priests, in spite of their mistreatment of many of the people, but thanks to a purported miracle of healing, had nevertheless managed to completely convert some and to divide the others. The peaceful people neither knew nor suspected the underlying motives of the priests and the Spanish government and were neatly taken in. Even the staunchest of the Traditionals were shaken and led astray. Complicating this was Maasaw's prophecy of another race of people that included a fearful warning. In fulfillment now, Spanish tactics confused and divided the people. For one perilous moment the keeping of the Covenant hung by a thread. Even though the invaders were eventually sent packing, confidence was restored, and there was a slow recovery, the effects of the Spanish visits continued to haunt all of the Hopis. Any complacency they might have had prior to the invasion evaporated now as they again and again discussed in their homes and kivas how close the escape had been.

The Oraibi people — those of the hallowed shrine and mother village — had their special memories to add to the Awatovi event. Just one plainly robed man — can you imagine that! — just one, with a small contingent of soldiers to protect him — carrying a cross and coming in the name of his Christian God — had walked into the middle of the village and in no time at all had nearly ended everything having to do with the Covenant and the survival of the North American continent and the world!

Their experience is packed into a few tightly knit remarks, and notice how the Elders and Katchongva unite fully in what is said. In the Covenant all Traditional Hopis are one, and what any generation experienced, all of the generations take the responsibility for, sharing accomplishment and acquittal, failure and guilt. So when they speak they use "we" and "us," rather than "they" or "them":

> *"This changed suddenly," they say.*
>
> *The priest's conquest took virtually no time at all...he suspected they would be, the quiet and generous Hopi were gracious hosts and easy victims. He set up his altar, unwrapped his chalice, wafers, and baptizing equipment, and went immediately to work.*
>
> *"He controlled us and treated us like slaves."*
>
> *The Hopi were not accustomed to such arrogance, especially in spiritual leaders. Their chiefs never ordered them around, and had they attempted to do so they would have been replaced. So they could not handle a situation like this, and did as they were told...which only emboldened the priest into taking what proved to be the step too far.*
>
> *"He prohibited our yearly ceremonial cycle."*
>
> *And, we can assume, replaced this with the Roman Catholic Mass said in Latin. It was a mistake that moved the priest onto perilous ground, for it declared, in effect, that the faith the Hopis had followed from the time of the Emergence and the Covenant with Maasaw were false, worthless, and should be thrown like worn-out household items onto the village trash piles. The priest had not the slightest idea as to what the Hopi believed or the meanings of what they practiced, but he could not have cared less. Hopi judgments were dismissed with a flip of the ecclesiastical hand, and the fact that the Hopi had survived beautifully for centuries by following their lifeway was entirely inconsequential. Nor did the priest bother to explain how his way was superior.*
>
> *All of this amounted to an imperious slap in the face that called Hopi judgments and intelligence into question and imperiled their ages-old relationship with the Creator, Maasaw, Mother Earth, and the rest of the Helpers. Remember this when we come shortly to the White missionary invasion of Hopi Land, for these are things they should have, and still should, think about before they seek to convert Hopis. Conversions are for unbelievers or those with false faiths, not believers with true faiths.*
>
> *The leaders knew the priest was wrong, and the divine beings would not approve of his teachings. Nature, tied fast to the Hopi by their entwined spiritual roots, quickly sent a message that told them they were right.*
>
> *"It stopped raining" and "starvation" occurred.*

The Hopi read this message as Mother Earth's stamp of disapproval. The cause being evident, the Hopi knew they could not survive more of it, and they moved to rectify the situation. Since it was the accustomed Hopi procedure to do

Spanish missionary

so, they first urged the priest to leave. When he refused, the clan chiefs gathered in the kivas and discussed ways to rid themselves of him so as to end the disruption and discourage any more priests from coming. Shortly thereafter, a unanimous verdict was reached and rendered. They simply threw him off the edge of the mesa onto the rocks below. The spot where this happened is known to Dan. The execution worked, for the time being at least. But as Katchongva tells us, the Hopi suspected that what had happened was not the end of it. Once again, though, they walked the narrow blade, eyes straight ahead and mind fixed on the Covenant vow.

"Then," the Elders say, "it started raining again."

The corn, the melons, and even the peach trees introduced to them by the Spaniards grew abundantly, and they accepted this as evidence that the divine beings were pleased with what they had done. The Covenant was once more secure, and the keeping of it would continue.

We can wish things had happened otherwise, and lament the murder at Oraibi as everyone does the massacre at Awatovi. In the light of the peaceful nature of the Hopi and the sacredness of the Covenant and its shrine, Hotevilla, these are difficult things to reconcile. But the acts were provoked by the Spanish and were a kind of treatment they had learned from those who were masters at it where Native Americans and others were concerned. Murder was a language the "Christian" Spaniards of the sixteenth and seventeenth centuries nourished to a high degree and understood well. In one instance at Awatovi, they set a recalcitrant Hopi on fire and made his friends watch while he was cremated alive. You remember, I am sure, your history lessons about the Spanish Inquisition. Here at Hopi, indeed in all of the Pueblo villages, the Spanish were ready and willing to remorselessly punish and slaughter both people and a millennias-old culture. In physical terms, the usually docile Pueblos endured something that was for them even worse than death. Death led only to rebirth in the Underworld. But in the name of God and the Roman Catholic Church, the Spanish performed group torture, cutting off hands and feet and leaving numerous helpless victims entirely dependent on others to survive. This was a crushing blow to the Pueblo belief in self-sufficiency and esteem. Yet sadistic torture was a common practice. And in spite of the positive things that were done to counterbalance their severe discipline, the Hopi encroachment proved for the Spaniards to be a lost cause. The unwelcome intruders contemplated this and shrugged their shoulders in resignation. They picked up their religious paraphernalia and left. There was no gold of consequence to be had at Oraibi anyway, and the coal was, they thought then, of limited value. Can you imagine a returning explorer unloading as booty a pile of coal from the Americas at the foot of the Spanish throne! They did not return, and over time the course of history mercifully removed them from the field of contenders.

From that moment forward, however, the succeeding generations of Hopi priests and Clan leaders watched and waited. Every year there were prayers and discussions concerning the past, the present, and what the future might be. What should they do when the Bahanna came again? — as surely he would, for the prophecies foretold it.

The Hopi people were left with a stinging reminder of what could happen when outsiders did arrive. Prophetic warnings had been right on the money. Even though they had survived another test, it was not without some of them being led astray. The interval was relatively quiet, but it was not uneventful. We know only that the testing of the Hopi continued at sporadic intervals. Maasaw did not make the unpleasant things happen, but he used them to hone and gird up his servants as he prepared them for the big test ahead.

Most scientists appear to think that the early Spanish explorations during Pueblo V had relatively little effect on historic Hopi culture, though the psychological effect was profound and continued to modify Hopi life in some respects. The Pueblo revolt of 1680 brought a temporary end to Spanish rule and a considerable influx of uneasy Pueblo people from the Rio Grande region to the Hopi villages. A group of Tiwa-speaking people settled on Second Mesa at Payupki. They remained until 1742, when they were removed by the Hopis and later resettled at Sandia in New Mexico. A Tewa-speaking group came to First Mesa, where they exist today as the village of Hano. Other refugees were probably incorporated into the Hopi villages, and it is believed that groups returned to the Rio Grande region at various times. A considerable amount of Hopi effort was spent in trading with virtually all of the Indian tribes of the Southwest, some tribes of the Great Plains, and even those of Mexico. Salt was an item in particular demand, but there was no available item that was not constantly bargained for at home or elsewhere.

Authorities do not know for certain exactly when the Southern-Athapaskan or Apachean-speaking tribes, including the Apaches and the Navajos, entered the Southwest. A round date accepted by most today is A.D. 1400. But everyone agrees that the newcomers were marauding peoples who found it easier to steal than to grow their own crops, and the Hopi fields and other useful produce became a primary source of supply. Eventually, the Apache tribes moved on, heading in different directions and settling down in mostly mountainous areas, from whence they could more easily strike at the southernmost Indian villages and those of northern Mexico. The Navajos settled down in areas bordering the Hopis, and with the encouragement of the United States government managed to surround the Hopis and steal their livestock, produce, and even women. Relationships between the tribes were seldom good, but they were not always bad either; there was some sharing, considerable trading, and intermarriage became fairly common. Since there has been contention and legislation about land borders between the two tribes, and since the Hopi Tribal Council is agitating for land return, you will be surprised to find that the Elders are perfectly willing to have the Navajos stay where they are. Later, they tell you why.

APACHE

NAVAJO

After 1680 the Hopi villages that were not already on the more easily defended mesa tops, moved up to them, and during this process a number of "satellite" villages developed, such as Sichomovi and Shipaulovi. The annual cycle of religious events was conducted without interruption, and without the rest of the world knowing how it was happening, the earth was kept in its proper rotation. Harmony and balance remained.

During the historic period, epidemic diseases periodically reduced the Hopi population. Navajo, Apache, and Ute pressures restricted geographical expansion, and occasional periods of famine led to temporary migrations of segments of the population to Zuni and to the Rio Grande pueblos.

The last vestiges of Spanish rule over the Pueblo Indians ended in 1821, when Mexico gained its independence. But internal problems plagued the Mexicans, and they paid little attention to the Pueblo Indians. No missionaries were sent north to the Hopis, and no aid was offered to them either. The Hopis were quite happy with that.

The United States terminated Mexican sovereignty over the southwestern and westernmost Indians in 1848.

KATCHONGVA
THE ARRIVAL OF ANOTHER RACE FORETOLD

Time passed on, people passed on, and the prophecies of things to come were passed from mouth to mouth. The stone tablets and the rock writing of the life plan were often reviewed by the elders. Fearfully they waited as they retold the prophecy that one day another race of people would appear in their midst and claim our land as his own. He would try to change our pattern of life. He would have a "sweet tongue" or a "fork tongue," and many good things by which we would be tempted. He would use force in an attempt to trap us into using weapons, but we must not fall for this trick, for then we ourselves would be brought to our knees, from which we might not be able to rise. Nor must we ever raise our hand against any nation. We now call these people Bahanna.

THE ELDERS

But again, Bahanna came, and destroyed our peace, this time known as the United States government. They wanted our children to go to their schools, to brainwash their mind. At first, all the villages refused to cooperate. We have our own ways to teach our children. But the government sent police to capture our men. Every village chief gave in to this pressure, including Lololmai, leader of Oraibi. He and his followers got the name "Friendlies." We who refused were called "Hostiles." Our refusal to abandon the Creator's law and our ways brought a serious split among our people, which destroyed our harmony.

THE WHITE BAHANNAS

The next invasion of Hopi country was at first not an organized one, but considering the impact it had, it might just as well have been.

Once the door opened, Americans came almost simultaneously at the Hopi from every side. Settlers, government officials, traders, scientists, educators, missionaries, painters, photographers, tourists — you name it they all swooped in at once. The intrusion was immediate, and far greater — even in the light of prophetic warnings — than anything the Hopi could have imagined.

Although it would be a prolonged and steady process, the deliberate execution of the culture was under way, and the bewildered Hopi leaders had only one defense to fall back on — Traditional life and the Covenant. No matter how well intentioned most outsiders were who shared in its construction, the coffin slowly and inexorably took shape. It remained only for United States government and industry to provide its last sideboards and bottom, render its final cover, and hammer in the nails to seal the coffin shut. I tell you again that this last part is happening right now. Before our very eyes the only fully existing Native culture left in North America, the wondrous one we have seen evolve and leave behind its sweeping panoply of magnificent markings and footprints, the heroes we have seen endure so much, all of this, is about to end… and we are about to be terminated with it…unless we — you and I — stop the process dead in its tracks.

Regarding the dissolution of Hopi Land as a whole, a general look at Hopi history will keep our chronology straight as we consider the detailed comments of the Elders and Katchongva in the chapters ahead. It will also help us remember that it was the invasion of White Americans that began and has continued it.

The first Americans known to enter were part of the James O. Pattie group, who spent some time with the Hopi in 1826, followed shortly by trappers, explorers and mountain men. After 1830, Anglo-American mountain men began to move into the area, causing at least one incident in 1834 when they raided some Hopi gardens and were turned away only after a loss of about twenty Hopi lives. Eventually Army exploring parties came, and after 1850 the Hopi would never again be alone in their world. When the land-hungry Americans came in the middle years of the nineteenth century, they brought with them their churches, traders, stores, soldiers, and their diseases. They brought their laws, courts, and an unquestioning belief in their own superiority. Energized by their faith in Manifest Destiny, the idea that theirs was a God-given right to take possession of all land regardless of the rights and nature of the people who were there before them, the lust of these fast-spreading Americans kept the Hopis in constant turmoil.

Many of these first visitors were only in the villages for one or two days, although some remained for longer periods. Most notable among the latter were anthropologists Alexander M. Stephen, who lived with the people from 1881 until his death in 1897, and Jesse Fewkes, who worked among the Hopi for long stretches between 1890 and 1900. Missionaries also came, two of the best-known being Mormon Jacob Hamblin in 1858, and Heinrich R. Voth, a Mennonite clergyman who entrenched himself at Third Mesa from 1893 to 1902.

Out of this early period, and increasingly affected by the completion of the transcontinental railroad, came the founding of satellite villages at the base of the mesas: New Oraibi (also known as Kykotsmovi), Toreva at Second Mesa, and Polacca at the base of First Mesa. As word about the primal Hopi culture and Pueblo culture in general continued to spread, to these villages came artists, tourists, and photographers, beginning with — to mention only the best-known — William H. Jackson, John K. Hillers in the mid-1870s; and later Edward Curtis, E.A. Burbank and Ben Wittick. Photographer A.C. Vroman was at Hopi Land several times during a nine-year period from 1895 to 1904, and the artist/photographer Joe Mora lived at Third Mesa from 1904 to 1906. All of these men were deeply impressed with the beauty, cultural loyalty and integrity of the Hopi. Unfortunately, some of these visitors behaved badly while they were there, and the overall encounter became, in many ways, an enlightening experience in human nature for both sides.

Interestingly enough, what enticed the majority of outsiders was a single Hopi dance — the Snake Dance! As we consider the Snake Dance here, bear in mind that it is no more significant to the Hopis than any other of their sacred dances.

It was first observed by Whites in the early 1880s, and even before 1900 numerous accounts of it had appeared in print. A description of the excitement caused by this news is provided by Vroman. Excited tourists streamed toward Hopi Land, he said, and then reported in his 1895 notebook that, at the base of First Mesa on the evening before the Snake Dance, "We found some forty white people camped, all to see the dance." He was surprised to learn these included artists of note, authors, sculptors, newspaper correspondents from half a dozen papers, and some dozen or more ladies. Two years later, Vroman reported there were more than 200 Whites in attendance. In addition, Navajos and other Indians would show up in large numbers to witness the performance.

Tourist fascination was stimulated by guidebooks and propaganda that emphasized what were described as the dance's "bizarre" features. Vroman's accounts of the ceremony are an exception to this view. He found it to be awesome, devout, and reverent. In his lectures and articles he frequently compared all of the Hopi ceremonials to major Christian observances, claiming that he failed to find the latter in any way superior. On odd-numbered years in those days, the ceremony was held at Walpi on First Mesa and Mishongnovi on Second Mesa; on even-numbered years it was held in Oraibi, then in more recent times in Hotevilla; the flute ceremony was held on the intervening years.

E.A. Burbank saw the dance several times and described his experiences in his book, *Burbank Among The Indians*, in a chapter entitled, "Dancing for the Gods." His description helps us understand why the dance, whose origin was ancient, was such an engrossing performance and attraction to people who could never have imagined themselves courting death by doing the same thing.

"All Indian tribes," Burbank said, "love ceremony involving religious dances, but none more than the Pueblos, who evolve a rite for every occasion of life. The Hopi people, in particular, were devoted to their ceremonies, the most famous of which was the Snake Dance. Although most of the dances of the Pueblo Indians were forbidden to white men's eyes, I was permitted to witness many of those of the Hopis, as I had been accepted as one of them. The Hopi dances were the most elaborate of the rites practiced by the Pueblos…Good luck awaited me when I arrived among the Hopis."

It was fortunate that the head of the Snake Clan among the Hopis at the time of my arrival was Kopeley, one of the most remarkable Indians I ever met. Kopeley was about twenty-five years old, a man of vigorous character and attractive personality. He was kindly disposed toward the white men and had won their respect by his industry and ability. Although he was conservative in character, he was open-minded toward innovations, welcoming every opportunity to improve the lot of his people.

So when I proposed to Kopeley that he let me paint him in the complete ceremonial costume of the Hopi Snake Dance, he agreed, after due deliberation. As he posed for his portrait, he was one of the most impressive figures that it has been my lot to encounter.

Kopeley wore on his head a bunch of eagle feathers stained red with sesquioxide of iron, the prescribed pigment of a warrior. To these feathers were attached those of a bluebird. The latter were symbolical of certain mystic adventures in the underworld from which the Snake Clan is supposed to have sprung.

The Snake chief's face was blackened. His cheeks were painted with iron. His chin was smeared with resin to represent a rain cloud. His kilt and buckskin thongs were stained red. Red was also the color used by the Snake priests to decorate their bodies.

He wore a necklace of badger claws to which were attached marine shells. The bandolier that hung over his right shoulder was decorated with stone arrow points and small seashells. To it were attached small pellets of clay which had been dipped in a medicine used by the Hopis to protect themselves from the bites of rattlesnakes.

In his right hand Kopeley carried a snake whip consisting of a wooden handle to which were bound turkey feathers. In the Snake Dance he used this whip to wave before the eyes of the reptiles. It confused them and caused them to uncoil when they had assumed a position for striking.

All of the objects worn by Kopeley in his Snake Dance costume had a special significance. They were not mere decorations, but were there for a purpose which only the Snake priests could appreciate.

Kopeley had inherited his position as chief from his uncle a few years before. He was the son of the oldest woman in the Snake Clan at Walpi. He was married and had one daughter.

The young chief took his responsibilities with great earnestness. When he learned that the Zunis were in the midst of an epidemic of smallpox, he considered it his duty to visit them and offer such help as he could. He did this over the protests of his friends. As was to be expected, Kopeley himself contracted smallpox and died soon after his return to Polacca. Several other Hopis who had handled Kopeley's effects contracted the disease, and the government finally was *obliged to send soldiers to destroy everything that was left of his possessions to check the epidemic.*

Kopeley's untimely death deprived the Hopis of a remarkable leader who, had he lived the normal span of life, might have become one of the greatest Indian chiefs of American history...The Snake Dance which has made the Hopi tribes famous the world over is presented on three different mesas. I have seen it on each of the three mesas. The only difference in the dance is that at Walpi the Hopis did not touch the snakes with their hands while they held them in their mouths. On the other mesas they did. The Snake Dance is an elaborate prayer for rain, which is as important as life itself to the Hopis. I once asked one of them what would happen if the dance failed to produce rain. He replied that it would mean that some one of them had not done his part correctly during the nine-day ceremony.

It is a strange but curious fact that shortly after the Snake Dance it invariably does rain throughout the Pueblo Indian country. So the Hopis have some reason for their faith in the efficacy of the Snake Dance... A legend of the Hopis states that the children of the marriage of the Snake hero and the Snake maid in ancient times were transformed into snakes. The snakes were regarded by the Hopis as earthly brothers. They were thought to be all-powerful in asking the water gods to bring rain. The ceremony is said to represent an agreement between the Snake and the Antelope clans to hold a joint celebration of their respective rites which conflicted when the clans originally came together. As the prayers are dramatized, certain roles are assigned to Snakes, certain to the Antelopes.

The dance occurs once in two years about the twentieth of August. More than 100 live snakes are used in the rites. Contrary to popular belief, no efforts are made to render the reptiles innocuous either by extraction of their fangs or by the use of drugs.

Six days before the ceremony begins, the men in the Snake Clan go down to the plains and hunt snakes. I have gone with them and have seen them use their eagle feather wands to distract the snakes and keep them from coiling to spring. The snakes were put in bags and brought to the kiva where they were given a bath. Bullsnakes, Gopher, King, and rattlesnakes are used without discrimination.

For nine days the priests of the Snake Clan never leave the kiva for any purpose. They eat and sleep with the snakes during that time. The snakes are kept in jars, but occasionally let out.

At the end of the ninth day of ceremony in the kiva, the Antelope men came up the ladder. They were followed by members of the Snake Clan. Some carried the bags that held the snakes. Then began the only part of the ritual which the public has been privileged to see — the actual dance itself.

After all the dancers were assembled, the Snake men went to the bags where each reached in and pulled out a snake which he placed (sideways) in his mouth and gently held between his lips, so that the head protruded on one side, and the rest of the body on the other. He began to dance, going around a big circle three times, each dancer stamping the board-covered hole as he passed it. If the snake dropped from his teeth, he picked it up and resumed his dance. If the snake coiled for striking, the gatherer touched it with his snake whip. During the dance, the Snake women continually sprinkled cornmeal upon the dancers.

As each gatherer picked up a snake, it was handed to one of the Antelope men, usually about twenty in number, who gathered on each side of a tree transplanted in the courtyard. One of the Snake men in the meantime drew a circle the size of a cartwheel upon the ground. Into this circle the Antelope men dumped all the snakes in a pile.

At a signal, the Snake men who had gathered around this circle seized several snakes apiece and ran in different directions from the mesa to the valley. There the snakes were given their freedom. They were to crawl off into the underworld to advise the rain gods that the Hopis needed moisture.

When the Snake men returned to the mesa they drank the snake medicine, which caused them to vomit violently… Although the formula was secret, I learned that one important ingredient is the juice of a small red bug.

The dancers were just as fearful of being bitten as any normal person would be, and all of them sidestepped a rattler if the reptile were coiled. Each dancer always carried a supply of medicine on hand to use at once in case he was bitten.

All of the members of the Snake Clan were sons of former Snake men, just as the offices in the Antelope Clan were handed down from father to son. Before they reached their teens the youngsters began to take part in the rites, preparing themselves for the day when they would become priests. [Dan Evehema participated in the Snake Dance at Hotevilla for a number of years.]

In the excitement of the occasion, it looked as though every dancer was following his own idea. But I learned later that each dancer had his special detail to perform in the ritual. The duty of Wick-ahte-wah, for example, was to hold at the door of the kiva a bow to which a red fringe was attached, warning all outsiders not to enter. To Kah-kap-tee was assigned the task of collecting colored sand to make the Snake pictures of the prayer emblems. He painted his skin, curiously, with zigzag stripes representing lightning. I was told that before the dancers left the kiva on the ninth day, the snakes were allowed to crawl over Kah-kap-tee's sand pictures to destroy them. Thus they carried the message of the prayer to the underworld.

For many years the Hopis were very secretive about their Snake Dance, being fearful that the government agents would prohibit it [which, of course, is exactly what the Government and missionaries attempted to do]. No pictures were made of the ceremony because the most important part of it was held just before dusk. At the conclusion of the dance thousands of visitors, not only white people, but Navajos, Apaches, and other Indians were permitted to witness it. As the Snake men dashed off to deliver the reptiles to their homes, the Navajos invariably made a rush to gather up the sacred meal which the Hopi medicine women had distributed, believing that this meal would bring them good luck.

FLUTE SOCIETY: Left, *member dressing for the ninth-day rite at the spring.* Right, *society priest.*

The photographer Ben Wittick, who is reputed to have been a great friend of the Hopis, died from a rattlesnake bite, fulfilling a prophecy made years before, to which Wittick often referred. Invited by a Hopi priest to watch a secret Snake ritual, he had been warned of his death by one of the Hopi elders present who resented a white man's presence there: "He has not been initiated!" the Elder shouted. "Death will come to him from the fangs of our little brothers." The fatal bite occurred while Wittick was packing a rattlesnake for shipment to his Hopi friends.

In many ways the extremely beautiful Flute Ceremony parallels that of the Snake, and it is regarded by Hopis as having great sacredness. Two societies participate, the Blue Flute and the Drab Flute.

Lacking any features that could be thought sensational, the Flute Ceremony never attracted the crowds that were drawn to the Snake Ceremony. A few years after Vroman's time the Flute Ceremony was abandoned, and only in recent times has it been revived.

Despite the great sacredness of the Flute Ceremony and the secrecy of most of its observances, Vroman was able in 1902 to make a photograph of the Mishongnovi Flute altar without, he stated, any protest on the part of the priests. He wrote that "No objection was made to our entering while the making of pahos (prayer sticks) and other preliminaries were in progress." One of the priests even permitted himself to be included in another view of the same altar. While the Hopi were still trusting, and did not know how easily news could and would be spread in the outside world, in 1908 Earle Forrest was invited into the house where the Flute altar was set up and was permitted to observe much of the ceremony. He was even given permission to photograph the altar. This kind of thing has not been permitted for a very long time and is not under any circumstances allowed today.

Since Hopi religion stresses the brotherhood of man with all creation, the idea of shutting non-Indians out of ceremonial observances seems inconsistent. The truth is that the ceremonies are so complex it is improbable that anyone outside of the clan members themselves would have much understanding of their meaning. That some of those who did not understand the dance would look on in mockery was and is certainly a factor in keeping the uninitiated out of certain observances, but the overriding factor has been the fear, sadly confirmed over the years, that the ceremonies would be suppressed if too much were known about them. It was a very serious threat at the turn of the century, it is a very serious threat now, and it has justified the secrecy of the Hopis about their religious life within the kivas.

The United States Bureau of Indian Affairs in North America Generally

Most non-Indians living in the United States at the close of the nineteenth century believed that the "Indian problem" had already been solved. Roughly two and a half centuries of slowly diminishing Indian resistance to White penetration and seizure of Indian tribal lands had come at last to its bloody end. For the White majority, military power was being replaced by the Congressional committee, political investigation, all-important budget appropriations, and the Bureau of Indian Affairs, abbreviated as the BIA. The time had arrived for the nation to recast the political and economic oppression of the Indian minority into a more permanent and more effective form. And the Bureau's assigned task was the rapid assimilation of American Indians into the dominant White culture.

Christian and Mormon missionaries' proselytizing energies added little-needed fire and brimstone to the Bureau of Indian Affairs campaign to wipe out Indian religious life. With their encouragement, a series of Bureau rulings begun in 1900 effectively suppressed, except for those rites Indians practiced secretly, Indian ceremonials for twenty years. Bewildering as it may seem, the American descendants of European immigrants who had fled their homelands in the seventeenth century to escape religious persecution, coming here to find and to found religious freedom in a new land, energetically denied it to the native residents.

In dealing with the Hopi, Washington itself simply never realized that in political terms the Hopi villages were neither single nor integrated units. During the long migration period they had become self-sufficient groups of cohesive but wholly autonomous peoples, sometimes at odds with one another and always expecting an equal voice in arriving at any decision. The only unanimous decisions they sought were those where tribal concerns were involved, and for a while at least they were staunchly united against the outside world.

The Concern for Indian Rights and Needs

Although vigorously defended by its supporters — in particular the religious interests and land speculators — the BIA came under deserved and increasing criticism. Steady streams of reports of misconduct and abuse in the bureau's treatment of its Indian charges in the Southwest stirred considerable demand for reform and for sympathetic understanding of Indian rights. These demands heightened an already growing concern among certain White Americans, and the outlines for an effective national movement in support of Indian rights and Indian needs began to emerge. Further stimulus came from Helen Hunt Jackson's brilliant document, *A Century of Dishonor*, published in 1881, and her second Indian work in 1884, the novel *Ramona*. Both of these detailed in succinct terms the endless abuses and outrages the Indians were forced to endure.

The Anthropologists, Archaeologists, and Ethnologists

Indian communities had next to endure the invasion of the sciences. Because of their professional training, the scientists were probably less ethnocentric than any other White groups in the United States and, in the short run, their impact upon the Indians less grievous. Nevertheless, with a typical White lack of concern for Indian sensitivities, they prevailed upon the natives' decency and hospitality to discover and report all they could of the intimate life of the people. The idea of using their energies for the preservation of the culture apparently did not, as a rule at least, occur to them in the early 1900s.

The truly wondrous thing for the scientists, of course, was that the Hopi living on the three mesa tips were precisely what their ancestors had been like for

thousands of years. Assuredly, the anthropologists had already been wondering about this for years, but upon seeing them now the mists of time were penetrated and the greater Anasazi/Hopi world came sweeping into view! Vexing questions were swept as rapidly away as if they had been hit by a flash flood.

It is important to recognize, though, that in light of what had already happened to other Indian tribes, the anthropologists also accepted that the Hopi would be assimilated as quickly as they had appeared. In their zeal to study and record Hopi life as completely as possible before this happened, certain of the scientists seemed to ignore altogether the Indians' right to humane treatment. While they wrote with great thoroughness of Indian religious rites, they lost sight of the words "sacred" and "privacy." The wholesale excavation of Indian burial sites was characteristic of this scientific blindness.

Buttressed by the evangelical pressures of organized religion, it became easy for the majority of White people to regard the Indian as simply an object of curiosity and welfare. He was not, in their view, another human being equal to themselves. From here it was but a small step to regarding him as an object to be improved upon, and his improvement became the official concern of the Bureau of Indian Affairs. Those who stood to gain financially or conversion-wise wholeheartedly approved of the bureau's work and policies. For the Indians, the view was unendurable.

Close behind the earliest explorers came four men whose work is of prime importance to outsiders. Something needs to be said about each one of them, for they, along with the outstanding later scholars Elsie Clews Parsons and Mischa Titiev, have contributed significantly to our knowledge of Hopi culture. Nevertheless, we must at the same time understand Hopi feelings about any work done by outsiders. While we who want to learn these things are fortunate to have this information, the present-day Hopi, and especially the religious leaders, find intrusions into religious rites to be matters of major consequence. You will see how these have affected the keeping of the Covenant, for they brought in on their coattails scores of people who determined, with no justification whatsoever, that the Hopi were heathens whose lifeway must be stamped out by suppression and conversion. In Dan's mind that risk still remains, and while he welcomes visitors to share in the public portions of religious events, he knows that among these will always be some who come to learn ritual secrets, to scorn, to suppress, and to convert. In proof of this, there are witnessed incidents where religious zealots, including Hopi converts, have inexcusably set up loudspeakers to harass the Hopi while they are in the very midst of their most solemn ceremonial dances! What would our response be if someone did this kind of thing during our worship services in our churches?

Alexander M. Stephen was a Scotsman who, from 1881 until his death in 1894, lived at Keams Canyon with the trader Thomas Keam. Nearly all his years in Hopi country were devoted to a study of Hopi life, especially to its ceremonial aspects. He spent a great deal of time with the people, mainly on First Mesa, where it is the general opinion that he was respected and loved. He kept a series of detailed notebooks that he profusely illustrated with eyewitness sketches and filled with minute descriptions of everything he saw. These notebooks were later edited by Elsie Clews Parsons and were published by the Columbia University Press in 1936, under the name "Hopi Journal by Alexander M. Stephen." They are by far the most authoritative and exhaustive compendium of data ever assembled concerning any Pueblo group.

The Reverend Heinrich R. Voth made his first visit to Hopi country in 1892. He returned in 1893 with his wife to establish a Mennonite mission near Old Oraibi. As his story progresses you will see why most Traditional Hopis remain angry about Voth and most of the others who came to the mesas to do research. Voth made no converts. When successors came to replace him at the mission, a few Hopi converts were at last gained, but, along with government interference, the successes joined in fueling a fire already kindling the division of Old Oraibi that would take place in 1906. After thirty years of work, the Mennonite converts numbered only about forty, and in the early 1980s the mission was no larger than before.

In any event, Voth, with or without the encouragement of the Hopi, was soon on his way to becoming an ethnologist. Even though at first he questioned the reasons for and the effectiveness of the Hopi practices, he was at the same time powerfully intrigued by them. During the 1890s he undertook a systematic study of Hopi social and ritual life — to understand, he claimed, their religious beliefs better. In time he would be forced to admit that, as a whole, "the ceremonies were devotional and serious." But lacking a proper understanding of their most important purposes, and making no effort to learn this — since he as a Christian "naturally" knew better anyway, he considered the "shows" of the clowns "degrading and filthy," and he thought the whipping of the children in the initiation ceremony was a travesty. In consequence, Voth asked the Government to prohibit some features of certain ceremonies, and the Government happily made every effort to comply.

By 1897, Voth was so deeply into collecting lesser material culture objects and information about the Hopi that he was able to provide George A. Dorsey with about 400 well-documented specimens for an exhibit. These included twenty-four sacred masks and a number of other kiva items that should have remained with the Hopi. From this point on, Voth provided Dorsey with a series of detailed and illustrated accounts of Hopi secular and ceremonial customs. The work in this instance was supported by the Stanley McCormick Hopi expedition, and it is published under that name. Included in Voth's contributions were a number of stunning life-sized altar reproductions he created for displays at the Field Colombian Museum. Hopi who saw the displays were astonished and dismayed at their accuracy. So much was revealed they had no idea what the consequences would be.

In commenting on Voth, one of Frank Waters' Hopi informants says, "They must have sent a German here because they wanted a stern man. That's what Voth was. He did not stay in the back. He always pushed to the front, anywhere he wanted to be, even in the kivas. Nobody could stop him. One time a Two Horn priest tried to stop him from going into a kiva. He kicked the Two Horn priest out of the way and went in…Most of the stories they told Voth is because they didn't want to tell him the true story." Another informant said, "I don't think it was right, what he (Voth) did. He came here to teach the Bible, to convert the people. Instead of doing what he was supposed to, being a church man, he got into all the secrets, stole them and some of the altar things too, and revealed all the sacred things in his books" (Waters, *The Fourth World of the Hopis*, p. 230). Yet when one uninstructed society member had to succeed his brother as kiva chief after the brother's sudden death, he was rescued by following Voth's account, translated by the new chief's grandson, which clarified details essential to the carrying out of the rituals.

The Voths entered into every phase of Hopi life and learned the language in order, they said, to convert more quickly what Voth called "immortal souls needing to be saved." In his writings, however, there is no evidence of contempt for the Hopi religion. On the contrary, there is impressive respect. In his final analysis of Voth, Fred R. Eggan concludes, "For all his interest in Hopi religion he never attempted to understand it in its own terms because he had already defined it as false," adding, however, that as an ethnologist of Hopi life Voth had no peers.

The task of interpretation, however, "has had to be carried out by others, and particularly Mischa Titiev for Third Mesa."

Among those who benefitted greatly from Voth's Hopi collections was Fred Harvey, who obtained in 1912 a superb, but perhaps in the light of history regrettable for the Hopi, display for his Hopi House at Grand Canyon. Although it lacked some culture items, it was a representative assortment, and in 1979, Northland Press, of Flagstaff, Arizona, published Barton Wright's *Hopi Material Culture*, which illustrates and describes most if not all of the collection.

In any event and as already indicated, the Voths had little success with conversions, and when his wife died in childbirth in 1900 Voth decided to leave the mission field. It was during this time that the relationship with George A. Dorsey flowered, and Voth began to make artifact collections for the Field Colombian Museum. Voth left Hopi in 1902 and became a home mission worker in Oklahoma. He died in 1927.

By any measure, Jesse Walter Fewkes was an extraordinary man. Despite the hazards of travel in the back country in the late 1890s and early 1900s, and during his years with the U.S. Bureau of American Ethnology in the Smithsonian Institution, he seems to have been everywhere at once, looking, listening, digging, recording, and speculating. He spent parts of many summers with the Hopi, mainly on the First and Second mesas; he was there while Alexander Stephen was alive, and the two shared notes. He also went to Oraibi to see Voth. Eggan says that Fewkes wanted comparative data from Voth, but that Voth was reluctant to release it, since it might weaken interest in his own accounts. Voth was probably right. Fewkes would have had it in print while Voth was still mulling over his introductory material.

Fewkes is admirable in his willingness to express openly his thoughts regarding the purpose and meaning of what he found, and to speculate about its historical development. This has never been a popular pursuit among archaeologists, since it is guaranteed to bring sharp criticism from other experts who dispute the views. But Fewkes put it all down, and he argued eloquently in his own behalf. Readers of any bibliography on the Hopi will find more than forty of his books and articles listed, and he is regularly cited in supporting footnotes.

As to his accuracy in what he deduced from his cherished experiences, many honors were bestowed upon Fewkes by foreign countries and at home, but those he prized most were his initiations into the Antelope and Flute societies of Walpi. Although some Hopis will dispute this assertion, it is said that both Fewkes and Stephen were welcomed to witness, record, and participate in many ceremonies in the kiva and in the public performances.

Albert Yava, who was born in 1888 in the Tewa village of Hano, on First Mesa, grew up in the context of both the Tewa and the Hopi worlds, and came to know the Hopi lifeway almost as well as any Hopi. He was initiated into the One Horn Kiva fraternity, where he learned the traditions of the clans and the essences of the ceremonial cycle upon which Hopi life is based. In his life story, *Big Falling Snow*, published in 1978, he speaks now and then of certain anthropologists, ethnologists, and archaeologists who worked among the Hopi. As a rule, he is not especially kind to these. But Fewkes is an exception. "What he tells is absolutely true," Yava writes. In regard to the One Horn ceremonies, Yava says that, while he is "honor bound" to keep the rituals secret, Fewkes was the only White man who became an initiate, and none of the One Horns "could find any fault" with what Fewkes wrote about the society. The One Horn people even suggested that Yava should get rid of his copy of Fewkes's book because it was so accurate. "Fewkes," says Yava, "had a brilliant mind." Jesse Walter Fewkes retired in 1928 and died in 1930.

A towering work on Hopi and Zuni is *A Study of Pueblo Architecture, Hopi Land and Cibola* by Victor Mindeleff, published as the BAE 8th Annual Report of 1886—87, although the field work was done in 1881—83. This astonishing collection of maps, sketches, commentary, and photographs presents a comprehensive display of the architectural accomplishments of the western Pueblo peoples as they existed before White influences began to change them. Some of these I have redrawn to augment the descriptions I give of the Hopi lifeway.

The Artists and the Photographers

Picture-taking in the United States was not merely a pleasant diversion in 1900. It had become a near mania among those who could afford it. Photography had become a big business, and the making of pictures had become an absolute must for tourists. At the pueblos and on the mesas it was no longer limited merely to the professional, and the taking of snapshots by hordes of curious tourists added new dimensions to old and vexing problems faced by the Indians. It was humiliating and degrading. The manic fervor of the tourists to get a "good shot" of Pueblo Indian life was so intense that simple courtesies were all but forgotten. The conduct of determined tourist photographers was especially disgraceful. They invaded the Indian's privacy and insulted him by their indifference to his pride and dignity. They even forced their way into the Hopi's kivas, and they desecrated shrines — those revered places where special roots were sunk into Mother Earth — photographing, handling, and even removing holy paraphernalia, frequently ignoring the restrictions the Hopi placed on photographing sacred dances and ceremonies.

As already mentioned, A. C. Vroman was one of the exceptions to this kind of thing, producing a collection of Southwest Indian photographs that are uncommon in vision and astonishing in execution. The plight and the abuse of the rights of the Southwest Indians affected him greatly. He was not the first photographer in the United States to photograph Indians, nor was he even the first to focus his talents so consistently on the Southwest Indians. His distinction is that he always thought of Indians as human beings of great worth. His experience is instructive, for it shows us the greatness of Hopi religion and what is there for us to understand as we think about the need to do what we can to keep their lifeway going.

Even some of the professed friends of the Indians, men who should have known better, proved to be sources of difficulty for the Hopi. George Wharton

James, an English journalist, author, and lecturer, and a skillful and talented photographer, was once strongly reprimanded by Vroman for invading a sacred Hopi kiva, unannounced and uninvited. By 1902, this kind of interruption was so common that the Hopi of Oraibi were forced to restrict photographers to a single area during the Snake Dance. James was incensed at this and described the restrictions imposed on White photographers by the Hopi as unacceptable. "Hitherto," he fumed, "every man had chosen his own field and moved to and fro wherever he liked — in front of his neighbor or someone else, kicking down another fellow's tripod and sticking his elbow in the next fellow's lens. Now, half a dozen or more Indian policemen kept us in line, so we had to go ahead and make the best of it."

The Bureau of Indian Affairs' ruling in the 1900s suppressing native religious life forced the Indians to move even more deeply into secretiveness. Official punishment for disobedience to Government edicts was swift and severe, and Indians quickly learned to be suspicious of most Whites who wished to see their ceremonies. Fearful of BIA reprisals, the Hopis forbade photographers entrance to certain ceremonies, kivas, councils, and sacred areas.

Vroman's encounter with Helen Hunt Jackson's book *Ramona* marked an important turning point in his life. The dramatic moment of a new vision, however, seems to have occurred in the summer of 1895, when he first witnessed the celebrated Hopi Snake Dance. He went there with great anticipation, but not with anything like what actually resulted. His first photographs of the picturesque village of Walpi present typical tourist scenes of the village itself and of organized groups of natives who consented to pose for him.

But here was Vroman, four days out of Pasadena, California, the burgeoning modern city he lived in, with the men of his party clad in hats, neckties, and business suits, and the women in fashionable travel outfits. They strolled along the dusty paths and streets of the village amid ragged dogs, naked children, and burros, while the shy women peeped out of their windows and doors at the strangers and giggled. It was hard for Vroman to believe he was still in America. Despite his attempts to remain calm, there was a growing excitement. Finally in the afternoon the Snake Dance began, and it proved to be an overpowering experience. It didn't last long, but when it ended Vroman and his friends stood stunned and tried to understand what had happened. In this single moment everything else in his life diminished to total meaninglessness.

He wrote in his diary that he absolutely must see the Snake Dance again, and he wished that others could experience it too. He even expressed a longing to be initiated into the Snake Society so that he might participate in the ceremony for the full nine days, but he must have known that was not likely to happen. Vroman did return in 1897, and during the ten-year period of his visits to Hopi country he managed to attend all but two Snake Dances. Those he did see came to occupy a crucial position in his personal philosophy. For the next ten years he devoted himself to the study of the Indians, trying to understand the complexities and difficulties in the relationship of the Indians and the Whites. He determined that through his photographs he could present Indian life to the Whites, establish respect for their religious life, their art, their precious relationship with the land, and at the same time he would be enriching the lives of his White neighbors. He finally did this, but he was long gone before it came to pass.

Most anthropologists have accepted that the Hopi ceremonies are conducted in order to produce rain. Recent and more sensitive thinkers have recognized that within these wondrous rituals there is a celebration with far more profound implications. Vroman may have been among the earliest to sense this, recognizing that the mere production of rain did not suffice to explain the profoundly involved symbolism and ritual. The Elders and Katchongva support this truth in the material included here.

As previously indicated, the White audiences that flocked to Hopi were for the most part intent only upon the sensational aspects of the Snake Dances, and the number who came despite the difficult desert journey and the absence of facilities along the way or at Hopi was impressive. No matter. The idea of watching men dancing with live rattlesnakes held in their mouths was simply too boggling to deny, and the fact that dancers were in rare instances bitten yet showed little effect from the deadly venom had people shaking their heads in a mixture of pleasure and disbelief. That the dancers seemed utterly blasé about this caused eyes to open even more and the head shaking to increase. Discovering why the Hopi did this was not really the concern. Like it is with seeing the fakirs, fire walkers and snake charmers perform their acts, watching the Hopi risk their lives with the snakes was everything, and in their wildness to see it the visitors turned the sacred dance plazas into zoos.

Photographing the Snake Ceremony presented a difficult technical challenge. Space was very limited. The public part of the ceremony began in the late afternoon, and waning light conditions caused severe backlighting problems and difficulty in getting depth of field and stopping motion at the same time. On the one hand it required complete attention to the proceedings — to the profound symbolism of the action, the chanting, the splendid body paint and costumes. On the other hand there was the photographic business itself — depth-of-field considerations, stopping the movement of the dancers, getting adequate exposure in the rapidly fading light, the constant changing of plateholders. Frequently, equipment had to be covered up quickly due to a huge downpour of rain. There was barely enough room for the Hopi dancers and Hopi spectators, let alone the outsiders who crowded in. Once the dance got under way, there was severe competition among the photographers with their ungainly equipment for the best positions, and more than one ugly squabble for a shooting location resulted in angry remarks and camera stands being kicked over. The Hopi spectators, and sometimes even dancers themselves, were shoved rudely aside as though they didn't belong there. The Hopis were far more amazed at the conduct of the Whites than anything the snake dancers were doing. Now and then a Hopi might even be cursed at, pushed, or struck. There was no regard at all for the sacredness of the moment, and even to this day there are Hopi who with every justification smoulder whenever they think about the disrespectful conduct of White spectators at some dances. Such bewildering behavior told them, and still tells them, more than they wanted to know about what the visitors really thought of their rituals.

The Missionaries

As one might anticipate, missionary groups played a stellar role in causing the greatest cultural disruption at Hopi Land, for it was their influence that pitted faith against faith, Hopi against Hopi, and family against family — fueling a far-reaching schism that continues to wreak its unfortunate consequences to the present day.

Since I am a Lutheran pastor, you may be wondering why I deal so harshly as I do here with the Christian missionaries. It is not because I think it is wrong to convert people. It is because I think Jesus would agree that it is wrong to forcibly and covertly convert people whose long-held faith has already proven it leads people to live as Jesus asks Christians to live, and who in fact do it better than most Christians do. Furthermore, the Hopi religion has shown itself to be so sufficient, beneficial, and effective in maintaining the relationship between the Creator and the people that the latter feel they do not need to be enlightened or converted and consider it an affront when Christians arbitrarily decide otherwise. Fortunately, a number of the mainline denominations have at last come to the same conclusion I did long ago, and have finally apologized to the Native Americans for past blindness and transgressions. You will find the documentation for this in Chapter 8.

It should be noted here that contrary to general opinion, the majority of Americans, including many in government service, and particularly those who invaded the West, were neither Christians nor Bible-believing people. We often blame the Christians for every unfortunate act, whereas the actual case is that many of the perpetrators were serving nothing but what they perceived to be their own best interests. God had no part whatsoever in what they did, and we, as well as Native Americans, should keep this in mind.

There were, however, more than enough Christians ready to do the "necessary" work at Hopi Land at the turn of the century. Thousands of years devoted to keeping of the sacred Covenant be damned and the happiness and satisfaction of the Hopi people ignored, the missionaries came, Bibles in hand, resolutely to the mesas. The fact that the Hopi Indians already had their own Creator-given religion was inconsequential to the missionaries. That it had served the Hopi wonderfully until Christianity only now became available did not matter. Explaining why God should permit this delay was beside the point. The missionaries did not ask themselves what kind of a God would, until Christianity managed to get to them, allow for thousands of years millions of people all over the world to languish in a false faith that would guarantee them an eternal place in Hell. Of course the missionaries meant well, and of course they labored sacrificially, and of course they believed they were carrying out the command of the Savior. But the missionaries were misreading Jesus's command to go forth and baptize. Jesus did say he came "to set a father against a mother, and brother against brother," but he was talking about making a choice between God and unbelief. He surely did not mean they were to go forth to disrupt those who already knew the Creator and were serving him. For such, it would be enough — if the missionaries were invited to — to let them know that Christians have been taught that Jesus is part of the Godhead, and the savior of all by whatever name anyone knows him. God…Creator…is a Being in common to be shared by everyone. The Hopi already knew and practiced that. No missionary had to tell them. You will see what Dan says about this in Chapter 8. It was presumptuous to think otherwise, and the missionaries then and now, as well as the Spanish priests, should have known better than to do what they did, for the Hopis need not in the least be ashamed of, or apologetic for, what they had believed and practiced since the Emergence.

It seems, though, to not have occurred to the missionaries that the Hopi might not agree with their conclusions or receive them with open arms. The lessons of the Spanish incursion was long past and not known to many Americans. Nor did it trouble the Americans that in those days the Protestant view was that Roman Catholicism was nearly as wrong as the Hopi were thought to be, and vice versa.

But the missionaries were like the good samaritans who felt compelled to help someone cross the street, even when they neither needed to nor wanted to go. They cringed at the Snake Dances, they were appalled at what they thought were moral indiscretions, they trembled with righteousness when the word "witchcraft" was even spoken — let alone the idea of its actually being practiced — they grimaced and were apprehensive when they thought about the secret rites going on in the kivas, they winced at the idea of spirits going to live in the Underworld after death, and the lack of hygiene was simply appalling. Something, they fervently believed, must be done about all of this, and they resolved to do it. Being totally ignorant about Hopi religion, and making no attempt to learn about it, there was hardly a single Hopi custom that was acceptable to them.

We can thank E. A. Burbank, who apparently was himself a devout Christian, for being one of the few who, in the appendix of his book, *Burbank Among the Indians*, has provided us with a first-person account, entitled "The Sunlight Missions at Polacca and Toreva," which describes how mission work began and proceeded at First Mesa, along with a graphic picture of the Traditional Hopi response.

Reference has already been made to Voth, the Mennonite missionary who was at work on Third Mesa, and how he was so fascinated by the ancient Hopi culture that he spent, if anything, more time investigating it and collecting artifacts than he did in the pulpit. There was no such fascination among the Baptists. They had no desire to collect artifacts or information about Hopi rituals; they wanted instead to get rid of them.

In a way we would not have expected, the gospel door, as did so many other doors at Hopi Land, opened on First Mesa in 1900, when some of the Kiowa Indian Christians in Oklahoma decided to share their new faith with a tribe that did not have missionaries. Accordingly, they sent money to the Women's Baptist Home Mission Society asking that it be used to open a new mission. Also, surprisingly, the Baptist venture at Hopi would prove to be largely a ladies operation. Some Indian tribes were still hostile, and perhaps the peaceful reputation of the Hopi tribe suggested it would be a safe haven in which to work.

Assuredly, though, the women were made of strong stuff. Miss Mary G. Burdette, who was the corresponding secretary of the society, made the arduous trip by buckboard to the Hopi Reservation with only an Indian driver who could not speak English, finally reaching their primary destinations of First Mesa and Toreva (whirling water), a place where the National Indian Association had begun work in 1894 and had so little success they were desirous of turning it over to any denomination that would take it. There had not been a single conversion during the six years they had been there. But that did not deter Miss Burdette. The mission home itself was nearly 2 miles from the place of the whirling water, where the government had a small day school. When she reached the site it was noon and the sun was at its brightest. On the one hand, this reminded her of Jesus as "the Son of righteousness," and she immediately christened it "Sunlight Mission." On the other hand, she thought the darkness among the Hopi was very great, and "added to their condition spiritually." There had also been five years of drought. The Hopi people were continually hungry, and she realized she could use this fact to her own advantage. She would convince them that their "mistaken" beliefs were the source of their troubles. The Hopi are superstitious, so they considered this possibility. Some decided she might have a point, and began to listen to the rest of what she had to say. It was a crack in the door that she needed, and one that could be widened if others would come to help her.

In November 1901, Miss Mary McLean was sent to Toreva. Six miles away by horseback trail was a group of three villages with about the same population as the three villages near the whirling water, and the government field matron, Miss Sarah E. Abbott, urged Miss Burdette to send workers to that place, known as Polacca. It was a little more than a year after McLean went to Toreva that Miss Ida M. Schofield was sent from the Comanche Indian mission and Miss Abigail E. Johnson was sent from the Cheyenne Indian mission to start the work at Polacca. They arrived the day before Christmas 1902. Now there were four pairs of hands to turn the wheels of conversion.

At Toreva, McLean found a number of Hopi who had been to school a short time, but none of them wanted the proffered job of interpreter. They knew there would be trouble. Finally one who had been to school for two years said he would try to tell the Hopi people what she wished to say to them. His name was Steve Quonestewa. McLean worked diligently with him to get him ready, and introduced him to Bible reading. He became a Christian during his first year's work, and immediately experienced a storm of persecution from the Hopi Traditionals. But he held on, and 37 years later was still a Christian when Burbank wrote his account in 1939.

Angry Hopis told Quonestewa they would take his children away from him.

When that threat didn't work, they told him they would take his wife. Steve said, "Even if you should take my wife and children away from me I will follow Jesus anyway." They replied, "You will have no rain on your field if you follow Jesus," but even that did not move him. These were strong and unusual positions for Hopi to take, and it should have signaled to the missionaries that there were deep reasons for the objections. One morning when Quonestewa came to the mission he was excited and his eyes were shining.

Miss McLean noticed this and asked, "Well, how is it this morning?"

Steve exulted, "It rained on my field last night."

"Did it not rain on other fields?" she anxiously asked.

"No," he assured her, "it only rained on my field."

The Hopi Indian men loved to smoke cigarettes, but the missionaries forbade them to smoke at church or in their presence. When the men came to pose for Burbank, they still wanted to smoke. He told them there was nothing in the Bible that read, "Thou shalt not smoke." So most of the men smoked without the White women's approval. For this and other reasons, the missionaries did not care for artists who went to the Hopi country to paint or take photographs. One lady missionary told Burbank that what he was doing was like putting a red flag before a bull. They also did not want the churchgoing Hopis to take part in any of the Hopi ceremonies, but some of them continued to do this on the sly.

During the time Burbank was there the Hopis refused to drink whiskey. They claimed it made a man crazy. And as far as he knew in 1939, they were still abstaining from any intoxicating drink. That, at least, was one thing the missionaries could not assail them for.

The proselyted Hopi came to church every Sunday and remained there all day long. They brought their lunch with them, and the lady missionaries furnished the coffee. The missionaries were well trained in clever ways to work the territory. They had a fine organ that they could power with a handle that turned. The Hopis loved to turn it and loved the music. On pleasant Sundays, some of them would carry this organ up to a mesa top, where the missionaries and the congregation would sing sacred music and the sound could be heard miles away.

They had the Hopi men make them a large stone tank and fill it with water, and they used it to baptize the Hopis who were converted. Even though it was located out-of-doors and close to the church so as to be immediately at hand whenever the opportunity for a baptism presented itself, it was called upon far less than the missionaries hoped would be the case.

After Kopeley, the head chief of the Snake Clan, died, his brother Harry took his place. Their mother, Sah-o-iok-o, continued to make the remarkable medicine which the Snake dancers drank after the ceremony to counteract the effect of being bitten by the snakes. This formula was a secret which the Government tried in vain for many years to secure.

Sah-o-iok-o was a remarkable woman, and Burbank felt privileged to paint her portrait. He thought she had an unusually fine mentality, and that like her son was open to new ideas. He was right.

While Burbank was still at Polacca, Sah-o-iok-o was converted and became a Baptist. After that she refused to make medicine for the Snake Dancers. This caused endless arguments between her and her husband, a fine old man named Shu-pe-la who belonged to the Snake Clan. In fact, he was the head of his Clan and held a position of great honor and influence among the Hopis, and her decision caused him great shame and embarrassment. It also brought her into disfavor with her son, Harry. But Sah-o-iok-o held firm, remained a Christian, and never again made medicine for the Snake Dance. The high cost of such a conversion as this to the Traditional Hopis is not difficult to calculate, but it appears the missionaries believed that what they were doing was so right that nothing else mattered. Do you suppose the missionaries ever asked themselves why the Hopi priests reacted so extremely as they did? After all, the Hopi were ordinarily peaceful and accommodating. But now, you see, the keepers of the Covenant had no other choice. It was the Spanish situation all over again.

A Miss Marrietta Reside came to Toreva and donated her services to do what she could to help the work along. It was while she was there that a lame Hopi man accepted Christ and was baptized. He too was being harassed by other Hopis. One day he came to the mission crying, his shirt torn to shreds, and riding on a burro, for he was too battered to walk any distance. He told her that Hopi men had caught him and beat him because he was a Christian.

Often, the Hopi leaders would bring an interpreter and come to the mission. Sometimes as many as fifteen of them would scold Miss McLean and order her to leave Hopi Land. But she always baked lots of bread and had it on hand so that when they came she could make them some coffee and give them some food. She also gave them the gospel about Jesus as Savior, "and" she claimed, "they went away baffled."

Along with their "need of the Savior and a clean heart," Burbank says, the Hopi women were taught to keep their homes, children, and villages clean. Since water was scarce at the mission station, as it was everywhere else, McLean talked a number of Hopi men into helping her dig a well. The site that was chosen was very sandy, and after they had gone down a number of feet one man was still down in the excavation when one side of it caved in and he was buried. She urged the other men to hurry and dig him out, and when no one did so fast enough she grabbed a shovel, jumped down into the hole, and began to work furiously to save his life. The impressed men soon followed her example, and the man was rescued. Her heroic act may have helped with subsequent conversions.

Sometimes White people who came into Hopi Land would laugh and say, "You will not get water enough to baptize these people by immersion. They will have to be sprinkled." But a short while before the time came to baptize the first converts, a little spring that was just over the line of the mission property and on Hopi Land closed up and then burst out on the mission property. Miss McLean considered this an act of God. She promptly had the spring cleaned out and walled up, and her next converts were baptized there.

When Miss Burdette took over the work at Toreva from the National Indian Association, there were two small frame buildings there. One was the house in which the missionaries lived; the other was a little building that was used as a laundry. Miss McLean had the Hopi women come there to wash their clothes, getting in this instance the water from an old spring that had been walled up by the Catholic fathers in the sixteenth century.

In that first year that the Christianizing work was started by the Baptists, an addition was built to the house. It was of stone and made the work much easier, since the larger room of the frame building could then be used for worship services. The mission had a bell, which was hung high up on an iron framework so that it could be heard by the villages up on the mesa tops. Since the Hopis did not have clocks or watches, it became a custom to ring the bell at sunrise Sunday mornings, so that no one could say he or she did not know it was Sunday and have an excuse for not coming.

Five years after the work started, McLean got a number of Hopi men to help her put up another church building. That was in 1906, and in 1939 they were still using the same building. The money for the construction work was provided by the Women's American Baptist Home Mission Society. Using other funds, McLean built a long, low building, which she planned to use as a hospital. This plan was not fully carried out by the mission, since the government had plans for a hospital of its own, although it was not built until several years later.

In the early years the missionaries traveled on horseback, and for a few years they had a buggy and used two horses. In 1925 they were provided with a car. In 1929 the community house was built, and repairs were made on the mission house and a Delco plant installed.

The church that was organized in 1907 grew until in 1940 it numbered between forty and fifty members, of whom, Burbank says, "many have gone home to be with the Lord." That number included the lame man who had suffered persecution, and Pliny, who was horsewhipped when he became a Christian, and in later years became an evangelist who "for several years did faithful service for the Lord."

In the fall of 1914, the mission house and a little laundry building burned down, and the W.A.B.H.M. Society sent the money to erect the present building. Rev. Lee I. Thayer, who was then at Keams Canyon, superintended the work. He was pastor of the two Hopi churches at that time.

Aside from the regular Sunday school, church services, and prayer meetings, the mission conducted two sewing meetings for women, one for men in the winter months, and one for children Saturdays during the months when school was in session. There were also "many other things of interest, such as stereopticon lectures, and so forth."

Miss McLean remained in the work at Toreva for ten years, then resigned. She was followed by a succession of workers.

There was a long, low, flat-roof building belonging to the Government, which opened into the court opposite the building Miss Abbott occupied. It had not been used for three years. For a number of days she worked to prepare that building for the missionaries.

Shortly before the arrival of Miss Schofeld and Miss Johnson, there was a snowfall that broke a long dry spell, and the Hopi people gave those new workers the credit for the change in the weather, saying, "Surely they must have good hearts." Burbank adds that "This was the opinion of many of the Hopi men and women."

The Government agent, Mr. Burton, at Keams Canyon, allowed the day school at Polacca to be used for Sunday services, and gave the missionaries permission to have chapel exercises with the schoolchildren each day. One teacher at Polacca had the children come down Sunday mornings to bathe, then to sing hymns and hear a Bible lesson. This went on for nearly a year. Many of the fathers and mothers stood listening while the message was given to the children, and after the children were dismissed, the parents sat in the seats and listened to a message which was interpreted.

"George Lomayesva and his wife, who had been in school four years at Keams Canyon, interpreted the word. The wife, Myra, took a strong stand for the Lord and was baptized before George was. She was a faithful interpreter for thirty-four years, then she went to her heavenly home."

Large numbers came to the services until they were told that God's word was against idol worship and against any other except that of worshiping "the Lord Jesus, the Son of God, then many of them stayed away; and every Sunday morning men were stationed at the head of the trails leading to the meeting place and told the people to go back home and not listen to the teaching anymore."

TEM— The suggestion here is that the Hopi worship idols. They do not, and you will see in the newsletters their actual beliefs. Reference has been made to certain deities who serve as helpers. These do receive great respect, but they are not equal to, or even like, the Creator.

"It was the custom," Burbank continues, "of the missionaries to bake bread, cook beans, and serve lunch to those who would go home with them and sing the songs they learned in the boarding school in Keams Canyon; for there they had used Gospel hymns. The hymns were explained and interpreted to those who did not understand English. Many rich gospel messages were brought out and sung into the hearts of the Hopi people."

When attendance at meetings began to diminish, the troubled missionaries went once a week to the villages, held a meeting in a home in one village in the afternoon, and after eating dinner in Hongovi's home, in the middle village, they would hold a service there that night. Since only those who already attended the regular services were coming to such meetings, the missionaries were forced to change their plans. They went from house to house holding services in each home, sometimes having as many as seven services in a single afternoon. George and Myra were still living in the middle village, and she always went along to interpret. A young man named Letseoma helped with the singing. Occasionally he used a "zobo" horn, and he would also lead in prayer. A guitar was used in those little meetings. "We knew the people were enjoying them," Burbank writes, "but finally we realized there had been more opposition, for the family would go out of the house always leaving a deaf person with us. So the little house-to-house meetings were discontinued."

Later on, several elders threatened to kill Letseoma if he did not stop going to the schoolhouse "to listen to the Jesus Road." A mild earthquake had caused a place on one side of the mesa to sink down, and rocks from it rolled into a peach orchard. The old men blamed Letseoma for this. They seized him and said to him, "You have been out there sprinkling meal and praying for that to take place," but he replied, "I do not pray that way with meal anymore, and I have not prayed to have the mesa fall; when I pray I talk to God in the name of Jesus." They answered, "But if you will not stop going to Sunday school we will put you in a dark room, and if you will not promise to stop we will kill you."

Letseoma replied, "I will not stop listening to Jesus's word. He has saved me and He will save you, too, if you will believe Him." Just then a young man came along, and although not a believer, he persuaded them to let Letseoma go.

When the Hopi people hold their ceremonies everyone in the village is expected to help in some way. Women have to cook for the dancers, and the men furnish extra flour and meat. Thus the believers saw that the only way to escape these duties was to move away from the villages and build homes. This they proceeded to do. We can be sure the missionaries encouraged the relocation since it further divided the people.

Some Polacca land had been set aside for mission purposes. As yet there were no buildings belonging to the mission. White people who saw that the Government buildings could not permanently be used gave money so that a small building could be put up. Because the Hopi people had very little corn due to the drought, Mrs. Gates asked Kansas farmers to donate corn to the missionaries for the Hopis. But to get the corn the Hopis had to work for the missionaries cutting out rocks to make this building.

There was constant opposition to what the Hopi called "the Jesus Road," and with every passing month fewer people came to services. It was thought best not to have meetings in the Government school building any longer, so those who still were brave enough to come met in the little mission houses. The Sunday dinners also were discontinued, and the people brought their lunches, with the missionaries furnishing coffee and sugar. "What a joy," Burbank emotes, "that was to see them come, one or two at a time, to join the prayer group, fully determined to leave all to follow Him at any cost."

In 1910, evangelist Reverend Lee I. Thayer came to Keams Canyon to do missionary work among the Navajos and to become pastor of the two Hopi churches. All of the Christians there had been baptized by Mr. Young and Mr. McCourtney. Mr. Young baptized the first six and organized the church at Toreva in 1907. Several of the female missionaries moved on to other places. In 1907, McCourtney baptized a number of believers and organized the church at Polacca.

Thayer had to erect buildings for that Keams mission and a building at Polacca. In June 1910 it was dedicated. In 1920 the community house, which included a laundry, was built. It was believed that contact with the Hopi women during wash days would further the work of giving the gospel. After limited success, it was deemed best to let the women go to the day school laundry, and the community house became a place where the women came to sew, hear the gospel, and where programs were held at Christmastime. The spring at the missionary house supplied the water for both missions and an electric plant was installed at Polacca.

Westward from the Baptist missions, the Mennonites established their missions among the Hopi people. The two denominations worked in harmony. They made translations of some of the scriptures and gave copies to both missions, which were used in teaching the believers and also in visits to the villages.

Despite the general antagonism toward the missionaries, Christmas became a time when crowds of Hopi people flocked to programs held at the festively decorated missions. Each year they were told that Christ had taken their place on Calvary's Cross so they might have eternal life with Him, and the Hopi were urged to accept this Gift of God.

In 1940, Sarah Abbott came to see Burbank and advised him not to go again to see the Hopi Indians. The people, she said, had changed dramatically, and were impressively different from what they had been forty years before. The Hopi country he had found so fascinating was disappearing. Their homes were modernized, they had radios and automobiles, and some of them were going places in airplanes. One Hopi even had a large and up-to-date store. Paved highways provided easy access to the different mesas, and all of the people were dressing in modern civilian clothes and speaking good English. Only a very few of the old Indians were still living, and those now living had been babies when Burbank was there.

How Hopi Prophecy Works

We continue now with our summary review of Hopi history, but at this point its handling in terms of prophecy and the Covenant becomes complicated. Most of the things that either have happened or are about to happen were prophesied, and therefore to be expected. So it is puzzling to discover that the Traditional Hopi, knowing what was coming, are often surprised, sometimes bitterly resentful, and oppose almost everything that is done to them. Why, it seems reasonable to ask, have they not just accepted what has taken place, been happy in knowing that the truth of prophecy is being confirmed by its fulfillment, and gone on doing what they promised to do for so long as changing circumstances allowed it? Aren't things the way they are supposed to be? Would that the solutions could be so simple! But in the midst of all of this, there are profound complications. A first one is that the prophecies and warnings associated with the Covenant are mostly general in nature. They do not specify times, places, and details. A second is that their enactment in every instance is influenced and manipulated by human reaction and behavior — something the Creator himself responds to, but chooses not, directly at least, to control. Why does He follow this course? Because He wants His children to participate in the grand plan, to contribute to its outcome, to know the joy of measuring up to challenges, and to feel needed and worthwhile. Out of this comes a reason to be, a sense of place, and a realization of self-worth. The Elders understand this. They have reaped the benefits and know that their contributions are worth everything it takes to accomplish them.

Certainly the Elders and their Traditional ancestors have at the same time experienced personally the trials and tribulations that accompany the process. While they have been able to anticipate and prepare for developments, they could only deal with them as they actually occurred. In essence, although the theme of the drama is written, its particulars are not. These only unfold as the actors improvise upon the theme. There is, then, always an element of mystery and the unexpected, so that it becomes a game of unpredictable fortunes wherein they know how the show is going to end but neither when it will nor the exact course it is going to follow on its way there. Like the winding and turbulent Missouri River, it year by year cuts its own channel and revises its banks as it makes its way to the sea. Furthermore, here on this epic stage of human progress in Hopi Land, one cannot even know who will be here to deal with given events when they do happen, let alone what exactly to do when they do.

In other words, no generation of Traditionals could know what part of the evolving drama they would be called upon to face, and in any event the drama would be in the process of evolving before they could recognize its existence. Caught in this dilemma, service and faith have served as rewards and shields to buffer some of the pain endured, but they by no means avoided it all. Neither do the prophecies provide ready answers to the vexing whys and wherefores of given incidents nor to the rights and wrongs of them. Who, for example, could ever have imagined that a Snake Dance, which meant no more to the Hopi than any other ceremony, would become the catalyst for an influx of Bahannas that would turn Hopi Land upside down. If then as you read the chapters ahead the Elders seem at times to be hurt and defensive, try to understand why this is so. They are vulnerable human beings who are running where the brave do not go, and they have done a magnificent job of it, but their ever-changing course has, in further complication, been filled with living obstacles, each of whom have born progeny — one thing leading to another — that have consistently made the keeping of the Covenant more difficult than the preceding thoughts, words, and deeds faced by their parents.

Where does this leave us? Dan and the others tell you how they have coped with the dilemma. And I tell you now that, except for the question of why the Creator has chosen to do it all this way, there are answers to these problems and questions. But to divulge these here would spoil your opportunity to follow the play as it unfolds, making your own guesses as to where it is leading and how it will finally turn out — an exercise that shows its vitality when I remind you of what I pointed out in Chapter 1: That we are on the stage with the Elders, and as such are a featured part of the cast!

The Hotevilla Hostiles and the Thunderstorm

Once you have considered the thunderstorm that swept across Hopi Land, you may ponder the consequences and rightness of the intrusion. You might also wonder what you would do if you were on the receiving end of such an assault, and whether the intense animosity many North American natives have toward the United States Government is in any way justified. Assuming that our Government has acted with the best of intentions and not wanting to believe otherwise, we tend to excuse it to the point where — as I also indicated in Chapter 1 — in the case of Hotevilla, more than a few outsiders have chided the Traditional Hopi for their "prolonged and unwarranted stubbornness." Our introduction to Hopi history will help you answer these questions.

As soon as the conversion process got under way, all of the Hopis who resented the high-handed things government and church officials were doing to them were punished in one way or another. As the most obstinate of all, however, the residents of Oraibi, and then Hotevilla, were routinely singled out for the harshest treatment and oppression. Was any of this deserved? If respect, fairness, and human rights are ignored you could answer "yes," since some of the people in Oraibi were in a very real sense "Hotevilla Hostiles" for twenty years before the actual September 6, 1906, Oraibi cleavage occurred. In both mind and heart they resisted with ever-increasing fervor every attempt to convert them to Christianity and the Bahanna way of life. Although never resorting to weapons — they threatened to but never actually used them — they did go to what can fairly be described as war against the United States. As such, the community of Hotevilla was actually born the first moment the Covenant needed to be defended — even when that meant going against members of their own families and clans who became "Friendlies" to the Bahannas.

But the Traditionalists did what they did with good reason, and that is still the case. They are people who have known that no one walks away from promises made to the Creator without paying the highest possible price. And this was no ordinary promise, for it involved the continued existence of humanity itself. In their minds, the Hostiles had no recourse but to keep the Covenant, and in doing so they found the only contentment available to them. Assuredly, in light of the above, the Traditionals could not, and are still not able to, understand how other Hopis can excuse their having done otherwise. Redundant as my use of this premise may be, what else but the Covenant could possibly account for a resistance so fierce it has been willing to endure the wrenching personal costs that have been paid by all of the Hopis during this last hundred years — first at Oraibi, then between the Hotevilla Elders and the other villages, and finally at Hotevilla itself.

In considering Hopi history, our inclination, because they have gathered so much attention, is to focus upon individual developments that tend to obscure this truth regarding the need to keep the Covenant vow — even to, as I said in Chapter 1, the point where we lose sight of it completely. The sciences themselves — including those who have known about the prophetic aspects of Hopi lore — have for the most part ignored the Covenant aspect, while for the Hostiles, the Covenant has been the beginning and the continuing justification for everything they have said and done. In another of history's strange twists, inept and diabolical Government actions have played their part in justifying the need for the ongoing Traditional response, beginning in the 1880s and continuing until now. How different the situation would be today if the Government had backed off and let the Hopi themselves work out their own destiny and accommodation with the White world — just as they did with other obstacles for millennia before White intrusion. What could once have been a fluid and workable situation was never given a chance, though. The Government unilaterally built its foundation forms, then filled them regularly with threats and actions that turned the mixture into unyielding concrete.

The following are highlights of what actually happened to the Hopi. In deciding what to think about them, it helps to link these events to the personal views and experiences of the Elders and Katchongva. Only then can we put ourselves in their places, asking how we would feel and what we would do if these kinds of things happened to us. And why should we do this? Because only then can we begin to feel their bewilderment, shame, and pain as they are systematically confronted by the relentless march of Bahanna intrusion, and only then can we know what we must do to help.

Until it was made a separate territory in 1863, Arizona was part of New Mexico, and the first Indian agent assigned there settled down in 1849 in the secure provincial center at Santa Fe. He learned a little about the Hopis, but the warlike Apaches and Navajos who roamed the area between Santa Fe and their mesa villages made it "too dangerous" to travel to them without the military protection the agent requested but never received. Nevertheless, it is interesting to note that without military escort the Hopis themselves managed to safely send two delegations to see the agent — one in 1850 and another in 1851 — to plead for his help against Navajo encroachment and raiding. But not until 1863, when most of the Navajos were rounded up and placed in a concentration camp at Bosque Redondo near Fort Sumner, did the Hopis obtain relief. Even that was short-lived. Utes and other Indians moved into the void and retaliated against every Navajo they found. At the same time, they also pillaged Hopi crops and livestock, and captured several women and children who were out tending crops or herding sheep. In 1855 a disastrous drought reduced the Hopi population by more than half.

In 1776, the Continental Congress resolved to civilize Indians by, among other things, converting them to Christianity. In 1858, the Mormons seized upon this opportunity by sending Jacob Hamblin, appointed Territorial Sub-Indian Agent for the Mormons by leader Joseph Smith, on the first of several trips to Hopi Land. Conversion was the primary motive, but they also — incredible as the presumption was — hoped to persuade the Hopis to move en masse to a location above the Colorado River, where they would provide a buffer between the areas where Mormons were settling and the Indian tribes to the north. The Hopi were friendly to the Mormons, but they were not about to leave their beloved land to which they were inexorably tied, and 99 percent of them were not in the least interested in becoming Mormons. A few did accompany a Mormon party to Salt Lake and other Utah cities, and their favorable impressions of some things such as flour and cotton mills led in 1878 to the establishment of the Mormon community, Tuba City, and a smaller one among the Hopis at Moencopi.

In 1864 another serious drought hit the Hopis, and they were forced to go to Santa Fe to plead for food to avoid starvation. Even with this assistance, many Hopis died. Smallpox erupted again, and a number of Hopis fled to the Zuni Pueblo in New Mexico, where they stayed for years before returning.

In 1869, the Navajos were released from the concentration camp, and some of them settled within Hopi country, using these locations as bases for launching raids against the Hopi. It was a pattern that would continue and cause numerous problems.

In 1870, Hamblin brought Major J.W. Powell to Oraibi. Powell was well received and developed a keen interest in Hopi culture, collecting numerous artifacts to take back to Washington D.C. and gathering an extensive collection of Hopi works for future study. He reported the Hopi population at about 2,200. At Shipaulovi, he was invited into a kiva and witnessed a night-long ceremony. His descriptions of his stay with the Hopis made fascinating reading for outsiders. It whetted their desire to visit the mesas, and the profoundly impressed Major became an influential friend of the Hopi in Washington, D.C.

Hopi isolation was becoming a thing of the past and disappeared entirely when the Atlantic and Pacific Railroad crossed Arizona just 60 miles south of the mesas. The number of visitors increased. In 1882, supposedly to protect the Hopi from excessive intrusion by Whites and Navajos, President Chester A. Arthur issued an order establishing a Hopi reservation. Its constricted borders not only turned the Hopi into wards, they ignored entirely the much larger area actually settled and claimed by the Hopi. The Hopi themselves were not consulted about the matter, leaving a festering wound in the Hopis' side that would be aggravated even more as Navajos quickly moved in to settle within the borders of the revised area.

At Oraibi, the keepers of the Covenant grew increasingly disturbed as their land base shrank and they were cut off from numerous shrines where in the migration time spiritual roots had been sunk by the rituals performed there. By these acts, a powerful spiritual bond had been established with Mother Earth, who had become a living part of their holy vow, and until now, there had been annual pilgrimages to these shrines, which was a necessary part of fulfilling the religious cycle. Understandably, the Covenant relationship was seriously affected, and the religious leaders did not know how to handle the situation. For their part, the Government officials did not ask the Hopi what they thought about all of this and ignored their protests. They could not have cared less.

Five years later, in May 1887, the first of what would be a succession of representatives of the United States Government established his residence at Keams Canyon, where he supervised the building of living quarters for himself and his staff, an office, and finally a school building. Hopis from the nearby villages, impressed with the wages and other gifts they received for laboring at the agency, responded by sending to Washington a petition signed by twenty Hopi leaders, including those of Walpi and Shongopovi, that stated they would gladly send their children to the school. What became a boarding school was opened on October 1, 1887, with fifty-two pupils enrolled. Considering Hopi attitudes at the time, this is an impressive number. If you had not already learned from Burbank that the school would cause intense problems, it would seem, for the agent and Hopi progressives, like a hopeful and positive turn. During this first year, the agent estimated the Hopi population at 2,206, and livestock counts at 20,000 sheep, 1,500 goats, 300 cattle, 750 horses, and 15,000 burros. In other words, the Hopis' needs were well provided for.

Traditionals knew from prophecy and common sense, however, that education in Bahanna ideas and ways would threaten the future of the Hopi and affect the Covenant. Just how it would do this they could not be sure, but they knew it would not be good. Certainly the Covenant was entering a new phase. So they calculated as best they could the various costs, bristled at the idea, and formulated ways to keep it from happening to their families. The Elders and Katchongva state in express terms their reasons for Hopi fears, but the premise of the Government in this and everything else it did was actually quite simple. It was to divide and conquer. Under the guise of giving individual benefits to all, one Hopi is set against another, first in one way and then in the next. If the first scheme fails to work, try a second. Where litigation or force is involved, Government funding is not a problem. It comes from the citizens themselves and is a bottomless pit. The tactics can be seen in action as they are put to work against the Hopis.

Where Hopi families were concerned, the children would now be separated for years from their parents and their culture. As such they could not help with the work at home or in the fields. Precious time for crucial education in the time-honored Hopi ways would be lost. And worst of all, the children would not be able to share in the great ceremonies and learn through the natural process of Hopi education what they must about them. At the same time, the children were being deliberately separated from their tribe. It was a calculated gesture on the Government's part, and not surprisingly, the first of many divisions among the people themselves got under way.

The various men who over the years represented the United States government to the Hopi, either as school superintendents or as superintendents of the

Hopi Agency at Keams Canyon, were given almost dictatorial powers. Especially in the early years, most of these were poorly trained for the work and surrounded themselves with political leeches. Nepotism and graft was a way of life. General Nelson A. Miles, the famous Indian fighter and commander-in-chief of the Army, wrote to his wife: "There has been no branch of the government so corrupt and disgraceful to the Republic as that which has had the management of our Indian affairs."

The annual reports filed by the majority of these men make it evident they came to the Hopis with deep-seated prejudices, intolerance, and a determination to do everything they could to turn the Hopi into imitation White people. It did not please them to discover that the Traditional Hopis refused to accept the schooling idea. And the greater the pressure applied to accomplish it, the more tenaciously the Traditional held to his ancient ways. It is equally clear that some of the agents serving the Bureau of Indian Affairs were sincere and honest. But their job was by no means easy, and much of their time was devoted to problems which had little bearing upon the Indians. Not the least of these was that of watching over the visitors who came to Hopi Land. For political reasons, it was prudent to house and feed these folks and to conduct them on tours of the reservation — especially to see ceremonial events. Some were just tourists. Others were there for specific reasons, being scientists, ethnologists, anthropologists, archaeologists, surveyors, geologists, biologists, writers, artists, and photographers.

Most of the men in charge at Keams Canyon were suspicious of visitors and often resentful of having to curry their favor and do the work entailed. Too many of these, they felt, sided with the dissident Hopi in their stand to preserve their own way of life. In confirmation, some of the visitors did write letters to their congressmen and cause trouble for the agents.

The language barrier was a principal cause of misunderstanding and friction. Interpreters who were fluent in both languages were scarce. But the single greatest source of trouble was that the control and management of the Hopi and their lands was set up without of any kind of agreement with the leaders of the independent Hopi villages. The BIA officials completely ignored the ages-old indigenous system of government the Hopi had worked out for their villages, for no attempt whatsoever was made to work through the Traditional leaders. Even to this day, radically different viewpoints regarding the land cause endless friction between Washington and the Traditional Hopi. In the Hopi mind their deeply religious concept of the land makes many things the Government has done with it sacrilegious. And since the White man's ideas of individual and corporate ownership are foreign to the Hopi, the giving of or granting the use of land to missionaries and traders was profoundly resented.

Although many of these village leaders did petition for a school, friction over spiritual matters developed almost immediately between school officials and Hopi parents. Since Hopi children did not have to attend regular school classes on Sundays and church festival days, Hopi mothers and fathers could not understand

YUKIUMA

why school officials objected when Hopi parents kept their children out of school for important Hopi religious celebrations.

To win this argument, the agents tempted the Hopis with various jobs such as freighting, road building, police work, construction work, and the like. By White measures these paid meager wages, but they were a substantial boost in the standard of living of those who wanted Bahanna goods. So the jobs were eagerly sought after, and not surprisingly became carrots used to persuade the people to accept both schooling for the children and conversion to Christianity — regardless of opposition from clan and religious leaders.

By 1890, a number of Hopi children had been taken to visit Washington and to the Carlisle Indian School in Pennsylvania. As might be expected, the agents declared that the students were very impressed with Carlisle and wanted a school just like it in their own country.

Because of its interference with their proper participation in Hopi religious observances, the people of Oraibi — the original Shrine of the Covenant — objected strenuously to their children's attending school, to the point where the school superintendent requested support troops from Fort Defiance. On December 28, 1890, soldiers entered the ancient village and captured 104 youngsters. They also evicted several Navajo families who were considered trespassers on Hopi territory.

The work of an 1891 survey party aroused profound apprehension among the Hopi Keepers of the Covenant. Not only was Earth Mother sacred and could not be owned in the sense Bahannas thought it could, their sacred shrines were being violated. So the religious leaders did the only thing they could think of — they pulled up the survey stakes as rapidly as they were set in place.

The agency people were not pleased, and by June, 1891, the situation had reached the point where a small detachment of cavalrymen led by Lieutenant L.M. Brett was sent to Oraibi from Keams Canyon. His report treating the affair to the assistant adjutant general in Los Angeles gives us a clear picture of what the Traditionals had to contend with:

"Came to Oraibi," Brett said, "to arrest several Oraibis, who have destroyed surveyors' marks and threatened to destroy the school. When we entered the village we were confronted with about fifty Hostiles armed and stationed behind a barricade. They openly declared hostility to the government, and a fight was barely averted. A strong force should be sent here with Hotchkiss guns, as I anticipate serious trouble if the hostiles are not summarily dealt with."

In a colorful and dramatic confrontation with ceremonially costumed Hopi men at the village, including a representative of Maasaw, Lieutenant Brett buckled and returned to Keams Canyon.

The next military move was the arrival at Keams Canyon on June 30 of Colonel H.C. Corbin with four troops of cavalry and two Hotchkiss guns — the semiautomatic machine guns of that day. Thomas Keam reluctantly agreed to accompany the detachment to Oraibi. After another dramatic confrontation, eleven Hopi prisoners were taken to Fort Wingate, and a small detachment with an officer remained at the agency until everyone had quieted down.

In spite of Colonel Corbin's suggestion that the people of Oraibi should accept the "friendly" Lololmai as their leader, the band of prisoners taken to Fort Wingate included him as well as Patupha, the leader of those opposing Lololmai. At Fort Wingate, the prisoners were put to work in the gardens of the officers and given plenty of clothing and food. Lololmai and some of the others were soon allowed to return to Oraibi, and by October, 1892, there were only five remaining prisoners.

Once Washington saw that its plan to divide the families through schooling was succeeding, they concocted a second plan to break up the villages. The superintendents had learned as they lived in Hopi Land that preservation of the Hopi way of life, and especially their religion, was rooted to a great extent in the social structure of their village communities. So the plan to break up the lifeway began in 1891 with the awarding of a contract for a survey designed to make it possible to allot farming lands below the mesas to individual Hopis. To encourage the Hopi to move to these allotted lands, the government promised to furnish lumber and other supplies for houses, and that year fifty were begun. In 1892, twenty-six of the houses were furnished with roofs, floors, windows, and doors. It was reported that 100 houses were well under construction and a number of allotment farms had been surveyed and staked out. The Government even established a model farm to teach the Hopi how to grow corn!

Also in 1892, the government of the United States acquired the tract of land known as Keams Canyon, which was within the Hopi Reservation, yet it was still another deal in which the Hopi were not consulted.

Throughout that year the superintendent was confronted by Oraibi objections to their children's attending the White man's school. Even the use of the troops to enforce attendance was not enough to cause them to return their children to school when the summer vacation ended. The superintendent threatened to use as much force as was required to compel their submission, and despite the objections and pleas of their parents eight children were sent away to school in Lawrence, Kansas.

When C.W. Goodman replaced Ralph Collins as superintendant at Keams Canyon on December 3, 1893, he found little to indicate that the Government's program was going well. In his annual report, he stated that two adobe buildings had been completed at Oraibi for a day school, which was opened in March by a doctor and a field matron. Even though a regular teacher took over the school in May, opposition continued. Only thirty children were enrolled, while attendance at the Keams Canyon School averaged ninety-three. He added that 120,000 acres of land had been surveyed and allotted to such Hopi as would accept allotment, and twenty houses had been equipped with stoves, beds, and so forth. But these were seldom occupied.

LOLOLMAI

TAWAQUAPTEWA

Of the Hopi population estimated at 2,029, one of these was Dan Evehema, born on an unknown day in 1893.   *104 yrs*

Only a year after the allotment program was completed, it was discontinued…supposedly because only a small number of Hopi continued their opposition to the allotment work, but in truth because a lot of them objected to it.

In 1893, a Government water development program began with the installation of "a good well" for the Polacca Day School at First Mesa, which opened officially on January 15, 1894.

Later on, a perceptive acting agent, first Lieutenant S.H. Plummer, reported there had been improvement in the condition of Hopis during the past year. He added that the plan to build houses in the valleys for the Indians, with the view of persuading them to abandon their overcrowded pueblo dwellings on the high mesas, was not as successful as desired. Many of the houses built in the valleys were unoccupied the greater portion of the year. The Hopis' habits, customs and general mode of living were so intimately connected with the conditions of life on the mesas that, in his view, it was doubtful whether anything else than compulsion would cause them to abandon their pueblo dwellings. It had been the custom for years for these people to cultivate their lands in common. Therefore, owing to the shifting nature of their planting grounds, it would be almost impossible to maintain any allotment to individuals. He believed it to be in the best interests of the tribe to grant their petition to abandon the allotment plan. He also recommended that a separate agent be appointed for the Hopi, a recommendation which was acted upon six years later.

The continuing divide-and-conquer policy deepened the crisis at Oraibi. For the first time, Hopi who acceded to the desires of the government officials and the missionaries were described in official reports as "Friendlies" and those who held fast to their Traditional Hopi way and the Covenant as the "Hostiles." So open had this division become that School Superintendent Samuel L. Hertzog reported the Hostiles at Oraibi and Moencopi were taking farming properties away from the Friendlies, and that troops from Fort Defiance had been called in to restore order.

Captain Constant Williams, acting agent at Fort Defiance, reported that the troubles at Oraibi resulted from the disposition on the part of the Hostiles to drive the Friendlies from their fields. In the fall they drove the Friendlies from the fields at Moencopi, and in the spring threatened to do the same thing at Oraibi. To prevent this, nineteen of the Oraibi ringleaders were arrested by U.S. troops and sent to the federal prison on Alcatraz Island, located in the middle of the San Francisco bay…a facility operated by the U.S. Government as a place to keep the most dangerous criminals in America! They arrived at Alcatraz on January 3, 1894, and were released for good behavior on August 7 of the same year. This stringent action ended the opposition for a while.

In 1894 a government day school was built at Polacca and a second school at Oraibi. A Toreva day school was completed in 1897.

When Collins returned to Keams Canyon and resumed the office of school superintendent, he reported in 1896 that the Hopis who had been imprisoned at Alcatraz claimed they had been told they would no longer be forced to send their children to school. But Acting Agent Captain Williams declared that the prisoners had only been released from Alcatraz on their promise to obey all orders given them.

Smallpox, brought in by Whites, ravaged the Hopi in 1780, 1840, and 1853, and in 1897 another epidemic began, which raged through the villages for several years and resulted in the deaths of hundreds of Hopis. Like other Indians, the Hopi had developed no natural immunity to the disease, and they could not cope with it. The government's program of enforced vaccination, which again was something done with no attempt to educate the Indians as to its makeup and purpose, led to still deeper rifts between the Government and the Hopi and also between the Hostiles and Friendlies. It was believed that the introduction of something Bahanna into the body made the body less Hopi, and therefore less able to be fully Traditional. It created another situation in which the intolerance and disinterest of the Government caused far greater problems than imagined. How the Covenant was kept while all of this was going on is nothing short of amazing!

There are indications that the official treatment meted out to the Hopi during these early years was being seriously questioned by many important government officials. Thomas Donaldson, for example, wondered about the legality of making prisoners of any Hopi who objected to sending their children to school or of imprisoning them without a court trial. He concludes his statement regarding the Oraibi campaign with these words:

"Are the lessons of history worthless?" he wondered. "…The shadows of murdered and poisoned priests and Spaniards hover around and about the Moqui country. They were killed because they attempted to civilize the Moquis in Spanish fashion. Why should we be more fortunate than the Spaniards, or shall we be compelled to keep a garrison of 250 to 300 men at the Moqui pueblos in order to educate 100 to 200 children at a distance from their homes? We began with soldiers and Hotchkiss guns. Are we to end in the same way? Such civilizing has not heretofore been a pronounced success."

When in 1900 School Superintendent Charles E. Burton also became the "Agent to the Moqui Reservation," he was only twenty-seven years old, impetuous, and without the required experience needed to supervise the work. He soon found that he had taken over a Pandora's box of trials and tribulations to which he quickly added more of his own making. These came to a dramatic climax in 1903 when Belle Axtell Kolp, a teacher at Oraibi school, resigned in disgust after having been in Hopi country only seven weeks. She was a niece of influential Samuel B. Axtell, one-time governor and later chief justice of New Mexico.

Agent Burton had issued an order stating that all Hopi men and boys who refused to cut their hair would be subjected to having it cut by force. The way this order was being enforced, the brutal treatment exercised by Burton and his assistants in their administration of the Hopi Reservation, and the general conditions Kolp observed during her brief residence caused her to burn with indignation. She went to Los Angeles and sought out Charles F. Lummis, the well-known writer who had spent a lot of time with tribes of the Southwest and who was a champion of their rights. Associated with him in his Sequoia League were some of the most respected men and women of that time, many of whom were authorities on the American Indian.

Beyond this, Lummis had become friends with Theodore Roosevelt while they were students at Harvard. Thus Lummis, more than anyone else, was responsible for gaining Roosevelt's interest in trying to get a decent deal for the Indians.

After listening to Mrs. Kolp, the writer realized that the situation on the Hopi Reservation was an ideal excuse for another crusade to bring justice and humane treatment to the Indian. In April 1903, Lummis began a year-long campaign to secure an investigation of Mrs. Kolp's charges with an eight-page illustrated article entitled "Bullying the Quaker Indians." In this he described the historical background of the Hopi and castigated Agent Burton as "the pinhead official... this oppressor... Czar over the lives of 1,800 Hopi... that bully."

In a second article, he printed the affidavit of Mrs. Kolp, which contained searing evidence that led to an investigation of Burton's administration. It is an important document that supports in every way the position of the Hostiles in responding as they did to the Government and their education methods, and it is worth quoting in full.

"As a teacher from the Government day school at Oraibi, Arizona; as one who has 'seen with her own eyesight' the cruelties inflicted upon the Hopi people there; as a sympathizer with these oppressed people; as an American — I offer, unsolicited by anyone but these poor, persecuted wards of the United States Government, my services in this fight for right, justice, and humane treatment for the Hopi Indians. In doing this I am but keeping a promise which I made to them. Among the last words they said to me were these: 'Tell our friends how hard it is for us — tell them to help us.' [The cry is reminiscent of Dan's own request that I tell the Elders' story today.]

"I began my work as teacher in the day school at Oraibi, December. 31, 1902; I resigned from the service February 5, 1903. I resigned that I might be free to speak and act according to the dictates of my own conscience with regard to the persecutions which the Hopi people were compelled to endure from those in charge of the school at Oraibi, John I. Ballinger and wife, and from the Reservation Agent, Chas. E. Burton. I left Oraibi February 17, 1903. Although there a trifle less than seven weeks, I witnessed more of 'man's inhumanity to man' than I ever saw before or ever hope to see again. And all done in the name of the 'Big Chief at Washington.' Whenever a punishment was threatened or carried out, it was represented to the Indians that it was by 'Washington's' orders. I have heard both the principal of the school, John L. Ballinger, and his wife, so talk to the children; and Mrs. Ballinger told me that 'Mr. Burton was going to get United

States soldiers to come on to the Reservation to put a stop to the Indians' dances.' By permission of Mr. Burton I attended one of these dances. I saw nothing immoral or improper. Most of these dances are religious ceremonies which have been carried on for hundreds of years. They are as sacred and as solemn to these people as religious ceremonies in our churches are to us.

"When I began work at Oraibi, the daily attendance at the school was about 125 children. When I left, there were 174 children in the school, and still two teachers — one of them having in her charge 96 children, whose ages ranged from less than four years to others who were 18 or 20. One of the latter — a girl — was said to have been married. There were, when I left, at least a dozen little ones in school who were not more than four years of age. They were not strong enough to walk the mile which lay between the village where the Indians live and the school-house. These children, with others, were taken forcibly from their homes by an armed body of Government employees and Navajo Indians under leadership of C.E. Burton — not for the purpose of 'making better Indians,' but for the benefit of those in charge. Mr. Ballinger wanted to establish a boarding school at Oraibi to take the place of the day school. This would permit drawing more rations and a better salary; also allow him a clerk — which position his wife was to take; so that instead of being school-cook at a salary of $30 per month, or teacher at $52 per month, she would draw from the Government $100 per month. I know these things, for it was all discussed in my presence.

"After consultations with Mr. Burton, a raid — or, as Mr. Ballinger called it, a 'round-up' — was planned and decided upon. About 10 o'clock on the night of February 2, 1903, the raiding party — consisting of Agent Burton, Physician Murtaugh, Carpenter Stauffer, Blacksmith Copeland, and a squad of Navajo Indian 'policemen' — arrived at the school grounds from Government headquarters at Keams Canyon. The Navajos, armed with rifles, were sent to surround the Hopi village in the night. The next morning — Tuesday — the white men previously named, and Mr. Ballinger, joined the Indian guards up on the mesa, about 5:30 o'clock. I do not know whether all of the white men were armed, but I saw revolvers on Burton, Ballinger, and Stauffer. The snow thickly covered the ground, and was still falling. Those children who could be found who were not already enrolled in the school were sent down to the school under guard. The attendance at school on the 4th was about 150. That was not enough. 'I know there are more children up there,' said Mr. Ballinger. 'We must go after them again.' The Indian police were reinforced by more Navajos — seven, I think, came up from Little Burro Spring – and this time the raiders made a 'clean sweep.' This took place in the early morning of February 5th. Men, women, and children were dragged almost naked from their beds and houses. Under the eyes and the guns of the invaders they were allowed to put on a few articles of clothing, and then — many of them barefooted and without any breakfast — the parents and grandparents were forced to take upon their backs such children as were unable to walk the distance (some of the little ones entirely nude) and go down to the school building, through the ice and snow in front of the guns of the dreaded Navajos. They were kept there all day, until after six in the evening, while clothing could be made or found for the children. Before being allowed to go back to their homes these orders were given them by Mr. Burton through his Indian interpreter — 'You must have these children in school every day. If the weather is very stormy, or if they are not able to walk to school, you must carry them here and come down and get them when school is out. They must be in the school. If they are not, we will take them away from you.' That same evening a meeting of the school employees was called, and I gave in my resignation. I could not be with those Hopi people and withhold my sympathy from them, as I was ordered to do by Mr. Burton. (You will find enclosed letter to me from Mr. Burton to that effect.) I never found that being sympathic and friendly made these people 'sullen and hard to manage.'

"On that Monday following the raid (February 9th), some of the little ones were not in school. The next morning they were not present at roll call. As I had been up to the village on Monday afternoon to visit some of the children who were ill, I knew the dangerous condition of the trail, and when I told Mr. and Mrs. Ballinger that those little ones could not walk down or up it — that I had carried three of those who had been brought down to school in the morning, and who had been turned out of school earlier than usual, up the steps, and that I had fallen several times (I found these children standing in the trail, crying and half frozen). That they did not have sufficient clothing, and would he please not insist upon their being in school until the weather moderated. 'That does not make any difference,' said he, 'they are better off here — after they get here — and they must come to school. Their parents or some of the larger children can carry them.' So he took the horses and wagons and with the school 'policeman' (father of Nellie Kiwani), rode up to the village, found the children, and made the parents go down to the school with the children on their backs, while he rode down in the wagon.

"Rations and clothing for about 125 children were allowed that school when I was there. When I left, bread for 174 children was made once a week from 150 pounds of flour. (Less than one pound of flour per week for each child.) And sometimes the bread was so poorly made that nothing save a hungry dog or a starving burro could or would eat it. The only thing many of their children had for their breakfast was a handful of parched corn. All that was allowed them for their dinners on school days was a slice of bread, a few stewed prunes, dried peaches or molasses, and a part of a teacup of boiled beans, cornmeal mush, or a tiny piece of boiled beef, goat, or salt pork. Absolutely nothing else, except a cup of water.

"If it were a rule to cut the hair of the Indian boys, that rule was never enforced while I was there (with the larger boys), except in case of punishment. One morning Mr. Ballinger came to me and said, 'I do not want you to sympathize with Bryan. I cut his hair just now, and I had to use him pretty roughly. He nearly got the best of me.' Bryan had indeed been used 'pretty roughly,' judging from his bruised face. Though he was a new recruit, he was one of the best boys in my school. The children were all truthful with me.

"A physician is provided by the Government for these people, but he is stationed at Keams Canyon, 40 miles away from Oraibi. I know of the death of two of the schoolchildren who died without having any attention from Dr. Murtaugh, although his attention was called to both cases. One of the school boys, Henry — about eight years of age — had his leg broken on the afternoon of Friday, January 30th, while on his way home from school, about two hours before the departure of Mr. and Mrs. Ballinger for Keams Canyon, where they went to plan with Mr. Burton for the 'round-up.' Mr. Ballinger saw the boy as his father was carrying him home from the place where the accident occurred; but neither Mr. Ballinger nor his wife paid any attention to the child further than to stop on their way and tell the missionary, Mr. Epp, of the accident. Dr. Murtaugh was notified on Saturday, but he did not come to Oraibi until Monday night with the raiding party; and then the boy was dead and buried. Another of the schoolchildren — Lena, aged about fourteen — was ill for five weeks or more, and died without having been seen by the doctor. A few spoonsful of cough syrup were sent to her from the school medicines. The doctor was at the village while she was sick; but I know that he did not see her, for I asked him what he thought of her case and he said he had not seen her. Lena died and was buried on February 15th. Though rations were drawn for these children, they never received them. All that Lena had from the school stores during her illness was a loaf of bread and one change of clothing, besides the cough syrup.

"An employee… told me that she had seen Mr. Ballinger break sticks on the boys' backs when whipping them in the school dining room.

"Mrs. Ballinger told me she whipped the children in her schoolroom when they needed punishing.

"In my room, which was my living room (as I did my own housekeeping at Oraibi), I had many pictures, paintings, and photographs which the schoolchildren took great delight in looking at and asking questions about. It was all new to them, and I enjoyed explaining things. One day, after they had been coming to my room for three or four weeks, Mr. Ballinger said to me, 'Don't you know that you are breaking school rules by allowing the schoolchildren to visit you in your room?' I replied that 'I knew that rule applied to boarding schools.' 'It applies to this school, if I want to enforce it,' said he. Then I asked him if he objected to their visits to me, and if so, why, since they were learning of things outside their little world. His reply was, 'We do not want them to know too much, and they must stay away.' And he gave those orders to the children, with threats of whipping if they disobeyed. I was told of these threats by several of the children, both boys and girls. It must have been so, for they did not come anymore, except to look in the doorway, smile, and shake their heads.

"A Hopi man — La-pu — who has a wife and two children — who lives, dresses and speaks 'American,' and who sometimes is interpreter at chapel services for the missionaries, was fined by Agent Burton for leaving the reservation to earn money to support his family. He was made to work out that fine by doing work in the Government school kitchen, and in the living rooms of the Principal's family-scrubbing, washing, etc.

"A few days after beginning my work at Oraibi, Mr. Burton came to me and said, 'The Indians here will find out that you are from Pasadena, and will ask you questions about Mrs. Gates. I do not wish you to talk with them about her.' On my asking him who Mrs. Gates was, and why I was not to talk of her, he explained that 'she was a lady from Pasadena who had been out there, and that she had done things which made it necessary for him to request her to go.' Subsequently, I learned that Mrs. Gates had done nothing but what was helpful in every way to the Hopi people, and the Hopi people all loved her. I have recently become acquainted with the lady, and know her to be a very superior woman, one who would do nothing but what was good. I was told by Mrs. Ballinger that if Mr. Burton heard me tell the Hopi that Mrs. Gates was 'paslolomai' (the Indian term for all that is good) he would discharge me.

"While at Canon Diablo, on my way back from Oraibi to my home in California, I met a missionary among the Navajo Indians. He told me of former troubles at Oraibi, and that he had bought from a Hopi Indian there a blanket which had been cut into shreds and had also seen remains of pottery which had been broken by H. Kampmeier — a former principal at Oraibi under the Burton regime. These things were destroyed because of parents not sending children to school.

"On February 18th, I was told by a trader on the Navajo Reservation…about what occurred up at the Indian village of Oraibi at the time of the school raid of February 5th. The Navajo assistants who went from Little Burro Spring told him 'what fun they had.' They also told him that Mr. Burton would not dare to do such things with *them* (the Navajos). Mrs. Ballinger also told me of some of the situations up on the mesa — (she had her information from the white men). While the raid was going on, she said to me, 'I'd like to have been up there this morning to have seen the fun when the Hopi woke up and saw the Navajos with their guns. I wonder what they thought?' What occurred at the school I saw for myself, I am grieved to say; and I only wish that those who have it in their power to change and make better the conditions for the Hopi people could have seen it as I did. When I asked Mrs. Ballinger why the raid was made in such a storm, she laughed and said, 'Why, so the Indians can't get the children away and hide them in the rocks. They can be tracked if they try to run through the snow.' These people need neither guns, clubs, force, nor brutality to make them 'better Indians.' Justice and mercy — kindness and friendship — will lead them any place. It will cost less; and these abused, embittered people will love, instead of hate, the name of 'Washington.'"

BELLE AXTELL KOLP

Subscribed and sworn to before me this 2nd day of June, 1903.

Immediately after Lummis's crusade, Agent Burton was reprimanded for neglect of duty in having failed to notify the department of Kampmeier's conduct or Ballinger's unfitness…also for his "ill-advised and improper method of carrying out the hair-cutting order." Furthermore, he was warned that in the future, no threats or force of any kind were to be employed regarding haircutting and that he must trust entirely to persuasion and example. The reprimand recommended that Kampmeier, who already had been transferred, be dismissed from the Indian Service, as he was in 1904, and that Ballinger be removed to a less responsible place. But Burton continued on the job. Basic policies were not changed, and harsh and brutal methods of enforcing ill-advised policies continued.

The national publicity given the whole affair did bring the Hopi to the attention of many people who may not have heard of them before, and the tenacity of the Hopi leaders in fighting for their traditional way of life brought them moral support from the Pueblo Indians of New Mexico. White scientists, artists, and writers who visited the Hopi after that did so with better awareness of what was going on, and many of these did what they could to help.

The situation as a whole for the Hopi did not improve overly much, however, especially at Oraibi, and in 1906 the flash point came where the Hostiles and the Friendlies could no longer occupy the village together. The final division and founding of Hotevilla is, of course, a primary part of our story, and it is considered at length in Chapter 6. Several perceptive versions of the division, especially that of Misha Titiev, are set forth in books — some by individuals who spent considerable time at Oraibi and talked with informants. But the Elders and Katchongva, who experienced it personally, give us here their intimate versions, and in so doing consider little-known matters that should be taken into account.

THE AFTERMATH

THE AFTERMATH OF THE THUNDERSTORM

Chapter 5 tells us why, of all the Hopi villages, Government vengeance fell most heavily on Oraibi. In this chapter the Elders and Katchongva share with us their personally experienced details of the division of Oraibi and what it led to. After this, chapters 7, 8, and 9 pick up the story in the early 1970s, and through the *Techqua Ikachi* newsletter articles bring us up-to-date. You will find that the sheer weight of the material eloquently supports the Elders' position and gives us rare insights into their reasoning. Yet as I stated in Chapter 1, the bulk of this material can, unless we are careful to prevent it, cause us to lose sight of the greater battle — which is the maintaining of the Covenant. The "Test," as Katchongva calls the Oraibi incident and its aftermath, is only one, although perhaps the most important, of a continuing series of obstacles the Traditionals overcame as they strove to keep the Covenant promises.

In all of this, the inevitable question has to be faced: Why must this engagement be so prolonged and so difficult? Dan's response, and mine, is that we are called upon to work out the solutions "with fear and trembling." It is the only way we have of strengthening ourselves and being enlightened for the ultimate test, which will come as the actual transition is made from this cycle to the next. Just as the migration period prepared the Hopi to settle at Oraibi and begin the great cycle of ceremonial and daily life, so too have the years of spiritual growth at

Oraibi and Hotevilla enabled the people to meet the Covenant needs of today and tomorrow. How else, without rendering humanity insignificant in the fulfillment of prophecy and history, could the Creator and Maasaw accomplish their purpose, which is to redeem and rescue both the earth and mankind — especially where rescuing us includes keeping us physically alive and at the same time forging us into worthwhile beings? Running where the brave dare not go involves more than the winning of a race. It is also about the building of human spirit and quality, and giving us a special reason to be here and alive!

MAASAW PURPOSE KEY

KATCHONGVA
THE FAITHFUL HOPI MEET THEIR TEST

Bahanna came with great ambition and generosity, eagerly offering his hand to help 'improve' our way of life, establishing schools to teach us the 'better ways' of his life. He offered us his medicine and health practices, saying that this would help us live longer. He offered to help us mark our boundary, claiming that in that way we would have more land. In all the villages we rejected his offer. He tried many ways to induce us, but failed to make us submit to his wishes, for we were all one unity at that time, believers in the instructions of Maasauu.

His next attempt was fear. He formed a police force consisting partly of certain people who had been tempted by his offers and given weapons. He threatened to arrest us and put us in prison, but we still stood firm. The threats of arrest and imprisonment were put into action. Villages panicked and weaker people began to submit. In Oraibi, our village leadership fell when Lololma (Bear Clan) made an agreement with the United States Government.

We who still had faith in Maasauu, including the main priests of the religious orders, gathered together, rejecting the Kikmongwi's request to submit. We sat down together and smoked and prayed that we would be brave enough to take our stand. We took out our stone tablet and studied it in every detail. We carefully reviewed the road plan written on the rock near our village. This is the plan we must always follow, for it is in order and complete. We recognized that the Fire Clan (meaning my father) Yukiuma must lead, for his symbol, Maasauu, stands to the right of the reed as he faces out. We also interpreted that since our way of life had been corrupted we must move to a new place where we would be able to follow the road without interference and continue our ceremonial duties for all beings.

We smoked and prayed again and reconsidered that this village, Oraibi, is our mother village. All our sacred shrines are rooted here and must not be left unattended. We knew that the

America still at war with Indians

SPECTATOR

STEPHEN TUTTLE
Special for The Republic

During the same week that President Clinton addressed the idea of offering a national apology for slavery, Rep. Bill Archer, R-Texas, a leading light in the so-called conservative revolution, was attempting to steal away 34 percent of Indian gaming revenues in the form of a new tax.

While the president publicly gnashed his teeth over an issue that was resolved, at least legally, five generations ago, we ridicule tribal people in Arizona who don't want a highway named after John Wayne in their back yards.

We have become the nation with a guilty conscience about almost everything. We build memorials to a European Holocaust we neither caused nor sanctioned. We endlessly debate our role in other ancient outrages, searching desperately for a way in which we might be able to accept at least some of the blame. Now the president wants to apologize for slavery.

Through all of this, we conveniently ignore a uniquely American bit of barbarism that has continued unabated since we first settled here.

When Europeans first arrived on this continent, the best estimates are that there were 10 million people already living here. We wanted their land. And so it began.

We can, one supposes, rationalize our behavior during the so-called Indian Wars by claiming they were just that — war. The butchering of women and children, the bounties on Indian bodies and scalps, the nonsense of Manifest Destiny were just part of the ugliness of war. These things happen in war.

Remember how many Native Americans were already here when we first arrived? By the time our Manifest Destiny was complete, less than 400,000 remained. The American Holocaust had wiped out 96 percent of the indigenous peoples. This was no vagary of war, but a concerted government policy to exterminate an entire people.

But we weren't done. We created a succession of government bureaucracies to oversee the newly created "reservations," to make sure they remained in abject poverty and to otherwise squander tax money.

We built Indian schools off the reservations, taking children away from their parents and trying a kind of mandatory re-education and assimilation program. When we discovered we had inadvertently put some tribes on land with oil and mineral value, we quickly tried to claim the mineral rights were ours alone.

There has never been a Rebuild the Indian Nations Act introduced in Congress, as there has been for almost everything else. There is no glorious but somber museum or memorial to remind us of this unpleasant part of our history. No lobbying group holds "never forget" candlelight vigils on the Capitol steps. Because the war is not quite over.

Even today we belittle their religious beliefs and devalue their symbols. We spout off when they complain about naming a road through their land after John Wayne;

of those wars is a bit harder to explain, especially in light of the way we generally treat vanquished foes.

We forgave and rebuilt the South after the Civil War. Twice helped rebuild Europe, friend and foe alike. We gave Japan a constitution and helped it emerge from the ashes. We have restored diplomatic relations with Vietnam, given most-favored-trade status to China and are trying to help most of the nations that spring forth after the collapse of the Soviet Union. We are very forgiving of our enemies.

But not so here at home. Defeated Native Americans, whose ancestors had lived here for 10,000 years, weren't so lucky.

We marched agrarian tribes off to land that couldn't be farmed, and hunting tribes to land with no game. We put cold weather tribes into the desert and warm weather tribes were marched north. We infected their bedding with smallpox, poisoned their water holes and banished their religions. We stole their children so white couples could adopt them and

could feed on them. We broke virtually every treaty ever made and found courts to tell us it was all right.

This was no vagary of war, but a concerted government policy to exterminate an entire people.

could feed on them. We broke virtually every treaty ever made and found courts to tell us it was all right.

movies, we say, but never explain how Mr. Wayne is important enough for us to name something after but not important enough for them to oppose.

We laugh at their earth-based Gods and dump grandpa's ashes in their lap. We wonder why they haven't assimilated like so many immigrants, and ignore the fact that they are not immigrants and have never shared an American Dream that ended their own.

Finally, after 500 years, the tribes stumbled on an income-producing idea that couldn't be stolen away by treaty or government chicanery. They would build casinos and white people would come and give them back all their money. Here was something the government couldn't regulate to death and the courts couldn't stop.

Then along comes Bill Archer of Texas, attempting to accomplish with taxes what regulation and court action could not — the death of Indian gaming. Fortunately, thanks in no small part to the efforts of Rep. J.D. Hayworth, R-Ariz., the Archer tax scheme failed. But it will likely be back, another shot in a war we won't let end.

While we consider whether or not we should apologize for slavery, we might at least consider the ongoing abuse of people who never asked for much other than to be left alone. Emerson once said, "Every man is entitled to be valued by his best moment." Native Americans have waited five centuries for our best moment. They are still waiting.

Stephen Tuttle is a Phoenix-based writer and political consultant.

with something
... s and situations
ns and positive

r comes on board
players in Valley
n their leadership
e to recommit to
gional economic
should be a time
w any new business
Valley community
It's also a time to
of retention and
pecially pertinent
lly built out.
made their point.
at this time and in
they have GPEC's
the opportunity to
ve in and support

---

that he has exposed the bankruptcy of constitutional government. A piece of paper protects no one. With or without the words of Thomas Jefferson, the words of Mao Tse-tung express the reality, "There are no rights, only power struggles," and "Power flows out of the barrel of a gun."

**— Kevin Walsh
Phoenix**

Only 21 words about D-Day

■ Unless I missed something in today's *Republic*, only the *Almanac* section carried 21 words on what was one of the most stressful days in American history.

At least Charles Schulz's comic strip "Peanuts" devoted his entire column to this day — D-Day in Normandy, France. Over 6,000 young Americans gave their lives when they started the downfall of Hitler's world, that eventually led to the end of the evil Japanese Empire. I

---

to teach her children at home, but it's too bad that she found it necessary to slander schools and professional teachers in the process.

**— Lee Root
Phoenix**

Columnists miss moral point

■ Re: June 6 Opinions Page columns by David Broder ("Military abandons common sense") and William Raspberry ("Adultery in America: So what?"):

David Broder doesn't know what he's talking about — simple as that. He writes: "Cohabitation was not unknown among his colleagues on Capitol Hill," "... his close friend Sen. Gary Hart ...," "... serious problems of sexual intimidation and abuse to ridiculous Puritanism that wrecks valuable careers."

It's the Washington way to never blame the individual: If a drunk driver strikes a tree and dies, it's the tree's fault.

---

teamwork and your life depends on it. Trust is everything. If an individual of shaky morality breaks an important "rule" still part of the 10 Commandments, I believe, they have broken a most important trust within their family. Would you want to trust your life to an individual who thinks so little of his family and expect them to think so much of you?

I don't think so.

I believe *The Republic* has been infiltrated by the morality of Washington, which is: If you like it, you do it at any cost to the other guy.

**Wm. H. Seely, Jr.
Scottsdale**

Eisenhower wasn't demoted

■ Tell Kay McKemy of Sedona (Letters June 7) we've always had adultery in high places. Was Eisenhower demoted?

**— Francys Merideth
Phoenix**

...ur state's children puts all in jeopardy

closer to us and wished for all children in the world to be safe and loved.

As members of the Arizona Supreme Court Foster Care Review Board, or FCRB, we also agonize over the failing of the system that was created to save our children.

We share the outrage of the citizens of our state as we, too, are citizens. The FCRB is made up of ordinary people appointed by the court to assist in making decisions regarding the best interests of abused and neglected children.

We are not part of the Department of Economic Security, as is CPS. Rather, the review boards are in place to make sure that children do not "fall through the cracks" of the system. The public is seeing only a piece of this ragged puzzle, yet needs to comprehend the bigger, far more disturbing picture.

Imagine this: A report is made to CPS. A terrifying, horrific report. A "priority one" report. It is investigated. It is substantiated. It is put in writing. What happens next is not what the public would expect. The children are left in the home. Another report is made, more terrible than the last. It is investigated, it is substantiated. The children are still left in the home. Picture that over and over, sometimes 18, 22, or 30 referrals on the same family. The bruises have been seen, the abuse has been documented.

This is what we see on the FCRB. Documented cases of abuse so severe that chills run down our spines. Cases of children not taken into protective custody until they are so psychologically impaired that even a "normal" foster-care placement is often out of the question. These children languish in hospitals and group settings until years later when they are dumped out of the system, too old for the continued allocation of state funds. Our hearts will break for them now, but tomorrow we will lock our doors in fear of them.

We contacted John Foreman, the presiding Juvenile Court Judge, about this very issue several months ago. Judge Foreman responded with concern for the "long-term damage to the children as well as potential liability to the state." The judge on the case appointed an attorney to investigate whether or not litigation should proceed on the children's behalf. To our knowledge, no lawsuit has been pursued.

Recently, in another state, two grown sisters sued their own state's child protective services agency for leaving them in the home of their abusive parents, despite one substantiated referral after another. They won. Millions. We can only hope that our children will have enough mental presence at the end of their childhood to do the same.

Lori Lichte-Brill and Sharon L. Graham are Valley residents.

road would be hard with many obstacles. We knew that we would still be troubled by the newcomer, and that we must still face all the tests of weakness, so we agreed to stay.

The trouble commenced its course. The Government wanted all of the Hopi children to be put into schools. They said it would do us good, but we knew that this 'good' would only be on the surface, and that what was under it would destroy the Hopi cultural life. Maybe they thought that with an education the children might be able to help the old people, but we knew this would not be so, because they would learn to think as White men, so they would never help the old people. Instead they would be indoctrinated and encouraged to turn against us, as they are actually doing today. So in order to be good according to the Great Spirit's instructions we refused to put our children into the schools.

So almost every week they would send policemen, many of them. They would surround the village and hunt for the children of school age. We could not be happy because we were expecting trouble every day. Fathers who refused to cooperate were arrested and imprisoned. Inhuman acts were imposed upon us: starvation, insults and humiliation to force us into submission. Still, over half of the clan leaders and religious society leaders refused to accept anything from the Government. Because of this we were mocked and treated as outcasts by those who had already submitted. Finally they decided to do something about us because we were keeping them from getting certain favors from the Government.

This was when Lololma's successor, Tawaquaptewa, became chief of Oraibi. It was under his leadership that the sad event, the eviction of the faithful Hopi from Oraibi, was touched off. Since we 'Hostiles,' as we were called by the missionaries and Government workers, refused to follow his wishes and accept the White man's way of life, he decided to evict us bodily. He figured that without our interference he would be able to take advantage of the good things offered by Bahanna.

On September 7, 1906, his followers, commanded by Chief Tewaquaptewa himself, entered the house where we were discussing prophecies and threw us out. We did not resist until rifles and other weapons were shown and they began beating us. Then we resisted only to the extent of defending ourselves from injury. I was knocked unconscious. When I came to, all my people were gathered to go. My father, Yukiuma, was selected to be the leader. The women and children, with a few belongings on their backs, a little food, and no shoes, were prepared to leave. Some tried to go back to their houses to get their valuables and some extra food, but they were turned back. (In 'Book of the Hopi' it is said we were allowed to go back and get some belongings, but this is not true. That book is not accurate.) After we had left we learned that our houses had been looted and that horses had been turned loose in our fields and had eaten our crops, which were just ready for harvest.

Thus we had to migrate once again to find a new home, leaving behind a corrupt world of confusion. We sought to start a new life, carry on our ceremonial cycles, and preserve our way of life without interference, but now we know that this was a dead dream, for the interference has continued right up to the present day.

THE ELDERS

Grandfather Titus: I am telling of my own experience. When we were banished from Oraibi in 1906, we were evicted by our own people who cooperated with the government; they were people of our village, who came into our houses and threw us out. They knew our leaders and caught them first. They had no respect, and were very rough. One of our men lay down, as if glued to the ground. They could not budge him. They drove us all to the north side of the village. There was a fight in which Katchongva was knocked unconscious. They even hit old people such as Yukiuma's father, and tore their clothing to pieces. Everyone known as Hostile was evicted. They dragged them by the hair through the dust of the streets to the edge of the village, where the women of the Friendlies were mocking, 'Ha Ha! Get out of here! Go west! Be like the Navajos, who never rest! Don't ever come back! Since you don't want Bahanna things, you don't need to wear their shawls,' and they took away any clothing that had come from white people. All of our women, and we children were chased from our homes, and the doors were bolted.

We wanted to get food, but they didn't let us. Without any supplies we were worried, but when we tried to get something, we were chased away. After some time, we were all forced to the edge of the village. Yukiuma made a line with his foot in the sand. Then he said, 'From here on all the land is under my care. You in Oraibi will only have the village.' Then he stepped over the line, saying, 'Thank you. Now we can go without fear. The land will provide us with food.'

They drove us over the hill like sheep. There our leaders gathered. 'Where shall we found our new village? Over there at Hukovi? No, this would mean we have to retaliate.' So we decided to move farther, to Hotevilla. But there was nothing there yet. Only cedar trees, no houses or food, nothing. It was September, and it was getting cold. The leaders decided to stay there, and we began building shelters, to get settled in Hotevilla. We dug pits in pro-

ENEMIES of
OUR OWN
household

tected places. *We used cedar branches for walls and roofs. This was our home for the winter. We had no doors, only blankets. It was a hard winter.*

We remember it with this song: 'Sad we are, poor things, chased from home, out of the village, here we sing, we are nothing. There in Oraibi they are so cheerful, to be rid of us makes them happy. They laugh at us as they take to the Cross because they depend on this source now for their support. We sing only of what truly happened. When they tell this story, they twist it around. They laugh at us outcasts.'

The village of Hotevilla was settled for one purpose, to stand firmly on the Great Spirit's instructions and fulfill the prophecies to the end. It was established by good people, one-hearted people who were actually living these instructions. Water was plentiful, and so was wood, from which we built temporary shelters in which we were to survive the cold winter with very few blankets. Food was scarce, but we managed to live from the land by hunting game and picking greens. We were united into oneness, but it would again be split into two due to extreme pressure from the outside.

Even today, nobody in Oraibi will admit that the Friendlies betrayed the Hopi way. We chose to follow Yukiuma because he wished to protect the land, and our life as Hopi. He became the leader of the Hostiles. When Hotevilla was founded, he was acknowledged as our village chief. He was truly faithful to the law the Hopi follow. All the other villages accepted Bahanna culture and were involved in banishing us from Oraibi.

Grandfather Dan: I was twelve years old then, so I remember well how everything happened. Here, too, the troops came and chased us out. They arrested our fathers and took them away to distant places. The government tried to break our resistance. They put our leaders into prisons such as Fort Wingate and Fort Huachuca, the jail at the Indian Agency at Keams Canyon, even as far as Alcatraz Prison in California. Some were sent to school at Carlisle, to be brainwashed into Bahanna thinking and taught their system of values. We all suffered much. I have seen it and experienced it myself. My own father put in irons!

Nasiwisima, who was there, tells it this way: As soon as we arrived in Keams Canyon, they threw us into a basement, six of us chained together. They starved us for five days. We got weak, and started to see things. Finally they fed us, but then we got sick, and each time one had to run to the outhouse, the other five had to come with him. As soon as we regained our strength, they put us to hard labor, blasting rocks to make the highway. We were lucky no one was hurt. Every day they came by with papers, saying, 'Sign them, then you can go home.' We refused to let them take our children away.

Grandfather Titus: My father was against the school. 'You'll learn a language with different meanings. They'll teach you their way to behave. Our culture will become strange to you. You'll never understand Hopi and never know who you are.' One morning the soldiers caught me. They cut off my way of escape — the back door. That is how they kidnapped me. I didn't know where I was being taken. It was to a boarding school in Phoenix. I didn't know English. When we spoke our own language, we were punished. All this force by the government made us suffer greatly. They tried every means to break us. Bahanna is indebted to us. We did nothing wrong to resist our oppressors without using violence. We suffered these prison terms because we stood up for the land and our life.

The people who later founded Bacabi village had come with us to Hotevilla at first. Maybe they feared more force from the Government. They tried to go back to Oraibi, but were refused there. So they searched for a place to settle. First they went to Gray Spring, where they were raided by Navajos. The same thing happened at Onion Spring. Finally they settled at Reed Spring, or Bacabi, which is close to our village.

Like bats they fluttered to the Keams Canyon agency of BIA to ask Mr. Miller's help in building their village. The superintendent said, 'Does Hotevilla agree that you settle so close by? You recently left them. Why do you settle in front of their noses? This will cause trouble if Yukiuma is against it.' The leader of Bakabi, Kewanimptewa, replied, 'Why should I ask them? It is my decision where I want my village.'

'So close. This isn't right. Do you intend trouble, and want me to back you up? I will not do this.'

'I only want material and tools, and I will let you build a school. And I want a pistol and a uniform, so my people will respect me.'

'This will give me nothing but problems,' said Mr. Miller, 'I won't support your lust for power.'

But Mr. Miller's successor, Mr. Crane, gave him everything, including a school. Kewanimptewa also wanted a church to be built; this lover of Castillians, the school and the Church were basic to his power. Alliance with them brought modern developments, as well as gifts for the people of his village. The Church was especially important in his scheme. He promised that when it was completed, he would proclaim from the rooftops, 'Get ready, my people, dress up and follow me. We all want to join the church, be baptized, and pray to Heaven!' But when the church [building] was finished, he did not join. One day a lady said to him, 'Hey, Kewanimptewa, it was your idea to have a church and all that comes with it. I believed you, and got baptized. Now, I expect it's your turn.' Did he get baptized? No. He knew no one would follow him now. The religious leaders had built a kiva, and were celebrating the Hopi cycle again. Kewanimptewa knew, and had to admit, what every Hopi knows: Bacabi has no land. They allow the things of modern civilization to be built on our land without consent. In this respect, they are just like the Bahannas. They take the land and say, 'It's ours. This is the law Bakabi follows now.' "

KATCHONGVA

Hardly had our footprints faded away in Oraibi, when early one morning we found ourselves surrounded by Government troops. All the people, including the children, were ordered to march six miles to a place below Oraibi. From there all the men were marched over forty miles to the U.S. Government agency at Keams Canyon, where they were imprisoned for about a year and one half for not accepting the generous offer of education for our children, among other things.

The first thing they ordered us to do was to sign papers. We refused. Then they locked us inside a building without food and with very little water for several days until we were very hungry. Again they tried to induce us to sign papers, promising to feed us and let us go, but again we refused. They tried other tricks to make us sign, but each time we refused. Finally they took us to a blacksmith shop, where they riveted chains to our legs with loops and hooks, and fastened us together in pairs. In this way we were forced to work on a road gang for long periods working dangerously with dynamite on the steep rocky cliffs near the agency. That road is now the foundation of a highway still in use today.

At night we were fastened together in groups of six by means of long chains. To add to our torture, soap was added to our food, which made us very sick. When one man had to go to the outhouse all six had to go. All this time the possibility of signing certain papers was left open to those who might weaken. During this period my father, Yukiuma, was being held somewhere else, so I was acting as leader.

While we were in prison, only the women and children, and maybe a few old men, were left out here. They had very little food, but as if by a miracle, there happened to be a lot of rabbits and other wild game, so on that meat diet they were able to survive the hard winter. It was very hard while the men were away. The old people used to talk about it. The women had to gather the wood themselves. My mother used to tell me how they would form hunting parties and get the dogs to help. We had a small flock of sheep which they tended while we were away. During the growing season they planted the crops, took care of the fields, and did all the work that the men would normally do, in order to survive.

THE ELDERS

Their leader even tried to convert Yukiuma. He knew it would be difficult to convince Hotevilla to change its life pattern, to make them into Bahanna there. <u>If we stray from the Creator's law, we are no longer Hopi, and must lose our land. The Hopi way is narrow as the blade of a knife. It is up to us to keep our balance. To let ourselves be seduced to either side would mean our end. But so long as we follow our path faithfully, we hold land and life in balance for all and everyone. This is the pattern we follow in Hotevilla.</u>

No trick could induce Yukiuma to forsake it. Kewanimptewa asked Tawaquaptewa of Oraibi, 'Would you help me make life miserable for them so they will be pressured into changing?'

'No, I gave them enough trouble when I banished them from Oraibi. I have tried in vain to convert Yukiuma and his people. You will not make them stray from Hopi law.'

Yukiuma's fundamental belief was well known. Never would he drop the original law. Never throw away this gift of divine wisdom. No, never could he do that to forsake his beliefs and lose land and Life, never he would do that. He is truly a Hopi, he is leading his people to keep this happy life in harmony with all living things. <u>A true Hopi must not deviate from this path. Oraibi originally had all these instructions, and was supposed to follow and fulfill them.</u>

But today, everything has changed. Our own people start to live by Bahanna ideas. Don't they see that Hopi life is good? This land was given to us. It is not Bahanna's land. We can build houses without money. Anyone can tend a field and feed the family. We are self-sufficient and need no economic aid.

The foregoing statements by the Elders and Katchongva present their vivid and eyewitness account of the famous split at Oraibi. Today we know that it did not come suddenly to pass, being instead twenty or more years in the making. At the time it started, Oraibi was by far the largest village on the three mesas, and its population was about 1,000 — nearly as much as the rest of the Hopis living in the other villages put together. Life, as it had been for three centuries since the Spanish incursion, was harmonious. But as the temptations and pressures by

YUKIUMA

The first temporary camp made on the way to Hotevilla

Hotevilla in 1907

Hopi prisoners at Alcatraz, 1895

Yukiuma held prisoner

Bahanna authorities and missionaries continued, an ever-growing number of Oraibi villagers, mindful also of the fact that all of the other villages were giving in, succumbed to their fears and decided to go along with the Bahannas. Watching this happen, the Hostiles who believed Hopis could not do this and remain faithful to the Covenant vow became increasingly anxious. Tensions rose and arguments ensued in homes and kivas, until it became too much for some to deal with, so they moved away. Foreign diseases took others, and by the time the actual split occurred less than 700 people still lived in the village. This population was almost evenly divided between Friendlies and Hostiles.

In 1901, the particularly determined efforts of the Government to secure pupils for the Keams Canyon school made any kind of harmony between the Hostiles and Friendlies impossible. The delighted Bahannas congratulated themselves, and drove the wedge in farther, each blow being a different program designed to widen the split and restrict independence — allotting the land in severalty, building homes at the foot of the mesas, distributing clothing and agricultural implements, controlling livestock and grazing areas, luring men and women to jobs, using force rather than persuasion. Since everyday life was rooted in the ceremonial cycle, the religious organizations began also to divide into opposing factions, holding independent performances and refusing to share their altars and other paraphernalia with one another. In the fall of 1900, the seceding members of the Wuwutcim fraternity, and in 1901 the Blue Flute Society, refused to participate in any ceremonies, an occurrence hitherto unknown among the Oraibis. In consequence, Wuwutcim was not held for many years, and no initiations took place. We can easily imagine what this did to the flow of the ancient lifeway of both the Hostiles and the Friendlies.

Dan, who was 13 years of age when the struggle on the historic day took place, did not witness it personally. His father, who was making him a pair of buckskin shoes when the final conflict erupted "about noon," made him stay home and told him about it later when the Hostiles reached the spring called Hotevilla. The reason for keeping him home was that his father and the other Hostiles knew, from the actions and words of the Friendlies leaders, that the ultimate confrontation was imminent and would be brutal. Dan told me that on the day the fighting took place, the Friendlies "acted crazy," because they had spent the entire previous night "eating medicine" — some plant that made them wild and gave them superhuman strength. Which is why, he believes, they were able to win the individual fights and the shoving contest and force the Hostiles out of Oraibi. You will see that the Friendlies also considered using weapons, including guns, but were dissuaded by outsiders who were present.

Despite the pain of this heartrending schism, Dan says that "We were happy as we left and then went to Hotevilla." This seems strange, until we remind ourselves that they were at last free of the endless arguments and able to put their full attention on keeping the Covenant. He added that "About sundown, the people started to put up crude shelters," and that for food "They mostly ate dried peaches."

To this day, 88 years later, Dan becomes introspective and makes futile gestures when the Oraibi division is discussed. His eyes mist and he grieves quietly. He knows that the Hostiles did the only thing they could do, but still wishes it could have been otherwise. For a long time there was extreme bitterness in the hearts of the people of both communities, and they would have nothing to do with one another. "Why," he asks plaintively, "does the Bahanna feel it is all right to separate us like this? We do not do anything to them." Disharmony is not the Hopi way, and Dan is glad that over the past few years the bitterness between Oraibi and Hotevilla has subsided, and some relationships have been restored between the two villages. This includes a few intermarriages. You will see in their comments that the Elders feel Oraibi remains a mother village and still has an important part to play as the fulfillment of prophecy takes place.

The *Land and Life* staff did not want the tragedy at Oraibi to be forgotten, as surely it will be if the Progressives fail to tell the story to their children. Whenever they addressed the issue of the divided village in their newsletters, the staff centered their remarks in Yukiuma, who was the acknowledged leader of the Hostiles while they were still at Oraibi, and then the Kikmongwi, or village chief, when they settled at Hotevilla. While some repetition is found in these accounts, every article contains vital information that contributes to the complete story.

It is especially interesting to learn the difference between the Government and Hostile views of Yukiuma. The former treated him with contempt and described him in vicious ways, while the latter treated him with utmost dignity and respect. He is still honored at Hotevilla today…and perhaps is the closest thing they have to an enshrined leader. The overall picture of the village division is instructive, for it mirrors what the generations of Traditionals have had to contend with as they have striven to keep their vows to the Creator and to his servant Maasaw. If what they have done is a criminal act deserving the overt censure it has received, then we must ask where the rest of us stand when we champion similar ends. Are we, in pursuing the Creator's cause, criminals too? I also wonder what there is about the Government's position regarding the Hopi that has been so insecure and wrong they could only accomplish it by deceit, derision, and force, rather than by persuasion and fairness.

We should also ask, since the collapse of the ancient Hopi lifeway has come so far as it has today: Where do you suppose the Hopi people would actually be without the stubborn defense of first the Hostiles, and then the Elders, their supporters, and Katchongva? Would there be anything worthwhile of the ancient way left, and what hope, Covenant wise, would there be for the Hopi — and our — futures? Dan and the other Elders continue to address this situation in Chapters 7 and 8, when they talk about present-day factionalism in Hopi Land.

As an aside to show how easily events in the outside world have overshadowed the news about Hopi developments — such as those that took place at Oraibi on September 6, 1906 — all we need do is point out that on April 18–19 of that same year the great 8.3 earthquake crumbled and burned the glamorous city

[handwritten margin note: Satan or the Negative force is always forceful X Not persuasive]

by the Golden Gate, San Francisco — after which its survivors were stricken by the bubonic plague, and there was economic chaos. Even though mention of the Hopi turmoil did reach into the communities of Arizona, New Mexico, and a few other places, it was San Francisco that still held the nation's attention. In the same way, if our book arrived in Los Angeles bookstores today — one week after our devastating January 17 earthquake whose damage estimate already stands at more than fifteen billion dollars, where thousands of people are homeless, and where our freeway system is down in many places — it would sit unnoticed on store bookshelves. Timing, perceived importance, and relativity are everything. And yet, the incident at Oraibi in 1906 and what is happening at Hotevilla today are, in the minds of the Elders, inextricably linked to natural disasters, which they see as among the signs to be manifested by Mother Earth of the portended end time.

Pursuing what they have already stated in their introductory remarks, Issue 28 of *Land and Life* included an article entitled "Hopi move to save their culture."

TI— "When," they wrote, "a new government was established upon Hopi land the Hopi knew this new establishment would be a threat to our land and our way of life. This threat was not long in coming. The first demand was to cooperate. At first all the villages resisted. Then pressure was applied and one by one the weaker villages fell, including our mother village, Oraibi. This was the beginning of friction among our people.

Yokiuma [an alternate phonetic spelling for Yukiuma], the caretaker of the sacred stone tablet, was appointed to lead the so-called Hostile Hopi. It became clear that people with widely different concepts cannot keep peace while living together. Chief Yokiuma made the decision to move his followers to a new location in order for them to follow the original Hopi path and maintain their belief that one day they will reach their goal of freedom and live according to the divine laws given by the Great Creator. The laws which Hopi believe are everlasting. Yokiuma was willing to sacrifice himself to overcome obstacles and resist oppressive forces in order to fulfill the writing on his stone tablet. If he was fortunate the reward would be delivered in the end.

Yokiuma founded Hotevilla, the last stronghold of natives on this continent. On this basis the Traditional Hopi accepted the help of the National Park Service, United States Dept. of the Interior, to be placed on the National Register of Historic Places as of October 1, 1984. We thank the NPS for their help..."

EVICTION OF HOSTILE HOPI

TI— "The following is one of the documents written during the period of the establishment of Hotevilla. It is a report by Gertrude Lewis Gates, who was among the first Bahanna employed in Hopi Indian Service by the Federal Government before the split in Oraibi Village in 1906, September 6th. This report was sent to the Commissioner in Washington, D.C. Since this report is too lengthy to quote in its entirety we print only the high points.

'Having been present at the culmination of disruption of the Hopi Village of Oraibi on date named above I write the following statement of my knowledge of the affair.

'One day in September 1906 we received word that Tawakwaptewa, Chief of the Friendly party, had the night before gathered his men at his house and spent the night in council and other preparations for an attack on the Hostiles the following morning. That he has announced to the village his intentions of driving out the Hostiles and all others taking their part.

'Early in the morning me and Miss Keith went up to the village to Chief Tawakwaptewa's house to tell the Friendly party not to engage in fighting with arms or else (there would be) consequences. They acknowledged having guns and revolvers. We left and as in Hostile house assembled with Chief Yukiuma, no arms were visible. Suddenly the door opened which filled with men crowding rabidly into the room led by Tawakwaptewa, and we white folks were ordered to leave the room at once. The melee was beginning when I, the last 'Pahana' going out, found myself jostled into the little plaza. Entering it seemed full of excited Hopis running to the house, where we just came. As I remained on the edge of the scrimmage I saw six or eight of the older Hostile leaders being dragged out of the house by their arms, legs, and hair. Three or more of the attacking party seizing one victim, dragged one Hostile aside from the center of excitement and there pounced upon him with fists and feet, kicking and beating him fiercely, a group of young men insulting and maltreating old Yukiuma, the Hostile Chief. I reproved them and was rudely shoved toward the wall by one of the progressive Friendlies. The Hostiles resisted such treatment but were overpowered by numbers. Soon a shout was heard, 'It is finished, Yokiuma's son is killed!' Proven untrue, just knocked out by pouncing feet upon his middle. I checked the wild behavior of the Friendlies somewhat and Yokiuma was released. I passed on Northward, the direction which a surging, struggling stream of humanity poured forth from the village. Shoved, dragged, pulled, those who (were) resisting had their clothing torn and getting bruised and scratched, women and children crying and frightened. Friendlies men and women shouting insulting remarks. Later informed were the words, 'Ha, ha, you are leaving Hopi world forever. You will become Navajo. Why you wearing Pahanna material? Take them off, for you choose not Pahanna life!'

'By high noon all Hostiles were gathered at the outskirt of the village. About 3 p.m. I saw Yokiuma quietly leave the knot of men surrounding him and work toward the Hotevilla trail, all of his people then moved after him as rapidly. I hung my head with shameful tears. What have they done, I pray our Almighty to watch over them. This is not a dream, it's real.

'Some weeks later outside most pahanna presses had an exciting heyday about the savage Hopi. Headlines crying, 'War Dances are said to be held nightly by members of Hopi tribe. Missionaries are leaving.'

'(San) Bernardino Herald, November 22, 1906. According to Robert Cooper and two nephews arrived here today from Oraibi on the Arizona-New Mexico boundary, bringing information that the settlers are fleeing from threatened uprising of the Hopi Indians.

'Robert Butler, one of the men, said that for weeks the Indians have been restless and last week they ordered the settlers to leave the region.

'Their warlike demonstrations caused general stampede. All the homesteaders who have not left the country have their families away and have united to protect their cattle.' "

Mrs. Gates also sent the following message to Washington, D.C.: 'Twenty years of factional strife between Oraibi liberal and conservative parties reached crisis today by liberals forcing ejection all conservatives from the Village. Agent Lemmon absent. Stanley Keith, Epp Gates secured concessions from aggressive party laying aside arms, granting right of removal of personal property and retention of crops and herds. None seriously hurt. Conservatives camping Hot Well Spring. Stanley Keith reported to agent. He advised both factions to observe Truce. Awaiting your action. Hoping for your speedy presence which I earnestly recommend. In possession of houses are aggressive Hopis. Subject to penalty under Federal or Territorial Law is it eviction? Courier awaits answer Winslow.'

Issue No. 4, written in December 1975–January 1976, was entitled "Retracing Our Steps."

TI— "In this sacred season, as we prepare quietly for the coming year, we would like to begin a series of articles on important Hopi leaders. We shall start with that stubborn, dedicated man whose name is identified with the struggle of the 'hostile' Hopi, Yukiuma.

An article in *Qua'toqti*, the Tribal Council puppet news (December 11), takes a glimpse of the storytelling tradition of this season, but what they say is misleading. The time is sacred, all motions must be slow and silent as possible, for all life is germinating as in the mother's womb, and nothing must be disturbed. In order to have a healthy village as well as a healthy body we must retrace our steps, to see how we came into the cycle of life with our father sun, our mother earth, and all children of nature. So the Soyal Ceremony is performed.

The stories told at this time are not all fables. It is true as *Qua'toqti* says, today stories can be written or recorded on tape, but contrary to their editorial this is not the best way to remember. To trust our memory to such methods can prove dangerous and humiliating, for we might still disregard the great laws of the Creator and lose his way of life, which will affect our future children. Even if we abandon the Great Spirit's path, many of our people may remain on earth for a time. It is said that if the future generations, even our own sons and daughters, find out through books and records that we did nothing to preserve the good ways, they will pull and box our ears and even throw us from our houses into the *yukiuma*

streets. Our suffering will be of our own making. So we are making our best effort to keep what little we have left.

    This is the story of Yukiuma, whom Alcatraz could not tame. It is for a great purpose that we recall his adventure to the Whitehouse. We bring this story to our readers around the world, as well as to our children of today, so that they may draw their own conclusions. Yukiuma's struggle grew out of his stubborn refusal to place the man made laws of Washington, D.C. above the way of the Great Spirit. We must each consider whether this struggle is bearing fruit in our life today. The fight against Yukiuma still continues long after his death through smears made against him by the 'puppet' Hopi of today, who mislead our children to rebel against us. Some try to say Yukiuma secretly accepted the school system and other programs. Some even mistake the prophecy that one day our children with short hair will become our ears and tongue. The original prophecy is meant to warn us that one day our own children may become our *enemies*. The meaning has been twisted to cover up the ways of the ones that have done that very thing.

    Still there are many among the younger generation who have a true Hopi heart but are forced into a difficult position by the government's influence. We hope the story of Yukiuma will help them retrace their steps."

YUKIUMA, THE "HOSTILE" HOPI

    TI— "The Traditional Hopi earned the name 'hostile' because they refused to bow to a foreign power. The United States Government thought that their resistance was just a sign of stupidity, and their chosen leader Yukiuma was even thought to be insane, but the government failed to see the high purpose behind this 'madness.'

    Why would the Hopi resist what the government thought to be benevolent offers? How did the Hopi earn the name 'hostile?'

    As early as 1883, when the anthropologist Frank Cushing, visited Hopi, to collect material for the National Museum, it is said he was turned away with the words, 'Stranger, you may as well attempt to scratch flint with your fingernails as to pierce our ears with your lying words. You will leave with all your brothers before morning, or we shall wipe you out as with a moccasin sole we wipe out bedbugs.' What could have provoked such a reply from peaceful people?

    Year after year, as Government Agents came to interfere with our life, the friction grew. When the agency was established at Keams Canyon and the Hopi were ordered to send their children there to the boarding school, great division was created among the Hopi. After Chief Lololma and chiefs from other villages made a trip to Washington where they were flattered into cooperating with the government, the seriousness of this threat was recognized. Because of the importance held by his clan, the Fire Clan, keeper of the sacred stone tablets, Yukiuma was chosen as the leader of those who refused to abandon the Great Spirit way.

    Government agents looked upon him as a crazy man who would rather wear a g-string than accept the comforts of modern life. He was even called 'a filthy, dried-up little old chimpanzee.' Rarely has a crazy man, especially a crazy Indian, received an appointment to visit the president of the United States in the Whitehouse. But Yukiuma got his appointment at 10:00 a.m. March 27, 1911.

What was the purpose of this? Clearly the government did not understand him, nor did they understand the prophecies for which he lived. But because of his stubbornness and his position as a leader, they regarded him as a key figure uniting opposition to the stated tactic of the government, to take leaders from each native nation and show them the power and glory of U.S. civilization. Even if these leaders were not attracted to the glory, they reasoned, surely they would be impressed by military power. They did not realize that such tactics would not work with a true leader. To their dismay Yukiuma was not impressed.

And even to this day he is ridiculed, not only in history books, but in the news media of the progressive faction which has knuckled under to the demands of the government. Last year, Yukiuma, among other traditional leaders, was the subject of newspaper articles calculated to diminish his true authority. This slander has a definite purpose, the same purpose for which he was brought to Washington, a purpose very much opposed to the Hopi way for which he stood.

No, Yukiuma was not crazy. He seriously believed with his whole heart that the old Hopi ways were the right way, and no amount of imprisonment or suffering, bribes or flattery could shake him from his stand. But would the government understand him?

His interpreter was Mock Setira of Polacca, accompanied by Mr. Lawshe, the government agent at Keams Canyon. Commissioner Robert G. Valentine accompanied Yukiuma to the Whitehouse. While waiting for the President, Yukiuma was told, according to government documents, that President Taft 'was a great big man as kind as he was big, as strong as he was kind, and as wise as he was strong.' Yukiuma was told that he should tell him about the problem of the Hopi children, and that the 'great white father' would decide what was best. But Yukiuma was not a bit astonished when he met President Taft face to face, for the statement of the Commissioner was a dead giveaway. The tactic was obviously to impress upon him the numerical and mechanical strength, and also the kindness, of the white man. It had been said that 'the surest guarantee of savage fidelity to any nation is through the conviction that government possesses the power of prompt punishment...By bringing the best-informed and most influential chiefs to the city of Washington, where they will have ample view of our population and resources, they will become convinced themselves and upon their return convince their people that it is fruitless to attempt to oppose the will of the government.' Many of the chiefs who visited the city under this policy were flattered and impressed to see what the white man wanted them to see. Few were so 'stupid' or stubborn as to wage actual battle after a visit to the 'great white father.' But the power of these representatives over their leaders and their people usually diminished upon their return from Washington.

Though Yukiuma must have had hopes, a real meeting of the minds was impossible. The stated policy of the government made it clear that this was not their intent. And to make matters worse, the language was a serious barrier. We know that Yukiuma's words were spoken in what we call high Hopi, which is used to communicate the deepest Hopi teachings. *There are important shades of meaning which cannot be known to a Hopi who has been denied his full traditional training.* The interpreter spoke English, as he had been educated in the government's schools, but by that same fact he was unable to fully comprehend Yukiuma's words. How foolish must have sounded Mr. Valentine's argument, as he tried to convince Yukiuma that by going to school, as his interpreter had done, the Hopi can make themselves heard by the government. Their argument was false, for not only was the interpreter not able to make the point Yukiuma wished to make, but the government didn't heed the warning anyway. The damage predicted by Yukiuma has already taken place, and is with us today.

Yukiuma is supposed to have said, 'great white father...' but we know he would not begin in that way, for our true father, the sun, is the highest. No doubt Yukiuma begins, in our customary way, by saying, 'Are you the chief or highest of your people?' He would then introduce himself as a chief and representative of his own people. Yukiuma's chief concern was that his people should be left alone to live as they wished, to roam free without the White man always there to tell them what to do and what not to do. The Hopi must be left free to teach their own children how to plant so they can survive as they have for centuries.

He wanted the Hopi to continue to meet their needs in their own way and to grow up in stages learning the ceremonies and prayers by which to preserve the sacred balance of life. He knew that the schools would destroy this, causing friction and division. They would interrupt the tradition and the people would forget the instructions of Masauu and the destruction would reach much further than our village. The whole earth could go off balance.

The predictions of Yukiuma concerned not only the village life but the life of mankind around the world. The U.S. Government's record of Yukiuma's conversation shows that he attempted to tell the prophecies, but it was all very confusing as it came from the lips of the interpreter, Setira, who did not rightly know himself what it was all about.

This was before the First World War, so even with the good translations our instructions regarding that event would be labeled meaningless or even crazy.

The President told Yukiuma that he understood his desires and wanted him and the other old men to live in the old ways. He also said that it was good for the Hopi to continue to raise corn and melon in the desert where the white man would starve, but insisted that the children must go to school. He told Yukiuma that unless he permitted the children to return to their classrooms soldiers would come again and there would be trouble. Still Yukiuma was stubborn. He knew that his people would be doomed if they accepted these new ways.

Another meeting was arranged for the next day. At that meeting the commissioner tried in every way to convince Yukiuma to yield, but was unable to convince granite-hearted Yukiuma.

Yukiuma refused to accept the written summary of what the President and the Commissioner had told him. The document was mailed to Yukiuma through his

Covenant

daughter, who had become a progressive. Yukiuma refused to accept it even from her. She returned the document to the Commissioner with the following letter:

> *Agent Lawshe,*
>
> *Dear Friend, my father came here last Monday evening and I read the letter and told him what the letter said. He said he did not want his children to be in school and that he had said to you: 'I want to take care of my own people.' I told him it is bad for them and that some of the children like to learn the white people's way, and I said to him that the President wanted the children of his village to go to school, but he said he did not want it. I give it to him, but he would not take it. And said it was because he did not know how to read. I was so sorry for him because he has never been to school, and he wanted his people to be like him. I talk to him but he does not want to put away his old Hopi way and so I have send the letter back to you, from your friend, Mrs. Myra George.*

As time went on, Yukiuma counted eight times that he was deported from his own land and imprisoned on the same charge without trial. Once he spent a year in prison on Alcatraz Island. The government could think of no better way to convince him, but all their attempts failed, so great was his commitment to his people.

On November 22, 1911, Colonel Scott and two of his aides left his soldiers behind and journeyed to Hotevilla to talk with Yukiuma. They camped there ten days trying to persuade Yukiuma to permit the children to go to school. Scott even threatened to call in his soldiers. On the fourth day, November 26, Colonel Scott composed a night letter to the Secretary of Interior, asking for instructions, one of the strangest letters to be sent over the telegraph wires. It reads in part:

'After four days constant observation the medical officer and I convinced that chief Yukiuma is a mild lunatic. He positively refuses obedience to any officer of the government. Nothing in the way of kindness and argument has been spared to influence him. To all argument he replies with talk of witches and spirits of underworld. He is perfectly sincere and is ready to die before he consents to the children going to school. He refused consent even if the school was in his own village. But if he is actually forced he cannot help it and the blame will rest with the government.'

The answer came directing Colonel Scott to take healthy children ten years or older. The soldiers came during the night and surrounded the village taking the Hopi by surprise. Yukiuma felt very much deceived by the President and doubted that he had ordered this move for he was supposed to be 'as kind as he was big, as strong as he was kind, and as wise as he was strong.' To confirm the claim that Scott had received presidential orders, Yukiuma chose Ray Rutherford Derranyema of Shungopavi to write a letter to President Taft:

December 10, 1911
W. Taft, President U.S.
Washington, D.C.

Dear Sir,

I take a great pleasure and writing to you while I am here with Chief Yukiuma as he is talking about his long tribe, and he said he was glad to visit you once, and speak to you himself, and so you are now all know him now. You know what's going over there for, about his people are not wanted to send their children to school, because they like to keep it their children, themselves, and the boys could help their fathers on the farm, and the girls could also help their mothers in their homes, that's reason they don't let them go to school. Of course we are Indians, the school is not our own business. The school is belong to white people. I think it's be alright, if you let the Chief Yukiuma alone. Let they staying at their home, it's only 600 of people, let their children stay home and not go to school. Chief Yukiuma wanted to his people must not lazy and to work on the farm and raise corn and oats and potatoes, vegetables, and they could sale them for money and pay for some cloth for own selves. That what Yukiuma wanted for his people to do. He didn't want any harm for his people. He wanted to do good take of his people, and children. I think we like to be stay Hopi way. Of course these friendlies peoples children must attend to school and those hostiles children must not allowed to school. And stay at home, and help their fathers or mothers that way they want. You American peoples must stay your own way and us Hopis Indians, stay our way too.

Last week ago are crying. Because superintendent from Keam Canon, Leo Grean (Crane) take the children to school, did you send the soldiers to Yukiuma? One company of soldiers came here with Grean. Who is that man came to Hodvealla to Chief Yukiuma asking what the old people saying. Then Yukiuma tell him all about what he knows. Then that man write all those things, and sent it to you. But I know this Supt. Grean and soldiers are making large trouble, and that man too. I don't know what is name. He said he come from Washington, D.C. Did you send that man to Yukiuma? You told him to come out here and make trouble out here? Yes or no. Yukiuma want you to answer this letter. Send to me, what you say. And I tell Yukiuma what you said tomorrow. I am going to Winslow, you must hurry to answer this letter. I guess this is all I say to you. Good-bye.

from Ray Rutherford Derranyema, Chimopovay, Toreva, Arizona.

Jail had failed, and the President also had no effect, so they took him back to jail. Since he never fought with them physically they gave him the run of the place. Mr. Crane recalls, 'Sitting on the porch floor hugging his knees in his skinny arms he would say, You see, I am doing this as much for you as for my own people. Suppose I should not protest your orders. Suppose I should willingly accept the ways of the Bahannas. Immediately the great snake would turn over, and the sea would rush in, and we would all be drowned. You too. I am therefore protecting you. Yes, I shall go home sometime. I am not unhappy here, for I am an old man of little use, and my chief work is ceremonies. Washington may send another agent to replace you, or you may return to your own people, or you may be dismissed by the government. Those things have happened before. You have been here a long time now, seven winters, much longer than the others. And you too may die.'

In 1921 Crane and Scott returned to Hopi for the snake dance. They found the old rebel Yukiuma in the guardhouse once more, and wrote, 'He looked half starved, and he was naked, refusing the clothing and food they urged upon him. He sat in the agent's swivel chair barefooted, his knees doubled under his chin.' Scott asked him whether he would promise to obey the agent if he were allowed to return home.

'No! No!' he said.

Scott was dumbfounded. 'I looked at the little monkey with what amounted almost to stupefaction. This was the result of twenty years of effort by the great American nation, or rather the Indian Bureau, to make that dried-up little monkey obey.'

Crane said of him that he was not malicious, but simply a 'deluded old savage living in a lost world of fable.' In Supt. Lawshe's opinion, 'One might as well have taken a piece of Old Oraibi sandrock to see the Pope, as the spider-like Hopi prophet to see President Taft.'

Yet he had more of the core of greatness in him than the man whose hand he shook in the Whitehouse. He lived unfalteringly in his light, and not for himself alone, but for his people and his children's children."

Greatest thing ANY human can do —

To the Government, Environmentalists, Humanitarians, and All People...

TI— "*Attention! There are certain species of life facing extinction on this planet because of environmental changes caused by foreign concepts and modern technology. These species are related to mankind, so it seems that the government, environmentalists and ecologists are helpless in saving them. We are talking about the first inhabitants, the Natives on this land. The Hopi are one group of them.*

Let us consider the facts which the Hopi have allowed to be known concerning our plight, and the creeping danger to all life and land on this earth. The time sign — the atomic bomb exploded in Japan — has appeared across the big waters. We realize that those outside our society will not know of the dangers, nor of the truth about Hopi, unless we make it known to them. We also know that a great deal of misinformation has been sown by the government press and by the publications of the early anthropologists who found the Hopi lifestyle so great in complexity, mysterious and confusing. Such early reports were published merely to fulfill their own motives of learning and fame, without concern for the survival of the cultures of the Hopi and other Native people. Their reports are mostly distorted out of proportion, for they are based on what they saw, or heard from those poor in English.

We hope you give the following words serious thought, for the survival of our village depends on these concepts. In this age it is not easy to sit down with our children to speak and teach, for intemperance, calumny, and rage are their means of rejecting what we say.

In the past we have frequently pointed out our claims to sovereignty and the purpose for which Hotevilla was founded. Without being boastful, we can say that it is true that Hotevilla still stands and has never been conquered by the mighty United States. But without support it will fall, honor will be lost. For understanding let us focus on this one particular village and explore a bit the insight of the leaders of this village and why it refuses to fall. A long time ago in Hopi Land the villages' social and ceremonial functions were healthy. Each in their own way knew much about future possibilities to serve as guidelines for action. Oraibi was our home at that time. In that village the care taken of the stone tablets, given to us by the Great Spirit to symbolize title to the land and power of authority, was every way in harmony — until the Bahannas' (white man's) arrival.

Before the Bahannas' arrival it was foretold that one day, if we are fortunate, we will meet up with another race of people of peace who will respectfully request the use of the land and who will accept our rules concerning the land without question. But if we are unfortunate, we will meet up with the wrong people. We will encounter many pitfalls, and once we are caught in them, we will be cursed forever. Remembering this, all Hopi villages at first resisted the demands to change their ways. However, when the pressure of imprisonment was applied, one by one the villages weakened and fell. Oraibi village itself was threatened, and corruption appeared. The important leaders and priests chose to leave and start anew. Through their knowledge they knew that the sacred circle would be closed and once caught inside, escape would be impossible. They also knew that if the important clan leaders did not participate in closing the circle, there would always be a pathway out. The circle could always be opened for those who wish to rejoin the people outside who may still have in their possession the original beliefs and Hopi ways of life.

So in 1906 they left. They were the true believers in the words of the Great Spirit, the Creator, carrying with them their most sacred possession, the stone tablet which was their title to the land and power of authority. Thus Hotevilla village was founded. *There they planted the spiritual power to keep all life and land and heavenly bodies in balance. The sacred pipe was passed and an oath of commitment was made to uphold the purpose upon which the village was based, to protect and defend them from harm.*

We know that this is all hocus pocus and melodrama to the Bahanna and the progressive Hopi governments. The oath of commitment is not written in words, but it is as good as the written constitution of the Bahanna. We hope some of you will agree. We know, and no doubt the Government and Puppet Tribal Council know, that Hopi is deteriorating. Sadly they don't seem to care."

TEM— Continuing our summary of Hopi history from where we left off in Chapter 5 (the Elders, Katchongva, and the *Land and Life* newsletters deal with some aspects of this in greater detail), Hotevilla is now established and beginning to function as an independent village. A semblance of normalcy is restored, and the ceremonial cycle is continued, albeit with problems caused by the divisions that resulted in having to either do without or construct replicas of some of the religious paraphernalia that remained behind in Oraibi and without some Clan members and teachers who had been essential to certain of the ceremonies. A few ceremonies were discontinued, but the majority survived. Oraibi itself was in even worse condition in this regard and apparently was not able to perform most of the major ceremonies.

In 1910 the Shongopovi Day School was built. Hotevilla parents still balked at permitting their children to attend school, and in 1911 military force was once again applied to gather in the children — an action that only intensified the anti-Government feelings of the Hostiles. Very slowly, positions solidified on the three Mesas, and day schools were built in other areas. The Bacobi Day School was opened in 1912. In 1916 its title was changed to the Hotevilla-Bacabi School. In 1913 the government opened a hospital at Keams Canyon to serve both the Hopi and surrounding Indian peoples. During the First World War, approximately one-tenth of the Hopi men served in the United States Army.

In 1926 the Lee's Ferry Bridge over the Colorado River was erected, bringing increased tourist travel into northeastern Arizona. The Hopi saw more and more outsiders coming into the villages, and the completion of the Cameron-to-Gallup road added to this contact and pressure. While tribal income in 1930 was primarily gained by farming, it was supplemented with a modest amount of agency and off-reservation work and by increased arts and crafts activities.

The Government continued its efforts to change the Hopi from an independent to a dependent people. Since it provided no income to pay for the tempting Bahanna goods and lifestyle, the traditional way of farming was downplayed. As wage work became an ever more important basis for the economy, and as automotive transportation became available, Winslow replaced Flagstaff as the key city in the Hopi world. The Great Depression of the 1930s affected Hopi economic life drastically, especially that of the Friendlies, usually addressed now as "Progressives," who are defined in a thesaurus as people who are dynamic, enterprising, reformative, broad-minded and liberal. These are opposed to "Conservatives," who are considered to be stagnant and otherwise none of the above. Can we say though that "the proof is in the pudding," and rather than by adjectives measure the Progressives by what they have actually produced? The Elders invite comparisons.

Previously, the Hopi were known as a tribe remarkably free from alcoholic beverages. But liquor was readily available in the cities, and for the first time drunkenness became a problem.

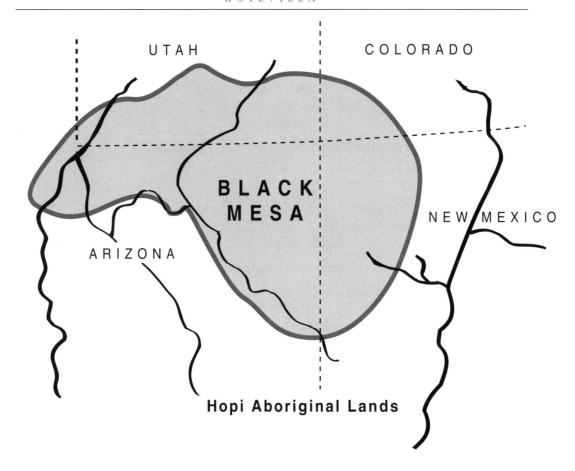

Hopi Aboriginal Lands

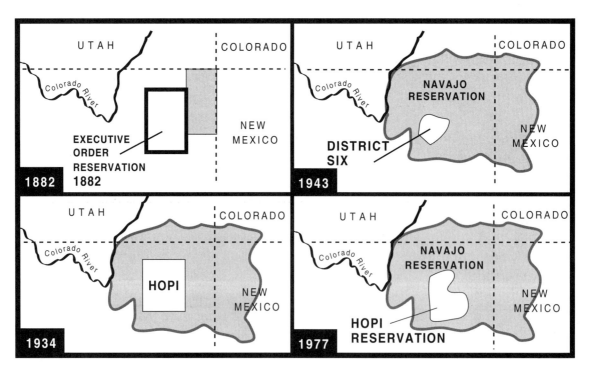

The Evolving Hopi Reservation

One of the greatest changes in the Hopi lifeway followed passage in 1934 of the Wheeler-Howard Bill, commonly known as the Indian Reorganization Act. This act offered a well-meant and certainly dramatic modification of federal attitude — but the statements of the Elders and Katchongva make it excruciatingly clear that the bill was not a blessing where the Covenant was concerned. In 1935, after consulting widely with Hopi people he knew, writer Oliver LaFarge, a longtime friend of Indian causes, drafted a constitution for the Hopi, and after a contrived election in which a tiny minority of Hopis voted to accept the terms of the Reorganization Act, a Tribal Council was established. The rest of the Hopi adults who were eligible to vote registered their disapproval by staying away from the polls. Almost from the beginning, it was recognized that the Council was not formed for the good of the Hopi. It was directly answerable to the BIA, and designed to provide the Government with a channel through which it could accomplish its use of Hopi land for industrial purposes. That is why the Elders refer to the Council as a "Puppet Government." Understandably, the perpetuation of factionalism was assured by the Council's existence. The nice thing for the Government was that from this point on it could operate from a distance, reduce the heat it had been taking, yet accomplish even more than it had before. You see, thanks to the surveyors, they had learned by now that under the surface of Hopi Land lay vast amounts of coal, water, and other valuable resources the corporations, states, and nation needed. Furthermore, since the Government played the lead role in establishing prices for the tribal lands being used and what is taken from them, it is far cheaper for the corporations to do whatever they do there than it is to use land elsewhere in the United States. To put this bluntly, the Indians were routinely cheated, and being so poor and desperately in need of funds, could do little about it.

Oraibi High School was established in 1939. It opened with about 200 pupils, and in the sense of equipping students to understand and deal with the outside world has proven itself to be a beneficial educational force. This same year, Hopi representatives met with Commissioner of Indian Affairs John Collier to enlist his support in confirming the boundaries of Hopi Land and enforcing the exclusivity of at least the 1882 reservation. The meeting produced no tangible results.

Hopi fears that the United States would not protect Hopis' special relationship to their land were heightened when the Hopi and Navajo reservations were divided into grazing districts. As the main administrative agency concerned with Indian lands, the Bureau of Indian Affairs assumed administration of the districts. In 1943, the BIA's Hopi Indian Agency took charge of District Six as its area, even though District Six included only 631,306 acres immediately surrounding the eleven Hopi Reservation villages.

Although Hopis were assured that District Six would not become the new Hopi Reservation, it in fact did.

A unilateral federal stock reduction plan introduced to the Hopi was strongly opposed, and the Hopi could do nothing about this either. It was another means of establishing control and dependency. We discuss this elsewhere, but what the Government did in effect was to establish an allotted amount of grazing land to each farmer, and then forced the farmers to reduce the size of their livestock herds to what the Government felt the new property could support. Dependency was incurred when the less than sufficient number of livestock diminished the Hopi economic base. An interesting way of dealing, don't you think?

The Hopi Agency said that it implemented stock-reduction to improve grazing potential only in District Six, but it left the rest of reservation stock reduction in the hands of Navajo agencies. For practical purposes, then, the Interior Department's interpretation of the stock-reduction procedures, together with a soil-conservation program, shrank the Hopi tribal, village, and individual land base to a token fraction of the enshrined area that had been venerated for thousands of years in Hopi ceremonies. My drawings on page 280 showing the successive changes in the size of the Hopi Reservation present a graphic portrayal of how devastating this was for the Hopis.

By 1940, the Hopi had seen tremendous changes in their social organization. Outside pressures had increased radically, and the world view of the Progressives had undergone new and probably irreversible alterations. Oraibi had declined in population from more than 600 in 1906 to 112. The village was spiritually lifeless, while Hotevilla was still strong. Several new and modern villages had developed. During World War II, many Hopi people left the reservation for work in the neighboring cities. Others registered as conscientious objectors and rendered alternative service. One of the few laudable consequences of the war was that missionary activities were reduced to a minimum, and the influence of traders waned.

Hopi population was increasing, and the subtle but steady movement of Navajos who were settling closer and closer to the Hopi villages brought reservation landholding problems to, at least in the mind of the Hopi Tribal Council, a boiling point. With their population superiority and political dominance, the Navajos were able to hold their positions, and this remained in the 1970s a key point of contention between the two tribes — or perhaps better said between the two tribal councils. As is seen in Chapter 8, however, the Elders have taken an unexpected and surprising position in the dispute.

Two issues that emerged as central focuses of Hopi concern in the 1950s and 1960s were land and resource use and cultural sovereignty. For reasons already stated, land, along with the Covenant, has always been the mainstay of Hopi culture. The Hopi ceremonial cycle, still practiced in varying comprehensiveness and ways at all three mesas, centers in the land and its generative powers. Hopi Elders of the 1960s and 1970s continued to speak reverently and emotionally of what in their migrations they had established as Hopi country, referring to it as a "shrine" that encompasses the Grand Canyon, the San Francisco Peaks, the northern reaches of Black Mesa, Zuni Salt Lake, and even territory south of Route 66.

Naturally, the United States government has never acknowledged this claim. The 1882 executive order reservation included only two and a half million acres and completely excluded the Hopi settlement of Moenkopi.

The postwar years brought increased government attempts to establish its presence in Hopi Land and also led to, for the first time, conscious action by Hopis to deal with the problems of non-Hopi jurisdiction over their lands. Two of the most important legislative actions accomplishing the government's intent were passage of the Indian Claims Commission Act of 1946 and the Navajo-Hopi Act of 1950.

The Indian Claims Commission was authorized to rule on claims for monetary compensation brought against the United States by any tribal entity recognized as representing a tribe or identifiable Indian group. By far the most common proceedings were those concerning lands taken by the United States without rendering just compensation or without due process of law. According to Indian Claims Commission statutes, once the award is made and the money is in the hands of the Indians, such payment "shall finally dispose of all fights, claims, or demands" that the claimants could make. Although the BIA officially had nothing to do with the Claims Commission, it did, however, disseminate information about the claims, called meetings, and supervised referenda. Teachers in the Hopi Day School at Kykotsmovi, referred to now as New Oraibi, were encouraged to talk about the claims in class, and the agency superintendent prodded the Hopis to submit a claim for monetary compensation. The Commission knew the award would not be sufficient, and that once accepted by the Hopis the money would soon be gone, but the Government's problem would be ended.

In 1950, the Hopis from Second Mesa who had already spearheaded one attempt to establish the Hopi claim to their land and shrines were joined now by Progressives from First Mesa and Moenkopi in a trip to Washington to see what they could do to press their land claim. In Washington they were told "that the only salvation for the Hopi people was…to revive the Hopi Tribal Council," which had been disbanded in 1940 after functioning sporadically and ineffectively for four years. With the aid of the agency superintendent, 7 of the 13 villages were persuaded to select representatives to the Tribal Council   which was resurrected in 1951 — just in time to retain a Bahanna lawyer and submit a claim before the deadline expired.

All of this took place at the very time Government attention was — for a very special reason — being focused on the Hopi and Navajo reservations. The Navajo-Hopi Act had authorized the expenditure of $88,570,000 for general improvement of both reservations. On the Hopi Reservation, these included such enrichments as schools, houses, roads, fences, wells, stock troughs, and flood-control dikes. Coupled with the revival of the Tribal Council, this act solidified the government's presence among the Hopi by providing jobs and services, by promoting indebtedness, and by encouraging Hopis to think of the United States and its agencies as part of the normal state of affairs. For everyone except the Traditionals, on the surface all of this looked promising…but what the Government was really after was not on the surface. It was underground.

As we said in Chapter 1, think "Machiavellian!" Think coal, oil, gas, uranium, water, and whatever else might be there. And in a supposedly innocent and well-intended way, the Tribal Council would become the paid channel to reach these things. *Bribery*

While those who pushed for the Council's revival generally supported the government's presence, the legacy of the ideological split of 1906 was reflected in a renewed resistance by the Traditionals to Government policies. This resistance was publicly expressed to the Indian world when two Hopis spoke against the Navajo-Hopi Act at the annual meeting of the National Congress of American Indians in 1949. They presented a viewpoint diametrically opposed to that of Council supporters which reflected a growing concern among Traditional elders that, without non-Hopi allies to counter Government influence, Hopi cultural sovereignty could easily be compromised and lost. In Chapters 7, 8 and 9, you will see how critical this matter is for the Elders.

In 1949, the needs and aspirations for the Traditionals' message were expressed in a letter sent to President Harry Truman. Later, they would send similar letters to other presidents, and to senators, congressmen, and to the heads of special Government committees. But the document sent to Truman should in itself have dispelled any thoughts that Hopi religious elders were lost in spiritual clouds and detached from everyday life. It rejected outright the notion of Hopis asking the Government through participation in claims proceedings for land that was already theirs. It refused to allow oil companies drilling access to Hopi lands. It denounced the Navajo-Hopi Act appropriations as an effort "to reduce the Hopi people under this plan," and it refused participation in any military action resulting from the North Atlantic Treaty Organization alliance. It stated, in part: "This land is a sacred home of the Hopi people…It was given to the Hopi people the task to guard this land…by obedience to our traditional and religious instructions and by being faithful to our Great Spirit Massau'u…We have never abandoned our sovereignty to any foreign power or nation." The document was signed by 24 ceremonial leaders from four villages and reflected the firm belief that Hopi prophecy was unfolding in a manner that necessitated action on their part. The two opposing political strategies with separate leaderships that had existed from a time before the 1906 split once more burst into the open among the Hopi, with each side communicating a different ideology to the agencies of non-Indian jurisdiction. Since the Hopi had never signed a treaty with the United States, the Traditionals asserted that each of the Hopi villages were an independent nation who had not even extended diplomatic recognition to the United States. The Council supporters, reflecting the influence of 60 years of Government persuasion and Christian missionizing efforts, asserted that as "the younger generation of the Hopis who are not baptized into Hopi ceremonial customs," they had in truth "chosen the civilized method of democratic government in dealing with others for the welfare of our people." It was a backwards way of saying that the Elders who had maintained their vows and the ancient ways were not using civilized methods. In this regard, we think that a proper definition of "civilized" is in order.

In the 1960s land was still the central focus of attention for both the Hopi Traditionals and the Progressives. Just as the Traditionals asserted their role in the Covenant and caretakership of Mother Earth, the Tribal Council, claiming also to be traditional in its actions, used its economic interest in Hopi land resources as a basis for political strength and influence. Naturally, the Elders heard the Council members make this claim, but knew, as was subsequently proven, there was an ulterior motive underlying everything the Council said.

After filing a claim with the Claims Commission, the Council next started negotiations with the Navajos over the areas of the Hopi Reservation outside District Six, which by 1953 had become occupied almost exclusively by Navajos. Several years of fruitless negotiations between the Hopi and Navajo tribal councils caused Congress to pass a bill authorizing the Hopis to sue the Navajos to settle the land question in court. Filed in 1961, the suit was resolved by a three-judge panel in 1962. They ruled that Hopis had an exclusive right and interest in District Six, but with the Navajos had only "joint, undivided, and equal rights and interests ... to all of the executive order reservation...lying outside...District Six." The Progressives were in no wise happy with the Elders or the decision, since it required them to pursue an aggressive strategy to enforce their rights and officially diminished their land base.

Not to worry, though. Despite limited access to once-exclusive Hopi territory, the Tribal Council has actively, and with a recent exception in the case of the Peabody Mine, in their view successfully promoted economic exploitation of land and its resources. The Elders say that an examination of what the Council has wrought calls into question any Council claims of success. In 1956 the Navajo-Hopi Act led to a report published by the Bureau of Indian Affairs assessing the economic feasibility of mineral exploitation. Between 1961 and 1964, and against the wishes of the Traditionals, the Tribal Council secured leases for prospecting, exploring, and drilling for oil, gas, and minerals. These leases brought the Council — not the Hopi people — $3,139,104.43 in royalties. This unheard-of income greatly bolstered the Council's image of itself, and in their view made it more like a real government. From this largess, the Council authorized an incredible payment of $1,000,000 for legal fees and services to their Mormon attorney, reserved about $500,000 to be used for operating expenses, built a new and modern meeting hall and headquarters at Kykotsmovi, and arranged for regular compensation for Council members. The latter cemented the relationship of the Council and the Government, and put the Council fully in the Government's pocket.

Once more rejecting the advice of the Elders of Hotevilla, the Council used the remaining $1,600,000 to construct an undergarment factory for the B.V.D. Company on lands donated as a "Hopi industrial park" by private individuals and the city of Winslow in that off-reservation town. After only two years of operation, the factory threatened to close down in 1971. Worker dissatisfaction, Hopi complaints of B.V.D.'s failure to pay rent, and lack of enthusiasm for either making the long drive over poorly maintained roads or relocating to Winslow indicated that the B.V.D. factory was destined to fail. Nevertheless, the Hopi and Navajo tribal councils, the Bureau of Indian Affairs, B.V.D., and the city of Winslow launched a cooperative effort and spent additional money in an effort to pump new life into this struggling venture — an important investment from the Council's point of view, because failure would reveal that the Council had made another unwise move. This attempt was not successful either, and in 1975 the factory closed. Nearly two million Hopi dollars went rushing down the drain.

At the same time as the Council began its B.V.D. venture, it also began to provide more services and employment for Hopis under the BIA's "buy Indian" policy and under various programs of the federal War on Poverty. Through a grant-loan from the Economic Development Administration and $144,700 of Hopi money, the Council constructed a modern motel, museum, and shop complex on Second Mesa. Known as the Hopi Cultural Center, the building opened in 1970, featuring excellent displays of contemporary Hopi weaving, carving, and visual art, and providing craft sales and a restaurant. It is probably the most rewarding investment the Council has made.

Judging by what has resulted from it, the largest and worst economic development scheme the Hopi Tribal Council has gotten the Hopi people involved in is, in conjunction with the Navajo Tribe, the 1966 leasing of a portion of the joint use area to the Peabody Coal Company. In 1970, Peabody began strip-mining the northern area of Black Mesa, agreeing to pay the Hopi Tribe an annual royalty of at least $500,000. Later on, and after renegotiation, this figure would rise substantially. In addition to coal, Peabody also obtained the right to pump 38 billion gallons of water from underneath Black Mesa to use in transporting the coal to power plants in Nevada. Although the mining operations guaranteed a steady income to the Tribal Council, and a worthwhile number of jobs to Hopis and Navajos, many Traditionals feared that runoff from the mining area could adversely affect Hopi crops, that Peabody's plans for reseeding and recontouring the mined area would not reverse the environmental damage to the fragile ecosystem, that no amount of money could undo the possible harmful effects of pollution from the power plants, and that pumping operations could seriously deplete accessible water supplies.

Once all of these fears and more became naked and stunning truth, the Hopi Traditionals mustered impressive opposition to the strip-mining. In 1970, kikmongwis and ceremonial leaders representing 10 of the 13 villages organized to file a lawsuit against the Secretary of the Interior and Peabody Coal Company. Following nearly a year of village meetings at which Hopis, environmental experts and advocates, lawyers, and anthropologists aired their opinions, the suit was filed in May 1971. There was much discussion of Hopi prophecy, the significance of Black Mesa as a portion of the Hopi holy land, and the advisability of subjecting

Hopi sovereignty to arbitration under United States law. The suit alleged that the Hopi Tribal Council did not constitute a proper quorum when it signed the lease, and charged the Secretary of the Interior with exceeding his authority when he approved it. A further basis for the suit was that the strip-mining violated "the most sacred elements of traditional Hopi religion, culture, and way of life." In a statement prepared for the complaint, six Hopi elders explained that Black Mesa was "part of the heart of our Mother Earth" granted to the Hopi to hold "in trust in a spiritual way for the Great Spirit, Massau'u." "Title," they asserted, "is vested in the whole makeup of Hopi life.... If the land is abused, the sacredness of Hopi life will disappear."

In 1970, the Navajo Tribal Council offended the Hopis by offering to purchase the Hopis' half-interest in the joint use area. The Hopi Tribal Council denounced and rejected the offer, and the Hopi Traditionals issued their own statement to the same effect, declaring that no part of Hopi land was for sale. Their reasons for the rejection differed considerably, however. The Traditionals were simply maintaining the position the Keepers of the Covenant had held for almost a thousand years at Oraibi and Hotevilla, and believed that the Tribal Council simply served as puppets who wanted the land so that the Government could obtain its use through them.

Although by the 1970s there were several hundred Hopis attending college, few could expect reservation employment from Federal or tribal agencies dependent on fluctuating government funding. Climatic factors limited agriculture to a subsistence basis, and the inadequate land allotments limited stock production. As late as 1975, however, efforts to solve the Hopi land problem and work out a legislative plan for relocating Navajos, enlarging the exclusive Hopi area, and including Moenkopi in a new Hopi reservation had not materialized.

As a whole today, Hopi isolation is completely gone. Except for Hotevilla, village independence has suffered greatly, and internal vitality and spiritual energy has, in the estimation of the Elders of Hotevilla, been radically reduced. Although fundamental behavior patterns and perceptual modes persist from aboriginal times, and on the surface the religious cycle appears to be intact, in less than a century there is almost no facet of Hopi life that has not been grievously affected. A number of ceremonies have been dropped. Others have been modified. The leadership supply has diminished. Elders who hold the precious knowledge of the ancients have dwindled down to a very few. It is a fragile situation, with nothing more than an egg-like shell to contain it. To accommodate those who do wage work, those ceremonies that are held are scheduled more and more on the basis of the European calendar. There is confusion about what to share and what not to share with one another and with the outside world. Architectural and transportation changes subtly affect home life, and utility-supply programs alter attitudes toward rain ceremonies in a negative way. Please pay particular attention to our comments in Chapter 8 regarding this. In varying proportions in each village, the economy has changed from a subsistence base with some cash supplement to a completely cash base with small subsistence support. Indebtedness is a grave threat. High school graduates and returning war veterans conclude quite naturally that there is a need for a sound education in order to harmonize with Anglo-American culture, as well as for political sophistication. All of this affects the Covenant, and you will see in the chapters ahead what its consequences are, as well as how the Elders have attempted to deal with it.

With the Hopi being more accessible than ever through railroad contacts and roadway development, and along with what is happening to the Elders, everything has borne in upon them as Maasaw predicted it would. With expanded schooling, most children can no longer comfortably converse in Hopi with their elders, particularly the grandparents. They tend to use English in their everyday life. Younger Hopi avoid the religious duties in increasing numbers, endangering the future of the ceremonial cycle. Economic, political, and social needs have been adjusted to the pattern of the outside world, and many of the basic certainties of the traditional Hopi have been badly shaken. The present impact of the Peabody Mine is small compared to what its future portends. Already, revenues from it are said to provide more than two-thirds of the income accruing to the Tribal Council. There are also cross-cultural complications that come from Hopi employment at the Peabody Mine. More is said in Chapter 8 about this enormous threat to Hopi well-being.

I have seen only a few of the church buildings on the reservation, but if these are typical, the churches are small and run-down. Conversions to Christianity are not rampant, but they do continue to take their toll. Although the total number is not proportionately large (a statistical summary is given in Chapter 8), the apostate group is militantly vocal and extremely disruptive. Their portable broadcasting systems have become effective disturbances at the performances of Kachina dances. Even more successful in their disruption are the everywhere-present automobile, pickup truck, television, and radio. In short, the general qualities of American life have invaded and had the same impact upon the Hopi as they have upon the rest of civilization. No one, including the Elders, denies the right of the Hopi to choose the course of life they want to follow. But we must not forget that they have had massive encouragement toward the White man's world. The Elders describe this process as "brainwashing" — in other words, they do not think that the choice has been an entirely free one.

Aside from the issue of the Covenant itself, Hopi dedication to the preservation of their culture has given them an artistic strength remarkable by any measure. Today, there are more than 100 identifiable painters and sculptors; well over fifty potters enjoy recognition throughout the ceramic world; and there are silversmiths who have changed and enhanced the direction of Indian art. In 1973, a group of young Hopi established Artists Hopid, an association formed to perpetuate the best of Hopi culture. There are also some excellent young photographers whose work has recently been published. It is comforting to see that the arts thrive. As a whole they are probably technically and aesthetically better than at any previous time.

The colorful and impressive Kachina dolls, so cherished by collectors, are a major source of income for many of the Hopi people, although problems are being created by four manufacturing businesses who hire Navajo craftspersons to produce kachina doll reproductions on machines that rapidly turn out large quantities. The quality of these kachinas is not nearly so good as that of the Hopi originals, but they can be sold cheaply in stores around the nation, and the mass sales cut deeply into Hopi income. Notice that while I normally capitalize the word Kachina, I use the lowercase "k" here for the Navajo dolls — indicating that these are a lower-class production, and that people who purchase them are receiving very little for their money.

Weaving is still produced, although not to the degree of earlier times when the Spaniards demanded and received an amazing 5,000 blankets as one year's tribute. They gave the Hopi sheep, let the Hopi herd them, and then took away everything the sheep produced. Although agriculture remains basic to the economy, tribal and nearby town employment accounts for much of the cash income. But even Hopi working in towns return to their home villages for ceremonial activities, and it is the ceremonial life which has proven to be the most resilient, resistant, and stabilizing quality of Hopi life.

We turn now to individual actions that have been taken by the Elders and which are described in the *Techqua Ikachi* newsletters. In these, the history of the Hopis shifts to a narrower focus upon Hotevilla and the Elders, which of course is our primary thrust and concern.

On November 20–30, 1980, Traditional leaders from Hotevilla went to the city of Rotterdam, in the Netherlands, to present its case before the Jury of the International Tribunal on the rights of the aboriginal natives of the Americas.

The following is a copy of the statement that was presented to the Jury. It is, in effect, a summation of the key points in the evolution of the Shrine of the Covenant. Further on, you will learn what resulted from the visit:

TI— "This is a special document in reference to one individual Hopi village group — the traditional community of Hotevilla Village, which is to this day one of the strongest symbols in the modern struggle for self-determination as it resists the foreign rules that are being imposed upon it by the U.S. government. These rules are imposed under the guise of acculturation and are gradually assimilating the Hopi into the mainstream of the American way of life, and have already damaged much of their culture as a whole Hopi nation. The focus now is called for on one particular village, Hotevilla, which herein presents its history and stand.

Much has been written about the Hopi in general, by anthropologists and other study groups, which always depict the Hopi as one nation. Because of the unique way Hotevilla was founded, this particular village was selected to present its case… Now it will be up to the Jury and the people of the world with an open mind to consider what is herein stated.

Do the people of Hotevilla deserve justice from the U.S. government? Should the government admit its wrongs and justify the desire of these people to self-determination by self-rule, and the practice of their own beliefs without interference from outside influences?

Should a portion of land be put aside for them so they can be self-supporting, with a firm traditional self-government?

There is not much time, but because of their strong stand the damages can be repaired with your help. [TEM— Please see chapters 9 and 11 for qualifications regarding this matter of repairability.]

So here Hotevilla Village speaks, from the mouth of its leaders and its people who have suffered from many ill-fated judgments by the U.S. government. Since their words in print would take many pages, the information presented here will be held to essential points.

Our village of Hotevilla is very young — it was founded in 1906, after we were forced out from our homes in Oraibi, our mother village. Those who left were under the leadership of Chief Yukiuma of the Fire Clan, a man of courage and strongly dedicated to his spiritual knowledge and wisdom in accordance with the sacred stone tablet bestowed to the Hopi by the Great Spirit, Maasauu. As its keeper, Chief Yukiuma understood the meaning of what is written on this stone tablet, the instructions regarding the path to follow. The Bear Clan is also a keeper of one tablet. Oraibi and no other village has these sacred stone tablets in its possession. They are very important, as will be seen further on.

Before our way of life reached the period of change, we were of one mind. The Bear Clan was highly respected, and recognized to carry on the leadership for the community. As stated previously, they too have a stone tablet to which they dedicated themselves. All Hopi have a doctrine, a leadership structure guideline and code of laws, forming a system practiced for ages by which the power of leadership is regulated. The line of leadership is firmly drawn in all the Hopi villages. The responsibilities for each village still rest with village leaders. The system still stands as years ago, and it still works to this day.

There are three ways a leader can retire from responsibilities — through death, retirement, or due to mistakes in leadership. But the successor must be well trained and taught, and usually would be of the same clan as his predecessor.

Now we will explain how the power structure of leadership is regulated. Once each year, around the time of the winter solstice, all the clan leaders would gather to review the past history of our ancients through other worlds, migrations, and meetings with the Great Spirit; to speak of the instructions and laws on the stone tablets they received from Him; and to discuss the prophecies, knowledge, and the penalties they would receive if they lost sight of their spiritual path.

The three important clan leaders would sit at the front before the fireplace. The Bear Clan leader sat to the right, the Fire Clan leader to the left, and back between the two leaders sat the Spider Clan leader. His duty was to correct and fill in what might be left out during the talk. Behind these three sat all the clan leaders. Since this session was important, pipes and tobacco were passed from man to man, symbolizing brotherhood of truth and honesty. Prayers were made for the benefit of all mankind. Then the Bear Clan and Fire Clan leaders would talk into the wee hours of the next morning.

At the conclusion, the two top leaders moved closer to the fireplace. This moment was very important to all present. What was said now must not be forgotten.

The head chief of the village (the Bear Clan) would speak first. He reached down and picked up his stone tablet and with both hands he lifted it up to the light where all could see. Then he turned to the Fire Clan leader, extending his stone tablet in front of him, and spoke thus: 'This is my power of authority, strength, and peace to all the land and life. Today I vowed to obey all laws that are within this stone tablet. This day I made my commitment, with the clear mind of truth and honesty, to lead all my people and all life on the righteous path toward good life and good health, abundance of food, and peace, *so that on this earth all life will continue.* I will not stray away from what we have said today, and leave my people in sadness. I will not change my course; l shall fulfill the tasks as a leader to the best of my ability. But should I along the way make a mistake and lose sight of the commitment I made here this day, I will surrender my stone tablet, my power of authority, on to you; and from there on you will have every right to use it as your power to lead the people upon this land. You will claim all the land into your possession for your children and those who will follow you along the spiritual path. I will deserve no land, for that is the penalty I will receive, along with those who follow me. Perhaps we would be allowed a small portion to rest our feet on, if you have pity and mercy.' 'Thank you,' the Fire Clan leader would answer.

Then the Fire Clan leader would speak likewise to the Bear Clan leader, with nearly identical wording. The Bear Clan leader in turn would thank him. Now they both turned back to the Spider Clan leader and spoke, 'If along the way we both make mistakes and stray away from our spiritual path as written in our stone tablets; if we forsake our commitments made this day, we will surrender the tablets to you for you to use to lead your people. If you do like we did along the way you must pass our power to any clan behind us to use, giving it to a person with a good heart and knowledge. Your penalty will be the same as ours.' The Spider Clan leader would answer, 'Thank you.' This confirmed and sealed their commitment.

The leaders went on to say, 'The conduct of man and nature changes in accordance with space and time. So in case the tasks we vowed to fulfill fail because of deceitfulness on the part of those to be successors to the stone tablets we hold here, then corruption and greed will develop, impostors will flourish as leaders, forsaking the whole structure of the leadership. What damage may be the result might not be restored. It will then be the time to await our white brother who traveled eastward across the big waters, who was to return when he hears we have difficulties. Then it will be his duty to place these stone tablets in the right hands. If this does not happen, our Great Creator with the help of Nature will pass on the judgment.'

These are the basic principles upon which Hotevilla village and its leadership were established — the only village in Hopi Land which is still strongly resisting the changes away from traditional leadership. This seed of the original must not perish.

Now let us explore the roots of factionalism and explain how Hotevilla was founded. We are aware that what we say will hurt and cause disharmony among those who in some ways have caused the friction and upheaval among the Hopi people in Oraibi. As foretold, all this information must come out into the open at the period when we are about to be overcome by harmful elements and can step no further.

When the first U.S. government agency was established on Hopi land, they first wanted to "civilize" the Hopi, because they looked upon us as savages. They offered to build the schools so we could learn better ways of life, up to the standard within their society, and to accept their superior religion as presented by the missionaries. They tried several ways to induce these changes, all of which met with complete failure and rejection in the villages.

In order to break the Hopi, they created fear by forming a police force, consisting partly of Navajos, and Tewa Indians of First Mesa village, because they were non-Hopi who would swing their weight without mercy. So when the threats of arrests and imprisonment were applied for noncooperation, the villages panicked. The weaker people began to submit as the pressure mounted, causing all village leaders to consider the problems developing in each of the village communities. It was now the time for the Hopi to negotiate with the President and officials at the White House. The arrangements were quickly made to take all of the village headmen to Washington, so they could see for themselves the Bahanna (white man) and his ways. Similar tactics had been used by the government with other native nations. They were received like kings upon their arrival, were given the best food and beds, and glimpses of U.S. civilization, its splendors and multitude of people. Many promises of good things were offered if they would agree to the government proposals, with the threat of punishment for those who might dare oppose the 'Great White Father.' So as to avoid further harsh treatment, and for their own comfort, all the chiefs signed the agreement to cooperate and to send their children to government schools. Chief Lololma of Oraibi was among those who made a trip to Washington, and upon returning he reported his findings. Many of the people in his and other villages were impressed and decided to take advantage of the good things that the government offered. Thus the frictions began to develop among the people.

The Fire Clan leader, Yukiuma, did not approve of Chief Lololma's move.

He pointed out his weakness in going against his commitment to follow the spiritual path, and destroying the leadership structure by not surrendering his stone tablet to him (Yukiuma). Because of Lololma's action, Yukiuma was now recognized by the majority of the people as a chief to lead the traditional Hopi. The name 'Hostiles' was given to those who chose to continue living in the Hopi way, and the name 'Friendlies' was given to those who wanted to live in the Bahanna way.

Chief Lololma died not long after. The last of the Bear Clan had no successor. So Tewaquaptewa of the Bear Clan was recruited from Shomopovy, a Second Mesa village, to be chieftain and to represent the so-called 'Friendlies' to the U.S. government. He held on to the sacred stone tablet for his own purposes.

Since the time the friction began, many dreadful events had taken place, which still remain in our memories. We were never at peace. The government and the Friendlies, by use of police and the military, tried to force the Hostiles into submission. The Friendlies became prejudiced and radical, and heckling became an everyday activity. Chief Yukiuma and other important leaders became prime targets; they were in and out of jail without court hearings, yet still they would not yield to the government demands.

Then, on September 6, 1906, the friction came to a head — the Hostiles were driven out of their homes. The Friendlies even tried to use arms, but were disarmed by missionaries, while Hostiles remained non-violent. They were driven to the outskirts of the village where Chief Yukiuma agreed to move out with his people, following a pattern that has been practiced by our ancients during their migrations, whenever the settlements became corrupt, and they would have to start out anew.

Chief Yukiuma marked a boundary line across a rock, and spoke when he stepped over the line, 'Thank you. From this day on, all the lands beyond are in my possession, for all the people who have chosen to follow me. To the best of my knowledge and ability I will defend and take good care of the land for my people and all life. Tewaquaptewa can have the village. Follow me without heavy hearts. We will rebuild.' What he meant was that he claimed the land for all people and life on earth and would protect it for those who have faith in all our Great Creator's laws; while the Bear Clan would meet his own end due to his choice to change his ways.

So the new village of Hotevilla was settled with hardship and grief. In spite of the problems, the foundations were laid, rooted deep into the earth and enshrined as the heart of the community. All paths within the village are linked to all the directions and to sacred places of spiritual power, for the delivery and receiving of prayers. Therefore the village is a shrine itself, a special holy place, identical to the Bahanna's church. This includes the layout of the village; clan duties; and the kivas where the chief important deities and symbols are placed and planted, and then blessed with certain powers to maintain the balance and directions for humans in relationship between heavenly and earthly forces of nature, complete with ceremonials and the ritual cycle. All shrines grew deep to all directions, weaving their roots into the earth like fabric and thus maintaining the balance and harmony with

[handwritten left margin: must experience these powers soon]

[handwritten right margin: would like to walk these paths with the elders]

all life. They are endowed with powers of self-protection, a weapon of mysterious power. Those who defy and disturb their roots without respect suffer great misfortune which can extend to the whole of mankind.

The founding of Hotevilla village did not mark the end of the suffering for the Hostiles. Many times its leaders were imprisoned and forced to work on chain gangs, and nearly starved. Meanwhile, the children were put in government schools against their and their families' wills. Some were sent to schools far away, for five to eight years, in the hopes that they would forget the old ways. Women were left alone to feed the old and the children and keep them warm during the hard winters.

Chief Yukiuma continued to resist and would not bow to the government. He even spent about a year in Alcatraz for wanting to maintain his traditional ways. At one time, he met with President Taft in the White House, and told him face to face why he wanted to continue living his own way. He knew that the government agents looked upon him as a crazy man, who had no desire to accept the comfort of modern ways. The government regarded him as an obstacle in the way of progress. When he met with President Taft, he talked of the Hopi problems and why he would not accept the white life, while President Taft in turn tried to convince him to change his mind. But Chief Yukiuma was not impressed by the Bahanna's ways, promises, and threats, nor by the food and soft beds, as were the Hopi leaders before him. The meeting was disappointing to both men, and no agreements were reached. He returned home, only to end up in the guardhouse once more. He refused to be defeated, and no amount of imprisonment, suffering, bribes, or flattery could make him forsake his stand; even the President of the nation had no effect. He was deported over eight times from his own land and imprisoned on the same charges without trial, and no doubt passed on happily and proudly. He fulfilled his task to the Hotevilla village, which still follows his pattern of philosophy.

After his death, Chief Yukiuma's clansman (Pongyayouma) was appointed to take over the leadership, and thus became the (keeper of the sacred stone tablet.) He quickly became very active in carrying out his task in accordance with his uncle Yukiuma's teachings. He was not very popular among some people due to his disposition and character, but in due time he was accepted.

During this period some of the government's hard-core policies were toned down, and the compulsory schooling was relaxed; but some new compulsory policies were enforced, causing more suffering for the people of Hotevilla. Other villages did not suffer as much because they complied with the government demands. Here are some examples of these new policies:

1) Matrimony by Native ceremonies became prohibited; often the bride and groom were jailed until they yielded to the Bahanna system.

2) Chemical sheep-dipping was enforced, and herdsmen had to comply or

they were arrested and jailed. Police and rangers were hired from other villages to come and herd Hotevilla sheep and take them several miles away to the dip, and many times sheep would be slaughtered for the rangers' feasts. Sometimes Hotevilla people who resisted this activity were themselves dumped into the chemical dips. This was accomplished by police from other villages who were hired alongside Navajo and Tewa Indians.

3) <u>Stock reduction</u> — those who refused to comply were jailed and all their stock was taken away, and divided among Friendlies and the schools — most of the stock was sold or even destroyed.

4) <u>Draft</u> — religious leaders and young men were imprisoned for refusal to submit to military service because of their religious beliefs.

These are just a few examples of the oppressive government policies enforced against Hotevilla and the other villages.

As predicted, Chief Pongyayouma <u>did not last</u>. It was said that he lacked judgment and <u>was too fragile to withstand pressure</u>. So when word leaked out that he had secretly involved himself with the demands of the government and in other scandals, he exiled himself to an Indian town in New Mexico where he stayed for seven years. Upon his return, he forsook his religious activities and became affiliated with the Friendlies, and was recognized by the government and Hopi Tribal Council as a chief of Hotevilla village. Like Chiefs Lololma and Tewaquaptewa, he did not surrender his stone tablet to the Spider Clan, who was still waiting to receive it, in accordance with their commitments to the leadership structure. <u>We are now awaiting our white brother who traveled eastward across the big waters long ago, who was to return when he hears of our difficulties. He will then deliver the sacred Hopi stone tablets into proper hands.</u>

After Pongyayouma's self-ejection, three of the high spiritual religious leaders took over the leadership — first, Chief Katchongva of the Sun Clan, a son of Yukiuma. After he died, Chief Tewangyouma of the Corn Clan, also a close relation to Yukiuma, took over, until he died. Both were very strong and wise leaders, following the footsteps of Yukiuma, and thus received similar punishment from the opposing forces.

In the same manner, religious leader (David) Monongye was recognized by the leaders and people to be acting regent for the community and has been functioning <u>as traditional chief of Hotevilla community to this day</u>, with the traditional type of government supported by the leaders and people. The affairs of the yearly ceremonial cycle and resistance against lingering pressure by the U.S. government and the government, instigated Hopi Tribal Council are very active and alive.

Now, to the jury of this Tribunal and the people world over: We have presented our case before you with clear minds of truth and honesty, as one of the last pillars for all Native people of the land, defending our aboriginal Native rights by struggling and resisting the total change of our ways of life. <u>The aboriginal seed must not die in vain</u>. The essence of this case is clear — the evidence of where we stand, as the Sovereign Hopi Independent Nation of the Traditional Community of Hotevilla Village. We ask for freedom, a self-stable government, to practice our own beliefs and control our own land and its resources, and to restore our self-sufficiency as in the past. We are speaking of a full autonomy."

TI — In the Words of Dan Katchongva...

"It was when I was just reaching manhood that the long road of iron came together between Winslow and Flagstaff...'

Dan Katchongva often recalled the great occasion in 1881, when the Santa Fe Railway joined east and west about 50 miles south of Oraibi. 'At that time the air was so clear that you could see it all the way from Oraibi, where I was raised. Some days we could actually see the machines move in the distance. Perhaps our eyes were better at that early age.'

Katchongva belongs to the Sun Clan, which took over the chieftaincy of Hotevilla after Pongyayouma of the Fire Clan neglected his duties and left the village. He is the son of Yukiuma, the chief who founded Hotevilla in 1906, and served as a spokesman and advisor up to the time he became chief.

'When I was growing up there was not much trouble,' he would tell us. 'What you see around Oraibi has changed a great deal! Down there to the southeast, that wash used to be flat with many cornfields, belonging to many clans. We had heavy rain, but there were no deep arroyos like you see now, for we could control it with our sacred knowledge, so the flooding waters would spread evenly throughout the fields. But we were upset and angered when our own people in Oraibi turned against us by choosing the white man's ways and evicting us from the village. We delivered our *pahos* and digging stick to the water spirits and commanded that deep wash to be formed, so the waters coming from above would be useless to those who disregarded the Spirit's laws. There was also sand down below Oraibi which is no longer there. With our sacred knowledge we took a handful of sand to Hotevilla when we moved, to make the land richer, so we would have plenty of food.' Such statements must seem unbelievable to people who have never experienced this type of power.

'I was young and strong when we had the clash between the 'hostiles' and the 'friendlies' in Oraibi. Only later did we learn the true meaning of that word. I was full of vigor, and felt no one could throw me. But when the factionalism erupted I was stormed by four or five men, each to one limb, and another jumped onto my midsection and knocked me unconscious. That convinced me that I was not so tough after all.'

Thus Dan Katchongva recalls his involvement in the famous split in Oraibi, out of which Hotevilla was founded as a sanctuary for the Hopi way of life. He was involved continually in countless efforts to protect our right to live according to the Great Spirit's instructions.

'Not long after we moved to Hotevilla, Government troops came and marched us, men, women, and children, to a place 6 miles below Oraibi and tried to get us to sign an agreement to join the Government Agency's flock, and be spared from further harassment. We refused, and the men were marched over 30 miles to Keams Canyon. There we were shackled and chained together, starved and forced to work to build walls and roads. I and many of the followers of Yukiuma did not weaken in spite of all we were put through to break our spirit. If they had shot us all then, they would have no obstacle crossing their road to riches, but for some reason they didn't.'

Katchongva withstood the trials along with the rest of us, and later emerged to take over the duties abandoned by Pongyayouma. As Yukiuma's son, he became the natural successor. 'I have protested against the hindrances to our ways of life for years, but the more I reject, the bigger the offers get. Some people think I am a crazy teller of fairy tales and doomsday stories. Since I became recognized as the leader of Hotevilla village, I have met many times with those who want to better our ways with material things, some who say we must meet such offers halfway, and those who agree that I must refuse entirely. I think the ones who refuse entirely are right, because they have experienced our struggle. Those still living through it are having a hard time, and will probably continue to as long as they live. Someday after I pass on all of my story will be written down. It will be long if written in detail. I have lived to journey to Washington, D.C., at least two times, and to the 'house of glass,' and on all occasions I found eyes and ears closed. Mouths were too tight to let out anything positive. I have lived to see and ride on the 'road in the sky,' the 'moving house of iron,' and the horseless carriage. I was fortunate enough to speak to many people through the 'cobwebs,' and through space as well, as our old leaders had predicted, to reach people with my message. I have lived to wear, and wear out, many pieces of white man's clothing, and eat many of his fine foods. I am getting old and will pass on someday. It makes me sad to think I may not get to meet our True White Brother in person, but it is prophesied that just two or three righteous persons will be plenty to fulfill his mission. Even one truly righteous would be able to do it.'

Katchongva passed on in February 1972. Unlike his father, Yukiuma, he didn't get to shake hands with the President in the White House. But in the late 1950's, when he was in Washington to attempt communication with the U.S. Government, the Commissioner of Indian Affairs, himself of native ancestry, asked him why, if he refused to support the white man's schools and way of life, he wore a White man's coat and rode in a White man's car. Katchongva replied, 'I have heard these words from traitor Hopi, but I never expected to hear them from you!' The Commissioner blushed and hid his face.

What Katchongva stood for is hard for anyone to face while trying to go the other way. That is why every attempt is made to discredit his authority, even today. But he saw, just as clearly as his father did, the grief and confusion that would strike Hopi soon after a few of the Government's tempting offers were accepted. He knew very well the tragedy that would befall our future generations once we sacrificed our land and our self-determination for a few handouts.

Sun chief.

Following the example of Dan Katchongva, his father Yukiuma, and many other dedicated Traditional leaders of today and of centuries long past, the true Hopi would rather die than see their children obliged to serve a dangerous system beyond their control."

TEM— In *Techqua Ikachi* issues 16, 17, 18, and 19, the Elders attempt to help Hopi youth and Bahannas understand, through Hopi eyes, the full measure of what happened to the people during the first years of the twentieth century. Entitled "Understanding the Hopi World," it is a story filled with marvelous insights into the life and ceremonial cycle, and into Hopi thoughts and feelings. I have modified it only a little by merging its four parts into a continuous narrative. It is, of course, a carefully shaped account designed to favor the Traditionals' position, and the deliberately happy ending is wishful thinking. This has not been the actual case for many Hopis. Yet it is true for the Elders, who actually experienced it in their personal lives. I don't know how the tale of Oraibi and Hotevilla could be told in a clearer way. It is filled with valuable lessons, speaks for itself, and requires no further comment from me.

"Let us suppose," the story begins, "you are Bahanna or even a young Hopi who is puzzled about the Hopi Traditional Society, regarding their behavior and their attitude toward Bahanna's ideals and about their resistance to adopt the Bahanna system. To help you reach a more clear understanding into the Hopi world, we will take you back to a time just a little before Bahanna appeared on Hopi land.

Now, you will be the character, so just imagine and pretend you are one of the Hopis. You are yet at the tender age of about five or six. You live in the Northern part of what is now called Arizona. The village where you live is atop the mesa, with houses built of mud and stones. You have a family, consisting of mother, father, and others that make your house whole and complete.

You love your home because from there you can see the endless desert with its mesas and yonder mountain reaching into the sky. You love to look at the sunrise and sunsets with prayers in your heart for your needs and protection. At sunset you give thanks as, like your father before you, you were taught by your elders.

All throughout the yearly cycle, your village is filled with magical activities during evenings — laughter, drums, singing, and clacking rattles. If it is a summer evening, you, together with your sister or brother, lay beside your mother and father on the rooftop, enjoying the sounds of activities. Now and then you ask your father about the stars and the moon. He points out to you certain stars, their names and meanings. At the end he sings you into deep sleep. During winter evenings, storytelling is at its best. It is Grandpa or Grandma whom you favor because they do not scold you. Their tales might be about anything — some

Handwritten margin note: I've had this vision from these mesas and have yet to go there —

funny, some sad, some scary, some of history, the history of your peoples' past. You learn not to be like the bad coyote who does stupid things. Rather you want to be like people in the story: good runners, hunters, and those who did good deeds.

Your uncle comes some evenings. You are afraid of him because somehow he always learns of your mischief and reminds you to be good. You remember that on two or three occasions he poured cold water on you for looking into the Ceremonial Kiva when you were not supposed to and for other mischief. So you behave when he is around. You all gather around the fireplace and he talks about prophecies describing the origins of clans and the Great Laws that we have inherited. If he is relaxed and in a good mood he may end up with a short tale. Sometimes you don't like to listen because he always tells the same thing over and over. But you brave it out and sit there like a good little child, with your old blanket wrapped around your body and head.

You are too young to know that your uncle is planting the seeds of Wisdom and Knowledge inside your body and mind.

The daylight hours too can be very enchanting, all the year round. All the do's and don'ts of life are laid out by your parents. If you do your best to go by the rules, your uncles will be sure to know about it. If you are a girl you help your mother around the house, or you can play with your Kachina dolls with other girls, and play house. If you are a boy you can play with your bows and arrows or explore the edge of the mesa — but be careful not to touch any sacred things or dangerous animals or plants. Often you accompany your father or grandpa to their fields. You did not do much, but by their happy faces you can tell they are very pleased that you came along. They will point to different plants, insects, and animals, and reveal their names and functions for you to learn. Little did you know that you are learning about and becoming part of nature. Then there are other parts to your world — the colorful dances and sacred ceremonials, the sounds of drums, rattles, and turtle shells, whose meanings are not yet clear to you. However, there are special days you love best — that is when your Kachina Friends come into your village with their gifts of Kachina dolls, bows and arrows, other toys, and food for you to eat. Sometimes the clowns will accompany them and will do many funny things to make people laugh and be happy.

As always you love their songs and dancing, their colorful costumes, and their colorful antics, and you love their movements, but your mind is yet too tender to know what their songs and movement mean.

When there were the winter months with their sacred ceremonials, those who observed the religion would spend hours in the kivas. You would miss your father and grandpa, because they slept and ate there and never came home. You can't wait till they come home and tell stories again.

So one early morning at dawn, your mother awakens you to walk the path of cornmeal toward the rising sun. There you will ask for blessing and pray for good health and long life. You do as you are told, which makes you feel good. Not forgetting your Kachina friends, you pray for more toys.

This is only a glimpse of your past world, and your short experience as a Hopi is starting to take root. But it will stay with you, no matter what changes come in the future, and your memories of it will linger on.

You will now enter the world of Bahanna (white race) during the period when the first Bahannas planted their curse in Hopi Land. The results of this curse have brought us to where we are now at this stage of life. Knowing this, the Hopi who are completely loyal to Maasaw refuse to even acknowledge the Bahanna's proposals or to be tempted to raise arms against any foreign powers. Our position is clear. All we want is to control our own way of life, and to have our land and freedom to practice our own beliefs. Maybe the Hopi do see into the future and are able to foretell the Bahanna's acts which will split the Hopi nation into two factions, or in the truer meaning into two paths. When this situation finally came to a head one faction had to suffer. Those who chose the original path were punished, imprisoned, and finally evicted from their homes. This is their sacrifice in order to keep to their ways. This is a brief introduction to the situation so you may find your way around as a Hopi in the Bahanna world.

Please, once again pretend you are a Hopi in your early years, in the period when your view of life is still somewhat blurred. Your home is in the village atop the mesa with a view to both the sunrise and sunset, a view to the wide deserts and the high mesas. At night there is the most enchanting view of the heavenly bodies. Here too is where you will view the first Bahanna through Hopi eyes.

From your uncle's lips you have been hearing a lot about the Bahanna as an elder brother of the Hopi who was to come someday. You often wondered what he looks like and when he will come. You did not know that you would have a chance to witness the historical event personally until the village crier announced that strange people were coming up to the mesa.

You are told to stay indoors until confirmation is made by the chiefs as to whether they are friends or foes. It is best to be cautious. They are believed to be Bahannas. 'Bahannas,' you say aloud to yourself, 'What will they be like?'

The arrivals do not take long in coming. They seem to be harmless and to want to be friends. With the other children you go out to explore what the first Bahannas are like. At first you peek at them from a corner, and when they come closer you run quickly to the next corner. By and by you come nearer to get a better look. You hear them speaking a strange tongue. 'Look,' you say excitedly, awed by such strange creatures, 'Look, their clothing is different. Look, they have hairs on their faces like dogs!' Very weird things happen that really astonish you. As you look at them with wide eyes, one of the Bahannas takes off his glaring eyes and puts them back on again after wiping them with a piece of cloth. Another pulls off the top of his head and replaces it without a show of blood. 'They must be witches,' you think to yourself.

The Bahannas have with them a black box with one bulging eye. They connect legs to this so it stands up, and then their behavior becomes very strange indeed. They flap their hands like birds' wings, and they offer you some kind of objects. They motion that the objects are to eat. You are too shy to come close so they toss a few to you. Naturally you grab for them. They toss more and more, and soon you all scramble to grab more than the other children, resulting in some friction among you. You notice that all during this time one of the Bahannas is always behind the black box with his head covered. You do not understand what he is doing, it is only your fun that matters. You do not know that the first seed of the curse is being sown by these Bahannas.

As time passes the scouts for the more ambitious Bahannas exploit the Hopi. From now on the life of the Hopi will be one of tension and fear. In spite of this, the yearly life cycle continues according to the Creator's plan. Before long the Bahannas make a proposal to set up a school to teach Hopis a better way of living. On the basis that we are satisfied with the Hopi way of life, Hopi leaders oppose these plans, but the Bahannas persist and build schools near each village.

Your young mind has not yet comprehended full Hopi knowledge, so you think it would be interesting and exciting to go to the white man's school. Perhaps you will get to eat more candies and cookies and other things you may like. Your whole family is totally against this. Your uncle will often gather all the clan members and preach to all of you about how it will affect your future. He will end up by saying, 'If we all turn into Bahanna, the great waves of water will swallow us all.'

Before long the factions began to form: some to stay with the old ways, some to learn the new white man's ways. It begins to affect the children, and some of your friends become your enemies. The schools open, and the parents who agreed to go along with the Bahannas plan of their own free will to enter their children. Those who oppose do not. Teachers come into the village to take you and the other children, but your parents and other parents refuse. The teacher tells them to reconsider and that he will return.

Now to avoid being caught you and your sister sleep each night in different places, and never sleep in the same place twice. Several times you have close calls but are able to outrun the Bahannas. They carry guns and shoot behind you to scare you into stopping, but you never stop running.

One morning you come home and your sister is gone. Your mother and grandmothers are crying because the Bahannas have taken her. Sounds of crying come from the other households nearby who also lost their children.

One day you walk right into them because the Bahannas are waiting in your house! Your father grabs you into his arms and the Bahannas try to drag you away, but your father holds you firmly. There is a struggle and your father lets go only because he is hit on the head by a Bahanna's club. Still struggling, they take you to the school. They take all your clothes and clip all your hair off, then they throw you into a tub of hot water and scrub you raw. Now a new kind of clothing is thrown to you for you to put on.

To keep you from running away, they take you on horseback two days' travel to another school. There you are given a bed, a blanket, and a meal. It is not candies or cookies, but something you have never eaten before. The first few days you are very sad and lonesome and you cry yourself to sleep. The other children are in the same shape.

In this new place there are many strict rules. You are not permitted to utter the words of Hopi or you will be punished with a whip. You are expected to be in bed at a certain time and to rise at a certain hour. There are many more don'ts than do's.

After months go by, you are taken to another school that is still farther away from your home. Here you will spend the next four to five years.

So far we have taken you on a journey through the Hopi world, before and after Bahanna came into Hopi Land; during the period when order within Hopi Land was disrupted by western ideas, as foretold. We led you through this journey in an effort to give you a clear understanding of what consequences the Hopi will face if we forget our ways and allow ourselves to be diverted into other life designs that are not ours. In fact, this is what has happened to the traditional Hopi. Only this handful who have refused to accept the new ideas have suffered prompt and continuing consequences at the hands of even our own people.

Now let us continue with your journey as a Hopi. You recall that before all this you walked the mesa top where your people live. It was a great feeling to do as you wished, unafraid, to play and dance with children of your own age.

You have grown up quickly during all the confusion. You begin to pick up the realities of life as your thoughts return to your elders and the knowledge of prophecies that established the pattern of life set out for you. You want to run away now because of your fear, but you also want to see it through like a brave Hopi. You realize your people are helpless too, that all of you are in the clutches of Bahanna.

Many things have happened during your captivity, and you have learned to accept the demands that come your way. One morning after early breakfast you and the other boys and girls are dressed in extra clothing and with blankets and sacks of food you are loaded onto wagons. No one has told you where you are going, but everyone is excited to be going on an adventure after being cooped up for several months.

All that day you travel without reaching your destination. It is cold and there are patches of snow on the ground. Some children huddle together to keep warm with what little covering they have. You and the other older boys run or walk beside the wagons to keep warm. You have the urge to run away, but you realize you could not escape the guards who are on horseback. Shortly before dark you are stopped and told to make camp. Cold, tired, and hungry, the older children are told to gather firewood. You are happy that you can do something to get warm, and you feel pity for the younger children who are in tears. Finally you are fed and allowed to warm yourself near the fire. Sleeping is almost impossible in the cold, but somehow you make it through the night and are ready to continue the journey the next day.

Late the second day you hear a shout and look off into the distance where you see smoke. Your spirits rise; maybe you are nearly there. It takes another three hours to reach the place, and you arrive just before dark. As you ride through the streets on the wagon you see that these are much bigger houses with many windows and lights. Many people are walking around who look like the first Bahannas you saw.

Soon you find yourself in a very strange place with roads of shining metal. Upon these roads are strange monsters who breathe through the tops of their heads and each have one glaring eye. They are monsters that howl like coyotes and hiss and grunt like giant snakes. These things are long and move on wheels like wagons. You are told to get inside the belly of one of these monsters through a doorway, and you do so reluctantly as you try to control your fear.

Once inside the monster you are surprised to find it is comfortable and warm with seats for you to sit on. The Bahanna who is going with you is nice. She gives you and the other children sack lunches and some sweet drinks. After the previous two hard days of traveling with little sleep, everyone is soon in deep slumber.

The next day you awake to find yourself in a much larger place with taller houses than you have ever seen before and many more Bahannas. You are taken to a place which will be your home for up to the next five or more years. You are separated from the other children, bathed, and given clean clothing, a bed, and a schedule for all the things you are to do. From now on your life is a mixture of loneliness and happiness. You are always under watchful eyes. No longer can you dance and sing your own way. No longer can you see Kachina dances in the plaza or in the kiva; no longer can you go exploring on the mesa tops.

As time passes, however, you begin to adjust to the new conditions by taking part in the activities. Soon you no longer think much about your country and people, about the ceremonial dances, or about helping your father and grandfather in the cornfields. All of this begins to dim in your mind. You no longer speak your own language. During the five years or more in captivity your mind has slipped into Bahanna concepts. You dream of the future with better and easier ways of living. Working the fields has no future, and the Bahanna ways seem much better. You can have electricity and water right in your own home. Why live the old ways, carrying jugs of water and wood to store in the barn on your back for the long distances, as you remember having to do as a child? Now that you have learned a trade and will be making a lot of money you plan to buy many of the good and beautiful things you have seen in the big stores. You even think about moving into town and owning your own home. That would certainly make you the envy of your people and your friends.

Unknown to you, about this time the crisis in your land has become critical and is causing much unrest and friction. Continually the children are taken away by force to schools by the Navajo and Hopi renegades under instructions from the agency. They act without mercy in dealing with your people, causing much disturbance and distress. Because you have by now spent so much time with Bahanna you do not understand why your people have made a firm stand to suffer for you and your future. You could not understand that Bahanna and your corrupted leaders have planned deliberately to destroy the minds of all the children as Hopi. But it has worked, and you and the other children are the victims. In our next issue we will show you how the victimized children accept Bahanna ideas and concepts and become traitors to their own people. Later one will discover that his people were right. Through his own experiences in exploring the inner cities and towns he realizes the false values of the Bahanna and denounces the Bahanna system to defend his own people.

Remember now that we have taken you through the period just before and after Bahanna came to our land. You were still a child, still free to roam the mesa tops and the valleys with the cornfields which nourish your people. Sadly, this freedom ended when you became a captive of the Bahanna and were sent far away to school. Your Hopi pattern of life was put aside while you had to follow the rules of Bahanna. There you forgot the rules and pattern of life set forth for you by the Great Creator.

As the time passed in captivity, you grew to young manhood and learned many things the way white people do them. You were taught a 'trade' by which your captors said you would tackle the world and earn your living. After five years you were released, free to go home to your people. You now have great plans for your future; you will work for Bahanna and make lots of money. With that you can get what Bahanna has, all the beautiful things you see in the stores, may even buy a lot and build a house on it like the Bahanna.

On your return to the village your family receives you with joy, admiring how you have grown. Now you can help with the fields and stock. Now you can participate in the ceremonials.

You notice many things have changed in your absence. People seem older, and there are new additions in the family. The most obvious change is that you have arrived in a different village, different surroundings. You are told that they had to move to the new place while you were gone and start out a new life after their old village had become corrupted. They did this in order to keep to their Hopi ways of life and not adopt the Bahanna ways.

You are dumbfounded, confused, as though the world has fallen on your future plans. You stay and help your family, but there are always nagging thoughts. Working the land, herding, the rituals, slowly drift from your mind, for they have no value like money. It is the money that buys nice things. Your life seems empty. After a year you make a decision to leave for the white man's world. Your family resents this but permits you to go with some warnings and advice. You are grown now and it feels good to be on your own.

Before dawn you leave with some food, a jug of water and a few of your belongings. Your father and uncle have also given you a few dollars. Being a good runner, you reach the nearest town by sundown.

It is a good feeling to get away from the old dead village. By contrast the town is filled with excitement and the promise of the life you have been longing to live, an opportunity to make lots of money. You treat yourself to a big hunk of ice cream and the cookies you missed so much. You learned to like them very much during your captivity, and they were not part of village life.

You now look for work and find it is not so easy in this small town so you decide to go to a larger city. You hop the freight and after two days' travel find yourself in the biggest city you have ever seen. Being a beginner, you don't know what to do and are lost. During the day you look for work, willing to accept anything. The first thing you realize is that what you were taught in the Bahanna trade school has no value. The money you had is gone so you sleep in parks and alleys. Soon you get so hungry that you start to depend on picking scraps from the slop cans.

Greed has produced Beggers

You are too timid to ask anyone for help, and no one comes forward to help you. It was not possible for you to know that this was the Depression, that everyone was looking only for their own survival.

One morning you are picked up by the police for sleeping in someone's hallway. Scared and confused, you are asked many questions. You are taken to a place you later find out is the Salvation Army. There you are bathed and given clean clothing and the first hot meal since you hit the big city. There they arrange for you to help on the farm.

On the farm you meet people like yourself, without jobs, without skills. There you work picking vegetables and fruit. It is hard work, but at least you have something to eat. Those you work with are very nice and live together in shacks nearby. Together you pool what little money you earn to get food. The vegetables and fruit are free to eat. This is where you learn many things you were not taught in school. Among other things, you are introduced to alcohol and 'women of profession.' You are having such fun that you forget about your goal of making lots of money.

Before long, this life loses its attraction and you begin to feel self-pity for your failure. You want to return to your people, but you are too ashamed and embarrassed to face them. One day though you decide to just pack up and leave. You hop a freight and in a couple of days you find yourself in the small town you left behind over a year ago.

The frustration and depression drop away from you, and it is a good feeling, since you are near your homeland you now know is where you rightfully belong. With your own experience you have learned a valuable lesson   that Bahanna's world has false values. What you were taught in school and elsewhere did not help you find happiness, make you lots of money, or fulfill your dreams.

Back in the village you are accepted without question despite your unsuccessful adventure. Within a year you are initiated into a higher order. You now realize the elders were right in advising you to learn inner wisdom and the knowledge of nature and man. You know it is true that it is important to protect what the Great Creator has given to us.

I must also learn this —

Thank you for coming with us on this journey and looking with us through the eyes of a Traditional Hopi. Perhaps it will help you understand the feeling of despair and uselessness that wells up in our hearts as our ways are being threatened and destroyed. Thank you — with our blessings."

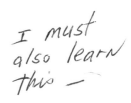

CHAPTER 7

Two-Hearteds: The Progressive Hopi and the Government

Two-Hearteds Who Today Impede the Keeping of the Covenant: Progressive Hopis and the United States Government

Progressive Hopis

The Traditional Hopis identify those who promised they would <u>live as the Creator told them to</u>, and then did so, as "one-hearted," or "one-hearts." These were <u>single-minded people who walked the narrow blade</u>, kept themselves and the <u>world in balance</u>, and <u>did not give in to temptation</u>. "Two-hearts" or "two-hearteds" were those who succumbed to temptation and stepped off of the narrow blade. In ancient times, these people were usually considered to be bewitched, and were <u>called "witches,"</u> people who held individuals under their evil spell and practiced witchcraft. This practice is still believed in today, although outside influences have caused its position in the culture to be less strongly held than before.

As the Traditional Hopi saw how the United Sta<u>tes Government officials</u> performed, they began to refer to them as "<u>witches from the east</u>" who said one thing but did another, and who employed deceitful practices to accomplish their goals. From there, it was an easy step to calling the "Friendlies" who embraced the Government and behaved like the Government did, "Two-Hearted," although the "Hostiles" of Oraibi did not usually carry this farther and call Progressive Hopis witches. We capitalize the word Progressive, since it pertains to an identifiable body of people as opposed to someone whose nature is to be progressive, or forward-thinking in simple, day-to-day affairs. These two-hearted Hopis have, though, attempted to live simultaneously in two worlds and serve two diametrically opposite masters. Logically then, when the "so-called Tribal Council" came into being the way that it did — and became a channel for the Government, whose members were Progressives and sometimes Christian converts who pursued materialism rather than the Traditional life — it too was an entity considered to be two-hearted. Of all those whose opposition hampers the Traditional people the most today in their efforts to keep the Covenant, the members and employees of the Tribal Council, because they are Hopi, are considered the worst.

Actually, there are five groups of opponents who fit into the two-hearted category: they are the Progressive Hopis who have embraced Bahanna ways and programs and are present in varying percentages in all of the villages; the United States Government and its departments — in particular the BIA, or Bureau of Indian Affairs; the Hopi Tribal Council; certain corporations, such as the Peabody Coal Company; and missionaries — in particular the Mormon Church. Notice in particular that the Elders single out the Progressives, and thus do not automatically include all other Hopis in the two-hearted category. There are exceptions, and the Elders know this, although some of these exceptions may have adopted some of the Bahanna accoutrements that are questionable.

I emphasize here what I have before, and will again — that as you read the *Techqua Ikachi* articles that follow you must not let the amount of material cause you to lose sight of the fact that the activities of the two-hearteds are considered here mainly because they have impeded both the Covenant relationship and the Keeping of the Covenant itself. To measure their success in this regard, and to show how right the Traditionalists have been in warning others about what the two-hearteds have been doing, all we need do is recognize that where only a little over a century ago every Hopi was Traditional and loyal, the steady disintegration has reduced the number of Keepers of the Covenant to a tiny fraction of what it once was, and in so doing has jeopardized both the fate of the Hopis and of the entire world.

What we are looking at then are not the innocuous doings of people who simply have different ways and opinions than those of the Elders. We are witnessing the planned and seditious destruction of a lifeway and culture the Creator himself chose to serve him in the preservation of the world. The gravity of the problem is not imagined. What you find in the *Techqua Ikachi* newsletters may on the surface seem like treatments of common political affairs, but between the lines are the two-hearteds coming from every side and cutting systematically away at something immensely beautiful and very special. To miss this in what you read now would be like going to a Kachina dance and seeing only the paint and costumes — never understanding and experiencing what is going on within the minds, hearts, and souls of the performers and the dance fathers. Or, it is akin to reading about the struggle for the land without probing the fact that without the land the Elders and other Traditional Hopi cannot do their appointed task of Keeping the Covenant. Take away the land and its elements, the spiritual roots are shredded, and the Keepers of the Covenant cannot function. Underneath every surface story being told here there is an accompanying and far more important revelation. Those who criticize the Elders for their stubbornness and for resisting progress cannot deny the plainest of facts. All of the things done to them by the Government, Tribal Council and Progressives have brought to pass precisely what Maasaw predicted they would: the virtual elimination — edge of extinction might be a better phrase — of the once magnificent Hopi culture.

THE ELDERS

The other villages have chosen Bahanna's way of life. They should have dropped their ceremonies. Maybe they don't have the courage to do this. Now even the Hotevilla people are influenced by American ways. Soon all the ceremonies will end here. When the elders die, the knowledge will be gone. Then whoever cares for land and life, and tends the fields to feed the people, will be recognized as our leader.

OUR PRAYER TO MAASAW THE GREAT SPIRIT:

HERE I AM ASKING YOU...
YOU WHO OWN THE WORLD...
THERE ARE TWO OF YOU.
IT IS YOU WITH THE SIMPLE WAY OF LIFE WHICH IS EVERLASTING THAT WE FOLLOW.
YOU HAVE THE WHOLE UNIVERSE,
WE DO NOT FOLLOW THE MATERIALISTIC GOD.
WE ASK YOU, WITH YOUR STRENGTH,
TO SPEAK THROUGH US.
WITH THE PRAYERS OF ALL THE PEOPLE HERE WE SHALL RECLAIM THE LAND FOR YOU.

In Issue No. 9, November/December 1976, the Elders ask the poignant question, "What is Hopi?" Can you imagine coming to the point in time where there is even a need to ask that!

TI— "What is Hopi? What does the word Hopi mean or stand for? These questions have been on the lips of many who have flocked to Hopi Land or who have encountered the Hopi visiting in their towns or cities. In the early days, when many anthropologists asked, we would proudly tell them Hopi means 'Peace' and that we are peaceful people. The word is used everywhere by people in high places around their negotiating tables such as the media, television, newspapers, films, etc. It must mean something, because peace is equivalent to our name. Actually, Hopi means many things, such as peace between yourself and others; or a word signifying obedience to the great laws and beliefs. Peace is a valuable element. Without peace, one cannot create harmony.

But that kind of peace was something we Hopis knew long ago, for at this moment in time Hopi has reached a sad state — interpreting it as peaceful today would not be positively truthful. The value of the word Hopi seemingly has declined, for peace has become a playful instrument and a defensive mask or cloak used to hide destructive thoughts, weapons and armies. Yes, Hopi was once our proud name, like a family tree. Sadly though, clever and ambitious men can find many ways to take advantage of the name Hopi in order to satisfy their personal desires. We have written about this topic in one of our past publications. We bring it up again in this issue so our readers will not be misled into believing the Hopi tribe is presently one big, peaceful family.

In the past, the news media, mainly the puppet press *Qua'toqti* (progressive Hopi newspaper), *strongly proclaimed that the Hopi Tribal Council and the Hopi leaders that support them have full authority over the entire Hopi tribe.* In fact, this group refers to itself as the 'Hopi Tribe.' One can easily be misled by their false claims and portrayals to the outside world. For there are in fact, two groups of Hopis — Traditional Hopi and the Hopi Tribe.

For many years, Traditional Hopi have maintained an organized body, controlling the functions of the yearly cycles, struggling for survival based on spiritual life and nature, and believing progress leads only to ruin. The so-called Hopi Tribe is something like a club which was organized just a few years ago. Only those that register can be members, but other methods of acceptance are used to keep the balance of political power in their favor. Besides, the Hopi Tribe is controlled by converted Hopi who, along the way, have abandoned their own original religion for greener pastures. Of course, what they have done is strictly against the Hopi Religious Code of Law. As in other religions, once this is done the name Hopi is lost to him or taken away automatically because he has lost trust in the Great Spirit.

Therefore, this newly established so-called Hopi Tribe is in this sense phony and has no right to use our name to make deals with outside interests. It would be better if, out of respect for the Great Spirit, this so-called 'Hopi Tribe' would find another name.

It is now more clear than ever that we cannot dismiss what we have grown into. We have learned that our feelings are more comfortable within the shadow of our own family tree, for it is a good shade producer, made by the Great Spirit in order to protect and defend us."

Why Are There Factions in Hopi?

TI— "Let us look into our immediate surroundings. At one time, the Hopi were stable and united. Why are they now continually breaking up into factions? We may refer to three sets of factions: **The Traditional Hopi, the Progressive Hopi,** and the **On-the-Fence Hopi.**

The **Progressives** consist of people who have accepted various sects of white-man's religion, and are usually considered to be more educated because they have spent more years in the Bahanna run schools. Some lean more or less on tradition and religion, and some do not participate in ceremonies at all. They frequently hold higher level offices of a nontraditional nature, tend to be domineering, and in some way reject Hopi teachings.

On-the-Fence Hopi still practice Hopi religion and tradition, are members, sometimes officers, in ceremonies, believe in adjustment through acculturation, and support the Progressives. Some are members of the so-called Hopi Tribal Council. Both recognize a certain Progressive as a super-commander over all Hopi villages, and over the entire Hopi nation. They likewise recognize an elected, law-making body which has courts, and jails, and judges, and lawyers to make decisions under the advice and influence of the Bureau of Indian Affairs (BIA) of the United States Government.

*The **Traditional Hopi** are those who strongly adhere to their aboriginal law, which they believe the Creator, or Great Spirit, laid out for them. As they see it, this is the most important thing. To stray from this pattern would be to stray from life itself. The Hopi believe that life and nature are of the same body, and that we must keep harmony with each other and keep the earth in balance. It is essential and vital that we care for the earth and all its unseen forces in order to keep a healthy environment. This is accomplished through religious ceremonial duties which required profoundest concentration, and can only be done rightfully without interruption and by remaining free from evil elements.*

Because of this the Traditional Hopi oppose all development programs, both cultural and environmental, and any encroachment by outside interests, such as the Progressives are promoting, without approval from the rightful Hopi leaders. This stand is based firmly upon the premise that the Hopi laid claim to this land through the Great Spirit before any other race set foot here, and that they were placed here to protect the land. Thus the Traditionals refuse to recognize the progressive Tribal Council, and reject the idea of being dominated by any other government, especially through this new system of leadership.

Traditional representation on the U.S. Government-sponsored Hopi Tribal Council has never materialized, for it has actually never been endorsed by the people or their leaders, with the exception of those self-elected for personal gain. These self-elected persons for obvious reasons frown upon the Traditional ways.

Now who would want to interrupt the Hopi way of life, and why? The white race wants to civilize the "Indians" because they see them as savages. They either kill them or Christianize them because they want what the "Indians" have.

Key to Hopi

Their boundaries and Landmark xxx

312

They didn't get all of it, so they formed the BIA through which they manage the native people and their natural resources. Still there stood another obstacle: the *Traditionals*, who are stubborn, but peaceful. They are even too stubborn to take up arms! So the attack took the form of forced assimilation under threat of punishment. One result of this was the eviction of the Traditionals from Oraibi in 1906. Still they would not yield. But the high officials did not have to scratch their heads for very long for a new idea; they simply formed a government within the tribe, one that would be more easily manipulated. The time was ripe, for by now there were enough educated Hopi, *and the prophecies foretold that one day Hopi children with short hair or bald heads would be the ears and mouth for the elders, and in time become the leaders.* So the Hopi Tribal Council was formed.

Still there was resistance. There was no support from the Traditionals, so this effort died. The U.S. Government saw that they needed something that would revive the Tribal Council, so the lawmakers came up with the Indian Reorganization Act. This woke up the dead Tribal Council. Under new leadership the whole tribe was to benefit. Anything asked would be done with honor, for all to enjoy, no strings attached, so they said. Still the old Hopi shook their heads — they had no confidence in the Council. Again the promoters of the Council were at their wits end.

So they once more put their heads together. This time they organized 'The Hopi Tribe,' and said that all "Hopi" must register to vote in an election of new leaders. Perhaps those who did not join would not be recognized as Hopi. The old Hopi still shook their heads — 'Why elect new leaders? We already have leaders.' So the Progressives decided to attract a following by creating jobs. Eventually large numbers of young people were attracted. No questions were asked as to where this would lead, and the job seekers automatically became members of 'The Hopi Tribe' without knowing everything they should. This is the stage we are in now.

So we know who *started* it — the United States Government. But who among the Hopi is to blame for the disastrous things that are going on now, the **Traditionals**, the **Progressives**, or the **On-the-Fence** Hopi? We shall try to answer this question in the coming issues of our newsletter."

Destruction or Survival — Old Dried Up Roots!

TI— "As we have said before, we have not rested since Bahanna (white man) encroached upon Hopi Land. We thought we might be able to rest when we moved from our mother village Oraibi — instead, Bahanna is resting because he has created his own flock of servants and slaves out of our own brothers and sisters to do his dirty work for him. Who knows, perhaps by the time this issue reaches the public, his work will already be completed.

Bahannas think everything is wonderful when they are hiding under the name of ecology. They think taking such care of the environment as is economically possible will be enough. But all things in the universe are tied together. They think all things such as earth and heavenly bodies will last forever, including the sun, moon and earth. But if even the functions of any one of these three were significantly changed, replacing the balance of the universe and world would be impossible. *For years our founding fathers have passed the knowledge of survival from mouth to mouth — which is 'to respect all living things, for we are all one and created by One.'* It seems most people have forgotten this concept of the right way of survival. They have replaced it with defensive tactics, and as a result are always running behind. They are racing steadily downhill to ruins — we mean all nations on earth are doing this. People must skid to a stop and look around. There might be an old dried-up root visible near you; get hold of it for support until you see the light. [Author's question: Could these 'dried-up old roots' be the Hopi Elderly Elders?]

We, the Traditional Hopi people, are at the stage now where we are not ashamed to say that every Hopi must choose whether it will be Hopi Traditionals or Puppet Traditionals that are followed. Perhaps we are at the point in time that this choice must come to pass; for one must follow his own philosophy to meet his own end. At Hopi, no one decides for others how it must be. We persuade, but we do not force. At Hotevilla, we have made our decision. We have followed the basis upon which our village was settled, which is to fulfill the Great Spirit's instructions. We are proud to say we are still struggling to do this, even though we are at the threshold of defeat and are suffering the inner pains of humiliations. But we believe enough of our strength must still exist, because our consciences are clear of guilt. We still live by the great laws, while others nibble at them. Soon we may have to stand entirely alone, because others, for their own reasons, want to hide the truth.

Recalling some of the memories and experiences of one of our elders shows us some facts that concern every Hopi today. He reflects on what Bahanna has sowed since he claimed dominion over the Hopi and other nations.

Thus he begins…'I often think back through the years to the times of my youth, when we were one people in our mother village in Oraibi. Our ceremonial pattern was still in order. The duties of the rightful clan leaders were being carried on as they were long ago. As if by magic the rain would come. There was an abundance of fresh corn and other crops. The land was green to feed the animals. I took this to mean we were being blessed, and thought this wonderful life would go on forever without interruption.

The elders would tell stories of the past. The prophecies of things to come were told and retold. But at this young age my inner mind was not fully developed. I was confused by what seemed like meaningless and idle talk, because the things of which they spoke did not yet exist. But as I grew older it was a sad fact to experience the things they talked about. As I relate my story I am sure someone will accuse me of lies and dreams of the past which cannot be lived again, and of prophecies that cannot materialize. Though many of the things that were foretold have come to pass, some we are now experiencing are part of ongoing prophecies. *Since the dimensions in time and space vary in accordance with the conduct of man and nature*, there are certain confirmations by which we can recognize the stage we are in. One such prophecy, for example, foretells that one day our land will be taken

man's chemicals have ruined the soil now

over for development. So today the housing projects are beginning. To some people this seems like a good thing, but to people of knowledge it is not good. Rather it is just another case of Bahanna's system of laws that lessen our hold on the land. The Creator's law teaches us that we must not yield to this, for it will break up our way of life and put the Hopi and other nations out of existence. For we are waiting for our white brother to help us, and he might come and find we have forsaken the sacred laws and instructions. Then he will whip us without mercy, either this or nature herself will take over, for we will have proved ourselves too weak to deserve what was promised to us by the Creator.

We knew that one day a strange people would appear in our midst, people who create man in their own image. Once given his language and knowledge, our own people will become the instrument by which he will try to rule over us and carve the rest of us into his image. Our own people will become his tools, and he will make certain they do a good job.

But if we remain strong and firmly rooted we will not be reshaped, whereas others will slump because they will be rootless. So when the tests come we must possess the strength to preserve ourselves.

[handwritten margin note: TRue Disciples Had all thing common]

As time goes by, for self-gain people will struggle for power to rule. But most of these efforts will be in vain, for whoever leads must allow for the distribution on equal value among the land and all life placed there by the Creator. In His plan, everyone shares equally.

Each race will create a different system to go by once their leadership becomes distorted by mistakes or destructive ways. The Traditional Hopi are prepared. For us the lines of leadership are already firmly drawn, for we know that along the way some rightful leaders and people may forsake and stray from their sacred duties, eventually using their ceremonials the wrong way for influence or commercial gain. *When this happens even the most important function must be discontinued until we find our way again and respect them rightly.*

It will often be asked in these uncertain years, 'Who will carry on the spiritual power and authority when the last of the present elderly religious leaders dies?' Although the leadership at Hotevilla will function normally without the Kikmongwi, since through the pattern of the life cycle bestowed on them and all mankind all of the religious leaders have the same power and authority to lead their people, the answer is that leadership will pass to some person who is clinging to the Creator's great laws — someone who is a strong and stable person ignoring the lingering pressures of destruction, and willing to die in honor of the Great Spirit — someone who knows this stand is not for himself, but for all people, land and life. When this does happen, as it surely will, the people of the destroyer will sieze upon this and use the word, *leaderless,* as a weapon they hope will bring the humble to their knees. In spite of this threat, all Traditionals must stand firm.

I was fortunate to witness and share in gatherings with the great leaders to review the instructions and prophecies that were often held in Oraibi before the division among our people caused by the intervention of Bahanna. At that time the theme of each gathering centered in oneness, and we all spoke in the same terms. The Bear, Fire, and the Spider clans occupied the authoritative seats in front of the others. Pipes were smoked and exchanged as a sign of brotherhood, symbolizing the understanding of our support for one another. The talk of the Bear Clan leader would be resumed by the Fire Clan leader, and the Spider Clan leader would correct any mistakes that were made. Meetings would last far into the night. Until my understandings were fully developed, I wondered why they always talked along the same pattern. As I grew older I began to understand the purpose. As we follow the pattern of life, our individual lifestyles might change, and some of us might become mixed up and even fall to the opposing forces who have their materialistic advantages. But there will always be resistance from those of us who stand together and adhere to the great laws.

As the authoritative leaders die out, people of bad intentions will seek out leaders with whom they can deal for their own ends. People with good intentions will also seek for the right leaders to help them regain what was rightfully theirs from the beginning.

Since both the Bear Clan and the Fire Clan have authority given to them by their stone tablets, should they ever make a weakening mistake, they exchanged vows concerning the manner in which their power would be surrendered. Should all three authorities fail, it would go to the next person in line; or to any person still traveling on the rightful path.

I have come to understand now that this doctrine has to be followed today as it has been followed since the dawn of time by people in power and authority. We can now look back and see our fallen brothers. In many cases we will fight for power by leaning on the hereditary value of our clan, but if one makes a mistake it is all in vain.

As far as I can remember, no words replacing the great laws were ever spoken. To forget or change them would lose the life they hold for all mankind.

I speak here of the doctrine followed in Oraibi, where we Hotevilla people came from. We have several mesas on which are situated many villages, each of which is independently governed. Perhaps they have their own system or pattern to follow in order to preserve themselves when faced with distorting or destructive influences.

Yes, I see, and I am aware of many things which were foretold. It was foretold that man's clothing would be taken over by women. Also skirts have been raised above the knee, as predicted, devaluing the sacred body of the female, indicating that many things will be devalued from the original. The lack of peace in our own spiritual being could trigger the revolution. So when the Hopi sees this his response is simple: 'We are now at the beginning of something!' Our character and conduct have changed. The respect we once had for each other is gone. We have forgotten how to greet, appreciate, and share with each other, and have become greedy to the point of competition. We are becoming militant against the weak, some resorting to Bahanna law here in our village for their own self-gain,

Love of man shall wax cold x

316

and without respect for the rightful leaders. Strong-arm tactics are employed. Our ceremonial dances and songs are waning spiritually. There are other signs too numerous to mention.

I need not look further. The landscape is dry. It has rained some but the plants and grass have not responded to it. Something is wrong. Let's look within ourselves. Perhaps we still have time to correct ourselves. For better or for worse we must try.

For example, I put a question to a young man who seems to be serious and always participates in ceremonial dances.

I asked him 'Why do you sing and dance?'

He answered, 'Because I'm Hopi and I enjoy dancing.'

'Do you know there are meanings in the songs and movements, that we hope will link our thoughts with the unseen forces so it will rain and grow our plants and we will have plenty to eat?' He looked at me with a smile and answered, 'Yeah, I know, but I have no field where I can plant. I dance to entertain so women and girls will enjoy my dancing.'"

Her Spirit Made Much Snow Fall

TI— "We respect and honor Mina Lansa, Kikmongwi of Old Oraibi in her passing on to the next life. Her spirit made much snow fall on our Mother Earth to give us strength to continue for the survival of the Hopi Way."

Hopi Identity — Our Appearance and Way Become a Sacred Symbol

TI— "We here in Hopi Land are always occupied with something throughout the year. The seasons themselves have their own way of keeping us busy and happy with Ceremonials, field labor, crafts, and much more.

All this continues, in spite of the never-ceasing encroachment of white man's culture, the ever-growing restrictions of their mind-bending laws which have begun to grind down the Hopi traditionals' strength and morale. The New Movement of the New Age (the Progressives) no longer respect true leadership; they rule and do what they see fit without the consent and guidance of their head leaders. To the people of the New Movement, we Traditionals are considered trouble-makers, dividers of people and obstacles of progress.

But we must carry on our purpose to protect the laws of nature and spirit which is our highest priority. Perhaps some of the (New Age) people understand *destruction* our position, but others think that what they're doing is harmless. We think they are destroying the link between Nature and Man. The warning signs are evident in many parts of the world. They had better consider the warnings signs that manifested themselves at Hopi this summer — if it means anything to them.

The harvest, we fear, will be very small, for we have had very little rain all summer long. The land and crops are as weary as we are. We can only watch to see what winter brings. If it doesn't snow, the spring will be drier. At the same time, in the coming winter months the feed will be scarce for the livestock and wild animals. *Drought*

There are always things of concern, and we must look upon them with open minds and hearts. Unless your focus is on personal enjoyment and persisting in efforts to kill the Golden Goose, unless you want to ignore the foolish laughter and you lack concern for others, you should focus your attention on determining why we are so concerned and down-hearted.

First, it is because all things are rooted to the Earth spiritually. While we were on our migrations we rooted our shrines into the Earth. Our villages, people and surroundings are all rooted with shrines and have been since we decided to settle permanently, in accordance with the instructions of the Great Spirit.

The markings we have left are our claim and testimony to our guardianship over this land as the first inhabitants to be placed here long before Columbus 'discovered America.' The truth is that he was merely one of the first Bahannas to step onto the shores of our land. All things have an identity, which is important for man. To Hopi, identity is found in a sacred symbol, in an emblem by which we know who we are. This is our proud possession that assures the survival of our future generations. It is an identity that must not, and so long as we can help it, will not fade away.

Our identity can be recognized in several ways. A Hopi is recognized by his language, customs and culture. Even the style of our hair and construction of our houses is important in this regard. Changing these ways would lessen the chances for our survival, for our long lost white Brother might be disturbed by this and decide not to return.

Sadly, most of us here have either forgotten or lack this knowledge, so our village identities are gradually being destroyed by the construction of white-man styled houses. Under the guise of false claims stating that the Hopis are in grave poverty, the construction of these houses has been prompted by the Tribal Council. We deny these claims and reject the project. As usual the boastful and the super rich take no heed of this, and they certainly know how to scramble with their bureaucracy to take advantage of us. This thing is wrong! No doubt the Progressives will look upon this story as a great step forward — but it could turn out to be a great step backward — a fading of our identity and independence because we are ignoring the wisdom of our head leaders.

Nevertheless, our readers can compare our present situation with those experienced by the ancient ones, for as happened with them our chances for survival are not yet gone. There has always been a group of people who survive to carry on. One difference today lies in the fact that the ancients did not know about nuclear warfare. Today's big powers have more powerful weapons, and they have exploited many newly revealed secrets of nature and used them wrongly. *They should remember that the Gods do not allow these kinds of secrets to become known unless the time has come for us to use them for the benefit of all living things. When the end is near we will see a halo of mist around the heavenly bodies. Four times it will appear around the sun as a warning that we must reform, telling us that all people of all colors must unite and arise for survival, and that we must uncover the causes of our dilemma.*

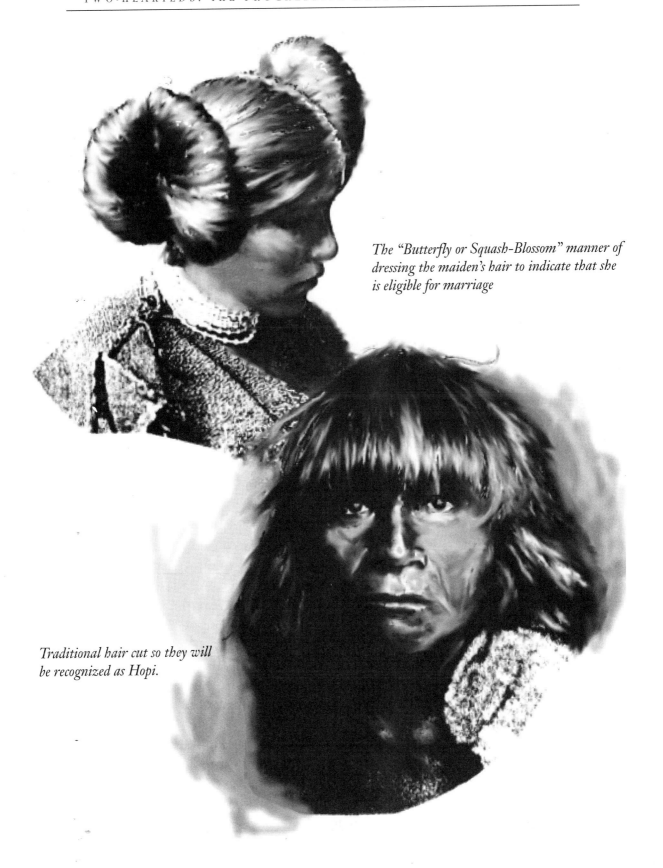

The "Butterfly or Squash-Blossom" manner of dressing the maiden's hair to indicate that she is eligible for marriage

Traditional hair cut so they will be recognized as Hopi.

Unless man-made weapons are used to strike first, peace will then come, and we must remember that <u>in all of man's history peace has never been accomplished through battle.</u>"

Changing Times in Hopi Land, and a Tribal Chairman's Belated Dream

TI— "Dear Readers, harvesting time is here again. Because of the dry summer months we doubted we would get very much from our crops, but it turns out that most of us will have our fill.

Still, the total harvest in Hopi land will be less this year than it should be. Many of the able Hopi farmers have let their fields lay idle in exchange for a wage salary base. This is gradually erasing our culture and our regard for the spiritual laws of nature, for rain and corn are the main important bases in all Hopi ceremonials.

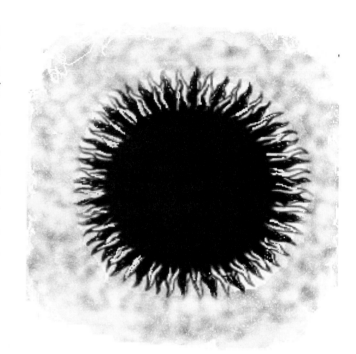

As we look upon the home scene, something is brewing within the Progressive Hopi society, which surprisingly is becoming 'born again' to Hopi tradition. This means they feel that they, the Progressives, can still participate in Traditional ceremonials and other activities which are a part of Hopi life. They think this is a way to keep the identity of the Hopi tribe alive.

Yet this idea is no consequence, because <u>most of the children, and even grown-ups, are forgetting their language</u> — so how can they understand the ancient songs and movement commands that are used? <u>Intermarriage with other tribes and races are depleting the identity of what we are.</u> All these things have been foretold repeatedly by our elders and taught us to beware that Bahanna education would lead us into pitfalls from which we will never escape."

Pipe Dreams and Control

TI— "The following article describes a Hopi Tribal Chairman's dream about the <u>return to ancient ways and a Traditional lifestyle</u>, a dream which may be far too late in coming.

It is Hopi Tribal Chairman Sidney's view that once Hopi reclaim their land from the Navajo the Hopi will return to their traditional life style. That in taking the lead on new land they have to respect the traditions of the Hopi people. He claims this message was relayed to him by numerous Hopi people and village leaders. <u>The young people who are moving to 900,000 acres of land are the beginning.</u> Someday there will be another village. Its blue print and design will be drawn in the near future.

where are these acres?

The tribal government will provide the people with guidelines and aid in financial assistance. The Hopi tribe has over 200 applicants for homesite use of the Hopi partitioned lands. Presently they are being effectively denied the use of this much-needed land by the BIA and the Navajo tribe.

The Hopi tribe needs the use of the land for the purpose of agriculture, grazing, homesites, and other forms of economic self-sufficiency. The Hopi are a growing tribe, Sidney says, and we need our land in order to continue to survive as a people and culture. The tribe will attempt to preserve their culture and religion, a belief system that is tied to our land. Land is food, family and the Great Spirit. The impact of intrusion will never be erased.

In another statement, Chairman Sidney declared in his keynote address that, 'The Hopi have been traditionally self-supporting. We do not want to rely on the Federal Government. I want to be the first Chairman to say to President Ronald Reagan, 'The Hopi people are self-sufficient. Thank you but we don't need your Federal Funds, social programs. Give these funds to those that do.'

Just give us back our land

What do we think of the Chairman's statement? We admit that, because in some ways it goes along with the traditional views, it sounded good to us. But after reflecting on it, as we see it from another side, we think it is a cunning way to gain support for his fight against the Navajo…a political tactic to sway Hopi and others to his side. It could all be just a dream, and we are not inclined to buy it. He may be opening up another Pandora's box.

Restlessness and complaints are now in evidence among us because of the strict rules coming out of the Tribal Council. One cannot own livestock without a permit and paying a fee for each head. Even the total number one can own is controlled by a limit on the number of heads of livestock anyone may have.

Reclaimed land will not be free to the applicants for homesites. The land and other things will be leased to them, and this spells debt. Large numbers of Hopi view this as anything but a traditional life style.

The Traditional Hopi system is that the land is free and open to those with enough energy and ambition to make a livelihood from the land. But Progressive Hopi claim that Traditional Hopi have never contributed anything of benefit to the Hopi people, that instead they prevent the Hopi from progressing together with the material world.

We will admit that this is true in some ways. But it seems to us that it is the Progressives who are blind to the benefits of the Hopi traditional system. Ours is a way of holding and protecting the land for the people and children to come, so that they can have land and use it freely. The traditional system is best because it alone can last forever and assure the best food that the land can offer, also the health and happiness for a better life. These are the benefits Traditional Hopi contribute. These and many more are the benefits by which Hopi have survived for thousands of years. Therefore the Hopi do not need to add a new ingredient — especially one that might not harmonize with what Hopi have had in their possession for ages. Which is a proof that this ancient system must be good.

Hopi prophecy says that if in the name of progress we link ourselves with a culture not our own it will become difficult to regain what we discard. Of course, we can go through the motions and continue to practice what we have lost, but it will have no value. What happens toward the end will be the consequences of our carelessness."

Will This Unity Movement End in a New Turn or a New Age?

TI— "In our last newsletter we talked about the friction sickness that exists within the Hopi Nations (individual villages). We realize of course that it is not only Hopis who are victimized. It has been a long time problem among other nations on our planet Earth. Blood has been shed daily in many violent ways, because of frictions among mankind. We believe the motive for this is that we often do not agree about certain things such as knowledge and beliefs.

Not long ago a meeting was called and a Unity Movement was introduced in Hopi Land. With caution we examined the details and found its basis was sound. It was clear to us that without unity the Hopi may not gain their goal, while with unity there is some chance. There is a possibility Hopi will succeed if all the Hopi villages unite. If the plan works out, Hopi will gain control and be able to live in their own ways, to control the land and its resources and to restore Traditional culture and beliefs — including those needed to maintain our identity as Hopi.

At that meeting all of the leaders from all the Traditionally established villages were present and agreed that this is a long awaited desire of the Hopi which has finally arrived. So with one exception, it was agreed to organize, and the name 'United Sovereign Hopi Independent Nations' was adopted.

However, the Traditional religious leaders and people of Hotevilla Village chose not to join. They chose to maintain their position as an independent nation as has been the case since the founding of the Village of Hotevilla in 1906. There was no sign of dispute or friction about this because everyone knew each village has a self-governing body.

People must understand that even though all Hopi Villages are already united on a spiritual level, the local political matters in each village are something else. Because their rejections are based on their knowledge and beliefs, the fact is that this is not the first time Hotevilla Village has rejected what may harm their stand.

We remind you that Hotevilla was established for a specific purpose, which was and is to protect and preserve their beliefs. Hotevilla has been looked upon with scorn because most Hopis, thanks to Bahanna education and Tribal Council brainwashing, think the people of Hotevilla believe and follow the impossible. We give you this glimpse into this new turn of events because there may be questions that arise.

Going back a bit to the U.N. meeting in New York, we are concerned that there seemed to be an awareness of disharmony among the Hopi delegation. This may be so, but the problem is not so serious that it cannot be mended. What saddens us most is the fact that in this instance we are not responsible.

Our conclusion: We hope you will understand and consider all the ancient Teachings we have passed on to you over the past years. We believe that through understanding we will succeed in preserving the Hopi tradition and culture. We are the only remnant of the Hopi people with the original faith. We were taught that our Great Creator does not depend upon numerical factors or material strength — that working under His banner is all of the strength needed to produce miracles."

Brief True Tales — The Bahanna Germ Is Even Among the Progressives Themselves

TI— "We often wish we could write something that would make you laugh and be happy, because we are mostly happy people and laugh a lot. But because we are always dealing with serious things here, it seems we always lay grief on your shoulders by telling tales of doomsday. We feel very humble about this, and know that you must be getting tired of hearing of our problems. We want you to know that it is OK for you to feel that way, because the efforts you put behind us are strong. You are like a cane we can lean on when the climbing is hard so that we won't fall.

But it does seem that since the Bahanna came there is always friction between the Traditional Hopi and the Progressive Hopi. It is like a sickness which refuses to heal. We call this the Bahanna germ, and it is a sure killer that has spread to every village. Does the Bahanna Government enjoy this? We were so contented once. Now when one family decides to bring into their home a Bahanna convenience, such as water or an electric line, it creates friction between the one who wants it and those who oppose it. From this situation the titles were born, 'Traditional' and 'Progressive' Hopi. The friction goes on and on until one of us falls, and because we have no material or political power it is usually the Traditional Hopi. Right now, only the Traditional Hopi of Hotevilla has the upper hand in their village: this you know.

It appears however that now the sickness has infected the Progressives themselves. Are you surprised to learn that there is now friction between Progressive and Progressive? You shouldn't be. But in one village the Progressive Hopi have had a dispute with progressive teachers over a school problem."

[TEM— As a matter of clarification I insert here, as I did earlier, that I capitalize Progressive when I am referring to those Hopis who have adopted and pursue Bahanna ways. They are a definable group as opposed to someone whose attitudes are progressive in nature, as in this case the progressive teachers in the schools are. In the same way I capitalize Government when I am referring to the United States Government, as opposed to government, which in the lower case can refer to any governing body, or a way of administering. In the *Techqua Ikachi* newsletters, however, the lower case is used for both the U.S. government and progressive Hopis. In quoting them, I leave it as they — their Bahanna typists to be more exact — I doubt that the Elders and their transcribers ever discussed the matter — rendered it.]

"So here friction has developed between the Progressive Hopi and the progressive school teachers. In this case the angry progressive teachers are even suing troublesome progressive Hopi. So the Progressive Hopi asked the Progressive Hopi Chairman for support, and the Progressive Chairman did not respond! So friction increased between the Progressive Hopi and the Progressive Chairman. In the meantime, the Progressive Hopi chairman made friends with his long time foe, the Progressive Navajo Chairman. He did this to settle the land question. Then the Progressive Hopi rejected this idea, so more friction developed between the Progressive Hopi and the Progressive Chairman. The friction has now become so bad that the Progressive Hopi have passed a petition to kick the Progressive Chairman out of office! At this writing the situation has not been resolved.

Meanwhile the Traditional Hopi can for once sit back and rest in leisure. We mean we are able to rest our minds from the troublesome problems — which we know naturally could reawaken any day. We are not exactly rested physically however, for there seems to be a wedding revolution going on in Hopi Land, and it seems Hotevilla weavers always get the job of weaving the bridal robes and making the buckskin moccasins and all that goes with them. Our robe weavers complain that they are tired and they must also tend their fields. So they wish the youngsters would slow down on their romances. Good day."

We Need to Tell You About the Day the Sun Stood Still

TI— "What we say here could offend many of our fellow men. But it does not matter, for we ourselves can be blamed for much of our shortcomings. We have a very sad feeling that the Po-wa-mu-ya ritual is losing its power and value. Something is wrong. Could it be that we are using it as a plaything, or is it that we are just not giving it our serious attention?

Just as was predicted by our Ancients, in recent years many problems have begun to form. They said this would come to pass when we get hooked into a lifestyle that is not ours. Maybe the Ancients are right. Some of us have adopted a Bahanna lifestyle with all of its modern technology, modern entertainment, sex, alcohol, and drugs. Even money-making labor has taken the front seat in our daily life and ceremonialism. This lifestyle has kept our youngsters away from the Kivas, where they should be in order to learn to help in the ceremonial functions and to help preserve them for a long time to come. With this new Bahanna lifestyle comes foreign law and order, political organization, and from the Bahanna view a good education. We wonder though, do you think that all these modern concepts will help balance the natural order on earth and in the universe? Enough of this! Now let us consider Grandpa's dream about 'The Day The Sun Stood Still.'

This day seemed to begin as usual. People and surroundings appeared normal, the sound of birds chirping was normal. There was hardly any breeze. It was a good day for a winter month. The morning meal in every household was proceeding normally.

In one home Grandpa was as usual talking while he was eating. Was it about the same old things, the prophecies? No. Not this time. He changed the subject to today's world. These are the tactics he used to avoid boring the youngsters who were now grown up and attending the Bahanna school.

'I know the times have changed,' he began, 'and I know my words are useless and will not change your attitude toward a better way of life, which is the Hopi way. When I was your age I listened to my elders. I learned that religion and the divine laws we follow are important. I want to remind you that you youngsters are ignoring the ceremonials. You did not participate in any of the dances this winter, and you put your mother and father to shame. You should pay more attention to the doings here and not to go to so many movies, ball games, and Bahanna type dances. You should cut down on your sitting here all hours of the night watching TV. If you could see it my way and go to the kiva once in a while you would perhaps learn something valuable and irreplaceable. The worst thing I have heard is that you have been boozing around with the other boys. This sort of thing is bad for you and bad for everyone else. Do you know some day the Bahanna's world might collapse? Then we will all starve to death when Bahanna food stops coming in' Grandpa scolded mildly.

The eldest boy could take no more of this, so he shouted back at Grandpa. 'Starvation is impossible in this age. We have lots of Bahanna friends who will provide food for us.'

Grandpa said, 'You might have me there. But I don't think I want to be totally dependent upon my meat and other food having to come from my Bahanna friends nor any other Bahanna. There is security in providing for myself.'

Their old battery-powered radio suddenly blared out the news describing the latest happenings in Hopi Land. Everyone became silent to listen.

'This station brings you the latest news about Hopi Land. There seems to be something extraordinary going on out there. We just can't believe our ears! Surely this can't really happen where 'peaceful people' are supposed to live. First of all, there is a report that many of the Hopi Progressives are hopping mad about the Tribal Chairman being seen dining with the Hopis' long-time enemy, the Navajo Tribal Chairman. The suspicion is that they are up to something no good, and the Progressives are wondering whether he should be booted out of office.'

Grandpa is still dreaming wishful dreams:
'The Tribal Council members,' the radio report continued, 'were not satisfied with the four new Tribal Representatives certified by the Kikmongwi of 1st Mesa Village, wondering whether they were acceptable for seating on the Council. The Kikmongwi group called a meeting with the 1st Mesa Election Board who claims to have a say. They failed to appear. The Kikmongwi's decision was to return to the traditional ways in appointing his own representative. Later on, the Election Board met with clan leaders. Since the Kikmongwi was not present, they voted to unseat the Kikmongwi's certified representative permanently.

Representatives from Second Mesa Village and Moencopi Village have reported that they were threatened with removal from Tribal Council membership because they had voted to support the retaining of the 1st Mesa representative.

There is a reported drop in the number of housing participants because they were not fully informed about the housing project land assignments and the responsibilities and obligation involved with the project.

The Tribal Chairman announced that there will be a meeting in Phoenix regarding the <u>water table decline in Hopi Land</u>. This decline could be resulting from <u>water withdrawals at Peabody Coal</u>. There is also evidence of unfair labor practices at the coal mine by the construction contractors.

The Supreme Court has supported a Circuit Court decision to allow development on the Hopi sacred San Francisco Peaks. Employment is dropping because of cuts in Tribal funds.

Hotevilla Community school is having some serious problems. Students are dropping out to go to other schools. There may not be enough funds available as a result of this.

The Village of Hotevilla is requesting a halt to land development activities in the Hotevilla and Bacabi area. Now we sign off, good day.'

A loud knock woke Grandpa with a jerk. 'Boy, what a dream!' he exclaimed! 'I wish the dream was real and all of these things really happened.' As he sat up rubbing his eyes, his grandson barged through the door sounding like a herd of running buffalo.

'Grandpa,' he yelled with excitement, 'there is fighting over the hill, I saw them firing guns in the air. These people are from Bacabi. They are mad because the Hotevillas say they are going to cut off the electric and water lines to the area.'

'I'll go over there and find out what is happening,' Grandpa said as he tried to calm the boy. It must actually be a conflict between the Progressive Hopis, he thought and scratched his head — the Traditionals would not use guns. Let the Progressives fight it out. So he flopped back and tried to resume his pleasant dream.'

'Now, let us get the sun moving again.' "

The Hopi Unity Movement May Already Be Dying Out.

TI— "A question has been raised about friction between Hopi Traditionals over the Unity Movement, about which news appeared in our last issue. We are very sorry this caused much confusion and saddened most of our readers. There is actually no hostility over this issue. All of us know that each village has their own guidelines to follow. The fact is, we see this as a political issue rather than a spiritual one.

What Hotevilla Village did was in accordance with space and time, and the guidelines set by our prophets long ago. They said that should we, as we travel along the way, find ourselves out of step with the Great Creator, we must stop and ask ourselves whether we have become careless. Then we must not follow those who become tangled in what we are told not to do. Remembering this, Hotevilla chose not to join the Unity movement. <u>Hotevilla is the only village which to this day is fighting to keep out modern conveniences</u>.

This may sound out of tune with modern life to most people, but it is a protective measure that defends our sovereignty and independence. Already, the Hopi Unity movement is failing. Four villages have bowed out, each for their own reasons."

A Welcome Moment of Relaxation

TI— "Greetings. No doubt many of you are anxious to hear how things are going here in our village. We are pleased to inform you that some of the worrisome problems have calmed down. So, after long years of oppression, we at last are more relaxed as we live our lifestyle in the way it should be. We are hoping this will lead us to peaceful ways of life. Perhaps someday the solution will be found to free us entirely from anxiety. We pray that a time will come when we will be free to be independent."

Wisdom of the Hopi

TI— "When we were youngsters our elders gave us plenty of advice, or perhaps a better expression would be, told us about the facts of life. Because of our lack of understanding at our early age we would rather play than listen to their old songs which we had heard many times before.

The songs would begin with words that said: 'Each of us are put on this earth to do some task, which is to fulfill our life purpose. We come at different times, with others to follow us just as we followed those who had gone before. They say we come to this world just to visit. Our behavior is tested and then we go on to the next phase or sequence of life. Some of us leave good marks, some do not. We are judged by what we leave behind. As we are fulfilling our lives, we search for the best way to satisfy our life style. Along the way, our elders said, the people and the world will change. Factions will develop in Hopi Land. The Hopi must search for and choose the path which will best satisfy his ideal way of life. The Hopi must compromise and adjust his life accordingly, hoping he has chosen the best way to achieve happiness. They say our life is one great play or drama in which we all take our part when our turn comes. We are the actors. We are all given different tasks to perform which will either bring benefits and good things, or will produce evil things.'

On this earth we are also gifted with different religions to guide us in good ways. Some will forget the right ways. Many will simply be pretenders. But our elders say the best way is not to forsake the Great Creator's divine laws. The time will come when many of us will put material laws above the Great Spirit's laws. Yet in time of need, the wealthy, the poor and the disbelievers will abandon these things and cry out to the Great Spirit for His help. This proves we cannot forever avoid the common belief that there is an unseen Power which affects our lives. Our elders say this Power exists so that we may work with this Power to do the tasks we are gifted with. Don't let the burden of worries trouble you into sickness. Let your hearts be filled with happiness, enjoy your lives to the fullest, for this is the best medicine for sickness. Live long, for there are great exciting adventures awaiting you. So time passes on and the prophecies of our ancient people begin to unfold. Many great events lie before us, and we are witnessing with astonishment today the fact that our ancients' words were right."

Sadness and Hope Seem to Go Hand in Hand

TI— "Greetings from Hopi Land. We trust everything is well with you. For some time now we have felt somewhat gloomy and dejected, but we know that sooner or later all good things come to an end.

Something happened to make us feel this way. We know that we should not grieve over the mistakes our youngsters made or let their insulting remarks hurt us. After all, they were inspired by older Progressives. And, they do not know what they are doing. This is about the repairs to the trail down to the spring. Because of the trail's sacredness, the procedure was improperly done through not consulting the religious leaders for advice.

After some years of friction between the young Progressives and the old Traditional Hopi, thanks to the incoming Bahanna elements the Progressives formed what they called the 'Hotevilla Village Committee.' Then they attempted to make improvements for the village without consulting the village leader. Afterward, they had a sudden change of heart. They wanted to establish the village as a 'traditional village,' and approached on their own a department of the BIA and the Tribal Council. Since at this time we were having trouble with a neighboring village (Bacabi) expanding into our land, we were delighted the youth decided to support the elders. Most of our people were swayed into believing they would even merge with the elders.

They proposed to repair the trail to the sacred spring. When the time came for the work to begin, the leaders expected them to come and seek advice — as is customary. Instead they started the work themselves and were confronted by the leaders. This was in vain. The elders had been deceived and it really broke their hearts. They were badly insulted, and told that they were useless now and should not interfere…that they had not after many years made any apparent progress for the village…that it is now time for the young Progressives to do it themselves. Many of the things they said were condemnations of the old order of the village and the top leaders.

So in their own way they have demolished the significance of what the trail represents. It is a sacred pathway used for religious ceremonial purposes. The result is that their actions have reawakened friction within our own village community. We trust this will heal soon so that we will again be able to depend on one another for the good of the Community.

TRuth shall make thee FREE. my heart is with the Hopi Ancients

Forgive them for they know Not

trail to the sacred spring

We are not happy to write about such things, but feel we should tell the truth about how things are here, that we should not let others believe that we are all one and agree about everything."

How a Traditional Hopi Works and Thinks

TI— "There has long been a misunderstanding of the Hopi — how he or she works and thinks. People who come here to learn about Hopi often leave disappointed. They quickly learn that a Hopi keeps their own values to themselves, and are reserved in manner. They discover that Hopi are sensitive about being boastful of their deeds or performance, and about the position they hold in the community. They find that a person believes humility is important in their ceremonies and prayers, and even in the politics they use to achieve their goals and rewards.

But the visitors are also surprised when they learn this reserved attitude does not mean that the Hopi will stand silently by and let outsiders take away from them those things that their life and hopes are rooted in. They are sensitive and always cautious of the dangers of seeming benefits coming mainly through foreign Government sources which would erode their own knowledge and wisdom to the point where they search for and find loopholes in prophecy which allow them to accept any new proposals. So to this day Hotevilla is still a village standing by itself, holding fast to traditional wisdom, and making the effort to follow the pattern of the Great Spirit's plans."

CONCLUSION: TO THOSE WHO ARE
WILLING TO STAND UP AND BE COUNTED

TI— "It may interest you to know that all knowledge and wisdom based on archaeological aspects (the ancient past) is respected by the Hopi. In this case the voice of the multitude is not important in making decisions regarding the keeping of the Covenant. The wisdom accumulated by anyone who is willing to stand up and be counted is respected. Anyone with a strong spirit and strength who is unafraid of reaching our goal of destiny, which is for the good of the earth and all life, can undertake the tasks involved, and can count on support from others. There is a saying, 'If one or two be strong, three or four will be greater under the banner of our Great Creator.'

We hope you are enjoying reading our free paper, and hope you have learned a bit about Hopi and support us in the cause we are struggling for. That is, in preserving Hopi culture for coming generations. Thank you with all our blessings. Good day."

THE GOVERNMENT AND THE BUREAU OF INDIAN AFFAIRS

Migration Story — Once Upon a Time in a Pure Land

TI— "The Hopi elders tell a story of the great migration which is very long and differs in certain aspects from clan to clan and village to village. Our Traditional Elders say that:

'Long, long ago, there were nomad-like people who had a sacred purpose as they roamed this continent. The land was pure and these people traveled by foot with their belongings on their backs, for they did not know about animals of burden to carry them and their goods. Harmony with nature was in full bloom — health was assured as food was plentiful and one could live off the land with little effort.

These people had a great knowledge of the teachings and prophecies for their sacred knowledge had not yet been twisted to mislead the masses as is reflected in today's age. They had learned from what was known about previous worlds that man brings about his own downfall by both forgetting and repeating his past mistakes. So the people were obedient to the great laws and instructions given to them by the Great Spirit, for these instructions were their means of guarding and protecting the land from all harm.

Through the inspiration and forewarning of the Great Spirit, man could foretell events centuries in advance and therefore knew that some day strange people would come ashore to take over the land. We Hopi remember the historical event of this first meeting with the stranger who came asking permission to share the land with us. Knowing that someone was coming, Maasaw put his footprints on the shore, perhaps as a test to see if the stranger would respect them and understand that the land was already occupied. The stranger did not respect the footprints and so Massau appeared as a person. The stranger then asked him, 'Are these your footprints and do you live here?' Maasaw confirmed this, so the stranger then asked his permission to stay and settle on the land.

The Great Spirit remained silent, and pointing offshore suggested that they should sit down on a log that extended out into the ocean. Again, the man asked for permission, but Massau replied, 'First move a little toward the water for I'm getting crowded, and then I will answer.' He repeated this command four times until the stranger was sitting above the water at the edge of the log. 'The land is already occupied and I cannot permit you to stay here — go back to the land that was given to you — this land was for a certain kind of people,' answered Massau. More words may have been spoken, but having no choice, the stranger kindly agreed to leave the same way he had come — perhaps by boat. But Massau knew that he would return — next time he would not come alone, but with others who would have great ambitions to take over the land.

These migrating people knew the importance of fulfilling Maasaw's instructions. They knew that they were to travel to all corners of the continent leaving rock writings and symbols as records of their migrations. Although they knew that others would come along, they trusted that these strangers would either leave or ask the first people's permission to settle. The people traveled on for years resisting temptation to stay too long in any one place where life became too easy and subject to corruption — they were to move on before a complete breakdown occurred. Their destination was EARTH CENTER — where all clans would gather and establish a permanent village and ceremonial pattern. After many years the people settled at what is now known as Oraibi, whose original and true name is *'Sip-Oraibi' meaning a place where the roots solidify.* Other surrounding villages were also established according to whatever instructions the people were given. All of these prophecies were retold from generation to generation. People with open minds can view today's events as being simply the astonishing fulfillment of these ancient prophecies. Even still, some people choose to disbelieve what is foretold, even when they see it come to pass. For them, these ancient signs do not appear to be the pathway to progress. So these old prophecies are avoided or ignored.

One might wonder what secrets our founding fathers have for survival. The secret is really very simple — anything that glitters with charm and lures one to promises and gain is temptation. The Traditional Hopi have made every effort to avoid such temptation by rejecting offers to improve themselves according to Bahanna standards. The True Hopi will not allow themselves to be induced by something foreign that could be harmful. So, they surround themselves with what appears to others to be superstition, taboo, bad luck, and even death in order to control and protect their key doctrines. Sadly, men who were unable to resist temptation gained powerful positions and found that no immediate harm came to them. Lacking clear vision, they were not able to see that their actions marked the beginning of gradual decline and the death of the Hopi way of life.

In connection with this story we find valuable the words of a wise man, "if good does not accumulate, it is not enough to make a name for a man. If evil does not accumulate it is not strong enough to destroy a man. But the inferior man thinks that goodness in small things has no value and so neglects them. He also thinks that small sins do no harm and does not give them up. So his sins accumulate until they can no longer be covered up and his guilt becomes so great that it can no longer be wiped out thus bringing him to ruin.'"

Tales of Horror Transformed into Tales of Greatness.
The Government and the Tribal Council Want To Get Us into Debt!

TI— "It is easily seen that we have been put through the mill ever since the coming of Bahanna. We knew that the white man's educational system would be fatal to the Hopi way. So, we refused to follow their path — which caused the government to strong-arm us by kidnapping our children and forcing them to be educated at gun point. In addition, tribal leaders were imprisoned and tortured for defending their children. Then, somewhere along the way, the U.S. government changed its tactics — perhaps because of pressure from certain powerful people who considered these 'sadistic' methods against the Hopis to be completely un-American. Unfortunately, other ambitious people found new ways to further harass the peaceful Hopi. Reduction of their animal stock was enforced and the

Economy is based on how much time a family spends cultivating in the fields and gardens.

TI— Maasaw: "There will come a time when you will come to two paths. Seek your wisdom for directions to lasting peace or the destiny of fate."

Hopi had to either oblige or suffer the consequences. Those refusing had their entire animal supply confiscated and sold for a dollar a head to people who cooperated with government agents. To make matters even worse, our young ladies were stripped naked and thrown into sheep-dip filled vats for amusement. Are these the actions by which the United States of America is considered a great nation? No wonder we Hopis look upon government services with dismay and suspicion, knowing that acceptance of any of these services continues to jeopardize our future."

[TEM— Enlarging upon references to this elsewhere, Dan inserts here a comment that shows how cleverly the BIA operated where livestock was concerned. Before land control was inaugurated, a Hopi, whose land was assigned to him by the kikmongwi of his village, could have as many livestock as he felt he could afford and successfully manage. Under the new policy, boundaries were set for each homeowner that reduced the size of his land. Then the Government decided whether it thought the herds were too large for the land to support. Anything over that total became the property of the BIA to dispose of as it saw fit. They would then either kill the excess, or pay the Hopi some ridiculously low price for it and sell it to a slaughterhouse, or if it was in excellent condition and had real value, it would be bought for next to nothing from the Hopi and then sold for a much higher price to a Bahanna rancher. In either of the latter two cases, the BIA would keep the proceeds as a just reward for the time and effort involved.]

TI— "When the old traditional Hopi leaders refused to knuckle under to government pressures, a new way of stealing from the Hopis was concocted. This new way was through the formation of the Hopi Tribal Council, an organization made up of only a very few Hopis who, motivated by personal ambitions, betrayed their sacred Hopi teachings by swiftly accepting all government services. Then with backing from the Bureau of Indian Affairs, the Hopi Tribal Council leased our sacred land and allowed it to be raped through exploration and coal-mining developments. Even worse, ignoring the voices of Traditional village leaders and chiefs, they sold a great portion of our Mother Earth for $5,000,000 dollars.

If these things aren't enough to do a Hopi in, then get him drunk and talk him into signing something called a mortgage — a procedure which the Indian didn't have before and did not at all understand. He had no experience in these things, and no one to guide him. He certainly did not realize that if he could not pay off this mortgage his property would be foreclosed and he would be shut out of his own land! Another point is that the indebtedness incurred becomes an attachable claim on both a person's house and farm land. Therefore, the BIA and Tribal Council gain control of both, and can then lease the farm land to outsiders who want it for its underground riches. This can be done to all Hopis, but especially to the Traditionals, who, if they want to continue living in the ancient way, can support themselves, but do not have the money to pay even the smallest of the bills.

All Indians are treated the same. So for the past 200 years all Indians have endured many bitter experiences under the white man's so-called justice. Here at Hopi, our Traditional people knew that to follow the whiteman's ways would indeed be a very poor thing for the Indians. You can perhaps begin to understand why the Indian did not progress under 'white' rule and, indeed, you may wonder how any of us were able to survive at all! Although the situation for survivors today is quite bad, our remarkable Indian people can still drum, sing, joke, and laugh as they maintain their traditions under such hardships. They have not given up. They do not want handouts or charity from the government as they continue to follow their old ways. They will attain their goals by holding to the ancient knowledge. If True Hopi continue to survive this pressure — all land and life in America will be enriched. If not, it is anybody's guess as to our collective chances for survival. We direct this statement to all our Indian and non-Indian brothers and sisters who are concerned.

The time has come when the government through bills like H.R. 9054 introduced by Cunningham, and S.B. 1437, a criminal code reform act introduced by Kennedy, will try to take away all our native lands and rights by promoting us from savages to citizens and by turning our reservations into real estate that is taxed and controlled by the Tribal Council, state and federal government. But beware, for it is a trick and at the same time a test to see who will stand with our Great Spirit's law, or stand with man-made law.

This very issue is what Hotevilla was founded upon, and will continue to hold fast to until the end. May the Great Spirit guide you and give you the strength and wisdom to take this message out to the world where it can be known and acted upon."

Equal Opportunity? Will People of Peace Ever Be Really Free Again? Choice, Choice, We Keep Saying "Make Right Choices!"

TI— "Awhile back we put out a flyer to alert our people of a certain prophecy put forth by our elders, hoping our people would consider what we have told them in past years and realize what it is all about.

A few comments have been made that our interpretation regarding this bill, H.R. 9054 is inaccurate. The bill is called, 'Native American Equal Opportunity Act.' For the benefit of our Hopi people and readers around the world, we quote the bill, and you may draw your own conclusions regarding it:

'To direct the President to abrogate all treaties entered into by the United States with Indian tribes in order to accomplish the purposes of recognizing that in the United States no individual or group possesses subordinate or special rights, providing full citizenship and equality under law to Native Americans, protecting an equal opportunity of all citizens to fish and hunt in the United States, and terminating Federal supervision over the property and members of Indian tribes, and for other purposes.

Be it enacted by the Senate and House of Representatives of the United States of

America in Congress assembled, that this Act may be cited as the Native American Equal Opportunity Act.

SEC. 2. (a) The President of the United States shall, as soon as practicable after the date of enactment of this Act, abrogate all treaties entered into between the United States and any Indian tribe.'

This bill leaves us with many questions. Will this move from Washington fulfill our prophecy? Will we, the original Hopi, claiming sovereignty, no longer be subjected to the laws of the Federal, state, and local governments?

In reference to the questions and how they apply to our prophecy, we maintain and continue to stand for our original purpose in defending our right to live in a peaceful manner, rejecting all borrowed patterns which do not blend with the original Hopi way — which is based on the Great Law.

To abandon these ways would mean our destruction. Therefore, we repeat for our people that these issues may actually be the fulfillment of our prophecy that says, 'One must pay, or one must not.' The time has come to make a decision as to which each person will follow — the Traditionals, or the Bahanna: this is your choice.

This move by Washington is no small thing. It will involve the entire world — and the tide will turn either to total rebirth or annihilation."

TEM— Having seen how the Government operated in its early days in Hopi country, it is not surprising to see it teaming up with the Hopi Tribal Council and the Hopi Progressives to continue its work today. In reading about this new and pernicious combine, it is important to pay careful attention to the fact that while there are subtle shifts in tactics, the original end, that of complete control, remains the same, and the assurance that it will be used as the basis for continued land exploitation is ever present. Accordingly, it is not surprising to find that the issue of a HUD housing project that was planned by others for development on Hotevilla land was a major focus in the *Techqua Ikachi* newsletters. On the surface, the land grab seems innocent enough and not a real problem for the Traditionals, but a careful examination of the project indicates otherwise.

The United States Department of Housing and Urban Development has a mandate to provide low-cost housing in areas of the United States where people could not otherwise afford to purchase it. Usually, these projects are solicited by state and local governments to solve housing shortages in economically strapped areas. A good thing, we would all agree.

But in this instance at Hopi, the spider spins its web. The project in question was jointly solicited by the Tribal Council and Bacabi Village — the latter being a natural for this since it is entirely Progressive in its lifeway. Because Hopi people were involved, the Government could claim it was only responding to an invitation, and in so doing being helpful to people who were in dire need — were it not for the fact that, as the Elderly Elders vividly remind us, we have a lesson from history to consider. They remember, as we should, that long before

HUD came into existence the Government built several housing communities at the foot of the mesas as a thinly disguised inducement to get people to move, and in so doing to divide and reduce the strength of the Hopi villages.

Accordingly, the Elders viewed this newly proposed project with great suspicion, believing it was not only illegal to use Hotevilla land, it was not being done for the best good of the Traditional people. The fact that Bacabi and the Council were the channels through which the project would proceed only heightened their distrust. Building there, in an area between the two villages that would to the unknowing observer connect them visually into one village, would usurp and intrude upon Hotevilla rights and privileges. Moreover, this ignoring of the existing resentments between Traditional Hotevilla and Progressive Bacabi promised to fuel constant hostilities between the two. Everyone involved knew full well that the housing issue was symbolic of the irreconcilable differences in the entire range of Hopi philosophy, and as such once again showed a continuing Government and Tribal Council disregard for Traditional Hopi culture and the need to do everything required to keep the Covenant.

For example, the HUD project would, quite simply, include utilities, and bring them onto Hotevilla land and ever closer to the existing traditional village itself, thus jeopardizing the spiritual power, or energy, needed to make the ceremonies productive and fully effective. The Elders and Katchongva make this danger very clear in all of their statements regarding utilities and the sapping of spiritual energies; a matter whose consequences are spelled out in detail in Chapter 9.

As one Traditional said to me, 'At Hotevilla you still feel the energy when the Kachinas dance. In other villages you feel nothing.'

Out of this housing development would come a further reduction in the influence of the Traditional village leaders, and even confusion for visitors from the outside who would be exposed to the modern Bacabi housing as they entered historic Hotevilla land on their way to the great ceremonial dances in Hotevilla. Bacabi is thoroughly upgraded and Council controlled. Would this stark contrast not clearly evidence itself in any new housing development? Of course, the Tribal Council knows both this and the rest of the associated list of concerns that goes on and on: such as indebtedness probabilities, the loss of self-fulfillment, further distancing from tradition, and the ever-looming consciousness of Council control. How could Hotevilla Traditionals, having to pass through this particular HUD housing, go in and out of their village without being acutely aware of the Council?

From the Elders' point of view, judgements concerning this are not difficult to make. The points expressed by the Techqua Ikachi staff and the situations they describe make it easy for us to understand why they had and will always have no recourse but to oppose the project, and any other project like it, at Hotevilla. They long ago gave up warning against such housing in other villages. In their eyes, most of the Hopi in those places have already become Bahanna who, where traditional life is concerned, have very little more to lose — or forfeit.

Hotevilla Land Threatened

TI— "What has been done for us with good intentions in the past has often backfired and must be approached cautiously.

On this basis we oppose the proposed housing program on Hotevilla land. The true promoters could be none other than the Bureau of Indian Affairs (BIA) and Hopi Tribal Council. Such a project has been completed in First Mesa. One in Second Mesa has been started but is stalled, and Third Mesa, including Hotevilla, has been surveyed in preparation for work to begin soon. The housing units planned for our area are to benefit the adjoining village of Bacabi, and have been approved by the governor of that village with the backing of the BIA and Council.

Among other reasons, we oppose the housing project because it will be on our land. Two attempts to meet with the people of Bacabi have failed, stalled by various excuses. This move was decided upon without common consent. For we claim this land by an order of sacred movement, according to the laws and instructions initiated and documented between the Bear Clan and Fire Clan long before the coming of the white man, and which was commemorated often until corruption in Oraibi led to the split in 1906. The document is in the form of a deed inscribed on each of their stone tablets. It was agreed that should one of them succumb to the invading forces, whoever is still strong will inherit the power and the land. Thus when Yukiuma was forced out of Oraibi, he drew a line on the ground that is still visible today, and made the statement: 'Thank you, now from this point all the land is mine,' whereupon he moved on to Hotevilla where he settled a new village in order to fulfill his mission in accordance with the laws of the Creator.

Bacabi village was established on October 27, 1909, under the leadership of Kawonuptewa of the Sand Clan, who with a group of people who had returned to Oraibi on their signature that they would yield to the new ruler. But they had to move out again because of the cool reception they received from Chief Tawaquap-tewa of Oraibi, thus Bacabi was settled.

Before Kawonuptewa died he admitted his wrongdoings. In his testimony he admitted that he had no land. He claimed only the ground as far out as the outskirts of his village. He said, in effect, 'To survive I have chosen the Bahanna way, his religion and the laws of his system. But in order to feed my people I have by force taken part of the land from the Hotevilla people. In order to make them suffer more I did this through oppression. But I made a big mistake that will hurt my people when I am gone. I did not accomplish what I promised, and I have deceived those who promised to follow me all the way. Not once did I enter the church that is built in my village, which I approved and ordered. I say again that I am wicked. I did not record any document or deed for my people. It was also with my approval that the Hotevilla School was built under the name I stole, *Yukiuma.*'

On these grounds we in Hotevilla will not permit any housing in the area surveyed. Today the Bacabi people are happy with all the conveniences of Bahanna. We would not have this trouble if they would avoid expanding into our land."

Housing. One More Threat to Traditional Hopi Life. How Can There Be Peace When Those We Must Deal with Are Not Peaceful?

TI— "Throughout history, the United States Government has refused to recognize the fact that the Hopi villages are religious farming communities, each with its own independent leadership established in a very careful way according to their ancient tradition. Yet since the first government contact with the Hopi villages, programs have been enacted in complete ignorance of the meaning of Hopi life. Over the years, this has caused serious trouble. The current HUD housing project which threatens Hotevilla land is no exception.

The recent assault on one of our elders illustrates this clearly, and provoked a meeting of several Traditional Leaders in our village who directed the following letter to the Secretary of the Interior, signed by three traditional leaders:

February 15, 1976

Dear Sir:

Your immediate action is requested on the following:

William Pahongva, a respected and learned Hopi elder over 90 years of age, was knocked unconscious when he was pushed from the doorway of the home of James Pongyayouma of Hotevilla Village, in the Hopi Independent nation.

The incident occurred about 10:30 p.m. following a meeting on the evening of Friday, February 13, in which traditional leaders sought to determine his true role in a proposed housing project which would affect the village land rights. It is typical of the trouble your programs frequently cause.

William identified his assailant as Charlie Sekyawuyuma. The meeting ended in violence when Charlie, accompanied by Percy Loma, a Hopi-turned-Mormon, began to forcibly evict the visitors in an angry outburst, according to witnesses.

Hotevilla was founded in 1906 in order to preserve the Hopi tradition. It has always been the Hopi custom that anyone wishing to live under another system must do so elsewhere, without interfering with the village life.

The housing project would require that village land be leased to the Housing and Urban Development Project (HUD) of the U.S. Government. Failure to make regular payments has resulted in the actual loss of aboriginal land title for native nations who have accepted such projects. The leases may later be transferred to banks or other business interests, who may demand unexpected increases in payments. These implications are very serious, yet they are not clearly explained to the applicants, who often think they are just getting a free house.

The traditional leaders were alerted to the imminent danger by Melbert Pongyaysvia who found several government workers in his orchard. Since James Pongyayouma's name appeared on a recent tribal council announcement of the project, the leaders invited him to a meeting to clarify his position.

James was once the kikmongwi (chief) of Hotevilla until he left for about seven years, neglecting his duties and ceremonies, which means he for-

there they go again.

feited his authority according to Hopi tradition. Upon his return he could not face his former traditional associates, because of his conversion to the more corrupt way of life. He even departed from tradition by switching to another kiva society, rather than face them. He has since denied his former responsibility in order to seek wealth through the white man's system.

James and several of his associates are known to have been promoting the installation of water and power lines into our village against the wishes of the villagers, and against the purpose for which the village was founded.

Also invited to the meeting was Nathan Fred, Sr., the progressive governor of Bacabi, the village responsible for introducing the project, who works with a group that seeks to recognize James as kikmongwi in order to gain access to government projects through the Hopi Tribal Council, which the traditional Hopi must refuse.

About fifteen of us waited at the house of David Monongye, but James, who has consistently refused to meet with the village leaders, failed to show up. Finally we decided to go to his home. We found him there with a few associates, more of whom arrived later.

When asked to account for the use of his name on the document he told us he did not know a thing about it. He insisted several times that he is not a leader, and denied any association with a group. He denied that he approved of the housing project, or that he was associated with the so-called Hopi Tribal Council, which has always served the U.S. Government which set it up.

Around 10:30 p.m. James asked the visitors to leave. Some of us are hard of hearing, and did not respond immediately, though nobody refused to leave. Then someone shouted that the owner wanted everyone to leave. Percy Loma and Charlie Sekyawuyuma started pushing people out very roughly.

William Pahongva said Charlie grabbed him by the collar and began to shove him backwards toward the door. He held on to Charlie's shirt to keep his balance. Charlie then pushed him hard through the doorway, causing him to fall to the ground, which knocked him unconscious for a short time. William found it hard to move. Later his feet and knees became swollen and bruises showed on his face.

This incident brings out the friction caused by the needless and insensitive introduction of such projects. We can build much better houses ourselves, as we have for centuries, with rock and mortar. There is no need for us to accept such interference from outside interests, especially when they work against our traditional way of life.

In formerly accepting the position of kikmongwi, James Pongyayouma committed himself to the purpose which Yukiuma, the founder of Hotevilla, suffered greatly to uphold. Perhaps the people behind HUD don't realize that we are still committed to this high purpose, which is the foundation of our village life. The sole power to select a kikmongwi still rests with the village, and must be carried out according to clearly defined principles and customs. James has ended his authority by his own choice. The fact that the Tribal Council chooses to recognize him to suit their selfish purpose does not change this. Responsibility for this village still rests with the village leaders.

We Hotevilla people do not want government housing, or any other projects which tend to place control of our land in the hands of outside interests.

We bring this to your attention so that you, and all other individuals responsible, may know the trouble your projects are causing, and be in a position to act with knowledge and a clear conscience.

To us the matter is very urgent. We are asking you to bring an end to this serious interference into our village life. May your good faith be shown by the steps you take.

The response of the Secretary of the Interior, if any, will be reported in the next issue of Techqua Ikachi.

TEM— If any replies to the letters sent in this and other cases were received, or if there was any investigation of this matter, no mention of this is found in the *Techqu Ikachi* newsletters…not a surprising circumstance I suppose when the perpetrators of the attacks were serving those who were called upon to consider and rectify the matter. When we consider the question of why the number of Traditional people has steadily declined over the years, we have here a perfect example of what they have been up against.

Elder's Attacker to Represent Village?
An Ominous Sign Pointing to Further Plans?
TI— "True to their established pattern, and in violation of the Tribal Council Constitution under which they operate, Bacabi Village and the Bureau of Indian Affairs allowed Charlie Sekyawuyuma to represent Hotevilla Village in a meeting regarding the transfer of the water-sewer system to Bacabi Village. This meeting took place February 10, three days before Charlie assaulted the 90-year-old William Pahongva. The reason he was chosen to represent Hotevilla Village: He was 'instrumental' in bringing water to Hotevilla! It is easy to see how outsiders are trying to choose our leaders for us."

Progressive Paper Gives False Report
TI— "Readers of the local anti-traditional paper, *Qua'toqti*, are urged to notice the fact that paper not only has failed to give any of the background of the Hotevilla land problem dispute, but carried only a brief statement based on Charlie Sekyawuyuma's claim that he was the victim, and not the attacker! He prefers, he says, not to 'press charges.' Of course, the Traditional Hopi do not use courts and jails, so the leaders involved will not 'press charges' either, but we welcome any move they or others might make to fairly investigate the incident."

Ex-Chief Used As Tool for the Proposed Land Theft by Bacabi
TI— "We now quote from the newsletter of Bacabi Village, dated February 6, 1976. It is one of the documents which made necessary the meeting at Pongyayouma's house:

'At the Board of Directors meeting on January 21, 1976, the members decided to continue the survey of the area for housing and development. The governor informed the members that although the council recognized James Pongyayouma as the chief of Hotevilla, it was not him who was protesting Bacabi's claim. Therefore, the board decided to go ahead with the plan for this area. If and when James Pongyayouma protested, only then would the governor and the board meet with him. Some members felt that the village should go ahead with the survey and other plans simply to resolve the jurisdictional problem between Bacabi and Hotevilla.

The area was designated last year in September as a housing and development area for Bacabi, and [construction] since then has been stopped by followers of David Monongye of Hotevilla. Monongye has requested several meetings with the authorities of Bacabi, but Bacabi has refused pending the council's reply as to who is the recognized leader of Hotevilla. Bacabi maintains that if and when it must meet with Hotevilla it should be with the recognized chief.'

In the light of history as well as Hopi tradition, we would like our readers to carefully consider the above proposal. As our letter to the Secretary of the Interior explains, the authority to govern the village and select the Kikmongwi (chief) rests with each independent village. Hotevilla has never relinquished this right to the Hopi Tribal Council, which is a recently established foreign institution that is basically opposed to our traditional form of government.

As a religious community the traditional people of Hotevilla are committed to a sacred vow to follow the instructions of the Great Spirit which have been handed down to us from the beginning of time. We do this not only because we want to, we do it because we must!"

TEM— Although the newsletters continued over several issues to address the HUD housing project, we feel we have included sufficient information regarding it, and skip now to a final article that contains thoughts that should be shared regarding the matter of Hopi self-determination.

Housing Programs Destroy Self-Determination. Who Gave the Government the Right to Punish Us? Who Gave Them the Right to Change Us? Who Gave Them the Right to Ignore Us in Making Decisions Regarding Ourselves and Our Land?

TI— "A close examination into low cost housing for Indian tribes, based on experience in Hopi and other nations, reveals nothing worthy of praise. Mostly we find expressions of grief and resentment, fears of meeting the coming monthly bills on the house, and the difficulty of keeping a job as it is done in the white man's system. Of course, flattering remarks are often made about the creature comforts, such as having a water hole at your fingertips or being able to answer the call of nature in comfort. Naturally we envy such an easy life, but the Indians who have gone through this mill have sad stories to tell. Manhattan, which we

New housing

have heard was bought for a few trinkets, is not very attractive to us Indians now. We know that the same terrible life will come to the Hopis who are blindly induced by the so-called 'Tribal Council' into accepting new housing.

Many who have accepted such housing in hope of reaping the rewards of progress have become trapped by the strange system of upkeep and continual expenses. They have lost their homes and their land through increased assessments and foreclosures they have not planned on.

"People," Dan inserts, "buy things and do not have the necessary income to keep or maintain them. The Tribal Council knows this, and counts on it as a way of obtaining land which they can then lease to outsiders for commercial purposes."

'Most important,' the newsletter continues, 'their tradition and culture is being ruined through neglect. Once-happy communities have been scattered out to the cities and towns, homes are broken, people are deprived of many things they wanted to have. The 'rights' that are supposedly theirs as wards of the government have only brought them heavier obligations. When they ask for help, they're told to stand 'on their own feet.' The correct word for this reply is *termination*…

It is very plain to us that we are better off being allowed to stand 'on our own feet' in the way we have been doing for ages, rather than to be dragged off our feet by this deceitful system. We may not be safe from this approaching monster, but we must heed the lesson of experience and do what we can to avoid it.

It was foretold that Bahanna would have all the tools necessary to protect our right to the exclusive use of Hopi Land for those who wish to live by the Great Laws without interference. But it was also prophesied that this person of white skin who would come among us might gather us under his wings, feed us and take care of us like a mother hen, only because he sees something underneath us which he wants to get. Then when we grow big enough to suit his purpose he would adopt us into his fold, and thereafter we would support him as his servants. We must certainly not allow ourselves to become his adopted servants in this way. We must not experiment with his system within our own land. In order to remain safe our land must be protected, so that those who wish to experiment may do so outside, and learn which life is best for them. Then they will be able to return when they have discovered the truth. If, on the other hand, we sell out our own land, we shall have nowhere to return. The Prophecy foretells that Bahanna would be very persistent, and eventually might force his ways upon us. But should he reconsider and correct his mistakes, he would then decide who will pay and who will not pay.

The Progressive faction accuses us of withholding the good things and of keeping our children from a better future — by which they mean the advantages of modern conveniences. They are enticed by gadgets run by electricity and public water for household needs. These things would be good if there weren't spiritual problems associated with them, and if one could get them freely without the danger of involvement in obligations that will later be regretted. Certainly these things seem to promise a nice future for our children, but our knowledge, as well as the clear voice of experience in the modern world, teaches us the danger of allowing our life to be controlled by outside interests. A person's life easily becomes ruled by his pocketbook and by foreign rules — even by jail.

Our readers far and near understand this fact, and we are grateful for the encouragement we receive in support of our way of life, a way which no amount of money could possibly buy. We have our own land free from foreign taxation, one that certainly guarantees a good future for our children! We have no need to pay rent or bills except by individual choice. We know how to run a happy community without allowing what they call 'law and order' into our village. It is not that we claim to be perfect, but we know it is possible for one to correct himself as is necessary as he becomes older and wiser. This too is a wonderful future, for it does not darken the character of those who choose to fit into our society and respect the Great Spirit's instructions. Yes, there are many good things we are trying to preserve for the future of our children. The best of these are what 'progress' wants to destroy.

We regret very much that we find it necessary always to accuse the United States Government for the wrongs done to us. If only they would correct these wrongs we would not have to point our fingers at Washington

When a Hopi says, 'I want the best of everything for my children and those to come,' he means, 'I want this land for my children, for it can last forever. I want for my children the best food which the land can offer. I want health and happiness for my children, and the best life which the land will provide. But I will not force my culture and religion on others, though we have survived for thousands of years, and know our ways must be good.'"

Little Things That Please Us — the Government Appreciates Our Newsletter

TI— "*Techqua Ikachi* has received an inspiring letter from none other than our old enemy the U.S. Department of the Interior, asking for our subscription rates in order to receive our publication on a regular basis: 'Thank you very much,' they say, 'for sending a complimentary copy of your publication, I found it extremely interesting and informative. And it does an excellent job of providing the understanding and knowledge which we are seeking in order to more effectively deal with the Indian nations.' We have gladly included the U.S. Department of the Interior on our mailing list free of charge. We thank the unseen and the people by whom our message is shared. We pray that this will benefit all people."

Forward and Back, Forward and Back, Like a Bahanna Tennis Game!

TI— "Our prophecies foretell that times will come when we will periodically recover our senses and find that some vital element is amiss. Then we will retrace our steps with fear, not bearing to look back at where we have been. So we will go forward, backward, forward and backward, our decisions uncertain. This is happening today in Hopi Land, as it is happening in the rest of the world."

Who Can Tell Us What We Are and What We Are Being Fashioned Into?

TI— "It is well known among Traditional Hopi that the Constitution of the so-called Hopi Tribal Council is a tool used to impose a system which violates the true meaning and purpose of Hopi. This document, imposed in 1936 by the U.S. Government, even seeks to *redefine Hopi identity* in order to serve a very different purpose.

In our language, the name, Hopi, has held the same meaning from our beginning. It designates those who live by the plan laid out by the spirit, Maasaw, and who today hold the land in trust for him. Although our bloodline is very important, the word refers to our whole way of life, as well as to the foundation of the authority of our traditional leaders, and our claim over the land.

But Article II of the Hopi Constitution gives a different definition of who a Hopi is or can be:

'Section 1

a) All persons, whose names appear on the Census Roll of the Hopi Tribe as of January 1, 1936, but within one year from the time that this constitution takes effect, corrections may be made in the roll by the Hopi Tribal Council with the approval of the Secretary of the Interior.

b) All children born after January 1, 1936 whose father and mother are both members of the Hopi Tribe.

c) All children born after January 1, 1936 whose mother is a member of the Hopi Tribe and whose father is a member of some other tribe.

d) All persons adopted into the tribe as provided in Section 2.

Section 2

NON-MEMBERS of 1/4 degree of Indian Blood or more who are married to members of the Hopi Tribe, and adult persons of 1/4 degree of Indian blood or more whose fathers are members of the Hopi Tribe, may be adopted in the following manner:

Such person may apply to the Kikmongwi of the village to which he is to belong, for acceptance according to the ways of doing established in that village. The Kikmongwi may accept him and shall tell the Tribal Council. The Council may then by a majority vote have that person's name put on the roll of the tribe [underlining is ours]. But before he is enrolled he must officially give up membership in any other tribe.'

Last July a diagram of how this works was printed in the newspaper of the progressive village of Bacabi.

We ask those of you who saw it, 'Is this really a definition of a True Hopi? Why it necessary to have a definition, unless it is needed to serve Government, Council and Progressive purposes? We do not need such a plan to live as true Hopi.' It is only valid for some who choose to give up being Hopi, and live from Government programs which include dividing, leasing, and selling the land. To accept such 'benefits' they need to be identified. But each True Hopi leader has vowed never to sell or cut up the land. Anyone who does this is *no longer Hopi*.

Now are we just being stubborn and old-fashioned when we take this stand? Perhaps there is some wisdom behind it. The truth is, we Hopi have no need to yield our self-determination to an outside power in order to prosper. We don't need to place the control of our land under foreign laws. We understand what is behind the 'easy-money' system, and we know how dangerous it is for us to adopt it. We look forward to the day when we may share things with others without being asked to give up all that we live for." *my heart is Hopi, skin is white.*

Cutting the Hopi Lifeline — Why the Government and the Hopi and Navajo Tribal Councils Really Want the Land in the Joint Use Area

TI— "Government, law, and industry are actively working as a team to break our hold on our sacred trust, our aboriginal homeland. This is nothing new, of course, but events described in a *Bacabi Newsletter* dated August 6 provide a very important lesson that all who are seriously interested in *true* Hopi law should study.

The newsletter tells us that John Boyden, attorney for the Hopi Tribal Council discussed the Phillips Petroleum Company's application to develop oil in the 'joint use area,' a section of Hopi land currently shared with the Navajo people. The letter states *that Phillips Petroleum Company feels that there is strong indication that there is oil in certain portions of land in the joint use area.'*

Mr. Boyden 'and a group of attorneys,' are apparently promoting a certain resolution (H-52-76) which contains 'three major objectives:

(1) To take to the U.S. Courts the matter that the Navajo Tribe should pay the Hopi a certain amount of money for charging joint use traders fees and related fees on joint use area,

(2) To take to the U.S. Courts the Navajo Tribe for damage to the land of the joint use area, and

(3) The Hopi tribe will sue the Navajo for other related relief to which the Hopi Tribe is entitled on the joint use area.'

The letter concludes with the announcement that 'Two new attorneys were hired to our ring of attorneys,' namely Boyden's son, John, and Michael Hunter. But this happy family, whose firm represents 'Utes, Paiutes, and other Zuni tribes' would not be complete without one more…US, the Hopis. It is interesting that these tribal attorneys are under the Congressional Act, which provides that, at first at least, they will be paid by the U.S.A.'

So the U.S. Government wants to pay attorneys to help the Hopi sell out their birthright and to fight their neighbors, the Navajo people (whose attorneys are probably paid to do the same to the Hopi), and to do this fighting in a court of U.S. law! How can the so-called Hopi of Bacabi Village and the Tribal Council be so gullible? Well, the Government wants them to feel proud to be the 'new leaders,' tempting them to fall off of the narrow path with crumbs from the table of the great oil company, and most of all to have them think the 'old way' is dead.

The Government works in this manner through the puppet Tribal Council because a true Hopi leader can never be paid to break that sacred vow upon which we were first allowed to hold this land. That vow is a real and binding agreement which will never allow us to lease it for oil profits.

In effect, the United States Government is telling us, 'That vow is all nonsense! Forget the past! The land is all ours now!' They must have a good reason for wanting everyone to lose sight of the fact that Hopi Land has never been given up — even according to their own Law. 'No war, no treaty' was the reason we traditional Hopi refused to fight. We also refuse to forget.

Is this just another of our sad stories? If we thought so, we would no longer do our part by continuing to live in the Hopi way, and continuing to speak out about these things. We have no powerful army, so it is only with the help of friends on this continent and throughout the world that we can be heard by those who are able to stop this attempt to replace our original leaders and cut us away from the land. So whether it remains a sad story is up to you as well."

The Question: Should We Save Our Aboriginal Ways?

TI— "Our late chief, Katchongva, recalled, 'Mr. LaFarge used to come to my house or to my field every day for a week. I guess he was very desperate to have me accept the Hopi Constitution. He followed me everywhere saying that others had already accepted it. I think he was a good man but very, very persistent. I did not yield, because if I accepted the Constitution, it would be the end of Hopi. Finally he came to my house with his bedroll — I suppose to wear me down to submission. But before he had spent one night, I was asked by my people to get rid of him by sundown. So I told him, through an interpreter, that he must not stay, and I told him that my final word was that I would not accept or sign anything. He did not persist and obeyed my wishes. Before he left he thanked me for my kindness, honored my courageous stand, and thought I did right in telling him my opinion of the Hopi Constitution he had drawn up. He told me that I did not have to follow it, that it may not be good for everyone, and that maybe it was useless for me or would someday become useless. So he apologized by saying that he had tried to persuade me — not because he wanted or had to — but rather because it was his job by which he earned his living.'

Now we are at the period where we must decide, and our conclusion will probably not fit everyone. Surely no Hopi will deny that Tradition is real, that it is our inherited cultural belief, our religious doctrine, our unwritten instructions to be used as our guideline. But most of us have forgotten the real thing and have substituted fabrications. We know our philosophical doctrines and prophecies vary from village to village, but when we really look at the core of Tradition we see that it has the same meaning for all. We all enjoy the social or Traditional gatherings, and we attend Bahanna religious things for reasons we need not spell out for you because we trust you will understand.

A survey about the Land Claim has been taken among the Hopi, but the majority of Traditional Hopi — 90% to 95% — have not even been consulted about confirmation of the Claim. Perhaps now the world will think the Traditional Hopi have confirmed the Claim, and accordingly both people of high places and common people will make the same assumption. Accordingly we now set our problem before the people who care about our survival, and who are trying to resolve it by helping to save our environment.

So, now it is up to each of us to confirm our stand as to whether we should save the aboriginal ways. It is not a simple decision, but one does need to decide which side to support — the Progressive Hopi or the Traditional Hopi — or to break free from both. Consult yourself and get your own pattern in motion."

Balance: A Rewarding Path, a Way To Travel, Like the Narrow Edge of a Knife

TI— *"Long before Bahanna (white man) came upon our land, when Maasaw, the Great Spirit, still walked among us, he gave the Hopi special knowledge. He gave us instructions and prophecies indicating that along the way many things would come to pass. Then He pointed out a path, a way to travel, that was like the narrow edge of a knife.*

Along the way, He said, we would face many evil obstacles, obstacles which would lessen our spiritual energies and the will to go on, causing us to stray off the path. But, if we reached the end of the path without weakening, we would be rewarded with a good, peaceful and everlasting life. Then Maasaw, the Great Spirit, would be our leader, for He is the First and will be the Last. This is the path our village, Hotevilla, the last remnant of traditional Hopi, has chosen to follow to this day."

But The Shocking Time Has Come When Our Ceremonials Are Fading

TI— "Many years ago our life was good and beautiful. We had much rain, the earth bloomed, there was plenty of food. The Ceremonial Cycles were in order according to the months. Natural forces within our Earth Mother were in harmony and balance. At that time we were one in heart and performed our prayers in the proper way in reaching the Spirits. So we were surrounded by peace with one another according to the divine laws of our Great Creator.

Upon the arrival of Bahanna in our land however, our minds became distorted by their activities. They changed our life pattern by exploring our ways of life and then contesting against the sacred Ceremonials. Then they began to bend our children's minds by educating them into Bahanna ways of thinking.

This was a clear sign of dangers yet to come. In earlier times initiation was important. It was the way for a child to become a member of the religious society, to learn a deeper knowledge of life — its meaning and function. Many of these things are secrets that only members may know, not the public. They are strictly guarded. Now in this age the educated and ambitious Hopi, along with anthropologists, have stolen and sold to collectors and museums religious objects such as altars and other important things. These are to be shown to the public, and they will be meaningless to them. These acts were forbidden, for eventually they will break down the religious orders.

To illustrate this truth, a number of earlier ceremonials which were of importance were ended. This was because of the coming of the white race. Also, today's educated and ambitious Hopi are using religious concepts and knowledge in improper ways for their own gain and for power in conflicts with others. Our knowledge is not for that purpose. The basis of our religion is for good things, for food, health and happiness. It is not to be used for weapons.

Sadly, because of Bahanna and the carelessness of our own people in creating corruption in our society, like we did in our previous worlds, many have forsaken Maasaw, straying from their commitments to live in His ways... in simple and peaceful ways. They have forgotten their promises. There is no other choice for us but to follow His instructions, unless we want to lose more of our Sacred Ceremonials. We are unhappy in saying this, but these are our ways and we must live by them."

'Fencing' — in the Purest Sense —
These Must Come Down, Say the Hotevilla Villagers

TI— "Recently, attempts have been made to fence certain Hopi fields against the wishes of the traditional authority. The true issue may not be apparent to the casual observer, and is not adequately explained in the so-called Hopi tribal news media. Actually, the friction behind the fencing can be traced back to the founding of the first government agency on Hopi land in the late 1800s. It was born out of a fierce and overpowering period of forced assimilation into the ways of the white man, or Bahanna, that amounted to a police state... Today, one of the arguments provoked by the Council is whether the Hotevilla fields should be fenced, or whether grazing cattle belonging to the so-called 'Hopi Tribe' should be moved entirely out of the area. The Hotevilla people argue that the land belongs to them, and that they will not allow it to be fenced. The so-called 'Hopi Tribe' says that it will solve the problem and keep the cattle out of the fields. The traditional people say, 'No! Once you fence that off you will keep the land outside the fence as your own. You move your cattle elsewhere, where you can be happy with them.' It can be added that once the Council has the land they will open it to Government arranged leases for commercial exploitation.

The so-called 'Hopi Tribe' insists that the fences will only be temporary, but the traditional people see them as a show of force, a wrongful claim of jurisdiction over their land, which the 'Hopi Tribe' knows very well it has no intention of regarding as temporary. Thus the Hopi shrines will be desecrated along with the spiritual paths, and the keeping of the Covenant will be seriously affected.

At a meeting many things were brought out in hopes of creating a better understanding for the benefit of the opposition, but it was useless, for the opponents were of a vastly different mind. Finally, out of anger and frustration the Agency superintendent rose to leave the meeting, announcing that the fence would go up whether they liked it or not, and that he would be responsible for the consequences… So the meeting came to an abrupt end. The signal was given that the offensive would roll without respect to any people or laws. The Hopi would soon be encircled with no place to run. But we will still stand our ground to the last, whichever way they drag us out, feet or head first. Remember how we pulled up the surveyors' stakes? Our last word here is that 'We will tear the fence down, we are ready!' In this regard a written ultimatum was issued to Superintendent Alph Secakuku, Hopi Indian Agency, Keams Canyon, Arizona, on June 30, 1975.

> *Dear Sir,*
>
> *You, as the representative of the Bureau of Indian Affairs, claimed responsibility for the present disturbance to the Hopi ways of life. The so-called Tribal Council associated with your office again disregarded our rejections to the fencing of our land. You have encroached by force, and without our approval, put the fence up, thereby once again violating the exclusive land use of Traditional Hopi people.*
>
> *How many times more must we reject this proposal? It seems to us that our past statements of explanation are quite sufficient for you to understand and respect our wishes and not create the confrontation.*
>
> *Giving this our fullest consideration, this hasty, one-man decision is unjust. We denounce your action on the grounds that you are not a member and representative of this village, and therefore have no business interfering with our village government.*
>
> *Your action seems to indicate that your office and your associate, the so-called Tribal Council end your negotiation with us, the lowly Hopi Traditionals.*
>
> *Therefore, since you are responsible, we want you to remove the fence. We have no confidence in your word, 'Temporary.' So we want it done by the month of August. If you fail to do so we will remove the fence in plain sight, not slyly. We will inform you and people of this country and the world the day we will make this move.*
>
> *Sincerely, Traditional and Religious leaders of Hotevilla Independent Village: David Monongye, Paul Sewemanewa, Amos Howesa, Lewis Naha.*

Copies of this letter were sent to Secretary of the Interior, Washington, D.C., Commissioner of Indian Affairs, Washington, D.C., Hopi Tribal Council, Oraibi, Arizona, and interested people."

George Washington — George Government

TEM— *Techqua Ikachi* included a long story about George Washington and the famous cherry tree incident, except that after experiencing how the United States Government dealt with them, the Hopi came up with their own ending — which provides a perceptive twist. We omit some of the story.

TI— "In honor of George Washington's birthday anniversary, we wish to fill you in about the famous cherry tree story and the bywords 'I cannot tell a lie.' We first heard this in our primary school days from our teachers years ago. Each

I cannot tell a lie, I did all this with my own little hands.

year we were reminded of Washington, the first president, on his birthday. We were told he was nice and honest; so when he chopped his father's cherry tree he admitted it and said, 'I cannot tell a lie.' We were always encouraged to be like him and always tell our parents and teachers the truth.

After reviewing the Cherry Tree story we found it very interesting. It clearly confirms the prophecy of the Hopi about the newcomers arriving in our land. Hopi called them "Bahanna," (the white race). It was prophesied that they would come in large numbers. They would be cunning and sly with forked tongues and sweet tongues. By deceit and fraud they would take over the land of the Native people. They would be ambitious in many ways and disturb the lives of the first inhabitants — disturb even the land and Nature. If we protested they would seize the land through superior force of weapons and would attempt to annihilate all Native people. But a remnant of these people would survive to carry on for the future. Bahanna would not end their conquests until the last Native culture disappears. This would be their goal. But if we were fortunate, the Bahanna Government might have mercy and refine their policies, using softer methods to induce the natives to give up their land. Their conquest would linger on without bloodshed and death. It would work in such a sly way that before we knew it, we would be caught in their web. Therefore we were warned to be cautious and to beware of getting fooled by their tricky words so as to not fall into their pitfalls and traps.

Just as predicted, the Bahanna Government did come to Hopi Land with what they said were good intentions, armed with a proposal to educate the children, with promises of many good things for the Hopi and for their children's future. After meeting to consider this, leaders from all the villages rejected the education idea, saying, 'Bahanna school is not good. It will not fit our needs or blend with our religious ceremonials. We will teach our children in our own ways, as we have done in the past.'

The religious leaders foresaw the whiteman's education process as trickery devised to destroy the minds of Hopi children. They foresaw the danger that the children would lose their traditional culture and identity, lose even their language and become the tool of the Government. They foresaw that through it they would destroy themselves and lose the Hopi way of life.

The Bahanna persisted but failed for a time. Then finally when threats of prison and imprisonment were used, all of the village leaders bowed to the inevitable.

Among the Hopi this created great division and friction. Discord erupted between those who yielded to the powers of the Bahanna Government and those who chose to keep their position as Hopi. Knowing they could not live side by side, the devoted Hopi decided to escape to a better world where the traditional culture and their religion would not die. Thus the village of Hotevilla was founded and firmly established to guarantee the protection of all life and land. *It is important to understand that at this place a sacred wall of defence was erected to wall-off the wicked and their attempts to annihilate the last remnants of the first native people. That those who dare venture to disturb this sacred barricade will cause a great misfortune to befall us all.*

This is how the United States Government has worked with the Hopi: 'When one day George's father came home he saw the fallen cherry tree and asked his wife what happened. She told him. After dinner he summoned George to the fireplace for a talk.

'George,' he said, 'your mother tells me you chopped down the cherry tree. Is that true?'

'Yes, father, I cannot tell a lie,' said George, 'I did it!'

This is the Hopi twist…

'Now George, do you know what's worse than chopping down your father's prize cherry tree?'

'Lying, father?'

'No George, admitting that you lied.'

'I don't understand father.'

'George have you ever heard the saying, 'The road to hell is paved with good intentions?''

'No I haven't father.'

'Well, that saying is quite true,' said Augustine taking his pipe and lighting it with a twig from the hearth. 'But equally true is the saying, 'The road to failure is paved with the truth. In here next to the fire it is warm and comfortable, but out there it is cold and bitter. A man must use his wits and his wiles to survive. If I had managed my estates in the light of truth we would be living on a patch of weeds in the backwaters of the river. The truth is a poor man's shackle, George. It is something we of the elite group must demand from the lowly in order to keep them where they are. Truth is the enemy of a good bargain."

Hotevilla Village Commemorates Founding — We Could Bring into Being a New World, or, THE TERRIBLE PURIFICATION DAY!

TI— "*Address by David Monongye, a religious leader of Hotevilla, to a gathering of Hopi and Bahanna friends on September 6, 1976, the 70th anniversary of the village.*

First of all, as you come here to my village of Hotevilla, I wish to welcome each one of you. At this time we are celebrating a time in our history which is both filled with joy and with sadness. I am very glad that you have come to share these feelings with us.

We are now faced with great problems not only here, but throughout the land. Ancient cultures are being annihilated; the people's lands are being taken from them, leaving them no place to call their own.

Why is this happening? It is happening because many people have given up their teachings and the Way of Life which the Great Spirit has given to all people. It is because of the sickness called greed, which infects every land, that simple people are losing what they have kept for thousands of years.

Here at home, it is the so-called Hopi Tribal Council which is stealing our land and life. We Hopis are a Sovereign Nation. We have never signed a treaty with the U.S. Government, or with any government. Yet the so-called Tribal Council has let the U.S. run over them and push them around. Now they, the so-called Tribal Council, push around their own people as if they have some kind of authority. But they do not have authority over Hopis. Hopis have their own authority and their own leaders who watch over all the people like a mother and father. But the so-called Tribal Council will not admit that this is so. Yet if it was not so, how else would we be able to still be alive today? We have managed for thousands of years to survive, without wars, without laws, and without outside authority telling us how to live our own lives.

Now we are at the very end of our trail. Many people no longer recognize the True Path of the Great Spirit. They have, in fact, no respect for the Great Spirit or for our precious Mother Earth, who gives us all life.

We are instructed in our ancient Prophecy that this would occur. We were told that someone would try to go up to the moon; that they would bring something back from the moon; and that after that, Nature would show signs of losing its balance. Now we see that coming about. All over the world there are now many signs that Nature is close to losing

its balance. Floods, droughts, earthquakes, and great storms are occurring and causing much suffering.

We do not want this to occur in our country and we pray to the Great Spirit to save us from such things. But there are now signs that this very same thing might happen very soon on our own land.

Now we must look upon each other as brothers and sisters. There is no more time for divisions between people. Today I call upon all of us, from right here at home where we are guilty of gossiping and causing divisions even among our own families; and reaching out into the entire world where thievery, war and lying goes on every day to recognize that these divisions will not be our salvation.

Only by joining together with love in our hearts for one another and for the Great Spirit, shall we be saved from *the terrible Purification Day which is just ahead.*

5th cycle
on v-shaped
stone

Those of you who have come here today are honest people. I know you, each one of you, and I know that you have good hearts. But good hearts are not enough to solve these great problems. In the past, some of you have tried to help us Hopis, and we will always be thankful for your effort. But now we need your help in the worst way. We want the people of this country to know the truth of our situation. This land which you people call the Land of Freedom has just celebrated its 200th anniversary. Yet in 200 years the original Americans have not seen a free day. We are now suffering the final insult. Our people are now losing the one thing which gives life and meaning to life: our land, which is being taken away from us.

I ask you this: Where is this freedom which you all fight for and sacrifice your children for? Is it only the Indian people who have lost it, or are all Americans losing the very thing which you originally came here to find?

Listen to us: We have no freedom of religion because others come to our homes and tell us that our religion is no good; that we should take theirs instead.

We don't share the freedom of the press because the only thing that gets into the papers is what the government wants people to believe, not what is really happening.

We have no freedom of speech, because we are persecuted by our own people for speaking our beliefs.

So you have come here to help. I hope and pray that your help will come. If you have a way to spread the truth through the newspapers, radio, books, or through meetings with powerful people, tell the truth! Tell them what you have seen here; what you have heard us say; what you have seen here with your own eyes. In this way, if we do fall, let it be said that we at least tried, right up to the end, to hold fast to the Path of Peace as we were originally instructed to do by the Great Spirit.

And should you really succeed, we will all face up to our mistakes of the past and return to the True Path; living in harmony as brothers and sisters, sharing our Mother, the Earth, with all other living things. In this way we could bring about a New World. A world which would be led by the Great Spirit and our Mother could provide plenty and happiness for us all.

God bless you, each one. May the Great Spirit guide you safely home and give you something important to do in this great work which lies ahead of us all."

Like a String of Beads…

TI— "The wisdom of Hopi tells us that while we would begin like a string of beads, all united, as time passes people will begin to unstring themselves from this true life line. As they see or hear temptations of pleasure and gain, the string will become shorter and shorter, until at last only a few with strong wills will be left hanging onto the life line to pursue their destiny as laid out by Maasaw, the Great Spirit. Yet there will be great joy if they achieve this goal, for it will purify the land and lead to peaceful ways of life. But if they fail, it will be up to the Great Creator to work through nature to do to us what we will deserve."

The Time Has Arrived to Do Something for the Traditional Hopi

TI— "Three people were named who were to help the Hopi when we reached the crisis of no return. The Paiute Indian was to help according to his wisdom, but if he is unable the Navajo Indian will help also, according to his wisdom. If their efforts fail then Bahanna will come to aid us. This is where we are now. The time has now arrived to do something for the Traditional Hopi of Hotevilla. Why only Hotevilla? Our answer is simply that it is time.

Today we stand alone according to our prophecy. We can only say that if you are interested in helping our cause — in preserving our Traditional Hopi culture — please write to your Congressmen and Senators to look into the so-called Joint Use Area between the Hopi and Navajo reservations. To support Senator Cranston's Bill S-2545, calling for a moratorium on funding for the relocation of Navajo. Both Traditional Hopi and Navajo must be included in their discussions in order to keep their voices separate from those of the Tribal Councils, or both tribes. The views of both Tribal Councils are western in nature. On December 26, 1986, Traditional Hopi elders of Hotevilla filed a complaint with the UN Commission for Human Rights in Geneva. It will help our cause if you write letters of support for our complaint. We ask you to write letters of support for our complaint. We ask you to write to Mr. Jacob Moller, Center for Human Rights, Communication Unit, Palais des Nation 121 1, Geneva 10. Express your support for the preservation of our aboriginal culture. We thank you with all our hearts."

TEM— It seems clear, doesn't it? We can rescue the Traditional Hopis, and they can save us. It is time to assault consciences in every way we can think of!

PEOPLE MUST BE
FREE TO CHOOSE.
BUT WHEN THE
UTILITIES ARE
RUNNING, WHAT
WILL WE DO?
OUR HEARTS WILL
NOT BE IN THE
CEREMONIES, AND
OUR ENERGY WILL
NOT BE THE
SAME...

CHAPTER 8

TWO-HEARTEDS: THE PEABODY MINE, NAVAJO RELOCATION, AND MISSIONS

TWO-HEARTEDS WHO TODAY IMPEDE THE KEEPING OF THE COVENANT: PEABODY MINE, THE EFFORT TO RELOCATE THE NAVAJOS, AND MISSIONARIES

At the beginning of Chapter 11, we summarize the probabilities of how the fate of the world and future will work out in the different circumstances that are possible at Hotevilla. But before we do this, there are other things of consequence to consider, things that already do, and will continue to, affect the keeping of the Covenant. Unfortunately, there are three of these, and as we would expect, they are among the matters that were addressed by the writers of the *Techqua Ikachi* newsletters.

THE PEABODY MINE AND BLACK MESA

Reference has been made in Chapter 3 to the early settlements of Hopi ancestors on the northern end of Black Mesa. Located in the Northeastern corner of Arizona, the mesa is a 2,500-square-mile plateau that rises approximately 1,500 feet above the valleys and canyons of the Navajo and Hopi Indian reservations. Up there are hundreds of square miles of high valleys, dry washes, and aspen-and-pine-laced–canyons that descend from a surrounding rim to a basin-like center. Abundantly rich in ores and minerals, Black Mesa is divided into four main geological strata. The highest of these is Mesa Verde sandstone. Next is Mancos shale. Then comes Dakota sandstone, and finally there is the lowest level, consisting of

Navajo sandstone. Coal seams 4 to 8 feet thick are found in the top strata, and seams as thick as 65 feet occur in the Dakota strata. Springs on the mesa top serve Navajo Indians who have gardens and graze their sheep and cows in the northern part. The southern end breaks away in a series of deep canyons that are interspersed by high peninsulas. It is here that the Hopi Indians have their farms, livestock, and villages. For these people, as well as for the Navajos who live on the mesa, the springs are their lifeblood. Without them, they cannot survive in this region.

In 1964 and 1966, respectively, Peabody Coal Company, a subsidiary of Kennecott Copper Company, negotiated Black Mesa coal mining leases with the Department of the Interior and the Navajo and Hopi Tribal Councils. Under pressure from the Department of the Interior and anxious for the lease money, the Tribal Council signed the leases. As is obvious today, their understanding and comprehension of the proposal was incomplete. Although the mine officials could not have helped knowing what was coming, they downplayed any possible problems, and the Councils of both the Hopis and Navajos did not fully understand the economic and ecological changes that would result. "It was done without adequate deliberation," said Keith Smith, a member of the Navajo Tribal Council during the period of Peabody negotiations. "The Council never had a good discussion on it," he said. "We were asked, in effect, to say 'Yes' or 'No' to the proposal."

At the time the information included here was gathered, the company had already ordered its turbine generators from General Electric — in December of 1967 — thus having ordered $100,000,000 worth of equipment a full two years before the Navajo had even given them permission to use it. The lease called for 337 million tons of coal — 220 million tons from the Navajo, 117 million tons from the Hopi — to be strip-mined from an area of 64,858 acres on Black Mesa. Promises of jobs were also made, and the shortage of these in Indian country guaranteed that, despite the possible hazards, the lure of Tribal wealth and individual employment would be far too great to turn down.

Attorney John S. Boyden of Salt Lake City, a Mormon, was retained by the Hopi Tribal Council to represent the Hopi people and expedite the project. Since any attorney retained by a tribe must be approved by the Bureau of Indian Affairs, the Peabody-Hopi-BIA Lease was negotiated by the Secretary of the Interior, under whose jurisdiction the BIA falls. Although Traditional leaders denounced his contention as a shameful lie, Boyden claimed to speak and act for all the Hopi villages. In addition to the coal lease, Boyden arranged a $3 million oil exploration lease with several oil companies, many of which were represented by his own firm, and for which work his firm was paid a million dollars by the Hopi Tribal Council.

Information from several reliable sources indicates that the following warnings were issued about the possible consequences of the Peabody Mine — all of which were completely ignored, as were the uneasy premonitions of the Hopi spiritual leaders:

Extending 275 miles southwest across the prominence of Black Mesa would be an 18-inch steel pipeline originating at the Peabody processing plant on Black

pipeline

Mesa. This pipeline would slurry a mixture of 50 percent pulverized coal and 50 percent water to the Mojave power plant across the Colorado River from Bullhead City, Arizona. Something between 2,000 and 4,500 gallons of water and 6.6 to 10 tons of coal would pass through the line each minute to the plant, where the slurry would be put into a centrifuge and the water separated from the coal. Peabody, using 7,500 acre-feet of water annually, would pay the Navajo and Hopi tribes $1.67 per acre-foot of water (in contrast to the $55 per acre-foot charged by the Central Arizona Project for Water Use).

While 23,000 tons of coal per day would be used at a plant near Page, Arizona, the rest would be slurried to the power plant near Bullhead City, using the water from deep wells near Black Mesa. According to officials of the Peabody Coal Company, this water was to be drawn from a lower water table that is separated from the topmost 500-foot table by a layer of hard, impervious rock. To ensure against readjustment of the natural equilibrium of the water level by seepage from the upper table into the lower, Peabody said they would line their wells with a waterproof casing. This was by no means sufficient insurance against faults and fissures that occur naturally in the rock strata, or against those which might be created by the disturbances caused by drilling and pumping. Besides these threatening factors, there was a probability that water would not seep through the porous lower table into Peabody's wells fast enough to satisfy their needs. The Navajo sandstone that holds the water table has the quality of only allowing water to pass through it at a slow rate. When Peabody found, as it no doubt realized it would, that the lower table was not providing enough water for its operation, there was nothing set forth in the lease contract to stop them from taking water from the upper table, thus directly ensuring a rapid lowering of the crop-supporting water level.

water

To anyone who really cared, and especially to the Traditional spiritual leaders, it was evident that the amount of water Peabody extracted for its use from the natural aquifer would result in the depletion of springs, dune hollow seeps, windmill-operated wells, and alluvial groundwater supplies, thereby drastically affecting the people, the livestock, and agriculture of an area whose annual rainfall varies between 8 and 15 inches. At a rate of 2,000 gallons per minute pumped to operate the slurry line, the natural water table would be depleted by 2,880,000 gallons of water per day. Over a period of 35 years, which is the time the coal was predicted to last, the number of gallons of water lost to the coal company could be as high as 36,792,000,000. If 4,500 gallons were pumped, the figure for a 35-year period would be 89,204,500,000 gallons. Deprived of this water, corn and other Hopi staples would die, the ages-old way of Hopi life would come to an end, and even the Hopi themselves would have no recourse but to leave the mesa and be absorbed by the outside world.

x Key

Elder David Monongye of Hotevilla warned, "They are not only going to destroy our family land, they will also destroy the life of the people and the way we are living now. The Hopi way is going to be destroyed. That's what they are after, so naturally we don't want it. Black Mesa is a sacred homeland of the Hopi people that should not be destroyed, because if they ever destroy it, we are destroying our Mother Earth, and we were strongly warned not to cut up our land in any manner. It is not for sale. We are not going to sell it, and we should be let alone because (we have no treaty with the government) or with any other nation. (We are still a sovereign nation.) Why should they try to take things away from us by force? And just on account of these Hopi Tribal Council members. They are the ones who are accepting things and leasing out our land without the consent of the real leaders. They are the instrument for the Indian Bureau, and they are not set up in a legal way.

Stolen Land + water No TREATY

"We were told that if the Hopi is defeated, then everything will have to go down. That was a strong warning not to accept anything to be in the village, and right now we are very much concerned about this Peabody Coal Company that is trying to dig up coal and putting up — if I understand it right — six power plants. They are going to build wells that would affect not only the Hopi people, it will affect other people, too. It would affect four states, we were told. And that it would draw all the water from under our feet and there would be no water left for us to drink, and that is something that we don't like. We don't want that. We want that to be stopped completely.

"He's [lawyer Boyden] telling the people that he represents all the villages, but he doesn't. And he is supposed to be a lawyer for only the Hopi Tribal Council, but he is also a lawyer for those who want to drill for oil. I don't know whether he's a lawyer for this Peabody Company too. They just gave a million dollars for just . . . So I told them at the meeting, Now we always do this. When something goes on, we holler and then they don't stop. Then we holler about it, then they say, 'Wait, we already started it. You should have said something before we started. But then, you know, things are going ahead. They [the Tribal Council] don't ever come to our meetings.'"

WINDOW ROCK N.M.

TEM— So what has happened and is happening today? Black Mesa, though topographically a highland, is geologically a structural basin, which, in terms of groundwater, makes it a low point. Skeleton Mesa to the north is higher, as are the Hopi villages and the springs that give them life. The main aquifer of the region, which is where the groundwater is, is the Navajo sandstone. This sandstone formation is 3,000 feet deep under Black Mesa. It is higher in the surrounding areas, but water flows downhill. Pumping 2,000 gallons a minute out of Black Mesa is draining large parts of the water that feeds the Navajo and Hopi reservations. Other than the groundwater, the Hopis and Navajos have only rainfall to depend upon. There are no accessible rivers.

Contrary to public-relations propaganda issued by the mine officials, there is no recharge of this area's Navajo sandstone aquifer from Lake Powell, the reservoir behind the Glen Canyon dam. Because of faulting and warping of the geologic strata, the Navajo sandstone there lies thousands of feet lower than at Black Mesa — and water does not flow naturally uphill. The only recharge available to the aquifer is rainwater, and it has taken millennia to stock the aquifer that exists today. At the 2,000-gallon-per-minute depletion rate, replenishment of any consequence is a hopeless proposition.

What becomes painfully clear is that in the minds of the U.S. Government and industry, the land, water, and people of Black Mesa are expendable. They are sacrificial offerings being exchanged for the unceasing Bahanna demand for electrical power.

As soon as this project was proposed, spokespersons for two Hopi villages, Old Oraibi and Shungopovi, asked: "Cannot this coal be moved to the power plant in some other way besides with precious water? Our religion and way of life say that water is the most important thing for life. Someday we Hopis and other people as well may need this precious water that is being pumped out of the ground, and will find instead that it has been wasted for industry. Someday we may find our springs dry if this drilling cracks the earth and drains our water table. A train or a truck can carry coal, but only the water can make our crops grow and put fluid in our bodies. If they ever put up that plant, it'll be just like California — there'll be smog, and there'll be a lot of trouble, and now that it's already going the trees and the plants will be drying up. See, that's what's gonna happen."

In regard to smog and other pollution, a mid-1970s report indicated that a power plant near Farmington, New Mexico, one not yet in full operation, was already spewing out daily hundreds of tons of flying ash and invisible poisonous gases. Aerial tracking of the visible air pollution revealed that this single plant soiled air, water, land, and peoples over an area of 100,000 square miles in the Four Corners region of New Mexico, Arizona, Colorado, and Utah. What then, the reporter asked, is going to happen when the Farmington plant is joined by its sister San Juan plant, by three more proposed in Utah, and by the two now under construction in Page and Mojave? The effect of coal dust on human lungs and bodies in general is well known to the inhabitants of most major industrial cities of the United States. Some alarmed cities — notably Pittsburgh, Pennsylvania; St. Louis, Missouri; and Los Angeles, California — have begun phase-out programs that will make coal-burning power plants illegal within a decade. Coal miners of Illinois, Kentucky, Indiana, Ohio, West Virginia, and other states are even more familiar with the illnesses associated with the constant inhalation of coal dust. It is a major cause of silicosis, or black lung disease, which is common among miners. Although open-cut strip-mining does not concentrate the dust as much as shaft mining does, the combined effect of smokestack soot from the 60-story towers, mining dust, and the pulverized coal that forms the slurry, has supplied the town of Page and an area for miles around with an awesome blanket of dirty air and haze.

The Salt River Project and Arizona Agricultural Improvement District and Electric Power Sales Utility, which was in charge of building the plant at Page, promised that the 750-foot stacks would be smokeless. They also said that the plant would generate 2,310 megawatts of power by the time it was completed in July 1976 — enough to furnish the electric needs of eight cities the size of

Albuquerque, New Mexico. Even though smokeless, the plant would emit 222 tons of sulfur oxide and 229 tons of nitrogen oxide each day. Experts know that even with a smokeless stack these clear-as-air gases emerge from the stacks. But in Los Angeles, nitrogen oxides — when mixed with hydrocarbons from vehicle-type brown smog and sulfur oxides — are known to combine with water vapor to form a sulfuric acid mist. <u>Across Lake Powell, 12 miles away from Page, is the chosen site for the biggest power plant in the world. It will use coal deposits from Kaiparowitz Plateau, Utah, to produce up to 6,000 megawatts of power</u> — six times as much as the entire state of New Mexico is currently using. As of 1976, Western Energy Supply and Transmission (WEST) had not yet committed itself to building the Kaiparowitz plant, but it is not doubted that one day they will, and <u>when all of these units are in operation the sulfur oxides in the Lake Powell area will be greater than they are in New York City</u>. The nitrogen oxides will be equal to Los Angeles emissions of those same pollutants.

Salt River Project officials, speaking only for the Page plant, said it would have precipitators working at 99.42 percent efficiency, which would clean the stack gas of flying ash to nearly the purity of Ivory soap. And, they added, its construction plant being erected at a cost of $360 million by Bechtel Corporation, the world's largest construction firm, left space for added chemical scrubbers to take out most of the sulfur oxides. They would do this if, of course, it became absolutely necessary.

Conservationists recall that the six WEST partners in the Four Corners generating station, the Fruitland plant, promised in their contracts to install the best equipment available to reduce air pollution from that plant, which has been blamed for reducing visibility as far away as the Rio Grande Valley. Yet when the Department of Health, Education, and Welfare did a pollution study of the Fruitland plant last year, they discovered that, although the contract said it would, the design of the electrostatic precipitators for units 4 and 5, the two newest units, did not incorporate the most effective, commercially proven electrostatic concept available under the technology known at the time of design.

TI— We Told You So… Our Water Is Disappearing… So Will Everyone!

"Not long ago there were many natural springs running through Hopi Land. Hopis knew all of their locations, so they could drink on long journeys. Hopis always had water, enough for themselves, and some springs even supplied flocks of sheep and other animals. As usual, a Bahanna from a government agency was sent to Hopi to make a proposal. This time it was to develop our humble springs into something more productive. He told us enthusiastically that by his methods we could produce more water. The religious leaders shook their heads, saying that it was not a good idea, for it would disturb the great water serpents, who would then stop the water from flowing. 'How foolish,' thought the agent, and sought out other Hopis who were more willing to cooperate. He explained his ideas and soon converted enough people to allow the development of the spring to take place. Many years later we find some of our springs drying up and others giving less water.

Time passed, and yet another agent was sent. This time it was with a proposal to build windmills. He assured the people they would pump the water from deep drilling holes made inside the earth, and that we would never run out of it. Of course, he knew then what we learned later — that the Peabody Mine was lowering the water table so drastically we would need to go deeper than we ever could with our hand-dug wells. The leaders once again shook their heads. 'No good,' they said, 'drilling will pierce the great water serpents and cause them anger, thus drying up more springs.' Again the agent thought 'How foolish they are,' and after thinking very hard, another idea came to him — he would ask the Hopi stock owners to do it, seeing that they had a lot of money tied up in their animals and could not refuse.

So the windmills went up, and more springs went dry.

It was during this time when a new tribal government was being formed — the so-called 'Hopi Tribal Council.' From the beginning, they were ready to welcome the industrial world. The Peabody Coal Company's strip-miners came and introduced themselves with a proposal to strip-mine the Black Mesa.

In their youthful folly, the Puppet Council readily agreed to the proposal and the money involved. No one bothered to seek the blessings of their elders.

Deep wells were drilled, and hundreds of thousands of gallons of water went into use daily to transport the coal to distant places. There were many protests by the chiefs, but all were in vain. The Council and Peabody Coal Company assured everyone that the drilling would not harm the Hopi or the environment. The chiefs shook their heads sadly and said, 'The Mother Earth is being raped. You are destroying the sacred shrines and the great water serpents. What will they do?'

'Why make such a fuss? Your claims are a hoax,' replied the Puppet Council. 'The old ways are long gone. This is the New Age.'

So now, 3,456,000 gallons are being pumped out daily to carry the coal to the processing plants. As time passed, some of the windmills brought up nothing and springs began to go dry. The water shortage became a problem, especially in the modernized homes of the Tribal Council members who lived in Kykotsmovi. In their outrage, they made attempts to stop and gain control over the Peabody Coal Company's continuous use of their water. Laundromats were hurting and the new latrines had to wait until every member of the family had used them before they could flush. Going behind bushes and boulders, as we have done since the old days, could be less painful and cheaper, but the Health Department won't allow it. Anyway, the Tribal Council members are still figuring out what to do about Peabody Coal. And so we write for their benefit, we told you so…"

The Black Mesa Story Is One That Will Grow
to Where It Will Dwarf the Horrors Already Present

TI— "In a 1972 report, we learn that the Black Mesa project, which involves land and resources located on the western Navajo and Hopi Indian reservations in northeastern Arizona, is only part of and the first step in a much larger undertaking spread throughout California, Nevada, Arizona, New Mexico, and Utah, which calls for development of an urban center in the Four Corners area, and construction facilities for producing 14 million kilowatts of electric power primarily for the proposed center itself and for the Southern California megalopolis stretching from Ventura to San Diego, and secondarily for other communities in nine western states. Plans call for at least seven power plants to be built in Page, Arizona; Bullhead City, Nevada; Kaiparowitz Plateau, Utah; San Juan, New Mexico; Shiprock, New Mexico; and Huntington Canyon, Utah. The plants will serve a total of twenty-three power companies, united in a system known as WEST—Western Energy Supply and Transmission Associates. The major participating power companies of the consortium are: Arizona Public Service Company, Tucson Gas and Electric Company, Nevada Power Company, Southern California Edison Company, Public Service Company of New Mexico, El Paso Gas and Electric Company, Utah Power and Light Company, Los Angeles Department of Water and Power, San Diego Gas and Electric Company, Salt River Project of Arizona, and the U.S. Bureau for Reclamation."

TEM— As of early 1994, not only has the water situation at Hopi Land become a grim one, the vast area already strip-mined has become a barren wasteland where, even though the mine officials said they would replant it with trees and other vegetation, nothing is growing successfully, and possibly never will. We were told recently by Hopis at Second Mesa that the water table has dropped nearly 60 feet from the point where it was when the Black Mesa mining project began. We don't know how they obtained that figure, but it sounds reasonable. Wells and springs have dried up in some areas, and the commonest sight on the reservation is that of rain symbols, as prayers for water, painted on the sides of buildings everywhere.

Since we do not have access to Tribal Council files, we do not know what exactly the Council is doing about the situation — although information in a *Washington Post* article that follows clearly indicates some action and Council concern. It has been rumored at the reservation that the Council members, who no longer have any illusions about the damage that is occurring, are greatly alarmed and have insisted that Peabody officials find alternative ways of transporting the coal to the generating plants. The *Post* article confirms this. In other words, they want water use to stop, but the coal mining to remain — for the lease money and jobs, naturally. Trucks and railcars are options, but in Peabody eyes not economically feasible ones. Any person who comes up with a practical solution will be deeply appreciated by both Peabody and the Hopis in general. It seems obvious that from the very beginning some plan for recycling the water, or for obtaining it elsewhere, should have been provided. Even though it would be expensive, water can surely be pumped uphill from Lake Powell, then, when separated at the end of its slurry journey, recycled back into the lake. What are human lives worth? Meanwhile, no one actually knows how much underground water there is left to draw upon, how difficult it will be to reach, or how long the supply will last.

It may already be too late to do anything of significance, and if withdrawal is continued until the coal supply is gone, the damage will be irreparable. What the Government has not otherwise accomplished, the previously mentioned coffin will be finished and ready to receive the body. The Hopi, as Hopi, will be gone, and Hopi efforts to balance the world and keep it in its proper rotation will disappear with them. As said before, if all of this and the prophecies are just delusions on their part, we need not be overly worried. As they always have before, things will work out. The problem is that if we choose to follow that course, and we are wrong, then it will be too late to stop the process. And the price — discussed in Chapter 10 — we will all pay is so high it is beyond calculating!

So where are we now with the Peabody situation? The contract should not, of course, have been signed in the first place, and it should be terminated as quickly as possible. The Elders wanted to do without it, and urged people to settle for lives built around a digging stick, some seeds, fresh, sweet water from bubbling springs, and a simple cloak. But neither that accommodation nor the end of Peabody is likely. In fact, the actions of the Tribal Council — which is almost entirely dependent upon outside money for its existence and usefulness — indicate that along with the previously mentioned taxes, fees, and more leases for oil, gas, coal, or whatever, are already in the works. As Dan put it, "Once the turkey begins to die, you might as well speed up the killing."

Having the necessities of life—be content.

There are other matters for we Bahannas to consider in regard to the minerals and water devastation of Hopi Land. Las Vegas, Nevada, along with, on a lesser scale, Laughlin, has built the grandest gambling casinos imaginable. Just now the media has been featuring in lavish accounts the grand opening in Las Vegas of the sumptuous Luxor Hotel. It has 2,526 rooms. The Treasure Island hotel, to open this year, will have 2,900 rooms. On December 18, MGM Grand Inc. will open with 5,009 rooms and will be the largest hotel in the world. The total visitor count to Las Vegas is expected to jump to 25 million. The Luxor, a 30-story pyramid-shaped resort, features a laser-lighted sphinx and shoots a beam of light from its peak that can be seen from airplanes as far as Los Angeles, 250 miles away. All of these new hotels are theme based, with extravaganzas that feast voraciously on electricity from, as you surely supposed, the power plants that feed on the water and coal taken from Southwest Indian country! We do not know which power plants do service Las Vegas. But does that really matter? If they are not being fed by Peabody coal, the fact that Peabody coal is taking care of other places in Nevada and California allows whomever does provide the power for the casinos to do its job. Accordingly, those fun-loving people who flock there to gamble and enjoy the entertainment might remember as they do so that their hours of pleasure are being provided for by the lifeblood of all of the Hopi and many of the Navajo people — by water that will continue to be their irreplaceable sustenance.

Out beyond this, there is still that previously mentioned giant community being planned for the Four Corners region. With all of its urban demands, what will it do to the Hopis? If by then the water shortage has not finished the job, the

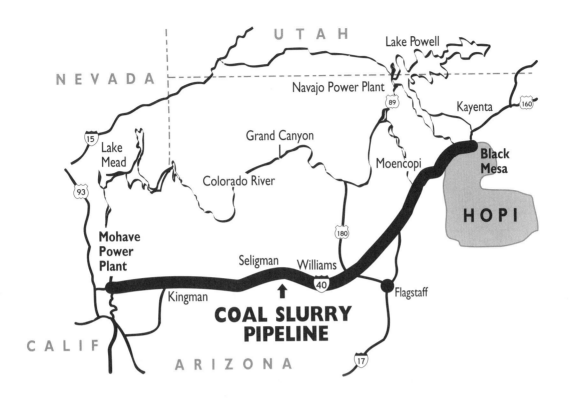

urban community will. Will we meet the displaced Hopi somewhere there in this metropolitan center — a few in professional capacities, others occupied in menial jobs — instead of living unparalleled lives in the villages and carrying out the ceremonial cycle? Think about the difference between that and keeping the natural forces and the world in balance. Anyone can paint this numbing picture as well as Dan and I can.

Bringing things up to date, *The Washington Post* of Wednesday, November 17, 1993, page A14, carried a beautifully done article by Tom Kenworthy, who is a *Post* staff writer. It is titled "Hopis Feel Their Lifeblood Draining Away" and subtitled "Arizona Tribe Blames Water Problem on Coal Being Transported to Nevada Power Plant." The sentences in italics are ours — something we have done to focus attention upon key and revealing points.

"At the base of a spring in northeastern Arizona," Mr. Kenworthy begins, "Hopi Indians have placed prayer offerings made of bird feathers.

"The Hopis depend on the pure waters that come from a deep underground lake to nourish their crops of corn, melons, beans, and squash. Their offerings are a poignant reminder that something is amiss in the village of Moenkopi, which in the Hopi language means 'the land is full of water.' In the past decade or so, that has become something of a misnomer as waters from the village springs and in an intermittent stream known as the Moenkopi Wash have become less and less plentiful.

"The Hopis believe something is terribly wrong with the aquifer that lies several thousand feet under their reservation. In this arid mesa country that has been the Hopis' home for many centuries, the aquifer is both a critical resource for farming and an essential part of the religious life of the tribe.

"The source of their trouble, many Hopi believe, is a huge coal mine to the northeast atop Black Mesa that annually uses more than a billion gallons of water to transfer pulverized coal through a pipeline to an electric plant in Nevada. Although they willingly leased rights to the coal and the water a quarter century ago to the Peabody Western Coal Company — and have, along with the Navajos, profited handsomely from the arrangement — *Hopi tribal officials now say that sharing their water was a tragic mistake. They are asking Interior Secretary Bruce Babbitt to deny the company a renewal of its operating permit, thereby pressuring Peabody to find an alternate [method] of transporting its coal.*

"It is a classic western water fight, in which Peabody Western cites government studies to support its view that the mine and the 273-mile coal slurry pipeline have a negligible effect on the aquifer. But it is more than that, too, because *the Hopis believe if they lose this argument they will face a kind of cultural genocide.* Babbitt's decision, they say, will be seen as a test of how he approaches his responsibility to Native Americans.

"Without the water that bubbles to the surface in seeps, springs, and washes, life would be almost impossible in this area, where it rains only about 10 inches a year.

"In Moenkopi, water has been relatively plentiful for untold generations. But now, the Hopis contend, the Moenkopi Wash, which drains into the Little Colorado River, goes dry in April, whereas it used to be deep enough in July for children to swim. The seeps in the sandstone cliffs above the highway have disappeared. And the springs that emerge from a hillside above the traditional garden plots yield far less water than they used to.

"'Everything is drying up now,' said Alton Honani, who has gardened below the springs for decades. Hopi tribal chairman Vernon Masayesva said it is hard for outsiders to grasp the importance of these precious waters to a tribe that dates its residence in mesa country back 2,000 years and still occupies a village, Oraibi, that was settled before the Magna Carta. The springs on the 1.6-million-acre reservation are sacred sites, central to many of the tribe's traditions and sacred ceremonies, he said.

"'If the water is depleted,' said Masayesva, 'The Hopis will be cut off from this holy land where they have a covenant with their creator.'

"The Hopis know, however, that their dispute with Peabody Western will not be won with emotional appeals based on their ancient way of life, but with arguments backed up by hard science and tough lawyers. So they have hired their own hydrologists and are represented by the Washington law firm of Arnold & Porter. Three years ago, the tribe won a preliminary skirmish when then-Interior Secretary Manuel Lujan Jr. overruled his own department's Office of Surface Mining and delayed issuance of a permit in order to allow further studies on the mine's potential impact on the aquifer and possible alternative modes of transporting its coal.

"These studies are now complete, and Peabody Western officers believe they support the company's argument that the aquifer is in no danger and that there is no economical alternative to the pipeline that sluices millions of tons of coal a year to the Mohave Generating Station in Laughlin, Nevada. Peabody Western maintains that without the water to slurry the coal, Black Mesa would become unprofitable and might have to shut down. That would be a severe economic blow to both the Hopis and Navajos, because Black Mesa and a sister mine provide hundreds of jobs and tens of millions of dollars in annual royalty payments. The Hopis alone reap about $10 million a year in coal royalties plus about $1.5 million for the water, payments that constitute about 80 percent of their tribal budget.

"But the Hopis argue that loss of the water from the aquifer shouldn't shut the Black Mesa mine. An alternative is available, they say: building a water pipeline from Lake Powell that they contend would raise the price of coal by just 80 cents a ton and electric rates for users in Los Angeles and elsewhere by 1 to 6 cents a month.

"The 100,000 acre-feet of water the Black Mesa mine will use during its lifetime, said Peabody Western President W. Howard Carson, represents just one-tenth of 1 percent of the aquifer's reserves and will be replenished naturally in a relatively short time after mining ceases. An acre-foot is the amount of water needed to cover one acre a foot deep and is equal to 325,851 gallons. Earlier studies by the Office of Surface Mining and the U.S. Geological Survey back Carson up and lend some credence to the company's position that it is a prolonged drought, rather than withdrawals for the pipeline, that has affected the tribe's water sources. But as in most complex resource fights — and this one involves a resource deep underground where study is difficult — the science is not always precise.

"For example, the Environmental Protection Agency, in reviewing an environmental impact study of the mine three years ago, found 'potential adverse impacts' of the groundwater pumping on the aquifer and said 'the wisdom of continuing use of this water for a slurry pipeline' was uncertain.

"And late last month, after being asked to review the model upon which earlier studies were based, the U.S. Geological Survey reported that 'the model is not well suited to address concerns about adverse effects on individual washes and springs.' Because of the uncertainty, the USGS said it 'cannot make definite statements about the effects of pumping for slurry transportation.'

"With their lifeblood at stake and so much uncertainty, Hopi officials argue that Babbitt should err on the side of caution.

" 'We've been here a long time,' said Nat A. Nutongla, director of the Hopi water resources program. 'And we want to stay a lot longer.' "

It is clearly seen from the *Post* article that what we have in the Peabody Mine is another, but as bad as it can be, example of Tribal Council ineptness, of their entering in managerially or politically where they are not equipped to go, and of the consequences that come from not letting the tribal Elders guide them in decision making. The Elders do not have the training needed to make Bahanna-type geological judgments either, but they do have the ear of Maasaw, who, as history has proven, can unerringly tell them where they should be cautious and what course they should follow for the best good of all Hopis.

There are many areas of service the Council can fill that are needed, and which would not require them to do many of the things they have done. Some of the things that the Council, and particularly the Office of Cultural Preservation, have accomplished in the attempt to curb the sale and theft of Hopi religious paraphernalia are certainly commendable, as is their cooperation with anthropologists in the deciphering of rock art at Hopi shrines — although when I asked Dan about their ability to do this, he replied that they lacked the necessary training to do it with any degree of competence.

Understandably, in light of serious mistakes the Council has made and its arrogant dealing with affairs in general, the Elders and all other Traditionals would like to see the Council gone. Yet in today's world, and in view of the fact that the transformed Hopis have little recourse but to deal with outsiders and a modernized Hopi Land, there is probably a need for a vigorous coordinating body whose entire goal is to protect and provide for the well-being of the Hopi people. If the Council would accept a continuing delineation of their jobs by the kik-mongwis and religious leaders of all of the villages, and one that either replaced or more carefully defined the present Hopi Constitution, the entire relationship could become a pleasant and advantageous one. They need to sit down together and talk — in Hotevilla, and not in the Tribal Council chambers.

Of course, if the "object" at Hotevilla has been, or is in the future, destroyed, any changes are a moot point. They could only affect the pace and manner of Hopi and world demise. They could not keep it from happening.

<u>Is Hotevilla a microcosm of the world</u>?

Consider just a few excerpts from our local Riverside, CA, *Press Enterprise* newspaper:

November 8, 1993, p. A3: *"Population growth drains world's freshwater supplies, report says*... People from Los Angeles to Beijing to Riyadh, Saudi Arabia, are having to look farther and farther away for fresh water... water scarcity is a spreading global problem... <u>By 2025, one out of three people will be living in countries with inadequate freshwater supplies</u>... Over the next three decades, between 46 and 52 countries will be either 'water-stressed' or 'water-scarce,'... Even in the United States, which has abundant freshwater supplies nationally, regional demand often exceeds supply."

November 10, 1993, p. A3: *"Water warning — World faces peril, National Geographic says*... Americans have squandered fresh water to the point of creating a national emergency... America's fresh water will continue to decline — with dire consequences — unless we all commit ourselves to reasonable consumption, preservation and conservation... Unlike energy, there is a finite supply of fresh water worldwide... there is no substitute... <u>all of the fresh water there ever has been or ever will be is on earth now</u>."

March 22, 1994, p. A3: *"40 years later, water cleanup set*... After 40 years, the oil company acknowledged it was time to stop covering up and start cleaning up. Unocal Corp. executives, embarrassed by evidence that employees for years hid petroleum leaks that killed sea lions and contaminated groundwater, hope to restore a stretch of Central California... Kathy Johannes recalled a gruesome die-off of seals and sea lions in 1988, when the company denied any spills... A state investigation found that as far back as 1978, employees were told not to call attention to spills of diluent, a transparent thinner used to dilute the field's heavy crude. The pollution was able to go unchecked for so long partly because most of the diluent seeped into the ocean..."

How many cover-ups like this — and much larger ones — do you suppose are going on daily all over the world, and what will the true cost really be?

RELOCATION OF THE NAVAJOS

In 1979 the Hopi Tribe wrote an open letter to the members of the United States Senate, the House of Representatives, their staff members, and to all friends of the Hopi people regarding the <u>relocation of the Navajos who have settled illegally on Hopi Land</u>. The letter sums up in a very efficient way the history of the

Hopi/Navajo problem, and ends with a poignant paragraph describing the present condition of the Hopi people and reservation. It witnesses well to my previous suggestion that there could be a healthy accommodation between the Council and the Elders. Yet you will also see that the solutions proposed by the two groups vary greatly. The Council seeks to solve the problem by what Dan describes as "Bahanna ways," while the Elders seek to solve it by placing it in the Hopi spiritual context that addresses the ending of the Fourth Cycle of the world and the beginning of the Fifth.

Excerpts from the Tribal Council's open letter:

"We believe that the 1974 Act was basically fair and consistent with both law and equity. We also believe that in the whole history of this case, our Tribe has clearly demonstrated its ability and willingness to follow a policy of reasonableness in its approach to the Federal Government... Based on that evaluation, we have proposed legislation which seeks to correct certain present inadequacies in an even-handed way and to meet the most pressing needs of both the Navajo and Hopi Tribes. We hope this Congress will carefully consider all proposals and effect improvements which will not offend the delicate balance achieved by the 1974 Act. The courts and the Relocation Commission should then be left to complete the task which Congress entrusted to them...

"With this information, we pray that *our leaders in Washington, D.C.,* and other friends of the Hopi will understand and support our efforts to work within the America System for Justice and a proper settlement to the long-standing Hopi-Navajo conflict... Throughout the history of the Hopi-Navajo land dispute there is one fact that has not and cannot be disputed. This fact, verified on page 10 of the Opinion of the Court in *Healing* v. *Jones*, is that no Indians in this country have a longer authenticated history than the Hopis. As far back as the Middle Ages the Hopis occupied the area between Navaho Mountain (Tokonavi) and the little Colorado River, between the San Francisco Mountains and the Luckachukas. The Hopi Village of Oraibi is considered by archaeologists to be the oldest continuously inhabited community in North America. The Hopi have lived in that area for more than 1,200 years. Other archaeological evidence of Hopi communities and religious shrines in the region predate even Oraibi by hundreds of years. Regular pilgrimages and gathering trips to these shrines and gathering areas are still made today. As a result, the Hopi have deep religious, cultural, and emotional ties to these lands as well as settled, long-standing legal rights. These are the lands which the Hopi formerly used in peace for centuries before the Navajo came to the Southwest.

"The establishment of reservation boundaries did nothing to halt the more numerous Navajo from intruding onto traditional Hopi lands and the new reservation. Repeated appeals by Hopis to the U.S. Government did not bring action. By 1934, the Navajos claimed almost all of the land surrounding the then-existent Hopi communities, depriving the Hopi of peaceful access to many of their hunting, farming, and traditional ceremonial areas... There were, and are, more than twenty times as many Navajo as there are Hopi people. When the Hopis attempted to use their lands for farming, grazing, wood gathering, and other purposes, they were frequently and violently prevented from doing so by the Navajo. This record of abuses extends back more than 100 years . . . This situation worsened in 1934 by direct action of the Bureau of Indian Affairs. In that year, the BIA illegally divided the Hopi 1882 Reservation into grazing districts and issued grazing permits to the Navajo throughout the Hopi Reservation, with the exception of Grazing District Six. Further, through administrative action, the BIA denied the Hopis the use of most of their other reservation lands. Ultimately, the BIA succeeded in confining the Hopi to Grazing District Six, about 25% of the original reservation.

"Over the years, the Navajos had forced their way into the Hopis' aboriginal lands, and government agencies, through illegal action, had virtually turned three-fourths of Hopi land over to the Navajo. Despite all this, the traditionally peaceful Hopi did not resort to violence or forced occupation. Rather they have pursued forums in Congress and the courts to strive to protect their rights and to receive justice. They have often been disappointed.

"On December 22, 1974, the President signed Public Law 93-531, the Hopi-Navajo Settlement Act of 1974. This act authorized the court to partition the land. It also provided relocation benefits, some continued litigation and, in summary, directed the courts to settle the dispute along the legal and equitable lines the courts had already determined... Due to constant Navajo delaying tactics, ascertained and condemned by the federal courts on several occasions, and due to the ineffective action by the Interior Department's Joint Use Area Administrative Office, the Hopis find themselves in 1979, more than four years after Congress declared its intent that the land be divided, without any additional access to and use of their land.

"Further efforts of Navajo leaders to block Hopi rights have worked to the detriment of even Navajo people... The Hopi Tribe is cognizant of hardships placed on potential relocatees and have supported many benefits for Navajos. The Hopi Tribe feels that delay makes relocation more painful for Hopis and Navajos alike and more expensive for the federal government. It is essential that the relocation process proceed more expeditiously and efficiently... It is now clear that the 1974 Act needs updating, if the objectives set forth by Congress over four years ago will ever become reality. It is necessary that jurisdictional timelines and goals and other amendments be added to the 1974 Act to help bring about an early solution to current problems... For these reasons, the Hopi Tribe has developed legislation for consideration by the 96th Congress."

"Because of its relative isolation, the Hopi Tribe has been able to retain the purity of its traditional and cultural past far better than other Indian tribes.

"Over recent decades, the factors of isolation, poor health services, an agrarian base, and confinement to ancient villages have had the effect of keeping the population growth of the Hopi Tribe relatively low. But changes in the form of mass communication, paved highways, tourist exposure, better health and education services, and a trend to a dollar-based economy are necessitating changes in Hopi life.

"The use for economic development of lands already partitioned by the court to the Hopi holds the key to tribal ability to maintain themselves and their culture, and to be able to function in the Western economic system. This is one reason why regaining the use of our land is so important to the Hopi.

"The Hopi are traditionally a patient and peaceful people. They are sensitive to hardship. They have endured more than their share at the hands of others. The Hopi believe that there must be a balance between sensitivity to relocation hardship to the Navajo and securing the Hopi people's equitable and legal stand interests, which are so vital to Hopi survival.

"Delay in implementation of the 1974 Act has grave consequences for the future of Hopi culture. Delay in implementation prolongs the anxiety, frustration, and uncertainty which the Hopi people have endured for over a century. Delay in implementation also creates additional hardship to Hopi and Navajo individuals alike.

"Time is running out for the Hopi. Because of continued deprivation their reservation is becoming a place populated by the elderly and the very young.

"Overcrowded households, the lack of a high school or medical center, and the lack of jobs force young adults to the cities and border towns. Lack of a sufficient number of challenging work opportunities keep educated Hopi adults off the reservation. But the Hopi always come back to the Mesa, their homeland, for observing and participating in their cultural events.

"Hopis won't expect miracles when they finally have access to their land. The first priority will be to restore their land to a usable condition, then over time homes will be built and new communities established. A place where young educated Hopi adults can earn a decent living and be close to their heritage will be a reality, not just a dream, only when the lands which the courts and the Congress have time and again determined to be rightfully theirs are restored to the Hopi."

We turn now to what the Elders have to say about the Hopi/Navajo land dispute, and immediately find an important difference of opinion.

Why Is There a Land Dispute? Because the Tribal Councils of the Two Nations Have Created It for Their Own Personal Reasons:

TI— "The United States Congress has made several attempts to 'solve' what certain vested interests have claimed is a 'land dispute' between Hopi and the Navajo. They do this at a great distance from the people whom their decisions affect. Their ideas of 'ownership' and 'jurisdiction' are alien to the way we live.

Public law 93-531 is a recent attempt which proposes negotiations between the 'Tribal Councils' of the two nations. If the negotiations fail, which is almost certain, being based upon ideas alien to both, the Secretary of the U.S. Department of the Interior will be given control of the matter, which involves a plan to declare a boundary, and fence the Hopi and the Navajo off from each other.

It is clearly evident that the so-called 'Hopi Tribe' is the thorn hurting the establishment's progress in solving the land problem. In the past, many attempts have been made through its press to distort the meaning of the Traditionals' actions, including the Hopi and Navajo unity movement, which the Tribal Council opposes in their fight to 'regain' Hopi Land through White man's law. They wonder why the Traditionals want to keep relations with the Navajo, who were once their enemy. They also claim that there is no such thing as a true Hopi leader in any Hopi village who can think for his people. They say it is a pity that the Traditional leaders take it upon themselves to solve the land problem, ignoring the labors of the Tribal Council governments of the Navajo and Hopi. 'Look!' says the Bahanna Council, 'I am the Supreme Chief of the Hopi Nation. You must obey what I say. I create jobs for you so you can make lots of money, and get cars, television, and everything that the White man has, courts and jails where you get justice.' This sounds glorious, but they don't talk about the disadvantages that always come when things are done their way.

The whole problem could have been avoided if the Tribal Councils of the Hopi and Navajo had sat down together to consider what their Traditional leaders want. They must cease exploiting the Traditionals and grabbing after the land. They should liberate those who want to live their original lives instead of downgrading them. Most of the people wish to live a simple life and keep their cultural heritage. This is the most important element which the Bahanna Council fails to see. Perhaps the U.S. Government has foreseen that if the leaders of both Tribal Councils persist, their struggle might end in bloodshed.

A startling conclusion by the Traditionals: It is in the prophecies of the Hopi that in a case like this the Navajo may help our cause. Also the Bahannas or the Piute Tribe may help. We doubt that the U.S. Government will easily concede our sovereignty. If possible both Hopi and Navajo Traditionals would like separation from those who want to be assimilated. Both tribes could thereby retain their identity and lay the foundation for a self-respecting community.

The Hopi were established long before the White race came to this continent. Their leadership is deeply rooted in their culture and traditions, and most important, in the Creator's law, which is everlasting. Every race in the world began this way, including the Bahannas. Therefore the Traditional Hopi do not base their authority upon majority rule. Instead, they stand upon the oneness of man's tradition throughout the world. Even the Bahanna Hopi still practice their ceremonies despite the fact that they spit upon their tradition. Yes, our heritage is powerful. One cannot erase by law a people's traditions and religious history that has been nurtured by centuries, and lies at the base of every phase of their lives.

As an example of this, one day Emery Sekaquaptewa came to a group of us near Hotevilla and announced that he and his wife were quitting the Hopi way, that he and his wife could not stand living under its system and were converting themselves and their children to the Mormon Church and relocating. But in spite of what he said, Grandma Sekaquaptewa was seen making piki bread and other traditional foods for the traditional wedding. A traditional wedding robe was made for the daughter. Just the other day Grandma Sekaquaptewa was seen watching traditional ceremonial dances, and her son Emery is making a lot of money teaching traditional Hopi culture and language to the White folks. We have heard that he wants Traditional schoolchildren to speak Hopi and learn the traditional ways.

What does tradition mean? We have concluded that it is power. To the Hopi it is a barrier protecting their independence against Bahannas' destructive efforts. The so-called Tribal Council has not seen the importance of this, so they have gone on a march for progress, leasing our land, making money, and paving the way for encroachment. Perhaps their most childish act was a gift of a million dollars to their Mormon lawyer for Christmas. As if in rebellion against tradition they mock and downgrade the Traditionals as primitives who must not use White man's clothing, or for that matter anything else made by the White man, and go back to G-strings and donkeys. We feel sad when such words are thrown at us, but we know they are foolish. The Progressives will come back crawling under the cloak of tradition when they come up against the stone wall. When they do, we shall not retaliate by stripping them of all traditional things.

Now as the so-called 'Hopi Tribe' tackles the land problem, they find they can't go over the hump and solve it without having the image of being 'real' Hopi. So the chickens come home to roost. How can they get land for the Hopis without being Hopi themselves! So they are backpedaling furiously. Hopi awareness programs now flourish throughout the schools. Hopi children are encouraged to speak their language and learn traditional dances and customs, which are a 'must' for special programs and activities. But even though the Council now leans heavily on tradition, they have nothing to do with the original Hopi. In fact, they diminish them and force them into extinction. They replace living beings with a written law to protect dead ruins, and pretend to be interested in the restoration of ceremonial kivas. While this is going on, their chairman and lawyers are busy behind the scenes scheming at ways to lick 'the opposition' in order to exploit the people and their natural resources. Are they really interested in saving the ceremonies, we wonder? They are, after all, Bahanna Christians. To them the ceremonies, kivas, and shrines are taboo — places where the work of devils is practiced by heathens. But they are willing to go along with the holding of ceremonials where there is money to be made.

They have lured into their fold some 'Traditionalists,' whom we shall call 'Bahanna Traditionalists,' some of whom hold office in Traditional Hopi society. This allows them to be Council members or job holders who have some insight into traditional knowledge, but little understanding of the Bahanna political system. Some of them cannot read English, yet they are allowed to hold a seat and make decisions and laws. Since the Council works through a one-party system, the voice vote is often 'Ayes' and seldom 'Nays.' It depends on how much sugar coating a proposition has. The means by which they are elected are in most cases questionable. In the case of Oraibi, the representative is self-appointed with no support from the people of the village. All Council officers are paid. The Bahanna Traditionalists are useful in creating a traditional image to the outside world, though they may in fact hold only inferior offices or none at all in the traditional

amen

Gold Fever White man's disease

system. Their function is to give false advice to the truly Traditional Hopi and to serve as a front — while the Council tells the outside world that its members are a different kind of Hopi, the 'true' Hopi, which they hope will lower people's opinion of the actual Traditional leaders.

But the authority of those who do this is null and void, according to Hopi tradition. Before entering the Bahanna world the True Hopi inherited the original Hopi wisdom and knowledge from his Great Chief Uncles with all the instructions as to what to avoid at this stage. He is supposed to be of strong character and deeply devoted to the Creator's law and instructions. Sacred vows are fixed to his office in order to protect his power and authority to lead his people until death. To disregard these vows is to become a traitor to the Great Spirit, to His religion, and to His people.

The traditional Hopi leader does not accept money for his office. He is too strongly and deeply devoted to do that, for the original Hopi came into this world together, and their instructions and teachings have remained the same to this day. He is therefore willing to follow the path set out for him and fulfill the prophecies — no matter what the consequences. He knows what help will come, for it has been planned by the Creator. If no help materializes from other people, it will come in the form of destruction by nature. If none of this materializes, then the True Hopi is wrong. This much we know . . . one day soon people everywhere will see with their own eyes how it will be."

The Progressive Hopi Chairman Speaks Regarding Hotevilla . . .
Think About This When You Wonder Why It Was Necessary
for the Traditionals to Write Their Own Newsletter

TI— "We would like to share with you the views of Progressive Chairman Ivan Sidney concerning the statements he made about our meeting with U.N. observers in our village, about what he thinks of our village leaders and their wrongdoing. This statement was made through the Tribal Council newsletter. We quote only part of what he says, but give your attention to how he thinks and works:

'There were only five Traditionals supporting and representing the Hopi position, and a house full of Big Mountain Navajos, their attorneys and non-Indian supporters. I cannot help but wonder what would have happened if the investigating team had met only with these people at Hotevilla. Who are these few Hopis who claim to speak for the Traditionals and try to dictate the future of the entire Hopi Nation? Just who are these Hopis who claim to speak the Hopi views and yet support the Navajo position? Either they are being manipulated and misled, but they do not speak for the Hopi people. They speak only for themselves. The activities of these Hopi individuals are becoming a concern among the Hopi people.

'At a recent village meeting the village leadership requested the Tribal Council to begin investigation of these Hopis who are advocating on behalf of the Navajos and involving themselves with Big Mountain Legal Office.

These Hopis are capitalizing on the land issue for their own personal and financial gain. Their activities jeopardize Hopi interests, hurting all the Hopi people. How much longer should we, as Hopis, tolerate their behavior? The same few Hopis are traveling nationally and internationally advocating for Traditional Hopi position.

'We, the Hopi people, have tolerated their outrageous behavior up to now. How many Hopi people have had enough? <u>Let us hear from Hopi villages how they feel about these Hopis who are trying to give our land away.</u> What should we do about these Hopis? There are non-Indians who are helping breed dissension and conflict within Hopi people. We must awaken to this fact and not allow such outsiders to further factionalize the tribe.'"

More About the Relocation of the Navajo

TI— "The first thing we want to make clear is the definition of Hopi. The Progressive Hopi Tribal Council is a <u>governing body elected to represent each Hopi village</u> — if that village chooses to do so under the constitution bylaws adopted from Bahanna.

progressive

Traditional

The Traditional lives under or in His own ways according to the <u>Divine Laws of the Great Creator.</u> The Traditional Hopi are independent of the Progressive Council and do not support the Progressives in the relocation issue.

Since the inception of this publication some years ago, this paper has never published anything about the Navajo and Hopi dispute over the land issue to inform the outside world about what is happening between the Progressive Hopi and the Navajo. The editor of this publication found this to be an impossible position to maintain. After a survey among the Hopi leaders and people, we find that opinions about supporting the Council's position in the Navajo problem are mostly negative. This is a finding that tells us that the Hopi should take a 'wait and see' attitude and not get involved too deeply. What we have gathered is that there is not really opposition to Navajo presence, but rather a sense of wanting to take a more modest approach, based on the agreement the Navajo and Hopi smoked over long ago, one which obligated the Navajo to work out with us matters they must fulfill.

All in all, if the Navajo do depart from the area, the Hopi Progressives will take over and the Traditional Hopi will be left out — unless we join in and get a piece of the pie or at least some of the crumbs.

As it has been for past years, the editor of this paper has been sitting on the fence about this in order to avoid unpleasant decisions and to stay away from controversy. This also has been due to a lack of understanding of the Bahanna ways of political dealing in such matters and the fear that once he involves himself in the issue he may become a devil's advocate who creates a nasty situation for both the Hopi and himself.

In any event, it <u>is not easy to keep up with the relocation problem.</u> Here, however, is the <u>latest news</u>... I will quote some lines hoping it will give some insight for you.

"BIA AIMS TO SOFTEN NAVAJO RELOCATION

The agreement which was signed by BIA and the Relocation Commission put the BIA in charge of the fate of hundreds of Navajo Indians who now face relocation and may mean that none of them will be forced off the land against their will. The immediate objective within the BIA is to try to persuade as best we can the 238 families still on Hopi-partitioned land that we can help them replicate their lifestyle. In Washington, D.C. Representative Udall, D.-Ariz., introduced a bill that would change the 1974 law that made mass relocation necessary in the first place. The bill, in effect, would nullify the BIA agreement. The bill would require the Navajo to pay the Hopi about $300 million from royalties on coal leases, would allow about 700,000 acres of land to be exchanged between the two tribes, and would settle all outstanding legal disputes over Navajo and Hopi Tribal Lands. The Hopi Council made no comment.

A memorandum of understanding signed set up procedures under which the BIA will provide housing and infrastructure for relocatees. Its role in providing those services was mandated by an appropriations bill by Congress. The BIA will take over the controversial job of convincing families that a decent future awaits them if they move. Humanely and sincerely they would work with them and not force anything on them they don't want. No one will be pushed off the land. There are a few older folks who probably will not want to move, but something will be worked out for them, something like leases. But there will be nothing happening on July 6, the deadline set by the court for relocation. Because of the slow process of relocation it has built up a natural rebellion.

This may be a bad law. A bright future could await the Hopi if they move to the new land. Only 30 families say they will not move. The area has been described by Anti-Relocation Activists as the home of hundreds of Navajos who are determined not to move. We want to start taking people down to the new land and grazing lands, if they agree to go; in two or three weeks we can start building there. But we have to treat these people like human beings. If they want we have to find them good homesites. We think people will be thankful for relocation if we build a home with water and other conveniences that are at least as good. We support the Memorandum of Understanding if the law has to be carried out, that is the way to do it. Too bad that it wasn't done long ago, so all the suffering would not happen.' "

The Moratorium on Navajo Relocation

TI— "During the Navajo relocation deadline of July 7, intended to be a showdown, there was no direct action taken. Protest marches of Navajo and outside support groups were in evidence, ending with the main event near Big Mountain of the cutting of more than half a mile of partition fence by the Navajos. At this time things are at a standstill. Promoters of relocation are at their wits' end, scratching their heads, figuring the next move that might work. The Hopi Tribal Council chairman demands a relocation plan in 30 days, insisting that

Navajos are trespassers subject to eviction.

Most impressive is Bill S. 2545, which Senator Cranston (California) introduced in condemnation of the relocation ruling (PL-93-531), since this ruling has not worked after 12 years. His bill calls for a moratorium on relocation. It also calls for the establishment of a Presidential Advisory Committee to study the remaining problems. The committee would consist of the Secretary of the Interior, four members of Congress, four Hopi Indians and four Navajo Indians. The Hopi and Navajo delegations would consist of two from each Tribal Council, two Traditional leaders, and two elders who are facing relocation.

If we understand correctly, the moratorium would halt all further funding for relocation through the fiscal year, 1987. So we expect nothing will happen for quite some time. This depends on the passing of the bill.

For firsthand information, write to or contact:

Big Mountain JUA, Legal D/OCOMM
2501 N. 4th Street, Suite 18, Flagstaff, AZ 86001
Phone (602) 774-5233"

Defining Hopi Nation and Hopi Tribe...

TI— "Which faction in Hopi Land deserves the name 'Hopi Nation' or 'Hopi Tribe'? These two important names have been crisscrossing between the Traditional Hopi and the Progressive 'Hopi Tribal Council.' We mention it here because it has caused much head scratching and confusion among outsiders who are unfamiliar with the Hopi. It is particularly noticeable in the Navajo relocation issue.

It seems these terms portray all the united Hopi tribe within the Hopi Nation as working together in trying to throw out the Navajo by their ears. We view this as misleading, for the Traditional Hopi are not involved in relocation so as not to tarnish our proud name of peaceful Hopi. As far as we know, the 'Hopi Tribal Council' was created by the BIA. We don't know from what substance, and they failed to give them a name, so they adopted the name 'Hopi Tribe.'

The Traditional Hopi were created by the Great Creator from spiritual seed, and received the name 'Hopi' long before the progressive council was ever heard of. We will let you decide which it should be."

MISSIONARIES

Earlier, the writers of the newsletters expressed their relief over the fact that missionary activities at the Hopi villages had, while not ceasing entirely, diminished, and conversion was in a state of remission. There has been one glaring exception to this condition — the Mormon Church. You will remember that they were the first of the missionaries who made their way into Hopi country, and even though their success during the last hundred years has been limited, they have never left. It is commonly known that the Mormon Church does not take "No" for an answer. It not only persists in its missionary activities, it seeks to expand its possibilities whenever the opportunity presents itself. Since Hopi converts to this church sit as members of the Hopi Tribal Council, the Council has cooperated with Mormon requests before and can be expected to do so again. You will recall that the lawyer, Mr. Boydon, was a Mormon, and that at least one tribal chairman was a Mormon convert.

If the Missionaries Had Only Taken the Time to Listen to Us, and the Mormon Church Would Listen Now

TI— "The issue of religious beliefs and prophecies is one most people frown on, yet it is most important. People the world over have been debating these issues, causing wars and destruction in the name of holiness. This need not be, if we look at our religious beliefs as a dominant guiding influence to peace and harmony. Otherwise the influence and gifts of the Great Spirit must be expressed by certain people who are willing to survive in order to keep life in balance.

Very often we hear the tune, 'Do the Hopi really hold the key to survival in their mysticism?' We do not want to undermine any religious groups. Hopi does not claim the key, for all people on Earth are responsible for holding the key to survival. A Traditional Hopi merely teaches alternatives by basing his knowledge on the past histories of humankind from previous worlds. We were instructed to tell of the Great Purification just ahead of a time when humankind would once again become highly civilized, tending to become careless and leading all of us to self-destruction. Survival is up to each of us to consider. Furthermore, we believe the instructions were given to all people long ago, according to where we are placed and how we were commissioned to fulfill our duties. Hopi brings this message to the world, hoping that there are pillars, however feeble these seem to be, still standing by the strength of His knowledge. Only His way will endure.

It is said there is only one Great Spirit, our maker, and that we, as His children, should be one happy family. But instead of equality, we develop caste systems and practice class struggle, glaring at each other in greed. Most religious groups boost their particular method of attaining perfection, while downgrading and undermining others in order to govern territories and people who wish to live in peace through their own inherent beliefs. *We worship one Great Spirit through many different names, and symbols of characters as varied as the lands of the earth. In this way we reach Him to get our strength by His blessing. We have also said the earth is like a spotted fawn, the spots being areas with a certain power and purpose. Each of us is provided with a different vibration and frequency which is designed for communicating with the Great Spirit, in order to accomplish certain life-supporting functions of Natural Laws in accordance with our own customary ways.*

Aware of this knowledge, we Traditionals have no intention of forsaking the Great Spirit's words. When the first missionaries came, the Hopi was respectful and did not attempt to interfere with their religion. We trusted they had come armed with knowledge, and would show the same respect by not interfering with Hopi religion. But as predicted by our elders, this would not be the case. It was said that only those who have made some kind of mistake in their past would forsake their original beliefs, then join other religions in order to cleanse their spirit and go to heaven — thus escaping the Hopi underworld after death. But this would be in vain, for we have our own original path given to us by the Great Spirit from the beginning. In respect to this, the Hopi do not twist the arms of others to get them to join their flocks.

Mormon

It was very disheartening that the missionaries did not take the time to understand our culture and spiritual ways. If they had, they would have seen that the Hopi believe there is one Great Spirit. Instead they used the time to convert our people from their native ways.

Conversion can eventually bring destruction to all humankind. Most of us Hopi have learned from our elders of the prophecy of the end… about a sea of water eating us up if we become converted into another religion which is not ours. With the Peabody Mine eating up our water, we might wonder where this water would come from, but if any Hopi is doubtful the prophecy can be tested (although we warn that the consequences cannot be undone once this is set in motion.)

We are pleased to say that the attempt to draw us into adopting other religions has greatly decreased, except for one group of Mormons who persist in building their church in the midst of our shrines and landmarks.

We reject this idea, for it will further imbalance the functional harmony between us and the natural forces of the Great Spirit."

World Council of Churches Supports Traditional Native Religion at a Time When the Whole Earth Is Glorified!

TI— "This may be bad news for the devil, but it brings out our brighter side. We received a letter telling us that the last assembly of the World Council of Churches in Geneva and in Nairobi agreed upon a resolution to support the vested original rights of the North American Indian in general, and to make a study about the very problem of the 'Traditionals.' It said that support will be given to groups or organizations of White people known to be in strong support of the traditional native nations.

We wonder whether we are dreaming. Could this mean us? We like to take for granted that we are not a forgotten race, but after a full century of unending interference we are weary of our surroundings. But we must not forget that this is a purification month (Powamuwa), and that everything has been purified, land and life, the unseen above and below. The whole earth is glorified! This may be a good omen.

Devil → On the other hand, the Mormon Church is requesting a land tract:

Wayne Sekaquaptewa, brother of the puppet council chairman, and president of the Oraibi branch of the Church of Jesus Christ of the Latter Day Saints, announced in *Qua'toqti* on March 11, 1976, that members of the LDS Church on Second and Third Mesas have petitioned the Hopi Tribal Council on February 5, for a 99-year lease on 5-acres of land about 1-mile north of Old Oraibi. The Church intends to construct a chapel and other facilities with a kitchen and classroom and special features for the preparation of Hopi food, such as oven pits and a piki house. The remaining land would be used for additional buildings as the membership expands.

Throughout recent history it has been our experience that Bahanna missionaries are always at the root of our problems. If these missionaries had not been so persistent in their efforts to convert us to their beliefs, the younger generation would have a greater under-standing and trust in their own teachings, and our way of life would not be disintegrating as it is today. Perhaps our attitude towards the Mormon Church would be less bitter if their conduct toward Hopi traditional-thinking people had been less excessive.

Any average person can easily see that it is wrong for them to construct their temples here without consulting the rightful people. That land might not appear to be in use now, but this area is already dedicated to a sacred purpose. There are many shrines there, some of which have already been destroyed by road construction.

So once more we look at this with suspicion. The establishment of this indoctrination facility, and the methods by which the land is being obtained, could be part of an attempt by the Mormon Church to take over all of our land. It is a fact that many key posts are occupied by Hopi Mormons, including those of the two Tribal Council attorneys from Salt Lake City.

It is very sad that the Mormons disregard our rightful leaders to get what they want. It is obvious that they follow this course knowing that they can get the land without question from none other than their own kind, by working with young Hopi who have no Hopi spiritual or earthly foundation, and have lately been brought to power by outsiders.

Upon hearing the proposal, Mina Lansa, Kikmongwi of Oraibi, and Sewe-manewa, a religious leader of Hotevilla, went straight to Wayne Sekaquaptewa's office, for they knew that he would not come before the Traditional leaders when invited. They both gave him a tongue lashing, but said later that it was as if they were talking to a dead stump.

'You listen to me carefully,' Mina began, 'I have come clear over here to look right in your eyes and speak to you. You must lack respect by not coming to us for proper approval to build your church between my village and Hotevilla. You know very well that the Tribal Council does not own that land. Who gave it to them? On what authority? We Traditional leaders and people desire no church on our land in that area. Please heed what we say to you here today. Do not intrude upon our land with your church.'

"Sewemanewa added, 'We are closely related brothers. I have spoken to our brother Abbott [the Tribal Council chairman] several times. Ever since you and your whole family became the ruling class, you do as you please, regardless of whether it is right or wrong. You are breaking up and dividing the whole Hopi nation. One day you will come to a dead end with your faithful followers. It may not be a good one, so I warn you both to be prepared for the consequences. We do not want that church there, and we mean it.'

More words were spoken. Although Wayne did not challenge them, he only promised to let them know the outcome of the proposal."

they have always been Greedy & make own Laws —

385

Dollars or Corn and Beans?

TI— "During the past several months our tempo has increased. Both Progressive and Traditional factions have been seeking support wherever possible — one through promises of gain, the other through religious commitment — aware that the unrest and difficulties we experience means that somehow our duties are not being fulfilled in accordance with the Great Laws. We seek support and strength from the Great Spirit.

Perhaps we need the help of little Du-sun-hoe-me-gee, 'dirty mouse.' We would have less worries if the self-appointed 'ruling class' would slow down on some of their ideas such as housing projects and adding other religions. These things look innocent enough at first, but most people are unaware that they are really ways to assimilate the Hopi by 'painlessly' rubbing out his 'Indian-ness.'

The effect these things would have on Hopi was already written on the rock walls before the landing at Plymouth Rock, so when the proposals for a housing project in Hotevilla and a Mormon church on nearby land were announced, we immediately opposed them. 'You cannot build there!' we protested, 'That's a sacred holding.'

But the progressive promoters cry in *Qua'toqti*, July 1, 1976, 'We still have to have a roof over our families and the wherewithal to feed them. But instead of growing corn and beans, we will be "growing" dollars with which to keep the family together, as we have already begun doing.'

They have been seeking information to support their attempt to claim the land for this purpose, but not from the traditional leaders who carefully hold the title handed down over many centuries. It is from their 'Bahanna Traditionalist' backers who are ripe and ready to confirm the favor.

The following letters were written by us to [both] HUD and LDS headquarters. You should know that no response has been received [from either organization.]

P.O. Box 54
Hotevilla Independent Village
Hotevilla, Arizona 86030
May 3, 1976

Church of Jesus Christ of Latter-Day Saints
Office-hdqrs of L.D.S.
Salt Lake City, Utah

Dear Sirs:
We the religious leaders of Hopi Land wish to write you directly concerning your members L.D.S. of 2nd and 3rd mesa, who proposed to build a chapel between Old Oraibi and Hotevilla village, headed by your member Mr. Wayne Sekaquaptewa, brother to Hopi tribal chairman.
Our representative and Mrs. Mina Lansa, chief of Oraibi, had lately has spoken with Mr. Sekaquaptewa and told him not to expand the Mormon

church further, the Traditional leaders does not want that. He did not put up any argument nor gave any promises to go along with the wishes of the leaders.

But up till now there is a show of persistence regardless who oppose to his desires. It seems unlike a good Mormon who should be preaching good thoughts and keeping peace among man, rather disturbing the good thoughts that is vital to good brotherhood.

We are not against the churches but it is not right when our own converted brothers and sisters shows disrespect and persist in getting their wants without asking, disregarding the sacred bindings that should be respected.

Now looking back to our past, we know foreign religion is always a cause of breakdown in our ways of life; assimilating into foreign religion has destroyed much of our cultural and religious ceremonial value. What we have left of today we must preserve, with the help of your open mind and understanding this can be done. By advising Mr. Sekaquaptewa to halt the procedure, drop the whole idea so all will be well and peace, or we surely will regret that you will hear from us again. Thank you.

Yours sincerely
Religious Leaders of Hotevilla Independent Village
cc: Mr. W. Sekaquaptewa

To the concerned and supporters for the Hopi cause:
Land and Church Struggle

Once again the Hopi Puppet Council and their supporters are granting lands to wayward neighboring Hopi and the Mormon Church — lands to which they have no title. The Council is disregarding the original Hopi native land holdings dating back thousands of years. By doing this the so-called Hopi Tribal Council, which came into being only a few years back, continues its harsh process of extracting power from Traditional Hopis by force or coercion in order to dominate all of Hopi village lands. While Traditional Hopi struggle on to protect environment and culture from destruction, efforts are under way to hasten exploration and progress by artificial means, causing great confusion for today's generation. The question now is which of these groups has more right to the land. It is clear that by signing the five-million dollar deal in favor of the Puppet Council, President Carter has failed in his promise to help the minorities. No doubt Carter's action has given Puppet Council much ego-power to use for quickly breaking down the Traditional Hopi. Their tactics and timing are almost perfected, and perhaps this is a test of whether or not the rest of the Hopis will follow them.

Oliver LaFarge, author of Hopi Tribal Council Constitution, says, 'Since the Indian race was a doomed and dying race, from time to time government policy must change about every 25 years — such as to de-Indianize by breaking up the tribe, destroying tradition, preventing group action, doing everything possible and impossible for the Indians to make themselves heard. Since they are foreign to our laws of process, the schemes applied cannot be understood or detected. As we see it, their task is almost finished, and acculturation is now in process as planned.'

Mr. LaFarge went on to say, 'By then the oldest and most conservative would die off, the young people would have civilized themselves, and the Indian problem would be ended.' So at this stage Hopi went back to Tradition, to a Tradition which they once degraded and spat upon.

Yet if you support Tradition today, you are looked upon as some kind of freak or lunatic, and so as time goes by Traditional and Bahanna systems are interwoven to accomplish acculturation. This prospect of acculturation always looks promising, because its basic ingredient is green stuff — not corn or other things that once fulfilled the basic needs of the Hopi. This is pitiful indeed, for money will not end the problems — it will only destroy the real purpose of Hopi, obstruct the religious principles, and even end the great laws of Maasaw. One cannot recapture the true values by half-hearted actions and expect them to bear healthy fruit. We Traditionals have accepted some of the Bahanna things — paying for it by the sweat of our brows — but only those that we know will not harm our system. But what we reject is those Bahanna things that we know will harm our ways and that we and our future children will be obligated to pay for.'

The following is a listing of Christian churches and memberships at Hopi as compiled in 1979 from *The Native American Christian Community*, Beaver, Dr. R. Pierce, ed., 1979, World Visions International.

Excerpts taken from general comments from book introduction, pp 37–38: "One of the oldest, largest, and strangest blocks of Christian parishes… are the Pueblo Indians, originally coercively converted by the Spanish conquerors… by 1630 there were reported to be 60,000 converts, but the serfdom and enforced Christian profession were intolerable… The Hopis in northern Arizona have been impervious to even a veneer of Christianity, but the Navajos, who surround them entirely, have since 1960 shown receptivity toward the Christian faith… Protestant Sunday church attendance on the reservation has increased from just a few hundred 25 years ago to 12,395 on any given Sunday in 343 churches under 203 Navajo pastors and 121 Anglo pastors."

Hopi, Arizona, population 6,567 (the Tribal Council gives it as 10,000 today)
American Baptist Churches: 3 churches, 41+ members.
General Conference Mennonite Church: 3 churches, 86 members.
Roman Catholic Church: 2 churches.
Widow's Mite Mission: 1 church.

Baptist

Keams Canyon Community Church. 1909. Hopi, Navajo. Hopi Reservation. Mem. 41, loss of 2 in 1977. Ab. in 1977 — 10. SS 100. YS 10. WS 5. Religious instruction one day per week. 250 children from BIA school. 7 Bible schools, attendance 350.

First Mesa Baptist Church. Hopi. Hopi Reservation. Polacca.

Sunlight Baptist Mission. Hopi. Hopi Reservation. Second Mesa.

Coalmine Baptist Church. Oraibi.

Church of Jesus Christ of Latter Day Saints

Information on the Indian churches is unavailable.

Mennonite Church, General Conference

Bacari Mennonite Church. Hopi. Hopi Reservation. P.O. Box 108, Hotevilla, AZ 86030. Elmer Myron, pastor, layman, Hopi. Attendance 8. Total Mennonite com. 20 adults, 2 children. SS 10–15. WS. Daily VBS.

Moencopi Mennonite Church. Hopi. Tuba City.* Mem. 10 adults. 2 children not mem. SS 10.

Oraibi Mennonite Church. Hopi Reservation. Oraibi. Karl Johnson, pastor, lay, Ind. Mem. 56 adults. Children 20+. SS 40–50. Prayer meeting. WS. VBS.

Hopi Mission School. 1951. Hopi. Hopi Reservation. New Oraibi. Administrated by a school board of six members selected by the four Hopi Mennonite churches, one independent congregation and two Baptist. Grades K–8. Five Hopi staff members. Other teachers are white mennonites. Boys 25, girls 16, total 61. There is a Mennonite Volunteer Service Unit assisting the school.

Mennonite Service Unit. Oraibi. Hopi. Activities: Two volunteers teaching at Hopi Mission School.

Roman Catholic

St. Joseph's Mission. Keams Canyon. Mission: Hopi Village.

Abbreviations:

Mem.	members	Ab.	adult baptisms	YS.	Youth Society
SS.	Sunday School or Church School	WS.	Women's Society or Ladies Aid Society	VBS.	Vacation or Summer Bible School.

---

* There are also churches listed for Tuba City.

TEM— It is helpful to contrast Mormon and other missionary efforts in Hopi country with some thoughts set forth in my book, *Fools Crow, Wisdom and Power*, published by Council Oak Books of Tulsa, OK, in 1991. I wrote there about welcome changes that were taking place in the attitudes of some mainline Christian churches regarding the Native American religions. It is worth repeating here, and being kept in mind as you think about the Elders' comments regarding missionary activities among the Hopi.

"Despite the legion of exceptional things that were accomplished through Fools Crow, the eulogies since his death have highlighted his profound love and concern for all races. People recognize both his fervent wish to share God's gifts with as many as he could reach, and the fact that he pitied others who did not understand why this must be so. 'The survival of the world,' he said, 'depends upon our sharing what we have and working together. If we don't, the whole world will die. First the planet, and next the people.' Then he added, 'The ones who complain and talk the most about giving away medicine secrets are always those who know the least.' He had little time for anyone who attempted to keep blessings to themselves."

While Fools Crow was remarkably open about passing on information regarding the ways given to him for curing, healing, and accomplishing things in general, he did so with the clear understanding that even when others sought to do these things, Wakan Tanka would not lead them to do it exactly as Fools Crow did, and the results would be different. He knew that Wakan Tanka and his helpers worked with people as individuals, and not as clones, so as to take advantage of individual gifts that could be shared for the good of humanity and the rest of creation. He did not for a minute think that even when someone had seen him do something, they could duplicate it exactly or diminish his gifts. They would miss the small things that play vital roles. They could not read his heart and mind. And they could not share his private communion with his God when he prayed and sought guidance. The individuality of the viewers colored what they saw too much for that. But in his great wisdom Fools Crow knew that the essences — the precious core understandings, insights and thoughts that permeated the different rituals — were a common ground to be shared by all great religions.

So too, while Dan's wish is to keep the Hopi kiva practices private from both outside and untrained eyes, it is not because he believes someone else could watch these and then duplicate them sufficiently well to obtain the same power, or even to subtract power from the Hopi rituals. It would take a lifetime of training to do that, and furthermore, the trainee would have to be a Hopi. Like the bean plants in the kiva, Hopi knowledge must be nourished within the receptive cocoon of continuing tradition.

No, it is not privacy that determines who enters a kiva when a ceremony is in progress. Dan's concern about revealing ritual things or having them on display in a museum arises from the continuing disrespect of Bahannas regarding them, and from the fact that misunderstanding has, and still does where the missionaries are concerned, led to the suppression of the rites and the unacceptable — in truth

white man view

ignorant — belief that Hopi religion is so wrong that it demands conversion. Who is there that, under those circumstances, would want to expose something so sacred as these magnificent Hopi rituals to scornful eyes?

Considering this, it is little short of a miracle that the Traditional people of Hotevilla welcome so wholeheartedly as they do outsiders to see their dances. It shows, however, their abiding love and concern for everyone in the world, and explains in one more way why Maasaw chose them to hold in their hands the fate of first North America, and now the world. Only someone so deeply spiritual, loving and so wise could ever do this under the circumstances in which it must be done. And so, while they share some things, they do not share everything. Nor should we expect them to.

New Age people have come under fire from some Native Americans for having entered in where the Natives do not feel they should. This is unfortunate, and it is not an attitude Dan supports, although he too grieves when outsiders come onto the reservation and place their prayer offerings on Hopi shrines, for these are among the things that must remain sacred to the Hopi themselves. The problem has arisen out of a New Age misconception, or illusion, that because they and the Hopi are profoundly spiritual people, the Hopi will recognize this and welcome this spirit of sharing. When it comes to sacred places the Hopi and the other Pueblos do not agree. Those who intrude should realize that the desecration of shrines has broad historic ramifications, that the centuries-long acquisition of Hopi Land by outsiders has not only cut them off from shrines where spiritual roots are sunk, the people who took over the land destroyed them because they did not care a whit about them or what the Hopis thought. Such insensitivity has bred a climate of distrust that carries into the present and makes the Hopi all the more cautious about what is seen or touched. I am pleased to say that although I have been on the Hopi and other Pueblo reservations for many years, I have never looked for or seen a shrine or grave. My only knowledge of what they look like comes from the few photographs of them that have been published. All outsiders should adopt this same practice, and particularly in this critical period of time should neither look for or intrude upon Hopi sacred places when they go to the dances. Stay away from these, including the sacred springs, unless a Hopi invites you to a certain place. And do not, as is so commonly done, stand or sit on the kiva roofs at Hotevilla when a dance is in process. It is disrespectful, and it cannot help but be disconcerting for those who are carrying out the necessary rituals in the kiva below.

You noticed, I'm sure, that the Elders have stated their recognition of the fact that there is "one Great Spirit."

The renowned Oglalla Sioux holy men, Fools Crow and Black Elk, were taught the same thing. They were convinced that the Supreme Being they worshiped was, simply by a different name, the same God we meet in the Bible — which was, in their minds, an even stronger reason to share spiritual and other gifts with all believing people.

"I shall explain," Black Elk said, "what our pipe really is; peace may come to those peoples who can understand, an understanding which must be of the heart and not of the head alone. Then they will realize that we Indians know the One True God, and that we pray to Him continually" (Brown, 1953).

Sadly, though, it has taken centuries for any of the Christian churches to recognize both this truth of a common God and the fact that Christians can learn a great deal about spirituality and God's ways from the Native Americans. For more than twenty-five years I have been stating this publicly with only limited response, therefore I am delighted to report that at long last some of the leaders of mainline churches are recognizing it. Consider, for example, the following portion of a stunning report:

On October 16, 1988, and where the Christian church is concerned more than three centuries too late, the *Seattle Times* carried a long article describing how the area bishops and other leaders of ten major mainline church groups (two Lutheran, two Catholic, Methodist, Presbyterian, Baptist, United Church of Christ, Christian Church, and Episcopal) had offered a formal written apology to native people for the churches' long-standing participation in the destruction of traditional Native American spiritual practices, and made a pledge to help Native American and Eskimo peoples reclaim and protect the legacy of their traditional religious teachings, asking for forgiveness and blessings.

"The spiritual power of the land and the ancient wisdom of your indigenous religions can be, we believe, great gifts to the Christian churches. We offer our commitment to support you in the righting of previous wrongs; to protect your people's efforts to enhance native spiritual teachings; to encourage the members of our churches to stand in solidarity with you on these important religious issues... We call upon our people for recognition of and respect for your traditional ways of life and for protection of your sacred places and ceremonial objects. We have frequently been unconscious and insensitive and not come to your aid when you have been victimized by unjust federal policies and practices. In many other circumstances we reflected the rampant racism and prejudice of the dominant culture with which we too willingly identified... May the God of Abraham and Sarah, and the Spirit who lives in both the Cedar and Salmon people, be honored and celebrated... "

What these church leaders do not say is that it has been mainly through church actions that most of the Native American religious traditions have been eradicated, are irretrievably lost, and that the consequent cost to Native Americans and the world is enormous.

When I attended Luther Theological Seminary (now Luther Northwestern Theological Seminary) in the 1950s, no one on the teaching staff ever once mentioned Native Americans. Today, the situation has changed considerably. Last year, the *Minneapolis Star and Tribune* featured a full-page article by staff writer Martha

Sawyer Allen that was captioned 'Indian, Christian Faiths Fuse.' Since the newspaper used my book, *Sundancing at Pine Ridge and Rosebud*, for its pictorial details, and without asking my permission (although they did credit the material), I cite portions of their very informative text.

The article mentions the Reverand Steve Charleston, a Choctaw who teaches cross-cultural studies at Luther Northwestern Seminary and who argues that Indians have a sacramental tradition that is as valid as — and in many ways similar to — that of the Old Testament Hebrew tribes, the fountainhead of Christianity. Charleston is considered by many to be the main architect for a new theology, and says, "he (Jesus) arises from Native America, claims the gospel for us, and now our job as Native American Christians is to evangelize the western world with a revolutionary and reformed vision of what the church will be in the next century… God came to earth once, in the form of Jesus, but came to all people." The new theology is described as a "hybrid religion" that "has roots in both Christian and traditional Indian beliefs and is evolving into a theology that binds people in sacramental kinship. Its adherents are Whites and Indians who are finding ways to combine holy and sacred elements from both traditions."

This new theology, the article continues, is being created by the second generation of Indian seminary graduates. These are deeply versed in traditional rituals and can talk with authority to White clerics. One of these (graduates), the Reverand Marlene Helgemo, a Winnebago, is associate pastor at University Lutheran Church of Hope in Minneapolis. She is quoted as saying, "…We [Christians and Traditionalists] all believe there is only one God, and we need to raise up the questions that new theologians need to be answering." Helgemo participates in a Sun Dance every year at the Rosebud Reservation, and is hoping that the new theology will follow the Sun Dance outline. "We need," she continues, "more coming of the human community in a circle, sharing concerns and prayer. The world needs more sun dances."

Featured also in the *Star and Tribune* article is the Reverand Virgil Foote, a Lakota and an Episcopal priest, whose Mazakute Memorial Church is in St. Paul. He practices both Christianity and his Lakota religion passionately, arguing that following his native ceremonies has made him a better Christian. "When I pray," he says, "I pray in Lakota and English. Our people need to hear there is truth in both. I'm a Lakota, I'm a Christian. I'm one in the same. I pray to one God."

Perhaps as you read this you can hear me sighing to myself: How many times over the past twenty-five years have I said this identical thing?… and that being able to look at spiritual truths through the eyes of medicine acquaintances has opened some Bible verses for me in ways that my seminary professors never did while I was there.

Foote has danced and even pierced in the Sun Dance at Rosebud — at that place where, at Fools Crow's and Eagle Feather's urging, I recorded its every detail for posterity… Those two foremost Intercessors (dance leaders) knew what they were doing in asking me, and clearly understood that the recording was Wakan Tanka's will.

"I wish," Foote says, "that I had done all this before I went to the seminary. I would have known the Bible better, understood the life of Christ in a much deeper way… At the Sun Dance… you get in touch with your physical and spiritual self and respect the sacred in everything."

The article closes with two more insights that deserve repeating. Both should be borne in mind as we consider what Fools Crow reveals.

"Many Whites in the ecology movement," the article says, "are attracted to Indian theology. Hundreds of others participate in sweat lodges in Minnesota and elsewhere . . . But these theologians worry that Whites may be attracted to bits and pieces of the theology without understanding the whole . . .The Reverand Jim Egan, a White Jesuit, cautions that Christians must respect Indian theology and not just siphon off the 'interesting' rituals for their own use without following disciplines required for participation. Egan was keeper of the sweat lodge fire at the Sun Dance and a former Rosebud missionary. The second insight is that the new theologians encounter enormous problems, legacies of our hundreds of years of attempts to eradicate Indian culture. They are caught between the two worlds, traditional Indians and Indians who profess only Christianity… The Indian rights movement of the 1970s spawned a concerted effort to preserve, honor, and practice Indian rituals and ways of life. More than half of all Indians now eschew Christianity, claim only their traditional ways, and bar Whites from their ceremonies… The new theology has a long way to go before it is accepted by Whites or Indians. A few of the Indian people mentioned in the *Star and Tribune* article were at Sun Dances I attended, and learned some things at these and other dances that were being led by Fools Crow or Eagle Feather. But all of those mentioned would have profited greatly by being Fools Crow's full-time students. He knew and practiced for nearly a century what the just-mentioned clerics have only recently begun to conclude. I also believe that Black Elk and Fools Crow actually originated the 'new theology,' since they were the first to clearly point out what the clerics are saying, and more. What they recognized, though, was the common ground just mentioned. They did not recommend the merging of the faiths."

And what, exactly, is the point of including all of this information about the Peabody Mine, the Navajo relocation, and missionary work? It is that in this awesome moment of time we must recognize that we have the obligation to walk together to have any chance whatsoever of surviving what is to come. If either we or the Hopi try to walk alone, we won't make it. This is true also for the Elders and the Tribal Council, the Traditionals and the Progressives. The time has come to hold out olive branches, and to let Maasaw show all of us the way. If we want to make it, and if we want our descendants to make it, we will put aside our differences, our desires to convert, our desires to dominate, and instead combine our strengths. The road ahead is already going to be difficult enough. What would be wrong with walking it side by side and being glad for a common faith and goal,

Key

supporting one another where necessary, and cherishing our triumphs when they come? I do not think the idea of seeking to merge the Native American and Christian faiths is either right or the best solution. Surely we can walk side by side and rejoice for one another without that.

CHAPTER 9

Two-Hearteds: The Tribal Council

Two-Hearteds That Impede the Keeping of the Covenant — the Hopi Tribal Council

The Elders

All Hopi villages have forsaken the original law, except Hotevilla. By doing this they have lost the right to be caretakers of the land. They all know Hotevilla holds title to the land. Bacabi has no land.

Nothing in our divine instructions tells us to give up our pattern of sovereign villages and elect a central government. The so-called Hopi Tribal Council is a puppet of the United States Government. All who accept it become its instrument. They deny Maasaw and his laws. They deny that our elders are our true leaders. By doing this they have lost the name Hopi! Hotevilla has never accepted the Hopi Tribal Council as its ruling body. We have never elected anyone to serve this American institution. We are not puppets. We were instructed not to join any other religion or system or we would lose our land. Yukiuma opposed the Tribal Council. Were we to become part of that system, we could never get out. The Tribal Council plays that role now. They have sold themselves, they have sold the land. The programs of the Council are just like the programs of the U.S. government. These witches of the East have hatched up such a tribal government to use our own people to finish us off. No true Hopi wants this to happen. When the U.S. Government urges our leaders to join the Council they refuse because they know the "Hopi Constitution" has nothing in common with the original law the Hopi follow. To accept it would mean to accept U.S. laws and order. We would lose our sovereignty. Their laws and concept of justice are not ours. When the Bahannas plan things they do it without regard for our way of life. They never ask us whether we want it.

I am not afraid to tell the truth. We asked and received permission to live here. Before Bahanna knew about it we set our landmarks and organized our society. But they came without permission. They put up their flag and said, 'This is our land.' If this is what they call lawful or just, how can we trust them? The law they used to form the Indian reservations shows what they mean by justice. It was the beginning of our end. They would allot a small portion of our own land, first to the tribe, then to individual families as private property. This makes us dependent. Then they ask for taxes, taxes, taxes. No complaint would ever change that. The Bahanna need taxes for their government to function.

First they deprive us of our land. If we set foot on such 'private property' they chase us off, these poor settlers. They offer no food, no place to sleep, just a kick in the rear. This is how most Bahannas treat us. We did not invent their money or its rules. <u>We don't want to earn our living as they do, forced to buy everything for our life</u>.   amen

We sing this song that describes our feelings:

'A katsina without rank am I, coming to you with this song. I see the land cut up and divided, and you, the people, fenced in. I am sad to see this happen, it will be like this from now on. <u>Let us sing to the clouds</u>. The crops need the rain, and we <u>need sweet melons</u>. Long ago it was foretold that you would no longer hunt together or run in festive races. Happy and satisfied after the feast, <u>you forget to sing to the girls</u>, and they have forgotten the sacred meaning of the butterfly hairdo.'

Yesterday was a sad day for our village. With the help of the BIA the progressives are putting in water lines and electricity. I went to the boss of the workers and asked whether he had the consent of our elders. 'Yes,' said the Bahanna.

'I don't believe you,' I answered, 'we don't want to depend on the government here and bow to their will. I'm sure our elders don't want this to happen.'

The Bahanna said nothing. We told our opponents that we don't want a paved road. The BIA agent spoke up: 'I follow a petition of ninety village people. It's their right to have some comfort here. Now we can bring in everything. First the street, then water lines, electricity, and phones.' He gave a sign for the machine to move. It ran over two of our sacred shrines and destroyed them. This was very mean. They had no respect for anything sacred. As soon as the first pole was set, we said, 'Take it out.' They replied, 'You can draw up your own petition. If you outnumber them, you can remove the poles yourselves.'

[Grandmother Caroline] 'We asked a preacher, Are you the one who promoted all this?'

'No,' he said, 'but I want people to be happy.'

'Why,' I asked, 'did you collect all those signatures from Hopis who live in the cities? They want the Bahanna life, that's why they left. We don't want you preaching in our village. Take your Bible and look into it. Where does it say, thou shalt create disharmony among people? Or, thou shalt make your neighbor unhappy?'

The hole for the pole was ready when I got there. We tried to prevent them from setting the pole. A woman was injured. A big truck was rolling toward us. We were running in front and blocking its way. The driver did not stop. 'Stop, stop, stop,' I shouted. But he kept on rolling. Some other ladies joined us. We clung to the truck as he dragged us toward the hole. I quickly got into the hole. The workers shoveled dirt on me. 'Stop this,' I shouted.

'No, I can't,' they said. Then the pole fell down and I was hit on the head. This is how they pass over our heads!

After this incident, we asked their boss to tell us his name. He just walked away. We know Bahannas' laws too. Contracting parties must be known to each other before an agreement can be legally binding. Who got our agreement? They don't go by their own laws. This Bahanna didn't even tell his name.

[Dan Katchongva] 'What the government tries to install in our village I do not want, nor do my people. I went to protest against it.

The truck driver said, 'You have nothing to say. You are not the chief. This is not your land.'

'The truth is,' I replied, 'we came to this land first. It was entrusted to us as its caretakers.'

Here someone from the village interrupted me: 'You'd better shut up, self-proclaimed chief. You have no power. You've been deluded by these Bahannas who support you old traditionals.'

I told him, 'It's you who are deluded. You live and think like a Bahanna. You have abandoned the title to the land. Hotevilla was founded so that we might follow what you call 'old-fashioned' Hopi laws. We still do this for all land and life. You have forsaken the original Hopi way. Like the people of Bacabi, you have no land and no power.'

As father of this village, I am concerned. I want my children to keep the good life. I oppose these comforts because they make us unhappy. I know the outcome. If we accept the Bahanna lifestyle, comfort will make us dependent. These developments are from Washington. Someday they make us pay. What is the price? I want my people to keep their land. Then we can live a good, independent life. New houses, running water, electricity, such programs are a sly way to trick us into an alien lifestyle with values opposed to ours. I resist, not just to defend Hopi, but the land and life of the whole world, so it may continue. If we are fortunate, someone will hear and understand this message: 'Together with all nations we protect land and life, and hold the world in balance.'

In the words of our present village father, Lamahoyma, of the bear clan: 'I am concerned. The Tribal Council is putting in modern things with the help of the government and the church. They never got our permission. The elders and the people don't want this. We want to have the simple Hopi life for which we established our village at Hotevilla. The whole area was set as a sacred shrine. We want to keep it that way. Simply because we want to remain Hopi, we have been imprisoned. We still reject control by outside forces. We must be allowed to rule ourselves in the Hopi way, as we have from the first, as an independent nation. We hope someone will see why, and bring this about. Otherwise, Maasaw will be the last to do the job. May the outcome be good! We do not reject people because of skin color. All who come may eat with us. We welcome everyone to our ceremonies. In Hotevilla we keep the circle open to all.'

I would like
to attend.

THE DISRUPTION CONTINUES TODAY

During this [1906] period a group under the leadership of Kawonurnptewa (Sand Clan), fearing even worse pressure from the Government, returned to Oraibi to follow Tawaquaptewa and accept the whiteman's way, but they were rejected and driven out. They settled about two miles from Hotevilla, where they founded the village of Bacabi. Unable to make out independently, they asked the Government Agency for help. The Agency happily obliged with such things as housing materials. Now they almost entirely accept the whiteman's way, along with his religion. According to the Great Spirit's law, they are now landless. Their only assets are their dwellings. But it is through them that the Agency obtained token permission to build a school on Hotevilla land, and with the Agency's backing they have committed land grabs against the Hotevilla people. It is also through them that the Government has built a water tower on Hotevilla land, which supplies running water to the school and to Bacabi village, while depleting the natural water supply of the Hotevilla people. Most of the people in Hotevilla refuse to use the water from this tower. Much of the trouble caused by the Bacobi people still exists today. I can recall much more than I hope will come to light.

When we left Oraibi and settled at Hotevilla, the Grey Eagle Clan came with us on the same condition they agreed to in Oraibi, which is still in force. They have created trouble again and are due to move out. They are the backbone of the disturbances in our village, selling out the Hopi nation by their inclination to bow toward more persuasive powers for certain favors. There are two roads for them to follow: the road of the Great Spirit, or the road of Bahanna, the whiteman. They are supposed to move on to Mushongnovi as agreed — in fact the people there are waiting for them, but they lack the courage to carry out their agreement. They are cowards hiding behind the man-made law of Bahanna.

At the present time we face the danger that we might lose our land entirely. Through the influence of the United States Government, some people of Hopi ancestry have organized what they call the Hopi Tribal Council, patterned according to a plan devised by the Government, for the purpose of negotiating directly with the Government and with private businesses. They claim to act in the interests of the Hopi people, despite the fact that they ignore the existing traditional leaders and represent only a small minority of the people of Hopi blood. Large areas of our land have been leased, and this group is now accepting compensation from the Indian Claims Commission for the use of 44,000,000 acres of Hopi land. This is in error, for we laid our aboriginal claim to all of this land long before the newcomers ever set foot upon it. We do not recognize man-made boundaries. We true Hopi are obligated to the Great Spirit never to cut up our land, nor to sell it. For this reason we have never signed any treaty or other document releasing this land. We have protested all these moves, but to no avail. Now this Tribal Council was formed illegally, even according to whiteman's laws. We traditional leaders have disapproved and protested from the start. In spite of this they have been organized and recognized by the United States Government for the purpose of disguising its wrongdoings to the outside world. We do not have representatives in this organization, nor are we legally subject to their regulations and programs. We Hopi are an independent sovereign nation, by the law of the Great Spirit, but the United States Government does not want to recognize the aboriginal leaders of this land. Instead, he recognizes only what he himself has created out of today's children in order to carry out his scheme to claim all of our land. Because of this, we now face the greatest threat of all, the actual loss of our cornfields and gardens, our animals and wild game, and our natural water supply, which would put an end to the Hopi way of life. At the urging of the Department of the Interior of the United States, the Tribal Council has signed several leases with an outside private enterprise, the Peabody Coal Company, allowing them to explore our land for coal deposits, and to strip-mine the sacred mesas, selling the coal to several large power plants. This is part of a project intended to bring heavy industry into our area against our wishes. We know that this will pollute the fields and grazing lands and drive out the wildlife. Great quantities of water will be pumped from beneath our desert land and used to push coal through a pipe to a power plant in another state [Nevada]. The loss of this water will affect our farms as well as the grazing areas of the animals. It also threatens our sacred springs, our only natural source of water, which we have depended upon for centuries.

Issue No. 4, Winter, December 1975–January 1976:
The Tribal Council Is Unlawful and Un-Hopi

TI— "What and who is the Hopi Tribal Council? Does it represent the whole Hopi Nation? How does it function? What power does it have over the Hopi Nation? Who draws its Constitution and By-Laws, and by what method? These are a few of the questions often asked about that strange new institution which the traditional Hopi leaders have named the "Puppet" Council.

In our first issue of *Techqua Ikachi* we defined three factions: Traditional Hopi (living under the laws of the Great Spirit, the Creator), On-the-Fence Hopi 'Bahanna Traditionalists' who support the Hopi Tribal Council as the ruling class over the Hopi Nation and recognize its chairman as higher than all the chiefs (while trying on the surface to cling to Hopi tradition), and the Progressives, who completely support that Tribal Council for whatever benefits they can get.

Let's turn our attention to the establishment of that organization. It only takes a little research to uncover serious mistakes and violations in its ambitious ventures. We ask our readers to think about these and consider whether it rightly rules the people it claims to represent.

For our first example we consider the original election. One morning in the 1930s we were all called together at the outskirts of our village. Before us was something that looked like a hot dog stand. A White woman was there with a few Hopi who were affiliated with the government's efforts. A blank piece of paper was placed in front of each person who approached the stand. At that point we noticed two markings (+ and 0). We were told to mark either + or 0 on our piece of paper. We were also told that both were good symbols. We asked the lady what this was all about. 'It's a secret,' she said, but she coaxed and insisted that we choose one or the other. We asked again what it was for, but she refused to give any information, saying that we were not supposed to know. We told her we would choose neither, because she refused to explain it to us. And we left.

We later found out that this was what they called 'voting,' the purpose of which was to establish the Hopi Tribal Council to act as our mouth and ears. Of 400 people here in Hotevilla, only 2 or 3 voted. Later we learned that the same activity was conducted in other villages, with the exception of First Mesa. Out of about 6,000 Hopi, very few actually voted. We heard that it was only 100 or 200, but in order to make the issue pass, votes were switched or stolen to make it look legal. In spite of this, the number of votes counted was far below any legally recognized percentage. One of the two Hopi who helped count the votes testified that they helped stack votes in favor of the establishment of the Council, which was promoted by the Bureau of Indian Affairs. In this way the so-called 'Hopi Tribal Council' was born. *out of deceit.*

 puppet council

Around twenty years later, Oliver LaFarge, the author and so-called father of the Hopi Tribal Constitution, described the Tribal Council as 'an unlawful body.' Now, what did the Government do wrong in this instance, and is there any penalty for their misdeeds?

In future issues we shall reveal some of the serious mistakes by which this organization not only violates our way of life, but is actually illegal according to its own laws. Until then, we would like our readers to ask themselves why a foreign government would establish such an organization, and how the Tribal Council that calls itself 'Hopi Tribe' has earned among us the name 'puppet.'"

The Rise and Fall of the Fire, or Spirit, Clan, and the Chief Who Is Not Our Chief

TI— "The so-called Hopi Tribal Council has chosen to recognize a certain Fire Clan man as the chief of Hotevilla Village. According to our ancient doctrines, this act is out of order. Looking at the past dealings of the Tribal Council, we see this move as a scheme — the latest in a long series — designed to topple the last stronghold of original Hopi government. The Council and the forces behind it find this present move necessary because of the past failures of their attempted conquest, and because of the mistakes they have made in failing to abide to their own constitution. *Sounds like U.S. Govern't –*

Article III, Section 3 of this constitution states: 'Each village shall decide for itself how it shall be organized. Until a village shall decide to organize in another manner, it shall be considered as being under the Traditional Hopi organization, and the Kikmongwi of such village will be recognized as its leader,' although in Section 1 it reads: 'The Hopi tribe is a union of self-governing villages sharing common interests in working for the common welfare of all. It consists of the following recognized villages…' [All nine villages are mentioned, including Hotevilla.]

We have never considered organizing in another manner. We are an independent village not subject to the laws made by the Tribal Council, and have no representative in that organization. Since this man has excluded himself according to our ancient system of government, and has even personally denied having any authority, the council violates its own constitution in forcing us to recognize him.

It is true the Fire Clan are the rightful people to hold the authoritative position in this village and are those from which a Kikmongwi might be chosen, because it was under their leadership that this village was established. They are also caretakers of the Sacred Stone Tablet, which is to be respected. But they are also bound by certain obligations in order to accomplish their mission. That is, they must strictly adhere to the Great Spirit's laws and instructions. They must not stray from the path. Then they would become the highest, for along the way they would gather and accumulate the powers of the fallen ones. But if before they complete this task, they become wayward, their authority and power will decline to nothing, and they will be spat upon. The power will then be given to the next person who still adheres to the Great Laws.

Keeping this in mind let's look at this man and compare him with his great uncle, Yukiuma. He took over the chieftaincy soon after Yukiuma's death, and without the regular ritual of ordination. No one objected because it was thought that, being of Yukiuma's blood line, he could be trusted.

But not many years after he took office, he secretly became affiliated with the agency's stock-reduction program. Many who did not cooperate were jailed and their stock confiscated by the agency — though this man himself escaped that treatment. In later years he became the victim of a scandal, and there were other signs as well that his image was tarnished. This caused him to exile himself to an Indian reservation in New Mexico, where he stayed for seven years. We learned from reliable sources that he was expelled from there for some offense. He returned to Hopi a changed man, a Progressive who supported the puppet council and a reactionary who opposes the views of the Traditional leaders."

Issue No. 21 of *Land and Life* Describes How an "Old Problem Becomes a New Problem"

TI— "We were shocked when word came that workmen were beginning something up on the hill part of Hotevilla land. It was hard to believe, and we wondered why we were not notified by whoever wanted to use the land for some purpose. Our reaction was not a happy one. We wonder when people will understand us and let us live in peace. If only they would listen to our reasons. But we know it is useless. From past experience over the years we know what we can do. The fact is, they know that within legal terms we are helpless. Which is to say that the Bahanna's help here is in doubt. They know the technicalities which often bar outsiders from helping us (the Traditionals), when they are helpless to act. There is also the expense involved. This is always a drawback for us in getting a legal defense, but not for them. The expenses involved in a court fight are more than we have. No government institution will help us because it is part of their program to destroy us, so they can do whatever they wish with our land. So in plain view of all are the pretensions of those in high places, even to their own race. This is so in spite of our ancient teachings that the Creator, the Great Spirit, is the highest, and in the obeying of His laws lies our true strength. ✗

Now, you may not know that *Qua'toqti, the puppet press*, has been reawakened by the same family of Mormons and Mr. Sekaquaptewe, the former Tribal Chairman. Within a few days it cried out about the new development. Here we quote in part:

'The erection of a 150,000-gallon water storage tank near the village of Hotevilla and Bacabi has brought on another round of talk among people trying to understand one another regarding new services to the village.' Then it continued: 'Hotevilla is resistant to accept such convenience within Hotevilla Village because of a strong belief that acceptance would mean indebtedness, down the road, to the dominant White society. This belief is strongly advocated by Traditionalists and their followers. Percy Lomaquahu states that this new service will benefit both villages. In regards to the land, that his concern is [with] future population growth that will expand into the area. The Hopi Agency, BIA and Public Health have fully agreed to support the project. The Hopi Chairman will support it on the basis that Hopi people must drink.'

During these hectic days we now learn that electric power lines will also be installed in the village, so we will have many fights on our hands this Spring and Summer.

In an effort to have people understand, and also hoping for support, we have replied in written form to challenge the promoter, explaining from our viewpoint why it is wrong. This document and letters are sent to the various departments through channels, and to institutions and key organizations, both in the United States and abroad. Copies of these documents are available. Write to this paper.

Subject: Land—Water storage tank, Percy Lomaquahu:
The Sovereign Hopi Independent Nation, Traditional Community of Hotevilla Village, wishes to contest proposed land giveaway and construction of a water storage tank made by Percy Lomaquahu, resident of Hotevilla, Bacabi, and the town of Winslow. We hereby challenge his action on the grounds of improperly assumed authority and land claim, for we know that the document which he drew up is fraudulent. On this day, March 25, 1982,

he was called to a meeting to explain his action to the leaders and people of Hotevilla Village but failed to appear.

These are the grounds upon which we challenge him:

1. That he does not hold any rank in village official status to authorize construction of water storage tank and sharing of land with Bacabi Village.

2. That he is in conflict with Hotevilla's doctrine or traditional code of laws concerning this land and the situation of Bacabi village also in accordance of their doctrine.

3. That his title to the land was not on file in office of Hopi Agency, supposed to be endorsed by the official of the village and the owner of the land as practiced by progressive Hopi.

4. That he did not receive the authority of Hotevilla leaders to give away Hotevilla land and construction of water tank.

5. That in any case, Talashongnewa would never have given the land to Lomaquahu and his brother without advice from Hotevilla Village authorities because Talashongnewa was fully pledged to Hopi religious code of laws.

6. The land in question, the time the proposal was drawn, 1977, was not used by Talashongnewa nor the large area claimed by Lomaquahu, therefore by the traditional rules it is being held in common by the Hotevilla Village and is not the property of any individual. Bacabi Village is excluded from this land, on basis that rules and doctrines for the village were already set at the time Bacabi was settled by Kewanumptewa, the leader and founder.

7. That none of the documents presented were signed by members of Hotevilla Village, traditionals or progressives.

8. That Lomaquahu is deliberately interfering in order to undermine the sovereignty of Hotevilla Village. He is self-proclaimed leader and owner of this land, without any support from Hotevilla Village. We challenge that the statements made in his documents are all fabricated.

If Hotevilla allows the water storage tank and well and land giveaway to occur, that land will be lost to Hotevilla. The members of Hotevilla Village who occupy and use the land in question will eventually be under the domain of Bacabi Village. We believe that no members of Hotevilla would want to merge with Bacabi Village — which is a different entity.

Truly and honestly, without fear in defending our village autonomy, we the leaders of Hotevilla Village Independent nation sign our names: SS....'"

Great Spirit's Peace, or Government Police?

TI— "For thousands of years we Hopi have lived happily in our villages by following a pattern established by the Great Spirit, whose teachings go all the way back to the dawn of time. Now all of the prophecies are being fulfilled, including that of a period of great trial in which the world will be engulfed by efforts to force one's will upon others. As predicted, these efforts have grown so great that mankind has reached the brink of self-destruction.

But some people are too fearful or impatient to deal with others face to face, regarding the truth. Instead they force their will on others through a police state and gladly reap the temporary rewards. Selfish people find this avenue of accomplishing their purposes very tempting. They think they have found an easy solution for life's problems, but they fail to see the harm they cause to their fellow men, to future generations, and even to themselves. And they are not aware that by falling for this temptation they place themselves at the service of a worldly power greater than themselves, which is at least as selfish, and which intends to gain at their expense?

Are they blind? Or are they just afraid to look? No true Hopi could ever agree to follow such a foolish way of life!"

Respect Requires a Good Example
A Look at an Editorial in *Qua'toqti*, April 24, 1975

TI— "It is true that respect requires good example, but who is really following the example set by countless generations of Hopi ancestors to whom we owe our life? They struggled long and hard to follow the life plan of the Great Spirit so that today's Hopi might have a chance to survive the destructive pressures of the modern world rather than yield to them totally. If those who so criticize their elders were still following that example, the land would still be paradise. Considering the shape the world is in now, surely it is not being followed.

The first paragraph, '…as if it has all happened before…' seems to indicate they are bored with their own tradition, hatred, and frustration. It is so childish for them to characterize their own elders as lowly and stupid because of their 'bowed heads.' In our opinion the bowed head indicates wisdom and knowledge. The greatest men on this earth still practice such behavior to increase their concentration, for it is said, 'Mind is the greatest lever of all things; human thought is the process by which human ends are ultimately answered.'

Although the meeting written about dealt with the issue of cattle and cornfields, nothing about this issue appears in the editorial. We think the Hopi people might want the issue analyzed for the benefit of their understanding, not covered up with a petty attack against those who raise it. It was only said that no one intended to come to terms with the opposing forces. Perhaps that statement would more accurately describe the article itself, which avoided coming to terms with the actual problems.

Instead it said that the young people just 'sat impatiently listening and waiting for something to happen, which they knew would not.' Why are they so blind to the happenings they witness at this very moment — which are the fulfillment of the prophecy about which these elders have been so concerned?

We agree with the statement that the Hopi philosophy is beautiful and always in the same pattern. It is indeed beautiful that the Hopi have lived by that pattern since the dawn of time. The survival of all people, their land and life, depends upon following that pattern. We hope it will continue to be beautiful, but that will happen only when people stop opposing it.

The editorial failed to analyze the subject that was not agreed upon, and the question of why the disagreement exists. What the Traditionals were trying to make clear has, as the article said, been explained in the same pattern many times. They oppose the fencing of the land because the plan appears crafty, and they also know that the path of such so-called progress has been marked with thoughtless destruction of land and life. The land grants, and the internal changes within Hopi communities, are often imposed against the will of the native inhabitants, and once imposed, persist, despite whatever opposition is raised.

Yes, we do indeed agree with the 'glorious' Hopi doctrine and philosophy laid out by the Creator Himself. Each Hopi has been born into it, grown up with it, believes it is sacred, and that it is a part of himself with which it would be wrong to part. Respect for elders would exist everywhere today if the world leaders would conform to their teachings, constitutions, and laws by which they originally intended to lead people We know that the Tribal Council often does not conform to their own written laws. They deviate in order to gain what they want for themselves. This is illegal by whiteman's law. Yet they argue that the old Hopi teachings are dead and that the U.S. Constitution is often good to lean on, or hide behind.

Meanwhile the Traditional Hopi wants simply to live his way of life without expense to anyone.

It has been argued, 'Let these young ones experiment with gentle things that would be good for their future, that will not hurt anyone, and can be easily canceled.' Unfortunately, the immature actions of the Tribal Council prove difficult, if not impossible, to reverse. The Progressives cry that the old Hopi hobble them, but we think our cold attitude toward the kind of change the Council wants is good, since it makes a person think deeply before he takes his next step.

We agree that the Hopi world is changing rapidly. So is the Earth and all its people. Each person has a right to change, and no one can control that. This is up to each individual. It is also right for a person to not change when one has already found the right way. But this editorial seems to imply that the Hopi way is extinct. On the contrary, it is very much alive. So it is not the resistance of the Traditional Hopi that puts the pressure on the young people, but rather it is the Tribal Council that has led them into a walled circle where they are vulnerable to unemployment and economic conditions. Personal assets for most Hopi workers have dwindled in recent years. Overdue bills cause pressure, and dead-end jobs drive them to drink. It's clear now where Bahanna's culture, with its money system, is leading our youth. It is up to the Council to help them out of the circle into which the Traditional Hopi foresaw and chose to avoid by holding on to their way of life. No doubt the glorious material promises they put out will win many followers, but we can assure everyone that their way is not all a path of roses.

If leadership is, as the article says, measured by the number of people willing to follow, and if people will follow a real leader even into Hades, then we Traditionals

TI— Look, we Tribal Council members are the true and real Hopi traditionals. We control the land and our tribe. This guy here is nothing, nobody. He is Bahanna!

must have had some real ones indeed, for we followed them out of Old Oraibi village into Hades, which is what the Friendlies called Hotevilla. We have that much trust in them. And though we hoped it wouldn't really turn out to be Hades — which it didn't — we have followed them even further, for their path is much wiser than the one Bahanna would force us to follow. This takes guts as well as trust. The followers of the Tribal Council had better hope that they aren't being led into Hades either!

But the Tribal Council and their followers are trying to turn the young against their elders by building an image of doubt. They create division, whereas the elders would have unity. They misrepresent themselves to the outside world as the leaders or 'Chiefs' of the Hopi nation, while twisting what the Traditional leaders say. For example, the Traditionals' complaint that the Council acts in the fashion of a dictator is misrepresented in the article.

We use the word 'dictatorial' to refer in this instance to an uncompromising attitude of leadership because we think it is a necessary thing. It is found not only in the traditional Hopi leadership, but in the leadership of all nations. But we Traditionals use that word in our article to refer to the way in which the Tribal Council forces its will, or rather the U.S. Government's will, upon the people when it is dividing and misusing their land, and without consulting them. Even though the Council represents themselves as the supreme leadership of the Hopi, they are not. But they play the part of a dictatorship very well.

It is true, as the article says, that it would be wrong to use a priesthood office in a Hopi ceremonial society for political purposes, but this is not what the Traditionals are doing. It is actually the fulfillment of their offices to uphold the prophecies, teachings, and instructions of the Great Spirit as they do. They defend land and life as we all must do in order to live. They hold to the Hopi Way because it is deeply rooted and stable. They do not see this as politics, but as the means by which the Hopi have survived from the beginning of time. Other nations around the world have made their own vow to protect the earth. The Hopi are obligated to not break theirs. The same is true of Bahanna, except that Bahanna has now obligated himself to a man-made law. If by this he neglects his original vow, it will mean not only his downfall, but terrible damage to the earth as well.

It is so strange for the editorial to claim that the loss of the green valleys and fertile fields we once had is due to teachings they are not receiving. These teachings are the very thing the Traditionals are offering in their meetings, but the article itself covers them up! If they wish to serve the Hopi people fairly, the *Qua'toqti* editors should clarify their statements for the sake of those less educated. This loss reflects not upon the priesthood, but upon the new leadership who act against the Traditional Hopi. They dim the spiritual minds of the leaders and the people, so there is no rain. The pressures they create interfere with the natural way of life.

So indeed people have gone astray. Many have left the Hopi way and joined foreign religious sects. Participants in ceremonials often use intoxicants, won't work in the fields, and don't speak the Hopi language or think like Hopi. In plain sight they are not Hopi — yet they claim to be. What are they actually?

Since a share in something great always arouses envy, there are always those who would rob the humble and meek of their great possession. They seek to rob Hopi, or destroy its meaning. But their enmity is in vain — its richness is assured in its own positive achievements, which no one can take away."

Issue No. 2, October 1975: Foolish as It Seems, Could Separation Be the Real Answer?

TI— "We apologize for being so late, but September was a very busy month, considering all the disturbances we have had to deal with.

We were hoping to bring some pleasant news. Visitors often ask us about our weather, crops, health, and daily life. It would be wonderful to say, 'Yes, we are happy because it rains often and our fruit, corn, melons and beans are growing well, there will be plenty of grass for the animals, and the U.S. Government and the Tribal Council which they set up have recognized our sovereignty and agreed to let us live our way of life without interference.'

These are pleasant dreams, but we regret that these happy words are impossible for us. We are not happy today because we did not have much rain. Some rainfall this summer was not good. The grass and our crops did not respond and are poor. Our planting season was delayed by a late spring. The enemies to our crops are many and strong. The value of our prayers is waning because of our lack of oneness and disturbances of every sort.

Our troubles come mainly from the Bureau of Indian Affairs and the so-called Hopi Tribal Council. Every day their propaganda machine is grinding away in an effort to belittle our tradition and indoctrinate our children into Bahanna's material laws while at the same time erasing the spiritual laws of the Hopi. This is a fact we cannot avoid and must face every day.

Despite all this, some of what the followers of the Hopi Tribal Council offer has a bright side, which is very appealing to the followers of the original Hopi prophecies. It is a certain suggestion that arises each time there is friction. We forget it sometimes because we know it is intended as mockery and foolishness, but at this stage in time the idea arouses our interest. Perhaps we should play out the game and explore its value, for it just might resolve the Hopi problem.

The BIA and Tribal Council propose that any Hopis who wish to continue their traditional life should return totally to the primitive life, living entirely in the old way without whiteman's clothing or food. Housing must not be made of whiteman's building materials. We must remove all our children from school, and all those who earn their livelihood from Government and Tribal Council employment must resign. Drinking and cooking with water from Bahanna's wells should be forbidden. We should not drive cars. We should use nothing made by Bahanna.

This means separation. Yet it might actually be the means we can use to fulfill the sacred mission for which we have lived and struggled all these centuries, for even at this stage it can only be accomplished so long as our life is based upon the original Hopi system. So those who like Bahanna's system should move away and into that society where they will be happy under his laws. This must, of course, be done voluntarily. This way we can remain related and still be happy. If such a plan fails to materialize, then it is up to the Hopi Tribal Council or Washington, D.C., to heal the pain of Hopi Land by correcting their own wrongdoings according to their own system. Otherwise, our grievances must be presented to the United Nations or to the World Court for a decision. Beyond them we still have three people standing behind us who are to come and purify us if this effort fails. After that, nature will have to take over and fulfill the remaining prophecies regarding it.

At this moment we are being overrun by the invading forces of our own blood brothers and sisters who are trying to deliver the coup-de-grâce to our village government, backed by the BIA and the Tribal Council who dominate through police power, which is an absolute violation of the Hopi way of life.

As a people we have always avoided such methods, for our ancient legends as well as our prophecies clearly warn us of the disastrous results. It does not take much common sense to see that this will destroy the very life of our culture.

Only within the past month there have been three incidents concerning the installation of water and sewage systems into our village without our approval. The first two were repelled with violence. The clashes were provoked by the puppet Hopi and supported by the puppet Hopi police. The Hotevilla 'Bahanna Traditionalists,' as we call them, finally won their round with the installation of a pipeline — though no arrests of any of them were made.

For the time being the installation of electricity was stalled but this does not mean it will stop. All it takes is a little ignorance, plus a police force to carry out your will (really the will of Washington, D.C.), and selfishness will overshadow the meaning of the traditional way.

If such people have their way they will persist until the Traditional Hopi is no more or until he is completely silenced."

The Tribal Chairman Opposes Traditionalists…Shows How Tribal Newspaper Is Used for Council Purposes, But May Have a Good Idea!

TI— "Regarding recent efforts of visiting Bahannas (white folks) to protect Hotevilla from the forced installation of utilities without regard for the wishes of the village leaders, or for the reason the village was founded, Abbott Sekaquaptewa, the chairman of the so-called Hopi Tribal Council, made in *Qua'toqti*, October 2, 1975, the following statement, which we feel should be set straight, and again shows the need for our own newspaper, *Techqua Ikachi*:

'The traditionalists claim they want to live their own way and not the white-man's way. Yet, they have adopted, without hesitation, one of the whiteman's least desirable ways—resorting to political propaganda pressure through the use of partisan letter-writing campaigns and media releases, without the support of the majority of the community members. There is not one Hopi soul who has not adopted the whiteman's way in one form or another, and there is no use in throwing that accusation back and forth. It will not stick to anyone.'

It seems the chairman has forgotten that he was born in Hotevilla, as were his brothers and sisters. He must also have forgotten that his blood relations were among the first who settled the village in order to preserve our way of life. They shared our burden of sadness and the compelling pressure that was exerted to bring us to our knees. They shared our imprisonment for simply refusing the offers of the government.

When the government failed to break us, other methods were used. We were induced to the money system to get food, clothing, tools, etc. But we knew that doing this would not hinder our stand so long as the money was earned through our own hard work, and not by becoming the tool of the ruling establishment. We knew as well that the money system would become a weapon in the hands of our own people, a means by which our culture could be destroyed. This is exactly what is happening to us now.

In making his statement the chairman is using a psychological trick to get our children to think we have already taken the whiteman's bait as everyone else has. He wants us to stop squirming and think we are licked. But we must disregard his argument, for it has no basis.

If he disapproves of our use of whiteman's materials while we defend our right to self-government by the Great Spirit's law, why doesn't he make a law against our using those things?

Of course he should then meet us halfway by relocating the people who want to live under the whiteman's government. Perhaps a good place to settle them would be in the Tribal Council-sponsored Hopi Industrial Park in Winslow, with its ill-fated underwear factory! Then these people could have the conveniences of the city, and we would be happy here in Hopi Land with our corn and beans, free from outside interference."

Why Do Traditional Villages Refuse Modern Conveniences?

TI— "Now as always the question arises: Why do Traditional Hopi refuse to have some Bahanna conveniences? Perhaps this has never been clearly understood by those who live in Bahanna's system or by people living in other countries. We Hopi are simply a group of people with similar languages living in villages which are actually independent from each other. The leaders in each village perform their part in the whole pattern of life through the cycle of their ceremonies which take place according to the sun and the moon. Through the performance of this cycle all land and life remain complete. Since we Hopis are placed upon this land by the Creator for a purpose, like all races of people around the earth, we are able to relate ourselves deeply to our environment: the waterless desert, rocks, woods, plants, animals, birds, and other creatures — many of which modern man has forgotten, surely to his great loss. If we allow our ways to be changed into the ways of modern society — even though strong-arm tactics are being used today by the so-called Hopi Tribal Council to force us to accept foreign leadership — we will be doomed and lost in the midst of unfamiliar surroundings. We will be forced into partitioning our land, paying taxes and bills we cannot afford — unless we give up our lives for whiteman jobs, in which case it would still be very difficult to adapt ourselves to the new environment.

Civilization can have many meanings. To some it means a lot of gadgets and comforts. People who visit Hopi Land agree we have good ways of life and a great possession. The true value of our own civilization lies in our peace with little or no war or crime, no jails or courts and law and order, all of which tend to lead to confinement, craftiness, and bribery. We are able to live without polluting the atmosphere or the water or destroying the environment in any other way.

All this would still be true today if the encroachment by outside interests, the law and order, and the Progressive promoters were absent. Yet the true Hopi way is not a thing of the past; the struggle continues today. We hope we are not wrong in denying ourselves and our children the good things that are offered, but we believe our way of life to be the best that man can achieve and that once lost it cannot be regained or purchased with any amount of money."

The Water Dispute Is Nothing New!

TI— "Water dispute erupts in Hotevilla," cried the eagle puppet press of September 25, 1975. People who have recently arrived here in Hopi Land from the Bahanna world might think this is a new issue, but it is nothing new to the Hopi people nor to many people in the outside world.

Recently new people have settled into Hotevilla village. Perhaps they wish to escape the monster of Bahanna society or have found it impossible to fit into the environment of 'a high standard of living.' Could it be that their conquest of the whiteman's world has failed? Perhaps they see a richer harvest to be made right at home by concentrating their wits on the humble and meek, while nourished by the words of those who say that nothing can be fruitful unless it is pulled up or built up. They seem to have no pity for the original settlers of the village, and the newcomers involved show no respect for the elders of a different tribe.

Mary Ann Felter, a full-blooded Hopi, born in Hotevilla, was married to Mr. Felter without approval from her parents. Both are employed by the Puppet Council. To quote her: 'Thinking back on the others [in other villages] who have water, I don't know of any one of those who have any kind of problem like this. I knew there would be trouble when we started work.'

Without regard for the rest of the village, the installation of a water pipe was requested. Before the project could be completed there were many clashes. *The Tribal Council police intervened to protect the puppet Hopi so they could complete their job.*

The Traditional Hopi, attempting to protect the independence of their village, were threatened with arrest, while at the same time these policemen failed to follow up on their own law and order, which would have required them to arrest the puppet Hopi who were obviously fortified with alcohol, which is a violation on the reservation land, according to the Government. The police have no jurisdiction on Hotevilla land. Why are they even here?

Mary Ann Felter went on to say, 'I hope that's the end of it. There are a lot of people who want water in their houses, and my advice to them is to keep at it, but I may be wrong, and I admit that I don't know much about the old Hopi ways. But I think I am doing right. When I am old I may say I should have listened to Katherine, but I am young and I want things. We all have our weaknesses! As the Bahannas say, it's not good to bite the hand that feeds you.' Unfortunately it will be too late to change things when Mary Ann is older but wiser.

Our readers who are new to the problem will be interested to know that over the past years there have been several similar incidents. We have explained each time to those who want water and other utilities why this village must oppose such things. But we were never heeded. We have had to dig up or remove pipes at least four times in order to make our point. Still, our reasons have not been understood. Mrs. Felter has said that the people who have water have had no problem like this one. That is false! It is not so. Usually the confrontation problem is avoided by connecting the utilities under cover of darkness when we are all asleep, or when we are at our ceremonial duties, at which time we must never allow such actions to dilute our humble prayers for mankind.

So we learn the hard way that it is not actually what we say but how we act that determines who we really are. It was only a few weeks ago that some puppet Hopi tried to terrorize Hopi elders and visitors at a meeting. One Hopi elder was held at gunpoint and kicked around. One round was fired but no one was hurt. The drunken gunslinger was not apprehended by the police. Is this a conspiracy, we wondered?

We would like to know what our readers think about all this. What are we really? And whose base is truly stable? Is it those who settled the village long ago, or those who are newly involved in disrupting it?"

The Progressive Press Welcomes the Traditional Newsletter

TI— "*Qua'toqti*, the puppet press, has welcomed our newsletter *Techqua Ikachi* with open arms describing it as 'political and religious,' although 'radical.' They say our writing 'sounds like something from the 1960s underground paper' but admit that they recognize a familiar Traditional Hopi 'song.' We all know that the trouble we face goes back much farther than 1960! We apologize, but the needle got stuck in the groove! And our song will continue in the same beautiful pattern, since the tone of truth cannot be printed by *Qua'toqti*, this we know.

We wonder why they sent a Bahanna reporter to inquire about our publication. We would have preferred a Hopi. It is amusing to see this 'establishment'-oriented newspaper grasping at straws as it speculates about the 'influence of young Bahanna writers' in our traditional newsletter.

Most of the September 18 *Qua'toqti* editorial entitled 'New Voice, Old Message' is not worth analyzing as it is only a defensive reaction, but we have to agree with their statement, 'when are we going to learn that it is not what we say but how we act that determines what we really are?' Though they claim they 'have the greatest respect for Hopi philosophy,' we shall leave it to the readers of *Qua'toqti* and *Techqua Ikachi* to decide for themselves whether this is true. We welcome outside opinions."

Who Really Is the Respecter of Hopi Philosophy?

TI— "Please consider this brief outline of Hopi values and decide for yourself: To begin with, the Traditional Hopi desires to live peacefully and uphold his name. He desires to live his own way of life according to his own laws as given by the Great Spirit without the influence of modern laws made by men.

As Traditional people we would not have become involved in our current conflicts were we not provoked by what we sense will overcome us and destroy our chosen way of life. Just as all forms of life on earth and in the universe have the sense to move in their own defense when they sense violence, we too must react strongly to defend our land and life.

While the defensive reactions of the Progressive Hopi appear to follow the same level of reasoning as ours, he desires to live under modern materialistic laws while at the same time practicing some of his tradition. Since he cannot get what he wants under the traditional system, his only alternative is to join the more forceful society with its jails and police. To accomplish this he must forcefully disregard traditional doctrine.

Compare this kind of action to that of the Traditional who must act in a peaceful manner to defend himself and his way of life from the constant threats of violence presented by the Progressive.

We hope everyone involved will consider this and decide for themselves what we really are by our actions. It should be easy to see whose fault it is that there is unrest within the Hopi nation, as we described it in our first newsletter. Are we wrong when we follow the way of our Maker and reject the blind schemes of men? What do you think?"

Yes, the Corral Gate Is Indeed Open!

TI— "The editorial went on to say that the essence of *Techqua Ikachi's* message is 'We are chiefs. We demand that you respect us.' But a True Hopi never demands. He merely teaches, hoping that people who have ears to hear will respect the ways of the Great Spirit that lead to a long and healthy life. He hopes simply that others will let him remain within his own environment, whereas Bahanna demands respect by using law and order to force people into his environment. The Traditional Hopi is not a prophet of doom. He merely respects the words that come to him from the mouth of the Great Spirit, and clearly warns us about what will happen if we do not wake up and correct ourselves.

Yes, as the editorial says, 'some shepherd has left the corral gate open.' But the fact is, it has never been closed!"

The Guessing Game Goes On!

TI— "So far, three editions of *Qua'toqti* have been devoted to a guessing game about the true origin of our paper that in truth looks more and more like a smear campaign. Perhaps their Bahanna reporter, unfamiliar with our ways, has jumped to certain conclusions about our staff, and their editor has snapped at these as ways to demean us.

In our next issue we'll explain more about how we operate, but for now we will tell you that all of their guesses are wrong! Our staff is definitely Hopi! Now we hope they will become as curious about the <u>real</u> issues we are raising!"

Message from a Blue-Eyed Hopi Who Helped with the *Techqua Ikachi* Newsletters

TI— "As one of several friends who help the traditional Hopi produce *Techqua Ikachi*, I wish to correct certain false rumors circulated against this newsletter by *Qua'toqti*, a progressive paper.

Techqua Ikachi was started by a traditional Hopi in Hotevilla, after consultation with his elders. The names of those whose viewpoint would be represented were suggested by David Monongye, who also reviewed the material for the first issue. He did not see the finished product before release, being out of the village at the time. Since copies were released as soon as they were ready, some reached *Qua'toqti* before TI's staff got theirs.

When *Qua'toqti*'s White reporter showed a copy to a staff member, he naturally did not recognize it. And when David, who is nearly blind, returned, he too had not yet seen it. *Qua'toqti* jumped at the chance to ridicule the newsletter as the work of outsiders, but they jumped too soon, for the staff have approved it as expressing their views and want it to continue as presently organized. And it is written by a Hopi after all, though the quality of writing confused *Qua'toqti*, since friends had helped with the grammar.

Contrary to accusations, we who help do not express our personal views, and we have nothing to gain. Our help is purely technical. We support no faction, only the teachings of the Great Spirit, which are simple and clear.

The followers of the Great Spirit have been imprisoned, silenced, and ridiculed, and we know why. The truth they speak is the enemy of those who get rich from Hopi, and gain by turning the Hopi against their own leaders. We know who are really involved in outside interference, and why they use tricks to try to silence Hopi leaders and create disunity.

For those who think it wrong to give voice to the followers of the Great Spirit, we offer the words of a respected leader, Dan Katchongva:

'We know that when the time comes, the Hopi will be reduced to maybe one person, two persons, three persons. If he can withstand the pressure from the people who are against the tradition, the world might survive from destruction...I must continue to lead my people on the road the Great Spirit made for us to travel. I do not disregard anyone. All who are faithful and confident in the Great Spirit's way are at liberty to follow the same road.' (signed: a 'Blue-eyed Hopi')."

whosoever will may come

Riley Sunrise Case Is Revealing About Tactics and Government Oil Leases

TI— "We thank *Qua'toqti* for recalling the incident with CORE in the early 1960s, in which Harry Chaca was supposedly stabbed with a railroad spike and the Agency Superintendent 'manhandled.' As we recall the incident, Guy Kotschaptewa, an eighty-year-old leader, was charged with assault because he challenged the Superintendent. Guy had made a move to lead the Superintendent out peacefully, with which the Superintendent cooperated, but Guy was then jumped by the police. Lewis Naha ran to his aid but was beaten severely. A man named Riley Sunrise responded but was arrested, so he put up a fight and was overcome and beaten. Both men were thrown in jail. Old man Kotshaptewa was charged with assault for touching the untouchable Superintendent.

Charges against Mr. Naha and Mr. Kotshaptewa were made but later dropped. Riley Sunrise was charged with assault with a deadly weapon, but was acquitted in Federal Court in Phoenix. The railroad spike proved to be a plant to make the case stronger against the traditional Hopi who were *only trying to defend their land against oil-prospecting leases negotiated without their consent*, which was the reason for the meeting with the Superintendent.

The friendly Bahannas who helped us were objecting to outside interference in Hopi affairs on the part of oil companies operating through the Tribal Council's Mormon lawyer, John Boyden. The Superintendent's testimony in the Phoenix trial revealed *an unethical conflict of interest on the part of Boyden, who represented at the same time both the oil companies and the Tribal Council with whom they were dealing.*

We also recall something comical that happened at the trial. The witnesses for the defendant were uneducated Hopi with traditional long hair and beads, yet they were able to make a statement in blunt English to the judge and jury — though they could have used their interpreter. On the other hand, the prosecution witnesses — educated, with short hair, white shirts, and ties — were too shy to speak English, and had to borrow the Traditionals' interpreter to make their statements. But we won in the end because we spoke the truth.

What, then, was really behind this police incident? Why did police chief Tipling and tribal judge Sekaquaptewa need to hire heavily armed deputies to guard a couple of helpless Hopi? Later, we heard they were afraid the radical Hopi and CORE might attack them. As for CORE, they were simply a nonviolent organization called in to help the Hopi as observers to see that the Traditionals would have a fair hearing. After all, the Traditionals are, the Progressives say, uneducated.

There have been many such acts committed against the Traditional Hopi that should be told someday — such as the time government workers stripped Hopi women and girls naked and threw them into sheep dip, and the time the U.S. Government enforced livestock regulations in our sovereign territory by imprisoning many Hopi simply because they refused to allow their livestock to be confiscated — which has been a recurring issue. Should anyone doubt what we say, we are sure these events are on record."

Two Kinds of Law…One for the Tribal Council Members When Outsiders Come to Visit Them, and One for Traditionalists When Outsiders Come to Visit Them…A Matter of Control.

TI— "We alert all our Bahanna friends to be aware of Hopi 'law-and-order' when they visit us. Anyone with long hair, beard, and beads, or in any way looking like a hippy, could be stopped for any excuse. Even short-haired people can be stopped if they hang around the traditionals too long. The progressive government knows what they can lose by being exposed, so they regard outsiders friendly to us as a danger to their stronghold.

There have even been laws passed which go deeply against our tradition, such as the shameful 'Anti-Hippy' law, which so far as we know may still be in effect. We present it here as an example of one of the many ways the puppet Council violates the spirit of traditional Hopi life:

> *Whereas, the Hopi Tribal Council has been informed that a group of California people known as "Hippies" is likely to visit the Hopi reservation in the near future, and*
>
> *Whereas this group is known to have radical ideas and practices which are incompatible with Hopi Culture,*
>
> *Now, therefore be it resolved by the Hopi Tribal Council that this group is declared undesirable and all members of the "Hippie" group shall not be allowed on the reservation.*
>
> *Be it further resolved that [the] Superintendent is hereby requested and authorized to employ whatever means necessary to remove individuals or group of "Hippies" from the reservation at his own discretion.*
>
> *Certification: I hereby certify that the foregoing resolution was regularly adopted by the Hopi Tribal Council on the 1 day of June, 1967, by a vote of 9 in favor and 0 opposed, the chairman not voting, after full and free discussion on the merits. (Resol. no. H-9-67)*
>
> *(signed) Logan Koopee, Hopi Tribal Council.*

Chief Katchongva of Hotevilla Village issued an immediate response which read in part:

> *Your attitude toward people is wrong and wicked. Removing people from my village by force is very wrong for the Hopi. I hereby reject…resolution no. H-9-67.*
>
> *On the grounds that this resolution was acted upon without my approval, nor none of the information concerning this resolution ever came to my attention, that the village of Hotevilla will be subject to it.*
>
> *Now for years I have retold my reasons to the people of the Agency as to why the village of Hotevilla refuses to accept all your programs. That is, by high reasons, the Hotevilla Village was settled in the traditional way from the beginning, and will continue to be. All your law enforcements must discontinue within the Village, during the ceremonials and at all times…*

This was the chief's way of telling them, 'You have violated the highest law of the land — the Great Spirit — by breaking the great link between men, the power of harmony, the very element by which mankind has survived. My village will not be bound by such inhuman law. Those who enter with a good mind are accepted. Stop interfering through your police force. Our ways have worked for centuries to this day. Thus I protect the Great Spirit's honor, as I have vowed to do.'"

Taxes Refused...the Descent into Debt and Dependence

TI— "It looks as if the puppeteers of the Puppet Council — the lawyers who work behind the scenes — have been working overtime on their new act. A letter dated January 8, 1976, was circulated 'To all persons doing business on the Hopi Reservation who are subject to the proposed Ordinance 17.' The letter announced a meeting on January 19 at the "Criminal Justice Department, Oraibi, Arizona," concerning the proposed tax on private income within our independent nation. The ordinance is the work of outsiders who know nothing of the Hopi way of life. The title page states that the ordinance is from the 'Hopi Indian Tribe, Oraibi, Arizona.'

We have reviewed the provisions of this ordinance and find them completely unacceptable to the Hopi way of life. Accordingly, the following letter of January 13, 1976, was directed to John Hennessy, coordinator of the 'Hopi Criminal Justice Department':

> *Our response and reaction to your letter — subject proposed Ordinance 17. Mailed to businesses throughout Hopi Land. Dated January, 1976. (Including — article of establishing Hopi revenue commission and providing revenue through taxation for the Hopi Tribe.)*
>
> *Upon going over the text, we feel this ordinance does not fit our needs. Thereupon, on behalf of our village standing and for people of Hotevilla we will not affiliate into supporting the Ordinance 17. We think it is undesirable; it will be our greatest mistake to support that which will be harmful and will hinder our ways of life. We have our own laws to go by that are far richer than man-made laws, by which we have survived thus far.*
>
> *On January 13, 1976, we are the leaders of the Hopi people gathered and declared not to adopt the Ordinance 17 of the Tribal Council, on basis we do not recognize the Tribal Council as our leaders and vice versa. Nor do we have any representative in the establishment. Therefore we are not under their domain. Only our desire that we live in peace and self-determination. Thank you.*
>
> *(Signed by religious leaders: D. Monongye, D. Evehema, W. Pahongva, L. Naha, J. Pongqyesvia, P. Sewemanewa)*

On January 18th, we sent a second letter with the same signatures, pointing out that:

> *The so-called Tribal Council purports to take its 'authority' from a document called 'Constitution and By-laws of the Hopi Tribe.' According to this document, 'This constitution is adopted by the self-governing Hopi villages.' This is a lie!*

The traditional self-governing village of Hotevilla never acknowledged the so-called Tribal Council for its continuing efforts to impose their ways upon us.

Furthermore, since the so-called Tribal Council has in the past leased our land without our knowledge or consent, we consider them traitors to the Hopi nation and its traditional beliefs.

As traditional people our religious instructions strongly warn us never to implicate ourselves in any organizational structure of a political nature.

It is for this reason that we have never sent a representative to the so-called Tribal Council and that we continue to look upon ourselves as a sovereign nation.

So far, the tax measure has failed to pass. Even the 'progressives' don't want to pay taxes. But our objection is far more serious. The whole thing was planned from outside Hopi (by white lawyers). It forces us to pay the very system that is destroying our independent and sovereign nation. It would have cost the United States absolutely nothing to just leave us alone."

Issue No. 6, April–May 1976: The Attack on Traditional Authority and the Issue of Village Sovereignty

TI— "We gathered the following information from a newsletter issued by Bacabi Village this March, to which we add our opinion.

The biggest item of the discussion was the water/sewer project at Shungopavi Village, which has been stopped by the Kikmongwi, Claude Kewanyawma, and some of his followers. Kewanyawma says that the water/sewer project was not approved by him, and that a group led by Alford Joshvaem and Fred Kaboti had no authority to go into an agreement with the Indian Health Service. So what happened was that this group, the Village Committee of Shungopavi, then asked the Tribal Council to go into the agreement with the Indian Health Services on their behalf.

This shows that the puppet committee will do almost anything on their own, trying desperately to get what they want — even if it means denouncing the authority of the Kikmongwi, the village doctrines, and the great laws of the Great Spirit.

The newsletter continues to report that several important questions were raised, including how much authority the Kikmongwi has under the present 'Hopi Constitution.' It was argued that the Tribal Council is the governing body for the whole tribe, and that the individual village has little or no power.

This is completely wrong. As we have pointed out many times, the Tribal Council is not the governing body for the whole tribe. This is no doubt a scheme being used to combat our true leaders' refusal to allow a takeover. Traditional authority, as we still practice it, is the most perfect form of government to be found anywhere in the world. The belittling of our religious leaders as "illiterate" cannot change this.

The article further points out that the Council Chairman believes that if this issue reached the courts, it would be decided in favor of the Tribal Council. The Chairman claims that if the Tribal Council were to enter an agreement on behalf of the 'Village Committee' of Shungopavi, it would signify that any group from any village could work through the council without going through the proper local authorities. In the case of Bacabi, for example, even the progressive 'governor' and his 'Board of Directors' would be bypassed. The Tribal Council agreed that representatives of the Indian Health Service, Richard Gruitt and John Martin, redraft the agreement for presentation at a later date.

The real issue is village sovereignty. By long established tradition, each Hopi Village governs itself, and the traditional village leaders represent this authority. The 'Tribal Council,' which the United States has forced upon us, seeks instead to destroy our traditional system, regardless of the fact that the Council's own constitution guarantees the right of a village to govern itself in the traditional way."

Shungopavi Sellout and Cover-Up by Bahanna Traditionalists

TI— "We feel obliged to comment on a very confusing article in *Qua'toqti*, the weekly newspaper of the 'puppet' Hopi who have abandoned their tradition. The April 29 issue ran an article which quoted 'leaders' in Shungopavi who claimed that the priesthood in that village is 'jeopardized by corruption.' Pretty strong words. Still, this statement would be music to our ears if it were not from the mouth of 'Bahanna Traditionalists,' who themselves have in fact abandoned their religious purpose.

We regret that we must intervene and defend our *traditional brothers in Shungopavi*. We've known all along that one day our old songs would become very popular, and that our pattern of life would once again be regarded as very beautiful — yet we would also need to beware of the danger hidden beneath such shows of 'tradition.'

The article stressed that several religious leaders were dissatisfied with the political affairs of the Kikmongwi of the village, Claude Kewanyawma. It claimed that his actions are not in harmony with his responsibility for the 'welfare' of the village, and that 'tradition' obliges them to reveal the 'confusion' now threatening their 'religious' way of life.

It went on to say that serious consideration was being given to informing the people of Shungopavi about the 'unfortunate situation,' and added that the Kikmongwi has become involved with 'outsiders' and Hopi from other villages who were breaking down the 'ancient custom' for some selfish political purpose.

This is a clever approach, but in reality the "puppet" Hopi who make these claims are not defending Hopi tradition — though they would like it to look that way! They smear the Kikmongwi because he has taken a stand in opposition to a housing project, which is in fact the work of *outsiders breaking down the ancient customs.*

They claim to act out of religious obligation, but they would not dare tell the truth, which is that the Kikmongwi is bound to defend the right of his villagers to own their land in common without allowing it to be leased or sold to the United States.

These so-called Hopi are only looking for Government hand-outs. The Kikmongwi and the true Hopi in Shungopavi know it is best to survive in freedom as our ancestors have by their own hands. All true Hopi deeply oppose handouts such as housing, sewers, water and power lines, because, among other reasons, we want to remain farmers of the land, not puppets looking for and dependent upon a job. (This is what is meant by following the Great Spirit's instructions.)

While it suits the purpose of these seekers of handouts to make it appear that outside 'radicals' are interfering with and corrupting the religious structure, it is actually the other way around.

Chief Kewanyawma has appealed to the Secretary of the Interior of the United States, asking him to review the decision of the so-called Hopi Tribal Council by which land below Second Mesa is now being developed for a HUD housing project. The houses are nearly completed, yet there are at least ten grounds on which this appeal is being made, mostly of which are violations of the constitution under which the Council is required to operate.

If by some change of heart the Secretary should recognize the illegality of the lease, it might make Watergate look like child's play compared to what is going on in Hopi Land.

The article fails to mention that these supposedly Hopi religious leaders are not Hopi, but Mormons in name if not in fact! What else could they be, considering their preference to follow the Mormon chairman of the Tribal Council rather than their Traditional chief! As we have said before, the Bahanna road is no path of roses. This is proven again and again by hard experience. It looks nice at first as the 'progressive' Hopi start to accept the handouts, but any Bahanna will tell you the road never ends. The bills keep coming, and they can't be paid with corn. That means giving up the Hopi life and looking for a whiteman's job. The word 'unemployment' meant nothing to us before such government programs were introduced .

In spite of experience, the progressives say, 'We know we have to deal with the present way of life for our children's sake.' But their true selfish motive keeps them from admitting that by speaking these words they are selling their children's birthright."

Indebtedness and the Matter of Evicting and Cutting Off Those Who Can Not Afford to Pay the Bills...Something That Never Happens When We Live the Traditional Way.

TI— "This summer the puppet press reported the eviction of two or three families from their low-cost housing by the Hopi Tribal Council. One of the evicted victims had a stroke because the family couldn't find another home, and the Tribal Council said they were powerless to help. What gives? Has the Council become unfaithful, or do they exist only to serve their own purposes?

Another report came our way. The puppet Council had shut off the water to their faithfuls, the Old Oraibi puppet residences, who have been getting water from the Council's tap. For what reason? The Tribal Council now pays for the water, and it was their decision to not share with their faithfuls, who now must carry water for miles to their homes. The Council feared their bills would be too high, so in their September 16 editorial the puppet press complained that the federal government has failed to respond to their local needs. Are they now biting their big brother's hand that feeds them? Well, we expected it would happen and told you so. Your big brother has raised you and spoiled you like a kind mother hen. Now you must go on your own and face the music."

The Dividing and the Diminishing Goes On in 1981

TI— "We are aware that many of our readers are anxious to hear about our present relations with the Tribal Council. At this moment we are not certain in which direction the newly elected Chairman, Ivan Sidney, will lean. We have heard rumors that he is not in harmony with most of the Council Members, and that in most cases he follows closely the Hopi Tribal Constitution, respecting the Traditional leaders and Traditional values. The latest rumor was that the hard-core Progressives wanted him to step down.

We wonder if he will keep his campaign promises by remaining in touch with us. So far he has defaulted twice by failing to meet with us as arranged. We hope that he lives up to his words and we will not need to use pressure.

The water line was forced into the village this past year, but no hookup has been attempted. Perhaps President Reagan's program of cutbacks has something to do with it. However, we fear that the coming warmer days will bring renewed problems.

Recently the Committee on *Education* of the so-called Hotevilla/Bacabi Community School made a survey seeking advice from certain Hotevilla people. The survey questioned whether the School should be run by the Hopi Tribal Council, the Bureau of Indian Affairs, or by Hopis themselves. This issue, based on what the Tribal Council calls 'the law of self-determination,' will decide how the School should be operated.

Funding is provided by the government, but no matter who runs the School, we traditional people of Hotevilla are refusing to cooperate. In the past, when the Oraibi leaders accepted a similar program, we were forced to accept the white-man's education. Whatever decision is made, the end result will be the same."

We Hear Our Earth Mother Through Our Spiritual Roots…
Listen to Her Cries!

TI— "We are all aware that here as well as in other places certain mystical changes are occurring in society that are causing us to question the very basis of our existence. Some of us know the sacred purposes and designs given to us by our creator, and realize that the Spirit dwells within all of us. But unfortunately, some other people, giving way to great ambitions, are trying to control others. Instead of

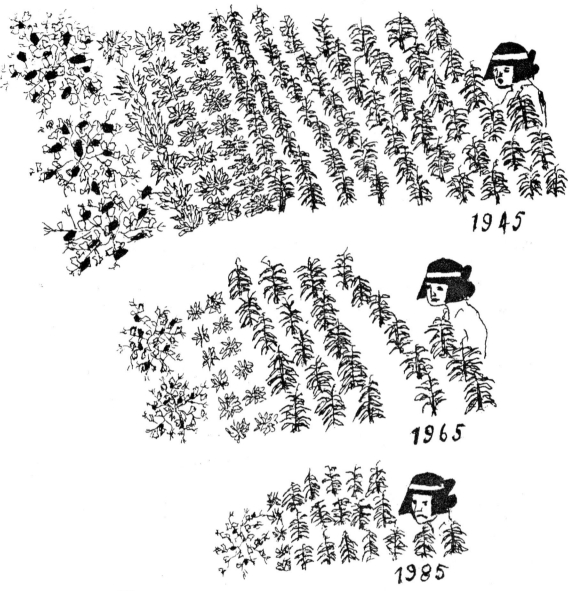

TI— 2000? What Or Who Is Responsible For Farm Decline?

correcting certain imbalances found in today's world, they are busy trading blame, which further drains our planet of spiritual energy. *These people are weaving self-destructive circles, causing great harm to all land and life.*

It is a fact that today's generation no longer relies on what was said by our forefathers. They have forgotten how to avoid temptation — a key by which man has survived thus far. And while it is true that we cannot escape new changes, we can at least use these changes wisely, so that we won't destroy those important elements which maintain our way of life. At this point in time we must awaken ourselves to our true destiny. We must not be deaf to the cries of our Earth Mother, for if we do not mend our ways our sacred purpose will have been in vain.

Looking at one of the more serious changes in our society, we come to the rather long and dangerous subject of the five million dollar settlement for 1.5 million acres of Hopi Land. This situation worries those of us within our traditional circle more than a little. It is also a subject of much interest to most world watchers, and therefore we thank our friends in Washington, at the Institute for the Development of Indian Law, for analyzing and simplifying the complicated language of the Land Claims Commission. We are printing this information for the benefit of those people who have doubts about what is really happening to the land. Hopefully this simplified language will help people understand the danger of accepting this award (money) settlement. It is stated in 'section 70v in law 25 of the U.S. Constitution' that 'payment and acceptance of an award made by the Indian Claims Commission is a complete bar to any other legal action to recover land for which the claim is made.' This five million dollar award would thus mean a complete settlement for already-appropriated Hopi Land, and accepting it would put an end to further petition any claim to the land itself.

This situation confirms a theory found in our prophecy telling us that the choice of what to do with the land is ours. Therefore, whatever choice is made will bring its due reward. We will see in the end what happens. When we look at our past history, we see the actual fulfillment of our prophecies, and know that amazingly enough many events were foretold centuries in advance. And even still some of us refuse to accept the reality of this ancient knowledge.

In our last issue we quoted some passages from the Hopi Constitution, written by one Oliver LaFarge, who for the Indians was both oppressor and protector. We feel that these testimonials will become a reality if we lose our struggle for survival of the Hopi way. What will our grandchildren say to us when they learn that we sold them out? From our recollection of facts contained in both the *Hopi Constitution* and *U.S. Constitution*, it was thought that for the U.S. to recognize Indians, they would have to find a group of native people numbering 6,000 or more who still retained a tribal life and organization. Since 1870 the U.S. has dealt with tribes as if they were individual little nations having limited sovereignty that was always subject to Federal jurisdiction. When the government wants to have new arrangements with Indians they simply make promises called treaties. It is a sad truth that there is not a single tribe with which the U.S. government has not broken its treaties. Most Indians still have the feeling that the tribes have never surrendered to Federal jurisdiction and therefore retain their original sovereignty.

The Hopi have long resisted all services from the Bureau of Indian Affairs — especially educational services — thus remaining in BIA eyes one of the most primitive and traditional of all Indian groups. In recent years, unfortunately, some of our people have neglected their struggle and are now dealing more with the Federal government. Since 1946 Indians were no longer considered to be wards of the government, and therefore the U.S. had no more or less authority over them than on any other citizen. By 1880 the Hopi tribe owned a total of almost 155,000 acres, at which point well-meaning people came to supposedly civilize the Indians. Their theory was that tribal ownership would allow certain allotments of land to

Bahanna Lies

Keep resisting

be given to strengthen the tribe, but in reality, this allotted land only bound the tribe to a limited reservation. This, then, was a process of giving Indians a home with a fence around it. Since they were considered a 'dying race,' if everyone got an immediate allotment of land, there would be no need to worry about having more land available for their future.

Unfortunately, some unscrupulous people saw great possibilities in using this allotment plan to further their own gains, with the Indian once again suffering. These people knew that if all Indians got allotments, then a lot of land would be left over and would be declared 'surplus land.' They then could buy this 'surplus land' very cheaply and could use it either for homesteading or for reselling at greater profit. Therefore to offer each Indian $3,000 for his land was usually more money than he had ever seen or heard of in his life, and he could imagine no end to this money.

Now comes the introduction of taxation — a means by which the government continues to control the Tribal Council. The Council's first attempt was to tax all local Hopi traders and those whose livelihood depends on selling their wares. This proposal was rejected by the people. The Council is now putting a lot of pressure on the local Hopi traders, and the other villages may go along with this plan. But Hotevilla Village will stand firm on the basis that this move will jeopardize our way of life. This tax system is something we know nothing about. We are neither members of this system, nor have we any representatives in their organization. Therefore, they are outside our jurisdiction and we feel that they have no right to dominate us. In spite of this, our local traders continue to be harassed and pressured to pay up. Were we to permit this to happen, then it would be the beginning of our gradual movement into the tax pot — where we will be lost. So, beware, brothers and sisters!"

A Unity Movement, and a Petition from the Hopi Religious Leaders

TI— "After many decades of oppression upon our own land from the U.S. Government and the Hopi Tribal Council (an establishment we have never endorsed), we, the Hopi religious leaders, and the people from all the traditionally governed villages, rise to challenge, through non violence, these most cunning oppressive forces. At our gathering within our Kiva over our sacred pipes, we have made a decision to unite and stand together to challenge the movement of the so-called Hopi Tribal Council toward destroying our Traditional leadership and authority. We ask all our people and those elsewhere to support our move. We are assured our stand is based on truth. We bring this before the people to make them aware that we have been deceived. Therefore, the so-called Hopi Tribal Council members are unworthy to be the leaders of the Hopi Nation. *They do not participate in Hopi ceremonial functions, the important factors which motivate the powers of the Hopi, thus they lack the wisdom and knowledge necessary to lead the Hopi in spiritual ways.* Because of this we demand several things which must be carried out. The most important are:

1. That the so-called Hopi Tribal Council cease their activities and planning operations.

2. That a full investigation be made into their cover-up of their activities, dealings, and wrongs.

3. That the Tribal Council's lawyer, Mr. Boyden, be discharged from his position.

4. That Mr. Boyden's activities be fully investigated.

At this writing, the Hopi Tribal Council is at a standstill, having the support of only three non-traditional governed villages while seven Traditionally governed villages support the Traditional leaders. None of the village Chiefs have certified their representatives, therefore the Tribal Council cannot function according to their Constitution, which calls for a full quorum. The Traditional Hopi leaders are now in an advantageous position to have their demands met, that is, if the other institutions cooperate. But, as foretold, they will be cunning and we are aware of it. This is as much as we can say at this time."

$5,000,000 Claim Hearing Excludes Traditional Leaders

TI— "Since the Land Claim Commission awarded five million dollars to the Hopi tribe on the land deal, Hopis have been undecided what to do with the money and are in disagreement as to whether it is a land sale or whether the funds have been awarded for wrongs done.

Several fruitless attempts have been made by the Hopi traditional leaders to meet with the Hopi Tribal Council about this question, all of which were declined. Instead Supt. Alph Sekakuku conducted his own five million dollar hearing on March 11, 1980. None of the traditional leaders attended because of his slanderous remark in the tribal newsletter, 'That they think it will be useless to attend his meeting because of his racist attitude.'

On the agenda was the question, 'Have the Hopi people sold their land as claimed by some people?' He says the winning answer was NO from the crowd of approximately 200 persons. Actually few agreed, so we are informed, because there were so many who remained curious and undecided.

His theme is: 'It is like paying a fine for something that you have done wrong. Because that is what the U.S. Government had been guilty of.' He claims that the Hopi tribe, under this Hopi Tribal Council, has owned the land under Indian title (who gave them the title?) for half of the 19th and the 20th centuries. We wonder why he made this claim. The Hopi Tribal Council was not around then and was not really organized until the Commissioner granted official recognition December 1, 1955. The traditional Hopi government has been organized for thousands of years before the Bahanna came, so actually we, the traditionals, have far more right to control our own land than the Hopi Tribal Council does.

The following is an interpretation by capable lawyers of Docket 196 of the Land Claims Commission:

'Accepting the money for the claim will have the same legal effect as selling the rights to the land. This is so because accepting the money will mean that the Hopi will no longer have any right to the land for which the claim was made.

'According to present U.S. law, payment and acceptance of an award made by the Indian Claims Commission is a complete bar to any other legal action to recover the land for which the claim was made. This is stated in Sec. 70U of the law, 25 USC 70U.

'The claim made in the Indian Claims Commission was for the taking of Hopi land, among other things. To say it another way, the claim asked for money, that is, for the value of the Hopi land. This can be seen by reading paragraphs No. 8–19 in the claim petition. The five million dollar award settles and puts an end to any claim to the land itself. This award is not simply compensation for past wrongs.

'In paragraphs 20–22 of the petition the lawyers make what is called an 'alternative' claim. In those paragraphs they take the position that the land still belongs to the Hopi, and that the claim is for depriving the Hopis of the use of the land. But as explained above, the claim also takes the contrary position, saying that the land was taken and making a claim for the value of the land itself.

'Accepting the award will settle and put an end to all the claims in the petition, including any further claim to the land itself.' "

Surprise! The Hopi Tribal Chairman Is Skeptical!

TI— "A month ago the Progressive Hopi Chairman announced that he was skeptical of Congressional hearings on the BIA concerning its mismanagement of education, health care, and other Indian issues. The hearings were scheduled to begin sometime in November. The Chairman was concerned that this might be the beginning of Congress's phasing out or abolishing funding for Indian Tribes. What would this mean to the Indians? The Chairman wanted to know. Will Hopi be left out in the street, or will the Hopi get attention? He said many tribes are ready to take control of their own programs, but the Hopis are not. This appears to be a quicker route to termination. The Chairman asked, 'What is the government obligated to do and for how long?'

Our Traditional Elders would simply say to the Chairman, 'Why worry and get upset? You have prepared yourselves for this day — or rather the Bahanna government has prepared you for it — by educating you to the Bahanna ways of life so that when the time comes you will be able to stand on your own feet and not need to rely on government help and handouts. You must think now about your own survival and that of your families. You have chosen your path. It is your own wish. If you are fortunate, you will succeed in reaching your goal in the Bahanna world.' "

A Proposal to Us from the New, Self-Proclaimed Hotevilla Village Committee…If We Can't Be Beaten One Way, Try Another

TI— "We received the following letter from the self proclaimed and so-called 'Hotevilla Village Committee' to the Traditional leaders of Hotevilla, inviting the following groups to their future meetings: Hopi Tribal Council,

Telephone Co., Indian Health Service, BIA Road Construction, BIA Superintendent and Chief Pongyayouma, who is affiliated with the Tribal Council and recognized by the Government, but who is not recognized as a chief by the religious leaders and people of Hotevilla:

You and members of your organization are invited to attend all future meetings which will be held at the Hotevilla Community Building. These meetings will be planning sessions. Surveys conducted indicated a majority of residents need such services as: water, sewers, telephone and better roads. Residents requesting such services are signing petitions to support these projects.

Do not confuse this letter as requesting your permission or approval of these projects. This is to inform you that these projects will be implemented based on the needs and the wants of the majority of residents. You will be notified once these meetings have been scheduled. If you are aware of other funding sources that could be utilized to improve the condition of our village, please stop by our office. We look forward to having each and every one of you at our planning sessions. Thank you.

Kenneth Quanimptewa CD
Village Committee
Hotevilla, AZ 86030

We wondered what this proposal really meant. Have they decided to listen to the elders' advice? Not hardly, we think. It could be an attempt to lure us into their fold. They did not mention electricity, but once people get hooked to the utilities mentioned above they will want electric power. But according to the prophetic instructions of our Great Spirit, nothing was supposed to enter the village that still exerts its inherent powers under the Great Spirit, Maasaw. After purification and when we reclaim our full independence or autonomy, then we will get full benefit from the land to use these powers wisely, in good ways, not to destroy and without fear of pitfalls."

Issue No. 33: Looking at Hopi Today

TI— "Greetings, we know many of you are waiting to hear about the goings on here in Hopi Land and in our neighboring Navajo tribe at Big Mountain. But first, let us give our attention to local matters.

We sense that most of our readers and people in general are not totally familiar with the position of the Hopi Traditionals and the so-called Hopi Tribal Council. This is because what comes to us through the Tribal newspaper is often misleading and creates confusion. There are questions in people's minds which must be clarified. Herein, briefly, we shall try to show where each group of Hopis stand, how the Hopi thinks, and how he looks at his problems.

It would be nice if we could write about pleasant things, but because of the frustrations and emotional problems confronting Hopi society we feel it is time to admit to our personal shortcomings in order that the outside public may understand our situation. At present the future of the Hopi looks bleak. But we also know that throughout our history crises like these have served the people well. With the Creator's help, bad things can sometimes be turned into good things. Crises cause people to stop and think and to find their way back to the good path. So we are hoping that all our mistakes can be mended and will lead to a brighter future. We are certain that those with open minds will understand what we are saying — that frictions and divisions within Hopi society make it difficult and complicated to voice personal opinions to a person with a different view. These create aggressive feelings toward fellow Hopis, often disturb clan relationships, and also cause hard feelings among leaders when the opinions of others do not agree with their own wisdom and knowledge. This problem exists in all of the Hopi villages, not only in our village of Hotevilla.

One good bit of news is that our Traditional spiritual wisdom has not declined much. Ceremonialism is one factor that still unites us for a day or two at a time as we help one another and share our food and happiness. This sharing makes our ceremonials complete.

Not long ago Traditional Hopi — mainly the people of Hotevilla Village — were regarded by some as a people with a wayward spirit, a backward people wanting nothing that was not Hopi and believing in dead wisdom and knowledge — like devil believers in doomsday prophecies. Humiliated by this, but refusing to buckle under the heavy pressure, the Traditionalists continued their ways because they believed the struggle was worth it and would enable them to continue to live their own way of life.

Our village continues to oppose and reject all the programs and proposals of foreign government. To the casual observer, Bahanna activities seem harmless, and while the promoters think good things will come out of the proposal which will benefit the village, the fact is that these programs are one more part of an ongoing attempt to force the village into assimilating western ways — just another effort to force us away from our tradition and culture.

We remind you that Hotevilla Village was founded in 1906 by Chief Yukiuma following his eviction with his followers from our mother village of Oraibi. The eviction followed his efforts to preserve the Hopi tradition and culture. He is the only Hopi Chief who shook hands with U.S. President Taft in the White House. The only Hopi Chief who defied the power of the great American Nation and was sent to Alcatraz Prison, who endured suffering, bribes, and flattery. The great American President could not convince him to bow to the greatest nation on earth. Therefore, to this day Hotevilla Village has been following the philosophy of Chief Yukiuma. Moreover, we do not forget his followers, men, women, and children, who suffered equal punishment and humiliation at the hands of Government Agents. We also do not forget some Hopis from other villages who stained their hands by committing sorrowful and disastrous acts against our village. In spite of this, and while we must not forget, it is our elders' advice that it is proper to forgive the incidents.

If we are fortunate this event in our past at Oraibi will, in the future, help fulfill some of our prophecies. Upon these foundations we must stand firm, and at a certain period of time we must even widen our distance from people who have a spirit unlike ours — else we will be tricked into the same pitfalls they have, and will continue to be caught in. All traditionally established villages have problems

similar to ours because of encroachment from one source or another. Since, however, they have their own guidelines, we are not in a position to give them direction. We mean, of course, in terms of Bahanna political matters where we are lacking in understanding. On the spiritual level, however, we have understandings in areas where we share feelings of good will and oneness. We know it can be difficult for outsiders to understand where each village stands and how we happen to be different. There is no easy answer to the question. So we will once again point out that each village is separate, something like Bahanna towns with their own leaders, except that, in the Traditional way, there is <u>no federal body that controls us all.</u> Each village has its own self-governing body whose size and influence depends on the number of traditional-thinking religious leaders and people who make decisions for the community.

Sadly, at the present time, Hopi lifestyles are changing at a rapid pace. The things we were supposed to avoid have made deep inroads into our communities. Electric power and water conveniences are now being installed in homes. Large numbers of Hopi now depend on the BIA-created Hopi Tribal Council for economic purposes. The unconcerned observer may think these activities are a great step toward progress, that they will do us no harm. Our view is that it only shows we are ignoring the wisdom and knowledge of our wise elders and ignoring the great laws of our Creator, that we are forgetting our Creator-given guideline to survival. *We are proud to say that our village, Hotevilla, still stands firm in keeping out modern things — at least those things which will break down our resistance. Hotevilla is the last traditional stronghold in Hopi Land and the Shrine of the Covenant, please help us keep it.*"

Considering the Rewards of What We Sow

TI— "*The Hopi elders look on with awe as the predictions of Maasaw and our prophets continue to unfold before their eyes. The fast life, the changes in attitudes and behavior of the world's people, contesting for power, boastfulness in know-how, increased immorality and materialism. The world's people do not realize these actions gradually diminish the life resources by opposing the laws of nature with our own designs. Clever as Man is, he did not see that his actions set nature in motion toward disastrous consequences.*

Upon this basis, our religious leaders have always opposed modernization. But for some years conflicting and distorted versions of our traditional wisdom and knowledge have been passed on by 'progressive' Hopi. Today, these distortions are confusing the minds of Hopi people and leading them into modern ways. People who don't understand the old teachings correctly are easily misled. Those with shortcomings are easily hooked into the very way of life that true Hopis are avoiding. These people are encouraged to follow the new system of a salary-based life and education. They are told that modern ways will not harm them, and those who lack the whitemans' education and technical skills are encouraged to become dependent on handouts, welfare, food stamps, etc. So these do great harm to the traditional principles of self-sufficiency through farming and handcrafts. This is a shameful and not a proud way to obtain necessities. It seems these who are deceived would know better, but they appear to ignore the problems of the present crisis as if it were unimportant. Devoted Hopi regard this crisis as an extremely serious one. *It could, in fact, be the harrowing last chapter of the true Hopi way of life.*

To show you how persistently willed the Hopi 'progressives' are in doing their dirty work, only a month ago they made another inroad into our village with telephone lines, and again without the approval of the village leaders. From informed sources we hear now that they are planning to install water and power lines into our village. Can we stop them? We have done it before, and we will try to do it again."

Regarding Our So-Called Childish Behavior and Attitudes...

TI— "Our greetings to all with good hearts. We are now well into the new year. We pray it will bring us prosperity and peace throughout the world. Also that it will bring us good health and happiness.

In the past year many of us have encountered some form of pitfall. These experiences are intended to teach us that our life is not always a path of roses. Especially in today's hectic world, there are pitfalls able to drain our minds and strength. The 'Rambo' style policies of world leaders and deceitfulness in high places has people puzzled the world over about what is going on, as well as concerned and worried.

According to our ancient prophecies, one day as we walk along our path we will arrive at a point of confusion because of the fast life resulting from the change from good to bad in our moral principles. Just as in our previous worlds, the lives of people and the leaders will become corrupted by greed and power. Honesty and truthfulness will wane. This will affect our children, who will hassle us with nagging and annoyances which will finally cause us mental distress resulting in the failure of our health, sending us perhaps even to our graves. Many other things will come about which will be cloaked with mystery, things which cannot be fully understood, and so will make it difficult to explain to others how exactly they will affect the world and people.

Maasaw: 'I only have my planting stick and my seeds. If you are willing to live here as I do, you may come and live here with me. Then you will have fruitful lives. There will come a time when you will come to two paths. Seek your wisdom for directions to lasting peace or the destiny of fate.'"

The Matter of Social Class and the Power Struggle

TI— "For some years now our little newsletter has been making the effort to keep active as an information source to the outside world. We also have our messengers going to distant places, informing those who will listen to be aware of our domestic problems, and of the problems that are emerging between Man and Nature.

All of us know that the people and the world have changed many times over, leading to many views being expressed. However, our view of this changing time in this era appears extraordinary. Perhaps it has a special purpose or function. To us it is frightening. With this in mind let us look at Hopi.

Hopi Land is undergoing a change or reformation of great consequence. Because of friction between the progressive Council and the Traditional Hopi, or conservatives, many Hopis are caught in the middle and looking for which path to follow. So this change has activated a new social class and power struggle.

Now, Hopis with little knowledge, along with the younger generation, lean toward progressive ideas because this path appears to offer some meaningful opportunities — if one joins the fold of the Hopi Tribal Council and their Hopi Constitution and Bylaws. This is a direct path to a whiteman's western lifestyle. This path also leads to rights for land assignment in the JUA, Joint Use Area, when the Navajo move out. No doubt this is a sister to the Allotment Plan which failed in the early 1900s. This is another instance where the Traditional Hopi are looked upon as an obstacle to progress. It is said that no value can be gained through us because we have no power or wealth.

But the Traditional Hopi follow the teachings of precaution, believing it is wise to take action beforehand in order to prevent those who are not Traditional from taking hold of our ways of life and land. In spite of the pressures, these are precautions that will protect and defend the land for you and me. Maybe we are far from achieving our goal. Or who knows, maybe our goal is nearer than anyone thinks!

Having come this far, and having held fast, we don't think of ourselves as being unworthy for this task. Actually we believe that no one is unworthy — because we humans are divinely created by our Creator. Therefore, we are spiritual beings. And divine rights cannot be withheld from any common man, for each of us is given a special role in life."

Traditional Hopi Meeting — October 10, 1976 — Regarding Corruption In Hopi Land

TI— *"As dawn appeared over the horizon in Hopi Land one would dimly notice movements of dark figures against the Eastern sky. There was an air of extra awareness and feelings for those who were up at that hour. One could almost feel the movements of the Mother Earth getting ready to care for her children and even the jogging feet of Guardian Maasaw returning home after an all-night vigil over Man. Dogs were barking; cocks and mockingbirds were sounding the arrival of dawn. Before long, Father Sun would take over the task he does every day.*

One by one, bowed darkened figures would whisper and breathe their prayers upon the cornmeal that their hand held: "Our Father Sun, all the Unseen Living, help us this day with your Supreme Power. Echo your voices into the ears of men so that they may hear and understand our purpose here this day. Protect and guide us in the right way. May our body, mind, and spirit be wholesome this day. I humbly ask Thee."

Yes, today is an extraordinary day. It may even turn out to be historical. From the housetop, the village crier will announce the gathering not only to people, but to all directions and unseen spirits, for the Hopi desires everyone's support in spirit and prayers.

The setting is Old Oraibi, the Mother Village. This 'issue' is 'Tribal Council,' the 'New Establishment.' Since it was born not very long ago, they have gotten out of control and became involved in corrupt dealings with the 'U.S. Government' and the 'BIA,' and other 'progressive interests,' leasing land, fencing lands for their own use, housing and church projects, plumbing, electricity, and pavement for our Ancient Villages, strip-mining and electrical power plants, 'industries,' and 'programs for economical and cultural development,' destruction of our Sacred Shrines, etc., which Traditionals oppose for obvious reasons. The 'Tribal Council Members' no longer respect the advice of the Old Leaders and, thereby, violate their own 'Constitution.'

Reliable sources alerted the Kikmongwis (Traditional Leaders) that if we Traditionals or they, the 'Tribal Council Members,' accept the 'big money offer' ($5,000,000) from 'Land Claims Commission,' we will lose control of all our land.

Shortly after our morning meal, the leaders from several Hopi Villages arrived, each a Village Leader or Representative Speaker. Two former 'Council

Members' also attended the gathering to inform us about the dealings and conduct of the 'Tribal Council.' The discussion lasted all day. The two former 'Council Members' opposed the move to dissolve the 'Tribal Council.'

A solution was proposed: Kikmongwis, or leaders of each village, should withdraw or refuse endorsement of 'Tribal Council Members' as 'Representatives' of Kikmongwis and Traditional Hopi people. Spokespersons of Walpi and Mushongnovi were favorable to this decision. On them this hinged, for they have 'Representatives' in the 'Council.'

So the meeting ended. Each man parted with different thoughts, for there are ways our opponents have for stopping this very important move, such as bribery, blackmail, or fear of being exposed. Will it materialize?"

Meeting with the Tribal Council, and Corruption in Action

TI— "This is the Hopi Traditionals' view of the statements and interpretations of the 'Land Claim Settlement' by the so-called 'Chairman of the Hopi Tribe,' Abbott Sekaquaptewa, when they met with him in their last desperate effort to voice their opinion that the 'vote' and 'move' of the 'Puppet Council' and their followers to accept **five million dollars** ($5,000,000) is ILLEGAL and improper. The Council says it is not.

The question is, by accepting the money, does it mean selling out or not? The Puppet Council says that it is only a matter of 'payment for wrongs done by the U.S. Government.' They add that the lands were taken away from Hopi; that there is no passage in the 'document' indicating that the Land is being sold; also that it would be the beginning of recovering our Aboriginal Hopi Land; that later, as 'progress' increases, suits for 'money' will be filed against the Navajo Tribe and White settlers. They also assure everyone that from the five million dollars there will be no offsets for 'helpful-aid-expenses' for the Hopi from the beginning of the takeover to 1951, or for 10 percent payment to 'Attorneys.' Because, Sekaquaptewa explained, the 'Settlement' was done by what he termed as 'friendly ways' ('Negotiation-Settlement') instead of by ways of 'Land Claims Ruling,' and therefore, Hopis will have the greater advantage of not being 'billed' as other Tribes.

We Traditionals conclude that there is nothing new in these promises. We already know about all of the 'greater future promises' for the Tribe; all of them boil down to 'no strings attached, all clear Money.' But unless there is a ruling to the contrary in Washington, the Attorneys will receive their fees. They go by whatever the 'fine print' says. So, we know that in the end we will lose control of our Land, for there are no bona-fide passages included that include the Traditional Hopi, or saying that Land is given back to Hopi for their exclusive use. All it says is that 'Money' will be paid for what the Government has taken, or done 'wrong.'

We Traditionals think that what they really mean is: 'my conscience has bothered me all these years for taking your lands like a thief. What I really want is the wealth underneath, so here are five million dollars. Now that I have paid you,

I will explore the Land without a guilty conscience. And, now and then, I will throw you a few crumbs to put on your table.'

The Puppet Tribal Council caustically remarked, 'What we're doing is proof that we are fighting for our Land. Now, we ask you, what have you got to show to prove to the People that you are trying to save them the Land. What have you got?'

We Traditionals answer, 'The Great Spirit gave us the Land to take care of. Now, who gave you the Land to sell?' Perhaps you too believe in who has given you the Land — the U.S. Government? Is it your Creator?

The Council Chairman replied by saying that he does not affiliate with any church or belief. Does this sound like a True Hopi?

For once we agreed with the 'Chairman' in that we would never unite, for our thought and beliefs are different. We say it is because they are people who have become a different product than we are, people who have been taught from birth to think and act only in Bahanna's Patterns. Bahanna Society has impressed these views upon the parents, who in turn impressed them upon their children. And together they have conditioned today's generation to reject the advice of the Elders.

But the question remains, 'Who has the Creator's Basic Principle giving them the Right to the Land?'

We conclude by asking, 'What if today's generation lives long enough to have grandchildren?' and they grow up to ask, 'What were you doing grandpa when all this could have been stopped?' What will be their answer to the children's questions?

From our long experience we can tell you that big promises, even when put in writing, notarized, and recorded, are not worth the breath that utters them.

A Letter from Members of the Hopi Independent Nation
Shungopavy Pueblo
Second Mesa, Via, Arizona 86043

October 19, 1976

Mr. Alph Secakuku
Hopi Superintendent
Keams Canyon, Arizona

Mr. Abbott Sekaquaptewa
Chairman, Tribal Council
Oraibi, Arizona

Mr. Secakuku and Mr. Sekaquaptewa:
Several meetings were held in Oraibi, Shungopavy and Mushongnovi Pueblos where there were representatives from all Traditional Pueblos includ-
ing members of One-Horn and Two-Horn Society Religious Leaders and

Clan Members whose religious duties are to protect Hopi Land, way of life and religion.

Kikmongwis from Walpi, First Mesa, Shungopavy on Second Mesa, and Oraibi on Third Mesa were also present. After hearing about the illegal and dictatorial manner in which the so-called Tribal Council and the Hopi Superintendent has been operating on Hopi Land, and since Mormon Lawyer, John S. Boyden, has proposed settlement of Indian Claims Commission Docket No. 196 to the so-called Hopi Tribal Council in which John S. Boyden and United States Government are now offering Hopi people for the land they took away but never paid anything to the Hopi people in the amount of $5,000,000, since this will involve all Hopi people, our sacred homeland, way of life, and religion it has become very necessary that these Hopi Initiated Traditional Headmen and Kikmongwis meet with you along with our People to look into this very vital issue. We as Hopi will never sell our Mother Earth, and we have been saying this for a long time. The so-called Hopi Tribal Council and Hopi Superintendent of the Bureau of Indian Affairs were supposed to protect all Hopi Land and life, but who is responsible for this present critical problem? This must be investigated by our Hopi people, so we want to hear from each so-called Hopi Tribal Member, Hopi Superintendent, and Tribal Council Chairman individually now.

We have set a date for Sunday, October 24, 1976, at 1:00 p.m. in the Kyakotsmovi Community Hall where Hopi people will meet with Abbott Sekaquaptewa and Hopi Superintendent Alph Secakuku, therefore, you are now invited to come to this meeting, without fail. We will not argue on personal matters but look into this issue of why we have to accept the $5,000,000 or to reject it.

KIKMONGWI OF SHUNGOPAVY:

CLAUDE KEWANYAWMA

KIKMONGWI OF ORAIBI:

MINA LANSA

KIKMONGWI OF WALPI:

NED NAYAWTIMA.

Doomsday and the Big Money. Quickly Here, Quickly Gone! How the Tribal Council Works

TI— "As 'Doomsday' approaches, the Tribal Council keeps silent. Then suddenly their Puppet Press comes forth with the notice of a 'Meeting' signed by 'BIA Superintendent' Alph Secakuku, including a report by the Claims Attorney to the Hopi people from the Council and regarding a vote to be taken on the 'proposed settlement, concerning the Aboriginal Land Title, or $5,000,000 big money offer.'

Hopi people were surprised. The villages had not heard of this important matter from their representatives. Some of us had heard of the 'Land Claim,' but we expected the 'proposal' would be explained and debated so that we could better understand it. So a few days before the deadline, most village people discussed the 'Issue,' but no doubt could not in such a short period of time understand its consequences. Many people think this notice is too sudden and unfair.

So on October 30, 229 out of 8,000 Hopi voted 'yes' to accept the $5,000,000. This 'settlement' was presented as payment for wrongdoings done to Hopi, but we Indians know that big money offers mean business as usual — in short, the matter of taking away land and life from us Hopi.

A big money offer — so what is the catch? We ask you. Who gives away money for wrongdoings or for nothing? If we 'Indians' were to be paid what is right for 'wrongdoings' committed against us by our 'Uncle,' the U.S. might go broke. So is our 'Uncle' really becoming generous?

In spite of Traditional Leaders disapproving and intervening to request more time to consider the 'proposal,' the Puppet Council feels that they have accomplished something and proudly wave their arms to celebrate the conquest they have just 'won': 'We still have one thing,' they shouted. 'We have the land, or what is left of it. We will be rewarded. Though we are sad that so few voted to decide such an important issue, what we did is proper and legal. After all, all leadership in the entire world is composed of only 5 percent, and this 5 percent leads the other 95 percent around by their noses.'

But the True Hopi know that our Mother Earth is sacred, and that this kind of 'deal' and 'leadership' is not the Hopi way taught to us by Maasaw."

Uncle Sam Sends a Contradictory Puppet to the Queen of England

TI— "We were informed that the Hopi Tribal Council Chairman, Abbott Sekaquaptewa, visited the Queen of England draped in Hopi traditional finery and Mon-go-ho and posing as the greatest chief of the Hopi Nation — while back home he had just finished threatening to have his police 'put the screws to' her countrymen, the ATV film crew, presumably to 'protect' Hopi Tradition. We wonder what makes him so nervous! Maybe he has a monkey on his back that is nagging him about his hiding of his guilty conscience. He must be worried that news of his own role in the attempted materialistic conquest of the Traditional Hopi might reach the Queen's ears.

On September 15 he traveled as part of a U.S. delegation to London for the opening of the United States Bicentennial Exhibition. Perhaps it is appropriate that he, rather than a true religious leader, should help represent the United States in what is actually a propaganda stunt.

If there is a joke in this, it is on him. To us leadership is something our Chairman is not — religious. As with all religious things the genuine article should never be used in a commercial venture!"

**Traditional Leaders Welcome Shocked British Film Crew That Was
Harassed by the Tribal Council Who Wants to Control Everything**

TI— "A crew of four filmmakers from England visited Hopi this spring. Their visit was the culmination of a plan that started about two years ago. Members of the group had read about our way of life and thought it would make an interesting subject for a film. They have filmed native people in other parts of the world, and are under a contract with ATV Television, London, to produce a certain number of high-quality documentaries each year.

But they were in for a real shock! Greatly respecting our tradition, they desired to work only through our proper leaders. But coming from a foreign land, and knowing us mostly from books, they innocently walked right into the office of the puppet 'Hopi Tribal Council.' Patiently they sat through long meetings and waited for assistance, growing suspicious and greatly disappointed. These were obviously not the spiritual people they had heard about! So where were they?

After two weeks all they had to show for their effort was a contract offer from the Council that demanded the right of absolute censorship of the entire film! 'Even Marlon Brando doesn't get that!' they told us. When they sent the contract back to London, the ATV staff just laughed at it and said they would frame it and hang it on the wall as a joke.

It was clear that the puppet government and their lawyers had something to hide, and themselves were shocked that news of their wrongdoings might leak out and be seen by the entire world.

The crew were so discouraged that they were ready to give up and call it quits. Perhaps they did think there were no real Hopi left! But somehow they came across a little booklet by Dan Katchongva called 'From the Beginning of Life to the Day of Purification.' 'It was Katchongva's words that turned us around and made everything clear,' they told us. Through the booklet they finally learned that the Tribal Council and the Traditional leadership are anything but the same thing. They decided to seek out the Traditionals.

They met John and Mina Lansa, Thomas Banyacya, and David Monongye, and began to work through them. Feeling encouraged, they spent two more weeks filming the spring planting and other neutral subjects which would not offend anyone, then left after promising to return for the harvest.

In September they returned for four more weeks. This time with the cooperation and approval of the Traditional leaders they decided just to work with individual people.

They showed us two films that were done by their director, Michael Pearce, which were very well received by we Traditional people. One of the films showed a South Sea Island tribe whose way of life was being destroyed by outside influences which were supposed to help them.

Once when Mr. Pearce was checking his mail in Kykotsmovi, the Tribal Council Chairman, Abbott Sekaquaptewa, had him picked up by a policeman and taken to his office.

According to Mr. Pearce, Sekaquaptewa claimed he had received complaints that the crew had been filming in Oraibi Village. Pearce denied this, and pointed out that since the Tribal Council had offered them an impossible contract the group had decided simply to work with individuals. Sekaquaptewa threatened to confiscate their film and equipment if he heard any more 'complaints.' He refused to identify the alleged complainant. A police officer threatened to 'cause trouble' with the crew's visas. Pearce later expressed amazement at finding such a 'police state' on the sacred Hopi land.

Sekaquaptewa's claim that his actions toward the crew were intended to protect Hopi tradition proved false when several Traditional leaders instantly rallied to their support. The leaders signed an agreement which Pearce later presented to the Chairman — who could then make no argument, but still threatened, 'If we hear any complaints we're going to put the screws to you!'

Though no equipment was officially confiscated, the crew had a very difficult time getting back a camera they had lent to a Council employee who had offered to take some shots for them.

Pearce explained that it was not the crew's intention to side with the Traditionals, but only to produce a good movie. To him, this means showing everything as it is. He thought it unfortunate that the Tribal Council officials acted in such a "devious" and "threatening" manner.

The difference between the two styles of government left the Englishmen with an impression they are not likely to forget. They became firmly convinced that the Traditional people had a lot to tell about the situation, and that the U.S. Government-sponsored Council had a lot to hide. They grew more determined than ever to show both sides exactly as they are.

They left at the end of the month, thankful for the cooperation they had received from the people, and pleased that they had completed almost everything that they had planned. They expect the film to be released internationally early next year."

The Film Crew Was Not the End of It, but Hospitality Is a Hopi Tradition

TI— "The Progressive newspaper, *Qua'toqti*, has criticized the efforts of friendly Bahannas who have opposed outside interference in Hopi culture. These friends tried to alert the Arizona Public Service Department that Traditional authority had been violated by the signing of contracts with the so-called Hopi Tribal Council, allowing the installation of power lines into Hopi villages. An editorial in the October 2 issue tries to imply that this is an interference in itself.

From our viewpoint, it seems that *Qua'toqti* is almost in tears with concern for the new establishment, the Tribal Council the newspaper serves, and seeks to hobble outsiders who interfere in any way to expose the misdeeds of that establishment. We Traditionalists defend the efforts of our Bahanna friends, and once again repeat, as foretold in prophecy, that the Paiute, or the Navajo, or even the

Bahanna who has an open mind, may make an effort to help us when we are at the last step and about to vanish from existence. This brings to mind that we were taught not to turn anyone away from our door. Humble or rich, we should feed them, even if water is all we have left. For someday we might be blessed as the Great Spirit allows us to get the rewards we deserve. Most of us forget that this is the most powerful element in our keeping of the Great Law.

Perhaps *Qua'toqti* distorts this fact for a reason — they don't want to give anything away. Sometimes it is not easy, but it is said that even if your house is gleaming with beauty and good food but not shared with kindness, it is empty, without spirit, and not worth anyone's envy. Likewise, the humble home that is shared is beautiful."

TEM— "As you have certainly noticed, in their every reference to the Tribal Council, the Elders use the phrase "so-called Tribal Council." They do this for two main reasons:

The first reason is that in their eyes the Council was not created in the ancient way of determining leadership. Instead, it was created illegally by the BIA to serve that institution's interests. From its inception in 1936 Hotevilla has rebelled against the Council, refusing to recognize it, and in no way admitting that it has authority over Hopi citizens and land — in particular the village of Hotevilla. Small as it is, Hotevilla remains a sovereign nation. It has the time-honored right to control its own affairs and, unlike other Hopi villages, it has steadfastly refused to send representatives to sit as Council members. Those Hopi members from other villages who do serve on the Council appear to rubber-stamp and endorse any programs put forth by the BIA and Council leaders.

The second reason is that the Council does not behave as the Elders believe true Hopis should. They use force to achieve their goals, they have no respect for village leaders, they do things arbitrarily, and they do things that are not in the best interests of the Hopi. They even violate the Constitution they have sworn to abide by. Worst of all, they are hypocritical. They say they put traditional life and the best good of the Hopis first, yet their actions belie this. Their income is dependent upon the continued existence of the Council. Many of the Council members and employees are not initiated in the traditional way, and few of them actually participate in the full ceremonial cycle. As has already been seen, some of the programs they have inaugurated have caused wide-ranging problems for the Hopi people, and what may be the worst of these are still to be treated in the next chapter.

One Council department in particular has, since its inception, waged an unrelenting war against the Elders. This is the Office of Hopi Cultural Preservation, whose director is the aforementioned Leigh Jenkins. We give his name simply because we know he would not like anyone else to receive credit for his contributions. Considering that the Elders are known to be the arch-defenders of the faith, this is, until you learn their primary reason for doing so, a bewildering thing for the department to do.

To put it as clearly as it can be put, what the Office of Hopi Cultural Preservation and Mr. Jenkins want is absolute control over what Hopis can say and do, and over what any outsider can say and do about the Hopis. This desire for control extends in particular to their final obstacle — the spunky and tenacious Elders of Hotevilla, for they have been the constant thorn in Mr. Jenkins side. Beginning with Manuel Hoyungowa's denunciation of Mr. Jenkins in his letter to me, we have shown repeatedly how this is so.

Actually, the Tribal Council scenario for the present and future is not a hard one to script. For Hopi members and employees, the pay is steady and very good. They will not need to worry about paying taxes and assessments. We do not for a moment doubt its sincerity. It consists of good people whose challenges and duties are sometimes more than they are equipped to handle. It is doing what it believes it is supposed to do, and accepts that the passage of time in office and performance has established its worth. Even though it has in fact abandoned the traditional way, it continues to think of itself as traditional, and it simply cannot, even though the reasons are so plainly there to be seen, understand why the Elders have opposed it so strongly. The Council knows that it has made mistakes in some of its projects, and wishes it could rectify these. For example, it knows belatedly that the use of the water-slurry to deliver coal to the power plants is a very bad idea, and it desperately wishes that the Peabody Mine could find another way to do it. You were given more detailed information regarding the magnitude of this nightmare in Chapter 8.

But in looking to the future, the Council sees itself, especially where economic issues are concerned, as the only realistic hope for the Hopis. Having steadfastly routed the people away from their traditional way of life, the Council may in fact be partly correct. They may have made it impossible for things to be otherwise. They have been, and are, making the Hopi wage-dependent and badly in need of jobs. Peabody is a source of survival now, but the day will all too soon come when the coal will run out. Then what? And if the water is also gone, what else? Even though we do not envy them their dilemma, we must still ask what practical reservation-wide job solution the Council has offered thus far?

With the end of their lucrative source of funding in sight, the Council's present move is to replace it by putting in place a tax and service basis for the Hopis, knowing full well that most Hopis do not have jobs and a steady income to accommodate these things, and that the Traditionals especially have only their crafts and their farms to depend on — the latter providing sustenance but no income of consequence. Where the accomplishment of this new program has been concerned, Hotevilla, most of all, has stood in the way. I am sure you have noticed how often the Elders have stressed the fact that they are the last of those to stand fast and keep Maasaw's Law. Unless Hotevilla is brought down, as the financial pressure spurs other villages on, they will surely take heart and join in anti-Council protests. You will shortly learn, for example, of things happening in Shongopovi that support this assertion.

Hence the present Council strategy, which in truth is no strategy at all. It was simply to plant subversives inside the village of Hotevilla who would clamor for service. In response, the beneficent Council has sent employees and workmen to knock the door down, cow the inhabitants, and, jettisoning the tentative thrusts of the past, it has begun to install those utilities that will make the villagers hostage to installation charges, monthly meter bills, and to the inevitable upkeep and improvement charges that all of us in the outside world are so accustomed to. The primary difference is — I will say again — that the people, and especially the Traditional people, who for the most part have only their farms to depend upon — cannot pay for these unwanted 'amenities.' Therefore, if things go as the Council hopes they will, the Traditionals will fall like ducks, with their property foreclosed because of unpaid bills. Along with the house will come the historic farming plots, which is where the real prize lies. Waiting patiently out there under the surface are the valuable oil, ores, and minerals, and waiting less than patiently are the Bahanna commercial interests who are rubbing their hands gleefully together in their desire to get at them.

Some claims have been made by the Council that part of Hopi salvation might be found in commercial farming. But anyone with a lick of sense knows that the land pattern of nature is not a kind that will support it. Moreover, the daily depletion of the water table by the Peabody Mine dooms the idea before it starts. Should the time ever come when rainfall is all there is, and if the displeased Kachinas fail to deliver enough rain, even private farming will only be a dream. Then there will be no option for the Hopi but to leave their cherished Hopi Land, and with it the ageless culture which for millennia has given them direction and life.

Are all of these criticisms of the Council and Mr. Jenkins something that exist only in our imagination? We think not. Already detailed in the statements of the Elders, Katchongva, and *Techqua Ikachi* newsletters are Council efforts to usurp village powers with attacks on village sovereignty and authority, the constant denigration of the Elders, the attempt to appoint their own puppet leader for Hotevilla, the fencing of private property, numerous efforts to intrude with utilities upon the sanctity of the Hotevilla village proper, the installation of a water tank and some utilities on Hotevilla land without Hotevilla authorization, the attempt to annex Hotevilla property for Bacabi HUD housing purposes, leasing land to the Peabody Mine, paying a Bahanna attorney an unconscionable amount for services, the ill-advised funding of a factory in Winslow, the acceptance of five million dollars in claim money for a huge slice of Hopi land, the attempt to lease oil and mineral sites, the use of Tribal Council police to enforce Council wishes, the use of a puppet press to support Council views and purposes only, the attempted exclusion by regulation of certain Bahanna visitors to Hopi Land, the imposition of taxes upon Hopi craftspeople who already barely make a living, the implementation of indebtedness and eviction policies, the rejection of Maasaw's Law, the attempt to entirely control what a British film crew could and would do on the reservation, and the attempt to make exclusive decisions as to how matters concerning the relocation of the Navajos will be handled.

There is more. Where control is concerned, the agile-minded Council is by no means bereft of ideas. During the last part of February of this year, two Shongopovi men who are spokesmen for certain of the Traditional village leaders, knowing Katherine's support of the Elders, contacted her and asked if they could meet with her. They were hoping she would assist them in their needs. During the first week of March they came to Dan's house, where they explained that they were Traditionals who endorsed what the Elders have been and are doing. Their reward for this, as it turned out, was that the Tribal Council had threatened to arrest Shongopovi youth for, in the traditional way, hunting rabbits for ritual use without having purchased a permit from the Council. We don't know what the permit was to cost, but the threatened fine was $200 per person! As you might suspect, the Shongopovi leaders were flabbergasted at this affront to traditional practices and declared that if the fines were imposed there would be real trouble.

At this, the Council backed off, but retaliated immediately by cutting off funding for special school projects, including the materials needed to assist children who have special education needs.

If they wondered about it before, these Shongopovi people now know for certain that what the Elders have said and done has been right all along.

Add to this — despite the fact that trash disposal has never been a problem for the Hopi in their wide-open spaces — the news that the Tribal Council has also enacted a $10 per house per month trash-hauling fee. Dan protested that many Hopis do not have the money needed to pay for this. Yet the trash fee is only a portion of what is coming once all of the utilities are in, and, as the Council also decrees, when hunting permits must be obtained for any game that is taken on the reservation, and taxes must be paid on all craftwork that is sold. By this simple gesture of hunting permits alone, several different ceremonies could be brought to a halt.

Got the overall picture? Well, that too turns out to be a more literal circumstance than one might hope. Dan relates that after the Elders made their two films several years ago, Mr. Jenkins sternly lectured him about how absolutely wrong it was to make any films or to allow any kind of literature to be written without the Council's, or more expressly, his, permission. Particularly unacceptable were films that included motion pictures of Hopi dances.

It turns out now that what Mr. Jenkins meant is that no films were to be made or no literature was to be written that he did not expressly approve of, participate in, and have absolute control over.

Just now information has come to us regarding a proposed and ambitious film whose principal consultant is — you guessed it — Leigh Jenkins himself. And the film, whose preliminary VCR shots I have seen, includes no less than — along with countless stills of Hopi life — motion picture scenes of the Snake Dance!

Frontier Films began research in December 1990 for a one-hour documentary film on Hopi history, ranging from mythological to modern times… "The Hopi formally restricted," they say, "passage onto the reservation and stopped permitting photography in 1917. This was done to eliminate the intrusive activities of anthropologists, photographers, and artists. It is a story of the Hopis' determination to maintain their privacy that inspired the making of this film, which will focus on the conflict between an ancient culture determined to retain their way of life and the intentions of a younger society anxious to impose its values in a remote desert at the turn of the century."

After the story of the film was determined, the support and guidance of Dr. Emery Sekaquaptewa, Professor of Anthropology at the University of Arizona, and Mr. Leigh Jenkins, Director of the Hopi Office of Cultural Preservation, was gained. *Mr. Jenkins assisted the project by facilitating a tribal research permit.* This permit enabled development of "a Hopi advisory committee made of Hopi elders representing diverse perspectives on the historical events of Words of Our Ancients." A sample film was made and presented to the elders regarding sensitive subject matter which, the producers claimed, "produced subsequent participation from the elders." Dan Evehema, it turns out, was the Elder they solicited most. They really couldn't do what they hoped to without him. But the fact is that, after learning who was advising them and seeing the sample, he — and so far as we know, all other True Traditional Elders — declined to participate. The film did not tell any of the Elders' story. Instead, it emphasized other aspects of Hopi life — the kinds that Mr. Jenkins would be most interested in.

Archival photographs are to be included, as well as motion picture archives.

"Since," the producers say, "there exists extensive public and private photo collections of outstanding quality by well-known (Bahanna) photographers of the time, and these images cover the full range of Hopi life, everyday activities, *elaborate public ceremonies, and private religious rites,* we will use these photographs to bring forth the movements, action, and feeling of Hopi life with sensitivity to subject matter *under the direction of the Hopi advisory council.*" Some of the earliest extant "actuality" film was shot at Hopi and will be used in this film. "Additionally, excerpts of numerous early fiction films which documented life on Hopi will be included. Traditional Hopi and American period music will create an elegant film sound track. First-person quotes from the period, read off-camera will express the variety of points of view expressed by and about the Hopi during the period of our story."

The producer, Paige Martinez, has more than six years experience in documentary filmmaking.

Meet the Co-producer, whose film experience, we trust, is somewhat limited. He is none other than "The Hopi Tribe Director, Office of Cultural Preservation, Mr. Leigh Jenkins, who is from the Third Mesa Village of Bacabi." He is, as you know, the one who tells other Hopi no films like this are to be made. "As Director of Cultural Preservation," the bio says, "he functions as liaison between the tribe's administrative body and individual Hopi citizens in cultural, historical, religious, and legal affairs. This has included saving numerous ancient burials from destruction through a re-burial program, fighting legal battles with Sotheby's over the sale of ceremonial masks that have reached an auction in New York, and reporting to and consulting with village elders regarding what steps must be taken to retrieve recently discovered lost or stolen religious objects. Mr. Jenkins will work directly with an advisory task force of Hopi elders to review the film at each major juncture."

The Associate Producer is listed as Phyllis Witsel, who is a Hopi from the village of Shipaulovi, of Second Mesa. Ms. Witsel formerly served as the administrative manager for the Hopi Tribal Court for approximately eight years. Ms. Witsel also served as a staff assistant under the administration of Abbott Sekaquaptewa, Hopi Tribal Chairman.

Consultant — Dr. Emery Sekaquaptewa is a professor of anthropology at the University of Arizona. As a Hopi, he maintains strong political, religious, and social ties with the Hopi community. He serves as a tribal judge and numerous other advisory capacities. Currently Dr. Sekaquaptewa is compiling a Hopi dictionary in conjunction with 'the Hopi tribe Office of Cultural Preservation.'

The editor, Tricia Reidy, is a very capable person, as is cinematographer Michael Chin, and the script consultant, Dr. Peter Whitley, who is a professor of anthropology at Sarah Lawrence College. For the past eleven years, he has conducted extensive research into Hopi ethnography and history. He has published two books, both specifically concerning Hopi ethnohistory from internal oral sources and external archival material.

"Frontier Films is," the film project bio says, "even coordinating with the Hopi Cultural Preservation Office and the Hopi Department of Education to provide training and internship opportunities for Hopi individuals. The specific areas of training and internship will be in production, coordination, photography, apprenticeship, archival research, participation in story development and rights, and permission of archival music material." This certainly sounds worthwhile.

Distribution plans for the film are impressive. It will be disseminated through several avenues, opening with a national public television broadcast and theatrical release. Frontier Films is currently negotiating co-production status with potential presenting stations. At this time several PBS stations have expressed great interest and letters of support of Words of Our Ancients. In conjunction with initial broadcast, the film will be highlighted at a Frontier Films-sponsored national symposium event. The symposium will tour major American cities for an examination of cultural rights and preservation issues. Foreign release will follow U.S. release. The following provides an outline of projected markets targeted for distribution.

Pacific Mountain Network — The Pacific Mountain Network administers PBS programming nationally by satellite and also broadcasts the Classroom Channel, the Sunday Exchange, the Division of Learning Services. The Classroom Channel reaches 10,000 secondary schools in the U.S. or 6.5 million students and educators. Division of Learning Services is available for broadcast by all PBS stations nationally, various educational agencies, and K–12 schools in 50 states.

The program will also be made available for PBS Home Video distribution, and foreign markets in Europe, as well as Spanish-speaking countries and the Far East, are targeted for distribution. A limited theatrical release will be timed to coincide with the symposium. Showings will be located at the same major cities as the symposium visits, including Phoenix, New York, Boston, Los Angeles, and San Francisco.

Previous fund-raising efforts have brought in $112,134 for the project, and numerous proposals for grants to businesses, organizations, private foundations, etc., have been submitted to fund it.

According to its latest production schedule, the film should have been wrapped up by now, and ready for release in the fall of 1994. There is, however, a not-so-minor problem. Regarding the inclusion of Hopi voices, the bio states that, "Several Hopi elders who were small children during the split of Oraibi are alive today. They live primarily in the villages of Hotevilla, Bacabi, and Kykotsmovi, all on the Third Mesa. These elders and some of their descendants will comprise the majority of the interviews for this documentary. It is extremely urgent that these interviews be conducted soon, as 1991 and 1992 saw the passing of many other valuable witnesses to our story."

It appears from this assertion that Mr. Jenkins, despite his mistreatment of the Elders, indicated to the producers that he could deliver them for participation. He couldn't. Katherine could. I could. But he, who in a letter to me accused the Elders of using their religion to cloak their political intentions, could not. And, while we do not know how reliable this information is, we have been told that since the Elders were vital to its success, the film project is not going ahead.

Believe me when I say that from what I have seen of the film it would/will probably be — except for its not telling the Maasaw and Elder story — a laudable and very good one. If it is not completed, I will regret that. I am not in the least bothered by the fact that Mr. Jenkins is working on it and is undoubtedly well paid for the effort. Nor do we discuss the film here because we have any problem with the production company. We discuss it to show how the Council and Mr. Jenkins consistently tend to serve only their own best interests, and in so doing are formidable obstacles to the Keeping of the Covenant. In proof of this, payback time for standing in their way has come once again.

We do not know what the actual status of the film is, yet this much is certain — and the nature of its action is supported by the retaliation of the Council where the Shongopovi rabbit-hunting incident is reported — almost immediately after the refusal of the Elders to participate in the film and its possible cancellation because of that, the following document appeared in Hotevilla and an all-out assault on the village was launched. Was this coincidence? We think not. The truth is that the Council believes it has succeeded in eradicating or disarming opposition to the point where, if offended, it is free to move whenever and wherever it wishes. I thought about them when I read David Broder's recent column The Press-Enterprise *Editorial Page, March 9, 1994. With minor alterations, this same thing could be written about the Hopi Tribal Council. where he asked, "What is it about working in the White House that breeds bad judgment and arrogance?"... "Part of the problem is simply the media-fed glorification of the White House... They are flattered and courted all the time — and they inhale the heady fumes of short-term celebrity...at a more sinister level, they come to believe that their own interpretation of a president's wishes is enough to justify evading the law and lying to Congress... When White House staffs are recruited primarily from those who proved most adept at swatting the opposition during the campaign, they bring their combat weapons with them. They tend to see everyone... as forces who must be subdued if the president is to prevail."*

Setting the Time Table

TI— *"The time has come to address a joint action on the part of the Government and the Tribal Council that either will, or has already, grievously affect the time table of the final downward decline to the end of the Fourth Cycle and the beginning of the Fifth Cycle of the world. More than a decade ago, the precedent was set for this foolish act, whose consequences are more grievous than the perpetrators could ever have imagined."*

The Water Tank and Its Consequences in Hotevilla

TI— "In order to reach this goal they (the Tribal Council and a small group of Progressives who lived in Hotevilla) formed the so-called "Hotevilla Village Committee," without the endorsement of the proper leaders. Thus they became self-proclaimed leaders. This action reawakens the old problem, which failed before in several attempts. Namely, bringing in the power line, water pipeline, sewer line, and paved roads into the Village. The water tank has already been installed without our approval. Because of the location, where it is now standing, we fear this will deplete our spring and wells, which are even now at lower levels than normal.

The following is our protest letter to the head of the project:

> *Mr. Orlan Tewa*
> *Hotevilla Village Committee*
> *Copies for all interested parties.*

> *Dear Mr. Tewa, C.D.S.:*
> *Every nation, State, City, and Village has its own Leadership to make decisions for the good of the people, according to their own agreed-upon laws.*

Hotevilla has its own agreed-upon laws. We feel that the proposal to bring water, electricity, sewer line, and telephone into our Village without the consent of our proper leaders was an improper action. We feel our first responsibility is to uphold our Creator's Laws, and that to bring water, electricity, sewer, and telephone into our Village will interfere with our ability to fulfill our spiritual duties according to the Hopi way. We challenge you to state to us what authority you have to come into our Village and change our ways of life without the consent of our leaders.

We ask you to respect our spiritual laws and our elders, who are our leaders, and not to disturb our traditional way of life, which to us is sacred.

We ask you to stop your effort to destroy our Culture.

(Signed by the elders and leaders of the Village)

Will our letter fall on deaf ears like all the others have in the past? Yes, we believe this will happen, because their minds are set to do what they please. Likewise our minds are set to follow the divine laws.

They are strong, clever, and sly since they receive their political leverage through the Tribal Council and other backing institutions. As for the facts, we have no part in the body of the Tribal Council because we have never elected anyone by voting to seat a representative for our Village in their establishment since they first organized. Therefore, we are a Sovereign Nation and not subject to their Constitution bylaws. Therefore, the desire of the Village can only be decided by the people and leaders through their own Traditional ways and in accordance with the laws and doctrines of long, long ago. This has been an unbroken law for survival from generation to generation. It is no secret that the BIA and the Tribal Council admit they have no power over our Village matters.

We know, however, that all of their words are deceiving. According to the prophecy the Hopi are to be the last target. We are to be conquered, not by the Army and their weapons, we are to be conquered by our own people. By our own sons and daughters, without us even lifting our hands. Their weapon will be what they learned through the education so kindly taught by the Bahanna. If we are lucky, they will be able to tell the light from the darkness. If not, they will continue marching until they topple us. The Bahannas will pat the backs of the conquerors while cheering and applauding. The Whites will be satisfied that they were not required to finish the task which they set out to accomplish. It is our own people who bring this about, and the Bahanna, therefore, cannot be solely blamed. The conquest will be over and all Native People will be finished. This is a sad ending and it is a pity that we might end this way.

Do you believe the unique religion and traditional ways of the Hopi deserve to be preserved? If so, do whatever you can to help us. This could be our last struggle for any hope of surviving."

TEM— And so the final assault commenced, but thanks to the Elders its effect was circumscribed, and the damage was contained. While seeming to accept this, the Government and Tribal Council simply bided their time and waited for the moment to press on. The Elders aged and diminished in number, to the point where Government and Tribal Council confidence returned, and given stimulus by an offense to the Council's ambitions, they are at this very moment striking again!

WHAT FOLLOWS NOW IS A BULLETIN OF ENORMOUS CONSEQUENCE FOR THE HOPI AND THE WORLD... SEEMS A STRANGE THING FOR A BOOK TREATING TIMELESS ISSUES TO INCLUDE, DOESN'T IT? BUT THAT IS EXACTLY WHAT IT IS!

During the first week in March 1994, copies of the following announcement, stamped as having been received at Hotevilla on December 3, 1993, were forwarded to me:

Consider now what these documents and actions that are underway signify. For more than 30 years the Traditionals of Hotevilla, and especially the Elderly Elders, have done everything they possibly could to keep utilities out of their village, so that the ancient ceremonial cycle could be practiced without the interfering energies that would be caused by this foreign presence. As we have already seen in previous documents, during these years several tentative attempts have been made by the BIA and the Tribal Council to penetrate the village, using every possible excuse and scheme to justify their doing so. All of these attempts were rebuffed, reversed, and failed — until now. As of this very moment the BIA and Tribal Council have invaded the village and begun, in a battering-ram kind of operation, to install every possible kind of utility. Recognize that even though the document cited here pertains to water and sewer, other utilities will follow. Dan's letter clarifying this fact is also included here. Unless something changes immediately, long before you read this bulletin the work will be complete, and its insidious consequences will be functioning to destroy the power of the ceremonies — which will reduce the Shrine of the Covenant to nothing more than a replica of the other villages whose spiritual powers are already grievously affected. And this will be only the first and lesser consequence for the village of Hotevilla. For if by some tragic chance the people doing the installations strike and destroy the buried object mentioned in Chapter 1, the forces necessary to end the power of Hotevilla will set to work, and the consequences of that will ripple out to put into motion the disastrous closing of this Fourth cycle of the world. All that may be left for us to do now is everything we can to assure some human survival and something of the earth's, thus making it possible for a new beginning and Fifth cycle. These are matters that we will focus our attention upon as we consider ever more closely prophetic fulfillment and actions to be taken regarding it.

To show how brazen this Council move has been, they even installed a water meter at Dan's own house in Hotevilla Village. Could anyone possibly believe that he, or any other Elder, would sign the necessary form to permit this? Naturally, he did move immediately to make them remove the meter — which the other Traditionals assuredly did also — but elsewhere in the village the work is proceeding. Remember now that even though it comes under the banner of the Department of Health and Human Services, it is actually according to the express wishes of the Tribal Council, the group that claims to be "traditional," that the installation is taking place, and, of all things, during the time of the sacred Powamuya Ceremony described in Chapter 4. The construction crew went to work at the very time the Hotevilla men were in their kivas doing the necessary rituals, and when the other villagers who know the sanctity of the ceremonial cycle were being especially reverent and quiet. Yet the work stopped only for the day of the public Bean Dance, when visitors were present who would have seen it and been upset by its irreverence. This, of course, is a technique previously used with success by the Council. You see, the BIA and Tribal Council know that once a ceremony is under way, the Hotevilla men will not interrupt their rituals to do anything of a confrontational nature.

Notice from the following how detailed and carefully thought out the installation plans are.

DEPARTMENT OF HEALTH & HUMAN SERVICES
Date: November 26, 1993
From: Erwin Tewa, Engineering Technician

Subject: Pre-Construction Conference PH 90-242 To: FILE

On November 23, 1993, a pre-construction conference was held
on the referenced project. In attendance were:
Kenneth Quanimptewa - Hotevilla CSA
Charlene Kyasyousie - Hotevilla C.D. Office
Amos Poocha Bacabi CSA
Erwin Tewa- Keams Canyon OEH&E Inspector
Daryl Melvin - KC/OEH&E Engineer
Robert Mahkewa - KC/OEH&E Construction Supt.

    Daryl Melvin started the meeting and introductions followed.
The following topics were discussed:
1. Keams Canyon OEH&E, personnel affiliated with the project,
   Construction Inspector, Construction Superintendent, Field
   Foreman, Equipment Operator and Laborers.
2. Phases of water main construction: Main lines, service lines, capping
   of all interconnection points, start and end point of construction

and verifying all existing water lines, tele., power, etc. Construction will begin at tank site and work toward the school.

3. Village approvals for fill material site and disposal of excess spoils site was requested. Kenny will submit to IHS in writing by December 6, 1993.

4. Temporary storage yard for duration of all projects in Hotevilla Village. Agreement between village and individual (Fred Koots) for use of land site (200' X 200') and written approval of site permitting IHS use. Kenny will complete by December 6, 1993.

5. BIA agreement pertaining to project, vault, and interconnection between both villages (Hotevilla & Bacabi) discussed. BIA to complete interconnection construction between all 3 entities, probably when school is out.

6. Notification of Hopi Tribe/Archaeologist, Kathy Johnson, for monitoring in arch. site area. One site recorded by first house near tank site. Technician will keep archaeology department informed.

7. Notification of utilities or organizations, affiliated with water system from start to end of construction (School, BIA, etc.) is required. Construction Superintendent will be responsible.

8. Notice to proceed date (December 6, 1993), and length of time to complete project (bulk 8 wks). Some items can't be completed at this time i.e. sewer service lines.

9. Hiring process: SF 171 through Phoenix Area. Phoenix Area pulling another panel on December 6, 1993. Expect crew size to be: (1) Construction Superintendent; (1) Field Foreman; (1) Operator; and (4) Laborers.

10. Storage tank construction - contract package to be in contracting in 45 days (Start of construction: Spring 1994).

11. Well Drilling: start of *Construction* (End of January, 1994).

12. Weekly Construction Report mailing list to include: Hotevilla School, Hotevilla CSA, BIA Facility Management and EADO.

13. OSHA's requirements to be followed on project: Safety Traffic Diversions, Daily Soil Analysis, Daily Log, Construction Signs, etc.

14. Village schedule for ceremonies: December - Pilgrimage, January - Night Dance, February - Bean Dance, etc., will be taken into consideration. Technician will notify construction superintendent of need to shut down construction at certain times due to ceremonies.

15. Tank: Height and diameter were sized with consideration to housing around tank location. Estimate that Hotevilla system will be 5 psi higher than Bacabi and school systems.

16. Installing of main lines around the village will take place on next phase of Village Project 312. Existing water services won't be shut off.

17. 242 individual requests for assistant application discussed. Some

home owners haven't signed off. Kenny to collect approvals by December 6th and submit to OEH&E.

18. Signatures and process of applying for electrical (APS) service to well site location is under way. OEH&E will submit application to Village/Tribe for approvals and then forward to APS.

19. MOA Amendment #1 pending BIA approval. Signature sheet was lost and was resubmitted. Village and Tribal approvals will be rec-ollected prior to submitting to Phoenix.

20. None of other entities notified of pre-con attended. UTI, BIA Roads, BIA Facility Management, APS, Tribe, EADO, HBCS, etc.

(SIGNED) Erwin Tewa

XC: EADO
Hotevilla CSA
Bacabi CSA
PH 90-242

BIA Superintendent, HBCS Principal, Hopi Tribe R & P, PG16-04

In addition to this main document, there were four other forms for each homeowner to fill out and sign — except that by some mysterious happenstance, even before contacting the residence owners, the forms were already filled out. All that was needed was the signature. As already stated, we have seen that even signatures did not matter, since Dan's meter was installed without his having asked for it. It would be fair to wonder how many others were installed on the same basis. To substantiate our charges of an all-out assault, we include here some of the information included on the printed forms, and a letter written by Dan.

Form No. 1, the "Request For Assistance," asks the homeowner to mark squares indicating what he or she wanted (remember that these were already marked for them), water supply, and waste disposal. Also requested were: the land status of the property — whether it was owned by Trust, Trust Allotments, or Other? Type of housing — existing, mobile home, newly built home and/or recent improvements? And, an indication of whether indoor plumbing was complete or not complete.

Form No. 2 asked for a detailed plot plan showing the house location and an indication of any special site factors that might influence the installation.

Form No. 3 asked the homeowner to sign and date the following agreement: "I understand that Indian Health Service will construct, as funds become available, water supply and waste disposal facilities starting at a distance of five feet from my home. I hereby agree to construct five feet water and sewer stubouts <u>through my own finances</u> (the underlining is ours). I understand no site work or construction is possible until all approval signatures are obtained and stubouts are constructed." Notice however that work started without the obtaining of the approval signatures.

Form No. 4, the "Individual Agreement Between the Head of Household and the U.S. Department of Health and Human Services" which is to be signed and dated by the "Head of Household," begins with these passages: "I have received and understand the guidelines for water and sewer services and agree to abide by them... I hereby agree to permit access to the Indian Health Service for installation of the facilities under the terms of the project Memorandum of Agreement... I hereby agree to accept upon completion of installation, the following described facilities to be installed on the premise located herein, and on land occupied by me, I also agree to operate, maintain and keep these facilities in good repair at my own expense."

If this installation were anything less than what we have described it to be, would all of this carefully worked-out paperwork be necessary?

Dan wrote and signed the following letter of alarm to be distributed among other Hopis and to concerned outsiders: It is entitled "Statement Concerning Hotevilla."

I am from the traditional village of Hotevilla and I have become very distressed — it seemed to me that the Hopis have to pay and pay to live, and this is contrary to our traditional way of life. The Department of Health has come into Hotevilla to put their laws on us about dumping our trash wherever we deem it is necessary in the village itself. They want to charge us $10 a month to take our trash in a big truck, but the Hopi do not have that kind of money and it is against our way of life to pay for things that are provided by the Great Spirit. Also the BIA with the approval of the Hopi Tribal Council has come into the traditional village of Hotevilla to install sewer and water and gas and power lines. We do not want this in our village. There will be a meeting of the people on Thursday, January 27, 1994, at 10:00 a.m. in the morning at Katherine's home in Hotevilla. This is a really important meeting, and if we do not take care of this then Mother Nature will take over and there will be more earthquakes, ice storms, and fires. It is up to us to save all life and land. We are calling on all the villages to come and meet with us to address these issues and the economic development that is denied us under the present system of government. We call for an abolishment of the Hopi Tribal Council and a return to our own self-government. We are also asking for legal aid and donations from lawyers or politicians to help us in this critical time to help us with our own government.

The sequel to this invasion? With excellent reason the Elders are anxious to stop this assault upon the village. Not having readily at hand the means to do this, and knowing the enormous consequences if they cannot, they are angry, confused and perhaps even panicked. As seen in Dan's letter, even a lawsuit is considered. This might result in a temporary restraining order, or it might not. Surely, time is against them. By the time a judge acts and appeals are considered, the job will probably be done, and the water will be turned on.

There is the matter of funding lawsuits, which the Elders, as the Council surely knows, have at best a limited ability to do. When Susie told me about this, I told her to tell Dan not to waste his time with lawyers. There is a greater power who can be addressed, and One who can, if he wishes to, send a solution. I was pleased to learn that the Elders have already gone into the kivas to pray with added passion in the Traditional Hopi way. My other suggestion was that the people just not use the utilities. Even if only some will do this it will weigh on the consciences of the others who do. There will still be, however, an attempt by the Tribal Council to levy prorated installation costs upon the villagers. They will not miss such a golden opportunity, that's for sure. One way or another now, they will keep at the villagers of Hotevilla, and through them try to get to the Elders.

With passions at a height not seen in the village for a long time, it is hard to keep things under control. Unfortunately, a small but highly vocal group of Bahannas who know how the Elders feel about the utilities have decided that the pipes must be removed by whatever means is required, even proposing the ridiculous idea that if necessary they would "blow them out of the ground." Not only is this foolish from the standpoint of potential damage and disturbance to the Shrine of the Covenant and the individual shrines within the village, it would stir up a hornet's nest of reaction, and give the Council an excuse to take stronger measures. More importantly, it violates the Traditional view which Dan and the others have stressed repeatedly — that matters like this must be settled peacefully. And if they cannot be settled in this way, then they must stand and have things play out as they will. The group asked Dan to approve their proposed action, but even though he desperately wants the pipes out, with Katherine's help in understanding the ramifications of what they were proposing, he did not give his approval.

We will not be thanked for what we are about to say now, but it must be said. If the pipes and meters are installed throughout the village, and if even only a portion of the villagers use theirs, this is what we can expect to happen. As the faithful dance and perform the other portions of their ceremonies in the kivas, the utilities will be running, and the telephones will be ringing. The performers will try to concentrate their minds upon the proper traditional thoughts, but the knowledge that the utilities with their negative kind of energy are there and functioning will edge in to disrupt them. "Who are you, really?" ghostly voices will ask. "What distinguishes Hotevilla from any other Hopi village?" The Elders will also be on the performers' consciences. Even when they are no longer physically present, the men and women will see them accusingly there in the audiences.

It will not be long before observable changes in Hotevilla will take place. The dances will lose their intensity, and Hopi and Bahanna visitors alike will feel this. The pervasive energy that marked them until now will gradually subside. The link to the past, the tension of the present, and the spell of the future will no longer be there. Like Old Oraibi, Hotevilla will begin to shrivel. The Council members and Progressives will like this. They will take it as vindication.

Whether their energy is literally sapped is a question of no consequence. If the Hopi people believe it is happening, it will happen. Sooner or later enthusiasm will flag, faith will crumble, conviction will give way to doubt.

Those villagers that served the Council by asking for the utilities will be happy — but only for a while. Unless there are reversals, it will not be long before the overall change in Hotevilla affects everyone. How long will it take for this to happen, and is it an absolute certainty? Dan says it is certain, but no one knows how long it will take. A surge in Traditionalism might influence the time frame and manner. It is also certain that the dampening effect will spread to all of those who had something to do with the planning and execution of the installation.

Is there a way that all of this can be rectified? Perhaps — if the "object" buried in the ground is not damaged. People can change their minds. The utility lines can be removed, and Hotevilla can be left entirely alone to fulfill its destiny. There would be limited shame in this for those who did the installation, since the removal would be seen by other Hopis as a vindication of Hotevilla's unique role in Maasaw's plan. But if the object is already damaged, or should that happen when the work proceeds, then the nature of the future is irrevocably set in motion. The final spasmodic twisting of the world's Fourth Cycle as it heads toward a cataclysmic event will have, as of that awesome moment, begun. What will be happening to the microcosm, Hotevilla, will happen on a larger scale to the entire world, and what we can do to survive and assure survival for our children and grandchildren will have become our dominating matter of consequence. As such, we address this eventuality and its consequences more fully in Chapters 10 and 11.

"Ah," you sigh, "surely the Creator and Maasaw will come through now and rescue us. Surely they can not let this happen to the Elders." But you must also ask why, in view of the Covenant, they should not let it happen.

Since I am writing about this alarming incident as it happens, I am becoming something of a "live" reporter on the scene…one who can tell you that, in light of documents just passed on to me by Katherine, the news is just what I expected it to be — neither promising nor good.

With some assistance, on April 1, 1994, Dan sent the following letter. You will find that the Tribal Council responses to it are typical:

Hopi Tribal Council
P.O. Box 123
Kykotsmovi, Arizona
Attn: Tribal Chairman
Mr. Ferrell Secakuku
86039

Dear Mr. Secakuku,

We appreciate your fast response to our request for a meeting, and the date you have suggested will be good for us as well. April 7, 1994 at 7 p.m.

There are many issues we have questions about, and as you requested we will outline some of them here for your review. We also would like to receive a written response to some of these questions prior to our meeting. This will assure all parties that the issues are covered and made public.

1: In the Tribal Council records, what agreements were originally intended regarding your support of the Hotevilla Pueblo? Please cite agreement.

2: Please cite the Hopi Tribal Council's legal jurisdiction over Hotevilla.

3: According to your best information, how many people reside in Hotevilla?

4: In your assessment how many Hotevilla residents are in favor of the water or sewage projects?

5: How many residents are opposed to the Hotevilla water or sewage?

6: By what means did you determine these statistics?

7: What is the construction schedule for the Hotevilla water or sewage projects?

8: How will water or sewage fees be assessed?

9: Will Hotevilla residents be charged or assessed for the construction costs of the water and sewage projects?

10: What are the civil or criminal penalties (i.e. fines, liens, etc.) for refusing (1) to accept the water or sewer lines, (2) to accept water delivery or sewer service or (3) to pay for the water or sewage bills (either before water is turned on or after water is delivered?) (a) What are the fees? Please list the exact cost of these sewers and water to the Hotevilla people in an itemized form and when will they begin. What are the regulations? Full disclosure.

11: Do you have an enacted ordinance or law regarding these penalties? When was the public hearing, and how do we access the public record? Do you have the ordinance?

12: Do you propose to enact one? If so, when is the public hearing?

13: Please state exactly how the water and or sewage projects will not interfere with or prohibit the religion and the religious practices of Hotevilla.

14: What are the plans for the alternative sewage service and water delivery? We believe it is imperative that this sacred ground and the pathways in which the spirits come for the ceremony must not be disturbed by digging in the ground. Have you thought of another way to accomplish this?

Please provide us with this information in written reply by 4/6/94 so we will also be prepared for the meeting.

Our hope is that you will live up to your campaign promise that you will be "the voice of the people" and that you will seriously listen to the original residents of Hotevilla. It is not our first choice to take legal action against the Hopi Tribal Council. Yet it is an option of last resort. I look forward to resolving our differences. May we talk good and speak the truth in the peaceful way of the HOPI.

Sincerely:

Dan Evehema
Eldest Elder
Hotevilla, Arizona

[As I have learned from personal experience, when faced with having to discuss a problem, the Hopi Tribal Council's tactic is to set a meeting, and then, having bought enough time to plan a new way to approach the problem, cancel the meeting. Having done this exact thing now, the further reply in the form of two letters came not from the Tribal Chairman; it came instead from the head of a Council-arranged-for community committee of Progressives at Hotevilla.]

HOTEVILLA VILLAGE
P.O. BOX 706
HOTEVILLA, ARIZONA 86030
(602) 734-2420

April 5, 1994

Mr. Dan Evehema
Hopi Sovereign Nation
Hotevilla, Arizona 86030

Dear Mr. Evehema:

This is in response to your letter to the Chairman regarding water/sewer installations dated March 23, 1994. Your invitation to a selected few to attend the meeting at Ms. Rena Murillo's home is not proper.

All meetings regarding community projects should be open to everyone, since it is the residents that are requesting these services. 98% of the residents have requested water/sewer services. I have posted your invitation to the Chairman at the Community Development Office, and I am also encouraging everyone from our village to attend.

This project, once completed, will benefit everyone wanting water/sewer service. Those not wanting service will not be forced to participate. In reality everyone has benefitted from the BIA-IHS and THE HOPI TRIBE; you are not excluded. This project will be completed as planned based on the wants and needs of the majority of the residents of Hotevilla.

Sincerely,
Kenneth Quanimptewa, CSM
Hotevilla Village

[A second letter from Mr. Quanimptewa went on April 5, 1994 to]:

Mr. and Mrs. Riley Lomatska,
Mr. and Mrs. Danny Lomatska,
Mr. and Mrs. Clef Honyaktewa,
Mr. and Mrs. Allen Pooyouma,

Dear Interested Parties:

This is to inform you that phase II of the Hotevilla community water/sewer line will begin Monday the [month not cited] 4th, 1994. Since your uncle Mr. Dan Evehema has been actively protesting water/sewer line installations, I am notifying you so that you can settle this matter with him before construction begins.

Please notify myself at the Hotevilla Community Development Office of your meeting with Mr. Evehema.

TEM— You will have noticed that none of the questions asked by Dan — all of which were appropriate and to the point— were answered by Mr. Quanimptewa, yet all of them are kinds that we in the outside world would demand answers to if such things were being so imperiously done to us. Obviously, the Council and BIA act as emperors once did when they considered themselves to be utterly unaccountable! Maasaw will hold them to account, though.

Nor were any of the questions answered by the Tribal Chairman or any Council member. The Tribal Chairman went one evening to Dan's house to see Dan, but only to tell him that he would not be at the meeting (the one he knew wouldn't be held anyway) because he was meeting with Secretary of the Interior, Bruce Babbitt, on the Peabody Mine question. Water, no doubt. The Council is working hard to rectify and cover that one up.

It is helpful to look briefly at this Tribal Council Chairman, Ferrell Secakuku, who has just been elected to the job. A Hopi businessman from Second Mesa, he is also a priest in the Snake Clan, and a former councilman, and states that "the Hopi are anxious to take possession of Hopi Partitioned Lands where Navajos remain"…but that "he is relying on the Hopi Tribal Council, which has decided not to return to the mediation table with the Navajo Nation"… he also says he "will listen to the voices of Hopi villagers… We have not inherited this land from our ancestors, but merely borrowed it from the future from our children." In his campaign speeches he stated that "The reality is that Hopis want good things. Today this means clean technology, good health, long life, and providing for future generations. We can do this by setting aside differences and working together." In the account of Mr. Secakuku's reception address it was noted that the Council members voted to grant themselves raises increasing annual salaries by $7,000, to $32,000 a year; also that fund shortages led to the elimination of funds for the tribe's public relations office and the Hopi newspaper, which resulted in the closure of the newspaper.

It is clear that regardless of opposition, and even though the statistics cited by Mr. Quanimptewa are untrue, (he could not produce the supporting signed orders to prove this if his life depended upon it), the Council, Progressives, and the Health Department intend to move ahead with the installation of all of the utilities as expeditiously as possible. We have told you what their motivations are.

Katherine talked with Susie by telephone today — April 7 — and was told that "The digging is going on." And Susie, who has real True Hopi gumption, even went alone to Tribal headquarters with her list of questions and demanded that they be answered. She received the feeble reply that "No one who was qualified to answer them was in the building." It is a very big building…

Mentioning Susie reminds me to tell you that the Traditional women who live in the village of Hotevilla have fought very hard in peaceful ways to prevent this latest installation of utilities. They can be proud of themselves.

News has also come that the aforementioned group who threatened to remove the utility lines by force, having been dissuaded from this for the moment at least, is now planning a massive rally at Hotevilla on May 22, 1994 to achieve "global awakening" about what is going on there. After four days of preparation, those who come — and the sponsors are hoping for a massive crowd with representatives from all over the world — will meet at Titus Lamson's farm and then march to the water tower at Hotevilla, where they plan to disable it. "In the event," their published announcement and invitation says, "the water system at Hotevilla is removed before May 22 as requested, come anyway! We would like to use our meeting for forming a strong bond that we all need to go through the difficult times of Global Purification… The three days after the action are reserved for follow-up meetings. During this time we will gather constructive ideas and information that can be used for abolishing the corrupt Hopi Tribal Council."

The invitation to the rally, along with an extensive accompanying letter, is signed by Titus, and was sent to the United States Department of the Interior; with copies to Hopi people; Hopi Tribal Council, Robert Carolin; Superintendent Hopi Indian Agency; President Clinton; Indian Health Service; and the media, and included such interesting words as these: "we cannot allow your ideal to destroy the

Heart of our Village… Just as the Watergate scandal opened a can of worms in your circles, the Hotevilla Water Tower will open the one we have here! The world has entered the DAYS OF REVELATIONS, and no government or earthly power can prevent this from coming full cycle. So if you want, we will be happy to help you go through the pains of opening that 'can.' Now it is up to you to undo the disruptions you have caused at Hopi Land… To begin with, immediately summon your Hopi Tribal Council and let them completely withdraw from Hotevilla, after removal of the whole water system… we will let you decide how to remove the water tower before May 22."

I must emphasize again that this letter comes from Titus and the group that is supporting him. Dan Evehema did not sign it. Much as Dan grieves over the installation of the water and sewer utilities, he does not support any kind of confrontation that requires or invites the use of force. With the letter already in hand, the Tribal Council is going ahead with the installation. And, we can be certain that they, together with the Government, are preparing for whatever emergencies that may arise. It could be ugly. And while the event will make news, it is contrary to what Dan feels is consistent with the Covenant. Since he knows what the use of the utilities will do to Hotevilla and the keeping of the Covenant, he wishes with every fiber of his being to have the pipes removed. But above all he believes that situations like this must be solved peacefully, and that individuals have the right to choose. The Traditional leaders' job includes the responsibility to tell people what the right choices are, and the need to urge them to be wise and choose well. They are also to be told what the consequences of the wrong choices will be. But once the Traditional leader has done this, every individual has the right to decide which way he or she will go, and to follow it. If the pipes and meters are to come out at all, the Hotevilla people and the Council should make and carry out this decision on their own.

Among the many things Katherine Cheshire and Touch the Earth Foundation does for Dan and his extended family is to arrange for Bahannas to go every year to Dan's farm to assist with the planting and the harvesting. Considering Dan's age, this is greatly appreciated, and it is a most rewarding experience for those who volunteer. You can make arrangements through the Foundation to do this too. As it happens, this spring the work crew will be at Dan's farm during the very week that the activists will be at Hotevilla to deal with the water tower and seek world attention. But in accordance with the view just stated, neither the work crew nor Dan will go to Hotevilla to join the protesters. They will be peacefully planting the corn and other vegetables, and celebrating as part of the cycle of life these wondrous and ancient moments with Mother Earth.

Isn't it fascinating to be part of these amazing events that are bringing the last great American Indian culture to its very end! Not many people can say they have shared in such intimate moments, let alone in those that set in motion the shape and timing of the ending of the Fourth Cycle of the world. Would you ever imagine that it would come about in such a prosaic way?

To be more precise, I pose for you at the beginning of Chapter 11 three "ifs." It is almost certain that you can discard the first and happiest one. Meetings among Traditionals are still going on. They still hope to change the situation. But that does not seem to be a viable probability any more. We have moved into the second phase. And if the "object" is struck, we move immediately into the third…which seems almost unavoidable — close to an absolute.

As for Dan, Susie, and the few other remaining Traditionals, they can still be pleased to have run their race — the one where the "brave" have dared not go, and they can pass on to the Underworld with joy. In the meantime, we will see that their needs, and those of the Traditionals who support and run with them, are cared for. The others, foremost of which are the Tribal Council, will learn soon enough what their real costs are. Not long ago, Leigh Jenkins led an alarmed group of Hopis in publicly decrying the theft by two Bahannas of the Taalawtumsi — sacred wooden figures that are used in and essential to the initiation ceremonies at Second Mesa. Even though the thieves did not know what they were taking, it was a reprehensible act. Mr. Jenkins and the others went on television and talked with newspaper reporters about the tragic consequences of the theft, and pointedly claimed that heinous "curses" would soon strike the thieves — which they did. They also talked at length about the need to save the Hopi traditional lifeway — its ceremonies, sacred teachings, and paraphernalia. Everything they said was true. Yet by what they are doing at Hotevilla, and expressly to the Elderly Elders, they leave us wondering about their sincerity and real intentions — for they are themselves committing a far greater crime and immeasurably greater harm.

In light of Hopi prophecy and the Covenant with Maasaw, will they walk away from this action unscathed? We doubt it. If what they say about curses is true, and if Maasaw's prophecies are true — and I would like any Council member to state publicly that he believes they are not — they are establishing for themselves a place in the history of the world that no one will ever envy.

What a threshold in time this is! When I began the book last year, I never imagined we would be at this plateau before it was finished, and I am wondering whether its timing is an accident.

A few days ago, I received a mailing from Time-Life Books announcing a book series that will be "an unprecedented event for collectors interested in the true history of the American Indian." It sounds great…lots of public interest in these wonderful people and their cultures. What struck me, though, were the opening paragraphs: "If we could turn the clock back, we'd see Sioux hunting grounds before they became cornfields. *We'd look into firelit kivas where Hopi elders tell their stories.* We'd walk Iroquois trails, learning the old ways…Of course, there is no such clock. But I can," the editor continues, "offer you something that comes surprisingly close…help you discover the world the Indians knew."

I leaned back in my chair at that, swallowed hard, and mused: "If we could turn the clock back... Is that really necessary? Doesn't the person who wrote this know they are not all gone, that of all the tribes whose cultures covered North America, one still stands — hanging by destiny's thread, of course — but as of today it still stands? The clock is still ticking at Hotevilla. Up there on the mesa we can still participate in what has been going on, cycle after cycle, for thousands of years. And if at this fatal instant those gritty few are listened to — those one, or two, or three that prophecy said it would come down to — it will be there to experience tomorrow."

So listen. The wind is blowing. It is going to touch your cheek. Somehow, some way, the Elders, the other Traditionals, and we, are going to join hands to peacefully save what we can of all this! Meanwhile, as time passes you will be wondering what is going on at Hotevilla, and you can find out by keeping in contact with the Touch the Earth Foundation. Information regarding them is given in the Appendix of our book.

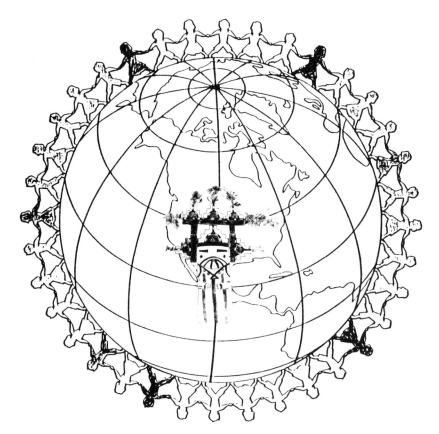

Together with all nations we protect both land and life and hold the world in balance.

Katherine and Dan exhibiting the happiness always found in working together at Dan's ranch.

The watering pond at Dan's ranch — dry now thanks to the Peabody Mine and the lowered water table.

CHAPTER 10

THE ONE-HEARTEDS AND HOPE

THE ONE-HEARTEDS — PETITIONS AND PROPHECIES

We have covered in previous chapters most of what the Elders and the other Traditionalists have experienced and done from the Emergence to the present. This chapter relates some of the other and special things the Elders and other Traditionalists have done recently to preserve their ability to keep their Covenant vows, and then reveals what they will be doing to maintain their faith and continue their work into the future. Here, they write about their struggle, emphasizing particularly the need for observing human rights, religious freedom, and common decency. Finally, they reveal to us what we are waiting to hear: the ancient prophecies having to do with the end and the beginning again of the world.

Over the past two decades, the Traditional leaders have gone many times beyond the borders of Hopi Land to present their message — to the United Nations, which they know as "The House of Mica," to the Geneva Conventions on human rights, and to Holland's Fourth Russell Tribunal. Each of these bodies has been asked to send delegates to Hotevilla and to the other traditional villages to see what conditions are like. You will see now what kind of a response the Hotevilla Traditionals have had. Since most of the *Techqua Ikachi* articles are not dated, it is not possible to keep the articles in chronological order. But that will not matter. What is important is to see their purpose, and the reasoning that is inherent within the passages.

I remind the reader that in all quoted material from the Elders, Katchonqva and the TI articles, I do not change their capitalizations and lower cases, or their spellings, to make them different from those I chose or to make them consistent. I believe that to do this would be a violation in procedure. Whatever they felt was adequate should be accepted as such.

A Journey of the Hopi to the United Nations

TI— "On September 16, 1986, Hopi elders were invited to the UN to present their message of peace and to participate in a spiritual ceremony.

Many people, old and young, were there to take part in this special day of International Day and Year of Peace.

The Hopi elders were honored to participate in a special fire ceremonial with other Native Americans. Exactly at sunrise the fire was kindled on the grounds of the UN by Iroquois Indians who blessed the fire with Native tobacco, with prayers to all directions. Hopi elders blessed the fire with cornmeal and with their own prayers. From this fire the Torch of Peace was lighted. This torch

The Dawn Kachina Spirit

will be carried around the world, passed from hand to hand by people of all races, ages, and beliefs, until it is returned to the UN on December 11, 1986. This will be called the First Earth Run. Later the Hopi elders presented the message of hope and love to the children of the world. In the late afternoon the Hopi met their appointment time with the Secretary General of the UN. Our message of peace was presented to him to be shared by other countries around the world. Since we were given an hour's time, not all the message was delivered. However, we left with them our video tape of our message so this will speak the rest.

Whatever did not fit within the allotted time, and which is too political to be heard in the House of Mica, will be put together in the near future for printing.

We were received with respect. Also our sponsors took care of us like VIPs, which we appreciate. This made our trip very exciting and interesting.

We pray our message will produce power and be heard throughout the lands. Perhaps along the way our voice will do wonders, that our struggle is not in vain."

Our Complaint Against the U.S. Government

TI— "On November 27, 1987, Traditional Hopi elders of Hotevilla Village filed their complaint against the U.S. Government through the UN Commission on Human Rights in Geneva, Switzerland. We feel this move is important to Hopi religious leaders because of the prophetic knowledge and instruction regarding the UN and because of its distinctive fitness in regard to the prophecy.

Hopis look with respect upon the UN as being of sacred symbolic significance. Various segments of religious orders dwell within the House of Mica which appear there for a purpose. That is, to look into world problems and into the problems of the weakest who are being pushed toward extinction by the stronger powers. Their duties are to resolve these problems if possible.

Hopi also have been given a duty to warn the leaders and people of coming danger. Also Hopi were to describe their suffering and their sorrowful experiences at the hands of stronger powers. When the A-bomb was dropped on Japan, the Hopi were prompted to warn the world leaders in the UN about the danger to land and life that lies in the advanced destructive technology. The Hopi were to test the wisdom and understanding of these House of Mica people, and ask for their help. Because the UN is linked with the prophecy, it means it will play an important role in fulfilling prophecy.

Four (the sacred number) chances were given the Hopi to accomplish their mission. The first three efforts were unsuccessful. The fourth effort succeeded to some extent, but the meeting with the world leaders was a failure. However, we were directed to the Commission on Human Rights, who might be able to help us.

Individuals at the UN were very kind and helpful in directing us and in advising us that it is possible to file a complaint against the United States for wrongs done to our Nation. Maybe, because of certain rules, the complaint can be made through the Commission in Geneva."

How Are We Doing with the United Nations?

TI— "No doubt most of you are wondering how our efforts are faring with the UN Human Rights Commission. Hopefully, we are making some headway.

We are working and following the knowledge of our elders according to the prophetic instructions regarding the United Nations. It was said this is where the final or decisive judgment will be made for us in reaching our goal, which is a full independence or autonomy.

We Believe the UN Commission on human rights will understand and help fulfill our prophecy. This could be our last and most important step because it will be in the House of Mica (UN) that we will find our position — whether or not we are worthy of existence. This will fulfill and conclude the prophecy we have been pursuing, with the help of our Great Creator.

Around July of this year, Hopi will attend the gathering of indigenous people from different parts of the world in Geneva. We find that most every country has been creating problems by violating the human rights of indigenous minorities. We think the Commission on Human Rights is doing a great job. They support us and believe we were born free and equal in dignity and rights. That we should be protected against genocide and discrimination. That we have the right to preserve our culture and tradition, the right to pursue our own cultural development, the right to practice our own religion, the right to protect and use traditional lands. The possibility of gaining these rights, among many other things, is encouraging and produces hope. But one thing is lacking: power. The Commission has little power. But they have had enough influence to help indigenous peoples in some countries regain their independence. So we will pray and keep strong as we await our cherished day of Independence."

The Traditional Hopi Visit to the UN was Successful

TI— "It was raining when the Traditional Indian delegation among the Hopi Tribe entered the great entry hall of the General Assembly building to the beat of the drum.

The spirit of happiness was there, good feelings were high with the hope that the UN would understand and accept the knowledge and wisdom from the mouths of Indigenous Native People.

The stage was set when the delegation entered. People of importance were waiting to welcome us. No doubt each of us had the feeling of pride and honor to be part of this extraordinary historical occasion…

Speakers: Sister Blaise Lupo, co-director, Clergy and Laity Concerned (CALC); Pir Vilayat Inayat Khan, Head of the Sufi Order of Islamic Tradition; Reverend Ambrose I. Lane, Minister and founder, Martin Luther King Jr. Community Church of the USA.

Prayer: Wallace Black Elk

Speakers: Native American Indigenous Medicine Council, Chief Leon Shannandoah, Six Nation Iroquois Confederacy; Caroline Tawangyouma, Sovereign

Hopi Independent Nation, Hotevilla Village; Thomas Banyacya, United Sovereign Hopi Independent Nations; Pandit Gopi Krishna, Yoga Adept.

Closing comments: Javier Perez de Cuellar, Secretary General of the UN, represented by Robert Muller, Assistant Secretary General of the UN...

Since we cannot print every word of the various speakers, we summarize them here as a whole. We believe all their statements have a common ground. Spiritually related doctrines laid out by religious belief regarding the survival of land and life which is threatened by nuclear catastrophe and wars, the environment threatened by pollutants, etc. That because of these threats all will not survive unless there is a complete change in social order and political structure. We must not forsake the Great Creator and all the great laws we received from Him which guide our thoughts in restoring harmony among all people, all living creatures and our Mother Earth. As a whole the speakers' voices were strong and inspiring and we pray they will bear fruit for the future to come.

Now it is up to us to make this real. We must perform self-analysis and change our behavior and character. We must not pretend to be something which we are not, which results in friction. We must not deceive our fellow men in any way. Let us become realistic and establish a goal to have faith in the All-Powerful Creator, for we are not above His laws. Let him be the Judge according to His plan.

Let us establish a goal of happiness and love. We must ready ourselves to serve and work for the Great Spirit, not making supremacy or superiority our goal. That aim would not succeed in reaching the purpose that we set out to achieve.

We trust our readers will understand and accept the brief description we give you here, and do so with an open mind. We recognize this assembly as a sacred event, for we, the Hopi, have a prophecy which foretold that one day a house built of mica (the UN) would appear on the eastern shore of our land. There the Hopi would visit the great world leaders within this house. The Hopi delegation would bring forth a message describing their dangerous situation, explaining that their way of life is threatened and may be demolished by lingering foreign encroachment. If for some reason they are not welcome, they must not be discouraged, for this will be the test of the prophecy. Four attempts must be made. If at the end of that time the door fails to open they were to put their disappointment behind them, toward the setting sun. So far three attempts have been made by Hotevilla religious and spiritual leaders.

On October 23rd (1983) during UN Disarmament Week, the Hopi, among other groups of Traditional Indigenous People, were invited to speak in the house of mica. So with eagerness and high hopes many came from far distances to speak or just to listen. Later the next day the delegations met together to exchange knowledge and prophecies. Free time was given to make new friends and meet old acquaintances. There we talked about the happenings in our homeland and about our families' health, etc. We all parted happy to report the results to our elders and people.

We wish all our friends to know that we are very happy and grateful to be part of this historical event. We hoped and prayed that this event will produce a closer relationship with the world leaders in the House of Mica, so that someday in the near future our prophecy will be fulfilled.

Perhaps some people will accept this as the final act of service in publicly fulfilling the prophecy. The fact is that according to our elders, fulfillment can be final if it is done according to the guidelines of the prophecy. Leaders in the House of Mica are supposed to recognize the Hopi as a living people who are endowed with all the human rights and equality of all mankind. They are supposed to receive and greet the Hopi with an open door. Within the House the Hopi are to speak freely and with feelings of equality with the world leaders. There are to be no feelings of superiority or inferiority. We are to speak brother to brother, in an atmosphere of harmonious respect. This is a large order, but it makes sense in a way. It may be what is needed to bring out the true value of the prophecies in regard to the problems of the past, and today's work for the future. What the Hopi say hinges upon divine laws and instructions for the future. Taking this position is not an act of pressure. It is a way of showing trust — so as not to tarnish the name, Hopi (peaceful)."

Standing in Sight of the UN … Just Looking At It and Wondering

TI— "In our last issue we informed you of the complaint we filed with the UN in New York against the U.S. Gov't. for wrongs done to us. This led us to a Geneva hearing for indigenous people. There we were not recognized to speak. During this time we received no response from any official member of the UN Since this situation lies within the guidelines Hopi received from Massau, we gave this our careful attention. We completed four trips there to speak to the General Assembly, all of which were failures. On reaching this point we became aware there is little hope we will ever fulfill the prophecy concerning the UN (One old Hopi leader wished to fulfill his duty, what he had to do concerning the UN. He passed on shortly after.) So the religious leaders decided that what they have to do to fulfill the prophecy, actually the final instruction, is to put their disappointments behind them. Hopefully this will help us reach our goal. From here on Hopi will rely on the three peoples who are supposed to stand behind them, upon the Great Creator, and upon natural forces. Any one of these could complete the purification according to His plan."

The United Nations — A Complete Failure?

TI— "Here we will briefly state our view concerning the United Nations. Because of our prophetic knowledge and instructions telling us we are to bring our message to world leaders, ever since the UN was established on our land we Hopi have, with respect, looked upon the UN as a place of sacred symbolic significance. For several decades Hopi have made constant attempts to fulfill this obligation. Since these have been a complete failure, we, with the help of the Human Rights Organization housed under the leadership of the UN in Geneva, made a formal complaint against the U.S. Government for wrongs done.

But we received no positive response from these world leaders, either. Our experience in the Geneva hearings was that activities there are political and are not based upon spiritual laws. Instead, things are controlled in a political way by the U.S. government, and by other world leaders, so it was clear that our case would linger on indefinitely, or perhaps become in the end fruitless.

We find that aggressive, violent activities are given top attention. So since Hopi are struggling in peaceful ways our plight failed to arouse any interest or sympathy, and we did not get our most needed help, which was having Hopi recognized as an independent nation.

In fact, as we looked on, the UN entered the Persian Gulf war, rather than following their supposedly neutral tradition of resolving problems in peaceful ways.

Therefore we have come to the conclusion that world peace is becoming hopeless. We still have our instructions to follow when we get to the point where leaders begin to corrupt everyone they can, and when relying on our leaders becomes impossible and our trust in them dims. Then not only True Hopi, but other devoted peoples as well, will choose to follow and struggle for their rights under the law of our Great Creator. This is a law that never changes nor breaks down.

How does this failure fit the prophetic pattern? Why would we be told to go there when we have achieved so little? It is because the principle of choice always prevails. The Creator and Maasaw give us opportunities to influence the course of the future. If we make wise choices, the future will be better. If they are unwise, they will be worse. The UN faces many problems and demands, so many in fact that it is confusing, and makes their job complex. So it gets caught up in these and is not able to focus upon the things it should. It works in a mist, or fog, and even when its best hope stands right in front of it, it cannot see it. So it is with the Hopi message — we had to try — we came, but they did not hear. All that is left now is the hope that enough of our message remains with them to jog them somewhere along the way, and make them think about it and act on it. But we are not optimistic about this. The problems will go on, and will continue to be in the way. Therefore the future does not look good."

The Mission to the UN — Promising At First

TI— "When nuclear technology was first devised and became known, we the people never gave much thought about the effects it would cause upon living matter and the earth itself until the nuclear bomb was dropped on the Japanese mainland. This ended the second world war. People hailed the outcome, and honors were bestowed, for this was thought to be the greatest invention ever made by man. People took it as a promising outlook for the future, believing that it would benefit the country in many ways and would be a strong defence against enemies.

The True Hopi was not impressed with this view. He was concerned and acted promptly to warn the world of its dangers, for he knows something about this device, termed in Hopi prophecy as **"the gourd of ashes."** Also according to the prophecy the house of glass or mica would be erected on the eastern shore of our land, where world leadership would be organized in the effort to resolve the world's problems. So they, the Hopi, decided that this would be the best place to take their message on the nuclear invention issue, and also to make the UN aware of the oppression confronting the Hopi from outside government efforts to break their way of life. This was the original plan they would present to the UN. Armed with all of their documents they journeyed to the House of Mica. Unfortunately, entrance was denied to them."

TEM— From the documents available, it is difficult to determine how many attempts, exactly, have been made. Thomas Banyacya and three other "appointed interpreters" made the first one in 1949, and they were refused entry. David Monongye made an attempt in 1962, and was also refused. The article we are in the midst of now states that an appointment was made to speak before the UN on September 30, 1985. Was one made on that date, or is it actually that Manuel Hoyungowa, David's grandson, made his recorded appearance on September 16, 1986, when he was refused entry, but left behind on the UN door a posthumous message from David? Another attempt was made on November 22, 1993, when Martin Gashweseoma, Manuel, and Emory Holmes, a medicine man from Hotevilla, were invited in to make a brief presentation, but the time given to them was "short." Then, in January 1994, another journey there was made, and an address was presented. The actual results of this trip are confusing. Although they did get in, Manuel was reportedly upset when he returned, and intends to put it all behind him and forget it. The Elders describe this as "throwing the case behind them," meaning they put it down as a lost cause and go on from there.

Dan Evehema went with several of the Hopi groups to the UN. Also, Thomas Banyacya played a central and important role in organizing these visits and in doing many other things to spread the message of the Hopi Traditionals. He deserves everyone's gratitude. On February 8, 1994, he wrote a long, informative, and touching farewell letter to UN Secretary General Boutros Boutros Ghali, which once again tells the Hopi story and sums up the ways in which prophecy is unfolding and will continue to do so. It is one everyone should read.

The *Techqua Ikachi* article continues:

"Their instructions, however, were to make four attempts, so during the last three decades a total of three attempts were made by Hotevilla religious leaders without success. Finally an appointment was made to speak before the UN on September 30, 1985. The reception was great. Our message was clear and simple. A prepared written documentary of the prophecy was presented, including a documentary videotape depicting the scenes and activities of our village. These were to be shared and viewed by all the UN members.

No political matters were discussed — this was not permitted — nor was our message demanding. The purpose of our message was to arouse the leaders and the people of the world and get them to look through the eyes of the Hopi and judge whether the message has value. Until we know how they react to this, we cannot say what we have accomplished. Of course, there are other human rights groups and others who are willing to serve us if needed. In a small way we symbolize the fulfillment of Hopi prophecy for our village.

Herein we wish to answer the questions about disagreements raised by supporters of the Hopi and the Hopi themselves before the UN presentation was made. Obstacles began to form almost immediately. Some argued that we should unite so that the Hopi would be stronger and more balanced for this special occasion of the meeting at the UN. Other Hopis claimed that only people with rank and chosen by the chief (Kikmongwi) should be eligible to carry out the mission, but we rejected this concept with doubt. We know that each village is independent and has its own governing body, or entity. We at Hotevilla think it is not proper to be obligated to what is not designed for our village.

We hope this brief comment is understandable. The thing we know is that sometimes the opposing forces use this tactic to tarnish one's image in order to shackle his ambition about doing an important task. This does not mean that what we accomplished closes the door to anyone. It can be done by anyone, and perhaps much better than we can. If so, we will wholeheartedly acknowledge their success."

What Will Tomorrow's Dawn Kachina Spirit Bring?

TI— "What are the thoughts of world leaders in the United Nations? What will tomorrow's dawn or the coming future bring? Will it bring us a New Dawn filled with splendor, peace, and happiness, or will the old divided spirit of the Hopi linger on until our life resources diminish in accord with the cycles of Nature or through the effects of mankind's technology? Which path will people choose?"

A Visitor from the UN, and Other Happenings

TI— "During August we had a dignitary visit from the United Nations. *Techqua Ikachi* was honored to have him and his wife in our home. They witnessed the Snake Dance in Second Mesa. During their two-day visit they met and talked with the Traditional Leaders in Second Mesa village and Hotevilla village. They were very impressed by village life and with the farming methods.

In October, Hotevilla Hopi made a trip to Frankfurt, Germany where a Spiritual gathering was held to present their statement and to meet with the Dali Lama of Tibet to compare knowledge.

There is still pressure from the BIA and the Tribal Council to modernize Hotevilla Village.

We have had a good corn harvest this year. The crows and blue birds which destroy the crops suddenly vanished. Only a few can be seen now and then. We wonder why?

Techqua Ikachi is doing its best to stay alive. Please be patient, we will make our best effort to bring you our message whenever enough funds are available. Thank you and good day."

The Geneva Conference

TI— "We are glad that Hotevilla Village was represented by David Monongye at the Geneva Conference this last September. The conference was held for all Indian leaders from North and South America, to protest, on an international level, against the United States. Monongye expressed a deep concern for the prophecies and the importance for all tribes to hold on to our lands and not give them up. 'Do not go for the money,' he said, 'for the money will soon be gone.'

The Hopi and Iroquoi nations went to Geneva on their own passports; we urge and support all our native peoples to do the same. It should also be acknowledged that Switzerland and Sweden have accepted the passports as being valid. Let this be an example for the world community to follow."

Hopi Traditional Village Presents Its Case to Holland's Tribunal

TI— "With much regret we delayed this issue — our apologies to our readers. Sometimes one must make a decision between two vital objectives. In this instance, in order to present our case before the international jury, we decided to bypass our newsletter for a time and respond to an invitation from Holland's Fourth Russell Tribunal.

We prepared two cases, the general problem in Hopi Land and a special document in reference to Hotevilla Traditional Village. We did this because of the different philosophic concepts and self-governing bodies of each village. We took this step because we feel and trust that they have similar purposes and goals to reach. We hope this move will not hinder the traditional concepts and efforts to resist the oncoming encroachment into our land.

At this time we are aware there are many people who are curious and anxious to know the outcome, if we shall succeed or fail. This we cannot predict or be boastful about, for it is like a seed put into the earth; we do not know whether it will bring forth a good harvest or whether we will face famine. We must be patient, for now all we can say from our viewpoint is that the gathering created deep strong feelings. We hope that it will bring a good harvest.

According to our understanding, the purpose and aim of the Tribunal is that it is a foundation, consisting of non-government organizations of different nations focusing on the rights of the native people of South and North America: seeking to further the observance of human rights, the rights of the Indians to have their own tradition, language, culture, and territory, without interference from outside sources. Asking that the governments of the countries and the tribal governments within (as well as any opposition) must respect their own constitutions and cease their violations of human rights and the autonomy of all the indigenous people so they will be free to seek their own self-determination. Asking that colonization, exploitation, and extermination must stop before all the aboriginal natives, the guardians of land and life, disappear from the face of the earth.

Upon these bases, the Tribunal's effort is aimed at mobilizing public opinion and arousing a consciousness of the Native problems by means of publicity, both on a national and international level. The documents they produce will be made available to or will be sent to the world's governments, institutions of higher learning, and others including those accused. This effort is to awaken and increase the pressure of public opinion, to make the problems known on a larger scale in order that they may be called to the attention of the various political and authoritative organizations.

The Tribunal was well attended by representatives from different countries. Anyone can feel the atmosphere of sacredness and honor among people with the same problems and the supporters who care and are dedicated to the Almighty, the Great Creator.

For several days after our case was presented before the international jury, key questions were asked of witnesses and experts for confirmation before the jury. Oppressed minorities of many countries had their cases heard. All of the cases had these factors in common: oppression, exploitation, extermination, genocide, etc. The accused or representative government institutions were also invited to present a clear understanding of their side to the jury and to the accusers, so that everything can be brought out into the open. Sadly, none of these appeared to challenge the charges brought by the Native peoples.

We have a hard struggle ahead of us. The opposition is very strong and it has no mercy. For over half a century the official Federal policy has been to assimilate the Indians by every available means. First, it attempted to outlaw the tribal religion and replace it with Christianity as the official religion. Then compulsory boarding schools were established for indoctrination. This had limited success, so the Federal policy toward Indians changed to fostering the Indians through economic development, modern conveniences, health care, religious freedom, cultural autonomy, and tribal self-government by election through denouncing the village leadership as a governing body.

In their folly, some Hopis took the bait claiming this was payment by the Government for making use of our land and resources. Reimbursement makes sense in some ways, but to set an example of the many ways it does not make sense, Hotevilla Village has, over the years, refused to be lured into the trap, and has maintained their stand.

Research by scholars regarding Hotevilla Village finds it is a special administrative problem because of our past. There are constant reminders of force and tension built up by persistent pressure by the Government which has caused them to cast themselves into an unyielding mold. They maintain that they have committed no crime, only to live in their own ways. This is true, but it is equally true that Traditional leadership is based on moral, non-violent, religious beliefs with respect not only for their own people, but for all land and life, rather than based on prestige and the power to dominate. To stray from this code of laws would destroy the Hopi way. Therefore acculturation is not the solution for the problems in Hopi Land.

We don't know what the future holds for us. But we will be patient. We will wait perhaps four days, four weeks, maybe four months, perhaps even four years. Whatever this seed produces — whether it is success or failure — our course must change."

To People of the Clear Nightime Sky

TI— "This world is in a terribly confused mess and faces grave danger. Almost all people are now without a genuine moral sense and have no spiritual discernment.

There is almost no limit to the hurt people cause each other, so much so that they consider it a virtue to not even feel or show emotions. They are, almost all of them, only interested in themselves — even where their benevolence is concerned.

Sex and physical expression is their major, fundamental, stumbling block — along with the pursuit of money, etc., — and these are the fundamental bases for the various ways of lying and hypocrisy. Much blame for the confusion in society must be placed upon the teachers of the divine knowledge of the old world (Europe and Asia) because of their confusion — sometimes acknowledged, but more often not — about the meaning and place of sexuality in the expression of human life.

Because these teachers were considered to be divine and perfect, their errors, ignorance and prejudices came to dominate the whole of civilization, upsetting balance and offsetting much of the good they accomplished. They themselves helped to corrupt and sometimes destroy millions of innocent people in their attempt to eliminate the mystery of sexuality from humanity. That is why they did not understand the wisdom behind our Hopi fertility rituals and the humorous antics of our clowns that taught us so much.

Unfortunately, there is very little that can be done at this time to change people, to correct the spiritual confusion and contradictions that saturate civilization. So many are the errors, both seen and unseen, that only through ultimate disaster can the situation be made straight.

At this time we wish to thank all those who support us with the expenses in putting out our publication. Most of all we appreciate all the letter writing to your elected officials. We are hoping the Congressional hearing will materialize here in Hopi Land so that the Traditional point of view will be heard concerning J.U.A. We have been waiting for so long and wish to be included, especially Hotevilla Village.

Now let us look at the brighter side of the picture. We include here more information about the UN observers' report that was gathered regarding the traditional Hopi and Navajo tribe. It was acted upon by the subcommission on prevention of discrimination and protection of minorities.

Since the report is sketchy, we put in writing here, according to our understanding, some of what happened at the Geneva hearing. The following organized tribes attended; Traditional Hopi and Navajo, Progressive Navajo and Hopi Tribal Councils, with one person representing each organization. Only the Traditional Hopi and Traditional Navajo spoke. The report is favorable, and the resolution of the Traditional Hopis was adopted. The proposal of an 18-month moratorium was offered by Hon. J. Bates, Congressman, and Honorable Senator Cranston. The idea was that more time should be given to Navajo and Hopi to relocate, and to form a new proposal commission to protect the human rights of both the traditional Hopi and Navajo. That advisory service should be made available to traditional Hopi people as soon as possible.

We think that thus far the result in Geneva is promising. We pray it will bear fruit, but we know it will be a long fight. We hope more information will be available for our next issue. In the meantime, we hope all of you will consider this and support the Congressman and Senator mentioned above, encouraging them to push the proposal through."

We See Light At the End of the Tunnel

TI— "This is only an alert signal for our readers to ponder. This is still on the drawing board and the project will focus on only one particular village, the Traditional Community of Hotevilla.

As all of you know, for many years we have been in search of ways by which our land base, our village, and our ways of life may survive before the encroachment of western influences overtake the whole foundation upon which our village was based. During many years of effort we have made many contacts and received much support. They have worked hard in helping us to reach the goal we have been working toward.

Not long ago, upon our request, we have had an important guest. A man from the National Park Service selected by the Park Director himself. He explained some of the systems they use to protect wildlife and parks. It was decided he would work on it and in turn we would try hard to work together to reach the goal of our desires. The basis of this project will be under the category of a Historical Site.

We don't know how this will work out. So we will be all ears to hear any opinions and suggestions. But at least we can see a little light at the end of the tunnel. We don't know how long the tunnel is and what it holds beyond the light... We have not yet received any reply to the questions we put before them. Below are a few of the questions.

1. Would the village of Hotevilla have to become Federal Land in order to become an historical site?

2. If the village did become Federal Land in order to be designated a historical site, what guarantee would there be that this land would always be preserved as such and not have its designation changed if the Department of the Interior decided to use the land in some other manner?

3. Since Congress has given itself permission to abrogate any trust agreement it has made with Native Americans, how can there be a safeguard against them breaking this agreement?

4. If this requires an act of Congress, what would a proposal presented to Congress have to include and what is the procedure?

5. How would the privacy of the villagers be protected? As a National Park

or Historical Site would there be some sort of cultural program for tourists, and, if so, how would it work with the residents?

6. Who would have to give permission for the Federal Government to acquire the village for this historical site? Would there be compensation for the land?

7. Is there a way for the village of Hotevilla to be designated as a Historical Site without signing over the land to the Federal Government? How can the village maintain its sovereignty?

8. Can Hotevilla become an Historical Site without having tourists in their village?

The Hopi tribe, both progressive and traditionals, are now entering the most critical period of their long history on this land. It is time now for the people of each village to recall and reflect on the prophecies handed down from our elders, which are the instructions, guidelines, and historical bases for this period of time. Because of the differences in knowledge among Hopi and the outsiders we expect critics and perfectionists will quickly jump on this move we have made. It may become controversial because of the feeling that top leaders everywhere are not trustworthy when it comes to keeping their promises. We are hoping this will not affect our conclusions, so that we end up dropping the whole matter. We are talking about a project we are considering with the help of the National Park Service. This might be the opportunity for us to become a fully recognized independent nation. Let us remind you of the questions put before the National Park Service in our last issue. Their response was that they gave careful attention to our questions, and gave truthful answers, but because of limited space we must omit the full response. Instead we will quote in part their replies, which we think will be sufficient, coming from an official staff meeting which stresses strongly the problems of Hotevilla Village:

From the directors:

> *It seems clear that the resolution to your problems do not lie in designating Hotevilla a National Historic Site, under which it would be acquired by the National Park Service and open for public visitation. Such a situation might actually increase the pressure upon Traditional ways rather than to protect them…'I have done considerable research in [an] attempt to give you an opinion on the desirability of naming your village either to the National Register or as a National Historical Site. The National Register would provide the best protection with the least amount of red tape. But it still implies that the Federal Government might be able to intervene and cause (you) to do something that you might not agree with. Finally, I think I have a solution which is better than both. Actually, we use the wording of the National Register Legislation to achieve what we want. The law says that if your site is considered eligible for nomination to the National Register then the same protection applies to it as if it were actually on National Register.'"*

Hotevilla Village Becomes Independent!

TI— "When the Village of Hotevilla made the bold move to become a fully Independent Nation (as it always has been since founded) we waited for the reaction when the Village became listed on the National Register by the National Park Service. The impact was as if the world came to a standstill. There was no opposition, people and the press were silent, even our well-wishers were silent. But we know and feel people are concerned, that this new turn in our lives stirs the people who have open minds.

Note: no thumb print appears on the document listing Hotevilla Village on the National Register. If this document serves to destroy us, likewise the document will be destroyed by our own will. A provision of the agreement is there will be no tourist visitation privileges."

The Commemoration of Yukiuma

TI— "On September fourth, fifth, and sixth a commemoration was held in the Traditional Community of Hotevilla Village, honoring the late Chief Yukiuma who founded Hotevilla September 6, 1906. His stand was unique, based on his belief and instruction from the Great Spirit, the Great Creator.

Against great odds he stood against the power of the U.S. Government and its military might. His strength was the sacred stone tablet received from the Great Spirit. To the end of his life, no amount of imprisonment, suffering, bribes, or flattery by the great American Nation could topple him from his beliefs. The spirit of His concept is still alive within Hotevilla Village.

People who came here from four directions completed the commemoration and made it a success. The main speaker was from old Mexico, who presented once again the 1848 Treaty of Guadalupe Hidalgo between the United States and Mexico. A study was made of the important passages which affect the Hopi people. The findings were very impressive and will be presented to the Geneva Conference, September fourteenth through the sixteenth of this year by the Hopi. Then we will learn what results from this, whether the essence of the treaty has had any effect."

Prophecy!

With their pleas to be left alone to live quietly and in peace as they kept the Covenant not only falling upon deaf ears, and their having to actually fight off constant attacks on their sovereign rights, the Elders and their supporters turned to selected Government officials and international bodies for help. Each time they did this, they patiently told the story of Hotevilla, not begging, but petitioning these individuals and institutions to support human rights and to push for the recognition of universal freedoms. They also presented summaries of their prophetic message, and in particular stressed the need for peace between nations and between individuals. They believed they had earned the right to make this presentation, having with less than a handful of exceptions sought peaceful solutions to every contentious issue they were involved in for thousands of years.

The Prophetic Role of the House of Glass

TI— "Just what are the Hopi prophetic instructions regarding the United Nations and what constituted fulfillment? Two misconceptions must be immediately dismissed. The Hopi are not asked by Maasaw to make just another appeal for peace, nor do they request membership in the UN. One more voice added to the chorus of those calling for peace would add little compared to the true significance of what Hopi tradition has to offer the modern world through this UN forum. When it was suggested that they join the UN, the Traditional Hopi — half jokingly — responded: 'No, we're waiting for the UN to join us.' This is not an arrogant reply. We speak with utmost humility and sincerity. Quite literally, we are waiting for other nations to return to that way of life which can continue endlessly, which is the deeper meaning of the name, Hopi. We trust this gives you a clue to the profound insights that are found in Hopi ancestral knowledge. If thoroughly understood, this single insight into the forces that shape the modern world would in itself enable those involved in the UN to bring an end to the arms race. The communication efforts of the Hopi and the developments that led to the existence of the United Nations are parallel responses to the invention of the atomic bomb. From the Hopi perspective, these first two efforts ought to enhance each other and work together for the benefit of the entire world. Can the UN say that its present way and course is solving the world's problems?

Centuries before the arms race began, the alternative to war was being put into practice by migrating societies in North America who slowly formed a spiritual political union at Oraibi, the oldest continuously inhabited village in the western hemisphere. To the Hopi, the UN has great significance, for it fits into this pattern.

Two monumental cultural factors have prevented the European immigrants from recognizing this process of widespread unification that we advocate: First, the presumption of racial superiority and the need to conquer and convert, and second, a recent tendency to discredit all knowledge which does not stand the test of scientific thought.

The Hopi insist that the coming of the light-skinned race, the invention of the atomic bomb, and the development of the UN were anticipated by their ancestral prophetic instructions, along with commands which were to be fulfilled by the Hopi. One of these is that they must make four attempts to gain a genuine hearing on the subject of their teachings, and concerning the efforts of the USA to eliminate their original form of government. If these attempts were unsuccessful, a rare opportunity would be missed, and could ultimately result in the elimination of most — possibly even all — human life on earth.

The basic premise is that humans cannot simply disregard natural order, make their own laws, and enforce them with weapons. The kind of enforcement violates natural order, causing precisely the suicidal situation we face today. Lest the Hopi be accused of being overly ethnocentric, we point out that all peoples once practiced the same alternative to war, and we are simply calling out for a return to our common heritage before it is too late. 'Perfect Consideration' could eliminate all war. A Perfect Consideration for one another will overcome all obstacles — both in the modern political sense, and in the seriously disrupted organization of Traditional Hopi government. These difficulties can be overcome. You recall that as in migration times the Hopi left their villages and moved on they were to break their pottery. For those who understand, this gesture has great symbolism. To many, there is saving grace in the pieces of the broken vessel of Hopi culture, in the 'broken off' persons of a few elders who still refuse to abandon their traditions, their understandings, and their hopes for a truly peaceful world for now and generations to come. In this piece of Hopi pottery lies a great hope for peace!"

Passing Prophecies and Future Prophecies

TI— "There is often the question of why the Hopi are so positive in their prophecies and claims of fulfillment. What proof do they have, people ask, and how do they see these things?

Here in a brief glance is how Hopi see when the prophesied events are coming to pass. The Hopi have been told that certain things are going to happen, but we do not have a definite day or year when these extraordinary events will occur. All we can say is, 'Maybe in your lifetime, maybe in your children's lives or their children's.' For your better understanding of this position we will provide some necessary background information.

Since all men are created as sacred, we humans were placed upon this earth for a purpose, which is to take care of the land, to protect the earth from harm, and to enjoy all the things it offers for a long time to come. If on the other hand we fail to live up to this law of creation, the consequence will be that we lose the land. This is the Universal Planned Structure laid out by our Great Creator.

It was foretold that one day a strange people will come upon our land. We were instructed that when they came we should walk cautiously and be watchfully alert to their ways of thinking and behaving. After many years they arrived — the white skinned people we call Bahanna. This event was the beginning of world decline.

The old Natural Order began diminishing, and it continues to do so up to this day, extending to all parts of the world, just as was also prophesied. This diminishment came about with the introduction of know-how [technology] and new life styles. For these things turned the hearts of people to new things from the

old, blemishing the old traditions and culture, so that we (Hopi) may even lose our identity because of the acceptance of English and the denouncing of our language, our Traditional culture, and our spiritual beliefs. As of this period of time, however, these things are not totally lost, and won't be until they become history. If we are fortunate, our ways of life will survive and we will continue the process of global balancing — proving that the words of our prophets are right.

We have said that Hopi predictions have no positive set date, but the Hopi do have ways of seeing what is coming. We do this by watching the natural balance of the earth, humans, and the behavior and activities of the wild species. We know that each of these factors has a power of sensitivity when it comes to detecting dangerous or unpleasant surroundings. The most important factor we were instructed to watch is mankind, because Maasaw told us man will become the most mindless and heedless foe of earth and nature. Therefore mankind is our chief source of information for seeing into the future — into what is about to happen. We were taught that through mankind's actions and deeds he will in time reach his desired goal, but he will at the same time gradually decide the future of the world by steadily lowering the important value of the Creator's law. It does

not matter whether his actions in ignoring the Creator's laws bring prosperity or disaster for mankind — man will still believe he can all on his own solve the world problems to better our way and bring us peace. Therein lies his greatest mistake.

Our views concerning the condition of the world today are similar to our views concerning the Hopi Lands situation. We are in a world of madness. Hopi have the proud name 'Peaceful,' which they seem to forget. What is happening around the world is disturbing for many reasons. We can look at it as if it were going on outside of our own world, but we must remember that our personal situation is like it and one of our own making. We have been sucked into it, but by our own free will.

Here are a few things for you to think about regarding the world as a whole: We see immorality flourishing and corruption everywhere. Men in high places are promoting destructive instruments of war which threaten to wipe out the world and its people. We see the earth being abused for its resources in order to gain wealth and power for destructive purposes. We see the polluting of the air, water, and land, and the depleting of the soil where once all plants grew healthy. We see the forests drying up and being destroyed. We see numbers of the earth's wonderful life species becoming extinct because of man's carelessness. The overall result is that the old, original natural order is badly disturbed, and this is causing climate changes to descend upon all parts of this country and the world.

What about a coming ice age and other frightful prophecies? These may be possibilities, but we can at least hope and pray that mother nature's computer is not being read correctly. It is interesting that our prophecies include many of the things the scientists see happening and are worried about today. What about Bahanna's nuclear bomb Armageddon ideology? It is possible the occurrence of this event depends solely on some Bahanna Chiefs pressing the button and starting it off. Do not worry. It might not happen in your lifetime. We Hopi believe that the Creator, together with Mother Nature, will themselves decide what the proper end is for the actual course we choose to follow. In other words, they will decide which ending fits the play we have self-directed. Keep strong."

A Prediction of Another Split

TI— "Our Prophets predicted that there would be another split like the one in 1906, when one side forsook the Divine Law and the advice of our religious leaders, and accepted cultural change away from Hopi ways. Then no solution could be found that would allow both factions to live side by side. This will lead to a second division, to what will be termed, 'One will pay and one will not,' meaning a time will come when some of the Hopi will choose to live the Bahanna way and the rest the Hopi way. This choice will be one that each of us will make — it will be a free choice for one or the other of the two paths. There will be no pulling or pushing to get one side to join the other side. If this prophecy is fulfilled the way we hope it will, we Hopis will once again live in harmony."

Grandpa Speaks

TI— "Now, let Grandpa speak from his knowledge and wisdom and advise us. 'What I say will not be my own words. They were passed down to me from my great-uncles and grandpas. I hope likewise that when I pass on you will pass my words on to your children and grandchildren so that they will receive them and understand as they grow.

'We are heading toward a difficult life. We have hastened our steps and are far ahead of time. I may not be here to share the excitement with you. It saddens me to think we may never recover our normal way of life. I also mean this for people everywhere. I think the world leaders carelessly tangle all the solutions for the betterment of the world in a web, like the spider, and I wonder if mankind will ever untangle the web. This is a sign of danger and I think the world leaders have strayed off the trail to peace. It was said if the leaders come to this point the people themselves are to take steps to shoo them back into the right path like animals. Then the people must awaken the leaders, the people of ability and those marked by greed, pinch their ears and make them open their eyes to the injuries they are doing our Mother Earth. They must be awakened to the consequences of the way they are leading the world's people. We must awaken them so they will cease their activities in developing destructive weapons which can destroy all life on earth. Awaken them to good thoughts of peace, happiness and love so they can be instruments to serve the world with loving kindness. Awaken them to protect and defend the earth, not destroy it, for there is no spare available for replacement. Awaken them to put away all evil thought and greed for this is the enemy of man. Write my words in your hearts so you will not forget.'"

THE ELDERS

Certain events show us that our prophecies are fulfilling. Consider starvation. Now most people buy their food in supermarkets. Our elders saw this coming. If there should be a serious drought the stores will be empty. We can't depend on them. So long as we raise our own food and store it up, we will be able to get through hard times. We must never forget why we pray for rain. Maasaw entrusted the land to us. We should follow his humble example, and live only with a planting stick and seeds.

Then the land will provide all we need. Maasaw knew our ambition for wealth and power. So he told us, 'If you don't forget to live by my law, you will reach the goal of a Hopi life. Care for the land, and it will care for you. Then you will reach me at the end of your path. After that I will lead you. For I am the first, and I shall be the last.' In saying this, he places all humanity between and within himself.

We have a Hopi life plan petroglyph. It tells us that we came through a reed from the underworld. Maasaw entrusted us with the land, which we spiritually rooted and claimed through our migrations. Two paths reveal the choice we would face. The figures above follow materialistic values.

Their path ends abruptly in confusion and horror. But on the path below stands a bent figure, meaning joy in old age, or a long, happy life. If we are led by selfish motives, we will lose the land and our life as well then we are Not-Hopi. The three circles on the lower path stand for three world-shaking events, which will purify the world. Only people who live by the original law will be recognized, and pass through this purification.

[Grandmother Caroline] 'When I was a child, Yukiuma told me much about the wisdom of the Hopi way. You cannot take both paths at once, he warned. The Hopi way and the Bahanna lifestyle do not blend together.'

We have travelled widely speaking for our village's sovereignty and protection. This may have been in vain, but we still hope someone will hear us, and in keeping with prophecy, take effective action to protect the Hopi way, to restore the rights of all native people, that they are respected by the human family. If you make your living at the expense of the earth and her children, you know it yourself. The consequences affect everyone. It is our own free choice whether we promote harmony for all living things, or contest with nature and war among people; wealth for a few, but hunger and grief for many. Every culture has its own guiding wisdom. As times get harder, we might recall this wisdom.

We don't know whether our warnings will reach people in time. The balance of life on earth must be restored. We have reached our last prophetic instructions. We have no more steps to take. All that remains is worldwide purification. Man made governments have not and will not change. Purification will cleanse them from the earth. Life is good when no one is oppressing others. For our life on earth to continue, the wicked must be weeded out. People of one heart will be recognized as Hopi. We will be fighting for our lives worldwide, one against another. When we reach this point, a brave person must stand up and tell the rulers, 'You deprive the very earth! You profit at the expense of all life! Come here and pay your debts!' No member of any government shows up here to hear the truth about how much they owe us. Instead, they are taking everything nature has, and wiping all indigenous peoples from the earth.

We still expect the help of our True White Brother, who took one of our sacred stone tablets to the rising sun. These tablets are our actual title to the land, given us by Maasaw when we met him at Oraibi. There our knowledge was complete. Fire Clan tablets came with us to Hotevilla. Oraibi was supposed to surrender all the tablets. It's foretold: A leader who forsakes sacred, divine laws will lose the land and the titles to it.

The duty to take over the sacred trust falls to any clan who is faithful and strong to use their power wisely.

The major threat to Hopi is the Tribal Council. The U.S. Government uses them as tools to break us down. It is said that when the Hopi are almost doomed, someone with courage will come to back us up. Three nations are to stand behind us. Protection

should come from Navajo and Paiute. If they fail to accept the task, or have no effect, the Bahanna must try. If they fail to rescue Hopi, three powerful forces will shake the world: the Swastika, the Sun, and the Red Symbol. Together they will bring worldwide purification. If we humans do not correct our attitudes and love each other and take care of the land, the Creator will complete the universal plan using natural forces to purify the world. This could be any collapse of natural order. The land could sink below the seas. After purification they say, a sister and a brother will start a new life on a new land.

KATCHONGVA

We Hopi knew all this would come about, because this is the Universal Plan. It was planned by the Great Spirit and the Creator that when the whiteman came he would offer us many things. If we were to accept those offers from his government, that would be the doom of the Hopi nation.

Hopi is the bloodline of this continent, as others are the bloodline of other continents. So if Hopi is doomed, the whole world will be destroyed. This we know, because this same thing happened in the other world. So if we want to survive, we should go back to the way we lived in the beginning, the peaceful way, and accept everything the Creator has provided for us to follow.

Whiteman's laws are many, but mine is one. Whiteman's laws are all stacked up. So many people have made the rules, and many of them are made every day. But my law is only the Creator's, just one. And no man made law must I follow, because it is ever changing, and will doom any people.

We know that when the time comes, the Hopi will be reduced to maybe one person, two persons, three persons. If he can with-

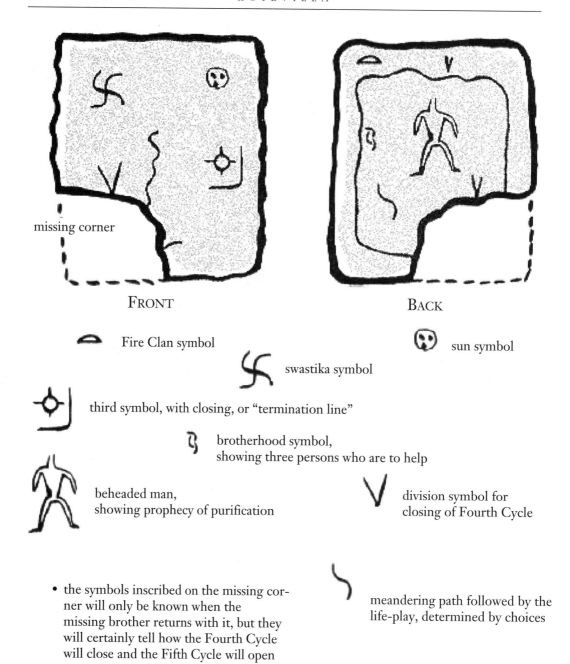

FRONT   BACK

Fire Clan symbol   sun symbol

swastika symbol

third symbol, with closing, or "termination line"

brotherhood symbol,
showing three persons who are to help

beheaded man,
showing prophecy of purification

division symbol for
closing of Fourth Cycle

• the symbols inscribed on the missing corner will only be known when the
missing brother returns with it, but they
will certainly tell how the Fourth Cycle
will close and the Fifth Cycle will open

meandering path followed by the
life-play, determined by choices

*Shown above is one of the tablets given by Maasaw at Oraibi to the Fire Clan. Dark
colored stone, it is about four inches square and tells in symbols the prophetic story that is
revealed in detail in our book. It has been told by the Hopi Traditional leaders for nearly a
thousand years.*

stand the pressure from the people who are against the tradition, the world might survive from destruction. We are at the stage where I must stand alone, free from impure elements. I must continue to lead my people on the road the Great Spirit made for us to travel. I do not disregard anyone. All who are faithful and confident in the Great Spirit's way are at liberty to follow the same road. We will meet many obstacles along the way. The peaceful way of life can be accomplished only by people with strong courage, and by the purification of all living things. Mother Earth's ills must be cured.

As we say, the Hopi are the first people created. They must cure the ills of their own bloodline so everything will become peaceful naturally, by the will of the Creator. He will cure the world. But right now Hopi is being hurt. To us this is a sign that the world is in trouble. All over the world they have been fighting, and it will get worse. Only purification of the Hopi from disruptive elements will settle the problems here on this Earth. We didn't suffer all this hardship and punishment for nothing. We live by these prophecies and teachings, and no matter what happens, we will not buckle down under any pressure from anybody.

We know certain people are commissioned to bring about the Purification. It is the Universal Plan from the beginning of creation, and we are looking up to them to bring purification to us. It is in the rock writings throughout the world, on different continents. We will come together if people all over the world know about it. So we urge you to spread this word around so people will know about it, and the appointed ones will hurry up with their task to purify the Hopi and get rid of those who are hindering our way of life. I have spoken. I wish this message to travel to all corners of this land and across the great waters, where people of understanding may consider these words of wisdom and knowledge. This I want. For people may have different opinions about some things, but because of the nature of the beliefs upon which this Hopi life is based, I expect that at least one will agree, maybe even two. If three agree it will be worth manyfold.

THE FORCES OF PURIFICATION

We have teachings and prophecies informing us that we must be alert for the signs and omens which will come about to give us courage and strength to stand on our beliefs. Blood will flow! Our hair and our clothing will be scattered upon the earth. Nature will speak to us with its mighty breath of wind. There will be earthquakes and floods causing great disasters, changes in the seasons and in the weather, disappearance of wildlife, and famine in different forms. There will be gradual corruption and confusion among the leaders and the people all over the world, and wars will come about like powerful winds. All of this has been planned from the beginning of creation.

We will have three people standing behind us, ready to fulfill our prophecies when we get into hopeless difficulties: the Meha Symbol (which refers to a plant that has a long root, milky sap, grows back when cut off, and has a flower shaped like a swastika, symbolizing the four great forces of nature in motion), the Sun Symbol, and the Red Symbol. Bahanna's intrusion into the Hopi way of life will set the Meha Symbol in motion, so that certain people will work for the four great forces of nature (the four directions, the controlling forces, the original force) which will rock the world into war. When this happens we will know that our prophecies are coming true. We will gather strength and stand firm.

This great movement will fall, but because its subsistence is milk, and because it is controlled by the four forces of nature, it will rise again to put the world in motion, creating another war, in which both the Meha and the Sun Symbol will be at work. Then it will rest in order to rise a third time. Our prophecy foretells that the third event will be the decisive one. Our road plan foretells the outcome.

This sacred writing speaks the word of the Great Spirit. It could mean the mysterious life seed: with two principles of tomorrow, indicating one, inside of which is two. The third and last, which will it bring forth, purification or destruction?

This third event will depend upon the Red Symbol, which will take command, setting the four forces of nature (Meha) in motion for the benefit of the Sun. When he sets these forces in motion the whole world will shake and turn red and turn against the people who are hindering the Hopi cultural life. To all these people Purification Day will come. Humble people will run to him in search of a new world, and the equality that has been denied them. He will come unmercifully. His people will cover the Earth like red ants. We must not go outside to watch. We must stay in our houses. He will come and gather the wicked people who are hindering the red people who were here first. He will be looking for someone whom he will recognize by his way of life, or by his head (the special Hopi haircut), or by the shape of his village and his dwellings. He is the only one who will purify us.

The Purifier, commanded by the Red Symbol, with the help of the Sun and the Meha, will weed out the wicked who have *disturbed the way of life of the Hopi, the true way of life on Earth. The wicked will be beheaded and will speak no more. This will be the Purification for all righteous people, the Earth, and all living things on the Earth. The ills of the Earth will be cured. Mother Earth will bloom again and all people will unite into peace and harmony for a long time to come. But if this does not materialize,*

the Hopi traditional identity will vanish due to pressure from Bahanna. Through the whiteman's influence, his religions, and the disappearance of our sacred land, the Hopi will be doomed. This is the Universal Plan, speaking through the Great Spirit since the dawn of time.

With this in mind, I as a Hopi do not make wars against any country, because if I do, the Purifier will find out and punish me for fighting. And since I am a Hopi, I am not sending my children across the ocean to fight. If they want to that's up to them, but they will no longer be Hopi if they do! Since I am Sun Clan, and the Sun is the father of all living things, I love my children. If they realize what I am talking about they must help me save this world.

The Hopi have been placed on this side of the Earth to take care of the land through their ceremonial duties, just as other races of people have been placed elsewhere around the Earth to take care of her in their own ways. Together we hold the world in balance, revolving properly. If the Hopi nation vanishes the *motion of the Earth will become eccentric, the water will swallow the land, and the people will perish. Only a brother and a sister may be left to start new life.*

I am forever looking and praying eastward to the rising sun for my true white brother to come and purify the Hopi. My father, Yukiuma, used to tell me that I would be the one to take over as leader at this time, because I belong to the Sun Clan, the father of

all the people on the Earth. I was told that I must not give in, because I am the first. The Sun is the father of all living things from the first creation. And if I am gone, the Sun Clan, then there will be no living thing left on the Earth. So I have stood fast. I hope you will understand what I am trying to tell you.

I am the Sun, the father. With my warmth all things are created. You Hopi are my children, and I am very concerned about you. I hold you to shield you from harm, but my heart is sad to see you leaving my protecting arms and destroying yourselves. From the breast of your mother, the Earth, you realize your nourishment, but She is too dangerously ill to give you pure food. What will it be? Will you lift your father's heart? Will you cure your mother's ills? Or will you forsake us and leave us with sadness to be weathered away? I don't want this world to be destroyed. If this world is saved, you all will be saved, and whoever has stood fast will complete this plan with us, so that we will all be happy in the Peaceful Way.

*People everywhere must give Hopi their most serious consid-
eration, our prophecies, our teachings, and our ceremonial duties,
for if Hopi fails, it will trigger the destruction of the world and all
mankind. I have spoken through the mouth of the Creator. May
the Great Spirit guide you on the right path."*

TI— *"When a Hopi is ordained into the higher religious order, the Earth and
all living things are placed upon his hands. He becomes a father to all. He is entitled to
advise and correct his children in whatever way he can. Together with the other religious leaders they decide the destiny of their children."*

Koyannisqatsi — An Awesome Power
of Temptation, Charming and Luring

TI— "At this time we will respond to the people who have asked us what our
opinions, views and interpretations are concerning the film entitled, *Koyannisqatsi*.

First, let us define briefly the word *Koyannisqatsi*. Warnings about it are
included in our prophecies. It can be expressed in many ways. It is a power of
temptation, a charm used to induce, almost without their knowing it, a change in
life from the old ways to new ways. It is a way of charming people into seeking
power and wealth without regard to the means they use to get it. Of charming
people into believing an Army and weapons will make peace. Or charming people
into immorality — into performing sex that opposes the natural laws. *Koyannisqatsi*
can be charming people into believing that there is nothing wrong in abusing the
earth and the universe. You name it, for you are living in the midst of *Koyannisqatsi*.

Our opinion is that, since each of us understands through a different level of
experience and knowledge, not everyone will be able to absorb the meaning. Since
the *Koyannisqatsi* film is based entirely on Hopi prophecy, understanding will be
difficult for those who are unfamiliar with, or have only a limited knowledge of,
Hopi prophecy. Nevertheless, the film is good and inspiring because it's intent is
to make people aware of the ways we live today, and to be cautious about our ways
of behavior.

We look at the film from a spiritual point of view, as if it were speaking
through the mouth of the Creator and his Assistants, reminding us of our past history and the mistakes we made in our past worlds. It reminds us that through our
cleverness we have destroyed our good ways of life and the land. The Creator and
his Assistants pity the human race because we have not learned from our past history and are gradually drifting back toward doomsday. They have watched our
activities and seen that we are living extremely fast and exciting lives, that we are
living in confusing and dangerous days with weapons of death and destruction
spotted everywhere over the face of the earth in the foolish belief that this would
bring peace to the world.

They see in our hearts our desire to fulfill a great plan. The plan is like a
drama or play. As they perceive us, the people of all nations will be the actors or

players. We will be positioned and readied so that the drama is in order before one of the nations will signal for the curtain to rise. This will be our world's last act. That is, unless we wake up and set our course away from *Koyannisqatsi*.

Herein we attempt to interpret the meaning of what came to us through the vision focused on by the film *Koyannisqatsi*. This will also give you some insight into our traditional religious views and teachings, for we saw what we already know. Its intent is to, through the mouth of our Great Creator, tell the audience of our past and of today's world.

Here He speaks, 'My dear children, I am the Creator and your Father. Beside Me are My Assistants; with their blessings you are what you are today. We are among you always in spirit and are watching over you. We saw in your hearts a great ambition. We appear here to warn you once more. We see you straying away from the Original Path which we gave you to follow. Your minds and actions are gradually drifting into folly, and you must find a way back to the Original Path. You have journeyed afar to all parts of the land, and have explored the unique features of the landscapes. You were inspired by the natural beauty of the scenery. You looked upon it with pleasure. You were awed by how attractive and beautiful it is. You gave whispers of thanks to the Maker, so others who come after you will share the scenic landscape with joy and happiness. Sadly, My children, you did not understand from your experience what I wanted you to. These unique formations were not created for your pleasure. They are there for a particular purpose. They are reminders of the past, of the wrong past deeds of mankind. They are the symbols of penalties and punishments received. What you see and understand in them is up to you. If you have received this message correctly and revise and remove the faults you created, we will give you extra time to make things right. Otherwise there will be no more time. We saw the conflict of Nations against Nations, of evil people fighting against those who saw and warned about the fast-approaching consequences. We saw the mystic fog covering the planet. We see today the world leaders whose tongues deceive you into following them, and into believing that they will bring peace with weapons and mighty armies. You are abusing the earth with your powerful tools. You are abusing the natural order of the soil for your own profit. You have in many ways violated the earth. Above all, the powerful weapons that are in your hands will doom the earth into becoming a likeness of the moon. Remember that we too have weapons of a kind that no man on earth can tame. We leave you now to the hour of your decision and judgment.'

To some people the above words may seem childish and have at best a thread of truth, so that it will be difficult to believe them. Even though this story about charming may give you a creepy feeling, it would be foolish to reject its words and good advice out of hand."

Universal Laws: Self-Sufficiency, Spirituality, Temptation

TI— "Let us take a look into the future through the eyes of our prophets. They say that a time will come when the industrialized world will have immense problems. Throughout the world, people will be uncomfortable because of the changing times. They will be deeply concerned about the woes people will be going through. To stay alive, they will have to make big adjustments to fit themselves into new life styles and environments.

The industrialized nations will become careless about the way they get the resources they need out of the earth — oil, coal, etc. Believing all these things will last forever, they will not use good sense about the way they do this. Natural resources will soon be depleted. Fuel shortages will occur, industrial machinery will come to a standstill. The machinery used for planting, harvesting and transport will become useless. Supermarket shelves will become empty of farm produce. The farmers and those who grow their own food will not sell their produce. They will keep it for themselves. Money will become worthless. With all his intelligence and technology the white man (Bahanna) will not be able to repair the damage.

Now let us pursue more of Grandpa's logical knowledge. He says there are higher laws than mankind makes for himself — the spiritual and universal laws which apply to everything in the universe, to all the people and to the world. One of these laws is the law of self-sufficiency. We must try to take care of as much of our own needs as possible, so that when here and in other countries other people have problems their troubles will not affect us so much.

Most of the Hopi are still working their fields and are not so far removed from their traditions. We must understand that these higher principles have sustained the Hopi through centuries. Since they do not change, they are still as good today as they were in the past. We think our position is much better than that of people in the cities when it comes to surviving a critical shortage of food and obtaining the necessities of life. We have land, we understand our land, and we know how to use it and the crops we know how to grow. We have fuel for cooking and for keeping warm.

At one time the Government tried to move us from these mesas. Our elders refused, saying 'We were put here spiritually to protect the land. The land is dry, but we get enough water from the springs to drink and cook. We pray through our ceremonials to get the water from the cloud spirits we need to grow our crops.'

Grandpa knows there is another principle in universal law. The key to this is spirituality. If one learns how to use this key, no one can prevent him from making it work.

We see the world worrying about what civilization has done. Today our land is being threatened by developers. But since we come from a spiritually devoted people and have the key, spiritual power will help us survive — just as it did our ancestors for thousands of years.

Yes, the money system is one way of self-sufficiency, but it is not stable and can break down at any time. Even we Hopi are forgetting what we receive from the earth. But as long as we don't forget to apply them, the higher system of principles about self-sufficiency and spirituality remains strong, and will continue to work and provide for us.

At one time, in order to live wisely the Hopi learned wisdom, knowledge, and prophecy through their elders. It is a pity that in these changing times the Progressives hear no more, see no more, nor do they understand. Yet these wise teachings remain the key to happiness and health.

There is another high universal spiritual law. The principle of this law is Temptation. It teaches that we must not be tempted into anything that will harm our way of life. So that we can maintain lasting peace and happiness, we must not be tempted into anything which will get us into trouble and produce problems. We are taught that temptation is evil, but desire is strong within us and is hard to control, so temptation will weaken us as we Hopi pass into the world of foreign ideas.

It was foretold that we will be introduced to many new things that will have many new advantages, but we must be cautious and accept only the least harmful of these things. Most importantly, we must not involve ourselves with foreign law systems, for they will destroy us. It was foretold that when we reach this period of time we must choose which path to travel: either the Bahanna way or the Hopi way.

If along our path we get careless and forget the vows we made to the Great Spirit and the spiritual laws He gave us when He permitted us to live on this land, it will be the sign that we have forsaken Him. So still to this day Hotevilla Village has continued to stand firm under the spiritual laws and is very cautious in accepting foreign ideas. Therefore Hotevilla is a unique village, and different from other Hopi villages… knowing that once we are lured by temptation into the Bahanna system it would be the end of the last true Hopi Village in Hopi Land.

Our ancients teach us that the law of Temptation is dangerous, that it can destroy. They learned this by their experiences as they passed through previous worlds where each world was destroyed by temptation. We believe that it is this law which is producing the worst of the troubles and unrest throughout the world today.

Here are some of the insights we have been given into two universal laws: that of Self-Sufficiency and of Temptation.

The teaching is that there are actually two Great Spirit Maasaws — a poor one and a wealthy one. The poor Massau lives in simple and humble ways. He travels the good path and teaches good ways of life. He only has a planting stick and the seeds for making his living. He is the caretaker of the land. When we destroyed our last world by our own corruption he permitted us to live on this land with him and to use the land for all our needs. And he protected the land from harm. We made a commitment to obey his laws. We asked him to be our leader. He refused, and said we still had great ambitions in our hearts, that not until we fulfilled the journey ahead to good or bad, would he be our leader. For he is the first, and shall be the last.

The wealthy Massau lives in carelessly evil ways. He is crafty and wicked. He is boastful and knows how to use his influence to sway people to his ways. He can destroy, and he teaches only hate. We must always be aware of his intentions.

We believe that in Bahanna terms the meaning of this knowledge and wisdom is that one Massau signifies moral law and the other signifies material law.

Perhaps few outsiders will accept what we say. The sad fact is that in this period of time not only Hopi, but people throughout the world, are forsaking the teachings of poor Massau and his laws for better things. They could be choosing doomsday by following the wealthy Massau. We are hopeful there may be one or two who still believe and are standing firm behind the poor Massau, the Great Spirit.

As we look on, many things have begun to happen and they change rapidly. Through the changed behavior and attitudes of mankind the world over, old-fashioned ideas are being tossed by the wayside as new generations go marching into the future armed with their technological know-how. We admit it creates many advantages, but on the other hand it has a chilling effect on our way of life. At this stage our life style and food is no longer the same as it was in years past. Farms have declined. Many of our religious ceremonials have vanished. And what is left is rapidly losing its value and power as old religious leaders pass on. Now, you tell us, what can be done to save the last remnants of devoted Hopi?

We trust those with open minds will understand that this means our good ways of life are near the end, and that our future children will not be able to enjoy them.

It seems to us that for those who are left who sincerely want to preserve what culture and tradition remains, the wise thing to do is to stand firm on what our wise elders teach and be aware of the elements that are out there to do us harm.

There is an entire philosophy of life behind this firmness. If people everywhere had respected the doctrines and philosophy laid out by our Great Creator, its wisdom would still exist today. Sadly, though, it seems that world leaders have ignored this great knowledge by which they were supposed to lead their people. Now it is time for each of us to consider which way of life is best.

As we all know, many things have come to pass in this era. We can say it is part of the cycle of life that has existed since the beginning of time. From then until now we have carried with us, planted, nourished, and harvested the seeds of crisis we must struggle and contend with throughout our lifetimes. The present crises in world events is an unfolding of a life cycle which we set in motion long ago through our own behavior. It has caused an imbalance which will bring to us many more and worse problems. We have learned now that once populations reach great numbers and become highly civilized, they become burdens upon each other. This creates disharmony, power struggles, conflicts, and wars.

When war started in the Persian Gulf, outsiders asked us what our views and feelings were about the war… what we think. They wanted to know whether we thought it related in some way to our prophecies. Our answer probably disappointed and mystified some of them, for it was that Hopi are supposed to be modest. He must not be boastful in what he says, for it might be deceiving. We do not have the answers to everything. Nor should a Hopi boast of the personal capacity he may hold among his people. For a good Hopi, humility is important. What he thinks personally about major issues is a private thing. But he can talk freely about what he has learned from his wise elders, about the ancient wisdom and knowledge, about the prophecies and spiritual instructions of our Great Spirit, Creator and Massau, and also about what he has learned from present or past oppressive problems which present truths that need to be heard. We also do not take sides in any war because we are peaceful people. We know that for ages men have always fought among themselves, and have accomplished nothing which benefits common people. In war, only the wealthy gain advantage and get richer. Fighting only brings destruction, sorrow, and increasing problems to the multitude of common people — no matter who wins the war. We have also been taught that those who are not given opportunities will sooner or later revolt and seek to gain attention, so that they will get their share and be like any people who are able to get it without revolting.

There is a Hopi prophecy which could easily come to pass that is related to the Biblical version of 'Armageddon.' It says that the time will come when common people will become concerned and frustrated because they no longer can cope with their hectic world. They will be particularly against bloodthirsty policies and the deceitfulness of world leaders. The unrest will become worldwide as people foresee that any possibility of living in peace has become hopeless. They will realize that their leaders have failed in accomplishing peace. Then the world over ordinary people will band together to fight for world peace. People in high places will be hunted down like animals — perhaps through terrorism. In turn, leaders will retaliate and begin hunting each other. This sickness will gather strength and spread far and wide. It will get out of control the world over. Revolution could erupt in our own land here in North America.

The liberators will come from the west with great force. They will drop down from the sky like rain. They will have no mercy. We must not get on the housetops to watch. They will shake us by our ears — like children who have been bad. This will be the final and decisive battle between good and evil. It will cleanse the hearts of people, and restore our mother earth from illness. The wicked will be gotten rid of.

Our prophecies even say a peaceful new world order will be drawn up in Hopi Land, that the people will live under one God and leader, that we will speak one language, the Hopi, and that the earth will bloom again.

But another side is also related. If what we have just described fails to materialize, our Great Creator will act through nature to do the task according to their plans. This could mean total destruction in any form. Only a brother and a sister will survive to begin a new way of life.

Since this prophecy is so frightening, it is perhaps of no value to most people. They will refuse to accept that it could happen — but we can wait and see whether or not it will become true. Ancient history teaches us that many mighty empires that people thought would last forever have fallen. The great Roman Empire is only one of these. When we decide how we should respond to our prophecies, we should not forget the lessons of the past."

The Warnings

TI— "With the arrival of Bahanna (white race) the old natural order of our Great Creator began to diminish rapidly. Not only in Hopi Land, it extended to all parts of the world. We all are to be blamed, for we are abusing our Mother Earth by our mindless actions and by our irresistible urge to better our way through our own inventive thinking. We have forsaken the warnings of our ancient fathers, gradually leading ourselves to ruin. We all should hang our heads in shame. What we say will pain most people, but we hope it will help them to understand themselves and reverse their ways toward better behavior for the good of lesser man and for the survival of our world for coming generations.

But first allow us to speak of our honorable fathers, the Ancient Ones, who have passed on and whom we have not forgotten. We continue to this day to honor them through our religious duties. It will be up to our readers to decide whether or not our claim of the ancient words is assured. However, we have faith and trust that these words are true. We have learned and believe that one cannot communicate with Nature unless your existence and behavior are in harmony with the will of the Great Spirit, that he who knows his part will also find his way in the future.

Long, long ago, before Bahanna appeared on this land, our Ancient Fathers were the masters of all spiritual knowledge because they dedicated their lives to the laws of our Great Spirit, and our Great Creator. Every part of their bodies and minds was filled with wisdom and truth. They knew and understood the balance of Earth and Nature and Life. They could see into the hearts of men and into the future of mankind. They knew the function of the earthly body and the heavenly body, of the forces controlling the relationship to Life and Nature. They knew man's actions are powerful, so powerful that it decides the future of man and earth, whether the great cycle of Nature will bring forth prosperity or disaster. So for thousands of years we have lived peaceful lives accordingly, avoiding those things which will destroy our good ways of life.

Yes, our Ancient Fathers were masters of all spiritual knowledge and judgement, for they were ordained by the breath of our Great Creator, commissioned to bring forth the great orders and teachings in the name of the One superior of all, He from whom the prophecies and instructions were handed down to us as a guideline to live by on earth.

So it was predicted by the prophets that one day we would encounter the presence of people of other races with ways different from our own. That they will erect their own kingdom upon our land. They will pose as good hearted. Their words will be charming and they will multiply like ants. We must not be deceived by them for the vines of their kingdom will spread throughout the land diluting and dissolving everything that gets in its way. We must be cautious and not covet or adopt any of their ways, for if we do it will forever be a curse upon our nation.

As foretold the vines emerged and expanded West, North and South, causing sudden changes throughout the country. Tragic events developed, causing unrest throughout the land. They came among the Native people with great ambition and force, they came with the belief of themselves as a super-race. The origin of their belief escaped their minds. Their lust was only for wealth and to claim our land as their own. They used treachery, cunning, and false promises; they did cruel deeds. We see their hearts are full of hatred. They have no understanding, they rape and slaughter our women and children to amuse themselves. We see their senseless actions, the fumbling of hands, a curiosity in thinking and knowledge that seems to know nothing. They have a forked tongue, two faces, two hearts both black and white at the same time. As their way of life unfolds we need none of it — our Ancient Fathers were right in their words.

The beginning of the new age of the prophecies of tomorrow has begun to unfold before our eyes. It was said, among Bahanna the people with the Cross will appear on our land. They will be kind and helpful with good hearts. Beware, for they will be the instruments of Bahanna's kingdom who will seduce you into forsaking the laws of our Great Creator. The wicked of our people will join their flock to clear their sins, but this will be in vain.

The new government order will be established on our land, our own people with short hair will take positions in this government disguised as the ear and tongue for our Nation. They will also be the tools influenced by the Bahanna's kingdom. They will, together with the Cross, help fulfill the desire of Bahanna to take over our land by diluting and dissolving our beliefs and traditional culture. The Hopi Land will be their last target, the test of survival for the Natives of this land. If we weaken and fall, the extermination will be completed by Bahanna's kingdom.

To this day we are shadowed with deep sadness. Our attempts to communicate with the Bahanna government have failed completely. Our words of honesty and truthfulness did not move the Bahanna, it seems he looks at us as creatures of the past, so-called stupid savages, smelling creatures who don't know how to develop the land. It seems the Bahanna has no understanding, their thoughts are entangled like cobwebs where nothing grows, where only destruction grows.

The Bahanna do possess high knowledge, they construct mighty tools, they drill into our Mother Earth and move mountains. They make mighty weapons and fly into the air like birds creating fear and terror in all around them.

But we don't think they believe in their Gods, their priests, their Bible. As a whole they do not have religion. We do not need any of that. We are satisfied with the order of our Great Creator, whose light does not blind us and does not lead us into confusion. Instead His light brightens the road, so that we can absorb its great wisdom and live like humans. While the Bahanna are destroying our world by their inventions they are blinded to such an extent that they do not even know their own origin. We do not make fun of or mock the Bahanna — what we say is only a reminder of their past, the terrible damage they have done to the minds of just people on this land and other lands which can never be repaired with all their wealth. We need none of that. Perhaps there is still time for this land to live on under the laws of our Great Spirit and our Great Creator. These are the things we desire. We are very sad for our life of today. It is heading down the direction you have created for us. The tide is gathering and the high tide which sweeps us away may not be far off.

The time will come when from the earth will arise a mystic fog which will dilute the minds and hearts of all people. Their guidelines of wisdom and knowledge will falter, the Great Laws of our Creator will dissolve in the minds of people. Children will be out of control and will no longer obey the leaders; immorality and the competitive war of greed will flourish.

Few will abide by their beliefs, and their attempts to transform darkness into light will be in vain. A sudden eruption will explode within the mist of their follies; this will be within or of other lands and will creep over the earth. Then men will destroy each other savagely. The period of this age will close by the gourd of ashes which will glow brighter than the Sun. The earth will turn over four times and mankind will end up in the lowest level of darkness where they will crawl on all fours forever. Then the spirits of our Ancient Fathers will return to reclaim the land. They will mock the lowly man for he will no longer deserve or be worthy of the land. Only those who are obedient to the guidance of the Great Creator's laws will survive. If it is the will of the Creator, if the surface of the earth is totally destroyed by the willfulness of man, the true sister and brother will give a rebirth to recycle the earth and renew its life."

Warnings: Previous Worlds, Present Times, and Decisions for the Future

TI— "The way in which human history began has always been a disputed question. So it has been with the origin of the Hopi. It is a question we need not dispute, for to do so might bring confusion, knowing that other cultures are closely related to what our ancient fathers passed down to us long ago.

We believe their testimonies are clearly explained, for their knowledge and wisdom includes a description of the origin of time, a time when man made his first serious mistakes in the previous worlds. We look upon our ancient teachings as a guideline used in order to avoid a downfall resulting from our mistakes. We have learned that through our conduct we can accomplish good and bad deeds. The old ones say that we have gone through at least three world catastrophes, and each of these worlds was destroyed by the same error in man.

Suppose a catastrophe happened today or tomorrow, what would you do or say?

The story we are about to tell may only be a legendary tale, but one does not have to look very far to find that it points to real situations that exist today:

'In the past our ancient ones lived at a time when people were at a highly civilized stage — greed and corruption were at their peak of controlling the so-called "lesser grade of man." Leaders and priests were branded with a disgusting evil, it was a time when people disregarded the Great Laws. People did as they pleased, they ignored the advice of their leaders. This was a time of sorrow and frustration, for the leaders loved and cared for the people as children. They warned them of the danger and tried many times to guide them on to the right road and to get them to repent. There were many violent signs in the sky and on earth that were given by nature. These were ignored with laughter, and the people answered that these things were only noticed by lunatics who wanted to create an obstacle of fear for those seeking pleasure and wealth.

Immorality and the greed for material gain continued to flourish, disrupting life for those who wished to live in peace according to the laws of the Creator.

The Great Spirit had been watching the hearts of all humans. His warning to the people ignored, He too was frustrated, sad, and felt betrayed, for His laws and instructions had been forsaken. It hurt Him to think that His own creation had turned against Him. He called together His servants of God who controlled the Earth and Universe. "What will it be?" cried the Creator sadly. "My children on Earth have betrayed the sacred vows they made with us. They now live beyond all bounds, ignoring all advice from their leader to correct themselves and get on the rightful path."

The servants of the Creator were grieved. Their hearts filled with sorrow and compassion for the wickedness of man, but they could only acknowledge the wrongs committed by the people. "The time has come!" they said. "We will punish them and re-people the Earth with Humans of good hearts!" Then they cried and cried. The Great Judgment began, the sky darkened and the great wind began to howl. Birds and animals were first to sense the full truth of the danger. All of these creatures fled in a desperate search of refuge — to the mountains and even to the cities. The people laughed in wonder at the strange behavior of the animals. But the earth and sky grew darker, the wind grew stronger, and the god of lightning lit up the sky, sounding a loud thunder call. The twin warrior gods at each of the Earth's axis released the great water serpents, and cracked the Earth releasing the fires beneath the crust. Lightning, thunder, wind and hail struck the people, and in awe they watched their stone houses and great temples crumble, falling on top of them. People panicked and ran through the ruined streets. Some of them ran to the priests, begging, "Oh, great ones — please help us and save us, we will reform!"

"We have warned you many times," the priests replied loudly, "Nothing can be done now, the time has come for you to depart, but all of you deserve one last pleasure: take your riches and your wealth that you wanted so much with you and go down!"

The scenes of this catastrophe were filled with frightening terror. The streets were strewn with ruins and the corpses of people who were killed by falling debris or fear. Yet it was still not over. Nature opened up with its worst fury, and in its wake the Earth swallowed everything.

Finally, the catastrophe ended. The Creator's warnings had been fulfilled, and Spider-Woman, god of Wisdom and Knowledge, had withdrawn all of her power. Those still alive had lost all of their reasoning abilities, and senselessly crept on all fours over hills and valleys. Some of them stumbled into cracks in the earth. Though physically still alive, their spirits were dead. They attacked each other and ate each other like animals. After many moons the water cooled and reseeded the Earth. The brightness returned and the Earth was re-peopled with righteous ones who had been saved for the purpose of carrying on the Creator's plan.'

This story is a glimpse into what happened in the past as the three previous layers of the wheel came to an end. As for the future, what do you think? Could it happen again? Do you want to be scourged from the Earth in the same way as our ancient ones? We hope not, but we have now entered the beginning of that very time period we have just described… maybe there is still a way of correcting our faults and avoiding this. No, not maybe, there must be a way!!!"

Warnings — The Time Will Come to Pass…

TI— "We were warned by the prophets of old that the time will come to pass when the minds of men will become deluded and the words of the wise will be ignored. When the influence planted by foreign sources has taken hold, then the spirit within the Native People of this land will wane, perhaps even be destroyed.

The Hopi will be the last target of the foreigners because the traditional ways embody a high level of knowledge and strong ability to resist. In the effort to accomplish his ends, the Bahanna will use many tactics. As time passes, we see more and more proof of this. And, there are increasing signs within the Hopi Nation that the oppressors are succeeding.

Yes, the Hopi have come a long way — through one obstacle after another — and many of the ancient prophecies have already come to pass. At this time the Hopi live in two worlds, our traditional one and that of the Bahannas. We are now at the point where each of us has to make his own decision as to which of these two worlds we will choose.

Our ancestors were right in predicting that dances and music that are not our own will, in this period of time, soon drown out the traditional teaching and knowledge of the Hopi. Our long tradition and customs of dress, our appearance, hairstyles, our traditional sports for children and adults, many things uniquely Hopi, will disappear. Most of our ceremonials will end.

In order to keep our village stable we must keep our thoughts on a spiritual level. This level becomes the most important base for our village to stand on. We must not forsake the laws and instructions of the Great Spirit, the Creator, from whom we received our teachings, and to whom we vowed to live according to them.

It has been said that if even only one or two stand firm it will accomplish the good result needed for the survival of all land and life. If we continue to weaken and fall under the mounting oppression of the Bahanna, as we did when we allowed our land to be cut up and put in writing and sold, then any possibility of recovery of our Tradition and our land is nil. When all that is ours — all that is Hopi — is taken away and all our powers of reaching the Spirits of heaven and earth are gone, we are as good as dead. We may stomp our feet to the beat of the drum and sing ever louder when praying, but, sadly, we will not reach the Spirits, the guardian Spirits and the producers of food and rain. We will know for certain then that our identity, our spirit power, and values have gone. Though we may still walk the crowded streets of our village, we will in truth, be dead.

A question: If it is all right for the True Hopi to become extinct, is it not all right for any other group of people in the world to become extinct also? To say no, is to say that we live by the rule arguing in favor of the survival of the fittest. But is that a Christian, or any other religious teaching? Is it a civilized view? It is certainly not the teaching of the Traditional Hopi!

Now we enter the time of testing which only the Great Creator can confirm, the alignment of the planets we were so kindly informed of by the star watchers. The Hopi have expected this to happen and have been waiting. According to ceremonial tradition of following the stars, one day certain stars will come together in a row as has happened thousands of years ago. This will mark a time of purifying the land. Changing climate and many catastrophes may occur as we pass through this stage. What may happen then no one really knows.

The alignment of the planets does not have an exact time associated with it. According to legend it may happen in your lifetime, your children's, or their children's. But the predicted behavior of the people that will show itself as the time nears accurately describes the people of today. Perhaps then the moment has come to repent and pray that our earth will not be totally lost. It has been said that this event may bring about one of two things: either destruction, or the prosperity of mind and soul needed to restore the earth to its original wholesomeness. This much we do know for certain."

The Claw Symbol

TI— "Could this be the claw symbol which the elders predicted will appear one day? It is now clear that our elders' words have come true. We were told to be cautious and alert, for along the way we will meet a white race who have a way of 'misunderstanding,' who will encircle us with claws like an eagle. This race of people will bide their time, waiting until the right moment arrives. Then they will clutch us tightly together with all our land and resources, and will rule us forever. There will be no escape.

What can we say? Sadly, some of us have forgotten the guidelines for defense against such things which have been passed on to us by our elders. Our actions have become so reckless and mindless that we have adopted the system and lifestyle of the very Bahannas who have encircled us.

The people who have become involved in the HUD housing operation units are now aroused because

509

they have trouble on their hands. There are many obstacles they must now hurdle. They risk losing their homes and land because certain legal matters included in the contracts were not made clear to them when they accepted the houses built for them. There are restrictions through which their homes can be lost, and which make it possible for rich outsiders to purchase them. Their view now is that they were deceived by the housing promoters who were backed by the BIA, the Government, and the Tribal Council. They demand that those who created this problem explain their actions. We wish those who have gotten themselves caught in the claws of Bahanna good luck... perhaps they may yet find a way to release themselves."

Worries About Butter and Bread

TI— "Greetings, we are sorry this issue is delayed. The summer growing months and harvesting took most of our time. Farming is hard work, but as usual we enjoyed our days in the fields. In caring for our crops we talk and sing to them so they can grow healthy and strong. Protecting the plants is another thing entirely.

Sometimes we are frustrated with pests who often outwit us as they eat up our crops and leave us with less to eat. Somehow though, we are always fortunate enough to get meals of fresh corn and other vegetables, along with having enough left over to store away some for our winter use. We are happy about this because we want to be self-sufficient and not rely much on supermarkets and having to work for wages. Nowadays getting other necessities with hard currency is out of reach for most of the Hopi who are without jobs. So many are worried about where their butter and bread will come from. They do not know how they will make the payments on household necessities, etc. And, the unhappy thing is that these problems will stay with us, all because of the inroads made by Western Culture.

This is another thing that was foretold by our elders. They said that the days will come when we will become weary and confused by the many complexities and strain which will bedevil us in our new Bahanna lifestyle. Even worse, these problems will deepen as we become careless in progressively adopting another culture not of our own making, thus straying farther and farther away from our original path of life."

Prophecy Warnings About Relying Upon Bahanna Government

TI— "The following statement contains a prophetic warning we need to be aware of during changing times. The warning is clear, but sadly most of us ignore it because we are tempted to rely upon new ideals. Because of some know-how we have learned through education by the Western Culture, we think we are ready to compete with the outside world. We think this know-how we have come to believe in will bring us prosperity and comfort. But only time will tell how long it will actually last.

For many years the Bahanna government has been good to us. They have pampered us and taken care of all our needs... even providing services at no cost.

We thought all the good things would last forever, didn't we? But there is one Hopi village with people who had open minds, yet were cautious in accepting favors. They knew how doing this would in the end lead them to self-defeat… they knew that one day the free services would come to an end.

According to prophecy, the Bahanna government will gradually end their self-assumed responsibility to care for Native people. The government will release us from their protective arms, and, even though they have taken away our ability to do so, will want us to stand on our own feet. They will want us to be just like any other citizen in their country… want us to become civilized quickly and join the main stream of the American way of life. In this way their responsibility over Indians will end. There will be no more 'Indian Problem.' Any mistakes we make after that will be our own doing, and the Bahanna government will not be responsible for them. Their influence will, naturally, linger on to make sure we run our government the Bahanna way and not by our own traditional ways.

Knowing this would happen, that this time would come, the Traditional Hopis refused to acknowledge the proposal of the Western concept of education and all the favors the government offered. Neither did Hotevilla Village recognize the Progressive Tribal Council. Consequently, Hotevilla Village still stands firmly in the original teachings and beliefs."

Prophecy Concerning Right and Wrong

TI— "Now let us review our knowledge briefly regarding the centuries old prophecies which warned us about what would happen when in our behavior we forget the principles of right and wrong. We will see extraordinary events taking place in Nature and all over the Earth, including extraordinary things happening to mankind; because modern man ignores the wisdom of ancient cultures and religion. Modern man looks upon old wisdom and knowledge as dead and useless, and he no longer respects it.

Modern man began to center his interests in the money system, and no longer looked to Mother Earth for simple foods. His view is that ancient food is poor man's food and the ancient ways of obtaining it are not productive. According to prophecy, when this happens Mother Earth will hide the nourishment which she provides.

When all food disappears, modern man will try to correct his mistake and to avoid the conditions he has caused upon the earth through his inventions. He will search for a way to heal the wounds, but once we have reached the point of no return, this will no longer be possible.

The survival of mankind and our planet Earth is only possible through peace — only if we, the human race, are willing to change and put peace first.

We know our ancients are right about what is going to happen. Perhaps we are even now entering a new phase of life. We are watching to see if this prophecy will be fulfilled. It is interesting that we have had less snow and rain during the spring and summer growing season. The land is very dry, our crops are very poor.

Most of us planted only parts of the field, wherever we could. A number of people didn't even bother to plant. So we will be lucky to get a sack full of harvest. A pity. Of course, this has happened before, so it proves nothing. But other things are happening too. Life has changed here, and promises to change a lot more."

Two Ways, or Paths, and the Power of the Land of Ice

TI— "You will notice that our prophecies usually have 'ifs' associated with them. This is because the Creator has given us two ways or paths we can follow in regard to each event or situation, and our choice decides what the end of the path we choose will be. He has also given us the information we need to make the right choices, but knows that temptation may lead us to choose wrongly. This is because He wants us have free will, so that our choices can be freely made and not forced. We then stand with Him not because we have to, but because we want to.

Most people will view this story, which also has ifs, as just another legend or myth. However, the Hopi were instructed not to forget this prophetic knowledge about the power of the land of Ice. It is a prophecy handed down to us from generations ago, and the Hopi still believe it has a true historical basis. No doubt critics will frown on our statements and take it as just another Hopi doomsday prophecy. Does that mean we shouldn't tell it? Do we want to be guided by critics, or by the Creator and Maasaw?

We will summarize our story so it will not be too lengthy.

When the first people emerged upon this land from the underworld they were met by Massau, the Great Spirit, the Caretaker of the land and His helpers. He saw they were identical, so He divided them into groups. To each group He gave a name and a separate language. Each group also received a religion and instructions. Each group was given a special food for nourishment, and shelters of different types. Later on, clan memberships were established within each group for mutual respect and for the carry out of different tasks which they must carried out for the benefit of all life and land.

From what was to become the Hopi group Maasaw selected four clans for special duty: the Bear, Fire, Spider and Snake clans. He endowed them with magical powers of warmth, and gave them taming powers over a cold climate. They were to go on a special mission to the Land of Ice. They were instructed to melt the ice with the Magic Songs and Prayers He taught them. They were told that the ice is growing, and that sometime in the future it will mature and travel southward — or worse, will explode, bringing grave misfortune, for this had occurred before.

They began their preparations: storing food, weaving coverings, and making other things needed for travel to the Land of Ice. Finally they started out and traveled Northward for some years. It took this long because they had to stop to rest, build their houses, and prepare fields for planting — so as to have food with them always. Finally, they reached the Land of Ice. First they made shelters, for it was very cold. Then they commenced to sing their Magic Songs and smoked and prayed. The ceremonial began with the Bear Clan. The next day it was performed by the Fire Clan, then followed the day after that by the Spider Clan. The Snake Clan was last to do the ceremonial. Each of these days the ice melted to some degree, until finally when their songs ended a thickness of only about four inches was left. But they had been instructed not to repeat the ceremonial. They had done their best, and must return to continue their migration. They were warned that the ice will grow again. Should the clans with the controlling powers vanish, or stray away from the great laws of the Creator, there will be no way of stopping the ice buildup. So the time will come when we will experience late springs and early frosts, and this will be the sign of the returning Ice Age!

Bahanna scientists and researchers are themselves doing their best to inform people and the top leaders of the world about the possibility of a new ice age. They claim it is absolutely essential to take action now to — if we even can — prevent a new glacial period. Otherwise we face serious consequences. Indeed, this message is frightening. Since our prophecy is closely related to what the scientists say, we read their articles with great interest. We are also pleased that in the past several years our prophecies have also drawn much interest, and have aroused much attention from the outside world. In this regard, we do believe another Ice Age is in the making. However, we also believe the most disastrous aspects of this event can be averted if all Mankind will return to the original divine laws of the Great Creator. Then He will tell us what to do to prevent them from happening."

Things That Help Maintain Balance as Life Passes

TI— "When we are young, most of us believe that the world is full of promise. This is true, but only when we can help ourselves fulfill that promise without hindering others. As we gaze with love upon our children, we, the parents, do our best to encourage them to live the good life and to avoid the bitter fruits of the fast and reckless life — which drugs the mind. We envy and support the youth who appear to fulfill the expectations of a loving environment, returning obedience in a helpful manner to meet the needs of his or her parents around the house and fields. A young person who sticks to the job and is an eager participant in community activities is looked upon with appreciation and satisfaction by family and community members. A young person who returns the love of his or her parents is regarded highly — even by strangers — and develops a wide circle of friends — which is a priceless reward that awaits them in the future. Of course, we all have our ups and downs. Life does not go smoothly. But living a responsible life is one certain way to walk in balance in the midst of changes. As parents, we are always responsible for the well-being of our children, and our desires for them should be rooted in this responsibility. We know it is difficult to retain perfect ways in this fast-changing world, but we must never forget that the foundation of society is based on a solid parent-child relationship.

What can parents and children of the world do to help our Mother Earth regain her health? How can we stop runaway technology from destroying her and all life? Has she not provided us with days to live, work, and enjoy our lives, and nights to rest? Has

she not provided us with seasons to seed the land and harvest its fruits for our nourishment, and provided water for our growth? With her love she gives us life, hope, and dreams of happiness, the ways for all of us to love one another.

Sadly, since technology has flourished, our nights and days have become a mixture of happiness, sadness, illness, and anger. Confusion is everywhere. It blinds us so we can't see what is beyond. We call things bad one day and good the next. Negative thoughts of both love and hatred are spread near and far. While nations spout words of peace and human rights, they at the same time stockpile weapons of war. The greed for natural resources creates friction among nations. Out of this comes retaliation, and for better or for worse marriages to richer or stronger nations until death do us part. We don't know whom we should love or whom we should hate. We are like masses of life milling around or piled up in a heap, confused and frustrated, waiting with fear for what will leap unexpectedly upon us.

It was said in our Hopi prophecies that when man loses sight of the Original Purpose and begins opposing the universal laws of the Great Creator, he will experience numerous problems. To mention only a few more, there will be wars, changing climates, man-made or natural catastrophes, and finally, a moral breakdown. Our behavior has already succeeded in accomplishing all of these things, and shows no promise of ending. As we analyze the theories of several different religious sources and their prophecies, we find their facts concerning how all of this will go and will end are similar to one another and to ours. For those who tend to shun spiritual beliefs, these happenings are confirmed by scientific study. So in this everyone agrees.

In Hopi spiritual knowledge, at the time of creation the Great Creator planned for the earth to be inhabited with life, but at first it was empty and covered with water. So He created four assistant gods to help put the world in order: A God of lightning and thunder; a God of knowledge and wisdom; and the twin brothers, Poqonghoya, God of hardness; and Palongwhoya, God of sound. Together they created life and earth. With their powers they rotated the earth, whereupon the water rushed to each pole, the land appeared, and at both poles the water was solidified into ice. The twin gods were given the duty of keeping the world in proper rotation by sitting atop the water serpent and keeping the poles in a stable form of solidity. They must never release the serpent entirely, only a little now and then, in order to warn man of his recklessness and disobedience by letting natural catastrophes occur. If mankind fails to heed the Creator's wishes and goes beyond bounds, the water serpent will be released and the water will cover the earth and swallow us. That will be the end of this age as well as the beginning of a new age.

If you know them, you will be aware that a few scriptures of the Bahanna Bible say almost the same thing as the following Hopi teachings:

'By the command of the Great Creator, earth was formed and water departed from some of the land. The Great Creator has created heaven, earth and life. He inhabited the earth with life, and for this purpose He gave instructions of a life plan and laws, which only He can give. He said, "I will box your ears for acting childish, for fighting for what is not yours. I will try and refine you with much suffering and sorrows; there will be famines and pestilence and earthquakes in different places."

He said, "I have planned for the day when man forgets his purpose and goes against My laws. I have reserved the water, in the form of ice and snow, for My own use as a weapon for punishment to be applied when mankind gets out of control. This will be a Judgment Day. Mankind will no longer deserve to live on this land which I made for him. Afterward, I will regenerate the earth."

The question on the lips of many is, "What shall be the signs of the coming end of this age?" Sadly, the signs which will unfold are not pleasant to think about. The reports of scientists, geologists, and other groups say that the earth is warming up, causing higher water in the South and lower water in the North. There are reports of sinking lands and disappearing islands at the southern tip of South America and elsewhere. They think that our changing climate could be the cause of droughts in some parts of the world and floods in other parts. Cold and hot spells are occurring in new patterns, so that vegetation is being affected. Corn is now being raised much farther north in Canada. The time may come when citrus fruit can be grown there.

New insects, animals and birds are appearing in different places as old habitats disappear. Supposedly, they are in search of their own cultural environment. If only one or two things were involved there might be some explanation, but when every phase of life, sea, earth, and air is feeling the same changes there must be something happening. Scientists believe the earth is tipping southward, because the melting ice is lessening the weight at the North pole. Their report says the ice is melting alarmingly because the earth's temperature is rising degree by degree as a result of pollution, due to the billions of tons of carbon dioxide put into the earth's atmosphere from internal combustion engines and the tons of fossil coal burned for power in factories and homes. They call this the greenhouse effect which traps more heat in the earth's atmosphere, averaging from one to three degrees a year. This in turn may melt vast antarctic ice fields, raising the ocean level 170 feet or more and flooding much of the land. That is, if nothing is done to correct or control the heat buildup. Chunks of ice weighing thousands of tons which have accumulated for thousands of years will break off and slide into the sea, which would cause the ocean level to rise to new heights. Some scientists predict this may begin to happen not long from now.

But this is too slow a pace for the technologists. Dropping the powerful A-bomb would speed the melting of the ice. They say we might defeat the communists by this act of war, or vice versa, but there is no power of man which can defeat the threat of flood. When God releases the surplus water, only God can stop it.

Is there a way of preventing this catastrophic upheaval of the earth? Or will we dismiss these warnings as a hoax and continue on living as we have? This is up to us, but we should not forget that the future of our children and those to come is

also involved. We may seem to be helpless against the powerful people in high places, but there must be a way to change this.

Since our Hopi prophecies predict different kinds of tragedies to come, some will think the things we Traditional Elders have said are so contradictory as to be useless. This is only true until we remember that the Creator has put different possibilities out there, so that man's free choices will determine precisely what form the end will take, and how long it will be before it arrives. But whatever form it happens to actually assume, *the fact is that an end and a new beginning will come.* That much we know. It is certain. Absolute. It will come to pass before our very eyes. All we can do is slow down the coming and do what we can to lessen the pain of the experience. We can get ourselves and the earth ready for it, and keep the earth enough in balance to survive and begin anew.' "

The Essence of Hopi Knowledge, Wisdom, and Prophecy.
The Gourd of Ashes and the Great Day of Purification.

TI— "How can there be peace, you ask, when nowhere is there peace, not even within Hopi peaceful society? In Bahanna society, in every nation on earth, from people in high places down to the lowest cast, there is no peace. How can peace be accomplished when weapons are made to kill? How can there be peace if people hate instead of love? Perhaps the only alternative now is 'Purification.'

What will purification accomplish? We will tell you, and we also tell you again now to not lose hope."

People often write to us and ask for more information about Hopi prophecy, but it is really not that simple and would take more pages to tell than we are able to write. Besides, what we are including in our newsletters is more than enough to give the world what it needs to know and to make the important decisions and choices. Let us look briefly into Hopi knowledge and wisdom concerning the 'Gourd of Ashes' (atomic bomb?), and the instructions regarding the UN that were often told by Hopi elders. The following is condensed from late Chief Katchongva's booklet '*From the Beginning of Life to the Day of Purification.*'

The Hopi play a key role in the survival of the human race through their vital communion with the unseen forces that hold nature in balance. It is a practical alternative to the suicidal man-made system and is a fulcrum of world events. The pattern the end will follow is simple: 'The whole world will shake, turn red, and then turn against those who are hindering the Traditional Hopi.'

Eventually, prophecy says, a 'gourd full of ashes' would be invented, which if dropped from the sky would boil the oceans and burn the land — causing nothing to grow for many years. This would be the sign for a certain Hopi to warn the world that the third and final event would follow soon after this. It could bring an end to all life — unless people correct themselves and their leaders in time to prevent this.

Hopi leaders now believe the first two events were the first and second world wars and the 'gourd full of ashes,' in one regard at least, is the atomic bomb. After the bombing of Hiroshima and Nagasaki, teachings formerly kept secret were compared and released to the world. The details presented here are part of those teachings:

The final stage, called '**The Great Day of Purification**,' has been described as a 'Mystery Egg' in which the forces of the swastika and the Sun, plus a third force symbolized by the color 'red,' culminate either in total rebirth or total annihilation. We don't know which of these it will be. But we do know that the choice is mankind's, and that war and natural catastrophe may be involved. The degree of violence will be determined by the degree of inequity caused among the peoples of the world, and by the balance of nature that is preserved. In this crisis, rich and poor will be forced to struggle as equals in order to survive.

That this event will be very violent is today almost taken for granted among Traditional Hopi, but man still may lessen the violence by correcting his treatment of nature and fellow man. Also, ancient spiritually-based communities, such as the Hopi, must be preserved and not forced to abandon their wise way of life and the natural resources they have vowed to protect.

The man-made system now destroying the Hopi is deeply involved in similar violations throughout the world. The devastating reversal predicted in the prophecies is part of the natural order. If those who thrive from that system — its money and its laws — can manage to stop destroying the Hopi, then many may be able to survive the Day of Purification and enter a new age of peace. But if no one is left to continue the Hopi way, then the hope for such an age is in vain.

The forces we must face are formidable, but the only alternative is annihilation. Still, the man-made system cannot be corrected by any means that requires one's will to be forced upon another, for that is the source of the problem. If people are to correct themselves and their leaders, the gulf between the two must disappear. To accomplish this, one can only rely on the energy of truth itself.

This approach, which is the foundation of the Hopi way of life, is the greatest challenge a mortal can face. Few are likely to accept it. But once peace is established on this basis, and our original way of life is allowed to flourish, we will be able to use our inventive capacity wisely, to encourage rather than to threaten life, to benefit everyone rather than to give advantage to a few at the expense of others. Then our concern for all living things will far surpass personal concerns, and it will bring greater happiness than could formerly be realized. Then all things will enjoy lasting harmony."

A Brief Insight Into Coil Basket Design

TI— "We have a coil basket symbolizing the road of life. It is called 'Boo-da,' meaning some great test which we will experience during our journey.

Hopi tradition says we started our travel from the center or beginning of life, and at a time when life was perfect. But soon we began to face new obstacles. Small groups of ambitious men wanted to leave the original path. There were only small groups of these at first, but as time passed they increased to great numbers. Those who wanted to maintain their original ways became fewer and fewer. Through the conflicts resulting from the new ways, mankind has lost the peace they once had with one another. So the Great Spirit, the Great Creator, has punished the people in many ways. Through all of this there has always been a small group who survived to keep the original ways of life alive. These groups are those who have adhered to the laws of the Creator. They are the ones who keep the spiritual path open, providing a way out of the circle of evil. But the movement out takes a long time, and according to our knowledge of what the prophecies say, we are not yet out of the circle.

Prophecy tells us that at the very end the number of men with ambitious minds will decrease, while the people of good hearts, those who live in harmony with the earth, will increase until the earth is at last rid of evil. If the Hopi are right, this will be accomplished and the earth will bloom again. The spiritual door remains open. Why not join the righteous people who are moving toward it?"

The Crisis of Today Seems to Be Moving Faster

TI— "Time seems to be moving faster in Hopi Land and elsewhere. Sometimes we feel that we are keeping up with it, then other times that we are not. Often, the thing that happens may look positive, like it would benefit man in his quest for freedom and hope. Then suddenly the same thing becomes negative, and there is darkness and no hope. We are talking now about the future of people and the earth. We can only say this: maybe this is a part of the cultural revolution that will go away if the global society becomes stable.

Perhaps most people frown on Hopi because of their doomsday prophecies. We understand this. The prophecies are not all happy things... such as the one dealing with the time when the first gourd of ashes (Atomic Bomb) was dropped on Japan, killing many innocent people in a few seconds. The Hopi had knowledge that this would happen someday, so we were not much surprised when it came about. Rather, Hopi took it as a sign that things were getting out of hand. As we were instructed to do, Hopi promptly warned the world that this powerful weapon must not advance further. If it did, mankind and all other life on earth would face disastrous consequences. Sadly, no one else heeds the warning, so we keep marching on thinking of our faithfulness as our personal defence measure, of our way of surviving. Do you think people would rather not know about these things, and not have to think about being caught unprepared when something terrible happens? Why wouldn't they rather do what Maasaw says they should, and stop it before it happens?"

The Matter of Helping Us

TI— "Greetings, with much regret we delayed this issue. There were a number of things which needed our attention. In addition to working our fields and attending to the ceremonials there were also political matters.

We again remind you we always appreciate your support and encouragement when our future looks gloomy. Often concerned people write or ask how they can help in preserving our culture and tradition. We do need help, of course, but there is no easy answer. Through our experiences over the years we have tried to make the Bahanna Government understand why we want to keep our culture and tradition alive. We reject all their proposals to help us by their own ways because Hopi know this is how they take control over our life and land.

To help, we usually suggest putting political pressure on the Hopi Progressive Tribal Council and the Government. As we know, this course has been taken a number of times and always came to a standstill. In other words, each time we have gotten support it has come to a stop. We understand why, but we continue to ask for it because we realize that the political pressure from our supporters has been having some effect. Some of the programs of the opposition have failed to materialize, and to this day we can still say we are alive as the last remaining village preserving Hopi culture and tradition.

And Now, With Regret...

TI—*"We regret to inform our readers that this is our final issue. The editor wishes to retire and rest due to age and handicaps of hearing and eyesight, in addition to a number of other things such as increased mailing and printing costs, etc. He wishes to devote his time to farming.*

This does not mean we give up resisting in order to continue to live our own way of life. We remnants of the devoted Hopi will continue to have faith in our all-powerful Creator, for from Him we receive our guiding thoughts in our efforts to maintain and restore harmony among all life and land. We will pray for success for the purpose we set out to accomplish on this earth. For years we Traditional Hopi have been actively informing the world's people of our plight in trying to survive, and based on our prophecies informing them of the future fate of mankind. Up to this time there has been no positive action, no response from people in high places. They heed us not, so nations the world over are in trouble. By their cleverness they have become involved in a world of their own design, believing a new design planned by world leaders would bring a peaceful world order, for everlasting peace.

For ages there have been wars and fighting because of corruption and greed among the nations extending down to common societies. In reality, we learn that wars have never accomplished any peace. We also have learned that land fights and domestic problems can be resolved by strength, for whoever has the meanest, loudest voice and the most muscle or financial resources will claim disputed property as their own. We can sit on our claims and fend off challengers, but no matter who says 'stop that,' they, the most powerful, usually get their way in the end.

We thank all our readers for their support and interest through all these years. Most of all we want to thank Onaway Trust of England, who helped make it possible for us to reach the outside world. In remembering you, all of you will be in our hearts. So please don't forget us.

Our mailing address will be open for questions.

Thank you."

CHAPTER 11

PROPHECY AND OUR RESPONSE

THE ELDERS
Our ceremonies are deeply connected with our tradition, history, and everyday life. They are a spiritual aspect of our culture that is difficult for outsiders to understand. Each ceremony is set according to position of the sun and the moon, to keep the natural forces in balance, and all living things in harmony.

We begin the yearly cycle in early winter. We pray (at Soyal) for a favorable climate everywhere, for abundant harvests, for health and happiness, for peace among people around the world. Our daily activities support these prayers. Through the ceremonies, all our actions become rooted in prayer, and life is spiritually nourished. Each individual creates harmony for all, so we can live together in beauty and joy. Some of the ceremonies were dropped during the period of Spanish influence; others were stopped more recently, as a protection against improper use.

The following will give only a glimpse of the traditional sights and sounds of traditional Hotevilla. Some of the ceremonies described here are already gone.

We sing this song: 'Is it really going to be like this? Empty gossip everywhere! They twist the language. They misuse women. They make laws just to suit their own desires. Science and the

Cross, partners in corruption, allowing these short-haired people to plan the future. They hide behind high positions. Poor things! Oraibi, you are there for a reason. It is your duty to wake people up, bring them to their senses. Crazy with greed, they distort sacred knowledge. Confused and deluded, they chase after truth, first here, then there, like herds of sheep. Blinded by desires, they are led astray. We must awaken from this madness, or perish. Poor things! Think about who you are and what you do! Our possessions make us boastful. No one will save us from destroying ourselves. Maybe we've sold the rain and the snow. The land dry, we'll seek water from little puddles. Poor things! The land is dry. Kachinas, bring us some rain, so our crops will grow and mature, and the harvest will be abundant. It will be a joy to share our meal. The animals living nearby will be happy to have flowers and grass. How beautiful the land looks after the rain! But now it is still dry. When you go home, take our prayers with you. There on the mountain, remember us always. Visit us in the shape of clouds. Let your blessings fall as rain, as flowing streams. Then new life will sprout and the land will bloom. Great is the power of the cycle of water. When you go home, think of us always.'

TEM— All they have really wanted is to be left alone up there on their barren mesa where no one else wants to live, left alone to fulfill their pledge to Maasaw to follow his lifeway, and in so doing to keep the natural forces and the world in balance and the earth rotating properly. This would bring harmony to everyone who would listen, and as the Hopi people sank their spiritual roots a parade of wonderful things would come to pass: closeness to the Creator, peace, love, beauty, joy, warm fellowship… every good thing we can think of, and more.

For centuries now, successive generations of Hopi Traditionals have honored their pledge to do everything necessary to keep the world in balance and the earth rotating properly. But others just would not and will not leave them alone. So then, in light of this new development at Hotevilla it is pertinent to ask whether the Elders still hold in their hands the fate of the world. They certainly do, and this will not change unless there is no longer a Keeper of the Covenant left. Or, until they lose in either a spiritual or a physical way the land they must have to continue their work. Remember that everything in the lifeway — the ceremonial cycle, the shrines, the sacred springs, the planting, nourishing and harvesting, the family life — melds together with Mother Earth.

How though, will the Elders and their supporters respond to this latest and in truth most critical of all developments? Will they do anything that is different than what they are already doing — and if so, what will it be? The answers to these questions will be determined either by what has already happened, or what happens next, and there are several possibilities to consider.

In Chapter 1, we emphasized that in Hopi prophecy our life follows a course whose directions depend upon the choices we make. In this sense we are continually involved in what will happen to us and to the world. Although the drama's closing is limited to one of several possibilities, which of those it will be, and the length of time it will run before it arrives there is left in human hands. In other words, there are things we can do to gain time, and we can influence how it all comes out. What is not left to chance is the moment when the very last act, or phase, of the final decline will begin. The installation and use of utilities in Hotevilla is the starting time for that. And the "object" that was buried in Hotevilla will determine the nature of its close. Once it is disturbed the die is cast. The end will be cataclysmic. How things will go during all of this will in part be decided by choices, and the time has come to make these. For the Hopis, this is quite simple. Individuals must decide whether they will follow the Traditional way or the Progressive way. Foolish as it may seem to believe that the fate of the world will actually pivot upon utilities and a mysterious object, that is what the Elders say was told to them a thousand years ago, and what they were told to tell us. The fact that this assertion is not scientifically verifiable (although it is psychologically verifiable) is beside the point. Whether the prophecy is fulfilled is what matters. The Creator is not likely to spend more time than He already has seeking to convince us. For a hundred years He has tried through Hopi teachers to do that. He will just let the "play" work itself out now, and we must make our individual judgements according to what we think we had better do as the scenery changes.

Even though the pressures and obstacles the Traditionals face in the present and future will be greater than those faced before, they will continue to do what Maasaw told them to. So long as it is possible, the established Pattern of Life must be followed, and the natural forces and the world must be kept in whatever balance is still possible. This chapter emphasizes how the Elders and other Traditionals adhere to their Pattern of Life on a daily basis. Should they for any reason lose their land however, all bets will be off. The closing process will intensify, and will speed up dramatically in every way.

As indicated, the future will be determined by one of three "ifs."

If Hotevilla somehow survives this latest encroachment by the BIA and Tribal Council, then the pattern will remain close to what it has been. For as long as even one of the male and female Elders is physically able, he or she will continue to lead and live the ceremonial cycle and pursue their accustomed course — aided and abetted as we would expect by both male and female supporters — including the Fathers of the Kachinas who share the ceremonies with the Elders today. When the last of the Elders is gone, the supporters will carry on in the manner Dan described to me during our conversations.

"The Elders who are still living," Dan said, "are Titus, Caroline, Paul Sewemanema, and another Elder (James) who is old, handicapped, and in poor health — not well enough to participate in the Covenant work any longer." The strongest of the present non-Elders is Manuel Hoyungowa. Dan has faith in Manuel's dedication and ability, and believes that an unseen person (perhaps Maasaw) is encouraging Manuel to hold on and go forward. "He will give Manuel the strength he needs to do what must be done." Recently, Manuel told Susie he is going to do more now than he has been doing.

Dan added — and I referred to this previously — that "When the Traditionalists held on to their faith in the early missionary times, the people started coming back and there was a resurgence of traditional life and practices. This will happen again if the people hold on now."

But saying this does not avoid the problems ahead. Following on the heels of the other villages who have gone over to Bahanna ways, Hotevilla has experienced disturbing changes, and it has lost, or in some instances deliberately put away, many of its ancient ceremonial practices. Unless by some miracle their situation is reversed, the thread they are clinging to is going to break.

"No one questions," Dan explained, "others in the village about where they stand — so people don't know for certain what others believe. Each is left to follow their own path and convictions. There is no discussion about this in the kivas. After the last three Elders of the Men's Society pass on, there will be no one left who can do more than the simple ceremonies. They are not able to do the things above and beyond this. But if they will just go on doing what they can do, the Covenant will be all right. There is only one two-horn priest still alive at Hotevilla. He is James' younger brother, and is perhaps 70 or so years of age. When an aged teacher tried to initiate more members awhile back, he found the training was too much work, and he couldn't complete it. Even," Dan added, "if all of the Elders are gone, the remaining two-horn priest will go to the kiva and do the necessary prayers — whatever he is physically still able to do. When he passes, others will just know when it is time to do certain things in the ceremonial cycle, and will do them."

So when they go now, these grand sources and conveyors of precious ancient knowledge will take their knowledge with them, and it will never again be available. What an indescribable loss this will be!

Regarding the "True Law" spoken of in the Elders' summary story, which is the Law of life, or Pattern of Life, people are to live by, Dan said there is no law in the Hopi way that is similar to the White man's kind of law. In the Traditional way inaugurated by Maasaw, and which the Traditionals have followed for the last millennia, each clan has a "housekeeper" who owns the house, and then a "crier" who gets on the roof, and is the "voice" of his clan. Every clan has their own "protector" of all the houses. Each clan also has special gifts for the people — in a spiritual way — and physical jobs to do. The last to do anything like this was the Greasewood Clan (Dan's Clan) — who were the only ones who had someone who filled the role of the crier. Now that pattern is gone, and there is only a single crier who serves everyone in the village. Even he doesn't get on the roof anymore. In earlier days, the kikmongwi would be the housekeeper, and the entire village would be his house, or responsibility. When it was time to do something during the ceremonial cycle, he would notify the crier. The older people still know about these things, but sadly, they don't bother to tell the younger ones. Accustomed to following the cycle from years of practice, when the time comes for a certain ceremony to be done, they will just do it.

The ancient system was a way of quietly assigning responsibility and keeping order. "The True Law is a way of functioning, of being respectful, of doing things right." It brought about a sense of security in which everyone played a role, and it assured a constant awareness of the Creator and Maasaw, the Guardian of the Earth. The pace was relaxed, and stress was minimal. The Hopi lived in the Creator's hands, and even in death the pattern of life and contribution continued. Beyond this, they even had their pivotal role to play in the destiny of the world. That brought a special sense of contribution. Everyone thought this was a good way to live.

I asked who the kikmongwi of Hotevilla was today. "Martin," Dan replied, "was supposed to be, but the stone tablet that should have been passed on to him was taken away by Martin's own family. They have joined with the Tribal Council in fighting against the Elders. So there is no kikmongwi at Hotevilla. The Elders are the ones who really fill this position."

So as do the Elders, we too must face with sadness the fact that Hotevilla, the Shrine of the Covenant, is no longer what it once was. It is countdown time, and they are barely holding on...shadows moving purposively about in a mist of once-greater glory...warriors who still hold ready their spiritual shields and weapons...still willing to fight...but unsure of where exactly the enemy is, and how long they can actually stand against him.

This is why the old people remember with particular feeling the ancient prophecy that says, "When we get near the end, a rock will roll down a hill crying as it goes." They look when a boulder rolls down the face of a mesa to see if its surface is wet and streaked. It ought to be. The rock will have seen a lot in its lifetime, and remembering this will have much to mourn.

Is it over then? Not yet. Don't you remember? As long as there is still one left to fight, the enemies cannot claim victory. The spiritual roots are still there, and more are being sunk every day.

In the ongoing process of sinking down of spiritual roots, Dan cites the following things as necessary to its success, and while there are five of these, they interweave to become a single force:

"Daily prayers;

"work with the land every day;

"ceremony cycles;

"special prayers for land and life;"

and **"runners to the directions to get water from the San Francisco Peaks above Flagstaff."**

For Hotevilla, Manuel's clan, the Water Clan, has possession of this water. When a ceremony is going on, runners from the participating kivas go to this

Clan home to get the water they need for the ceremonies. "No one else knows where — what spring or springs exactly — the water actually comes from. And they are not told."

Even though the ceremonial cycle has suffered losses, Dan maintains that "It is accurate to say that 16 days out of every month are still devoted to the religious cycle, and approximately 200 days out of every year. Nearly all ceremonies take up 16 days. A few are shorter, lasting only a day."

When the Elders are in the kiva, the prayers are constant. When he is at home Dan's daily prayers are made silently, and weather permitting offered outside. He says a morning prayer to "Father Sun for the daily things you need to help you out." At night, his prayer is to Maasaw "To protect you through the night," which is another way of pointing out that Maasaw, despite the ferocious mask he wears, is something other than malevolent. He is more like a devoted parent.

When Dan is working with the land, as the plants are planted he prays for rain. As the plants grow, he "is out there singing up the plants — it's like a baby" to him. Often, "early in the morning, there are little waterspouts that rise up and pass over the plants dropping teardrops into the corn. They are accompanied by little rainbows." He used his hand to indicate that the height of each spout measures about thirty inches.

Dan carries with him a little pouch filled with cornmeal. During the day, whenever he takes anything he needs from Mother Earth he puts or sprinkles a pinch of cornmeal at that place as a thank offering. By this gesture he pays homage "to the Source of all life and survival."

Prayer feathers, he pointed out, are made at Soyal for all people everywhere, for those who are known personally to the Hopis, and for those who are not known. These prayer feathers are placed out in major shrines on the San Francisco Peaks, and in other holy places maintained for this purpose.

Essentially, what the Traditionalists will be doing under these new circumstances is buying time in which to reclaim and improve all of life, and calling out to the world to hear their message and respond to it in the same way.

If the utilities situation at Hotevilla goes ahead and is not corrected, and if people begin to use the utilities, then the pattern of life will be what we have already indicated in Chapter 9, with the village shriveling spiritually and with other aspects of life lagging behind the fading ceremonial cycle — but nevertheless experiencing the same thing. The Elders and other Traditionals will struggle on, doing everything they can to fulfill their responsibilities. In spite of this, the day will come when Hotevilla will be like Old Oraibi is today. This being the case, the Elders and their supporters have already intensified their ritual practices and duties, as well as their individual prayers for the well-being of the world. As a whole, things will change significantly, and for visitors Hotevilla will not be the same place that it is now. Individual differences will not be so pronounced that casual observers will notice them. Only as they accumulate will they finally become so apparent that their total effect cannot be missed.

If the "object" is destroyed, the pattern of life will be the same as that just described, except that there will be a piling-up of trials and disasters that will eventually bring about a third world war whose magnitude and catastrophic consequences will dwarf anything before it. We note that the Elders place this harrowing experience under the heading of **Purification**, and the prophecies spell out what that time of cleansing will mean for us.

In telling their story, the Elders and Katchongva frequently say their way of life is about to disappear. I asked Dan what exactly it is they are missing, and expected a long answer. Instead, I received a surprisingly succinct reply.

"There are some people turning back to Hopi," he said. "What is missing is independence of bills and growing own foods. But it's hard to tell who is who."

Having looked now at the newsletters and other statements, I am impressed by how neatly this sums up the core issues. To begin with, even though some Hopis have indicated they are returning to the faith, the Elders do not know how many they can count on. Next, the huge change from being debt-free to indebtedness alters the entire complexion of life at Hopi Land. And finally, the lost ability to grow their own foods makes them constantly vulnerable to outside interests. Resolve these three things, and the Hopi would be close to living again as they did before intrusion.

What about the Elder Brother? He will come. But it appears that if he does not come soon, Hotevilla will have changed so much that he will not recognize it — recognizing being understood in the sense that he will know what village it is — but the people will not be known to him as those who are keeping the Covenant. He will exercise, then, a degree of purification, but not the full measure of purification that will be meted out to both the Hopi and the rest of the world as the final decline narrows sharply down.

We need to look carefully at the prophecies to see what exactly they tell us about this time period. Because they were not instructed to, Dan and the others have not sought to put them into some neat and organized form. Nothing in Maasaw's teachings indicates that the True Hopis would be required to smooth out and make coherent the closing-time prophecies. Disappointed as we might be by this, we find a precedent in the Biblical accounts dealing with the day when Jesus will come again. He presents a vivid account of what it will be like, and the terrors attending it are very similar to those of Hopi prophecy. But the scriptural accounts are not so smooth that today's scholars — theologians included — are able to agree about its portents and meanings. As for dates, Jesus describes signs that will attend the final stage, but states that no one knows the final day or hour the close will come. There are indications too that the time factor is influenced by the decisions we make. So all in all the Biblical account parallels to a considerable degree Hopi prophecy. Ultimately though, what acceptance of these claims comes down to is the element of faith. We will either believe the prophecies, or we will not, and we will fill our roles in the great stage play accordingly.

To me at least, reading some of the Hopi prophecies at first seemed to be so outlandish as to lack substance, and they appeared to follow a maze of sharp turns and confusing passageways. Some even seemed to be the wishful kind of thing people would concoct as they dreamed about a time of getting even with those who have done unseeming things to them. Perhaps most prophecies are deliberately shaped like this, so as to cause us to look at them more intently and to ponder more carefully the meanings of individual words and passages. We do know that when we do this they come alive to haunt us and keep us thinking about what we might do to prevent or reshape their fulfillment.

In chapters 1 through 9, we cite the Hopi prophecies that have already been fulfilled. Most are set in italics. The Hopi prophecies that are yet to be fulfilled are given in Chapter 10. These tell how the closing of the cycle will come to pass once the utilities are functioning and/or the desecration of the "object" has occurred. It is important to understand that even if the "object" is not desecrated, the end will still come. What will change is the time factor — which will be longer in order to give us more time to do something about it, and to make the closing of the cycle less painful and catastrophic — offering especially those who are alive at the closing an opportunity to open the next and Fifth Cycle on a better footing than would otherwise be possible.

It should be clear by now that in Hopi prophecy, where the climax of the fourth cycle is concerned, using the noun "end" poses an unnecessary and an untrue problem. We ordinarily think of an end as just that — as a terminal moment after which there is no more. In neither Hopi nor Biblical prophecy is that the case. The end is simply a transition point from one cycle to the next whose manner differs according to the circumstances attending it. It can be extremely difficult, or it can be Armageddon. But in no sense is everything over. Life will be affected, but not gone. It will continue. Remember that the Hopi speak of four layers of the wheel. This means that three previous cycles have already closed. But they were also followed by the openings of new cycles — this last of which we know from personal experience has had its problems, but also been filled with blessings, joys, accomplishments and opportunities. After this time of transition, it will happen again. And, as we keep saying, WE CAN MAKE THE TRANSITION EASIER AND BETTER. Another significant fact is that where dates are concerned the Hopis talk in approximations. They do not pin down the times of actual occurrences.

Except for Biblical prophecies, which I assume anyone would expect a pastor to be interested in, I have paid little attention to prophets such as Nostradamus and Edgar Cayce. But in glancing now at what they and some others have predicted, I must admit that they compare in startling ways with the predictions of the Hopis, who, we should once more remind ourselves, could not at the time Maasaw delivered them, possibly have known anything about these other prophets — what they said, or the kinds of worlds they lived in.

Here in Los Angeles on March 1, 1994, a television program was aired on the predictions of the most notable prophets of recent history. After the January 17 earthquake, it struck a nerve, and viewer ratings were very good. The time frames for forthcoming events given by these prophets were, to say the least, intriguing. One said there will be only two more Roman Catholic popes after this one, and that the last of these will be named the same as the first pope. Seems a simple enough prognostication to pin down in the near future. Nostradamus, we were told, predicted there would be three world wars and gave dates for them. He gave closely approximate names for both Napoleon and Hitler, and said the third of the "anti-Christs" would be born in 1962 and will become known to the world in 1995. His name is "Mabus," and he will come from the Israel area, but will not be a Jew. Seemingly peace oriented at first, he will change radically and begin to do the things that will bring about in July of 1999 the great catastrophe we call Armageddon — only five years from now.

Another prophet predicts that a realignment of the planets will cause the earth to twist on its axis, and cause a great shifting of all of the countries of the world.

Edgar Cayce, born in 1877, predicted that "the poles of the earth will shift and the frigid lands will become the more tropical. The coastlines of many of the lands of the world will become part of the oceans. San Francisco will be destroyed... before New York even. Western nations will be broken up, and half of Japan will disappear into the sea."

Gordon Scallian (Sp?) had a prophetic vision in which a deluge of natural disasters covered the earth in the year 2001. The earth will become very quiet, he said, then will reverse directions while the oceans "well up." He foresaw in other visions a 7.4 earthquake in the San Bernardino, California area, the Landers quake — also in California, Hurricane Andrew, and foretells a large quake for the Riverside, California area in 1998. (This is very close to where I live.) Ridiculous, isn't it?

In their numerous visions, four European girls saw a time of terrible heat coming, when people will search desperately for water without finding it. During what was called "their night of screams," an end date was given to the girls, but they are not to release it until eight days before the event happens that sets into motion the circumstances bringing it to pass. Among the information received was the statement that "If people will change, we can hold back the time."

Well, what to make of this? I don't want to accept it any more than you do. I like happy endings. But we cannot avoid the fact that the details of these prophecies support those of the Hopi in startling ways.

The illustration below shows in graphic form what the Hopi prophecies predict for the closing of the Fourth Cycle and the opening of the Fifth Cycle. As you consider it now, I sum up for you the probabilities based upon what either has happened or will happen at Hotevilla.

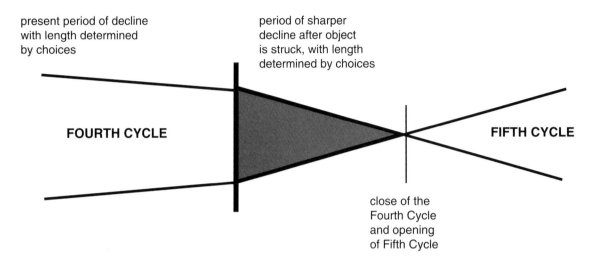

present period of decline with length determined by choices

period of sharper decline after object is struck, with length determined by choices

FOURTH CYCLE

FIFTH CYCLE

close of the Fourth Cycle and opening of Fifth Cycle

If the utilities are installed in Hotevilla and used by any of the residents, as it certainly seems will be the case, then at the moment the faucets are turned on a sharper closing down will commence for both the village and the world. The length of time from then until the transition point will vary according to the choices people make. It could be a few years or it could be many years — although the Elders' statement that "It could be in your lifetime, your children's lifetime, or in your children's children's lifetime," is no longer applicable if the "object" in Hotevilla is destroyed. Then it will happen sooner rather than later, and it will correspond to the times given in the prophecies by others just cited and the Mayan prophecies. And, the nature of what actually happens — how bad conditions will actually become on a worldwide scale — will be determined by our personal choices and actions, and by whether or not Traditional Hopis exist to carry out their Covenant duties.

Whatever does happen, once the downward spiral is under way our actions can delay the end but will not discontinue the process. The world — both its citizens and the environment — will gradually deteriorate and succumb to ever more grievous problems — until at last it reaches a point where it is no longer able to sustain itself. Those who survive the crises of this final time will be people who are loyal to the Creator. At some final point, He will enable them to begin again, to start over in a world whose condition will be similar to what it was at the beginning of this Fourth Cycle, but whose comforts are far different than those we in the western world have become accustomed to. In other words, we will have lost much of what we have gained in material ways, and our social and religious attitudes will have been cleansed of most of their undesirable aspects. Eventually, the world will be restored, and for a time at least it will "flower" again as it did before corruption and greed entered in. Come to think of it, that was a very long time ago, wasn't it?

With these exceptions, if the "object" is destroyed the just-described course will remain almost the same. The first is that the period of decline will be marked by continually occurring natural disasters of record magnitude — such as those already experienced around the world over the past two years. The problems associated with environmental demise will mount at an ever faster pace. Population will continue to increase. Food will not be available where it is needed most. Meanwhile, the internal struggles of countries will intensify, and there will be endless frictions and warfare between countries. Other social problems will flourish, as will immorality of every kind. Tensions and stress will be everywhere present. The accumulation of these things will eventually bring about a third world war, whose magnitude will dwarf any of the wars before it, and its catastrophic consequences will bring the Fourth Cycle to its ultimate finish — out of which those relative few who survive will make their painful way into the Fifth Cycle. This play will end, and a new one will begin. Interestingly, the Hopi were given no information about the Fifth Cycle, and are left to speculate about it just as we are.

There is little point in saying these things to frighten anyone. Doing this has never worked before. We include it only as evidence of prophetic fulfillment.

A few national items from the *Press Enterprise*, Riverside, CA., will stimulate our reactions:

April 13, 1994, p. A-3: Deutsche Presse Agentur —*"Think-tank study says future is now and the world is not prepared for it…*The future may be spinning out of control because of uncontrollable high technology, access to weapons of mass destruction and a breakdown of nations, especially in the developing world — according to a 600-page study, 'Global Engagement,' published by the Washington think tank, the Brookings Institution…a number of issues are coming together in a critical mass in a way that had never been anticipated. First is the explosion of technology, both militarily and in information-sharing…Soon, all technology, including military, will quickly spread around the world without constraint. This is occurring at a time when there's a rising rate of growth of the population, adding one billion people for every decade. That population growth, especially sharp in the developing world, means great stress on natural resources such as water. More importantly, if present patterns hold, it means a greater divergence between the world's rich and poor."

January 16, 1994. p. A-9: Washington —*"Food supply growth slows; group sees world at brink*…. Slowed growth in world food supplies provides real evidence that the planet's biological limits may have been reached, an environmental group says…Without radical scientific breakthroughs, large increases in crop yields that have allowed production to keep up with 40 years of rising consumption will probably not be possible…human demands are approaching the limits."

April 7, 1994, p. A-8: New York Times —*"Will we kill the planet trying to feed 12 bil-*

lion people?... Will all those people be able to provide decent lives for themselves without doing irreversible damage to the croplands, water resources, forests, fisheries and other ecological resources on which life ultimately depends?...we are in a race between need and ingenuity...but ingenuity can be blocked by a number of factors arising from a country's political and social institutions...No one can say what the carrying capacity of the earth for people may be, since it depends on unknown changes in technology and on the unknown ability of economies to substitute new resources for ones that are running out."

February 22, 1994, p. A-5: The Associated Press —*"Ecologist says world population must fall to 2 billion for prosperity*... Earth's land, water and cropland are disappearing so rapidly that the world population must be slashed to 2 billion or less by 2100 to provide prosperity for all in that year, says a study released yesterday. The alternative, if current trends continue, is a population of 12 billion to 15 billion people and an apocalyptic worldwide scene of absolute misery, poverty, disease and starvation, said the study's author, David Pimentei, an ecologist at Cornell University... If people do not intelligently control their own numbers, nature will. That we can count on... In the United States, the population would climb to 500 million and the standard of living would decline to slightly better than in present-day China... There are no more technical solutions to be found. There's no way out of it. There are just insufficient resources for these people to live like we do today. There is no technology I know of for creating more fossil fuel...land degradation will lead to a 20 percent drop in world food production during the next 25 years; world reserves of coal, oil, natural gas and uranium will be mostly depleted by 2100, and most countries are consuming ground water several times faster than it is replenished."

April 2, 1994: Deutsche Presse Agentur —*"Putting price on ecological collapse*... A continuing rise in world temperatures and toxic emissions will cause billions of dollars in damage in addition to multiplying human misery, researchers say...a bleak picture: Mass migration of the poor and bloody war between the remaining nations over depleted resources are inevitable..."

April 9, 1994, p. A-6: *"Many reasons why troubled Africa is coming unglued..."*

January 16, 1994, p.A-2: *"Death of life — among the vanishing species are the lost tribes in human history..."*

February 22, 1994, p. A-2: *"North Korea balks at nuclear inspections..."*

There is more — so much more it is wearying:

The prophecies of the Hopi describe the terrifying aspects of the final days, and as they do so we need to remember that the information was given to them at a peaceful time and place and hundreds of years before they knew anything of the world being described to them. Whenever we consider the validity of the predictions, we must not forget this, and the fact that the stories are etched in stone and there for anyone to see. Do you suppose they ever said to themselves as they pecked away at the rock surfaces, "Why are we doing this, and what is it all about?"

Consider just this: "The main thing," Dan said, "is that kids are wild and everything. If things don't go back to our peaceful way, the underground persons, the water spirits who are holding us up right now…when they get angry they might decide to separate, and then the oceans will turn over and cover the land again. If we allow this to happen, that will be the end of the people as we know it today. But we don't know how long it will be before the ocean carries us under."

Extreme perhaps, even though it has the disturbing ring of truth about it — possibly articulated like this just to get our attention. Nevertheless, every time I pass on to you these things I recoil even from the idea. It is repugnant to me. No matter how I come at it, its terrors are unacceptable. I am concerned about you, and I have loved ones who will be here to experience whatever happens. Even when I ask myself whether humanity truly deserves better, and I find myself doubting that it does, I hedge, trying to excuse my saying "yes" by concentrating upon the wonderful and decent people there are in every community. But nagging away at me at the same time are those whose manner of life and thoughts justify every bit of a bitterly painful end…Is it not fair, I muse, that a time will come when people such as these reap what they sow, even though others deserving better will pay the price with them? How do we excuse or in any wise accept the deaths of the hundreds of thousands of men, women and children who are being senselessly slaughtered in Bosnia and Africa, and in smaller but equally unacceptable numbers in dozens of other countries — even on the streets of United States communities? It would make a compelling debate, would it not, for someone to sum up the negatives and the positives of our present world, put them side by side in two columns, and then have a debate about whether or not the world deserves to survive.

It is plain in their newsletters and other statements that the Elders have thought about this too, and as you have seen in their writings they touch upon the same feelings as those I have just expressed. They beg people to change, and to make the right choices. There is still hope in the sense that we jointly control the time span and happenings from here to the end. They don't want this horrible scenario of prophecy to happen either. Therefore they, as I do, find particular joy in the prophetic announcement that the Creator will rescue those who hold fast to him and continue to serve him throughout this troubled time. As the ship sinks, He will be gathering in the lifeboats and delivering them to shore. Our hope has within it the same propensities as the "Rapture" spoken of in the Bible, and of the eventually beautiful millennial period that follows. Yet with the world wasted and ravaged, the survivors will be forced to rethink their goals, and to struggle upward until at last happiness reigns.

Can we live happily here with this information hanging over us? Yes. The Traditionalists have for the last hundred years, and we can too. And is there a way we can turn this alarming circumstance into a good thing? The solution is partly

Ryan Mails

in our hands — there already are things we are doing and can do more of that will make a substantial difference. I trust you noted we have already considered some, and will consider others further on in this chapter. They are all part of survival. But much of the answer lies with what happens to the Hopi themselves. The Elders will continue to do what Maasaw has asked them to. When they are gone, the other Traditionalists at Hotevilla and elsewhere will carry on as best they can. But the way will be extremely hazardous, and somewhere along it, when the Creator and he believe the time has come to do so, Maasaw will step in to take over and begin the Fifth Cycle.

Dan tells us what Maasaw's plans are for the final time of transition from this cycle to the next: "When the last of the Hotevilla Elders is gone, Maasaw will take back the land." Dan did not say what this means exactly, so we are left to speculate, but it seems clear that Maasaw will rule as the Fifth Cycle begins, and we certainly know what his attitude about life is. As to whether the Elders will be the last Keepers of the Covenant, or others will be carrying on the relationship at the time when Maasaw comes to do this, Dan tells us that "Up to now Maasaw is still watching over us. After the Elderly Elders are gone, Maasaw will still help others, even those who have not been initiated into the Men's Society. So when prayer feathers are made at Soyal today — and even for unbelievers — other Hopis are being encouraged through prayer to believe and to carry on. Maasaw showed himself at the founding of Hotevilla in the form of a fireball bouncing around. On occasion, He still shows himself to us this way, and late every night throughout the year He assumes the form of a fireball in the sky and circles the entire world four times, each time getting nearer to the earth. If you happen to be too close to him when he passes by, all of your energy is taken away and you black out until he is gone. He is also carrying with him his own gourd of ashes, and one day he will drop it. When he does, all fighting will cease all over the world. Enemies will just go to sleep. And when the enemy comes to Hopi, Maasaw will drop ashes on everyone, so they won't have to fight." So, while some Hopis associate the gourd of ashes of Hopi prophecy with the atom bombs that were dropped on Japan, Maasaw too has a gourd, and that in fact may prove to be the only gourd there is.

When I first learned about the association of the gourd with the bombs, I was greatly troubled by it, for it did not fit the pattern of the three signs. If the first two signs are associated with World Wars I and II, and there is a next and far greater war to come, then why would the gourd of ashes be linked to World War II, which already has its sign? It was when I raised this question that Dan told me about Maasaw's own gourd, and then indicated his agreement with me that the gourd should not be tied to the atomic bombs. I can only conclude that the linking of the bomb and gourd of ashes in the newsletter prophecies is the result of accepting the conclusions of some earlier Elder who made the association, and at the time it sounded reasonable to the others. Recall that the prophecy of the "three signs" does not itself align the signs with any definite events. It leaves that for the Hopi and us to speculate about.

"At the end," Dan concluded, "all who are of one heart, together with the Underworld people, will be safe and secure!" I have put this in the book twice now. I like the sound of it.

Susie listened to Dan for a few minutes, and translated what he said. "He says the world probably will start all over again, a whole new world, start all over again, back to the first time when it was when we all could speak the same language and love one another. He says there are four layers of the wheel. This is the fourth layer, and he said that the Hopis created the moon and the sun. Without the sun it was kind of dark, so the Hopis created the sun and the moon and the stars. Hopi people have experienced everything already — you know, like discovering, like going to the moon, but they went into the clouds, and they experienced going to the people down into the Grand Canyon, the Underworld, how they live. Now all of these elders, when they die they go home to Grand Canyon... Only big cliffs and a canyon... and life goes on forever there. If they looked for God to take them up he says, God would never put them up there, because the great eagle spirit would eat them.

Christians think they have God there in heaven, but the Hopi Underworld is not God's kingdom. There is no God there. It is not where He lives, only the young kids and other people are there. That's why, after journeying there, the Hopis and Dan even understand what's going to happen in the future... and the elderlies talk about this together. We are going through what they say is going to happen, and we're going through it right now. The True Hopi of Hotevilla are still fighting to live their old ways, so if this Tradition is not broken, then they will have the way [power] to help all Indian natives to go back to their Traditional Ways."

As a tangible example of the kind of thing Maasaw can do to curb fighting among people, Dan added that "When the soldiers of the King of Spain came to Old Oraibi, they brought along a cannon. When the leader ordered them to fire it to frighten the Hopis, Maasaw did something to keep it from firing. All they got was silence and embarrassment."

When Dan told me about Maasaw turning into a fireball, I recalled a time in the 1970s when I visited Henry Crow Dog at his home on the Rosebud Reservation. When I arrived he was in the midst of a meeting being held in his huge, rectangular living room, which had a dirt floor and no furniture. I was invited in, and sat on the floor with my back against the wall as the forty or so Sioux guests were doing. Henry sat at the end opposite me and underneath a window. He was burning

The Hemis mana and Kachina at the Home Going Dance

The magnificent costume of the Sio Hemis Kachina

Long-haired Kachina Dancers

The man called the "Hugger" accompanies The Snake Dancer, using an eagle feather fan to hold the snake's attention and keep it from biting. This does not always work.

Plaza Kachina Dancer

The Sacred Corn Meal

Female Buffalo Dancer

Plaza Kachina Dancers

Plaza Kachina Dancers

Plaza Kachina Dancers

Paliko Dancers

Maasaw Kachina Dancers

sweetgrass and chanting when suddenly through the window — without breaking it — came a fireball that was perhaps three feet in diameter. What it looked like was a burning tumbleweed. As we watched in fascination it bounced like a ball down the middle of the floor to the end where I was sitting, then back and out the window again. I don't recall feeling any heat. There was a moment's silence to acknowledge what to the Indians was a minor miracle, and which apparently was a sign Henry had requested to guide him in making some decision. Then the meeting continued. Since I did not feel it was appropriate, I neither asked for or received an explanation. It was only when I was with Fools Crow later on that I learned such things happen regularly with holy people. Do you suppose that the Sioux have their own Maasaw, called by some other name? The point is that however implausible things like this may be to the intellectual western world, they are fairly common among Native American tribes. It doesn't prove anything, but accepting such things opens the mind and allows us to be taught wonders that we would otherwise be closed to. Jesus taught that unless adults become as children we shut ourselves off from many of the things he wants to teach us. And, the Traditional Hopi, coming from their own direction that is completely independent from Christianity or any other religion, have the simple faith of a child, which has enabled them to be taught how to construct one of the most intricate and profound religions ever known.

The following is an outline of the Hopi Ceremonial Cycle, showing the individual ceremonies and the approximate times they are held.

	KACHINA CEREMONIES
Late November	Wuwuchim— initiation
December	Soyal
January	Pamurti, Night Dances
Late February	Powamu, Bean Dance, Soyoko
March	Night Dances:
	Puppet Dances
	Shalako Grinding Maidens
	Water Serpent Dance
Late Spring	Plaza Dances
July	Niman—Home Going Dance
	NON—KACHINA CEREMONIES
Summer	Snake Dance or Flute Dance
Early Fall	maturing crops:
	Women's Oaqole
	Lakone
	Mamzrau
at initiation time of Mamzrau:	Palhk Manas
	Howenai
	Butterfly Dance

We do not know how many of these ceremonies are still celebrated at the different villages. At Hotevilla, the major rituals are done, and many of the other dances too, so that the calendar is full, although the Snake and some other dances have been discontinued. But, the fact is that the ceremonies are going on, and even though they will be affected by the utilities, they will continue into the future. They are wonderful in every way, and a joy to experience as a spectator — especially when you know something about the purpose of the dance, the meanings of the colors and costumes, and the role each dance fills in the ceremonial cycle. This being the case, rather than present here a more scholarly analysis of the ceremonies, we can by good fortune turn once again to the *Techqua Ikachi* newsletters, where, as usual, the writers anticipated the need to address this, and over the course of several issues, presented readers with an insider's picture of ritual times on the mesa. They began with Issue No. 4, and entitled it **"Ritual Memories."** You will find much to think about here, and a kind of warmth that is absent from outside observers' accounts.

'Boom! Boom! Boom!' sounded a drum at dusk somewhere. 'What is that, Grandpa?' asked the excited children who gathered around the old man listening to the stories he quietly told each year at the time of *Ka-mu-ya* (December), a tradition among Hopi for both young and old. Coyote tales and stories of the past are told and retold year after year. Some of the stories are fables from which one can learn, and some are true history. Most of our readers who know about ancient traditions readily understand the purpose. 'Go outside my children,' he answered, 'and look west above our village! Perhaps the new moon has appeared.' The old man feels happy, yet a little sad that the sacred month has gone and his storytelling will end. He will miss the children. But before he dismisses the thought, he silently prays for strength that he will still be there to tell his stories to the same children and perhaps a few new ones next year. Knowing that the children will now find other things to do, he recalls the time he was their age, how he looked at Ka-mu-ya long ago. It seemed such a cold, long, and boring month. There was nothing to do. He also thought of it as a fearful month. Customs were carefully respected. Many things were not permitted such as playing ball, running, loud talking and singing, playing the drum, dancing or digging in the earth. One must be home and indoors by sundown and mark his cheeks with ashes before venturing outdoors after dark, a protection against evil spirits lurking everywhere ready to cast a spell over you.

'Why all this hocus-pocus?' one may wonder. The modern world finds it difficult to understand such practices, but in the ancient traditions throughout the world this time of the year has a special meaning. It is a time of careful preparation for the new birth. A new life may not be born normally if the mother is disturbed when brooding. The seeds of the coming year are sown during this month. Our Mother Earth must be free from disturbance to produce normally.

'So you see the moon!' confirms Grandpa. 'When will the Kachina come Grandpa?' 'What kind will come Grandpa?' another asks excitedly. 'Well,' he answers, scratching his head and looking at the anxious faces, 'it depends on the religious leaders. Before long they will gather in their kiva and make prayer feathers with their blessing and smoke tobacco. The Kachinas will come.' 'But we hear the Kachinas dancing in the kiva already,' says the smallest child. 'But what you heard could be something else,' Grandpa replies. 'Have you forgotten? This month is also for boys and girls to dance, and one of you might even take part. What you hear may be the men in the kiva rehearsing their songs... or it could be Kachinas practicing way underground and preparing food to bring to you as friends when they come.'

Yes, *Pa-my-ya* (January) is the time for Kachina ceremonies and social dances. The Kachinas are activated by the religious leaders. There will be great numbers of them in six groups from six kivas beginning at sundown and lasting into the night. Everyone will enjoy it, especially the children. Our Mother Earth is especially happy and peaceful at this time, protected from evil elements, what is in her womb will produce an abundance for all living things.

We hope we have you wondering what would take place with our excited and anxious children and our friendly Kachinas. Just as our Grandpa said, drums could be heard throughout the kivas. It has been seven months since our friends the Kachinas left to go to their underground resting place for the winter. Now familiar sounds cause much excitement among both children and grown-ups. This is also a month of togetherness, the right time not only for boys and girls but also for grown-ups to dance and have a good time. All of this activity has a special meaning and purpose.

Early one cold morning, Grandpa came home for breakfast from the kiva, where he had spent most of his time smoking and praying (which is not heeded today, and accordingly much damage has been done).

One of our little children took part in the Buffalo Dance from her Uncle's kiva. It was her first time and she enjoyed it. She need not fear, for she is yet so pure that hardly anything could pierce her heart.

Po-wa-mu-ya, the purification month (February), has many activities and many special meanings. Entering into the new moon a sacred ritual is performed to purify all life on Earth. The evil elements we have accumulated over the past months must be washed away in order that we may blend with nature. We must be free from contamination to emerge from the Earth Mother in colorful beauty, glorifying and creating harmony for her and all her children.

It is also a month of initiation for the children who have come of age. They are introduced into membership in a higher order, the second stage of life following the birth ritual with which they came into the world. This is regarded as a very sacred ceremony. Those who abide by it respectfully can learn much about the Hopi way of life, through its functions and the power it holds.

Colorful gifts are given to the children with the fresh green plants, symbolizing the introduction of the first fresh nourishment. Right at sunrise, Kachinas come out of all the kivas (ceremonial chambers) to bring gifts to all the houses: Kachina dolls, rattles, and woven plaques for the girls, bows, arrows, and rattles for the boys, and maybe balls and sticks later in the day when the Kachinas come to entertain the people. Each of the toys is designed with special meanings.

That night will be a sleepless one. The men in the kiva will smoke and pray for the success of the coming year. After midnight, dances will commence and continue until dawn, symbolizing the passage from new to old, or from creation to the fulfillment of life. But it would take many pages to tell all of the symbolism, so let's return to our children.

As usual Grandpa returns from the kiva early one morning for breakfast. Smiling, he tells the children, 'Get up! Get up! Go outside and look! It must be spring already, for I just saw *doo-gots-ka* (small black bird) walking eastward wearing green moccasins, announcing that it's time for planting!'

'Where? Which way?' They get up quickly and rush toward the door, rubbing their eyes.

'Down the street a ways! If you hurry you may be able to catch up with it and see it going by the next kiva,' he replies with a smile, knowing they will never find the bird with green moccasins. This is a code message used to get around the children's prying ears with a hint that man must now prepare for spring.

Seeds must be sprouted in the kiva, and in about sixteen days the main ceremony will be at hand. While the children are out looking, Grandpa discusses the possibility of initiation with their father and mother. Grandpa informs them that this year there will be no regular ritual, but possibly a short form will take place. Mother hints that maybe the oldest daughter, Mano, should be included, for she has been getting curious lately, asking things she is not supposed to ask.

By this time the children rush back indoors, shivering and excited. 'Grandpa,' yells the smallest, 'we've seen it! It was flying far off down the canyon.' 'Innocent liar,' Grandpa thinks to himself.

After dinner the Kachina mother comes out again, going from kiva to kiva with her crowd of children growing larger all the time. They each bring gifts, dolls, bows and arrows, some have balls and sticks to give to little boys.

Later in the afternoon Mano's godmother came to prepare her for the initiation. The children would soon gather at a certain kiva. Her godfather would come for her when it was time. They dressed her in a black handwoven dress, red, green and black belt around her waist, and a cape of red, white, and black, but no shoes.

Mano was fearful, but her godmother encouraged her, telling her not to be afraid, for it would not hurt her as much as the boys who would be naked.

Her little brothers would make remarks that were not so funny now that she felt so anxious. It was a relief when her godfather finally came for her.

She followed him proudly into the kiva where the children of age were already gathered to wait for the whippers. Visitors and parents also waited outside the kiva. 'Mother,' whispered two little boys huddling under their mother's shawl, 'they are coming closer to the kiva where our sister is. Will they hurt her much?' 'She's got a dress on, it won't hurt much,' she reassures them.

It took some time for all the Kachinas to enter the kiva, for there were many. All of a sudden they heard screams and yells mixed with the voices and sounds of the Kachinas. After a while the screams stopped and the Kachinas came out, pleased that they had fulfilled the task of bringing new members into the fold.

The children who are not initiated will not be permitted to witness the dances tonight. The new initiates will occupy special places in the kiva under the watchful eyes of their godmother, and from midnight until dawn they will watch the mystical drama unfold before them. Then they will return to the houses of their godmothers where their hair will be washed and they will each be blessed and given a new name. Thus they become full-fledged Hopi.

There will follow activities such as ball games, games with bow and arrow, and stone races by men and boys from each kiva, not just for competition, but for their symbolic significance.

After lunch one warm sunny day in the spring, everyone in Grandpa's household is resting. Grandpa is lying against the wall on a sheepskin, father is sitting by the door repairing his torn moccasin, mother and Mano are lazily clearing up the noonday dishes. The children are out playing. Now and then there is a little idle talk, but each person is mostly wrapped up in his or her own thoughts:

Grandpa sees himself making a windbreaker in his field, thinking that in a couple of days the job will be done. Visions of big melons and corn, which he hopes will be ready in time for the Niman Kachina ceremonial in summer, are already there in his thoughts. 'If it rains...' he muses.

Father is thinking of all the things to be done in the kiva and hoping that they will finish the wedding robes and sashes which he and the men have been weaving for almost five days. If his prediction are right, they should be finished in a couple more days. The bride will go back to her house about that time. He will then look over his fields to see if anything had to be done before planting time. 'It won't be long before my oldest son finds someone to wed, if he hasn't already,' he thinks, and it gives him a shiver as he imagines one night hearing someone's mother announcing her daughter from the doorway.

Mother is thinking of too many things! She and a group of women are weaving baskets, but she must let that go for a while for she has heard that there will be another wedding. She must get the corn grinding done to help out her relations, so they will help when her own older daughter gets married, which won't be very long. Growing up comes mighty fast! She also thinks of her younger ones, and the meals for tonight and the next morning. She knows that a woman's work never ends.

Suddenly there is a commotion and yelling outside. Father and Grandpa look toward each other and nod knowingly about the secret they have kept to themselves. 'Grandpa! Father! Mother!' the children yell bursting through the door. 'Kachinas with long yucca whips are coming into the village,' cries the older child. 'Are they coming to whip us?' asks the smaller one. 'No, they come as friends,' father replies calmly. 'They might have remembered you as good boys and brought you gifts,' adds Grandpa, 'better run over to the plaza where you can be seen.'

Yes, today is the day of challenge, a test whether we are in shape, and have the strength to outdistance these Kachinas in a race of a hundred yards or more. Those who are sure of their ability to run may challenge them, because these Kachinas are in shape and ready for this event. In the first round they are allowed to use their whips, which will then be taken away by the Kachina Father, depending on how he feels. Thereafter each racer must catch his challenger around the waist after he overtakes him.

They come in different representations, but the most feared are the one who rips your clothes off, the one who clips hair from your head, and the one that feeds you hot chili pepper. There is also one that feeds you animal droppings. But the ones especially feared by men are the kokopelli manas, or 'sexy girls.' When caught by them and once laid, it is very hard to get away, unless your aunts come to the rescue and drag them off you. Just the same it causes great excitement and fun for the women.

Strings of corn and tamales, sho-me-vicki, are placed at the starting point. Each challenger gets his reward from these, and most of them are given to the children as gifts. The children are half hidden under their mothers' shawls, all the time in fear, hoping the kokopelli mana will not see them and attack them as she does with the older boys and men.

'Mother, where is our big brother? He should have been here to get those prizes!' the smaller child boasted. 'Our brother can run faster than anybody!' 'He went herding sheep this morning and won't be back until later,' she answered, to cover up for the older brother who is participating as a Kachina.

Thus another event passes so that the spirit of life will be strong and bring blessings for the coming spring.

The Niman, going-home dance. One mid-summer morning, the household was very active. Mother had already made piki bread and cooked mutton that Grandpa and Father had gone to their Navajo friend's house to trade for. Early that morning Mother had also started the fire in the pit oven to make the special pudding for the next day. By sunup both men returned from the field for breakfast, and while eating Grandpa complained about the rats and rabbits eating up all his corn and melon patch. He doubted they would be able to get a meal from it. But it is the Hopi way to respect Nature and not get ahead of it through boastful ways. It is better to accept whatever it has in store. After all, that might not turn out to be as bad as one feared.

Father and Grandpa spent most of the day and remained until dawn the next day smoking and praying in the Kiva. Early, before the sun rose, mother awakened the children, reminding them to be good since she heard the Kachinas come while they were asleep. She washed their hair with yucca root.

'We did not cry or make a fuss, did we mother!' they said.

This reminded her of how much they disliked hairwashing.

'You acted very nice,' she replied, 'and I'm sure the Kachinas will recognize you with clean hair... let's hope they have made you something as a gift.'

Shortly after sunrise, Kachinas enter the village plaza, arms full of toys and cornstalks, blending beautifully. They are a sight beyond description. Little boys and girls eagerly eye the most beautiful ones, as the youngest one exclaims to the oldest, 'I bet the one at the end will be given to me,' and the older one replies, 'I bet you won't get any since you've been a bad boy lately.' 'But I helped Mother carry water yesterday and washed my hair,' the child answers tearfully.

After a dance, gifts of kachina dolls and bows and arrows are given out to the lucky ones. Later on at home the children and family admire the presents. The oldest 'mana' did not get anything. Maybe later in the day she would receive a gift, but this would be the last, for she was initiated last winter.

'Mother, these few ears of corn are not enough for all of us,' complained the children.

'Perhaps you should take it in the back room along with some cornmeal and pray to the corn to give birth, then go outside and pray to Father Sun. Don't come in until I tell you to,' directs mother.

Thus as if by magic, a few ears became enough for all including relatives, guests, and friends that will gather in reunion to honor the Niman (going home dance) and send all the Kachinas on a good journey until they return in midwinter.

At the end of the day the Kachinas will be blessed with prayer feathers, in all directions, and be given the messages to take back home. They are told not to wait long, but return in the form of rain, for the land and all living things are thirsty. So ends the Kachina Ceremonial for the summer. For a few moments we spectators are sad and silent as though we lost our last beloved friend forever. But we know they will return.

Because of the disrespect encouraged by the new culture that has been forced upon the Hopi, few people in our villages truly respect the silent and sacred month of December today. Storytelling is replaced by many new things, such as radio, television, and books. We no longer walk softly, our movements are fast, and the noises are ear-splitting and earth-shaking. Ball games, cars, airplanes...we stay out all night, as our Mother Earth is being pierced and scraped by the new inventions of today. As a result we are no longer normal. Things are out of balance. Look at your surroundings and draw your own conclusion. The outlook seems dim. But we have known all along that the temptations of today's world would be very strong, and that it would take great strength to keep the world in balance. Dreaming again? Yes, this was when our hearts were one not very long ago. The Bahanna (white man) system is destroying what was once beautiful and good. Our children are induced into Bahanna activities through the efforts of the

United States Government, its school system and its so-called 'Hopi Tribal Council.' Children are forced to spend much of their time in schools where their only chance for fun is in such activities. Before long they seem to know nothing else. Then they are easily encouraged to join night ball games, which have taken a great toll, as well as Bahanna dances and other programs. As a result, most of our children who are old enough to participate in ceremonies have lost interest. They have been taken from our hands by this foreign system and deprived of their chance to grow in their understanding of the sacred ways which have brought us prosperity and peace for countless centuries.

We wish only to be given the freedom to continue our tradition. This is our prayer during this most sacred of seasons.

In the early 1900s it became the stated objective of the United States Government to allow only the elders freedom to continue the full cycle of ceremonial life. The children were removed by force, and those elders who objected were imprisoned. The true ceremonial cycle was destined to die out with the elders. To the casual observer, the various Bahanna cultural activities seem harmless and those who promote them think they are doing good, but in reality they are part of a tremendous effort to force us from the path of the Great Spirit. We must face the fact that our vital link with Mother Earth has almost been destroyed.

The world is changing rapidly, and mankind is now in serious trouble. What we see today has been predicted all along, which is the reason the true Hopi have never stopped resisting.

We know it is possible for our children to see once again the importance of preserving the Hopi way. The troubles of the world showed this more clearly with each passing year. Our respect for the ancient way that has given us life is not merely a dream of a beautiful past. It is a dream of a beautiful future.

Our life was filled with such ceremonies not long ago, but today fast feet are being replaced with fast-moving wheels. Perhaps our wonderful lifeway will only be restored when we learn that wheels are dangerous to our health.

TEM— You noticed, I am sure, that the Elders say the cycle of ceremonies is their "vital link with Mother Earth," and you can project what life for them would be like without it. Dan added that, "Up to now, all these Elders are almost all gone. And then only the Bean Dance will be going on, because all the... because nobody knows what is to be done on that certain day. The Kachinas will still be dancing, but you know, it will probably be done in a certain way because the wise men aren't there to guide them in the right way, the way they are supposed to be done. These Kachinas and the Bean Dance will still be going on, but the other dances will probably just go to an end."

Susie: "Aha, but then right now he said, even if these Elderlies are gone, they still might know enough, they will just name a person to put on the dances. They're gonna go on, but they're not initiated into the Men's Society. It'll probably still be going on but the reason they are not doing this initiation anymore is because of the separation in the village. You know, hardly anybody believes in these things anymore, and they are pushing these Elderlies away. And they don't want to learn anything anymore. And by doing that, they are completely stopping everything, they don't want to learn. See, all this is supposed to be from the Society men. Everything comes from those who were initiated in there. And a lot of things we don't know about because we don't know how they are initiated. Maybe these guys don't want to do it because they don't believe in it, because the younger people don't believe in it. Even if they are initiated, it is hard to say whether they are doing it willingly, or they are just wanting to experiment. So in the future they won't do the promised things they are supposed to do."

Then I asked whether the Homegoing Dance we had seen in 1993 didn't speak well for the Traditional Elders, and didn't the whole village appreciate the fact that so many people were there and participating in the dance — didn't that bring the village together any? Susie replied, "To me, when there's a dance, we all have to get together, no matter who, because the Kachinas aren't the problem, they are supposed to bring more spirits to us then. Even if they don't believe in traditional ways, if they still want to participate in the dance, they're welcome."

Considering the youth of today, I wanted to know what Dan thought they can adopt of Bahanna's ways. How far can they go without breaking with the old way of life? Can there be any compromises?

"Everyone is different," he replied. "The children can do this because they are to be our eyes and ears, and speak for us. But when they walk against us that is going too far, and that includes working for or with the Tribal Council or the Government. There are a lot of people that are trying to come back to the traditional ways, but it won't really work out for them because they already haven't walked the straight line, and went off. And they can't have the whole spirit to themself when they're separated from the traditional way. But that is how it is — off and on, off balance, off to the traditional way."

"Can there be any compromises?" I repeated.

Susie answered, "I guess everybody's different. It's just that from my side I would see to it that the kids get an education, right, and like he said they would be our ear, our mouth, you know. But if they still stay with traditional, with traditional people, they are traditional people then, but if they go off and fight against them, then they will be with Bahanna and want things for their houses."

Forethoughts Always Lead To Afterthoughts...Just Suppose...

TI— "Suppose the world leaders in the United Nations had honored the message of the Hopi prophecies about the bomb four decades ago and had accepted them as truth. Suppose world leaders had wholeheartedly acknowledged their message regarding nuclear technology, that the invention is dangerous to the health of the earth and all living things. What if they had then decided to pass a law prohibiting further experiment? What would our world situation be like today? We think the world would be in a better peaceful condition in some ways, although it would still not be stable. Leaders can always think of something to oppress people — especially the poor.

Today many of us no longer abide by the laws that the Great Creator provided for us to follow. Instead we look up to the human governments of the world to provide the economic systems and scientific methods that hopefully will provide hope for us. It is true that at this age of time civilization is prosperous, but there are also terrible forces threatening our life and our earth. Do you think mankind has any chance of solving these problems?

Our view is that in this age no one has ever governed for the greatest good of everyone. Clever as man is he cannot govern himself successfully.

Many of us think that with modern science and technology everything is possible. We have come to think that any mistake can be corrected by our improved inventions. This is where we are now, But this idea could be self defeating. We could go too far in the wrong direction and not be able to come back."

We Are The Last Stronghold!

TI— "Our elders were right to resist and oppose what came their way from the Bahanna. With this in mind, let us focus upon one particular village, the last stronghold of the Hopi people. It may well be the last stronghold of all Native People on this land.

This village was founded in 1906 by Chief Yukiuma after the split in Oraibi. Ever since the beginning of Government Agency occupation on Hopi Land, Hotevilla Village has a long history of resistance. This history is filled with the suffering and sorrow that was created for the Hotevilla Hopi by the Agency and the Government troops. The Navajo and other Hopi villages have also shared in this abuse. We Traditionals did not turn to violence or weapons because we are Hopis, the peaceful ones. Instead we used our knowledge and wisdom in opposing the Agency demands. We knew that if we resorted to violence or the use of weapons it would cause our downfall. Then we would be conquered and perhaps have to sign a treaty. Whatever treaty we made would not be fulfilled by the Government. They would break it. That we know from painful experience.

The Hotevilla Hopi accepted and endured all the punishments demanded by the Government. But the provocation techniques used by the Bahannas did not work, at least not as well as they hoped they would, and so were a complete failure in that they did not get rid of us. In our view, we are being punished today simply because we want to live in our own way — the Hopi way. We have neither harmed anyone, nor have we stolen anyone's belongings. The actions of the Government are completely improper toward us.

Yet the harassments continue to this day. The same techniques of divide and conquer are being used, only they are being applied in a different manner. Our elders were right. Education in foreign concepts is wrong for all Native People. The foreign education cannot blend with our culture and traditions, into which we have been molded since ancient times. This 'education' will pollute our minds and do great harm to our culture and tradition. Our spiritual values, identity, and language will be lost. Most important, all our land will be lost.

What is happening today as a result of these things is as predicted. There is a loss of respect for the elders and leaders by a small group of hard-core Progressives who, although they have a limited education in traditional values, hold no official capacity within our Village Community. Their intent is to acknowledge the Bahanna system of rules and lifestyle for our Village."

Will We Stand Alone Or Will Bahanna Help Us? Prophecy Says He Will

TI— "Three people were named who were to help the Hopi when we reached the crisis of no return. The Paiute Indian was to help according to his wisdom, but if he is unable to do this the Navajo Indian will help, also according to his wisdom. In other words, they will not help us in physical ways. In their wisdom which comes from their ancients, they will give us some guidance as to how we might work together, and as to what direction it might be best for us to go. In this wise, we have been meeting with them. If their efforts fail, then certain Bahannas will come to aid us. It seems that this last place is where we are now.

The time has now arrived for the Bahanna to do something for the Traditional Hopi of Hotevilla. Why only Hotevilla? Our answer is that it is because we stand alone according to our prophecy. We can only say that if you are interested in helping our cause — which is preserving our Traditional Hopi culture — please write to your Congressmen and Senators, asking them to look into the so-called Joint Use Area between the Hopi and Navajo reservations. Support Senator Cranston's Bill, S-2545, calling for a moratorium on funding for the relocation of Navajo. Request that Traditional Hopi and Navajo be included in all discussions in order to separate their voices from those of the Tribal Councils of both tribes... Tribal Councils whose views are based on western concepts of material gain.

On December 26, 1986, the Traditional Hopi elders of Hotevilla filed a complaint with the U.N. Commission for Human Rights in Geneva. It would help our cause if you write letters of support for our complaint. Write to Mr. Jacob Moller, Center for Human Rights, Communication Unit, Palais des Nation 1211 Geneva 10. Express especially your support for the preservation of our aboriginal culture. Thank you."

Our Prayers For One Miracle At Least May Be Answered

TI— "Our elders taught us that through prayer a miracle is often possible. Because we have been praying constantly, and because of what has been happening this past month, we feel something good may be coming our way. We hope it is what we have searched and waited for. It could be a powerful force if we guide it in the right direction. As of this writing, three authoritative organizations are interested in helping us and getting involved in our struggle for independence. We pray these attempts will materialize favorably.

The first two involve persons with whom we have already met:

1. a man representing the Senate Investigating Committee on Indian Affairs.

2. a man representing the U.N. Sub-Commission, Protection of Minorities, has been an invited guest of Hotevilla Hopi elders.

Since space is limited, we briefly summarize the meetings. In both, related matters about Hotevilla Village concerns were discussed. Our position and stand we need not repeat. As for the rest, Navajo people of Big Mountain shared the meeting and expressed their views about forced relocation. We discussed our treatment by the Hopi Progressive Council and the police force, and our concerns for the future.

The meeting was a success. *The only problem arose when the Hopi Tribal*

Council hostilely raided the meeting in an attempt to disrupt the meeting. There was no violence — perhaps only shame for themselves in the presence of U.N. Sub-Commission witnesses.

Here now we wish to make a clear understanding of the True Hopi position. Outsiders are often misled about this by various sources — even by Hopi themselves.

Outsiders often think that the Hopi tribe is one Nation. This is not true. There are several Hopi Villages in Hopi Land. And the fact is that each Village has its own self-governing body with its own religious leaders. Each Village is independent from the others. Each has their own guidelines to follow. Therefore we have no central government. This rule is very important, for it keeps each Village out of the affairs of other Villages.

Following this system, we were happy and in peace — until the Bureau of Indian Affairs, under the Federal Government, encroached upon our land and followed this with the creation of the Hopi Tribal Council. Ever since that time we have had problems, conflicts and unrest, because the Hopi Tribal Council adopted foreign concepts, such as leasing out the land to mineral developers, creating programs that spell 'progress for economy's sake alone,' land grabbing, etc. And in all of this, they paid no attention to the resistance of Traditional Leaders and their reasons for it.

Now we have received news from an informed source that a new mineral development plan has been drawn up by the Federally recognized Hopi Tribal Council. This is planned for the area from which Navajos were forcibly relocated. Much coal mining is planned for the Big Mountain area, plus a large addition to the strip-mining already under way further north at Black Mesa. A great increase in water use is also considered.

This situation would not exist if the Hopi Tribal Council would listen to the Traditional Leaders' advice and learn why they are rejecting this program. The Traditional Leaders foresee further harm in depleting water tables and springs — which our farming and domestic uses depend upon for self-sufficiency. Hopi and other Native People possessed the land for thousands of years before the Hopi Tribal Council was created. Looking at it from a spiritual point of view, the Hopi Tribal Council has no basis in controlling our land. We believe their purpose is to use scheming ways to tarnish our cultural and traditional patterns, and by this to destroy our leadership structure.

According to the wisdom and knowledge of our elders, we received Divine Laws and identity as Hopi (peaceful) from our Divine Creator. These told us that so long as we use them wisely, we will have a long and peaceful life as a people. But if we carelessly adopt a foreign system of laws, we will then face unfortunate situations. *These warnings came before Bahanna, so we wondered why they were given. Now we know the answer. It was to give us time to prepare ourselves to meet the challenges.*

So we looked on from the spiritual point of view as the so-called Hopi Tribal Council adopted their own man-made bylaws and constitution. In so doing they cast away the laws of our Creator, our Traditional leadership, and also our religion. Therefore they are no longer Hopi. Their identity is lost. Even if they wanted to, they are no longer able to be caretakers of the land. Consequently their only interest is in projects like the Peabody Mine and other leases that abuse the land, our mother."

An Announcement About Our Film, and a Possible Other Miracle

TI— "The film titled *Techqua Ikachi* will make its first appearance in West Berlin beginning in July, 1989. It is produced and directed by Swiss filmmakers Mano Productions, from Paspels, Switzerland, with the help and personal participation of the Hopi Traditionals of Hotevilla.

It will be a unique film in that it tells the Hopi story of emergence to this world, migration, founding of Old Oraibi, the Ceremonial Cycle, the political war between progressive Hopi and Traditional Hopi, and more.

This documentary film is *especially made for future Hopi children*, so that they can see portrayed the true story of our lives and traditional views. They will not get this from the Tribal Council and in their puppet press.

We have not mentioned that the World Court has said they will send an observer to the hearing. They may even visit our Village for a talk. At this writing we don't know when. We don't even know what the reason is for this suddenly appearing miracle. However, our prophecy stated someone will appear one day and look into the wrongdoings at Hopi, going places where we, the Traditionals, cannot step anymore. We hope this means that the Tribal Council and the Government will be punished.

Now is the time you can help us push all of these things through. Any organizations or individuals anywhere in the world can help us. Arouse public opinion to help us regain our independence. We trust this can be done. Write to the organized establishments we have mentioned. We would be happy to get letters of support, so that we know you are behind us.

Thank you."

We Express Our Gratitude

TI— "The Hopi, over the years, are fortunate in meeting and making contact with many people from domestic and foreign countries. Many of you we know only through your letters. When we needed the most help, many of you came to visit us to see firsthand our situation with the forces of opposition. Your letters and petitions have helped much in taming our problems. We hope our way of life becomes more stable as we approach what the future holds in store for us and the whole world. At this time we give thanks to all those who helped us. We are truly grateful.

Over the years we have given our best of efforts to provide those who come here our hearty reception. All we expect from the visitors is their respect for our village, our people, and also the surrounding shrines. We hope you will also show respect by obeying the rules of the village.

If one is fortunate in coming to Hopi Land at the right moment, one can freely witness the Sacred Ceremonial dances and share the happiness and prayers."

At this point, Dan and I hope you are ready to accept Hotevilla as the battleground where the most awesome contest in history is being waged by this tiny handful of essentially peaceful people. Even if you are still not prepared to do that, being aware of what is going on in the world, you should at least be ready to admit that the battle must be fought. Changes of an ominous nature and proportions are so frequent today that anyone with good sense is beginning to wonder what their consequences will be, and what, if anything, can be done about them. We are, as Fools Crow said we would, starting to listen to those who are warning us. In 1975, he told me about a wondrous vision he had during a quest in 1901. He was carried by a spirit helper around the world four times. The first time the world was pristine and peaceful, and he was shown a walled-up place where a wind was contained that had within it priceless information people would need to know when the end of this cycle of the world was near. On each subsequent trip the world deteriorated further and experienced greater crises. On the fourth trip, it was in serious trouble, nearly gone, and as he passed overhead, the wall crumbled and released the wind. As it spread out and touched people they began to look around and listen. And the words they heard, Fools Crow said, came from the only tribe still carrying on their full traditional life in North America — not always but mostly gentle people who have never abused, misused, wasted or polluted the place where they live —people who have communed and lived in concert with Earth Mother over an unbroken period of time — and who want to and can tell us how to do the same. Although he did not name this tribe, who could it be other than the Hopi and other Pueblos? Have you felt an unusual wind touching your cheek lately?

When I asked the holy man whether he could project an end date, he answered, "The fall has already begun, and the end should come about 150 years from the time of the vision," which would put it at about A.D. 2050. In their prophecies concerning a closing and new beginning, the ancient Maya cut it shorter, setting it at A.D. 2011. Since we are all aware of recurrent "prophets of doom" who have predicted end dates that have not materialized, let me remind you again that the Elders are entirely different. They do not speak of specific end dates. They talk in broad terms about closing and beginning-again times, during which life, while seriously affected, nevertheless goes on.

People who want to argue against prophecies usually find it is easy to poke holes in them, although it should be pointed out that their doing so does not keep the predicted events from happening. Regarding those cited herein by the Elders, however, we must understand that they are not so much testifying about specifically detailed fulfillments as they are asserting that what the Creator says will happen will happen in its own time and way. Their prophecies are of a general nature, sometimes only having to do with human behavior, and are not to be pinned down to a certain day or hour. Also, as I have already said, it is not the Hopi practice to work out seeming contradictions or obscurities and make neat packages of them. To do this would be to question the Creator, and seek to force him, whom they know must remain in control, to bend to human wishes. We notice that they say certain events may be the fulfillments of prophecies, but are quick to admit that they might also be reading the signs incorrectly. This is not a cop-out, and it does not worry them. If they are mistaken in their conclusions, it will not matter, for in spite of their inadequacies the predicted things will still take place. The Elders make reference to world events, but they do not keep in tune with these or search for details so they can shape their prophecies to fit them. They know in a general way what is going on, and they will cite evidence that appears to support their contentions. But their aim is not to say that because certain things have happened it proves their case. Other than to demonstrate a pattern would it really matter? As physicist Steven Hawking says, "Not only does God play dice, he sometimes throws them where they can't be seen." Of far greater importance where the Elders' message is concerned is the fact that world transitions as a whole should be forcing us to face the fact that we are in serious trouble. Unless we make immediate and drastic changes in our attitudes and actions we are speeding toward an untimely closing and an unnecessarily difficult new beginning.

Optimistic and successful as we citizens of America and the other major countries have been in dealing with past crises, the combined magnitude of current man-made problems, together with a series of natural disasters of record proportions, is such that we are either close to or have already exhausted our means to deal with or control them. Where just one of the main dilemmas, the environment, is concerned, some respected authorities say flatly that it is already too late... that our global reactor has ruptured, the meltdown is under way, and while its end can be shaped and slowed, it cannot be reversed. Moreover, they add, the acceleration of events increases day by day as the combinations of factors simultaneously snowball the process in a hundred different areas.

The August 29, 1993, *Los Angeles Times Magazine* featured an extensive article entitled, *Apocalypse Soon*, that describes the impressive and passionate efforts of Nobel Prize-winning Professor Henry W. Kendall of Princeton University as he seeks to convince everyone who will listen—and listening his graduate students are, that overpopulation and environmental catastrophe are closer than we think. If nothing is done, these problems will converge in the next 50 years and plunge the world into terrible suffering... there will be a level of pain — starvation, disease, anarchy, a scarred landscape — more horrific than anything humanity has seen before. "In the United States," Kendall adds, "we think these problems affect people living far away in breechcloths, but overpopulation may spread suffering and chaos to the developed nations as well. If we wait until we see the damage here, it will be too late." "Although his message may seem extreme," the writer, Michael D'Antonio, says, "thousands of elite scientists have joined what amounts to an international campaign to convince us that a global disaster is impending."

Against Kendall, and therefore the Elders also, are those who always point out that similar warnings were raised in the 1960s, '70s, and '80s, and the apocalypse never came — an argument intended to suggest that people are numb to the overworked message.

Add to that the protests of the '90s: The December 13, 1993 issue of *U.S. News & World Report*, pp 81-91, carried an article entitled, "The Doomsday Myths 2," in which it was claimed that "By exaggerating environmental dangers, activists have undermined their credibility and triggered an anti-environment backlash." The author, Stephen Budianski, sets forth what he claims are four myths being propounded by leading scientists and environmentalists: 1. That fifty thousand species a year are being lost to extinction; 2. That forty million acres of tropical rain forest are destroyed each year; 3. That the ozone hole is spreading; 4. That no serious scientists doubt predictions of global warming... "But such warnings of impending doom," the author says, "are now coming under furious counterattack. Recent months have brought a spate of books and articles, most written by conservative academics and columnists, that dismiss all warnings of environmental doom as hoaxes and scaremongering. What's driving the backlash? Certainly, none of the global environmental issues now under attack is a hoax. Nor is the political agenda of many of the anti-environmentalists very hard to find. But some environmental researchers now concede that at least part of the blame lies with themselves for overstating evidence — by presenting hypotheses as certainties and predictions as facts to create a sense of urgency, scientist-activists have jeopardized their own credibility... A review of the scientific literature and interviews with researchers suggest that while none of the threats to the global environment can be dismissed, many oft-cited 'facts' used to paint a picture of impending ecological disaster are more myth than reality. Only by confronting these myths can environmental scientists hope to retain their credibility in the face of mounting skepticism and get on with addressing *the real environmental challenges the world faces.* Keeping the water clean, in other words, is the best way to make sure the baby doesn't get thrown out with it.

"While sweeping generalizations about impending extinction catastrophes may get attention, they don't do much to help a conservation planner figure out where to focus his efforts. Worse, they tend to discredit the work of scientists pushing for practical conservation measures that virtually all researchers agree are needed to protect the species that are threatened by a loss of habitat. Yet the political climate has made it difficult for scientists to challenge the more politically correct views of Wilson... The downward revision of the total deforestation rate undercuts the argument that the issue is a crisis that demands immediate and drastic action. But the edge effect greatly reduces the area of pristine forest, suggesting a need for sweeping curbs on development and that more attention should be paid to how forest land is developed... the Antarctic ozone hole is the product of two factors: man-made chlorine and extreme cold. Although man-made chlorine is distributed throughout the stratosphere, extreme cold is confined to polar winters.

So the existence of the Antarctic hole does not in itself prove that severe ozone depletion also will occur in more temperate regions...Much depends on the answer. The industrialized nations have agreed to terminate CFC production by 1996, but China, India and Brazil have been given an additional ten years to comply, and all three will be potentially huge producers as they industrialize over the next decade. It may turn out that the stratosphere can absorb the blow and the damage will remain confined to the Antarctic in winter. But if not, the damage will persist for a very long time. The stratosphere flushes itself out very slowly, and the chlorine already there will persist for hundreds of years...To environmentalists, global warming is 'a holocaust' or 'the end of nature.' To the political right, it is a Trojan horse for expanded government powers. Yet doubts about the likelihood, intensity and consequences of global warming extend far beyond a few fringe scientists or industry hirelings... Nevertheless, even some of the strongest skeptics agree that it is sensible to reduce carbon dioxide emissions for reasons that have nothing to do with the greenhouse effect. All of them support an increase in the gasoline tax, energy conservation and improvements in energy efficiency all make sense under any circumstances. That kind of common sense, they feel, is much less dramatic than predicting 'the end of nature.' But it may serve both science and the environment better in the long run."

Also cited where problems like this are concerned, is humanity's boundless ingenuity in dealing with previous crises. On November 13, 1993, it was reported in the press that food supplies are growing faster than the increase in population, and that population growth is slowing. Yet while food production is up in some countries, it is failing in those places where it is needed most, and we have no distribution system established. Contrasting thoughts were included earlier.

Of course, food is hardly the only problem we face, and it is the accumulation of problems that matters. Moreover, there is today a disheartening difference in magnitude to consider: All of our problems have grown to gargantuan proportions, and give no indication of slacking off. "The scientific elite seems almost unanimous in its fear. Last year, the National Academy of Sciences and Britain's Royal Society issued a rare joint statement on the dangerous trends in population and environmental degradation... Last November, the Union of Concerned Scientists published a 'World Scientists' Warning to Humanity' on the same topics. Signed by more than 1,500 experts, including 104 Nobel Prize winners, this document warns that humanity faces 'spirals of environmental decline, poverty and unrest leading to social, economic and environmental decline.'"

Dare we, as we have continually done, shun these so-called "prophets of doom," trust the optimists, or "realists" as they often call themselves, drag our feet any longer, and continue to put other concerns ahead of this before we act decisively? Coming from another direction than the scientific, and without any of the measurement or analysis tools the sciences use, the Hopi Elders at Hotevilla do not, on the basis of prophecy, think so.

For his part, to overcome such resistance, Kendall assaults his audiences with statistics and projections that ought to chill anyone... foremost of which are, the world population doubling in just 60 years to about 10 billion, food production declining, ozone depletion and global warming, destruction of plant and animal species, deforestation and pollution threatening agriculture worldwide, and eighty nations now experiencing water shortages with Americans pumping "fossil water" out of the ground faster than it can be replaced.

We can add to these menaces their disturbing offspring that are common everywhere — economic regression, desperate immigration from third to first world countries, inescapable tensions, frightful anger and disdain for life, and awesome violence and genocide. Interestingly, Kendall and the others do not include natural disasters in their prognostications, assuming apparently that they are just the regular course of things that happen at historic intervals, and that Divine intervention does not cause them. Along with other Native American peoples, the Hopi Elders disagree, and since they were predicted by Maasaw long ago, believe that the worst things happening today are signs accompanying the cycle end times, and therefore not accidental. They accept them as warnings that ought to be heeded, and when we consider their views concerning the violation of Earth Mother we can easily understand why. What mankind is doing to the environment is causing natural balances to shift in dramatic ways.

Is any of this Divine retribution? The Old Testament describes situations where Divine retribution happens. But most of these are connected to God's actions in history to bring redemption to pass. The Hopi Elders do believe in it, and they also believe that God does not step in to protect people who choose to do foolish things. The individual who decides to build his house on a floodplain or near an earthquake fault cannot blame the Lord when a flood or an earthquake comes. They know that just now, after a 10-year effort, the United States and 36 other nations voted to ban nuclear waste dumping in the oceans. This moment arrives, however, after decades of pouring in millions of gallons of waste — and Belgium, Russia, Britain, France and China abstained from voting — which means their dumping will continue. Should we blame the Creator for the consequences of this kind of act? If humankind chooses to flaunt and waste nature for whatever reasons, should we expect God to protect us — even though he is working through people like the Elders to tell us how to avoid such things? The sciences have learned that catastrophic natural changes have taken place at various intervals since the beginning of creation. Therefore, the fact that some record changes are taking place now does not in itself signal that the Creator is stepping in to wind down the world. But it is interesting to note how many of these things are taking place at the very time we have gotten ourselves into terminal trouble. However we look at it, Mother Earth is calling our attention to something we have got to recognize and do something about — all of which may well be an awareness sent down from above! The point is that it is prophesied that at the very time all of these other predictions accompanying the winding down of the world take place, there will also be record-breaking disasters occurring... which is exactly what is happening today! I think that is, at the very least, interesting. Would it not pose an entirely different picture — one skeptics would welcome — if the other things were happening, but the predicted disasters were not?

United Nations efforts, scientific appeals and growing media attention give Kendall and others reason to hope, but he is by no means optimistic. Governments, he says, must focus upon and enact economic development, education, conservation and pollution-reducing technology. Naturally, we have no choice but to do these things, and people everywhere are pitching in. But, the Elders ask, are we making the kind of progress that is required? If these needs are not fully addressed, then won't everything else we are worrying about and planning be of little or limited consequence as the world spirals down and the transition occurs? The Elders know, and make plain in their statements, that we have come to where it is a matter of priorities now — we are in a pitched battle and there is no room for complacency.

Since our message from the Hopi Elders includes a number of prophecies, warnings, and solutions, we knew you would want to know everything they say about it, including how they were able to learn so much hundreds of years before the first White person came to America, what they believe about the present status of the world, where they fit into all of this, what they say the end will be like, and what they can do about the overall situation. We have given you this information. The "story" has been told. The fact that they are not able to provide us with the things powerful governments can means little. Unless they change their ways drastically, most of what governments offer will be compromise and stopgap measures that will be hampered by selfish interests. Procrastination is rife in government and industry. A comment by Sen. John Glenn in the September 21, 1993, p. A-10, *Press-Enterprise*, is only one — yet a typical — example of the far broader problem as he accuses "the Interior Department yesterday of placing America's health and safety at risk by its inattention to environmental concerns... The Interior Department has allowed the environment to be trashed, permitted its workers to face dangerous conditions and run up a $200 billion cleanup bill, according to a Senate committee report to be released today." Among the problems identified in the report: "Dangerously high levels of soil, air and water contamination from mines and smelters. Some of this pollution has killed grazing horses and cattle. Department employees suffer chemical exposure injuries and illnesses with alarming frequency. Unexploded ammunition on public lands is a growing problem. Mercury contamination from oil and gas wells may be widespread. Interior has the worst occupational, safety and health record of all federal agencies." Every single day, our newspapers, magazines, radios, and television carry stories about how we have been deceived about the amount of damage this or that company has wrought. If this is what we learn about, what do you suppose the real problem is here and in the rest of the world? Know the truth or not, every single minute the consequences are piling up and closing in.

While entire books and countless articles are being devoted to the problems faced by the world, and to possible ways of addressing them, the Elders' solution — their Pattern of Life — is by far the best. It offers something unique and vastly more important, because — let them say again — it comes from the Creator, who being infinite and all-powerful is able to do what mankind cannot. In this book, they have told you what this is, and it is the only real hope that we have. All we need do is follow their advice and put the simple steps they observe to work each day in our own lives. If you have not thought to do so, re-read the book and this time look for the core things they warn against and practice. Make notes, and then adapt them to your life and the place where you live and work. Meanwhile, they are not sitting up on a mountaintop and waiting for the end to come. They are continuing to do what they were called to do, and will persevere in this until they are no longer able — dancing, running their fingers through the silken soil of Earth Mother, keeping the natural forces and the world in balance, and pushing the global calendar back.

Before any of us can dismiss any part of the Elders' message, it is necessary to ask ourselves several questions: Their information, warnings and prophecies predate contact with the outside world by at least 500 years. If this unique information did not come from the Source to which the Elders attribute it, where then did it originate? The story is even inscribed in pictographic form on the rocks! Could the ancestors have plotted, fantasized and made all of this up? If what they say is false, why have the successive generations of Traditional people continued to believe it, denied themselves so much, and clung so tenaciously to the Covenant? Have what we describe as primitive people been so different from us that they are incapable of having a full relationship with the Creator and learning truth? To sustain their faith, they have coped with a parade of challenges whose magnitude boggles the mind, and the worst of these are taking place at this very moment. How would it help them to live a lie and to fabricate any part of the story, especially when it has required such strenuous and essentially thankless effort on their part and gained them nothing of tangible value? There is little personal reward to be had up there on a remote and economically starved reservation whose entire population numbers something less than 10,000 citizens. They have always known how foolish their message will sound to the outside world, and that everyone will wonder why, acting through Maasaw, the Creator chose, of all people, them to be his special servants. Why did they not long ago, as nearly everyone else has, just give up and give in to the pressures? At their advanced ages today, anyone would excuse them for resting easy now and going quietly into the twilight. The winning of the battle means more to their descendants and to the entire world than it does to the Elders themselves. They will be out of harm's way and wearing the cloud mask long before it comes to fruition, and they can meet the Creator with their heads held high.

Observe also that it is common for those who prophecy a cataclysmic end for the world to believe that divine justice will spare them, but the Elders make no such claim. They not only face extinction now, their descendants will also reap the whirlwind when it comes. The exception will be at the very point of transition. In the meantime, they are working patiently to slow it down, and should it be possible, even to keep the worst from happening. All of this, and yet their detractors would have us believe that for countless centuries a small group of stubborn elderly Hopi people have done what they have done and said what they have said for nothing more than the sake of an outmoded religious view, a little status, a few barren plots of farmland, an absence of utilities and modern conveniences, and the right to go on battling the elements and their opponents as they have for their entire lives. Can we accept that? And, what do Professor Kendall and those who support him have to gain by their protests — other than an opportunity to go on living?

At this point it will not surprise you to learn that when I think of Dan and his lilliputian group I see them resolutely, but with fear and trepidation, binding up a thrashing giant, or filling the unlikely hero's role in the inspiring stage play, *Man of La Mancha*. They know full well that Hopi like themselves are suspect candidates for the job, but also have learned through exposure to history that the Creator usually chooses unlikely groups and individuals to carry out the most difficult tasks. The rest are too busy fulfilling their own needs, or wasting too much time looking for alternatives and asking questions.

Almost, but happily not entirely alone up on their high and demanding mesa the Elders are facing terrible odds, and like Don Quixote, are dreaming the impossible dream... fighting the unbeatable foe... bearing the unbearable sorrow... running where the brave dare not go. For again like the noble hero, that is their quest, to follow that star, no matter how hopeless, no matter how far... for this is exactly what they are doing, even though they are not dreaming and the foe is vastly more real and daunting than anything the windmills of Quixote represent.

The reality of this crucial engagement truly seizes us as we learn that we too have a key role to play in both the Covenant and the battle. It involves you, me, all creatures great and small, our quality of life, the air we breathe, the fuel we burn, the food we eat, the water we drink, personal and international relationships, every aspect of the globe itself, and the universe we live in. Having read the entire story of Hotevilla, Shrine of the Covenant, Dan and I believe you will have no choice but to agree with this conclusion. And, what you will do about it and the Elders is something we hope you will want to consider carefully. They have told us what the solutions are, but, while they continue to do what they covenanted to do, only we outsiders have the ability to execute our part of the solutions — which are disarmingly powerful, intriguing, and Maasaw's of course — on a worldwide scale.

You see, this is another way in which the Elders' message differs so significantly from that of others who also have personal complications and needs. The Elders want — I am going to repeat this also — nothing other than to be left alone to do what must be done for the rest of us. In other words, they want, Lord knows why they should, to save our necks, including those of the very people who are doing them the most harm! In this regard, I think it fair to ask what manner of person would want to destroy the very individuals who hold in their hands that person's life? Is this not an extravagant kind of dumbness?

This then is a call to join with awareness in the battle, knowing that our only opportunity lies in the choice between surviving in difficult circumstances so that life can continue on in the new cycle to come, or a catastrophic end so terrible as to defy comprehension. The Elders cannot stop what is coming, but they can regulate its timing, and they can make the ending and beginning again far less painful than it will otherwise be. The hope the Elders hold out to us is in no way idyllic, but it is far better than the alternative, and the Elders believe that without their assistance there is no way out at all.

Will life in the years ahead be worth living? Yes indeed — for those who are listening and following the Elders' advice! Despite all of its frightening portents, there is a special kind of peace and joy in what we learn from the Elders. In spite of their responsibilities and losses, they have enjoyed the satisfaction perseverance brings, and they have had their victories too. Perhaps the greatest one of all lies just ahead. Their closeness to the Guardian Spirit of the Earth (who is still present and often seen at night as he prowls around with a torch in his hand, appears at planting time in the fields, and participates in dances too), their knowledge and understanding, and their rewarding life as servants have brought them a very special kind of happiness. Like Fools Crow, they know they are special little hollow bones in and through whom the Creator is working. For them, "the true Hopi culture," as they say in their opening statement, is "good," so good they will not think of trading it for any other! Even though most of us live in vastly different circumstances than theirs, we can share this good life, and in this book the Elders have told you how.

Throughout their history, Oraibi — generally referred to today as "Old Oraibi" because some who moved from there relocated in what is called "New Oraibi" or Kykotsmovi, which is the headquarters of the Tribal Council — and Hotevilla have in a very real way been microcosms of the world. What they have experienced we have experienced, and what is happening and will happen to them, both negative and positive, will also happen to us — in a direct proportion but a far greater way. For example, even their once-invigorating and healthy air is polluted today by that commercial coal-mining plant at Black Mesa, and we have seen that the same mining operation has lowered and contaminated their water table to where it is in varying but ever-worsening ways affecting everyone on the reservation. So hold in mind this somber truth about microcosms as you reflect upon the story, and you will see how accurate it is!

The Hopi who yearn for another kind of life should know that while the United States and other industrialized nations look good on the surface, underneath they are steadily eroding away. If things continue as they are, by the time today's dreams are realized, there will be precious little opportunity to enjoy them. Any prizes that are gained will melt away before their very eyes. Only bitter memories will remain, and they will have wasted energies that should have been spent saving what we can of the earth and life. If another example will help, current reports tell us that population growth is draining the world's freshwater supplies — like Peabody is draining the freshwater supplies of the Hopi — and in America we have squandered fresh water to the point of creating a national emergency... "we must," the reporters say, "wake up while we still control our destiny and commit ourselves to reasonable consumption, preservation and conservation" (*Press Enterprise*, November 10, 1993, p. A-3). A further point in this regard is that even if the pundits of decline are wrong, we must ask ourselves what exactly we have to lose by doing everything we can to end waste, pollution, overpopulation, overconsumption, etc., since once it is accomplished our world will be far better off?

Everyone on the reservation already knows the Hotevilla story, and most take pride in it and are sympathetic to it. They are glad that someone is doing what they are not; that the Elders are standing firm. But they will not like having soiled laundry displayed in a book that anyone can read. So Dan wants readers to know that while they feel the way they do about the Covenant and are adamant in their refusal to break it, they also accept that, as the annual religious cycle is carried out everywhere on the mesas, all of the Traditionalists in all of the villages are with good hearts contributing mightily to the effort to keep the Americas and the world in balance, and thus are in many ways remaining obedient to Maasaw and the other deities. Some of what the Elders have said in previous pages appear to contradict these good feelings, but treating their statements in proper context clarifies the situation. The Elders freely admit they too have embraced some White customs and advantages. But they are the only ones who have not gone too far and crossed the forbidden line.

In considering the question of how far one can depart from the Covenant without breaking it, we will find that the answer lies in the intent. Is the reason a self-justifying or selfish one that will lead to something contrary to Maasaw's wishes, or is it something being done in such a way as to not violate the Covenant? A farming tractor can cut its grooves in Mother Earth for entirely different reasons. In earlier chapters we have seen how this plays out in actual life, especially when we compare the objectives of the Elders with those of the Tribal Council and the United States Government. The point is that in some respects full loyalty to the Covenant is something only the Elders and their supporters can claim. Even the others must admit this, for the majority of them have embraced everything they can of modern conveniences, and they have succumbed to and endorsed many Anglo views, customs and habits that have intruded heavily upon the ancient lifeway.

Another balancing factor is that people who are unacquainted with Hopi Clan and kinship relationships should understand that because of their close-knit nature the people are united in most things. Some Hopi dissension can be attributed to the separate migration paths by which they came to Hopi country, and this was considered in earlier chapters. However, the religion that has been practiced on the mesas in the annual cycle is not among these. For example, whenever a ceremony and dance is held in any village, including Hotevilla, the residents of other villages are welcome to share in it. Women relatives from different villages provide food and partake in the women's dances, and if a man is properly initiated and trained he need not even ask whether he can participate in a ceremony at another village. He simply takes his religious paraphernalia, goes to the active kiva, and joins in.

How We Can help the Elders, Their Supporters, and Ourselves

We have emphasized the fact that, although we are in our period of decline, and perhaps have even moved into the sharper downturn, we can, together with the Traditionalists slow the clock down and gain the opportunity we need to brighten the future. This aspect of the Hopi prophecies is simply wonderful, and it poses a great opportunity. By developing positive attitudes and focusing our attention upon the things that need to be done, we can push back the transition point, so that younger people can still have hope and a reason to go on, and so that their children and children's children can look forward to something better than they can look forward to now. In essence, what we need to do is to take upon ourselves the attitude of the Elders, while at the same time continuing to carry on here in the outside world. In addition, there are also specific Hopi kinds of things we can do each day to broaden our understandings, deepen our convictions, and produce results.

As Dan and Susie do, we must sow our own spiritual roots by:

Praying each morning and night.

Touching Mother Earth with our hands and with what we personally plant, nourish, and harvest. Be as self-sufficient as possible.

Carrying out our own ceremonial cycle within the realm of our own relationship with God.

Saying special prayers at regular intervals for the well-being of the land and all life.

Using pure water to purify ourselves, and thus know we are clean and fit to step into the presence of God so we can be taught the things we need to know.

We must also do everything we can to assure that the Elders and other Traditionals be left alone and untroubled to continue their holy work of balancing nature's forces and the world. In this way we can show our gratitude for these great and exceeding gifts they have given us, and be happy in knowing they are being taken care of.

Here in the outside world, books are filled with information regarding individual things we can do to slow down the world's problems, and we can be grateful for and encourage the commendable and important things that are being done in many places.

What the world needs to solve the major systemic problems confronting it is daunting, yet both available and affordable. Admittedly, the overall problem is huge and complex, but the scope and strategy of our efforts must address the following major problems where the environment and basic human needs are concerned. In light of current progress, we must not ever be so naive as to think we can achieve any of these fully or soon. In fact, considering human nature we may not come even close to accomplishing any of them. But those who are wise will try, and will continue to work at it until the close of the Fourth Cycle comes. The list has no preferential order. All of these should be addressed at once:

Make peace our goal.
Learn to love the unlovable.
Stand together.
Stabilize the world's population.
Protect aboriginal life.
Preserve wildlife.
Ready ourselves for what is coming.
Reverse soil erosion.
Reverse deforestation.
Reverse ozone depletion.
Stop acid rain.
Stop global warming.
Stop pollution.
Provide clean and abundant water.
Increase renewable energy.
Eliminate starvation and malnourishment.
Provide adequate health care.
Eliminate inadequate housing and homelessness.
Eliminate illiteracy.
Increase world efficiency.
Decrease crime and violence.

Beyond what has been required of them to simply keep the Covenant, the lengths the Elders and other Traditionalists have been forced to go to hold on to their land and lifeway are to me astounding. In looking at what the Elders have been doing over this past century, they seem like damage-control experts plugging one hole after another in a constantly threatened dike. No sooner has one leak been stopped, than another has sprung up. The mystery has been why this situation exists at all. Why is it that this sea of outside forces keeps pounding upon the adobe wall that the Hopi Traditionalists have erected to preserve themselves and their ever-shrinking land base? Why couldn't these once-contented and happily occupied people have been left alone to live a life that is so simple, and in the modern world's view so materialistically naive, that no one else would want to duplicate it? And why are they still not left alone today? As the king in *The King and I* would say with a huge sigh, "It's a puzzlement!"

Dan and Katherine

Dan's house

Actually, we do know some of the reasons offered by the offending parties, and we have addressed these. Yet underneath them all there seems to be a greater and more pervasive force, as if evil really does rise up to confront good wherever it manifests itself. Perhaps this is why in the end the Creator and Maasaw must deal with the culprits so harshly as Hopi prophecy, and that of the other prophets mentioned herein, tell us they must.

All anyone would need to do is visit Dan and Susie in their humble home and farm to learn that, excepting those beckoning energy supplies underneath the ground, there is nothing there that most of us would trade our own homes and properties for. Aside from the quiet and the wide-open spaces with their imposing vistas, there is nothing of consequence we would associate with our modern conveniences and world. The house is crowded with much-used furniture and appliances. The ceilings are unfinished. There is no central heating or air conditioning. A gasoline generator powers for short periods of time a small television set and a radio. There are no electric lights. There is no refrigeration, running water or a washer and dryer, and a small wooden outhouse set some distance from the house satisfies bathroom needs. Dan and Susie laughed when I wondered out loud how they accommodated themselves to this arrangement in the winter. Their answer was that it had this redeeming quality: no one stayed there very long to tie it up. The planting, protecting, and harvesting of the corn, vegetables and fruit is demanding and hard. Adding this to the ceremonial and family duties leaves little time for leisure. And yet they love it. Even though they have traveled beyond the wall and seen what the outside world has to offer, they would not for anything trade what they have — which includes above all their service to Maasaw — for anything any of us have.

I vividly recall that, after Dan, Susie, Katherine and I had spent a short time together in a motel in Flagstaff while we worked on the book, Dan was chomping at the bit and obviously ready to return home. When I told him we were done, he clapped his hands gleefully together, smiled broadly, and said — this indomitable 101-year old man — "Got to get back to work!" Katherine and I just looked at one another and shook our heads. That's the way Dan is, and that is the way all of the True Hopi and Keepers of the Covenant are. Susie has been several times to visit Katherine at her home on a cliff above the Pacific Ocean, but the best part of every visit is the day she returns to Hopi Land.

Why does the sea keep hammering at the wall, and why do the Elders not just walk away and let it in?

Perhaps, having experienced some of what they have through our book, you can answer that ...

This much does come clear. Saying you will be a Keeper of the Covenant is one thing, being one is another, for once you begin you will be tested in every possible way in order to keep your strength and vigilance up. If we were to make our presentation here without establishing this fact, we would be derelict in our responsibility. We would be placing every reader in peril if we just said that the

Between himself

GOOD

BAD

Within
himself

Elders hold the fate of the world in their hands and let it go at that. Those who wish to receive the blessings of the balance they achieve — who wish to survive what is coming, and indeed has already begun — must understand from seeing what has happened to the Elders that doing so will not be an easy ride. Learning about the things the Elders have faced, and with Maasaw's help triumphed over, should tell you that survival has its price to pay, and that it is a price of no small consequence. The ride is going to be very rough. You may indeed feel like Indiana Jones does on one of his adventures, and now and then you certainly will be holding on for dear life to the sides of whatever you are riding in. Moreover, there will not be so many welcoming hands as you might hope extended to assist you along the way. That is all right though. The challenges you will face will turn you into the kind of steel that Susie and Dan, Yukiuma, Katchongva, David, Paul, James, Caroline and Titus have become... those gritty little Traditionalists who have run where the brave dare not go. Then whatever hits, you will not break, and you and yours will endure.

And we become a seed

In their messages, the Elders and Katchongva include two very mysterious statements. You may have wondered about these when you read them earlier, and tried to figure out what they meant. The first mystery is that "Maasaw places us between himself, and within himself." How can we be between and in both? And the second refers to a "seed within which there are two."

Within which there are two

It was not until I learned about the two Maasaws, and the matter of making a choice between good and bad that the message became clear. And, it is a wonderful one to leave you with as you ponder what we have told you within these pages, something to think about when you need assurance that you can look forward to a more promising tomorrow.

There are two Maasaws — a good Maasaw, and a bad Massaw. They place the Hopi and ourselves between themselves, and having done so, each of them "koyanisquatis" us. That is, they charm us with temptations toward themselves — each of them hoping that we will chose him. Whichever one we choose then places us within himself, where we become a seed, and as a mother does her child in her womb, he nourishes us with his viewpoints and encouragements. In other words, he deepens our experience, and makes it grow. If we choose the good, which is the Creator's side, we are cultured within that atmosphere and grow steadily stronger in it. If on the other hand we choose the bad, or direction away from what the True Hopi believe and practice, then we are nourished within those viewpoints and encouragements, with their evident consequences.

Whichever we choose, we become a seed within that good or bad Maasaw. Still, within this seed are two seeds, which are our continued Creator-given ability to go on choosing the good or the bad. So our gift of choice remains with us. We can stay in, or we can opt out. Even if we make the wrong choice in the beginning, the Creator does not take our opportunity to change away from us. If you are worried about that, forget it. Restoration and Renewal remains the foundation for every major Native American celebration.

Therefore, our situation remains a freely chosen one, and not something that is ever coerced. To be genuine, love must be freely given. So, if you have chosen wisely already and are within the good Maasaw, rejoice greatly in this and make the most of it. Your chances of survival will be very good. Even if you have chosen the bad Maasaw, there is still hope. A change of course is always open to you. You can seize it as it passes by like we do the ring on the post at a merry-go-round. You can return to the good Maasaw on whatever day you decide — although this is neither an invitation or recommendation to vacillate continually within the two. Each time you leave Maasaw, something is taken away, and you cannot ever quite come back to where you were before. So, listen to the music of what the Elders and Katchongva have told you. Make your choices wisely, and do everything you possibly can to get those who have hampered the Keepers of the Covenant to leave them alone to live out their lifeway up there on the Mesa. However foolish it may seem to some, each and every day until the closing of the Fourth Cycle comes, the fate of the world turns upon this.

THIS HOPI PRAYER FOR PEACE WAS OFFERED AT THE HOUSE OF MICA

Great Spirit and all unseen, this day we pray and ask You for guidance, humbly we ask You to help us and fellow men to have recourse to peaceful ways of life, because of uncontrolled deceitfulness by humankind. Help us all to love, not hate one another.

We ask you to be seen in an image of Love and Peace. Let us be seen in beauty, the colors of the rainbow.

We respect our Mother, the plant, with our loving care, for from Her breast we receive our nourishment.

Let us not listen to the voices of the two-hearted, the destroyers of mind, the haters and self-made leaders, whose lusts for power and wealth will lead us into confusion and darkness.

Seek visions always of world beauty, not violence nor battlefields.

It is our duty to pray always for harmony between man and earth, so that the earth will bloom once more.

Let us show our emblem of love and goodwill for all life and land.

Pray for the House of Glass, for within it are minds clear and pure as ice and mountain streams.

Pray for the great leaders of nations in the House of Mica who in their own quiet ways help the earth in balance.

We pray the Great Spirit that one day our Mother Earth will be purified into a healthy peaceful one.

Let us sing for strength of wisdom with all nations for the good of all people.

Our hope is not yet lost, purification must be to restore the health of our Mother Earth for lasting peace and happiness.

Techqua Ikachi — for Land and Life!

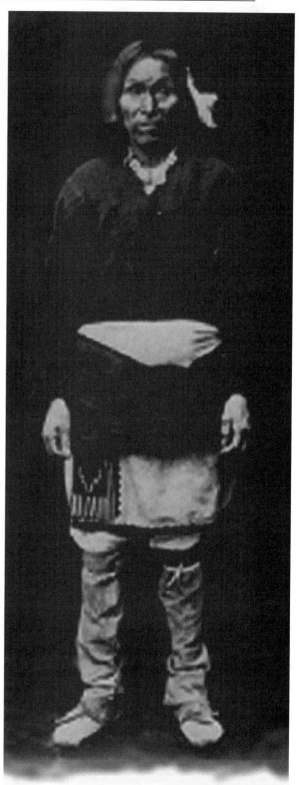

YUKIUMA
LEADER OF HOTEVILLA

"We want to be left alone to live as we wish, to roam free without the white man always there to tell us what we must do and what we cannot do. You see, I am doing this as much for you as for my own people. Suppose I should not protest your orders — suppose I should willingly accept the ways of the Bahannas. Immediately the Great Snake would turn over, and the sea would rush in, and we would all be drowned. You too. I am therefore protecting you."

In this time of crises at Hotevilla, Susie Lomatska has become a champion of the Covenant and Traditional rights. She is also a renowned maker of Kachina dolls, and her works are prized by collectors.

Some of Susies's Kachina dolls. The details are spectacular—done with only a pocketknife, paint and a paintbrush.

September 30, 1994:

Our book is typeset and will soon be on its way to the printer. We have told you what has been happening at Hotevilla, and that the village is a microcosm of the world. This is a progress report:

The village remains divided regarding the completion of the utility lines. Dan and the other Elders have proposed a compromise, asking that the ceremonial plaza and kiva areas at least not be invaded in any way. While no formal answer to this proposition has been received, work has for some unexplained reason stopped. Everything just sits. This may be because the Tribal Council and Housing authorities are disturbed by the adverse publicity their actions are generating, or it may be because villagers are having second thoughts and beginning to fear the spiritual consequences. The Elders wait to see what the outcome will be.

Families, however, are sorely divided, and the effects of this are painful. For the first time in her life Susie did not attend the July Home Going Dance. Dan himself is hurt and disillusioned. You can imagine his agony when, after a hundred years of faithfulness, he made only a couple of obligatory appearances at the performance. Villagers were stunned. It is probable that other Elders shunned the dance as well.

Shortly before the Home Going ceremony was held, Dan predicted that the Kachinas would be angered and not bring rain — a prediction that has proven to be harshly true. The corn stalks are only two feet tall, and the situation is so severe there will be no harvest. Corn is always stored in reserve, but the Hopi Tribal Council and the BIA will soon be faced with the problem of having to care for people who have inadequate supplies. Shortages of all kinds of goods are sure to follow, making it difficult for the Council to pursue their case with the Peabody Mine officials.

Employing the microcosm principle, we can expect that record droughts are already underway in some parts of the world. Extreme food and water shortages will soon exist in many places. Internal divisions will intensify and spread. Human energies will diminish. Environmental groups will face whole new challenges in financing and promoting their programs. Immigration problems will multiply, and the burden of meeting third world needs will mount until demand exceeds the willingness to supply it. The downturn toward the closing of the age is underway, and its signs will become clearer and clearer. So look for opportunities to join with those who are working to affect its timing and severity. The most encouraging thing for the moment is that the "sacred object" buried in Hotevilla has not yet been disturbed.

You can contact the Touch the Earth Foundation for continuing reports regarding developments at Hotevilla.

BIBLIOGRAPHY

Amsden, Charles Avery
1949   *Prehistoric Southwesterners from Basketmaker to Pueblo.*
            Southwest Museum, Los Angeles

Brew, John O.
            The First Two Seasons at Awatovi, *American Antiquity*,
            Vol. 3, pp. 122–37.

Burbank, E.A., as told to Royce, Ernest
1944   *Burbank Among the Indians.*
            The Caxton Printers, Ltd., Caldwell, Idaho

Colton, Harold S.
1939   *Prehistoric Culture Units and their Relationships in
            Northern Arizona.*
            Museum of Northern Arizona, Bulletin 17, Flagstaff

Courlander, Harold
1971   *The Fourth World of the Hopis.*
            University of New Mexico Press, Albuquerque

Dockstader, Frederick J.
1983   *The Kachina and the White Man.*
            University of New Mexico Press, Albuquerque

Dutton, Bertha P.
1963b   *Sun Father's Way, The Kiva Murals of Kuaua, a Pueblo Ruin,
            Coronado State Monument, New Mexico.*
            University of New Mexico Press, Albuquerque

Ellis, Florence H., and Hammack, Laurens
1968   The Inner Sanctum of Feather Cave, a Mogollon Sun and Earth Shrine
            Linking Mexico and the Southwest, *American Antiquity*, Vol. 33, No. 1,
            pp. 25–44.

Fewkes, Jesse Walter
            Numerous publications covering the period from 1891–1927.
            A complete listing of these is given in my book, *Pueblo Children of
            the Earth Mother*, Vol. 1.

Gumerman, George J., and Skinner, S. Alan
1960   Synthesis of the Prehistory of the Central Little Colorado Valley,
            American Antiquity, Vol. 33, No. 2, pp. 185–99.

Hargrave, Lyndon L.
1931   Excavations at Kin Tiel and Kokopnyama, Smithsonian Miscellaneous
            Collections, Vol. 82, No. 11, pp. 80–120, Washington, D.C.

Hough, Walter
1903   Archaeological Field Work in Northeastern Arizona, Expedition of 1901,
            Museum–Gates Expedition. Report of the U.S. National Museum of 1901,
            pp. 279–358.

James, Harry C.
1974   *Pages from Hopi History.* University of Arizona Press, Tucson.

Judd, Neil M.
            Numerous publications covering the period from 1916–64.
            See *Pueblo Children of the Earth Mother* for a complete listing.

Kidder, Alfred Vincent
1934   *An introduction to the Study of Southwestern Archaeology.*
            Yale University Press, New Haven & London

Lummis, Charles F.
1892   The Indian Who Is Not Poor, *Scribners*, Vol. 12, pp. 361–71.
1925   *Mesa, Canon and Pueblo.* Century Company, New York & London

Martin, Paul S., and Plog, Fred
1973   *The Archaeology of Arizona.* American Museum of Natural History.
            Doubleday & Company/Natural History Press, Garden City, N.Y.

Mindeleff, Victor
1891   *A Study of Pueblo Architecture: Tusayan and Cibola.* Smithsonian Institution,
            Bureau of American Ethnology, 8th Annual Report, 1886–87, pp. 3–228,
            Washington, D.C.

Pepper, George H.
1920   *Pueblo Bonito.* Anthropological Papers of the American Museum of
            Natural History, Vol. 27. New York.

Roberts, Frank H.H. Jr.
1939   *Archaeological Remains in the Whitewater District,* Eastern Arizona.
            Smithsonian Institution, Bureau of American Ethnology Bulletin No. 123.
            Washington, D.C.

Simmons, Leo W., and Talayesva, Don
1942   *Sun Chief, the Autobiography of a Hopi Indian.* Yale University Press,
            New Haven and London.

Smith, Watson
1952   *Kiva Mural Decorations at Awatovi and Kawaika, with a Survey of Other Wall
            Paintings in the Pueblo Southwest.* Papers of the Peabody Museum of American
            Archeology and Ethnology, Vol. 37. Reports of the Awatovi Expedition,
            No. 5, Peabody Museum of Archeology and Ethnology.

Titiev, Mischa
1944   *Old Oraibi: A Study of the Hopi Indians of the Third Mesa*, Papers of the
            Peabody Museum of American Archeology and Ethnology, Vol. 22, No. 1,
            Harvard University, Cambridge, Mass.

Waters, Frank, and Fredericks, Oswals White Bear
1963   *Book of the Hopi*, Viking Penguin Inc., New York.

Wright, Barton
1979   *Hopi Material Culture, Artifacts Gathered by H.R. Voth in the Fred Harvey
            Collection.* Northland Press, Flagstaff, Ariz., and Heard Museum, Phoenix.

Yava, Albert
1978   *Big Falling Snow*. Edited by Harold Courlander, Crown Publishers, New York.

ACKNOWLEDGEMENTS:

Special thanks are due *The Press Enterprise* of Riverside, CA., for its diligent reporting of national and international events having to do with environmental, population and other concerns facing the world as we near the end of the 20th century. Their coverage of situations facing the Native Americans is also outstanding. Readers will have noted that in researching documentation in these areas for our book, I seldom needed to look farther than this excellent newspaper.

Special thanks are due also to two cherished friends — first to Karin Elliott, owner of the wonderful Rainbow Moods bookstore and Native American art shop in Tucson, AZ, who shared with me the event that brought this book into being, and who supplied articles from varous publications that were useful in its production; and equally to Pamela Crawford, known to all her friends as "Sierra," who also sent me important environmental information that is used in the book — in particular the photographs found in the Peabody Mine section of Chapter 8 — even defying the corporation's "keep out" signs, and going into restricted areas to take them.

While substantial revisions to them have been made, including having to alter backgrounds and convert them from dark to lighter images so that details can be seen, most of the Kachina dance illustrations used herein come from black and white photographs taken by artist-photographer Joe Mora during the period from 1904 to 1906.

The color plate line of Massaw dancers and the Sio Angak, or Long Hair dancers are adaptations from black and white photographs taken by Emry Kopta in 1924.

A few of my illustrations, and some of the text included in chapters 2, 3, and 4 of this book appeared originally in my two volume series, *The Pueblo Children of the Earth Mother*, originally published by Doubleday in 1983, and scheduled for reprint in 1995.

Volume 9 of the Smithsonian Handbook of North American Indians, published in 1979, was extremely helpful in filling in gaps in Hopi history during the period from 1900 to 1974.

Appendix

While it is not within the province of our Hotevilla book to include such information in it, knowing what we face in the years ahead I have prepared a small book, entitled, **The Hopi Survival Kit.**

As a rule, survival kits provide us with items we need to carry on for a short period of time during or immediately after a natural disaster. This kit is different. Employing the ages-old wisdom and experience of the Traditional Elderly Elders of Hotevilla, it sums up and analyzes the prophecies, warnings, and instructions, and provides us with the understandings we need to survive the coming close of the Fourth Cycle of the world, whose final phase, according to Hopi prophecy, we have now entered. It also tells us how to prepare ourselves for the beginning of the Fifth Cycle by describing the unique actions we can take each day to influence the way in which the world will travel, and the things we can do to influence its timing. There is no other book like this one. It is for you, your children, and for your children's children — a manifesto of hope and joy to hold fast to — what some will inevitably call "a doomsday book," but if so, it is with a shining escape route for you and yours.

In the United States, you can obtain **The Hopi Survival Kit** by sending your name and address with $14.95, plus $2.50 postage, to the:

Touch the Earth Foundation
P.O. Box 257
Solana Beach, CA 92075
1-800-4BE-HOPI

To learn what the current status is at Hotevilla, and how you can help the Elders and the other Traditional people of Hotevilla and elsewhere in Hopi Land, call or write the foundation at the above address. For more information telephone 619-481-9824 or fax 619-481-9841.

Touch The Earth Foundation is a nonprofit organization. You can also obtain additional copies of the Hotevilla book from them.